Fair Opportunity and Responsibility

Fair Opportunity and Responsibility

DAVID O. BRINK

CLARENDON PRESS · OXFORD

OXFORD
UNIVERSITY PRESS

Great Clarendon Street, Oxford, OX2 6DP,
United Kingdom

Oxford University Press is a department of the University of Oxford.
It furthers the University's objective of excellence in research, scholarship,
and education by publishing worldwide. Oxford is a registered trade mark of
Oxford University Press in the UK and in certain other countries

Published in the United States of America by Oxford University Press
198 Madison Avenue, New York, NY 10016, United States of America

British Library Cataloguing in Publication Data
Data available

Library of Congress Control Number: 2020951172

ISBN 978-0-19-885946-8

DOI: 10.1093/oso/9780198859468.001.0001

Printed and bound in the UK by
TJ Books Limited

Links to third party websites are provided by Oxford in good faith and
for information only. Oxford disclaims any responsibility for the materials
contained in any third party website referenced in this work.

In Memoriam

David Ryrie Brink
1919–2017

Contents

List of figures

1

Prolegomena

Many of our reactive attitudes and practices of praise and blame reflect assumptions about the agency and responsibility of those who are targets of these attitudes. It would be odd to praise someone's actions if we thought she was not responsible for them, and it would seem unfair to blame someone, and especially sanction her, if we didn't think she did anything wrong or we didn't think she was responsible or culpable for her actions. Though assumptions about responsibility play an important role in our practices of both praise and blame, they come into especially sharp focus with negative reactive attitudes and practices, including guilt, resentment, blame, and punishment. Negative reactive attitudes and practices are often quite consequential for their targets, as is reflected in their role in the operation of the criminal law, where both stigma and incarceration can be attached to culpable misconduct. These and other negative reactive attitudes and practices are responses to wrongdoing of some kind—some sort of failing in conduct or attitude—for which we think the agent was responsible and, hence, culpable. These reactive attitudes and practices are deeply woven into the fabric of our dealings with each other—our everyday moral interactions and assessments of each other, our philosophical assumptions about agency and responsibility, and criminal law doctrines about responsibility, excuse, and punishment.

1. The Reactive Attitudes, Responsibility, and Fair Opportunity

Moral psychology and criminal jurisprudence share several important and interrelated concepts, such as responsibility, excuse, culpability, blame, and punishment. Even if these shared concepts play somewhat different roles in these two domains, there is clearly significant overlap in their nature and demands. In fact, given the importance of moral ideas to the formation and reform of criminal law principles and practices and the effect of well-settled criminal law doctrine on our moral assumptions and beliefs, we should expect mutual influence and interaction between these two domains. This book

Fair Opportunity and Responsibility. David O. Brink, Oxford University Press (2021). © David O. Brink.
DOI: 10.1093/oso/9780198859468.003.0001

works at the intersection of moral psychology and criminal jurisprudence to explore issues about the nature of responsibility, excuse, and culpability and their bearing on both the theory and practice of blame and punishment.

Many philosophical discussions of responsibility focus on the foundational question about whether we are ever responsible for anything we do. Those debates are often framed in terms of the compatibility of freedom of the will and responsibility with the truth of causal determinism—the thesis that every event is determined or necessitated by the laws of nature and the prior history of the world. *Compatibilists*, sometimes called *soft determinists*, insist that freedom is compatible with the truth of causal determinism, whereas *incompatibilists* insist that the two are not compatible. That means that incompatibilists who are also determinists are *hard determinists*, embracing *skepticism about free will and responsibility*. However, some incompatibilists are *libertarians*, rejecting determinism and embracing indeterminism and the idea of uncaused or contra-causal agency. But whereas some regard libertarianism as one way to vindicate free will and responsibility, others think that indeterminism cannot ground responsibility, because we cannot be responsible for uncaused choices. On this version of skepticism, free will and responsibility are incompatible not only with determinism but also with indeterminism.

In his influential article "Freedom and Resentment," P.F. Strawson proposed to sidestep traditional debates about whether free will is compatible with determinism and indeterminism by pursuing an intimate link between our *reactive attitudes* and responsibility.[1] Strawson focused on moralized reactive attitudes, involving praise and blame, especially negative reactive attitudes, such as indignation, resentment, and guilt. *Strawson's thesis*, as we might call it, claimed that the moralized reactive attitudes are fitting or appropriate just in case the targets of those attitudes are responsible. However, Strawson's thesis can be interpreted in two very different ways, depending on whether we assign explanatory priority to the reactive attitudes or to responsibility. On a *response-dependent* interpretation of Strawson's thesis, there is no response-independent justification of our attributions of responsibility or the reactive attitudes. Responsibility judgments simply reflect those dispositions to respond to others that are constitutive of various kinds of interpersonal relationships. By contrast, a *realist* interpretation of Strawson's thesis stresses the way that the reactive attitudes make sense in light of, and so *presuppose*, responsibility. A realist reading promises to justify the reactive attitudes in a way in which a response-dependent reading cannot, but the realist reading

---

[1] P.F. Strawson, "Freedom and Resentment" *Proceedings of the British Academy* 48 (1962): 187–211.

also makes the justification of the reactive attitudes hostage to the existence of a plausible conception of responsibility that can be specified independently of the reactive attitudes. Because the realist interpretation of Strawson's thesis promises to ground and justify the reactive attitudes in a way in which the response-dependent reading cannot, we should try to defend a realist reading if we can, treating the response-dependent interpretation as a fallback position if the realist reading fails.

According to the realist interpretation of Strawson's thesis, negative reactive attitudes, such as guilt, resentment, and blame presuppose that the target of these attitudes is responsible for her conduct. These reactive attitudes are justified and fitting insofar as the target of these attitudes engaged in some kind of wrongdoing for which she was responsible. If so, two important points follow. First, the dependence of the reactive attitudes on responsibility supports a broadly *retributive* conception of blame and punishment according to which blame and punishment are fitting responses to misconduct for which the agent is responsible or culpable. This implies that culpable wrongdoing forms a *desert* basis for blame and punishment that provides *pro tanto* reason for us to blame and, sometimes, punish culpable wrongdoing. Second, Strawson's thesis means that we can treat our reactive attitudes and practices as *evidence* about the nature of responsibility. In particular, the conditions under which we suspend the reactive attitudes, recognizing *excuses*, indicates our beliefs about responsibility. Responsibility and excuse are mirror images of each other—excuses deny responsibility, and responsibility implies the lack of an excuse. This means that we can articulate and test our ideas about responsibility against our ideas about excuse, and vice versa.

When we approach responsibility and excuse in this way, we will find that moral responsibility and criminal responsibility, despite some significant differences, share important *architecture*. Here, settled criminal law doctrines about excuse are instructive. We blame and sometimes punish agents who are responsible and, hence, culpable for their wrongdoing. The criminal law recognizes two kinds of exculpatory defenses—*justifications* and *excuses*. Justifications deny that the conduct in question is in fact wrong. Perhaps I need to use lethal force to defend myself from a culpable aggressor, or I need to trespass on someone's property in order to secure emergency medical attention for a critically injured companion. In these cases, conduct that would otherwise be wrong is in the circumstances permissible. By contrast, excuses concede wrongdoing but deny that the agent is culpable or responsible for the wrong. Perhaps I was unable to tell the difference between right and wrong at the time of my wrongdoing, or I was coerced into wrongdoing by threats to myself or loved ones if I fail to comply. Because excuses deny responsibility, they provide a window onto responsibility.

The criminal law recognizes two main kinds of excuse—those that involve significant impairment of an agent's *capacities*, as reflected in cases of insanity or immaturity, and those in which an agent's circumstances compromise her fair *opportunity* to exercise these capacities free from wrongful interference, as reflected in cases involving manipulation or duress. These assumptions about excuse tell us something about responsibility. Roughly speaking, responsibility is a matter of an agent having the requisite capacities, which we can conceptualize in terms of *normative competence*, and suitable opportunities to exercise the capacities free from external interference of certain kinds, which we can conceptualize in terms of *situational control*. Normative competence itself involves a kind of reasons-responsiveness that factors into *cognitive competence*—the ability to recognize moral and criminal norms—and *volitional competence*—the ability to conform one's conduct to this normative knowledge. Normative competence and situational control are individually necessary and jointly sufficient for responsibility, because significant impairment of either condition results in an excuse. These forms of impairment are excusing, because blame and punishment, despite these forms of impairment, would violate the important norm that blame and punishment are appropriate only when the agent had the *fair opportunity to avoid wrongdoing*.

The fair opportunity conception of responsibility represents responsibility as consisting in the agent having appropriate capacities and opportunities (see Figure 1.1). This conception of responsibility and excuse is attractive for several reasons. It provides a plausible principled reconstruction of our reactive attitudes of praise and blame, and it fits our considered judgments about

Figure 1.1 The Fair Opportunity Conception of Responsibility

when agents are responsible and when they should be excused, both in moral assessment and in the criminal law. It also draws on and synthesizes the best elements in two intellectual traditions. Within philosophy, the fair opportunity conception draws on the reasons-responsive wing of the compatibilist tradition about free will and responsibility, which reconciles responsibility and determinism by grounding responsibility in the capacities of agents to respond to normative requirements that bear on their conduct.[2] Within the criminal law, the fair opportunity conception draws on the fair choice tradition in criminal jurisprudence, which understands responsibility in terms of the choices of agents with rational capacities and the fair opportunity to exercise those capacities.[3]

The fair opportunity conception of responsibility vindicates the realist reading of Strawson's thesis. The moralized reactive attitudes presuppose and are justified insofar as the targets of these attitudes are responsible. When we appeal to the reactive attitudes—in particular, our practices of excuse—to illuminate responsibility, we are led to the fair opportunity conception of responsibility. The fair opportunity conception provides a response-independent conception of responsibility, because it represents responsibility as consisting in agential capacities (normative competence) and opportunities (situational control) that can be specified independently of the reactive attitudes and that can justify these attitudes.

Moreover, though it is possible to endorse the fair opportunity conception of responsibility from a variety of philosophical perspectives, it supports an attractive form of compatibilism. In its traditional form, hard determinism implies that we are never responsible for our actions, because determinism is true and is incompatible with responsibility. This would mean that any and all wrongdoing should be excused, because no one is ever responsible for her conduct. But when we look to our actual practices of excuse, as modeled by fair opportunity, we find that we deploy excuse *selectively*. In particular, we excuse for various kinds of incompetence, such as insanity and immaturity, and for

---

[2] See Susan Wolf, *Freedom within Reason* (New York: Oxford University Press, 1990); R. Jay Wallace, *Responsibility and the Moral Sentiments* (Cambridge, MA: Harvard University Press, 1994); John Fischer and Mark Ravizza, *Responsibility and Control* (New York: Cambridge University Press, 1998); Dana Nelkin, *Making Sense of Freedom and Responsibility* (Oxford: Clarendon Press, 2011); David O. Brink and Dana K. Nelkin, "Fairness and the Architecture of Responsibility" *Oxford Studies in Agency and Responsibility* 1 (2013): 284–313; Michael McKenna, "Reasons-Responsiveness, Agents, and Mechanisms" *Oxford Studies in Agency and Responsibility* 1 (2013): 151–83; and Manuel Vargas, *Building Better Beings* (Oxford: Clarendon Press, 2013).

[3] See H.L.A Hart, *Punishment and Responsibility* (Oxford: Clarendon Press, 1968); Michael Moore, *Placing Blame* (Oxford: Clarendon Press, 1997); and Stephen Morse, "Culpability and Control" *University of Pennsylvania Law Review* 142 (1994): 1587–660 and "Uncontrollable Urges and Irrational People" *Virginia Law Review* 88 (2002): 1025–78.

lack of situational control, such as duress—not whenever actions are causally determined. Of course, these assumptions and practices about responsibility and excuse could be mistaken. But skepticism about responsibility is an *error theory*, claiming that our assumptions about responsibility are systematically mistaken. To justify an error theory, the principles that entail skepticism must be more plausible than the assumptions that they require us to forego. Especially when the assumptions in question are widely held and deeply entrenched in our practices, this burden is difficult to discharge. The assumption that normal, mature adults are, for the most part, responsible for their conduct is a pervasive one. As Strawson reminds us, this assumption is implicated in many of our reactive attitudes, especially those involving praise and blame, such as pride, resentment, and guilt, and it underlies our practices of punishment. Though these assumptions and practices could be systematically mistaken, we should accept this conclusion reluctantly, only if we can identify no viable conception of responsibility. The fair opportunity conception supplies this need.

Though the fair opportunity conception of responsibility seems to have compatibilist implications insofar as it recognizes excuses selectively, it differs from forms of compatibilism that reconcile responsibility and determinism by denying that responsibility requires freedom. On one such view, responsibility does not presuppose freedom, because it does not require the sort of alternate possibilities that determinism denies.[4] However, unlike compatibilist conceptions of responsibility that deny freedom of the will and alternate possibilities, the fair opportunity conception seems to assume that the responsible wrongdoer could have done otherwise. Is this commitment to alternate possibilities defensible and consistent with determinism? Are these the same kind of alternate possibilities denied by some compatibilists? Consideration of the voluntarist principle that <ought> implies <can> suggests a plausible conception of alternate possibilities in terms of capacities and opportunities that is different from the conception that is incompatible with determinism. The truth of determinism does not prevent agents from having capacities and opportunities to avoid wrongdoing. Explaining this compatibilist understanding of fair opportunity requires saying more about the nature of capacities and opportunities.

Fair opportunity says that an agent is responsible for wrongful conduct insofar as she was normatively competent and possessed situational control at the time of her conduct. This formulation of fair opportunity has an important

---

[4] See Harry Frankfurt, "Alternate Possibilities and Moral Responsibility" *Journal of Philosophy* 66 (1969): 829–39. I discuss Frankfurt's view in Chapters 2 and 4.

synchronic quality. Responsibility is a function of structural features of the agent at the time of deliberation and action. However, a synchronic conception of responsibility might seem inadequate. Responsibility and excuse may seem to be essentially *historical* concepts. We may think that we can't reliably determine responsibility and excuse by appeal to synchronic or structural facts alone. In some cases, it may seem to matter how those structural facts came into existence. Is an agent who was reasons-responsive at the time of action responsible for her action if she was reasons-responsive only through the manipulation of others, or does the history of manipulation defeat her responsibility? A synchronic version of fair opportunity says that sufficient normative incapacity is excusing, but is it excusing in cases of culpable incapacity in which the agent bears responsibility for becoming incapacitated? Can an agent be responsible for her actions if she does not have a history of taking responsibility for her actions and instead views herself as buffeted about by external forces? Should we recognize an excuse, whether full or partial, when we learn that a culpable wrongdoer was the victim of systematic abuse and neglect during her formative years?

These issues raise the question about whether our conception of responsibility should have an historical dimension and, hence, whether fair opportunity should take an historical form. Fair opportunity can take an historical form, if need be. However, we will see that an ahistorical version of fair opportunity has the resources to explain cases and intuitions that might seem to call for historical analysis.

2. Fair Opportunity, Desert, and Culpability

Fair opportunity has an important role to play in criminal jurisprudence because of its implications for our understanding of the justification of blame and punishment, the nature and significance of culpability, and the theory and practice of exculpatory defenses.

Punishment combines blame and sanction. We can contrast *forward-looking* rationales for punishment that appeal to deterrence, rehabilitation, norm reinforcement, and communication with a *backward-looking* rationale that appeals to *desert*, where the basis of desert is wrongdoing for which the agent is responsible and, hence, culpable. Desert is an important constraint on blame and punishment, because it is impermissible to blame and punish in the absence of culpable wrongdoing. But desert also provides a *pro tanto* justification of blame and punishment. If so, retributivism must be at least part of the truth about punishment. Some form of retributivism is defensible, once we clarify misconceptions about retributivism. This leaves a choice between pure retributivism and a mixed conception that includes both forward-looking and retributive elements. That choice is best resolved in favor of a mixed conception in which retributive elements *predominate*.

Fair opportunity can also shed light on the role of culpability in the criminal law. Culpability is not a unitary concept within the criminal law, and it is important to distinguish different culpability concepts and the work they do. *Narrow* culpability is the mental ingredient in wrongdoing itself, describing the agent's elemental *mens rea*—whether she intended the wrong, tolerated the wrong without aiming at it, was reckless with respect to causing the wrong, or was negligent about causing it. Narrow culpability affects the seriousness of the wrongdoing. For instance, we think that it is worse to intend a wrong than to cause it negligently. *Broad* culpability is the responsibility condition that makes wrongdoing blameworthy and without which wrongdoing is excused. *Inclusive* culpability is the combination of wrongdoing and responsibility or broad culpability that functions as the retributivist desert basis for punishment. Each of these kinds of culpability plays an important role in a unified retributive framework for the criminal law. Moreover, these different forms of culpability have implications for our understanding of the nature and permissibility of strict liability crimes, because strict criminal liability would be liability for criminal sanction without culpability.

Finally, fair opportunity influences how we can and should understand exculpatory defenses. The two main exculpatory defenses in the criminal law are justifications and excuses, and they deny different components of the retributivist desert basis for punishment. Whereas justifications, such as self-defense and necessity, deny wrongdoing, excuses, such as insanity and duress, deny broad culpability or responsibility. We will be assessing inclusive culpability in several contexts—involving structural injustice, situational pressures, insanity, immaturity, addiction, and provocation. To do so, we have to understand distinct kinds of exculpatory defenses and the division of labor between justification and excuse. This involves understanding—and sometimes questioning—existing criminal law doctrines.

3. The Fragility of Fair Opportunity

Though the fair opportunity conception of responsibility has much to be said for it, it may prove fragile in light of certain pervasive social influences that may seem to challenge our assumptions about fair opportunity and individual responsibility. I have in mind two sources of concern—*structural injustice* and *situationist psychology*. Structural injustice and situationism pose challenges to any conception of responsibility, but they may seem to raise especially serious problems for the fair opportunity conception. For structural injustice may seem to deprive victims of injustice of the fair opportunity to succeed without resort to criminal activity, and situationism may seem to raise questions about whether agents ever possess the sort of situational control required by the fair opportunity conception.

Structural injustice obtains in societies in which material inequalities and discriminatory animus by in-groups against out-groups conspire to deny a significant segment of the population of the *fair equality of opportunity*. We might call members of out-groups with lower socio-economic status who lack equal opportunity the *marginalized*. A significant portion of criminal activity by the marginalized—for instance, non-violent drug offenses and other forms of participation in underground economies—are direct responses to inequalities of opportunity created by structural injustice. We might think that in societies that are structurally unjust, the state loses its authority to hold some agents responsible for their crimes, and we might doubt that victims of structural injustice are fully culpable for at least some forms of misconduct responsive to this injustice.

Fair opportunity and responsibility may well be fragile in circumstances of structural injustice, providing significant mitigation for some criminal activity by the marginalized. But we need to be clear precisely when and how structural injustice can mitigate, and there are limits to the fragility that structural injustice exposes. The fair opportunity conception of responsibility has distinctive implications for the bearing of structural injustice on individual responsibility. Mitigation will only extend to crimes committed by the marginalized that are directly responsive to structural injustice, such as participation in underground economies, and will typically not extend to crimes by members of non-marginalized groups or to violent crimes by the marginalized. Moreover, at least typically, when structural injustice excuses, it provides at most a partial excuse or mitigation, rather than a full excuse, justifying acquittal, because structural injustice typically compromises, rather than destroys, the fair opportunity to avoid wrongdoing.

Structural injustice raises questions about the responsibility of the marginalized. But situationist psychology raises questions about whether anyone is responsible. The fair opportunity conception of responsibility assumes that responsible agents have control over their behavior and that their conduct reflects their character and choices. However, situationist psychology claims that subtle and non-salient features of the situations in which agents find themselves and the architecture of their choice play a more powerful role in explaining their behavior than we normally assume and that individual character and choice play less of an explanatory role than we normally assume. If so, we might think that situationism undermines situational control and, hence, fair opportunity and responsibility.

Surprisingly, the biggest threat from situationism is not to situational control, because situational pressures do not involve genuine duress, but rather to normative competence, because situational factors may cloud an agent's judgment or his volitional resolve. However, in normal cases, situational factors affect performance, not competence. Like urges and temptations, situational factors affect how people actually behave, but they do not normally deprive agents of the capacity to recognize and conform to reasons. Nonetheless, there are unusual circumstances, such as wrongdoing committed in the heat of battle, where situational pressures may compromise cognitive and volitional capacities sufficiently to generate an excuse, whether full or partial. However, the scope of this excuse is limited in important ways and does not support a general excuse for wartime wrongdoing.

4. Fair Opportunity and Partial Responsibility

The fair opportunity conception of responsibility can take on board structural injustice and situationist psychology without capsizing the boat. Because responsibility and excuse covary, we can both apply and test the fair opportunity conception by looking at cases of potential excuse in which normative competence or situational control seems to be impaired. In particular, it will be worthwhile to examine cases of *partial responsibility* involving insanity and psychopathy, immaturity, addiction, and provocation and crimes of passion. These cases of partial responsibility and excuse are often discussed independently of each other, and they are often treated differently by the criminal law in various jurisdictions and by the Model Penal Code, which is a model statutory text of fundamental general and specific provisions of the criminal law designed to serve as a set of best practices for criminal law design and reform in various jurisdictions.[5] Though it will be valuable to see what fair

---

[5] The Model Penal Code (1985) is a model statutory text of fundamental provisions of the criminal law, developed by the American Law Institute (ALI) in the 1950s, first adopted in 1962, and

opportunity implies about each issue, treating them together within the framework of fair opportunity allows us to see and explore common themes and draw general lessons about the nature of partial responsibility and excuse.

Insanity is the primary criminal law excuse denying normative competence. Fair opportunity supports the broader Model Penal Code conception of insanity, as having both cognitive and volitional dimensions, against the narrower M'Naghten conception, which requires a bare cognitive capacity to discriminate right from wrong. It also supports modifications to the Model Penal Code, expanding its conception of insanity in some ways and contracting it in others. On the one hand, it's not clear that we should require that incompetence be caused by a mental disease or defect, as all extant insanity conceptions do, at least if mental disease or defect is understood as a separate clinical category that would restrict the cases of incompetence qualifying for insanity. On the other hand, incompetence should not be excusing if the agent is culpable for being incompetent, as she might be if her incompetence is successfully managed by medication and, while competent, she chooses to go off her medication and ends up engaging in wrongdoing as the result of her incompetence.

Though the criminal law does not recognize psychopathy as a form of insanity, several writers have recently argued that psychopathy funds an excuse of cognitive incompetence, often appealing to the empathy deficits of psychopaths to argue that they lack the moral concepts necessary for cognitive competence. However, the fair opportunity conception of incompetence supports skepticism about whether psychopathy excuses. Because there are other modes of cognitive access to basic normative requirements that are not empathetic, empathy deficits do not absolve psychopaths of moral or criminal responsibility.

Immaturity is developmentally normal, not pathological. Nonetheless, it involves diminished normative competence that presents an interesting and familiar case of partial responsibility. Developmental literature documents ways in which adolescents are cognitively and emotionally immature. The reduced normative competence of adolescents implies that, all else being equal, they are less responsible for their crimes than their normal adult

---

subsequently updated in 1981. The ALI consisted of experienced judges, lawyers, and legal academics who sought to create a principled conception of best practices in the criminal law that could be used to design and reform criminal codes in various jurisdictions. The Code has proven more influential on some criminal law topics than others. It's often useful to focus on the Model Penal Code rather than local criminal law (whether common law or statutory), both because local criminal law is variable and the Code is a uniform code and because the Code often represents a more principled conception of criminal law doctrines than local criminal law.

counterparts. Recognition of this fact explains the evolution of a separate juvenile court to better assess the culpability of juvenile offenders and tailor blame and punishment to make it commensurate with their just deserts. Against this background, it is worth examining two recent trends in juvenile justice. Immaturity argues against trends in American juvenile justice that assimilate juvenile crime to adult crime by transferring juvenile offenders to adult criminal court on account of the magnitude of their wrongdoing. This ignores the fact that culpability and wrongdoing are independent variables in the retributivist desert basis for blame and punishment and that, all else being equal, youthful offenders are less culpable than their adult counterparts. Several recent Supreme Court decisions recognize sentencing limitations for juvenile offenders—in particular, the unconstitutionality of the death sentence for juvenile homicides and of life in prison without the possibility of parole for juvenile non-homicides. On the one hand, these cases only arise because of the existence of the transfer trend in which juveniles can be tried and sentenced in adult criminal court. On the other hand, they involve recognition of the reduced culpability of juvenile offenders. Insofar as these sentencing limits are categorical, they also raise interesting questions about the tension between categorical sentencing rules and individualized justice. In the right circumstances, fair opportunity may support adoption of such categorical sentencing limitations for juvenile offenders.

The nature of addiction is disputed, and its implications for responsibility are complex. Two models of addiction seem especially promising. One model likens addiction to akrasia or weakness of will. On this view, akrasia involves *dynamically inconsistent attitudes* on the part of the agent in which she toggles from a distal prospective judgment that it is best not to consume the addictive substance, to a proximate prospective judgment that she should so consume, and back to a distal retrospective judgment of regret that she did consume. Addiction, on this model, involves recurrent weakness of will that results in the long-term frustration of one's mostly stable preferences and goals. A second model of addiction is best seen as a reaction to the extreme models of *compulsion*, according to which the addict is a slave to her cravings, and *choice*, in which addiction is the rational policy of someone with unusual preferences. The alternative model of addiction is one of *impaired self-control*, in which addiction makes one susceptible to cravings that make self-control especially difficult, but typically not impossible. Insofar as addiction involves simple akrasia, it should not be excusing, because temptations do not as such deprive the agent of reasons-responsive capacities. Because addiction can generate strong impulses, it is sometimes likened to duress. But these hard choices are best assessed in terms of whether they compromise cognitive or volitional dimensions of normative competence. An addict's disordered appetites may compromise her ability to recognize normative requirements or make it difficult to conform her conduct to this knowledge. Such impairment may mitigate, but it typically does not incapacitate sufficiently to provide a full excuse. Moreover, even partial excuse is limited if the agent is responsible for becoming addicted in the first place or remaining addicted once the addiction has been acquired, because even if addiction did incapacitate, these would be cases of culpable incapacity, which do not in general excuse.

As a general matter, American criminal law is *bivalent* about responsibility and excuse, treating them as all or nothing. There is a threshold of competence and control above which one is fully responsible and below which one is fully excused. The provocation defense is usually treated as the principal exception to this generalization about the bivalent character of responsibility and excuse, because provocation provides a partial justification or excuse for crimes of passion, reducing what would otherwise be murder to manslaughter when the homicide was suitably provoked. Relative to the fairly narrow kinds of provocation recognized by the common law, the Model Penal Code has relaxed the standards of provocation, recognizing it as the result of extreme emotional disturbance. Indeed, under the Model Penal Code juries are allowed to consider whether a spurned lover who kills his partner for exercising her rights to separate is entitled to a provocation defense. In this respect, the provocation doctrine shows a very regressive side to the Model Penal Code, at odds with its generally progressive influence.[6] This raises a number of interesting questions about the provocation defense. One question concerns the apparently disparate treatment of homicides involving provocation and homicides involving battered women. The Model Penal Code discounts punishment in crimes of passion, rewarding aggressors (almost always men) and penalizing victims (almost always women) for unreasonable responses on the part of the aggressor to perfectly reasonable and legal behavior by the victim. By contrast, in battered women cases courts are highly skeptical about recognizing justifications or excuses for the abused (almost always women) pre-emptively killing or harming their abusers (almost always men). A principled criminal jurisprudence should criticize this double standard. Another question is whether provocation and battered women defenses are better conceptualized as partial

---

[6] The case for this assessment of the Model Penal Code's provocation defense is made persuasively by Victoria Nourse, "Passion's Progress: Law Reform and the Provocation Defense" *Yale Law Journal* 106 (1997): 1331–448, which we will examine in Chapter 14.

justifications, reducing the wrong done, or as partial excuses, reducing culpability for the wrong. Closer analysis shows that both provocation and battered women defenses factor into two camps—those in which the provocation and history of abuse make the homicides less wrong than they would otherwise be and those in which agents commit the homicide as the result of impaired competence. Whereas the former justify, the latter excuse.

With the exception of provocation, American criminal jurisprudence is bivalent about responsibility and excuse, treating them as all or nothing. However, responsibility and excuse, conceived in terms of fair opportunity, are *scalar*. Both normative competence and situational control are matters of degree, as our discussions of incompetence, immaturity, addiction, and provocation confirm. Factors that tend to excuse but fall short of a full excuse are recognized, if at all, only as mitigating factors at sentencing. However, though sentence mitigation can sometimes soften the edges of bivalence about excuse, it is an imperfect way to do so. First, there is often little or no discretion at sentencing. Mandatory minima and sentence enhancements often eliminate or severely restrict discretion at sentencing. Second, even when sentencing discretion exists and is wide, it is nonetheless not mandatory. If the criminal law does not recognize partial excuses, it punishes more than retributive justice permits. One might admit that an ideal moral accountant would be fully scalar about responsibility and excuse, rather than bivalent, but insist that the non-ideal human beings that serve as judges and on juries need to make more coarse-grained assessments of responsibility and excuse. While we do need to distinguish the needs of ideal and non-ideal theory within the criminal law, there is reason to be skeptical that bivalence is optimal even for non-ideal theory. Instead, we should explore various different ways of modifying the criminal law to take seriously partial responsibility and excuse.

5. Methodological Commitments

This project is guided by three methodological commitments—working at the intersection of moral psychology and criminal jurisprudence and exploring the relevance of each domain to the other, exploiting the complementary relationship between responsibility and excuse, and appealing to pathology or otherwise suboptimal functioning to study proper functioning.

Philosophical and jurisprudential perspectives on responsibility and excuse stand to benefit from mutual engagement. Moral psychology and criminal jurisprudence share several concepts, such as wrongdoing, negligence, responsibility, culpability, excuse, blame, and punishment. Even if these shared concepts play somewhat different roles in moral and criminal assessment, there is clearly significant overlap in their presuppositions and demands in these two domains. As we have already noted, we should expect mutual interaction and influence between these two domains. The formation and reform of criminal law principles and practices are often driven by moral principles and assumptions about responsibility, and settled criminal law principles and doctrines exert an influence on our moral assumptions and beliefs about responsibility. Given this interaction between moral philosophy and criminal law, each domain stands to benefit from attending to the other.

On the one hand, moral psychologists working on issues about responsibility, blame, and punishment would do well to attend to settled criminal law principles and best practices, because these embody common assumptions about these concepts that have been implemented and tested in various ways. Here, I have in mind especially principles of American criminal law and of the criminal law in other common law countries (e.g. England, Wales, Scotland, Ireland, and Australia).[7] This isn't to say that moral philosophers must follow existing criminal law doctrines slavishly or uncritically. There is plenty of inconsistency in the criminal law and need for reform of particular doctrines and practices. As we will see, various ways in which American criminal law is overly punitive are problematic—including mass incarceration, mandatory sentencing minima, the trend to transfer juveniles to adult criminal court, the use of disenfranchisement and other post-incarceration penalties for felonies, and the bivalent character of responsibility and excuse. But reform of these and other problems can and should often be driven by principles that are already deeply embedded in the criminal law, such as retributive principles about making blame and punishment proportionate to culpability, where that is understood in terms of both wrongdoing and responsibility. Some of the most effective criticisms of criminal law practices involve *internal critique* that these practices are not faithful to or consistent with the criminal law's most fundamental principles.

On the other hand, the criminal law and criminal law theory would do well to attend to work in moral psychology about the presuppositions, nature, and implications of moral concepts that figure centrally within the criminal law. There won't always be a philosophical consensus on these concepts to which

---

[7] Though our focus will be primarily on American criminal law and secondarily on the criminal law in other common law systems, criminal law principles in European systems will play a brief but important role in the argument of Chapter 15.

the criminal law can appeal for ready-made answers to its own questions, but on many topics there will be philosophical problems to which the criminal law should be alert and philosophical insight on which the criminal law can draw in dealing with its own difficulties. For instance, in fashioning a sensible insanity doctrine, the criminal law would be well-advised to build on work in moral psychology about the structure and prerequisites of normative competence and reasons-responsiveness.

This methodological maxim enjoins mutual engagement between moral psychology and criminal law. With some notable exceptions, work in these two domains often proceeds in parallel with fairly modest interaction. Many philosophers writing about free will and responsibility tend to focus on foundational questions involving skepticism about responsibility, asking if we are ever responsible for our actions. By contrast, criminal law theorists tend to assume we are responsible in standard cases and patrol the border of responsibility via the doctrine of excuse. But these different starting points and concerns don't make disagreement inevitable. The fair opportunity conception of responsibility, developed here, provides a common architecture for moral and criminal responsibility and excuse that requires both normative competence and situational control. On this conception, moral and criminal responsibility have the same structure and differ primarily in the different norms— moral and legal—to which the competent agent has to be responsive. The fair opportunity conception of responsibility can appeal to both philosophical and criminal law sources—the reasons-responsive wing of the compatibilist tradition about responsibility and the fair choice conception of responsibility in the criminal law.

In drawing on both philosophical and criminal law sources, we transcend some limitations in each source. On the one hand, moral philosophers working in the reasons-responsive tradition have tended to focus on the agent's capacities, ignoring or at least downplaying the significance of her opportunities to exercise these capacities free from wrongful interference, which criminal law theorists have recognized. On the other hand, criminal law theorists have often appealed to the agent's rational capacities without analyzing them very much. Indeed, early philosophical discussions of reasons-responsiveness were similarly coarse-grained. But we can and should demand a more detailed account of the structure of the capacities constitutive of responsibility. More recent work within the reasons-responsive tradition and related ideas in moral psychology allow us to provide a more satisfying picture of normative competence and its role within responsibility. In this way, the fair opportunity conception not only builds on insights from both moral psychology and criminal law but has implications for cases of partial responsibility involving incompetence, immaturity, addiction, and provocation that are of interest to both moral psychology and criminal law.

A second methodological maxim emerges from Strawson's thesis about the connection between responsibility and the reactive attitudes. When we suspend the reactive attitudes, we excuse. An attractive working hypothesis is that responsibility and excuse are *inversely related*—if one is excused for one's wrongdoing, one is not responsible for it, and if one is responsible for one's wrongdoing, one has no excuse for it. The truth of this hypothesis implies that responsibility and excuse should have corresponding structure and that we should be able to study either in light of our beliefs about the other. As Michael Moore likes to say, "excuse is the royal road to responsibility," but we do well to remember that this is a two-way street.[8]

This working hypothesis is not beyond question. One might think that duress is an excuse that does not impugn the agent's competence or responsibility. If I commit wrong only because you have wrongly threatened me or my loved ones, I seem to act responsibly and reasonably in acceding to your threat. Duress is not an incompetence excuse. It does not compromise the wrongdoer's normative competence or her status as a responsible agent. But it does challenge whether she is *responsible for her wrongdoing*. This shows that we need to distinguish between *being a responsible agent* and *being responsible for one's wrongdoing*. Being normatively competent is sufficient for being a responsible agent, but it is necessary but not sufficient for being responsible for one's wrongdoing. The duressed wrongdoer is a responsible agent, but nonetheless she is not responsible for her wrongdoing. If so, our working hypothesis about the inverse relationship between responsibility and excuse is compatible with the way in which duress excuses. Though it's a defeasible hypothesis, it is a plausible working hypothesis.

This second methodological maxim recommends a third. Because responsibility and excuse are inversely related, we can study responsibility by studying excuse. In particular, we can employ the familiar strategy of understanding normal functioning by appeal to pathological or otherwise imperfect functioning. When we see why the incompetent or the duressed are excused, we learn something about the capacities and opportunities required by normal agency and responsibility, and when we see the different forms that incompetence might take, we learn something about the demands of normative competence. This is true both when the impaired competence is pathological,

---

[8] Moore, *Placing Blame*, p. 548.

as it might be with psychopathy or addiction, and when the impairment is a part of normal development, as it is in the case of immaturity. Moreover, impaired capacities and opportunities tell us something about normal capacities and opportunities, whether that impairment is complete or only partial.

6. Disclaimers

This book articulates a conception of both moral and criminal responsibility, examines threats to responsibility from structural injustice and situationist psychology, and explores the implications of fair opportunity for cases of partial responsibility involving insanity and psychopathy, immaturity, addiction, and provocation. As such, it is wide-ranging and has a significant interdisciplinary dimension, engaging work in moral philosophy, criminal law, and empirical psychology. The interdisciplinary character of this project is exciting and gives it wide relevance. But it also brings risks. It is hard enough to be fully conversant with the literature and issues in one discipline; it is even harder to achieve this kind of facility in multiple disciplines. I am acutely aware that my own expertise is limited and that I have at best partial knowledge of these multi-disciplinary issues.

Fortunately, intellectual progress does not require individual omniscience. Instead, it requires that we each bring some expertise to interdisciplinary work, that we be conscientious consumers of the expertise of others, and that we maintain a healthy fallibilism and intellectual modesty about our interdisciplinary contributions and conclusions. At least this is the sort of interdisciplinary work that I aspire to conduct here. Though trained as a moral philosopher, I have learned a good bit of relevant criminal law and aim to be a reliable consumer of empirical work on the psychological issues that I address here. My views are still evolving and, in some cases, remain unsettled. But the fair opportunity conception of responsibility is an important perspective that deserves proper articulation, and it provides an illuminating framework for analyzing cases of partial responsibility that are often discussed independently. I hope that the benefits of treating complex interdisciplinary issues together compensate for the need to be selective and sometimes impressionistic about complex issues in some cases.

I know my own contributions stand on the shoulders of others. Though there are no doubt limitations in the present study, involving errors of commission and omission, I hope that it too provides a foundation on which to build. The prospects for progress, I believe, lie chiefly in this sort of collective intellectual enterprise.

7. Origins

Though I came to issues about responsibility and excuse from philosophy, rather than the criminal law, I had little interest in traditional debates about freedom and responsibility and the foundational question about whether we are ever responsible for our conduct. As I've noted, skepticism about freedom and responsibility must take the form of an error theory, implying that we are systematically mistaken in our assumption that normal mature adults are generally responsible for their actions, in our reactive attitudes to each other and ourselves, and in our criminal law practices and doctrines. Error theories are hard to justify. To justify an error theory, skeptical principles would have to be more compelling than the beliefs, attitudes, and practices they upset. The error theorist's burden is difficult to meet in most domains, but it is especially difficult in this domain given the way assumptions about responsibility are entrenched in our reactive attitudes and criminal law practices.

Responding to skepticism about responsibility seemed no more interesting to me than responding to skepticism about knowledge or the existence of the external world. By contrast, I was quite interested in questions about *when*, not *whether*, we are responsible. These are questions that ordinary people address in their own moral assessments of family members, friends, and strangers and that the criminal law takes very seriously. In this way, I found criminal jurisprudence perspectives more congenial than many traditional philosophical perspectives. However, deciding when we are responsible and when we are excused requires standards of responsibility and excuse. For this reason, I was especially interested in the resources of compatibilist conceptions of responsibility to shed light on excuses and partial responsibility.

This interest took a practical form because of changes California made to juvenile justice. In 1995, Tony Hicks was 14 years old, and as part of a gang initiation ritual, he shot and killed 20-year-old Tariq Khamisa, who was delivering pizza. Hicks became the first juvenile under the age of 16 in California to be tried as an adult. He was tried and convicted and sentenced to 25 years in prison. He was paroled in 2018, after serving 23 years in prison. I learned of this case, after Hicks was sentenced, through friends involved in the Tariq Khamisa Foundation.[9] In 2001, California carried this trend to try

---

[9] Tariq Khamisa's father, Azim Khamisa, felt that Tariq was not the only victim in this situation and reached out to Ples Felix, Tony's grandfather, to help him work to avoid youth violence and promote principles of restorative justice. The result is the Tariq Khamisa Foundation (https://tkf.org), which sponsors workshops that educate children and parents about the importance of non-violence and forgiveness.

juveniles as adults further when it passed Proposition 21, which provided, among other things, that juveniles aged 14 years or older accused of certain serious or violent offenses must be tried as adults.[10] This was part of a national trend to get tough on juvenile crime. This transfer trend struck me as fundamentally misguided and unjust insofar as it held juveniles accountable solely on the basis of their wrongdoing, ignoring their reduced culpability on account of their immaturity. This seemed like a clear case for internal critique, because changes in juvenile justice were not consistent with the broadly retributivist foundations of the criminal law. This was my first foray into criminal jurisprudence and led to my article, "Immaturity, Normative Competence, and Juvenile Transfer."[11]

While I was working on this essay, I agreed to organize a roundtable entitled Responsibility at the Margins at the University of San Diego School of Law in 2003. The idea was a forerunner of the themes in this book, covering readings on responsibility and excuse and their application to partial or diminished responsibility involving insanity, immaturity, addiction, and provocation and crimes of passion. I didn't know the relevant literatures well and viewed this as an opportunity to educate myself on disparate topics that seemed importantly connected. I needed guidance, and I received patient, generous, and excellent advice from my colleague Dana Nelkin on the moral responsibility literature and from Stephen Morse about general criminal law principles and the treatment of insanity, addiction, and provocation. The roundtable was a success and launched a set of research and teaching interests for me.

In 2008, Dana and I co-taught a graduate seminar on these issues about partial responsibility, and I revisited many of the same issues in a 2011 graduate seminar, which Dana regularly attended and which led to many discussions of the material. In 2016, Dana and I co-taught a seminar on blame, which partially overlapped with issues addressed here. In all three cases, I learned a great deal from Dana and our graduate students. In the 2008 seminar, Dana and I first articulated the fair opportunity conception of responsibility, which eventually led to our article "Fairness and the Architecture of Responsibility,"[12] and has served as the foundation for much

---

[10] Some of the most regressive aspects of Proposition 21 have been modified, though some of these modifications are themselves subject to constitutional challenge. I note some of these developments briefly in Chapter 12.

[11] David O. Brink, "Immaturity, Normative Competence, and Juvenile Transfer," *Texas Law Review* 82 (2004): 1555–85.

[12] Brink and Nelkin, "Fairness and the Architecture."

of my subsequent work on these issues, and the 2016 seminar led to our article "The Nature and Significance of Blame."[13]

8. Acknowledgments

In developing the ideas in this book over many years, I have acquired a number of intellectual debts, which it is a pleasure for me to acknowledge. Four debts stand out, above others—to Dana Nelkin, Gary Watson, Stephen Morse, and Michael Moore. My greatest debt is to Dana. She has patiently shared her expertise about the moral responsibility literature with me, gently correcting my mistakes and pointing me toward relevant literature. Moreover, I learned much from her own rational abilities conception of moral responsibility, with which I have considerable sympathy.[14] We have a shared interest in the intersection of moral psychology and criminal law, which we have pursued in conversation, in the classroom, and in two research collaborations—one on the fair opportunity conception of responsibility and one on the nature and significance of blame. I doubt that this book would exist without Dana's intellectual and moral support. Gary's writings have exerted a tremendous influence on me. He has produced a remarkable stream of substantive and rich essays on various aspects of responsibility that have helped shape the agenda for many of us and whose influence will be readily apparent at many points in this book. As I mentioned above, Stephen provided invaluable orientation and advice about the criminal law literature at an early stage, just as I was getting started thinking about these issues and organizing the 2003 conference at the University of San Diego Law School. He has continued to be warmly supportive as I have gradually shed my intellectual training wheels. His own work on many of the topics discussed here has been very influential for me, both when we agree and when we disagree. Both the substance and systematicity of Michael's own work on the normative foundations of the criminal law have served as an important influence and model for me, and his friendship, both personal and professional, has sustained me over the years in working through the nature and implications of the fair opportunity conception of responsibility. I've certainly learned more about the structure of the criminal law from Michael than anyone else, and I hope he sees his influence here.

---

[13] David O. Brink and Dana K. Nelkin, "The Nature and Significance of Blame" in *The Oxford Handbook of Moral Psychology*, ed. J. Doris and M. Vargas (New York: Oxford University Press, 2021).
[14] See Nelkin, *Making Sense of Freedom and Responsibility*.

Unfortunately, the University of California, San Diego does not have a law school. However, I've been fortunate to have been affiliated with the University of San Diego Law School for over 20 years. Their Institute for Law and Philosophy, established by Michael, Heidi Hurd, and Larry Alexander, has been an ongoing source of jurisprudential ideas and inspiration for me. Through the Institute, I was introduced to a group of philosophically minded criminal law theorists, including Michael, Heidi, Larry, Stephen, Mitch Berman, Doug Husak, Peter Westen, Gideon Yaffe, and Kim Ferzan. They have generously included me in many of their conferences and have exposed me to important ideas in the criminal law. I'm sure that I have not learned as much from them as I could or should have. But equally important, I think, is how much I have learned from them already.

A recent but extremely significant source of influence and inspiration are my new colleagues Manuel Vargas and Monique Wonderly. Both came to UCSD only in the last few years, but their presence has already had a transformative impact on the department and my own work. Manuel and Dana attended a graduate seminar I taught on these topics in the fall of 2017. Manuel had many probing questions, which the three of us pursued inside seminar and outside at weekly coffees. I also learned a lot from attending Manuel's own seminar on the social ecology of agency in the winter of 2018 and from attending a seminar co-taught by Manuel and Dana on freedom of the will in the winter of 2020. There is considerable overlap in the views about agency and responsibility that Manuel, Dana, and I hold, and I learn as much from our differences as from our similarities. Monique arrived one year after Manuel, but it's already clear that I have much to learn from her expertise in developmental and moral psychology and from her constructive feedback on my own work and the work of others. Anchored by Dana, Manuel, and Monique, UCSD now boasts an excellent program in moral psychology, agency, and responsibility that has attracted a talented group of graduate students and hosts a stimulating series of workshops. I've learned a great deal from these interactions and look forward to learning much more in the future.

I would like to thank several groups of students at UCSD and USD for serving as willing and responsive guinea pigs as I tried out ideas here. In particular, three graduate seminars (2008, 2011, 2017), one law school seminar (2012), and five undergraduate courses (2015, 2016, 2018, 2019, and 2020) provided useful feedback on issues and readings covered here. In this connection, I would especially like to thank Craig Agule, William Albuquerque, Dallas Amico, Amy Berg, Matt Braich, Zack Brants, Rosalind Chaplin, Kathleen Connelly, Emma Duncan, Cami Koepke, Joseph Martinez, Per

Milam, Kaeley O'Shea, Erick Ramirez, Liberty Sacker, Michael Tiboris, Shawn Wang, and Honglin Zhu for sharing their own ideas and discussing mine.

Ideas in this book were tried out and discussed with audiences at various venues over the years, including philosophy departments at Ohio University, the University of Illinois, the University of Calgary, Cornell University, the University of Western Ontario, the University of California Davis, the University of California San Diego, the University of Edinburgh, the University of St. Andrews, and the Chinese University of Hong Kong; law schools at University of Bologna (honoring Michael Moore), the University of California Irvine, the University of Michigan, the University of Texas, and Yale University (honoring Larry Alexander); and at the Murphy Institute at Tulane University, the New Orleans Workshop on Agency and Responsibility, a Social Philosophy & Policy Conference on Moral Philosophy at the University of Arizona, the Rocky Mountain Ethics conference, a Moral Philosophy Seminar at Oxford University, a Forum for Legal and Political Philosophy at Cambridge University, and as a Lindley Lecture at the University of Kansas.

On these and other occasions, various people provided useful commentary and feedback. They include Craig Agule, Sarah Aikin, Larry Alexander, Dick Arneson, Amy Berg, Mitch Berman, Sarah Bernstein, Samantha Berthelette, Matt Braich, Reuven Brandt, Michael Bratman, David R. Brink, John Broome, Sarah Buss, Rosalind Chaplin, Pat Churchland, Randy Clarke, Kathleen Connelly, David Copp, Ann Cudd, Cory Davia, Dale Dorsey, John Dougherty, Linda Eggert, Ben Eggleston, David Estlund, Barry Feld, John Fischer, Guy Fletcher, Stephen Galoob, Jeff Helmreich, Scott Hershovitz, Gail Heyman, Richard Holton, Robert Hughes, Heidi Hurd, Doug Husak, Terence Irwin, Aaron James, Erin Kelly, Cami Koepke, Adam Kolber, Charlie Kurth, Brian Leiter, Robert Leventer, Hon Lam Li, Elinor Mason, Michael McKenna, Jeff McMahan, Gabe Mendlow, Richard Miller, Michael Moore, Stephen Morse, Dana Nelkin, Victoria Nourse, Marina Oshana, Derk Pereboom, Hannah Pickard, David Prendergast, Theron Pummer, Erick Ramirez, Sam Rickless, Michael Ridge, Tina Rulli, Daniel Russell, Tim Scanlon, Karl Schafer, Fred Schauer, Chip Sebens, Tommie Shelby, Ben Sheredos, David Shoemaker, Ken Simons, Paula Sliwa, Steven Sverdlik, John Symons, Jada Twedt Strabbing, Matt Talbert, Michael Tiboris, Evan Tiffany, Miles Unterreiner, Gary Watson, Peter Westen, Stephen White, Nellie Wieland, Gideon Yaffe, and Michael Zimmerman.

This book builds on and extends, sometimes with significant modification, ideas in earlier publications: (1) "Immaturity, Normative Competence, and

Juvenile Transfer" *Texas Law Review* 82 (2004): 1555–85; (2) "Retributivism and Legal Moralism" *Ratio Juris* 25 (2012): 496–512; (3) (with Dana K. Nelkin) "Fairness and the Architecture of Responsibility" *Oxford Studies in Agency and Responsibility* 1 (2013): 284–313; (4) "Responsibility, Incompetence, and Psychopathy" *Lindley Lecture* 53 (2013): 1–41. (5) "Situationism, Responsibility, and Fair Opportunity" *Social Philosophy & Policy* 30 (2013): 121–49; (6) "Partial Responsibility and Excuse" in *Moral Puzzles and Legal Perplexities*, ed. H. Hurd (New York: Cambridge University Press, 2018); (7) "The Nature and Significance of Culpability" *Criminal Law and Philosophy* 13 (2019): 347–73; (8) "The Moral Asymmetry Between Juvenile and Adult Offenders" *Criminal Law and Philosophy* 14 (2020): 223–39; (9) (with Dana K. Nelkin) "The Nature and Significance of Blame" in *The Oxford Handbook of Moral Psychology*, ed. J. Doris and M. Vargas (New York: Oxford University Press, 2021); and (10) "Responsibility, Punishment, and Predominant Retributivism" in *The Oxford Handbook of Responsibility*, ed. D. Nelkin and D. Pereboom (New York: Oxford University Press, 2021). I would like to thank the publishers of those essays for permission to make use of that material here.

I began to turn these ideas into a book manuscript while I was a Visiting Fellow at Magdalen College at Oxford University during Trinity Term 2018. I am grateful to Magdalen for providing me with the opportunity to begin drafting the book in the picturesque setting of the college and the stimulating environment of the university, free from all but the most welcome distractions. During the 2018–19 academic year I was privileged to workshop the book manuscript on four different occasions. I discussed the chapters on punishment and responsibility at a law and philosophy workshop at the University of Texas Law School and the whole manuscript at specially convened workshops at Lund University, UCSD, and Oxford University. I would like to thank the organizers of those workshops—John Deigh and Larry Sager, Matt Talbert, Dana Nelkin and Manuel Vargas, and Lisa Forsberg and Anthony Skelton— for arranging those events, which provided me with extremely valuable feedback on the project. In addition to the organizers, I would like to thank the participants in those workshops for their thoughtful comments, especially Craig Agule, Lucy Allais, Dick Arneson, Saba Bazargan-Forward, Gunnar Björnsson, Reuven Brandt, Rosalind Chaplin, Kathleen Connelly, Roger Crisp, Cory Davia, Gabriel De Marco, Tom Dougherty, Tom Douglas, Andrew Franklin-Hall, Mattias Gunnemyr, Terence Irwin, Kathryn Joyce, Alexander Kaiserman, Robert Kane, Jonathan Knutzen, Jeff McMahan, Dana Nelkin, Karen Margrethe Nielsen, David Prendergast, Janet Radcliffe-Richards, Sam Rickless, Paul Russell, Victor Tadros, Clinton Tolley, Caroline

Torpe Touborg, Manuel Vargas, Shawn Wang, Gabrielle Watson, Monique Wonderly, and Keyao Yang.

My editor at Oxford University Press, Peter Momtchiloff, provided judicious encouragement and patience on the project. I am grateful to him for securing Matt Talbert and Derk Pereboom as readers for the Press. They provided exceptionally careful, thoughtful, and constructive feedback on the penultimate draft of the book. I'm sure that I've not met all of their legitimate concerns, but their comments and concerns led to significant changes and improvements. I appreciate their encouragement and enthusiasm all the more, because the three of us are attracted to very different conceptions of responsibility. I am also grateful to the staff at the Press—especially Céline Louasli, Dharuman Bheeman, and Jen Hinchliffe—for their sensible and efficient help navigating the production process. Finally, I would like to thank Samantha Berthelette and William Albuquerque for their invaluable help in various stages of preparing and proofing the final manuscript.

Though I was able to draft the penultimate version of the book surprisingly quickly during my visiting fellowship at Magdalen in 2018, the path to the final version contained speed bumps, both anticipated and unanticipated. The workshops on the penultimate draft were spread out over the 2018–19 academic year, and they gave me many issues to think about and address. Professional and personal commitments and developments made it difficult to undertake revisions before the 2019–20 academic year ended. Then came the coronavirus pandemic of 2020, which has been deadly and disruptive for so many. But for some of us who have not been ravaged by infection, who do not work on the front lines, who have secure employment, and whose children are already grown the pandemic has simplified life and removed distractions. This discipline made it possible to complete final revisions during an intense period in the summer of 2020.

This book is dedicated to the memory of my father, David Ryrie Brink, for many reasons, but especially for showing me that the law can be intellectually rewarding and a force for good. He was a New Deal liberal whose career reflected the belief that the law can and should combat inequality, promote democracy, and secure justice and human rights. Sadly, in 2020 those are embattled ideals. I very much hope that we can restore those ideals to ascendancy.

2

The Reactive Attitudes and Responsibility

P.F. Strawson's essay "Freedom and Resentment" is a touchstone for many contemporary writers on responsibility, especially those who conceive of responsibility's natural home as in moral psychology, rather than, or, at least as much as, metaphysics.[1] In particular, Strawson's exploration of connections between responsibility and our reactive attitudes and emotions, such as guilt, indignation, and resentment, has proven extremely influential and is a useful starting point for our own discussion of responsibility and excuse.

9. Strawson and the Reactive Attitudes

Strawson's appeal to the reactive attitudes is reminiscent of eighteenth-century British moralists, such as Bishop Joseph Butler and Adam Smith, who appealed to fitting moral emotions and attitudes as a window onto virtue and vice.[2] Though Strawson laments that "talk of the moral sentiments has fallen out of favour" (79), he shows little interest in his historical antecedents. Perhaps this is understandable inasmuch as he wants to put the reactive attitudes toward somewhat different use. Whereas Butler and Smith appealed to fitting moral responses primarily as evidence about real moral distinctions between virtue and vice, Strawson sees fitting moral responses as a window onto responsibility.[3] Moreover, he believes that retrieving the connection between the reactive attitudes and responsibility promises to avoid the stalemate in the metaphysical debate between compatibilists and incompatibilists and make responsibility a part of moral psychology. Strawson's thesis linking

---

[1] Strawson, "Freedom and Resentment" 187–211. Parenthetical page references will be to the reprint in *Free Will*, ed. G. Watson (New York: Oxford University Press, 2003).

[2] Joseph Butler, *Dissertation on the Nature of Virtue*, an appendix to *The Analogy of Religion* [1736] reprinted in *Butler's Fifteen Sermons and A Dissertation on the Nature of Virtue*, ed. W.R. Matthews (London: Bell & Sons, 1953) and Adam Smith, *The Theory of the Moral Sentiments* [1759], ed. D. D. Raphael and A.L. Macfie (Oxford: Clarendon Press, 1976).

[3] However, Butler also thought that our differential reactive attitudes to the conduct of one with "mature and common understanding" and one who is an "idiot, madman, or child" reflected differential desert and revealed the connection between desert and an agent's capacities. See Butler, *Dissertation on the Nature of Virtue*, pp. 249–51.

Fair Opportunity and Responsibility. David O. Brink, Oxford University Press (2021). © David O. Brink.
DOI: 10.1093/oso/9780198859468.003.0002

the reactive attitudes and responsibility provides fertile ground for a number of different, sometimes competing, claims about the nature of responsibility and the justification of the reactive attitudes. The most important lessons to draw from Strawson's thesis have some anchor in Strawson's discussion but may not always accord with how Strawson is usually interpreted or his own considered view.

Strawson begins by introducing two opposing views about the relation between determinism and responsibility: *pessimism* and *optimism*. Pessimism is an *incompatibilist* claim, because it sees the truth of determinism as inconsistent with responsibility. Notice that pessimism needn't be pessimistic or skeptical about responsibility if it rejects determinism and embraces libertarianism. Pessimists who think that neither determinism nor indeterminism is compatible with responsibility are *skeptics*. Optimists, by contrast, are *compatibilists*, because they claim that moral responsibility is compatible with determinism. Notice that optimism, in this sense, could come in many versions, corresponding to different ways of making out the compatibilist claim.

However, Strawson also focuses critically on a particular optimist claim, one that reconciles determinism with responsibility by focusing on an *instrumental* justification of practices of praise and blame. On this view, praise and blame are justified in a *forward-looking* manner by the way these reactions minimize future harm by the wrongdoer, deter wrongdoing by others, and shape the attitudes of wrongdoers and others so as to produce better behavioral outcomes in the future (60–61). Strawson may have in mind the views of Moritz Schlick, B.F. Skinner, and J.J.C. Smart as examples of instrumental optimism.[4] In any case, he is famously critical of this instrumentalist variety of optimism. His claim is that the instrumentalist appeals to *the wrong sort of reason* for praise and blame (61–62).

To see Strawson's point, consider Amia Srinivasan's claims about the aptness of anger.[5] Anger can be a fitting response to culpable wrongdoing, such as policies or acts of political injustice. In such cases, anger seems a fitting or justified response on the part of anyone, but perhaps especially on the part of the victims of injustice. Here, anger is a backward-looking attitude, directed at the wrongs done and the attitudes of the wrongdoers. Its fittingness does not depend on the downstream consequences of expressing or even experiencing

---

[4] See Moritz Schlick, *Problems of Ethics* (New York: Prentice Hall, 1939), pp. 141–58; B.F. Skinner, *Science and Human Behavior* (New York: Macmillan, 1953); and J.J.C. Smart, "Free Will, Praise, and Blame" *Mind* 70 (1961): 291–306.

[5] Amia Srinivasan, "The Aptness of Anger" *The Journal of Political Philosophy* 26 (2018): 123–44.

anger. Even in circumstances in which it would be counter-productive to harbor or express anger, that doesn't gainsay the fittingness of anger. Similar claims apply to other reactive attitudes. They are backward-looking attitudes that appear to be fitting in virtue of someone's past conduct and the circumstances of that conduct, including the agent's quality of will and capacities. Though forward-looking considerations may be relevant to whether it's all-things-considered best to harbor or express those attitudes, they don't seem relevant to whether the attitudes are fitting. In this way, purely forward-looking rationales for the reactive attitudes may seem to provide the wrong sort of reason.

Indeed, insofar as the reactive attitudes are a window into responsibility, one might think that a purely instrumental rationale for the reactive attitudes is best understood as a kind of *fictionalism* about responsibility that is skeptical about responsibility but nonetheless treats our practices of praise and blame as useful fictions, worth preserving. If so, we might doubt whether instrumentalism is best conceived as a form of optimism.

One question is whether forward-looking rationales for responsibility, as such, involve the wrong sort of reason, or whether the problem is with a specifically instrumental rationale. This issue may affect our assessment of Strawson's own account of whether and, if so, how the reactive attitudes can be justified, which has some broadly consequentialist aspects.

Strawson apparently wants to defend a non-instrumental conception of optimism and do so in a way that bypasses traditional debates about freedom of the will and determinism. Often, that debate is framed in terms of the compatibility of freedom of the will and the truth of causal determinism—the thesis that every event is determined or necessitated by the laws of nature and the prior history of the world. Compatibilists insist that freedom is compatible with the truth of causal determinism, whereas incompatibilists deny that the two are compatible.[6] Incompatibilists who are also determinists are hard determinists, embracing skepticism about free will and responsibility.[7]

---

[6] A fuller discussion of incompatibilism would need to distinguish between *leeway* incompatibilism, which insists that determinism precludes the kind of alternate possibilities required by freedom and responsibility, and *source* incompatibilism, which insists that determinism prevents agents from being the ultimate source of their actions. For discussion, see Derk Pereboom, *Free Will, Agency, and Meaning in Life* (Oxford: Clarendon Press, 2014), p. 4 and Kevin Timpe, "Leeway vs. Sourcehood Conceptions of Free Will" in *The Routledge Companion to Free Will*, ed. K. Timpe, M. Griffith, and N. Levy (New York: Routledge, 2017).

[7] This is a traditional way of thinking about hard determinism. However, some hard determinists distinguish different kinds of responsibility and claim only that determinism precludes some kinds of responsibility, not others. For instance, in recent writings Pereboom claims that whereas determinism does preclude the kind of responsibility necessary for "basic desert," it does not preclude other kinds of responsibility, such as instrumentalism about responsibility or attributive responsibility. See, e.g., Derk

However, some incompatibilists are libertarians, rejecting determinism and embracing indeterminism.[8] But it is not entirely clear how indeterminism, in the form of uncaused actions or contra-causal agency, can ground responsibility. If an agent's will is not itself causally determined by past events or states of the agent, it's not clear why we should impute actions and their consequences to her, much less treat her as a legitimate target of praise and blame. Strawson refers to libertarianism as "panicky metaphysics" (80). If these worries about libertarianism are well founded, it will not be a promising way to defend realism about freedom and responsibility.[9]

Many parties to the traditional debates associate freedom of the will and responsibility; they either identify the two or understand freedom of the will as whatever quality of the will is needed for responsibility. So many compatibilists believe that both freedom and responsibility are compatible with determinism, and many free will skeptics are also skeptics about responsibility.

However, some later writers, such as Harry Frankfurt, distinguish between freedom and responsibility and combine skepticism, or at least agnosticism, about freedom with realism about responsibility.[10] We'll discuss the details of Frankfurt's position later (§28). For present purposes, the relevant point is that Frankfurt associates freedom of the will with the principle of alternate possibilities. Freedom requires the capacity to act otherwise than one does. If so, freedom seems incompatible with determinism, because determinism seems to rule out alternate possibilities. Frankfurt describes cases in which agents seem to be responsible despite lacking the freedom to do otherwise. If an agent is inclined to act in a certain way for certain reasons and does so of his own volition, then we are inclined to view his action as responsible, even if there is a *counterfactual intervener* who would have intervened in the agent's life to

Pereboom, "Responsibility, Regret, and Protest" *Oxford Studies in Agency and Responsibility* 4 (2017): 121–40. This needn't force us to revise our conception of hard determinism, because we can represent Pereboom as a hard determinist about the responsibility required for desert and a compatibilist about determinism and instrumental or attributive responsibility. The interesting question is whether those are forms of compatibilism worth wanting or the best we can do. I don't think so, as I argue in this book. First, there is a direct explanation of the fittingness of the reactive attitudes in terms of desert. Desert presupposes only accountability, and fair opportunity provides a plausible compatibilist conception of accountability and, hence, desert. Second, I think that instrumentalists either provide the wrong sort of reason for responsibility ascriptions or that these ascriptions depend on unnecessarily indirect and speculative claims about the benefits of making them. Third, I think that attributive responsibility is insufficient to establish accountability.

   [8] See, e.g., Robert Kane, *The Significance of Free Will* (New York: Oxford University Press, 1996).

   [9] Realism about free will and responsibility has an ecumenical sense in which it is simply the denial of skepticism about freedom and responsibility and a specifically meta-normative sense in which it treats facts about freedom and responsibility as response-independent facts. My own view about responsibility is realist in both senses. I discuss the meta-normative thesis in §13. Here, I'm concerned with realism in the ecumenical sense.

   [10] Frankfurt, "Alternate Possibilities" 829–39.

ensure that he acted that way, had he decided not to. Such cases seem to show that there can be moral responsibility in the absence of alternate possibilities and freedom of the will.

Where does Strawson fit into these debates? On one reading, Strawson is a certain kind of compatibilist about freedom and responsibility, who eschews both libertarian incompatibilism and instrumentalist versions of compatibilism. However, on another reading, we might see Strawson as implicitly agreeing that responsibility does not require any metaphysical claims about freedom of the will, because responsibility and freedom are distinct concepts and responsibility is tied to the reactive attitudes.

10. The Reactive Attitudes

Though Strawson's sympathies lie with a non-instrumentalist conception of compatibilism, he seems to want to bypass traditional metaphysical debates about compatibilism and incompatibilism. His proposal is to focus on the reactive attitudes and the way they mediate interpersonal relationships. The reactive attitudes are or involve emotional responses typically directed at someone in the context of something that person has done. Many reactive attitudes are directed toward *another*, such as resentment, indignation, and blame. But they can also be *self-directed*, as reflected in cases of guilt, remorse, and shame. Strawson includes among the reactive attitudes malice, contempt, love, pride, gratitude, anger, resentment, indignation, and forgiveness (62–63, 66). But these seem to be examples of a large and potentially very heterogeneous class, rather than an exhaustive list (64).

Not all reactive attitudes have a direct connection with moral responsibility. Consider *regret*. Bernard Williams describes the case of a conscientious truck driver who, through no fault of his own, hits and kills a child who has darted into the street.[11] As Williams claims, it is appropriate for the driver to feel a kind of agent-regret at being the instrument of the child's death, which is distinct both from the regret or horror that bystanders might feel in witnessing the accident and from guilt for having been responsible for wrongdoing. Agent-regret seems to be one reactive attitude that does not presuppose responsibility. Nor is it clear that love, gratitude, or anger presupposes responsibility.

---

[11] Bernard Williams, "Moral Luck" reprinted in Williams, *Moral Luck* (Cambridge: Cambridge University Press, 1981), p. 28.

To understand responsibility, we should focus on a subset of reactive attitudes that are *moralized* and involve praise and blame.[12] Consider the difference between anger and resentment. As we observed, anger can be a fitting response to culpable wrongdoing, such as acts of injustice. In such cases, anger seems a fitting response on the part of anyone, but perhaps especially on the part of victims of injustice. It is common to treat cases of anger that are responsive to moral wrongdoing as a special category of anger, such as blame, resentment, indignation, or moral outrage. However, although anger can be a fitting response to culpable wrongdoing, not all fitting anger is moralized in this way. It may be fitting for me to be upset and angry if the home I have just built is destroyed in an earthquake or if I am laid off from my job as the result of a viral pandemic. In such cases, no one in particular is the target of my anger, but anger seems justified or fitting. In other cases, there may be a target without the anger being moralized. I might be justified in momentary upset or anger if a small child or an exuberant puppy damages a treasured keepsake, but it would be inappropriate to resent or be indignant at the child or puppy. Blame and resentment seem inappropriate inasmuch as neither the child nor the puppy is responsible or accountable for the damage he does. Unlike anger, which can but need not be sensitive to accountability and perceived desert, blame, resentment, and indignation do seem sensitive to accountability and perceived desert. They are essentially moralized forms of anger. Appeal to the reactive attitudes promises to shed light on responsibility only if we focus on moralized reactive attitudes that involve praise and blame.[13]

It might also help to distinguish within the class of reactive attitudes between those that are *thick* and those that are *thin*. Thick reactive attitudes, such as gratitude or pride, are ones that are tightly tied to particular contexts and relationships and have fairly determinate descriptive content. By contrast, thin reactive attitudes are more invariant with respect to contexts and

---

[12] Wallace rightly recognizes that we can only use the reactive attitudes as a window onto moral responsibility if we restrict our attention to some subset of reactive attitudes. His proposal is to focus on reactive attitudes to breaches of expectations, demands, or obligations. See Wallace, *Responsibility and the Moral Sentiments*, ch. 2, esp. p. 33. However, I don't think that this is the right restriction on the reactive attitudes. First, many interpersonal relationships involve expectations and demands without obviously involving moral responsibility. Second, breach of obligations won't always involve moral responsibility; paradigm cases of excuse are cases in which an agent has engaged in wrongdoing but is nonetheless not responsible. I think we do better to restrict our focus to the reactive attitudes that involve praise or blame.

[13] This will be a problem for Shoemaker's response-dependent interpretation of Strawson's thesis, which grounds responsibility in anger responses. See David Shoemaker, "Response-Dependent Responsibility; or, A Funny Thing Happened on the Way to Blame" *Philosophical Review* 126 (2017): 481–527. A response-dependent conception of responsibility that appeals to anger will encounter problems of extensional adequacy; in particular, it is likely to yield an implausibly over-inclusive conception of responsibility.

relationships and apply to very different kinds of behaviors. Condemnation is a comparatively thin attitude, as are praise, blame, and punishment. This distinction is one of degree, but Strawson's link between the reactive attitudes and responsibility seems to apply to both thick and thin attitudes.[14]

Blame and praise are not complements. Blame seems fitting for *suberogatory* actions and attitudes for which the agent is responsible. But praise is not fitting for all non-suberogatory actions and attitudes for which the agent is responsible, because praise may not be fitting for many merely permissible actions, no matter how responsible the agent is. To be praiseworthy, it is not enough that the agent was responsible for performing her duty, it seems that the conduct must be *supererogatory* or that the performance of one's duty involved difficulty or sacrifice.

Though responsibility can be studied by looking at reactive attitudes involving either praise or blame, there are several reasons to focus on those that involve blame. Strawson is interested in our practices of excuse, and excuse is only appropriate for actions that would otherwise be blameworthy. We may suspend positive reactive attitudes toward actions that are supererogatory but for which the agent is not responsible, but we do not excuse such agents. Moreover, it is reasonable to count criminal law principles and doctrines as expressing our reactive attitudes and practices, but the criminal law concerns alleged wrongdoing of some kind, for which the agent is potentially blameworthy.[15] So, the criminal law is essentially concerned with negative reactive attitudes and practices involving blame.

11. Excuse, Exemption, and Compatibilism

In discussing negative reactive attitudes involving blame, Strawson asks us to distinguish two different kinds of cases in which we might *suspend* the reactive attitudes—cases in which the agent is otherwise normal but nonetheless acted wrongly due to some specific feature of the case in question, such as inadvertence or compulsion, and cases in which the agent lies outside the scope of the reactive attitudes quite generally, say, because she is immature or insane

---

[14] My distinction between thick and thin reactive attitudes is similar to and draws on the tradition of distinguishing between thick ethical concepts, such as bravery and honesty, and thin ethical concepts, such as the good, the right, or the obligatory. See Philippa Foot, *Virtues and Vices* (Los Angeles, CA: University of California Press, 1978) and Bernard Williams, *Ethics and the Limits of Philosophy* (Cambridge, MA: Harvard University Press, 1985).

[15] Strawson discusses punishment in "Freedom and Resentment," p. 78.

(64–66). Strawson suggests that in this second kind of case we not only suspend the reactive attitudes but also adopt an *objective attitude* toward the agent. The objective attitude, it seems, can include the sort of forward-looking concerns with behavior management that are characteristic of instrumentalism, though it's unclear if the objective attitude reduces to an instrumental one. One might identify the first sort of case as involving *excuse* and the second sort of case as involving *exemption*. These are not Strawson's labels. But others, including Gary Watson, have suggested this way of understanding the contrast.[16] A few observations about this contrast are in order.

First, we should not assume that exemptions are not excuses. Strawson includes insanity among the exemptions, but the criminal law treats insanity as an excuse. As we will discuss at greater length below, the criminal law censures and sanctions wrongdoing for which the agent is culpable or responsible. These institutionalized responses to culpable wrongdoing themselves involve reactive practices and attitudes, but presumably they also influence our more informal interpersonal attitudes. So, appealing to criminal law practices of blame and punishment can be instructive. Blame and punishment are treated as fitting responses to wrongdoing for which the agent is culpable or responsible. There are two main sorts of defense that an agent might invoke in response to potential blame and punishment. *Justifications* deny wrongdoing, whereas *excuses* deny culpability or responsibility. But that means that excuse and responsibility are inversely related, as we postulated in our working hypothesis (§§1, 5).

- *The Responsibility-Excuse Biconditional*: An agent is responsible for wrongdoing iff she is not excused for it.

According to this biconditional, an agent is responsible for misconduct for which she has no excuse, and she is excused for misconduct for which she is not responsible. But, on this way of thinking, all failures of responsibility, or at least all failures of responsibility for wrongdoing, are excuses. This means that exemptions, if they are systematic failures of responsibility, must also be excuses. So, we should not assume that exemptions and excuses are disjoint classes.

Second, Strawson's examples are not exhaustive of the possibilities. Strawson partitions cases into those in which the reactive attitudes are generally disabled in regard to a particular agent and those in which they are selectively, not

---

[16] Gary Watson, "Responsibility and the Limits of Evil: Variations on a Strawsonian Theme" reprinted in Watson, *Agency and Answerability* (Oxford: Clarendon Press, 2004), p. 224.

generally, disabled due to some specific feature of the case, such as inadvertence or compulsion. But the reactive attitudes can be disabled in other ways, in particular, in other ways that are selective but nonetheless variable in psychological or temporal scope. Perhaps an agent is temporarily incompetent due to dehydration, depression, or hypnosis. Or perhaps she is disabled in an ongoing but selective way because she is subject to specific irresistible urges or paralyzing fears. If a glutton had genuinely irresistible urges, he might be disabled in contexts involving food, but not in other contexts. Children may exhibit generalized incapacity that is not just episodic, but nonetheless the incapacity is a developmental phase and, hence, temporary in nature.

One response to both kinds of issues is to consider all the cases as ones involving potential excuses with varying degrees of generality or selectivity. On such a proposal, exemptions are just comparatively global or standing excuses.

Strawson notes that excusing and exempting conditions depend on specific failings, either in individual cases or with the agent in general. As such, they don't presuppose the falsity of determinism, which is a thesis that applies to all cases (67–69). But if our excusing practices don't depend on the falsity of determinism, then neither do the reactive attitudes themselves. To put it another way, if hard determinism were true, we should suspend all retributive reactive attitudes and excuse everyone, because no one is responsible. But the criminal law and our moralized reactive attitudes are *selective* about when to excuse. We excuse for particular kinds of incapacity, such as insanity, immaturity, or duress. But then our reactive attitudes and associated practices of excuse presuppose some version of compatibilism. This presupposition could be mistaken, but it would be a deeply embedded mistake, requiring an error theory to overturn (§1).

Suggestive as Strawson's discussion is, it does not provide a *comprehensive theory* of excusing conditions. He cites examples of excuse involving insanity, immaturity, and duress. But he does not explain why these conditions are excusing or say if this list is exhaustive, and there is no reason to think that it is. In any case, we need to know *which* conditions excuse and *why* or *how* they are excusing. Articulating a comprehensive conception of excuse is one major goal of this book. Without such a theory, it's hard to know if our reactive attitudes and their limits, as reflected in our practices of excuse, are justified.

12. Justifying the Reactive Attitudes

Strawson's own position on the justificatory issue is frustratingly elusive. He seems to recognize the possibility for *internal or local* justification or skepticism, but not the possibility of *external or global* justification or skepticism.

Inside the general structure or web of human attitudes and feelings of which I have been speaking, there is endless room for modification, redirection, criticism, and justification. But questions of justification are internal to the structure and relate to modifications internal to it. The existence of the general framework of attitudes itself is something we are given with the fact of human society. As a whole, it neither calls for, nor permits, an external 'rational' justification. [78]

Strawson does not say here why external or global justification about the reactive attitudes is impossible. He does suggest at a couple of points that we cannot give up on the reactive attitudes altogether (68–69), in which case he might think that the question about justification has no point.

Is this true? Watson points to Mahatma Gandhi and Martin Luther King as examples of people that led personally and politically engaged lives that were not mediated by retributive reactive attitudes of blame and punishment.[17] But even if this is a fair description of Gandhi and King, it shows only that they avoided particular reactive attitudes. Indeed, Watson says only that they managed to live without "vindictiveness" and "malice." But one can hold others responsible and even blame them without being vindictive or malicious. Indeed, Gandhi and King clearly recognized and condemned injustices that required correction, and it's hard to believe they could stand firm against injustice without sentiments of indignation. But one can be indignant without being vindictive or malicious. And, of course, there's no reason not to attribute positive reactive attitudes such as pride and gratitude to them. So even if Gandhi and King illustrate how it's possible to forego selected reactive attitudes, they don't show that it's possible to live without the reactive attitudes altogether.

Is a more systematic suspension of the reactive attitudes possible? That would seem to require a form of *abolitionism* about the reactive attitudes or at least those involving moral responsibility. What would it mean to live lives in which we interact with others not mediated by attitudes such as praise, blame, resentment, indignation, guilt, and shame? As Strawson suggests, abolitionism may not be consistent with the sort of interpersonal relationships with which we are familiar and which we value.[18]

Even if we could not help but participate in the culture and practice of reactive attitudes, that would not show that the practices and attitudes were

---

[17] Watson, "Responsibility and the Limits of Evil," pp. 257–58.

[18] For attempts to explore the possibility and significance of abolitionism, see Pereboom, *Free Will, Agency, and Meaning in Life* and Per Milam, *Abolitionism about the Reactive Attitudes* (UCSD Ph.D., 2013).

justified. In *A Treatise of Human Nature* David Hume famously says that he finds he cannot sustain his skeptical conclusions about the external world, causation, or personal identity outside the confines of his study.[19] Perhaps wholesale skepticism about the reactive attitudes is a skepticism that cannot be lived, at least not outside the confines of one's study. But I'm not sure that shows external or global skepticism to be incoherent, as Strawson sometimes suggests.

At other times, Strawson suggests that the question of global skepticism is coherent and tries to answer it by appeal to the value the commitment to the reactive attitudes adds to our lives.

> This commitment [our natural human commitment to ordinary interper-sonal attitudes] is part of the general framework of human life, not some-thing that can come up for review as particular cases can come up for review within this general framework ... [I]f we could imagine what we cannot have, viz. a choice in this matter, then we could choose rationally only in the light of an assessment of the gains and losses to human life, its enrichment or impoverishment; and the truth or falsity of a general thesis of determinism would not bear on the rationality of *this* choice.   [70]

This suggests that a broadly forward-looking justification of the reactive attitudes is possible, one that appeals to the value of the interpersonal rela-tionships in which the reactive attitudes are constituents.

A natural worry is that this forward-looking response to external or global skepticism invokes the wrong sort of reason, just as Strawson himself suggests that the instrumentalist optimist invokes the wrong sort of reason for the reactive attitudes and practices. I see two ways for Strawson to reply to this worry.

First, he could try to distinguish the nature and adequacy of different kinds of forward-looking rationales for our practices. Perhaps he could say that the forward-looking rationale he has in mind is that lives lived in ways regulated by reactive attitudes are necessary for various familiar interpersonal relation-ships without which our lives would not be worth living or otherwise severely impoverished. He might try to contrast this kind of consequentialist argument with the one the instrumental optimist provides, which appeals to values such as security, safety, and deterrence. But it is not immediately clear how

[19] David Hume, *A Treatise of Human Nature* [1738], ed. P.H. Nidditch (Oxford: Clarendon Press, 1978), Book I, Part iv, § 7 (I.iv.7).

significant this contrast is. This strategy needs to be spelled out further before it can be evaluated.

Alternatively, Strawson could claim that it's not so much *which* consequences matter as *when* you appeal to them. Perhaps he thinks that consequences cannot be appealed to in justifications made within the framework, but they can be invoked to justify the framework as a whole. If so, his claim would be very much like the claim John Rawls makes in his important article "Two Concepts of Rules" when he introduces a rule utilitarian justification of punishment.[20] Rawls asks us to distinguish the *legislative* issues of whether to punish conduct, which conduct to punish, and how to punish such conduct from the *judicial* issue about the conditions under which particular individuals ought to be punished. He thinks that forward-looking utilitarian considerations are relevant to addressing these legislative issues, but that only backward-looking retributive considerations are relevant to addressing the judicial issue.

> The decision whether or not to use law rather than some other mechanism of social control, and the decision as to what laws to have and what penalties to assign, may be settled by utilitarian arguments; but if one decides to have laws then one has decided on something whose working in particular cases is retributive in form.[21]

Here, Rawls asks us to distinguish the reasons for having a practice in the first place and the reasons that support certain applications of the practice. He thinks that by recognizing this distinction we can reconcile retributive and utilitarian perspectives on punishment. The practice of punishment is such that the justification for punishing offenders within the practice is backward-looking and retributive, rather than forward-looking. But if we ask why we should have a system of punishment that operates this way, Rawls thinks, forward-looking utilitarian considerations become relevant. Perhaps Strawson is making a Rawlsian claim here about how consequentialist considerations are not relevant within the framework of the reactive attitudes but are relevant when addressing external or global skeptical challenges.

It's not clear why Rawls thinks that prospective or legislative issues can be neatly sequestered from retrospective or judicial ones. The legislature may

---

[20] John Rawls, "Two Concepts of Rules" *Philosophical Review* 64 (1955): 3–32 and reprinted in John Rawls, *Collected Papers*, ed. S. Freeman (Cambridge, MA: Harvard University Press, 1999).
[21] Rawls, "Two Concepts of Rules," p. 684.

make law pursuant to various purposes or principles, which it becomes the judiciary's job to interpret and apply. But the process of judicial interpretation of legislation frequently involves appeal to the legislature's purposes or principles in enacting legislation. So the judicial perspective is not insulated completely from the legislative one.[22] Likewise, in the case of reasons for a practice such as punishment and the reasons for punishing individuals within that practice. Presumably, the prospective perspective asks what's the optimal set of laws and judicial institutions and practices for enforcing them, and it's not clear why optimal institutional design wouldn't allow the judiciary to depart from retributive constraints when it would be clearly optimal to do so. It's doubtful that utilitarian reasons for having a practice will justify a practice that operates in a strictly retributive fashion.

One might defend consequentialist sequestration with an analogy from officiating in sports.[23] It might seem that officials in athletic contests can and should apply the rules of a game strictly in all cases, without invoking the reasons for adopting the rules in the first place. Perhaps some rules are adopted to ensure player safety, promote competitive contests, or elicit player strategy and skill. But once the rules are in place, so the analogy holds, officials should apply the rules as written and not resolve contested plays by direct appeal to the reasons for adopting the rules. But this ignores the way in which officials in sports can and do appeal to the principles rationalizing the adoption of rules to determine whether and, if so, how to apply the rules in hard cases. For instance, the interpretation of rules concerning penalties and fouls often becomes lax near the end of competitive games, especially in a playoff context.[24]

13. Realism and Response-dependence about Strawson's Thesis

One might avoid the consequentialist response to skepticism without ignoring the skeptical worry altogether. One could undertake what Strawson does not,

---

[22] This is a recurrent theme in Dworkin's conception of adjudication. See, e.g., Ronald Dworkin, *Law's Empire* (Cambridge, MA: Harvard University Press, 1986). For discussion, see David O. Brink, "Originalism and Constructive Interpretation" in *The Legacy of Ronald Dworkin*, ed. S. Sciaraffa and W. Waluchow (Oxford: Clarendon Press, 2016).

[23] Thanks to Manuel Vargas for suggesting this analogy.

[24] For discussion, see, e.g., John Russell, "Are Rules All an Umpire Has to Work With?" *Journal of the Philosophy of Sport* 26 (1999): 142–60; Mitchell Berman, "On Interpretivism and Formalism in Sports Officiating: From General to Particular Jurisprudence" *Journal of the Philosophy of Sport* 38 (2011): 177–96 and "Let 'em Play: A Study in the Jurisprudence of Sport" *The Georgetown Law Journal* 99 (2011): 1325–69.

THE REACTIVE ATTITUDES AND RESPONSIBILITY 39

namely, a comprehensive theory about excusing conditions that not only shows that they do not track determinism but also explains why and how familiar excusing conditions excuse, hopefully providing a more systematic account of the excuses. That is a program that Strawson suggests but does not himself pursue.

As we have seen, Strawson links responsibility and reactive attitudes, such as those of resentment and indignation, in a biconditional fashion.

> *Strawson's Thesis*: Reactive attitudes involving blame and praise are appropriate just in case the targets of these attitudes are responsible.

As we noted earlier (§1), Strawson's thesis can be interpreted in two very different ways, depending on which half of the biconditional has explanatory priority. We can see this if we distinguish the biconditional just in case or if and only if <iff> and the explanatory biconditional if and only if and insofar as <iffi> in which the second *relatum* grounds and explains the first.

(a) Agents are responsible for their actions iffi they are apt targets of the reactive attitudes.

(b) Agents are apt targets for the reactive attitudes iffi they are responsible for their conduct.

A *response-dependent* reading of Strawson's thesis embraces (a) and claims that it is the appropriateness of the reactive attitudes that explains when and why their targets are responsible. By contrast, a *realist* reading of Strawson's thesis embraces (b) and claims that it is the responsibility of agents for their conduct that grounds and explains the appropriateness of the reactive attitudes toward them. In particular, the realist is committed to claiming that responsibility can be specified in response-independent terms.

However, (a) is necessary but not sufficient for response-dependence.[25] The response-dependent interpretation of Strawson's thesis cannot simply say that

---

[25] I take Todd to be agreeing when he notes that a libertarian could accept (a). See Patrick Todd, "Strawson, Moral Responsibility and the Order of Explanation: An Intervention" *Ethics* 127 (2016): 208–40, esp. pp. 217–20. In effect, Todd poses a dilemma for response-dependence about Strawson's thesis. Either (1) response-dependence takes a *reductive* form in which responsibility is grounded in our *actual reactive dispositions*, or (2) it takes a *non-reductive* form in which responsibility is grounded in *fitting reactive dispositions*. He thinks that (1) has counter-intuitive consequences because it implies that children or the insane would become responsible if only our reactive attitudes were to change, and he thinks that (2) fails to avoid the sort of metaphysical issues in the debate between compatibilists and incompatibilists. I agree with both claims, but I think that to be a genuine response-dependent view, it

we explain responsibility in terms of appropriate reactive attitudes, because that leaves open the possibility that what makes the reactive attitudes appropriate or fitting is itself a response-independent feature of agents or their conduct. To be genuinely response-dependent, there must be no response-independent justification of our attributions of responsibility or the reactive attitudes. Responsibility judgments must simply reflect those dispositions to respond to others that are constitutive of various kinds of interpersonal relationships. Particular expressions of a reactive attitude might be mistaken as inconsistent with a larger pattern of responses, but the patterns of response are not themselves corrigible in light of any other standard. Similarly, particular ascriptions of responsibility might be mistaken in light of a larger pattern of ascriptions of responsibility, but the patterns themselves are not corrigible in light of any other standards. Responsibility judgments simply reflect those principled dispositions to respond to others that are constitutive of various kinds of interpersonal relationships.

If so, the response-dependent reading of Strawson's thesis must claim that individual reactive attitudes by individual members of a moral community are apt iffi they conform to relevant patterns in the reactive attitudes of members of that community. It follows from this conception of response-dependence that fitting reactive attitudes and responsibility may need to be relativized to different communities or perhaps even different individuals. This relativism underscores the restricted sense in which the response-dependent conception of Strawson's thesis permits the justification of the reactive attitudes and ascriptions of responsibility. Response-dependence licenses local fallibility and justification, but not systematic fallibility and justification.

By contrast, a realist interpretation of Strawson's thesis embraces (b) and stresses the way that the reactive attitudes make sense in light of, and so *presuppose*, responsibility. According to the realist interpretation of Strawson's thesis, negative reactive attitudes, such as guilt, resentment, and blame presuppose that the target of these attitudes is responsible for her conduct. These reactive attitudes are justified and fitting insofar as the target of these attitudes engaged in some kind of wrongdoing for which she was responsible. A realist reading promises to justify the reactive attitudes in a way in which a response-dependent reading cannot, but the realist reading also makes the justification of the reactive attitudes hostage to the existence of a plausible conception of responsibility that can be specified independently of the reactive attitudes.

---

must be reductive. For a discussion of reductive and non-reductive forms of response-dependence, see David O. Brink, "The Significance of Desire" *Oxford Studies in Metaethics* 3 (2008): 5–46.

This contrast between response-dependent and realist readings of Strawson's thesis parallels contrasting accounts of the priority of *holding accountable* and *being accountable* and between *treating as responsible* and *being responsible*.[26] In these cases, response-dependence asserts the priority of holding accountable or treating as responsible, while realism insists on the priority of being accountable or being responsible. According to response-dependence, being accountable or responsible is ultimately grounded in our practices of holding accountable or responsible. By contrast, realism claims that our practices of holding accountable or responsible are only justified when they track response-independent facts about accountability and responsibility.

Part of the background to this debate between realist and response-dependent interpretations of Strawson's thesis is the Euthyphro problem. In Plato's dialogue *Euthyphro* Socrates and his interlocutor Euthyphro discuss the virtue of piety, which they both conceive as a part of justice.[27] At one point, Euthyphro defines piety (and, by extension, justice) as what all the gods love (9c–11b). Socrates accepts the biconditional claim that something is pious (just) iff it is loved by all the gods. But he thinks that this biconditional relationship admits of two different interpretations, and this leads Socrates to pose the Euthyphro problem. Does the love of the gods make something pious or just, or do the gods love that which is pious and just because it is pious and just? If what explains and grounds piety and justice is the love of the gods, our conception of piety and justice is voluntarist and response-dependent. Alternately, if the gods love what they do because it is pious or just, our conception of piety and justice is realist, because piety and justice are prior to and independent of divine attitudes. Socrates defends a realist response to the Euthyphro problem. He believes that the voluntarist or response-dependent response makes piety and justice depend on the contingent and arbitrary attitudes of the gods. On this conception, if the gods were to change their attitudes, piety and justice would change. Socrates rejects this picture of both morality and the gods. He thinks that the attitudes of the gods are principled and responsive to real moral features of the objects of their attitudes. On this realist conception, the moral worth of actions and individuals is what renders divine love fitting.

We can see these issues replicated in the debate between response-dependent and realist interpretations of Strawson's thesis. The response-dependent

---

[26] Wolf, *Freedom within Reason*, pp. 15–16; Wallace, *Responsibility and the Moral Sentiments*, pp. 87–93.

[27] Plato, *Euthyphro* in *Plato: Complete Works*, ed. J. Cooper (Indianapolis, IN: Hackett, 1997).

interpretation grounds responsibility in patterns in our moralized reactive attitudes and our dispositions to have these attitudes. To be truly response-dependent, these attitudes must not be explained as perceptions of the responsibility of the targets of those attitudes. Response-dependence makes responsibility depend on contingent psychological facts. If appraisers were to change their reactive dispositions, the facts about responsibility would change. Moreover, we have no way of making sense of the idea that the reactive dispositions of appraisers might be mistaken in a systematic way. Alternatively, we might be realists and claim that our reactive attitudes are or at least aspire to be principled, responsive to facts about when the targets of our attitudes are responsible. This represents responsibility, or at least our beliefs about responsibility, as prior to and independent of our reactive attitudes. But the realist owes us an explanation of what these response-independent facts about responsibility are that render the moralized reactive attitudes fitting.

The crucial question in deciding between these two different interpretations of Strawson's thesis is whether our study of excuses and exemptions leads to a conception of responsibility that can be specified independently of our reactive attitudes and that can serve to ground or justify those attitudes. If so, this favors a realist conception of responsibility. If not, it favors a response-dependent conception.

One question is how Strawson understands his own thesis and whether he is attracted to response-dependence or realism about the relation between the reactive attitudes and responsibility. Strawson is often understood as embracing response-dependence, and with good reason.[28] First, response-dependence fits with Strawson's view that our reactive attitudes and ascriptions of responsibility, as a whole, do not admit of external justification—they are the ultimate ground of responsibility. By contrast, realism implies that the reactive attitudes are justified iffi their targets are in fact responsible, which depends on facts that go beyond our reactive attitudes. Second, response-dependence provides one explanation of Strawson's belief that his appeal to the reactive attitudes avoids the stalemate between compatibilists and incompatibilists. The response-dependent interpretation of Strawson's thesis promises to do this, because it grounds responsibility in our reactive attitudes and practices, independently of any metaphysical commitments. By contrast, the

---

[28] Watson understands Strawson as endorsing the response-dependent reading; see Watson, "Responsibility and the Limits of Evil," pp. 220–22. Wallace attributes the response-dependent reading to Strawson and endorses it himself; see Wallace, *Responsibility and the Moral Sentiments*, pp. 19, 87–93. For a recent defense of response-dependence, see Shoemaker, "Response-Dependent Responsibility."

realist reading implies that the legitimacy of the reactive attitudes is hostage to the existence of a plausible conception of responsibility that is prior to and independent of our reactive attitudes.

But even if Strawson's sympathies lie with response-dependence, rather than realism, we might reach a different conclusion on the philosophical merits. For it does seem, as the realist claims, that the fittingness of the reactive attitudes depends on the responsibility of the targets, not the other way around. Moreover, it does seem that we can make sense of the possibility that the reactive attitudes might be mistaken if there are no response-independent facts about responsibility in virtue of which those reactive attitudes are fitting and that, as a result, we can ask for the justification of the reactive attitudes. But to be fallibilists about the reactive attitudes and to seek a justification for them requires accepting realism. A realist reading promises to justify the reactive attitudes in a way in which a response-dependent reading cannot, but the realist reading also owes us a plausible conception of responsibility that can be specified in response-independent terms. Because the realist interpretation of Strawson's thesis promises to ground and justify the reactive attitudes in a way in which the response-dependent reading cannot, we should try to defend a realist reading if we can, treating the response-dependent interpretation as a fallback position if the realist reading fails.

Actually, response-dependence is just one meta-normative response to skepticism about the prospects of realism. Normative realism is committed to the existence of response-independent facts in a given normative domain. As such, it is committed both to the existence of facts within that domain and the response-independence of those facts. Response-dependence preserves facticity but sacrifices response-independence, representing a skeptical solution to skeptical challenges.[29] But other meta-normative responses preserve response-independence and sacrifice facticity, in effect conceding that the skeptical problem cannot be answered. *Abolitionists* do without facts in the relevant normative domain and reject the associated normative discourse, whereas *fictionalists* embrace the normative discourse but treat it as a useful fiction. So, if one were to embrace skepticism about the prospects for a response-independent conception of responsibility, one would still have to choose among

---

[29] Response-dependent conceptions of responsibility are verificationist conceptions that offer skeptical solutions to skeptical worries about responsibility, denying any gap between the facts in question and our evidence or responses. For general discussion of skeptical solutions to skeptical problems, see Saul Kripke, *Wittgenstein on Rules and Private Language* (Oxford: Blackwell, 1982), pp. 66–67. In my view, skeptical solutions in general concede too much to the skeptic and are, at best, fallback solutions to be entertained only after straight solutions have clearly failed.

abolitionism, fictionalism, and response-dependence about responsibility. Fortunately, we don't need to decide among these anti-realist conceptions of responsibility. A central argument of this book is that fair opportunity provides a plausible response-independent conception of responsibility.

Indeed, part of Strawson's position is fully consistent with the realist reading of the link between the reactive attitudes and responsibility. Strawson's thesis says that the reactive attitudes are fitting just in case their targets are responsible, which allows the realist to take the reactive attitudes to be *evidence* about the conditions under which targets of these attitudes are responsible. Realism, unlike response-dependence, implies that this evidence is defeasible, but it is evidence nonetheless. Moreover, our practices of suspending the reactive attitudes—that is, our practices of excuse—are evidence of when agents are not responsible. This supports our working hypothesis that responsibility and excuse are inversely related, which allows the realist to study responsibility by studying excuse. If this methodological maxim leads us to a plausible conception of responsibility, whose conditions can be specified independently of the reactive attitudes, this will vindicate realism about Strawson's thesis. This is a process Strawson begins, but does not complete. We will pursue this process further than Strawson did. When we do so, attention to our excusing practices supports a conception of responsibility that consists in agents having the right capacities—normative competence—and opportunities to exercise those capacities free from interference—situational control. This is the fair opportunity conception of responsibility, sketched earlier (§1), which will be elaborated and defended in the rest of this book. If successful, the fair opportunity conception will vindicate the promissory note issued by the realist about Strawson's thesis.[30]

14. Quality of Will, Attributability, Accountability, and Answerability

Strawson suggests that the reactive attitudes are responses to the agent's *quality of will* (67, 70). But it is not immediately clear what he means by

---

[30] In effect, Shoemaker defends a response-dependent conception of Strawson's thesis as a fallback position, because he thinks that no response-independent conception will be extensionally adequate. To avoid intolerable revision, he thinks we must abandon response-independence and embrace response-dependence. See Shoemaker, "Response-Dependent Responsibility," pp. 498–508. But his critical claims about the extensional adequacy of response-independent conceptions rest on a brief and selective assessment of response-independent conceptions, which does not include the fair opportunity conception of responsibility. The argument of this book is that fair opportunity provides a plausible response-independent conception of responsibility.

this. He might understand quality of will in a way that is ecumenical, indicating simply whatever psychological features of agents that ground responsibility for their actions. However, more recently, quality of will has become associated with one particular kind of responsibility, which is sometimes called *attributability*.

To understand and assess this proposal, we need to distinguish three responsibility concepts: *attributability*, *accountability*, and *answerability*. In "Two Faces of Responsibility," Watson distinguishes between attributability and accountability.[31] Though his distinction has proven influential, it is not immediately obvious how best to understand it or whether everyone understands it the same way. One reason for this uncertainty is that Watson offers multiple characterizations of each kind of responsibility. For instance, he associates attributive responsibility with action that expresses the agent's real self, with an aretaic perspective on action, reflecting its virtues and vices or excellences and defects, and with the agent's own evaluative commitments. By contrast, Watson thinks that responsibility as accountability involves liability to sanctions, raises questions about the fairness of imposing sanctions, and presupposes that the agent had control and a fair opportunity to avoid sanctions. It's not entirely clear if these characteristics of attributability and accountability are exhaustive or if the characteristics of each always coincide.

We might provisionally identify attributive responsibility with an agent's quality of will where that signifies something morally significant about his attitudes and his evaluative orientation with respect to the rights and interests of others. If an agent acts wrongly and in the process displays a bad quality of will, he is attributively responsible for his wrong. But if the agent acts wrongly through inadvertence or in some other way that does not manifest a bad will, then he is not attributively responsible for his wrong. By contrast, we might say that an agent is accountable only for conduct that deserves praise or blame and over which he had control. For this reason, we might think it unfair to blame and sanction someone for conduct that it was not within his power to avoid.

This way of understanding the distinction between attributability and accountability contrasts quality of will and capacities and opportunities. This gives attributability an important *extensional* aspect, describing various properties of the will that an agent actually manifests in acting. Attributability appeals to features of the *actual sequence* linking the agent's actual attitudes and will with his action in order to impute that action to him. By contrast,

---

[31] Gary Watson, "Two Faces of Responsibility" reprinted in Gary Watson, *Agency and Answerability*.

accountability has an important *modal* aspect, describing not just how an agent reasoned and acted but also his abilities and capacities to act in certain ways, whether or not he does so. Accountability is *capacitarian*.

Watson's view is that both attributability and accountability are important but that attributability is inadequate for purposes of establishing fair treatment and accountability. For example, a psychopath's callous and malicious disregard of the legitimate interests of others might reflect a vicious or reckless quality of will, but if this quality of will is the product of the right kind of cognitive or emotional deficits, he may not have had adequate opportunity to avoid wrongful conduct. If so, the psychopath would be attributively responsible for the harm he causes, but not fully accountable for it.[32]

We can say more about attributability and quality of will. We hold an agent attributively responsible for her actions and the foreseeable consequences of those actions based on the quality of her will, where that discloses her character or true self or reflects her fundamental evaluative orientation. We might not hold an agent responsible for harm that she causes to others if this was beyond her control, for instance, if she was manipulated by natural forces or the will of another. But we do hold someone responsible in this attributive sense if the harms she causes reflect her will in certain ways, for instance, if she intended the harm or was aware of the risks she posed to others and was indifferent.

Different conceptions of quality of will are possible. First, we might understand quality of will in *characterological* terms as a will expressing the agent's stable character traits. On this view, an agent is responsible for actions just in case they are in character for her and excused just in case those actions are characterologically anomalous for her.[33] Second, we might understand quality of will in terms of a *mesh* between the agent's motivating desires and her other attitudes. Following Frankfurt, we might understand it as a mesh between the agent's first-order motivating desires and her second-order or aspirational desires.[34] Alternatively, following (early) Watson, we might understand quality of will in terms of a mesh between the agent's first-order motivating desires and her evaluative assessment of those desires.[35] On this view, an agent is responsible for her conduct in cases in which she endorses her motivating

---

[32] For a fuller discussion of whether psychopaths are responsible, see Chapter 11.

[33] David Hume, *An Enquiry Concerning the Principles of Morals* [1751], ed. P.H. Nidditch (Oxford: Clarendon Press, 1975), §VII, Part II.

[34] Harry Frankfurt, "Freedom of the Will and the Concept of a Person" *Journal of Philosophy* 68 (1971): 5–20.

[35] Gary Watson, "Free Agency" reprinted in Watson, *Agency and Answerability*.

desires and excused when she does not endorse her motivating desires in the right way. Third, we might understand quality of will in terms of the *regard and concern* the agent displays for the interests and rights of others.[36] On this view, an agent is responsible and blameworthy for actions that display insufficient regard for the rights and interests of others but excused if she behaves wrongly without insufficient regard for the rights and interests of others, for example, in cases of duress. There might be different grades of blameworthiness corresponding to different forms of insufficient regard—all else being equal, intending wrongful harm might be worse than reckless disregard (indifference to an unjustifiable risk), which might be worse than negligence (ignorance of an unjustifiable risk).

However, it is not clear that we should limit responsibility and blame to culpable states of mind that express an agent's stable character traits or motivating desires that she endorses, for then we could not hold agents responsible for wrongs that were out of character or for familiar forms of weakness of will, in which the agent acts on desires she does not endorse. It seems more reasonable to identify an agent's quality of will with the kind of regard she has for the interests and rights of others. Tim Scanlon develops this sort of conception of quality of will and attributive responsibility in terms of the regard that the agent shows for the rights and interests of others. Like Strawson, Scanlon thinks that reactive attitudes, such as blame, reflect our relationships with others and that blame is the appropriate response to an unjustified breach in these relationships. In assessing such breaches, Scanlon thinks we attach significance to the motives and intentions of the agent. On this view, A is justified in her hard feelings toward B and in blaming B if B injures A through malice, indifference, recklessness, or negligence. Here, our reactive attitudes are supposed to track the insufficient regard that B shows A's interests and rights. By contrast, we excuse, Scanlon thinks, just in case the agent wrongs others without displaying poor quality of will.

Pure or predominant attributionism holds that quality of will and attributability can do all or most of the work required by a theory of responsibility and blame.[37] It seems right that some reactive attitudes track this conception of

---

[36] T.M. Scanlon, *Moral Dimensions: Permissibility, Meaning, and Blame* (Cambridge, MA: Harvard University Press, 2008), ch. 4, esp. p. 202. Also see Angela Smith, "Attributability, Answerability, and Accountability: In Defense of a Unified Account" *Ethics* 122 (2012): 575–89.

[37] I would include as pure or predominant attributionists Scanlon, *Moral Dimensions*, ch. 4; Angela Smith, "Control, Responsibility and Moral Assessment" *Philosophical Studies* 138 (2008): 367–82 and "Attributability, Answerability, and Accountability"; and Matt Talbert, "Blame and Responsiveness to Moral Reasons: Are Psychopaths Blameworthy?" *Pacific Philosophical Quarterly* 89 (2008): 516–35, "Accountability, Aliens, and Psychopaths: A Reply to Shoemaker" *Ethics* 122 (2012): 562–74, and

quality of will. However, it seems implausible that quality of will and attributability can do all or most of the work required by a theory of responsibility and
blame. Extensional information about quality of will seems insufficient to
justify blame and sanction in absence of the agent's ability to do otherwise.
An agent might display a defective quality of will in the form of malice,
indifference, or negligence with respect to the rights and interests of others,
which would be sufficient to attribute wrongdoing to him. But if the agent
lacks the ability to recognize that this way of relating to others is wrong or is
unable to conform his conduct to knowledge that this is wrong, then the agent
lacks the ability to control his conduct and avoid wrongdoing. In such cases,
B might owe A compensation for harm he causes, and, if he is a continuing
danger to others or himself, he might be subject to civil commitment. But it
would be unfair to blame and sanction B for his malicious behavior if he lacked
elementary understanding of the rights of others or sufficient impulse control.
Since, by hypothesis, B was attributively responsible for the harm he caused,
the sense in which he is not responsible must be a different sense of responsibility. This is Watson's sense of responsibility as accountability.[38] As we will
see, it is responsibility as accountability, not as attributability, without which
the agent is excused.[39]

Several philosophers have identified a third sense of responsibility—
responsibility as answerability.[40] As with attributability and accountability,

---

"Attributionism" in *The Oxford Handbook of Moral Responsibility*, ed. D. Nelkin and D. Pereboom
(New York: Oxford University Press, 2021).

[38] Though Wolf did not have Watson's distinction in mind (it came later) and focused on the
inadequacies of "real self" conceptions of responsibility, she was, I believe, the first to recognize that
quality of will is insufficient for accountability. See Susan Wolf, "Sanity and the Metaphysics of
Responsibility" in *Responsibility, Character, and the Emotions*, ed. F. Schoeman (Cambridge:
Cambridge University Press, 1987) and *Freedom within Reason*, pp. 37–45.

[39] Whether, or how much, I am disagreeing with Scanlon here is unclear. On the one hand, he seems
to predicate blame, as such, on attributability and quality of will. On the other hand, he allows that
"hard treatment" and punishment require accountability and fair opportunity, and not just attributability and quality of will. See Scanlon, *Moral Dimensions*, pp. 202–04. If Scanlon accepts this second
claim, he can admit that attributability is not sufficient for accountability and claim that whereas blame
requires only attributability and quality of will, punishment requires accountability and fair opportunity. But blame often carries with it informal sanctions, and informal sanctions involve a kind of hard
treatment. If so, Scanlon's exception that hard treatment requires accountability and fair opportunity
might threaten to swallow his rule that blame only requires attributability and quality of will.

[40] Though Watson's distinction is a bipartite distinction between attributability and accountability,
the title of his collection of essays—*Agency and Answerability*—suggests that he sees connections
between his two faces of responsibility and answerability. Some writers have sought to expand Watson's
bipartite distinction into a tripartite one involving attributability, answerability, and accountability. See,
for example, Angela Smith, "Attributability, Answerability, and Accountability" and David Shoemaker,
"Attributability, Answerability, and Accountability: Toward a Wider Theory of Moral Responsibility"
Ethics 121 (2011): 602–32 and David Shoemaker, *Responsibility from the Margins* (Oxford: Clarendon
Press, 2015), chs. 1–3. In a more recent essay, Smith has expressed skepticism about the distinction
between attributability and accountability and proposed to analyze responsibility exclusively in terms
of answerability. See Angela Smith, "Responsibility as Answerability" *Inquiry* 58 (2015): 99–126. I don't

the literature contains different characterizations of answerability, not all obviously equivalent. We might understand answerability as a capacity to engage actual and potential interlocutors in appropriate normative conversation about one's attitudes and conduct—a capacity that requires abilities to provide accurate moral assessments of one's own attitudes and behavior and to respond to potential challenges and criticisms from others in various ways, for instance, by providing and exchanging reasons, justifying one's conduct, adducing mitigating circumstances, or repenting and seeking forgiveness. Answerability seems to have an essentially relational and retrospective dimension. In this respect, answerability is downstream from both attributability and accountability, because whereas attributability and accountability concern the agent's psychological relations to her conduct at the time of action, answerability concerns an agent's ability to answer later for her earlier actions.

Though we are often concerned with moral responsibility outside of the criminal law, we can see differences between attributability, accountability, and answerability reflected in different parts of a criminal trial. The trial itself occurs after the alleged wrongdoing. The guilt phase of a trial has two parts. In the first part the prosecution must prove that the defendant actually committed an offense. Whether and, if so, what offense the defendant committed can depend on the agent's quality of will, for instance, whether he intended to cause a wrongful harm, whether he was aware that he would cause a wrongful harm, whether he was reckless with respect to the risk of causing wrongful harm, or whether he was negligent with respect to that risk. As I will explain later (§56), the agent's quality of will often enters into a determination of whether he is attributively responsible for an offense. But the second stage of a trial permits the defendant to concede that he committed an offense but offer an affirmative exculpatory defense. He might either justify his conduct or provide an excuse. Whereas a justification denies that the conduct in question was in the circumstances all-things-considered wrong, an excuse concedes wrongdoing but denies responsibility or culpability for that wrong. Excuses can reflect impairment of the agent's capacities or opportunities and are exculpatory. So an agent might be excused for conduct for which she is attributively responsible. The kind of responsibility that excuse denies is accountability. Answerability corresponds to a defendant's competence to stand trial by responding to charges, participating in the trial, and, if

---

see how to dispense with attributability and accountability or how to reduce either to answerability. Westlund gives answerability an important role to play in her relational account of autonomy in Andrea Westlund, "Selflessness and Responsibility for Self: Is Deference Compatible with Autonomy" *Philosophical Review* 112 (2003): 483–523.

appropriate, mounting an affirmative defense. As such, answerability is down-stream from and independent of accountability. Competence to stand trial is a later ability to address earlier accountability, and the two can come apart. One can be competent to stand trial at a later time, whether or not one was competent at the earlier time the offense was committed, and one can be incompetent to stand trial at a later time, whether or not one was competent at the earlier time the offense was committed. Competence to stand trial and answerability are important parts of a criminal procedure, but the substance of a criminal trial concerns attributability and accountability. Attributability is insufficient for guilt; guilt requires accountability and culpability, and excuse is a denial of accountability.

Strawson's claim that the reactive attitudes track the agent's quality of will may be purely ecumenical. But more recent writers sometimes understand quality of will as standing for attributability, rather than accountability. In this sense, quality of will won't be an adequate basis for many reactive attitudes and practices; many retributive attitudes and practices, especially those embedded in the criminal law, seem to presuppose accountability, and not just attributability. Answerability is an ability to address retrospectively one's earlier accountability. In this way, accountability emerges as the central responsibility concept in the criminal law. If, as I will argue, the architecture of moral and criminal responsibility is relevantly similar, then accountability will also be the central responsibility concept in moral assessment.

3

The Fair Opportunity Conception of Responsibility

Realism about Strawson's thesis linking the moralized reactive attitudes and responsibility claims that the reactive attitudes, including blame, are apt or fitting if and only if and insofar as (iffi) their targets are responsible. As such, realism about Strawson's thesis implies that the reactive attitudes can be justified, provided we can identify a suitable respondent-independent conception of responsibility. Moreover, realism about Strawson's thesis also implies that we can study responsibility by attending to the reactive attitudes and blaming practices, both when we apply them and when we suspend them. This reflects our working hypothesis that responsibility and excuse are inversely related. This hypothesis implies that we can articulate and test our ideas about responsibility against our ideas about excuse, and vice versa.

When we approach responsibility and excuse in this way, we will find that moral responsibility and criminal responsibility, despite some differences, share important *architecture*. Responsibility requires that agents have certain *normative capacities* and suitable *opportunities* to exercise those capacities free from undue interference. These capacities and opportunities are individually necessary and jointly sufficient for responsibility, because they are both required by the principle that an agent is an apt target of blame when and only when he had the *fair opportunity to avoid wrongdoing*.

This fair opportunity conception of responsibility and excuse fits well with our considered judgments about when agents are responsible and when they should be excused. It also draws on and synthesizes the best elements in the reasons-responsive wing of the compatibilist tradition about moral responsibility[1] and the fair choice conception of criminal responsibility.[2]

---

[1] See, e.g., Wolf, *Freedom within Reason*; Wallace, *Responsibility and the Moral Sentiments*; Fischer and Ravizza, *Responsibility and Control*; Nelkin, *Making Sense of Freedom and Responsibility*; Brink and Nelkin, "Fairness and the Architecture of Responsibility"; McKenna, "Reasons-Responsiveness, Agents, and Mechanisms"; and Vargas, *Building Better Beings*.

[2] See, e.g., Hart, *Punishment and Responsibility*; Moore, *Placing Blame*; and Morse, "Culpability and Control" and "Uncontrollable Urges and Irrational People."

Fair Opportunity and Responsibility. David O. Brink, Oxford University Press (2021). © David O. Brink.
DOI: 10.1093/oso/9780198859468.003.0003

15. Responsibility and Excuse

Our working hypothesis that responsibility and excuse are inversely related implies that they co-vary in a systematic way.

> *The Responsibility-Excuse Biconditional*: An agent is responsible for wrongdoing iff she is not excused for it.

This hypothesis implies that responsibility and excuse should be mirror images of each other and that we can study either by attending to the other. If so, excuse is a window onto responsibility, and vice versa. If excuse is the "royal road to responsibility," we do well to remember that it is a two-way street.[3]

This methodological hypothesis allows us to draw on our practices of excuse to model responsibility. To do so, we could attend to our practices of moral excuse and to our criminal law principles and doctrines about excuse. Though we should not ignore either source of evidence, I propose to begin with criminal law principles of excuse, whose conceptualization is more settled and better understood.

Excuse is an affirmative defense in the criminal law. Affirmative defenses concede that the agent behaved in a way proscribed by legal norms but nonetheless cite grounds for exculpation and acquittal. As we noted in §1 and will see at greater length in Chapter 6, the retributivist desert basis for blame and punishment is culpable wrongdoing, that is, wrongdoing for which the agent is responsible. The two main affirmative defenses are justifications and excuses, and they each deny one of the two independent variables in the retributivist desert basis for blame and punishment. Justifications deny wrongdoing, claiming that although the agent's conduct satisfies the conditions of a criminal offense, nonetheless in the circumstances in question the conduct is not inconsistent with the law's larger aims and purposes and, hence, is all-things-considered permissible. Excuses concede wrongdoing but deny that the agent is blameworthy for her misconduct by denying the agent's responsibility or culpability for the wrongdoing. These claims about the criminal law have moral analogs as well. In response to moral blame, a target might defend herself, claiming either that her conduct was in fact justified or that, though wrong, she was not responsible and, hence, not blameworthy for it.

---

[3] See Moore, *Placing Blame*, p. 548.

The criminal law recognizes two main kinds of excuse—those that involve significant impairment of an agent's *capacities*, as reflected in cases of insanity or immaturity, and those in which an agent's circumstances compromise her fair *opportunity* to exercise these capacities free from interference, as reflected in cases involving manipulation, coercion, or duress.[4] These assumptions about excuse tell us something about responsibility. Responsibility is a matter of an agent having the requisite capacities, which we can conceptualize in terms of *normative competence*, and suitable opportunities to exercise these capacities free from external interference of certain kinds, which we can conceptualize in terms of *situational control*. Normative competence and situational control are individually necessary and jointly sufficient for responsibility, because significant impairment of either condition results in an excuse.

Criminal law theorists, working with a fair choice conception of responsibility, have recognized this general picture of the requirements and structure of responsibility based on the criminal law's patterns of excuse. For example, in "Negligence, Mens Rea, and Criminal Responsibility" H.L.A. Hart insists that punishment is conditioned on the agent's capacities and opportunities.

What is crucial is that those whom we punish should have had, when they acted, the normal capacities, physical and mental, for abstaining from what it [the law] forbids, and a fair opportunity to exercise these capacities.[5]

More recently, Michael Moore has endorsed Hart's analysis.

Hart thus subdivides the ability presupposed by his sense of "could" into two components. One relates to the equipment of the actor: does he have sufficient choosing capacity to be responsible? The other relates to the situation in which the actor finds himself: does that situation present him with a fair chance to use his capacities for choice so as to give effect to his decision?[6]

The fair opportunity conception of responsibility employs this analysis of responsibility into capacities and opportunities and claims that blame or

---

[4] For a different conception of criminal law excuses, see John Gardner, "The Gist of Excuses" *Buffalo Criminal Law Review* 1 (1998): 575–98.

[5] H.L.A. Hart, "Negligence, Mens Rea, and Criminal Responsibility" reprinted in Hart, *Punishment and Responsibility*, p. 152.

[6] Moore, *Placing Blame*, p. 554.

punishment in the absence of capacity or opportunity violates the norm that agents must be afforded the fair opportunity to avoid wrongdoing.

16. Normative Competence

If someone is to be culpable or responsible for her wrongdoing, then she must be a responsible agent. So, we need to distinguish between responsible and non-responsible agents. Our paradigms of responsible agents are normal mature adults with certain sorts of capacities. We do not treat brutes or small children as responsible agents. Brutes and small children both act intentionally, but they act on their strongest desires or, if they exercise deliberation and impulse control, it is primarily instrumental reasoning in the service of fixed aims. By contrast, we suppose, responsible agents must be *normatively competent*.[7] They must not simply act on their strongest desires, but be capable of stepping back from their desires, evaluating them, and acting for good reasons. This requires responsible agents to be able to recognize and respond to reasons for action.

It is common to contrast *motivating* and *justifying* reasons.[8] A justifying reason for action is a consideration that counts in favor of performing that action, whereas a motivating reason is a consideration that actually moves someone to do something and so explains her behavior. An agent's motivating reasons may include her beliefs about her justifying reasons, but they need not if she is weak-willed or acts on passion and impulse. The reasons-responsive tradition appeals to justifying, rather than motivating, reasons. A normatively competent agent must be able to recognize and conform to justifying reasons.

---

[7] Both Wolf and Wallace use the phrase "normative competence" and recognize that it has what I am calling cognitive and volitional dimensions. See Wolf, *Freedom within Reason*, p. 124 and Wallace, *Responsibility and the Moral Sentiments*, pp. 1, 86. However, neither explores the structure of normative competence in as much detail as one might like. This is what is especially significant about the extended treatment of reasons-responsiveness in Fischer and Ravizza, *Responsibility and Control*. However, several of their assumptions about reasons-responsiveness require rethinking (§§19, 21, 22), and it is important to connect the requirements of normative competence with criminal law principles about responsibility and excuse. Wallace tries to link responsibility and the excuses in *Responsibility and the Moral Sentiments*, ch. 5. But he makes controversial assumptions about the relation between justifications and excuses and does not engage with criminal law doctrines. I can better explain these problems in Chapter 7. Finally, it is important to note that normative competence is necessary but not sufficient for responsibility and needs to be supplemented with situational control.

[8] Hutcheson distinguished between "justifying" and "exciting" reasons. See Francis Hutcheson, *Illustrations on the Moral Sense* [1730], ed. B. Peach (Cambridge, MA: Harvard University Press, 1971), Introduction §1. For contemporary discussion, see Jonathan Dancy, *Practical Reality* (Oxford: Clarendon Press, 2000), ch. 1 and Maria Alvarez, "Reasons for Action: Justification, Motivation, Explanation" *Stanford Encyclopedia of Philosophy* (2016).

Present purposes do not require us to settle on any particular conception of the ground or content of justifying reasons. Importantly, familiar moral demands to respect the rights and interests of others are among the justifying reasons responsible agents must be able to recognize and to which they must be able to conform.

Non-human animals have a kind of rationality or reasons-responsiveness insofar as they can and do act on beliefs, desires, and intentions that are sensitive to their environment in certain reliable ways, enabling them to represent their environment accurately enough, to avoid predators, to seek shelter and security, and to forage for nutrition. Since these outcomes are good for them as individuals and as members of genetically linked groups, they can be seen as responding to a range of reasons, even if they do not represent these outcomes as good or as providing them with reasons. They typically act on cognitive and behavioral scripts that have proven selectively advantageous or that they have learned to be reliable, rather than engaging in deliberation about how best to secure safety, shelter, and sustenance. These scripts are reasonably reliable in the contexts for which they were developed, but they may not be reliable in novel situations or circumstances in which existing scripts offer conflicting guidance.

Importantly, brutes are not responsive to normative demands about the rights and interests of others. There is an important philosophical tradition, including John Locke, Bishop Butler, Thomas Reid, Immanuel Kant, and T. H. Green, that distinguishes between the biological kind *human being* and the forensic or normative kind *person* and treats persons as agents who can distinguish between the *power* and *authority* of passion and desire, exercise impulse control, deliberate about appropriate conduct in light of the relevant norms, and regulate their conduct in accord with these deliberations.[9] On this view, persons are agents who are normatively competent and reasons-responsive not with respect to any justifying reason but specifically with respect to moral justifying reasons concerning the interests and rights of others. In this tradition, responsibility is tied to moral personhood.

[9] See John Locke, *An Essay Concerning Human Understanding* [1690], ed. P.H. Nidditch (Oxford: Clarendon Press, 1979), Book II, Chapter xxvii, §§8, 15, 17–21, 23, 26; Butler, Joseph. *Fifteen Sermons Preached at Rolls Chapel* [1726] reprinted in *Fifteen Sermons Preached at Rolls Chapel and A Dissertation on the Nature of Virtue*, ed. W.R. Matthews (London: G. Bell & Sons, 1953) Sermon II, para. 14; Thomas Reid, *Essays on the Active Powers of Man* [1788], (Cambridge, MA: MIT Press, 1969), Introduction, Essay II, Chapter ii, Essay IV, Chapters iv and vi; Immanuel Kant, *The Groundwork for the Metaphysic of Morals* [1785] in *Kant's Practical Philosophy*, trs. M. Gregor (Cambridge: Cambridge University Press, 1997) (Prussian Academy pagination), 4: 446–48, 457, 459–60; T.H. Green, *Prolegomena to Ethics* [1883], ed. D. Brink (Oxford: Clarendon Press, 2003), §§86, 9296, 103, 107, 122, 125, 220.

Normative competence, on this conception, involves two forms of reasons-responsiveness: *cognitive* abilities to recognize reasons for or against conduct, in particular, to identify normative requirements and distinguish right from wrong and *volitional* abilities to conform one's will to this normative understanding. Both dimensions of normative competence involve norm-responsiveness. As a first approximation, we can distinguish moral and criminal responsibility at least in part based on the kinds of norms to which agents must be responsive. Moral responsibility requires capacities to recognize and conform to moral norms, including norms of moral wrongdoing, whereas criminal responsibility requires capacities to recognize and conform to norms of the criminal law, including norms of criminal wrongdoing. Though there will typically be considerable overlap between moral and criminal norms, especially in morally legitimate criminal systems, there is no reason to expect the coincidence to be perfect. Indeed, in most liberal regimes there will be many moral norms that the legal system will not criminalize. For the most part and with some exceptions, in morally legitimate legal systems, criminal law norms will be a proper subset of moral norms—in particular, especially fundamental norms of interpersonal morality related to people's rights.

It is important to frame this approach to responsibility in terms of normative *competence* and the possession of these *capacities* for reasons-responsiveness. In particular, responsibility must be predicated on the possession, rather than the use or exercise, of such capacities. We do excuse for lack of competence, not for lack of performance. Provided the agent had the relevant cognitive and volitional capacities, we do not excuse the weak-willed or the willful wrongdoer for failing to recognize or respond appropriately to reasons. If responsibility were predicated on the proper use of these capacities, we could not hold weak-willed and willful wrongdoers responsible for their wrongdoing. Indeed, the fact of wrongdoing would itself be exculpatory, with the absurd result that we could never hold anyone responsible for wrongdoing. It is a condition of our holding wrongdoers responsible that they possessed the relevant capacities or competence.[10]

This important point about responsibility depending on competence, not performance, is sometimes obscured by the language of reasons-responsiveness,

---

[10]   Henry Sidgwick famously objects to Kant's conception of autonomy as conformity to principles of practical reason that this would prevent us from holding criminals responsible and would allow us to recognize only morally permissible behavior as responsible. See Henry Sidgwick, *The Methods of Ethics*, 7th ed. (London: Macmillan, 1907), appendix, pp. 511–16. The solution to this problem, as Green noted, is for Kant to define autonomy in terms of *capacities* for conformity to principles of practical reason. See, T.H. Green, *Collected Works*, 5 vols., ed. P. Nicholson (Bristol: Thoemmes, 1997), vol. II, pp. 95–97, 134–37.

which can display an ambiguity. When we speak of someone being reasons-responsive, we might be signaling that she has the capacities to be guided by reason or, alternatively, that she exercises these capacities well. To avoid confusion, it will be helpful to make the former claim by describing her as *reasons-responsive* and to make the latter claim by describing her as *reasons-responding*. Perhaps some who describe themselves as sympathetic with the reasons-responsive tradition have reasons-responding in mind. But that leads to the paradoxical conclusions that weak-willed actors and willful wrongdoers are never responsible and, indeed, that all wrongdoing should be excused. The reasons-responsive tradition should insist on distinguishing competence and performance and claim that responsibility depends on being reasons-responsive, rather than being reasons-responding.

17. Cognitive Competence

Normative competence requires the cognitive capacity to make suitable normative discriminations, in particular, to recognize normative demands and distinguish between right and wrong. If so, then we can readily understand one aspect of the criminal law insanity defense. As we will see when we discuss the insanity defense in Chapter 11, most plausible versions of the insanity defense include a cognitive dimension, first articulated in the M'Naghten rule that excuses if the agent lacked the capacity to discriminate right from wrong at the time of action.[11] For instance, this cognitive conception of competence and insanity is reflected in the Federal insanity test in American criminal law.

> It is an affirmative defense to a prosecution under any Federal statute that, at the time of the commission of the acts constituting the offense, the defendant, as a result of a severe mental disease or defect, was unable to appreciate the nature and quality or the wrongfulness of his acts. Mental disease or defect does not otherwise constitute a defense.[12]

Cognitive competence is a requirement of normative competence, and sufficient impairment of cognitive capacity is excusing.

We just said that we excuse for incompetence, but not for performance errors that are not due to incompetence. Is this true with respect to the cognitive dimension of responsibility? Ignorance is a kind of performance

---

[11] M'Naghten's Case, 10 Cl. & F. 200, 8 Eng. Rep. 718 (1843).   [12] 18 U.S. Code §17 (2005).

error. Does ignorance excuse, independently of cognitive incapacity? It is sometimes said that ignorance excuses, whether that is moral ignorance, ignorance of the law, or ignorance about non-normative prosaic factual matters.[13] Certainly, recognition of particular normative truths, for instance, that an action would be wrong will typically depend on the recognition of both normative truths about the wrong-making features of actions and recognition of non-normative truths about whether those wrong-making features are present in a given situation. However, if we scratch the surface of claims that ignorance excuses, we find that this claim must be qualified in an important way. *Culpable ignorance* does not excuse; at most, *non-culpable ignorance* excuses. But when is ignorance non-culpable? Arguably, ignorance is non-culpable only when the agent was not in a position to correct her cognitive mistake at the time she made it.

1. Non-culpable ignorance excuses; culpable ignorance does not.
2. Ignorance is culpable iffi the agent was in a position to correct it at the time.
3. Hence, ignorance is non-culpable iffi the agent was not in a position to correct it at the time.
4. If the agent was not in a position to correct her cognitive mistake, then she did not (in the relevant sense) have the capacity to do so.
5. Hence, ignorance excuses iffi the agent lacked the cognitive capacity to recognize the truth at the time of her mistake.

If this argument is right, the truth in the claim that ignorance excuses respects the *capacitarian* analysis of the cognitive dimension of responsibility.[14]

---

[13] There is a further question of whether there is an asymmetry with respect to whether normative and non-normative ignorance excuses. For instance, it is sometimes said that ignorance of the law is no excuse, whereas ignorance of (non-legal) fact is excusing. For skepticism about the claim that ignorance of the law should not be excusing, see Douglas Husak, *Ignorance of Law* (Oxford: Clarendon Press, 2016). Some writers embrace an asymmetry about when ignorance excuses, claiming that non-moral ignorance excuses in a way that moral ignorance doesn't. See, e.g., Elizabeth Harman, "Does Moral Ignorance Exculpate?" *Ratio* 24 (2011): 434–68. But if ignorance excuses iffi it is non-culpable, and ignorance is non-culpable only when the agent suffered a relevant cognitive incapacity, then it will be hard to justify this asymmetry, because cognitive incompetence with respect to moral (and legal) norms does excuse, as is reflected in the insanity defense.

[14] It is reasonably common to think that moral ignorance can excuse. See, e.g., Gideon Rosen, "Culpability and Ignorance" *Proceedings of the Aristotelian Society* 103 (2003): 61–84; Michael Zimmerman, *Living with Uncertainty: The Moral Significance of Ignorance* (New York: Cambridge University Press, 2008); and Husak, *Ignorance of Law*, esp. ch. 3. While I agree that non-culpable ignorance excuses, I disagree with those who think that awareness is a requirement of culpability. For instance, Rosen thinks moral ignorance excuses anytime that it cannot be traced back to akrasia or

There are interesting and difficult questions about the demands of cognitive competence, the various forms of cognitive incompetence, and the possibility of reduced or partial cognitive competence. These issues will be addressed later in this book, especially in Chapters 4, 11, and 15.

18. Volitional Competence

However, normative competence requires more than cognitive competence. It also requires volitional capacities to form intentions based on one's practical judgments about what one ought to do and to execute these intentions over time, despite distraction, temptation, and other forms of interference. Volitional impairment might take many forms. Some volitional impairment involves irresistible urges or paralyzing phobias that are insistent and resist attempts to override or control them. Severe depression or listlessness might make it difficult to summon focus, attention, and resolve necessary to execute complex or difficult plans. Moreover, abnormalities in the prefrontal cortex of the brain, whether congenital or arising from injury or lesions, can cause a kind of systematic weakness of will in some patients that undermines executive function, as in the famous case of Phineas Gage. Phineas Gage was a nineteenth-century railway worker who was laying tracks in Vermont and accidentally used his tamping iron to tamp down a live explosive charge, which detonated and shot the tamping iron up and through his skull, damaging his prefontal cortex. Though he did not lose consciousness, over time his character was altered. Whereas he had been described as someone possessing an "iron will" before the accident, afterward he had considerable difficulty conforming his behavior to his own judgments about what he ought to do.[15] In these and other cases, pathologies involve volitional impairment and threaten volitional competence.

Volitional competence requires the ability to manage psychic resistance and interference with acting on one's normative judgments so that these forms of resistance and interference don't derail those normative commitments. As Alfred Mele puts it, a competent agent must be able to *conquer* or *circumvent*

---

weakness of will—knowing that what one is doing is wrong and doing it anyway. Similarly, Husak thinks that awareness is a condition of blameworthiness. By contrast, I think that moral ignorance excuses when the agent lacked cognitive competence and that an agent can have a duty of inquiry and the capacity to recognize facts of which she is unaware. A capacitarian conception of normative competence that insists on responsiveness, rather than responding, will be less exculpatory than those that require awareness. For a similar capacitarian analysis, see Fernando Rudy-Hiller, "A Capacitarian Account of Culpable Ignorance" *Pacific Philosophical Quarterly* 98 (2017): 398–426.

[15] The story of Phineas Gage is discussed, among other places, in Antonio Damasio, *Descartes' Error: Emotion, Reasons, and the Human Brain* (New York: Putnam, 1994).

these wayward influences.[16] A temptation is conquerable when one can resist it in the moment through an exercise of willpower and circumventable when one can act prospectively so as to render the temptation less likely to arise or make succumbing to it impossible or at least more difficult. Conquerability is mostly a matter of willpower, whereas circumventability is mostly a matter of foresight, strategy, and precommitment. For instance, the alcoholic who simply resists cravings conquers his impulses, whereas the alcoholic who throws out his liquor and stops associating with former drinking partners or won't meet them at places where alcohol is served circumvents his impulses. Conquering one's wayward impulses can be heroic, but it is often a difficult and fragile achievement. As a result, circumventability often plays an important role in assessments of volitional competence.[17]

As we will see at greater length in our discussion of insanity in Chapter 11, recognition of a volitional dimension of normative competence argues against purely cognitive conceptions of insanity, such as the M'Naghten test, and in favor of a more inclusive conception, represented in the Model Penal Code, which conceives of insanity as involving significant impairment of *either* cognitive or volitional competence.

> A person is not responsible for criminal conduct if at the time of such conduct as a result of a mental disease or defect he lacks substantial capacity either to appreciate the criminality [wrongfulness] of his conduct or to conform his conduct to the requirements of law.   [MPC §4.01]

If so, normative competence involves *both* cognitive and volitional competence, and significant impairment of *either* warrants an excuse.

19. Degrees of Responsiveness

Reasons-responsiveness is clearly a modal notion and admits of degrees— one might be more or less responsive. This raises the question of how responsive someone needs to be in order to be responsible. This is an

---

[16] See Alfred Mele, "Irresistible Desires" *Noûs* 24 (1990): 455–72.

[17] When an agent is responsible by virtue of the circumventability of her temptations to act wrongly, her responsibility is grounded in facts about what she could and should have done earlier. This may seem to invoke the concept of *tracing* by which we hold an agent responsible at a later time, even if she does not then otherwise meet the conditions of responsibility, provided we can trace the later conduct to earlier choices for which she does meet the conditions of responsibility. But, as we will see in Chapter 5, the same verdicts can be reached without tracing, holding the agent responsible only for her earlier failure to circumvent and its reasonably foreseeable consequences.

important and difficult issue, which will concern us in various ways through-out this book. For now, we can and should make some preliminary remarks, which can be refined as we gradually assemble more resources for addressing this issue.

Because sensitivity and responsiveness are modal notions, it makes sense to specify the degree to which an agent is responsive to reasons in terms of *counterfactuals* about what she would believe or how she would act in situations in which there was sufficient reason for her to do otherwise. An agent is more or less responsive to reason depending on how well her judgments about what she ought to do and her choices track her reasons for action in different possible circumstances.

In specifying responsiveness in terms of counterfactuals, we can remain agnostic about whether capacities or counterfactuals have explanatory prior-ity. On some views, normative capacities are real psychological structures that ground the truth of certain counterfactuals. On other views, what it is for an agent to have a capacity is just for certain counterfactuals to be true of him. A third possibility is that there is no explanatory priority between capacities and counterfactuals. I have some sympathy for the no priority view inasmuch as I find both claims of explanatory priority plausible. However, as far as I can see, our concerns about responsibility and normative competence do not require taking sides in this metaphysical debate. We can be ecumenical about whether capacities ground counterfactuals, counterfactuals ground cap-acities, or there is no priority between these two concepts.

We might begin by distinguishing different *grades* of responsiveness. Here, it will be useful to adapt some ideas from John Fischer's and Mark Ravizza's defense of a reasons-responsive conception of responsibility in their book *Responsibility and Control.* They frame their discussion in terms of the responsiveness of the *mechanisms* on which agents act, rather than in terms of the responsiveness of *persons* or *agents.* I will discuss this difference later and defend focusing on the responsiveness of persons or agents, rather than mechanisms (§21). But we don't need to engage this issue now and can adapt their discussion of the responsiveness of mechanisms to our discussion of the normative capacities of agents. Adapting their discussion in this way, we might begin by distinguishing two extreme degrees of responsiveness.

- *Strong Responsiveness*: Whenever there is sufficient reason for the agent to act, she recognizes the reason and conforms her behavior to it.
- *Weak Responsiveness*: There is at least one situation in which there is a sufficient reason to act, and the agent recognizes that reason and con-forms her behavior to it.

Once these possibilities are made explicit, it seems implausible to model normative competence in terms of either strong or weak responsiveness.

Strong responsiveness is too strong for the same reason we gave for focusing on competence rather than performance. We do not require that people actually act for sufficient reasons to do otherwise; it is their capacities that matter. For instance, the weak-willed are, at least typically, responsible for their poor choices. Moreover, if strong responsiveness was a condition of responsibility, wrongdoing itself would indicate that the agent was not responsible, with the absurd result that we could never hold anyone responsible for wrongdoing. Wrongdoing would be per se excusing, because wrongdoers necessarily fail to be strongly responsive.

Moreover, weak responsiveness seems too weak. It treats someone as responsive in the actual situation even if she did not respond in the actual situation and there is only one extreme circumstance in which she would recognize and respond to reasons for action. Suppose that I am cognitively limited and recognize my obligations only in extremely favorable circumstances, for instance, with lots of help from others, and don't recognize them in other circumstances. In these other, less fortunate, circumstances, I don't seem to have the capacity to recognize moral norms, even though I do recognize them in some possible circumstances. Or, suppose that an extreme agoraphobe will only go outside her house under immanent threat of death, for instance, if her house is on fire, but not otherwise. Assume, moreover, that she recognizes reason to leave her house, perhaps as a means to help an injured passerby. It seems implausible to judge whether she has the capacity in normal circumstances by whether she can conform her conduct to her normative knowledge in very unusual and dire circumstances.

The Goldilocks standard of responsiveness evidently lies somewhere between these extremes. Of course, there is considerable space between the extremes—the gap between always and once. We might stake out an intermediate form of responsiveness in something like the following terms.

- *Moderate Responsiveness*: Where there is sufficient reason for the agent to act, she regularly recognizes the reason and conforms her behavior to it.

Moderate responsiveness is deliberately vague; it specifies a *range* or *space* of counterfactuals that must be true for the agent to be responsive. Ideally, we would be able to specify a preferred form of moderate responsiveness more precisely. As we will see, one central question is whether to identify some *threshold* level of responsiveness that is necessary and sufficient for responsibility or to treat responsiveness in a *fully scalar* manner. In Chapter 15, I will argue that as a matter of *ideal theory* responsibility and, in particular, normative competence should be fully scalar, with the result that excuse should also be fully scalar. However, we will see that human limitations in tracking scalar inputs reliably might justify the adoption of thresholds for administrative and pragmatic reasons associated with *non-ideal theory*. If so, it would be important to identify where to set the threshold of responsiveness for purposes of responsibility. What is important for present purposes is that reasons-responsiveness is a matter of degree and that if there must be a threshold it should be some form of moderate responsiveness.

So far, these remarks about responsiveness lump together cognitive and volitional dimensions of responsiveness. But if they are independent aspects of normative competence, then we may need to assess responsiveness along these two dimensions separately. It is at least conceivable that we might require different degrees of responsiveness for cognitive and volitional competence. For instance, Fischer and Ravizza distinguish the cognitive and volitional dimensions of reasons-responsiveness in terms of "reasons-receptivity" and "reasons-reactivity" (respectively). Their conception of reasons-responsiveness is *asymmetrical*, because it requires different grades of responsiveness for cognitive and volitional dimensions of competence. They combine moderate receptivity and weak reactivity.[18] I will discuss their case for treating volitional responsiveness differently than cognitive responsiveness shortly, as part of my discussion of skepticism about volitional competence (§22). But I think it is hard to motivate anything more or less than moderate responsiveness for either cognitive or volitional dimensions of competence, and so I think our provisional view of normative competence should treat the degree of responsiveness for cognitive and volitional competence symmetrically.

This initial formulation of responsiveness is also somewhat coarse-grained in assuming that we consider together all situations in which there is sufficient reason for an agent to act. But we may find it more informative to partition possibilities into groups, depending on the kinds of reasons at stake and other aspects of the situations in which agents find themselves. For instance, in deciding whether an agent had sufficient volitional capacity to overcome fears that stood in the way of her performing her duty, we may think it best to restrict our attention to those counterfactuals in which she faced threats or fears of comparable kind or magnitude. For these reasons, we may need to make our assessments of the degree of an agent's responsiveness more fine-

---

[18] Fischer and Ravizza, *Responsibility and Control*, pp. 81–82.

grained as we proceed. But perhaps this is sufficiently fine-grained to help us fix initial ideas about normative competence.

20. Reasons-responsiveness and Deliberation

So far, responsibility seems to require normative competence, which has both cognitive and volitional dimensions and requires some kind of moderate reasons-responsiveness with respect to each dimension. We said that responsible agents are persons—able to step back from their passions and desires, to exert impulse control, to deliberate about the merits of their options, and to regulate their conduct in accordance with these deliberations. This may suggest that reflection and deliberation are essential to agency and responsibility. But this may seem to over-intellectualize our conception of agency and responsibility. Indeed, much recent literature on the role of automaticity in our cognitive and behavioral processes may seem to imply that we are not especially reflective agents and that any intellectualist conception of agency and responsibility is empirically inadequate.[19] Is any conception of responsibility that requires normative competence problematic in these ways? This question raises large and complex issues that cannot be addressed satisfactorily here. But I think we can say enough to sustain the importance of normative competence to responsibility.

It seems problematic to assume that every act of responsible agency requires a prior act of deliberation, because that assumption seems to lead to a regress.

1. Every act of responsible agency requires prior deliberation.
2. Deliberation is itself an act of responsible agency.
3. Hence, every act of deliberation requires a prior act of deliberation, and so on.

This regress is supposed to represent a *reductio* of the first premise.[20] But this regress does not threaten the appeal to normative competence, because normative competence does not insist that responsible action always proceed from deliberation. It requires only that responsible agents must have the

[19] For discussion, see John Doris, *Talking to Our Selves: Reflection, Ignorance, and Agency* (Oxford: Clarendon Press, 2015), esp. chs. 2–4.

[20] For discussion of related kinds of regress involving deliberation and reflection, see Hilary Kornblith, *On Reflection* (Oxford: Clarendon Press, 2012). My thinking about the regress discussed here has benefited from conversations with Dana Nelkin, Matt Braich, and Cory Davia.

capacity for deliberation and presumably that they sometimes exercise this capacity. Moreover, that capacity can often be exercised at significant temporal remove from individual expressions of agency, as when I act from a plan or habit that I adopted much earlier as the result of deliberation or that I acquired without deliberation but that has persisted because I deliberatively endorse it, explicitly or implicitly.

Even if normative competence does not lead to a regress, it still might seem to over-intellectualize responsible agency. Much action that is reasons-responsive is guided by automatic and unconscious processes and not the result of explicit deliberation. This reflects the operation of dual process models of cognition in which System 1 involves cognition that is fast, driven by heuristics and scripts, non-deliberative, and (often) emotionally encoded and in which System 2 involves cognition that is slow, effortful, and deliberative. According to these models of cognition, much of our ordinary cognition involves System 1, and System 2 mainly comes online in novel cases or cases in which System 1 heuristics and scripts give conflicting guidance. Moreover, this division of labor between System 1 and System 2 represents, for the most part, an efficient use of scarce cognitive resources.[21]

While some philosophical and psychological commentators treat automatic processes as non-rational, a number of commentators argue that we have good reason to regard them as rational and reasons-responsive.[22] Though not reliable for novel situations and circumstances, cognitive and behavioral scripts are broadly reliable for the contexts for which they were developed. Moreover, beliefs, desires, and affect are potentially rational insofar as they are capable of dynamic updating and attunement in response to feedback from the world, including outcomes of the agent's own conduct. On this view, a significant portion of human action can be represented as reasons-responsive, despite not being the product of explicit and conscious practical deliberation. This kind of automaticity is well illustrated in the sort of fluent performance of skilled athletes and improvisational musicians, though we all engage in this sort of non-deliberative agency in more mundane tasks and activities, such as

---

[21] For accessible presentations of dual process models of cognition, see Cass Sunstein, "Moral Heuristics" *Behavioral and Brain Sciences* 28 (2005): 531–73 and Daniel Kahneman, *Thinking, Fast and Slow* (New York: Farrar, Straus, and Giroux, 2011).

[22] See, e.g., Peter Railton, "Practical Competence and Fluent Agency" in *Practical Reason*, ed. D. Sobel and S. Wall (Cambridge: Cambridge University Press, 2009); "The Affective Dog and Its Rational Tale: Intuition and Attunement" *Ethics* 124 (2014): 813–59; "Learning as an Inherent Dynamic of Belief and Desire" in *The Nature of Desire*, ed. J. Deona and F. Lauria (Oxford: Clarendon Press, 2017). Railton gave a unified presentation of ideas in these and related essays in his 2018 Locke Lectures at Oxford University.

navigating our way home from work. Indeed, this sort of largely automatic reasons-responsive agency is characteristic of much of the epistemic and practical conduct of non-human animals too.

There is much that it is attractive about this picture of automatic agency, and it implies that we shouldn't think that responsible agency always requires reflection and deliberation. However, to say that rational action does not always require explicit deliberation is not to say that explicit deliberation is unimportant to rational agency. To jettison deliberation from our picture of rational agency would be to throw the baby out with the bathwater. There are important moments to suspend cognitive heuristics and behavioral scripts and engage in effortful deliberation. These include cases in which multiple heuristics support conflicting verdicts in a situation and cases in which it's reasonably clear that the agent faces a situation for which a given heuristic, while reliable in other contexts, is not reliable. In such cases, a rational agent needs to be able to step back from her cognitive scripts and engage in deliberation about her options and the comparative merits of those options.[23] While this sort of deliberation can be cognitively demanding, it is psychologically realistic, provided it doesn't occur too frequently.[24]

Of course, System 2 deliberation suffers its own dangers, including motivated reasoning and implicit biases. But if we become aware of these threats to deliberation, we can combat them. Blindspots and biases are threats to rationality insofar as agents proceed solipsistically, relying only on introspection for information about their own psychological attitudes and trusting only their own cognitive resources to evaluate the options and their merits. But suitably socially embedded agents, who are aware of the operation of heuristics and biases and make use of institutional and interpersonal sources for identifying and correcting bias, are positioned to engage in deliberation that better tracks their reasons for action.

Even if rational action per se does not require reasons-responsive deliberation and is exhibited by non-human animals, it is nonetheless true that, as far

---

[23] For interesting work on the role of practical uncertainty and anxiety in helping agents identify situations that call for switching from automatic processes to explicit deliberation, see Charlie Kurth, *The Anxious Mind: An Investigation into the Varieties and Virtues of Anxiety* (Cambridge, MA: MIT Press, 2018).

[24] Historically minded readers will no doubt see parallels between these claims about the value and limits of System 1 heuristics and biases and Mill's claims about the value and limits of secondary principles or precepts. The definitive edition of Mill's writings is *Collected Works of John Stuart Mill*, 33 volumes, ed. J. Robson (Toronto: University of Toronto Press, 1965–91). The importance and limits of secondary principles are issues Mill discusses in many writings. Two important sources are *A System of Logic* VI.xii.7 (*CW* VIII 951–52) and *Utilitarianism*, Chapter II, paragraphs 19–25 and Ch. V, paras. 32–38 (*CW* X 219–26, 255–59). For discussion of these issues and their significance for Mill's moral philosophy, see David O. Brink, *Mill's Progressive Principles* (Oxford: Clarendon Press, 2013) §24.

as we know, only normal adult humans display deliberative rationality, especially the capacity for normative deliberation about the good, the right, and the rights and interests of others. Normative deliberation is only part of rationality, and it is a fragile achievement, but it is nonetheless a distinctive and important dimension of moral personality. It is our capacity to engage in this sort of deliberative reasons-responsiveness that marks us as responsible agents and persons.

21. The Person as the Locus of Responsiveness

I have been writing as if responsibility requires that persons or agents possess reasons-responsive capacities. Indeed, persons just are normatively competent agents. This seems like a natural way to formulate these ideas. After all, it is persons or agents whom we hold responsible and blame or excuse.

But not everyone within the reasons-responsive tradition agrees. Fischer and Ravizza defend a conception of responsibility in which they ask whether the psychological mechanisms on which the agent acted were reasons-responsive. Of course, they don't deny that we hold persons responsible for their actions or that persons are the targets of the reactive attitudes. But they think that persons are responsible or excused and subject to the reactive attitudes in virtue of facts about whether the mechanisms on which they acted were reasons-responsive. Thus, their conception of reasons-responsiveness is mechanism-based, rather than agent-based.[25] This mechanism-based conception of reasons-responsiveness is somewhat idiosyncratic, but it is worthwhile seeing why we should avoid it.

First of all, it is odd to locate reasons-responsiveness at the sub-personal level inasmuch as persons, rather than mechanisms, are responsible and normatively competent. As we've seen, an important philosophical tradition identifies persons as reasons-responsive agents. Persons are held accountable and the subject of praise and blame. Our reactive attitudes are directed at persons, not their mechanisms, and we punish, sometimes via incarceration, persons, not their mechanisms. If only their mechanisms are responsible, punishing whole persons would be grossly overly punitive.

---

[25] See Fischer and Ravizza, *Responsibility and Control*, p. 38. Fischer and Ravizza link their mechanism-based conception with their acceptance of Frankfurt's focus on the actual causal sequence.

A mechanism-based conception might concede that we hold persons responsible and accountable but insist that we do so only in virtue of some facts about the responsiveness of their psychological mechanisms considered individually. This is a coherent position, but it requires a rationale. If persons are the bearers of responsibility and excuse and the proper objects of the reactive attitudes and practices, then we need some reason for thinking that this is true in virtue of quite limited facts about proper parts of them, the particular mechanisms on which they act. I think that this creates an explanatory burden for the mechanism-based conception that is hard to discharge.

If this was the only issue raised by mechanism-based conceptions, the debate might not be important to settle. However, a focus on the agent's actual mechanisms makes the mechanism-based conception of excuse implausibly promiscuous. Consider a weak-willed agent who acts on strong urges, say, for drink. Perhaps these urges are in the relevant sense irresistible insofar as the agent couldn't conquer her temptations by an exercise of willpower. In such a case, the agent's actual mechanism of impulse resistance was insufficiently reasons-responsive, and a mechanism-based conception of reasons-responsiveness should deny she is responsible and excuse her. But this conclusion reflects only conquerability, ignoring circumventability. The agent's actual mechanism was to rely on willpower, but she had available other mechanisms on which she could have acted so as to *work around* her inadequate willpower. In a cool prospective moment, she could have thrown out the alcohol in her house or avoided meeting her old friends at the bar. The availability of these alternative mechanisms shows that she was reasons-responsive and should not be excused just because her actual mechanisms were not reasons-responsive. Our ascription of responsibility should be sensitive to all of the capacities and mechanisms available to the agent.

These claims generalize to other cases. Agents often act on implicit biases and blindspots, which may reflect the operation of mechanisms that were not sufficiently reasons-responsive. But if the agent had available alternative strategies or procedures that provide workarounds for these defective mechanisms, then she is responsible and should not be excused. But this conclusion requires locating reasons-responsiveness at the personal, rather than subpersonal, level. In Chapter 11 we will encounter arguments for excusing psychopaths that appeal to the effect of their empathy deficits on their moral understanding. This kind of argument might show that their empathy-based mechanisms for acquiring moral knowledge are insufficiently responsive to reason, but that needn't show that they lack responsibility or should be excused if they have available alternate, non-empathetic forms of access to moral and legal requirements. Here too, a mechanism-based conception of reasons-responsiveness will be more promiscuous with excuse than a person-based conception in a way that seems problematic. We should be reluctant to excuse an agent if she had the capacity to recognize the limitations of her actual mechanisms and employ other reasons-responsive mechanisms to circumvent the non-responsive mechanism and avoid wrongdoing.[26]

22. Skepticism about Skepticism about Volitional Competence

So far, it seems that responsibility consists in normative competence, which involves moderate responsiveness along both cognitive and volitional dimensions. This conception is reflected in the Model Penal Code conception of responsibility and excuse. However, it's worth looking at challenges to these assumptions about volitional competence. *Strong skepticism* about volitional competence rejects the very idea of volitional competence as a requirement of responsibility. By contrast, *weak skepticism* says that, unlike cognitive competence, which requires moderate responsiveness, volitional competence requires only weak responsiveness. This is a form of skepticism insofar as weak responsiveness will leave one skeptical that there are many cases of volitional impairment. Stephen Morse expresses sympathy with both strong and weak skepticism about volitional competence, whereas Fischer and Ravizza endorse weak skepticism. It's especially interesting to examine their forms of skepticism, because they are otherwise broadly sympathetic with the general approach to responsibility defended here.

Does normative competence require volitional competence at all? Morse writes within the fair choice tradition of criminal law conceptions of responsibility that analyzes responsibility in terms of rational capacities and fair opportunities to exercise those capacities. Rational capacities might seem to be purely cognitive capacities, in which case one might think that volitional capacities were not necessary for responsibility. But that would be a poor rationale for skepticism about volitional competence. On the one hand, if we do restrict rational capacities to cognitive capacities, then it becomes eminently plausible that normative competence requires more than rational

---

[26] For other defenses of an agent-based, rather than mechanism-based, conception of reasons-responsiveness, see Nelkin, *Making Sense of Freedom and Responsibility*, pp. 64–79; Vargas, *Building Better Beings*, ch. 7; and McKenna, "Reasons-Responsiveness, Agents, and Mechanisms."

capacities. For if I know what I ought to do but am unable to conform my conduct to that knowledge, due to irresistible desires, paralyzing phobias, or severe depression, then I am not responsible for my conduct and should be excused, despite possessing rational capacities. On the other hand, this is a narrow way to think of rational capacities. There might be more to rationality than correct belief, knowledge, or cognitive capacity. For instance, one might not count as practically rational unless one's appetites and passions are sufficiently under control to enable one to conform one's will to one's normative judgment. This would argue for a broader conception of rational capacities that includes both cognitive and volitional elements.

In his essay "Uncontrollable Urges and Irrational People" Morse critically discusses proposals to treat wrongdoers with irresistible impulses as excused for lack of control. He claims, not implausibly, that many with emotional or appetitive disorders are nonetheless responsible, because they retain sufficient capacity for rationality. However, in discussing excuses that appeal to uncontrollable urges, he makes clear that his conception of rationality excludes volitional components.

> This ... Essay claims that our ambivalence about control problems is caused by a confused understanding of the nature of those problems and argues that control or volitional problems should be abandoned as legal criteria [for excuse].[27]

But why should we abandon a volitional dimension to normative competence and control? Morse focuses on the alleged threat posed by irresistible urges and makes three distinct claims: (1) we cannot make sense of irresistible urges; (2) we cannot distinguish between genuinely irresistible urges and urges not resisted; and (3) there are no irresistible urges, because under sufficient threat of sanction we can resist any strong urge. Notice that these are not just three different claims but that they actually support incompatible conclusions. The first two claims support skepticism about the coherence of volitional competence, whereas the third supports the conclusion that volitional competence is a comparatively easy standard to meet. The first two claims support strong skepticism, whereas the third supports weak skepticism. It will be helpful to separate these two lines of argument.

Morse's skepticism focuses on irresistible urges, which might already raise questions about the generality of his conclusions, because it ignores the

---

[27] Morse, "Uncontrollable Urges and Irrational People," p. 1054.

varieties of volitional impairment, which include not just irresistible urges but also paralyzing fears, depression, and systematic weakness caused by abnormality in the prefrontal cortex.

But consider what Morse does say about irresistible urges. A majority of the Supreme Court in *Kansas v. Crane* justified civil detention of those who are dangerous to themselves or others on account of control problems that are the result of mental abnormality.[28] In discussing irresistible impulses, the Court claimed that it was crucial whether the urges were sufficiently irresistible to present a control problem. A control problem can be understood as a significant impairment of relevant volitional capacities. In criticizing the Court's volitional test, Morse claims that we don't know what it would mean for urges to be irresistible and that, even if the concept was coherent, we could not distinguish between irresistible urges and urges not resisted. This second concern is the problem of distinguishing between can't and won't. Morse is not the only one to have doubts about distinguishing when an agent can't conform his conduct to norms and when he simply won't. In *United States v. Lyons*, Judge Gee expressed a similar concern about the Model Penal Code requirement of volitional competence and our ability to distinguish can't and won't.[29]

However, these two objections to the very idea of volitional competence are unpersuasive. First, there seems to be no conceptual problem with irresistible urges. We have already analyzed irresistible desires as ones that are neither conquerable nor circumventable. What is true of irresistible urges is true of volitional impairments more generally, so that paralyzing emotions and phobias, severe depression, and systematic weakness of will involve volitional impairments when they are neither conquerable nor circumventable. Conquerability and circumventability are modal notions. So, there is a question about how unconquerable or uncircumventable psychological interference must be to be excusing. But the concept of volitional impairment does not seem problematic.

Can we distinguish can't and won't? First of all, this appears to be an evidentiary problem, not a claim about the ingredients of normative competence. Moreover, this evidentiary problem seems no worse than the one for the

---

[28] *Kansas v. Crane*, 534 U.S. 407 (2002).

[29] *United States v. Lyons* 731 F.2d 243 (1984). In challenging the distinction between can't and won't with respect to resisting impulses, Gee was expressing skepticism about the volitional prong of competence, as recognized by the Model Penal Code. Significantly, this part of Gee's opinion was dicta, not endorsed by the concurring opinions. We will encounter this issue again when we discuss addiction and responsibility in Chapter 13.

cognitive dimension of normative competence, which requires us to distinguish between a genuine inability to recognize something as wrong and a
failure to form correct normative beliefs or attend to normative information at
hand on a particular occasion. Neither Morse nor Gee questions the importance of cognitive competence because of the difficulty of distinguishing can't
and won't there. Why should these difficulties pose a greater problem for
volitional competence? Making the distinction between can't and won't is a
challenge, but not an insurmountable one, in either the cognitive or volitional
case. Counterfactual evidence is relevant to establishing both cognitive and
volitional competence, and among the evidence for the truth of these counterfactuals is evidence about an agent's responsiveness in the past. We decide
whether an agent had cognitive or volitional capacity on a given occasion in
part by seeing if he recognized the relevant norms in the past and conformed
his conduct to them previously. Past history does not always answer questions
about current capacity definitively, but it is certainly relevant and probative. If
an agent has a history of control problems, that is defeasible reason to think
that he might suffer from volitional impairment. If there is little or no such
history and no other reason to suspect volitional impairment, that would be
defeasible evidence that current volitional failure does not reflect volitional
incapacity. Finally, there are various empirical tests of volitional engagement,
for instance, there are neurophysiological tests for various forms of affective, as
well as cognitive, sensitivity, such as electrodermal tests of empathetic
responsiveness.[30]

Skepticism about the very idea of volitional competence is not very plausible. But how demanding is volitional competence? If the requirements of
volitional competence are very weak, then we might be skeptical that volitional
impairment excuses very often. This would be weak skepticism about volitional competence.

Morse also claims that even if we could make sense of irresistible urges and
distinguish between irresistible urges and urges not resisted, we would find
that in actual cases the urges in question would almost always be resistible. In
discussing whether an addict's cravings are irresistible, Morse argues that they
are not because if you hold a gun to the addict's head and tell him that you'll
shoot him if he gives in, he can resist.[31] For historically minded readers, this
will be reminiscent of Kant's similar comments in *The Critique of Practical*

---

[30] See, e.g., James Blair, Derek Mitchell, and Karina Blair, *The Psychopath: Emotion and the Brain*
(Oxford: Blackwell, 2005), pp. 49–50.
[31] Morse, "Uncontrollable Urges and Irrational People," pp. 1057–58, 1070.

Reason, when discussing whether someone contemplating sexual assault could plead irresistible desires.

> Suppose that someone says his lust is irresistible when the desired object and opportunity are present. Ask him whether he would not control his passion if, in front of the house where he had this opportunity, a gallows were erected on which he would be hanged immediately after gratifying his lust. We do not have to guess very long what his answer would be.[32]

Morse and Kant assume that if you can resist temptation in one circumstance you can resist it in any circumstance. This position bears comparison with that of Fischer and Ravizza, who defend moderate responsiveness for cognitive competence (reasons-receptivity) but only weak responsiveness for volitional competence (reasons-reactivity).[33] In defense of weak reactivity, Fischer and Ravizza claim that reactivity is "all of a piece"—if you can conform in some cases, even one case, that shows that you can conform in any case.[34]

There are two problems with this defense of weak volitional responsiveness. First, weak skeptics about volitional competence are committed to an asymmetry between cognitive and volitional capacities. Yet, if reactivity were "all of a piece," then why not say the same thing about receptivity? If one can recognize moral reasons in some circumstances, then one can recognize them in any. No one is proposing to accept weak cognitive responsiveness. But if this is a fixed point, then there is no principled defense of weak volitional responsiveness. Second, as we have already noted (§19), weak volitional responsiveness is implausibly weak, because it claims that one has the capacity to conform one's conduct to norms that one recognizes, provided there is at least one circumstance in which one would so conform. If an addict can conform to norms against consuming the substance he craves only under threat of death, it seems wrong to assume that he can thereby refrain from consumption in any circumstances, including those involving less serious threats. In effect, these writers seem committed to claiming that one can't have weak responsiveness without having moderate responsiveness. Anyone

---

[32] Immanuel Kant, *Critique of Practical Reason* [1788] in *Kant's Practical Philosophy*, trs. M. Gregor (Prussian Academy pagination), 5: 30.

[33] It is worth noting that Fischer's and Ravizza's view is *doubly* asymmetric insofar as they require receptivity to at least some *moral* reasons, but require reactivity only to reasons in general, not necessarily moral ones. See Fischer and Ravizza, *Responsibility and Control*, p. 79. I don't see a principled rationale for this sort of asymmetry either.

[34] Fischer and Ravizza, *Responsibility and Control*, p. 73.

who can resist an urge in one extreme situation can resist it in others. But I see no reason to accept this psychological stipulation.[35]

23. Situational Control

An important part of an agent's being responsible for wrongdoing that she chose and intended consists in her being a responsible agent. This we have conceptualized in terms of normative competence and analyzed into cognitive and volitional capacities. Evidence for this view is that one seems to have an excuse, whether complete or partial, if one's cognitive or volitional competence is compromised in significant ways. This conception of the normative competence aspects of responsibility and excuse fits the Model Penal Code conception of insanity, and it builds on work in the reasons-responsive wing of the compatibilist tradition in moral philosophy.

But there is more to an agent being culpable or responsible for her wrongdoing than her being responsible and having acted intentionally. Excuse is not exhausted by denials of normative competence. Among the factors that may interfere with our reactive attitudes, including blame and punishment, are external or situational factors. In particular, duress can induce an agent to engage in wrongdoing that she would not otherwise have performed. The paradigm duress excuse is coercion by another agent, as when one is threatened with significant physical harm to oneself or a loved one if one doesn't participate in some kind of wrongdoing, for instance, driving the getaway car in a robbery. The Model Penal Code adopts a reasonable person version of the conditions under which duress excuses, namely, when a person of reasonable firmness would have been unable to resist, provided the actor was not himself responsible for being subject to duress (MPC §2.09).[36] The duressed person is coerced into engaging in wrongdoing that she wouldn't otherwise have engaged in. In this way, duress denies agents the fair opportunity to act on their own deliberations free from wrongful interference by others.

Duress is not an incompetence excuse. It does not compromise the wrongdoer's normative competence or her status as a responsible agent. Indeed, it's

[35] For some related concerns about the case Fischer and Ravizza make for weak reactivity, see Gary Watson, "Reasons and Responsibility" reprinted in Watson, *Agency and Answerability*, esp. pp. 293–300.

[36] For present purposes, I accept the Model Penal Code assumptions that duress involves hard choice whose source is wrongful interference by another agent and that duress is an excuse, rather than a justification. Interesting questions can be raised about both assumptions. I address these issues in Chapter 8.

plausible to claim in the paradigmatic case of duress that the duressed person is not just reasons-responsive but also reasons-responding in acceding to the threat. But even if duress does not challenge the duressed agent's status as a responsible agent, it does challenge whether she is responsible for her wrongdoing. This shows that we need to distinguish between *being a responsible agent* and *being responsible for one's wrongdoing*. Being normatively competent is sufficient for being a responsible agent, but it is necessary but not sufficient for being responsible for one's wrongdoing. The duressed wrongdoer is a responsible agent, but nonetheless she is not responsible for her wrongdoing. Responsibility for wrongdoing requires both normative competence and situational control. Or, to put the same point another way, being a responsible agent is a matter of having the right capacities, but being responsible for one's conduct requires both appropriate capacities and appropriate opportunities.

The fact that duress is excusing shows that responsibility for one's conduct is a matter of both capacities and opportunities, as Hart and Moore insist. Some early modern philosophers, such as Hobbes and Locke, recognized the importance of freedom from coercion, but many recent moral philosophers in the reasons-responsive condition have ignored or at least downplayed the importance of suitable opportunities and situational control, focusing on normative competence and reasons-responsiveness. This is a point where philosophers working on moral responsibility would benefit from attending to criminal law concerns with duress. Recognition of the need for the right opportunities, as well as the right capacities, requires recognizing that responsibility requires situational control, as well as normative competence.[37]

24. Interaction between Normative Competence and Situational Control

So far, the picture of responsibility emerging from this discussion treats normative competence and situational control as essential for being responsible for one's conduct. This picture is quite attractive. But how, exactly, are these two elements related? Are normative competence and situational control completely independent conditions of responsibility?

---

[37] Interestingly, Wallace expressly denies that responsibility requires opportunities as well as capacities. See Wallace, *Responsibility and the Moral Sentiments*, pp. 187–88.

On one conception, normative competence and situational control are individually necessary and jointly sufficient but independent factors in responsibility. On this conception, there is an appropriate degree of competence and an appropriate degree of situational control that can be fixed independently of each other and that are both necessary for responsibility, such that falling short in either dimension is excusing. On this picture, we assess an agent in each area separately. We figure out whether she had the relevant capacities—whether they were normal or sufficient—and then we figure out whether she had the fair opportunity to exercise them free from undue interference. This is a natural interpretation of the conception of responsibility that I have defended so far.

However, an alternative conception of the relation between normative competence and situational control is possible that treats them as individually necessary and jointly sufficient but at least potentially interacting. On this picture, how much and what sort of capacities one needs can vary according to situational features. So, for example, there might be situations in which the wrongdoing in question was especially clear, such as a murder or an assault, and in which there was no significant provocation, duress, or other hard choice. We might think that culpable wrongdoing, in such cases, requires less in the form of cognitive or volitional capacities than in cases in which the normative issues are less clear or in which there is substantial provocation or duress. Or suppose we hold constant the wrongdoing in question and compare the interaction of situational factors and competence in different individuals. It's plausible to suppose that normative competence requires an ability to make one's own normative judgments and hold to them despite temptation, distraction, and peer pressure. It's also plausible to suppose that adolescents have less independence of judgment and ability to resist peer pressure than their adult counterparts. But then we might be more excusing of adolescent wrongdoing committed in groups than of comparable adult behavior committed in groups. If so, differential competence may explain why the same level of situational pressure may be excusing for some and not for others.[38] But then we might prefer a conception of normative competence and situational control in which they are potentially interacting, rather than necessarily independent, dimensions of responsibility. Such a conception would also imply that the requisite levels of normative competence and situational control

---

[38] These ideas are explored in Brink, "Immaturity, Normative Competence, and Juvenile Transfer" and in Chapter 12.

are not invariant, but rather context-dependent. We will return to these issues in Chapters 4 and 10.

25. The Fair Opportunity to Avoid Wrongdoing

So far, the conception of responsibility emerging here is a two-factor model twice over. Responsibility is factored into normative competence and situational control, and normative competence is factored into cognitive and volitional capacities. This kind of two-factor model seems plausible, in significant part because it promises to fit our practices of excuse in both moral assessment and the criminal law pretty well. Incapacity excuses deny normative competence, whereas duress excuses deny the opportunity to exercise those capacities free from inappropriate interference by others. But it would be nice if there was some unifying element to its structure.

One possible umbrella concept is *control*. Freedom from coercion and duress, cognitive competence, and volitional competence all seem to be aspects of an agent's ability to control her actions. But control seems important, at least in part, because it seems *unfair* to blame agents for outcomes that are outside their control. This suggests that the umbrella concept should be fairness, in particular, *the fair opportunity to avoid wrongdoing*, because failure of either normative competence or situational control violates the norm that blame and punishment should be reserved for those who had a fair opportunity to avoid wrongdoing. If we treat the fair opportunity to avoid wrongdoing as the key to responsibility, we get the following picture of the architecture of responsibility (see Figure 3.1). This diagrammatic representation of the fair opportunity conception differs from the one introduced earlier (§1) only by allowing for potential interaction between normative competence and situational control.

In "Legal Responsibility and Excuses" Hart suggests that the criminal law conditions liability on culpability out of respect for "the efficacy of the individual's informed and considered choice in determining the future."[39] This might be described as a concern with autonomy, but it also implicates considerations of fairness. This is evident in the fundamental legal principle of *legality*. Legality is the doctrine that there should be no punishment in the absence of public notice of a legal requirement. The principle of legality is

---

[39] H.L.A. Hart, "Legal Responsibility and Excuses" reprinted in Hart, *Punishment and Responsibility*, p. 46.

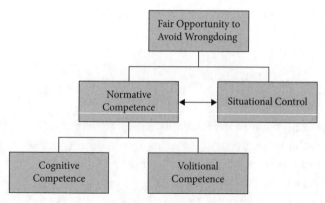

Figure 3.1 Fair Opportunity, Revised

usually defended as part of fair notice. *Ex post facto* or retroactive criminal law would be unfair, because it would punish those for failing to conform to behavioral expectations of which they had not been apprised in advance. In this way, *ex post facto* law not only threatens individual autonomy but is unfair because of the way in which it upsets people's reasonable expectations about the standards to which they will be held. The principle of legality articulates the demand that blame and punishment be conditioned on the agent having the fair opportunity to avoid wrongdoing. In this way, the fair opportunity conception of responsibility and excuse rests on principles of fairness deeply embedded in the criminal law.

26. Fair Opportunity as a Point of Convergence

Strawson's thesis links the moralized reactive attitudes with responsibility. For this reason, it licenses us in appealing to our reactive attitudes and practices—in particular, our practices of excuse—to provide evidence about the conditions of responsibility. Adopting this methodology suggests that we look, at least in part, to criminal law doctrines about excuse to shed light on responsibility. The criminal law excuses for sufficient impairment of either the agent's capacities, as in cases of insanity or immaturity, or opportunities, as in cases of duress. This tells us that responsibility requires both suitable capacities and opportunities. We conceptualized the requisite capacities in terms of normative competence, conceived as having both cognitive and volitional dimensions. We conceptualized the requisite opportunities in terms of situational control. This conception of responsibility not only fits well with our practices of excuse in both moral assessment and the criminal law but also appeals to an important normative idea that blame and punishment are legitimate only when the agent had the fair opportunity to avoid wrongdoing.

This fair opportunity conception of responsibility will structure much of the rest of this book. It provides a powerful lens through which to examine concepts central to both moral psychology and the criminal law concerning blame, punishment, culpability, justification, and excuse. In doing so, fair opportunity also provides a unified framework within which to address issues about partial responsibility that are forced on our attention by structural injustice, situational pressures, incompetence and psychopathy, immaturity, addiction, and provocation and crimes of passion. Each of these topics raises its own issues, which might seem to preclude a unified treatment. But, despite evident and important differences, these topics all raise issues of responsibility and excuse, and the fair opportunity conception allows us to see common themes about the fragility of fair opportunity and the need for an analysis of partial responsibility and excuse.

Embracing the fair opportunity conception of responsibility and excuse means rejecting an error theory and abolitionism about responsibility. But, otherwise, fair opportunity can be reasonably ecumenical and can serve as a point of convergence among disparate meta-normative and metaphysical views. Though our reactive attitudes and practices supply *evidence* for fair opportunity, the capacities and opportunities in which fair opportunity consists can be specified in response-independent terms.[40] We can specify the requirements of normative competence and situational control without recourse to the reactive attitudes. This supports the realist reading of Strawson's thesis according which responsibility—now conceived in terms of fair opportunity—grounds and justifies the reactive attitudes. We can take seriously the need to justify the reactive attitudes, and we can succeed in justifying them when the targets of those attitudes possess suitable normative competence and situational control.

Are normative competence and situational control compatible with determinism? They certainly seem to be insofar as we deploy fair opportunity excuses selectively to compromised capacity or opportunity. We do not excuse

---

[40] Here, my position contrasts with the otherwise similar position in Wallace, *Responsibility and the Moral Sentiments*, esp. pp. 1, 88–117. Though Wallace wants to understand responsibility in terms of a conception of normative competence that is supported by moral commitments to fairness, he embraces a response-dependent interpretation of Strawson's thesis. I'm not confident about the content of his fairness norms and their relation to my principle about the fair opportunity to avoid wrongdoing. But it seems clear to me that normative competence can and should be interpreted in response-independent terms, even if its importance is motivated by considerations of fairness.

every action as we would need to if hard determinism was true. This presupposes that capacity and opportunity are compatible with determinism. Though I don't aspire to address and answer the skeptic about responsibility or to defend compatibilism against libertarianism, Chapter 4 does try to explain how capacity and opportunity might be compatible with determinism. Realists who are skeptical that an acceptable compatibilist version of fair opportunity can be given can defend fair opportunity on libertarian grounds. I leave that project to libertarians. They are free to accept the fair opportunity conception of responsibility and should be able to accept most of my substantive analysis about the implications of fair opportunity for moral psychology, the criminal law, and partial responsibility and excuse.

Only if we conclude that fair opportunity can be given neither compatibilist nor libertarian foundations should we turn to a response-dependent conception of fair opportunity. Response-dependence says that what makes capacities and opportunities constitutive of responsibility is the fact that that is how we are disposed to react to others and to ourselves. Response-dependence must deny robust fallibilism about the reactive attitudes and either reject the coherence of demands for global justifications of the reactive attitudes or offer purely consequentialist reasons for maintaining them. That's a possible way in which to maintain fair opportunity, but it's hard to distinguish from fictionalist versions of an error theory about responsibility.

4

Fair Opportunity, Capacities, and Possibilities

The fair opportunity conception of responsibility seems to have compatibilist implications insofar as it recognizes excuses *selectively*—as the result of significant impairments of normative competence (e.g. insanity or immaturity) or situational control (e.g. duress)—rather than for all those actions that are causally determined. Though many discussions of free will and responsibility assume that these two concepts stand or fall together, some compatibilist views distinguish sharply between freedom and responsibility, defending responsibility without freedom. In particular, freedom may seem to assume that alternate possibilities are available to agents, and this assumption may seem incompatible with causal determinism. For this reason, some compatibilists defend a conception of responsibility that does not presuppose the sort of alternate possibilities that freedom requires and determinism precludes. However, the fair opportunity conception of responsibility does seem to assume that the responsible wrongdoer could have done otherwise. Is this commitment to alternate possibilities defensible and consistent with determinism? Are these the same kind of alternate possibilities denied by some compatibilists? Consideration of the voluntarist principle that <ought> implies <can> suggests a plausible conception of alternate possibilities in terms of capacities and opportunities that is not precluded by determinism. In this chapter, I motivate this different version of alternate possibilities and provide further explanation of how we should understand capacities and opportunities. I conclude by responding to an influential incompatibilist argument that appeals to manipulation cases and difficulties deciding when strong desires incapacitate and exculpate.

My aim in this chapter is not so much to advance new and decisive arguments in favor of compatibilism and against incompatibilism—a task for which I have little taste or aptitude—but more to explain the sort of compatibilist assumptions that the fair opportunity conception makes and show them to be reasonably plausible. As I have said (§1), skepticism about responsibility presupposes incompatibilism and must take the form of an error

Fair Opportunity and Responsibility. David O. Brink, Oxford University Press (2021). © David O. Brink.
DOI: 10.1093/oso/9780198859468.003.0004

theory about our reactive attitudes and practices. As such, the skeptic has a heavy burden to justify incompatibilist claims. I'll be content if the assumptions fair opportunity makes about capacities, opportunities, and alternate possibilities seem plausible and promising.

27. Freedom, Responsibility, and Alternate Possibilities

Many philosophers associate freedom of the will and responsibility, either identifying the two or understanding freedom of the will as whatever quality of the will is needed for responsibility. So, many compatibilists believe that both freedom and responsibility are compatible with determinism, and many free will skeptics are also skeptics about responsibility. However, some philosophers deny this interdependence of freedom and responsibility. They distinguish between freedom and responsibility, and at least some of them combine skepticism, or at least agnosticism, about freedom of the will with realism about responsibility. Famously, this is the position of Harry Frankfurt in his influential article "Alternate Possibilities and Moral Responsibility." Examining his argument will be instructive.

Frankfurt describes a case in which someone seems to be responsible despite apparently lacking the freedom to do otherwise. In the standard such case, the agent is inclined to act in a certain way for certain reasons and does so, but there is a failsafe or backup device, unbeknownst to the agent, in the form of a *counterfactual intervener* of some sort who would intervene in the agent's life to ensure that he acts in that way and for those reasons if he wasn't going to do it of his own accord. In Frankfurt's case, Jack is a neuroscientist intent on killing the mayor and assumes the role of the counterfactual intervener in Sam's plan to kill the mayor, since he is willing to intervene neurologically to ensure that Sam does kill the mayor should Sam try to decide not to. The classic Frankfurt-style case is when Sam decides to kill the mayor and proceeds to do so of his own accord, without any intervention by Jack. In this case, Sam seems to lack *alternate possibilities*, because there's no alternative in which he doesn't kill the mayor—either he will kill the mayor of his own accord or else Jack will ensure that he does. But Frankfurt insists plausibly that we judge Sam responsible for the killing in the actual scenario in which he acts of his own accord with no intervention from Jack. Such cases seem to show that there can be moral responsibility in the absence of alternate possibilities and freedom of the will. Frankfurt is responding to something like this argument for incompatibilism.

1. Moral responsibility requires freedom of the will.
2. Freedom of the will presupposes the principle of alternate possibilities (PAP), which says that a free agent must have been able to act otherwise than she in fact did.
3. Causal determinism is inconsistent with PAP.
4. Hence, causal determinism is incompatible with moral responsibility.

Importantly, this incompatibilist argument assumes that moral responsibility requires freedom of the will—premise (1). Frankfurt-style cases supposedly give us reason to reject (1) and so avoid the incompatibilist conclusion.

1. In Frankfurt-style cases, the agent is responsible when she chooses to act of her own accord, despite the fact that the existence of the counterfactual intervener means that she could not have acted otherwise.
2. Freedom of the will presupposes PAP.
3. Causal determinism is inconsistent with PAP.
4. Hence, responsibility does not require freedom of the will.

If we associate freedom with PAP and assume that alternate possibilities preclude actions that are necessary, then freedom is incompatible with determinism. If we want to be realists about responsibility and accept determinism, or at least remain agnostic about its truth, then we should deny that responsibility presupposes PAP.[1]

28. Responsibility and Quality of Will without Alternate Possibilities

How can we defend responsibility without alternate possibilities? Frankfurt proposes that we attend to the *actual* sequence of deliberation and choice, rather than alternate possibilities. In "Freedom of the Will and the Concept of

---

[1] One way to push back against Frankfurt cases is to note an ambiguity in the claim that one can do otherwise. The presence of the counterfactual intervener may deprive Sam of the possibility of not killing the mayor, but it does not seem to deprive Sam of the possibility of performing the mental act of trying not to kill the mayor. Call such mental acts *attempts*. Because they are upstream from the point of counterfactual intervention, they can be free. If so, one might locate freedom and responsibility at the level of attempts, relegating bodily movements with worldly consequences to the realm of moral luck. One problem with this response to Frankfurt cases is that if determinism is true there is no point upstream from counterfactual intervention. For this reason, it's better to rethink whether alternate possibilities are incompatible with determinism than to find mental acts that preserve the possibilities that determinism precludes.

a Person" Frankfurt suggests that responsibility involves a mesh between the agent's motivating desires and her other higher-order attitudes. Responsibility requires a mesh between what one wants (at least one's motivating desires) and what one wants to want. To this extent, Frankfurt agrees with the philosophical tradition that claims that responsibility requires personhood and that personhood involves a kind of self-conscious endorsement. In particular, Frankfurt claims that responsibility requires a mesh between the agent's first-order motivating desires and her second-order or aspirational desires. The "wanton" who does not have second-order attitudes toward her motivating desires is not self-conscious in the way that responsibility requires. Nor is the unwilling addict, who has second-order desires but regrets and does not endorse her consumptive desires, responsible. By contrast, the willing addict, who reflectively endorses her consumptive desires, is responsible for her consumptive behavior. This conception of quality of will is open to friendly amendment. In "Free Agency" Watson thought that Frankfurt's appeal to second-order attitudes was right but that second-order desires lacked the right sort of authority to ground responsibility. He proposed that we understand quality of will in terms of a mesh between the agent's first-order motivating desires and her *evaluative* assessment and endorsement of those desires. On this view, an agent is responsible when she judges her motivating desires worthwhile and she is excused when she does not evaluatively endorse her motivating desires.

Though I am sympathetic with the assumption common to both versions of the mesh view that responsibility requires self-consciousness and higher-order attitudes, I think that we need to understand this, as I think the philosophical tradition involving Butler, Reid, Kant, and Green does, in terms of an agent's *capacities* to reflect on and modify one's motivating states in ways that are reasons-responsive (§16). In particular, I think that we should deny that a mesh between motivating attitudes and higher-order attitudes is either necessary or sufficient for responsibility. A mesh is not necessary, because a failure to mesh does not per se excuse. Prototypical cases of akrasia, or weakness of will, in which one acts against one's better judgment, involve a failure to mesh. The akrates acts against her better judgment and so fails to endorse her motivating states. But we do not in general excuse the weak-willed person. Provided the agent had capacities to recognize what she ought to do and conform her conduct to those norms, her performance failure to conform to her normative commitments is not excusing. A mesh is not sufficient for responsibility if the agent lacked the power to act otherwise. The agent who is indifferent to the rights and interests of others and endorses this indifference is not responsible if she lacked the ability to recognize indifference to the rights and interests of others as wrong or the ability to conform her conduct to this knowledge.

This shows that Watson's amendment to Frankfurt will not be able to provide the authority that he correctly sees Frankfurt's version lacks. Wanting to want what one wants and what motivates one does not ensure that one can appreciate what matters and what reasons for action there are. Substituting evaluative beliefs about the good and the right for second-order desires is a step in the right direction. But Watson doesn't require that the agent's beliefs be true or reliable. Perhaps some insane actors judge their malevolent motivating desires to be worthwhile or good. That's not enough to make the insane accountable for their actions. Agents have to have the right relation to genuine justifying reasons for action concerning the good and the right. But we don't want to make it a condition of responsibility that the agent possesses and acts on justifying reasons, because that would confuse reasons-responding with reasons-responsiveness and make wrongdoing per se exculpatory. Instead, we should focus on reasons-responsiveness and the capacity to recognize and conform to justifying reasons.

29. Fair Opportunity and Alternate Possibilities

These concerns about mesh views suggest that it may be difficult to understand moral responsibility without the alternate possibilities required by an appeal to the agent's capacities. Capacitarian conceptions of responsibility, such as the fair opportunity conception, that appeal to normative competence or reasons-responsiveness seem committed to alternate possibilities. In particular, to explain how agents can be responsible for wrongdoing, we need to appeal to cognitive and volitional capacities they have that would have allowed them to avoid wrongdoing. But this assumes that responsibility depends on contrary-to-fact possibilities.

We might assume that if responsibility for wrongdoing requires alternate possibilities, so too does responsibility for permissible and supererogatory actions. However, two prominent reason-responsive theorists deny this symmetry. Both Susan Wolf and Dana Nelkin claim that the underlying capacity is one of being able to be guided toward the good and right. But, they maintain, what's actual is *ipso facto* possible, with the result that responsibility for doing the right thing does not require alternate possibilities in the way that responsibility for doing the wrong things does.[2] So, for instance, both Wolf and Nelkin would view the agent with an irresistible orientation and mesh toward the good and the right as responsible but the agent with an irresistible orientation and mesh away from the good and the right as excused.

Should we accept this asymmetry? It seems to imply that whereas responsibility for wrongful action requires *two-way* powers to act contrary to the way one does, responsibility for good or right action requires only *one-way* powers to act as one does. But we might think that agency and responsibility require two-way powers in all cases.[3] If orientation toward the good and the right were genuinely irresistible, perhaps one would not be responsible for acting well. Thomas Reid holds this sort of view. In *Essays on the Active Powers of the Human Mind*, he claims that accountability and blame presuppose that the agent has the *active power* to distinguish between the intensity and authority of desire, to recognize the demands of the good and the right, and to conform her conduct to those demands. He thinks that this kind of active power must be a two-way power, because the power to produce an effect implies the power not to produce it (*Essays* I 5). Reid concludes that the person who acts well from necessity is not responsible and praiseworthy.

> By *necessity*, I understand want of moral liberty . . . If there can be better and worse in actions on the system of necessity, let us suppose a man necessarily determined in all cases to will and do what is best to be done, he would surely be innocent and inculpable. But, as far as I am able to judge, he would not be entitled to the esteem and moral approbation of those who knew and believed of this necessity. What was, by an ancient author, said of Cato, might indeed be said of him. *He was good because he could not be otherwise.* But this saying, if understood literally and strictly, is not the praise of Cato, but of his constitution, which was no more the work of Cato, than his existence.   [*Essays* IV 1]

This debate about symmetry raises interesting questions about whether divine beings with holy wills, who are necessarily oriented toward the good and the

---

[2] See Wolf, *Freedom within Reason*, pp. 79–81 and Dana Nelkin, "Responsibility and Rational Abilities: Defending an Asymmetrical View" *Pacific Philosophical Quarterly* 89 (2008): 497–515 and *Making Sense of Freedom and Responsibility*, pp. 3–4, 15–19.

[3] For some discussion of the assumption that responsible agency requires two-way powers, see Maria Alvarez, "Agency and Two-Way Powers" *Proceedings of the Aristotelian Society* 113 (2013): 101–21; E.J. Lowe, "Substance Causation, Powers, and Human Agency" in *Mental Causation and Ontology*, ed. A. Gibb, E.J. Lowe, and R. Ingthorsson (Oxford: Clarendon Press, 2013); and Thomas Pink, *Self Determination* (Oxford: Clarendon Press, 2016).

right, would be responsible and praiseworthy. One might embrace symmetry here too, claiming that divine beings with holy wills are perfectly good and merit admiration and veneration, though they are not responsible and praiseworthy for the good they can't help doing. This would involve distinguishing between aretaic and responsibility assessments of holy wills. Perhaps responsibility requires two-way powers in a way in which virtue and admirable conduct do not.

These are complicated issues, and I'm not confident what to say. Fortunately, we need not resolve this issue for present purposes. If our focus is on wrongdoers and whether they are responsible or excused, the implications of symmetrical and asymmetrical capacitarian views will be the same. In such cases, the capacities for avoiding wrongdoing do seem to require some kind of alternate possibilities and two-way powers.

Does this mean that responsibility, as well as freedom, is incompatible with determinism? That depends on whether the alternate possibilities required by fair opportunity are incompatible with determinism, which depends, at least in part, on what kind of possibilities we are considering. Are these logical, metaphysical, physical, or psychological possibilities? On most ways of understanding these different modalities, they range from broader to narrower—for instance, whereas logical possibility is whatever is not inconsistent with the laws of logic, physical possibility is whatever is not inconsistent with physical laws of nature.

It seems clear that PAP, which Frankfurt denies is necessary for responsibility, concerns metaphysical possibility. For Frankfurt assumes that determinism implies the falsity of PAP. So, PAP seems to assume that among the possible worlds with the same prior history and laws of nature as the actual world in which Sam chooses to kill the mayor is at least one world in which he does not in fact do so. But it's not obvious that metaphysical possibility is what responsibility requires.

Consider a potentially related question about how best to understand the sort of possibility required by the *voluntarist principle* that <ought> implies <can>. Voluntarism conditions obligations or requirements on possibility— you can only be obligated to do something if it is possible for you to do it. But what kind of possibility is this? It would be surprising if voluntarism conditioned obligation on the falsity of determinism.[4] Most voluntarists, I think, see

---

[4] Earlier, I recognized the need to distinguish the kind of alternate possibilities that determinism denies and the kind of alternate possibilities that voluntarism requires. See David O. Brink, "Moral Conflict and Its Structure" *Philosophical Review* 103 (1994): 215–47, esp. p. 228. However, at that point,

the implications of voluntarism as both *variable* and *selective*. Voluntarism, on this view, implies that not everyone is under the same obligations, because what is possible for one person in one circumstance might not be possible for another person in another circumstance. But, for this to be true, voluntarism must appeal to something other than metaphysical possibility, because if determinism is true, no one can ever act differently than they do and so no one can be obligated to act otherwise than they do. So, if voluntarism is a principle with variable and selective implications, it must appeal to a different sense of possibility.

Voluntarism presumably appeals to a narrower conception of possibility, such as what is physically and psychologically possible for a given agent at a given time. This is arguably the sort of conception of possibility the criminal law has in mind when it appeals to an agent's capacities and opportunities to ground his responsibility (§22). Physical or psychological incapacity defeats responsibility for wrongdoing, as does lack of opportunities to exercise these capacities free from interference by others. Indeed, both capacity and opportunity appear to be scalar. Impossibility is the limiting case of difficulty, and there are degrees of difficulty. So, impairment of capacities or opportunities can be a matter of degree, and the criminal law recognizes significant impairment of either as excusing. We will be discussing and refining this scalar aspect of responsibility throughout this book. The important point, for present purposes, is that the criminal law conception of responsibility and excuse seems to presuppose a conception of alternate possibilities in the form of physical and psychological capacities and opportunities that agents have to a sufficient degree to behave other than they do. Importantly, these are capacities and opportunities that agents can possess even when they don't exercise them. We might think of capacities and abilities as *dispositions* that tend in the right circumstances to issue in conduct. Something can have a disposition without always manifesting that disposition in behavior.[5]

Indeed, this is the heart of the distinction between competence and performance. At any given time, I possess many capacities or abilities that I don't

---

I had not identified the sort of alternate possibilities apparently required by voluntarism as consisting in the opportunities and capacities that are part of fair opportunity.

[5] For dispositionalist developments of these claims about capacities and abilities, see Kadri Vihvelin, "Free Will Demystified: A Dispositionalist Account" *Philosophical Topics* 32 (2004): 427–50 and *Causes, Laws, and Free Will* (New York: Oxford University Press, 2013) and Michael Fara, "Masked Abilities and Compatibilism" *Mind* 117 (2008): 843–65. For critical discussion of the new dispositionalism, see Randolph Clarke, "Dispositions, Abilities to Act, and Free Will: The New Dispositionalism" *Mind* 118 (2009): 323–51 and "Abilities" *Philosophy Compass* (2015): 1–12 and Ann Whittle, "Dispositional Abilities" *Philosophers' Imprint* 10 (2010): 1–23. I address some of these concerns in §§30–31.

exercise—my capacity to make a short putt for par that I missed, my capacity to speak French to my philosophy class today, or my capacity to begin today to plan a family vacation for the next holiday. Of course, morality and the criminal law are especially concerned with capacities to recognize and respect the rights and interests of others. As long as my cognitive and volitional capacities are not sufficiently impaired, it seems that it was possible, in the relevant sense, for me to have avoided wrongdoing. So, we might key the relevant alternatives to the sort of sufficient physical and psychological capacity and opportunity recognized in morality and law, rather than to metaphysical possibility. Call this the *moralized* reading of alternate possibilities.

We might appeal to something like this moralized modality to understand and defend the voluntarist requirement. But notice that the criminal law does not support a moralized reading of the voluntarist requirement on duty or obligation. As we have seen, the criminal law is broadly retributive insofar as blame and punishment are *pro tanto* fitting responses to culpable wrongdoing. There are two independent variables in the retributivist desert basis for blame and punishment—wrongdoing and culpability or responsibility. But in the criminal law, capacities and opportunities condition culpability or responsibility, not wrongdoing. Excuse is an affirmative defense that concedes wrongdoing but denies responsibility for wrongdoing. Insufficient capacity or opportunity is the basis for an excuse. So, in the case of a paradigmatic excuse, the lack of morally relevant alternatives precludes blame, not wrongdoing. The excused agent violates normative requirements and demands, but is not blameworthy for doing so. This means that blame is sensitive to possibility in a way that wrongdoing and obligation are not. This is a feature of the criminal law that sounds in morality as well. In both morality and criminal law we should reject voluntarism as a principle about obligation, duty, and requirement but accept it as a principle about the conditions under which blame is appropriate.[6]

---

[6] For this reason, I am also skeptical of conceptions of responsibility as accountability that tie accountability to requirements, demands, or expectations. See, e.g., Gary Watson, *Agency and Answerability* (Oxford: Clarendon Press, 2004), pp. 228–29, 273; Wallace, *Responsibility and the Moral Sentiments*, ch. 2; Nelkin, *Making Sense of Freedom and Responsibility*, ch. 5 and Dana Nelkin, "Psychopaths, Incorrigible Racists, and the Faces of Responsibility" *Ethics* 125 (2015): 357–90; and Pereboom, "Responsibility, Regret, and Protest," esp. pp. 132–37. Wrongdoing, not responsibility, is tied to demands. So, breach of demands might be at most a necessary condition of accountability for wrongdoing insofar as it is what explains wrongdoing. But excused wrongdoing violates demands as well, yet it involves the denial of accountability. So, demands and their ilk cannot, I think, be the key to responsibility as accountability.

30. Fine-tuning Capacities

Perhaps the capacities presupposed by the fair opportunity conception of responsibility involve moralized alternatives. But there are other issues we need to address about these capacities and possibilities before we can ask whether they are compatible with determinism.

We can and should distinguish between *actual* and *potential* capacities. Ascription of capacities must always be indexed to an agent and a time. An actual capacity is one that the agent has at a given time. Drawing on that capacity, the agent could then reliably perform the relevant actions. At this moment, I have the actual capacity to speak English and (limited) French, to perform simple arithmetic, to skate forward and backward, to get up from my computer and stretch, and myriad other things. A potential capacity is a capacity that is not actual at the time in question, but which I could acquire—make actual in the future—with suitable training and effort. Though I now lack an actual capacity to speak Russian, I presumably have the potential capacity to speak Russian. I may lack the actual capacity to hold my breath for more than one minute, but presumably I have a potential capacity to hold my breath for more than one minute. When fair opportunity claims that responsibility and excuse depend on normative capacities, that means they depend, in the first instance, on the agent's actual capacities. As we will see, an agent is excused if she lacks the relevant actual normative capacities, unless she is culpable for her actual incompetence.

Though we have said that capacities are indexed to agents and times, we have so far spoken as if these were otherwise *general* capacities—general normative cognitive and volitional powers to recognize norms, including requirements concerning the rights and interests of others, and to conform one's conduct to these norms. Though such capacities might vary among individuals and over time, we might think that they were otherwise *context invariant*. This is a common way to read the reasons-responsiveness literature.[7] But once we make this idea explicit, it begins to look less attractive.

Normative competence is really a suite of *specific* recognitional and volitional capacities that vary along two additional dimensions—the *kind* of normative reason or requirement at stake and the *circumstances* of recognition and conformity. Though we can talk in general terms about appropriate

---

[7] See, e.g., Wallace, *Responsibility and the Moral Sentiments*, pp. 182, 233n. Though it is easy to read much of the literature in the reasons-responsive tradition as assuming that capacities are context-invariant, I don't think that this is necessary.

concern for the rights and interests of others, we are subject to different kinds of normative requirements in different sorts of relationships and contexts—duties to family and friends are special obligations, different from what we owe to comparative strangers; duties to partners in cooperative schemes are different from duties to those who are not; fiduciary duties are different from those owed to any member of civil society. Cognitive and volitional competence with respect to one set of requirements does not guarantee facility with others. For instance, addiction and compulsive disorders may present problems of volitional control, but these problems may affect compliance with some norms more than others.

Even when we keep these distinct kinds of competence separate, we should not assume that competence is context invariant. Recognition or conformity might be more or less difficult with respect to any one kind of normative demand in different circumstances. We touched on this earlier, in noticing the potential interaction between situational context and competence (§24). For instance, cognitive autonomy might be more fragile in group situations, especially for juveniles. Moreover, as we will see in discussing situationism in Chapter 10, cognitive and volitional capacities might be more robust in some social contexts than others. For instance, general or specific capacities might be impaired in the heat of battle, when time is short, there is a barrage of stimulus, and uncertainty is rampant. If so, we should not expect the relevant normative capacities to be contextually invariant. Instead, we should expect normative competence to be potentially *contextually variable*.[8] In particular, we should index capacities not just to agents and times but also to kinds of normative demands and circumstances of action. Indeed, we might see the contrast between general and specific capacities as one of degree. If so, we might begin by assessing normative competence in terms of general capacities but be prepared to assess these capacities in a more fine-grained way, distinguishing kinds of norms and circumstances for their application, if this yields differential assessments.

---

[8] In recognizing and emphasizing the contextually variable character of normative competence, I have been influenced by Manuel Vargas, *Building Better Beings*, ch. 7 and "The Social Constitution of Agency and Responsibility: Oppression, Politics, and Moral Ecology" in *The Social Dimensions of Responsibility*, ed. M. Oshana, K. Hutchinson, and C. Mackenzie (New York: Oxford University Press, 2017).

31. Capacities and Counterfactuals

With a somewhat clearer picture of the normative capacities required by fair opportunity, we can ask if they are compatible with determinism. It would seem so, provided that we can make sense of agents having, but not exercising, a normative capacity.

Remember that we said that we can measure capacities counterfactually (§19). The greater the agent's capacity to recognize and respond to normative demands, the greater the range of counterfactual circumstances in which there is a normative demand and the agent recognizes it and conforms his conduct to it. However, if we invoke the distinction between general and specific capacities, we might think that fair opportunity faces a dilemma.[9] We can see how general capacities might fail to manifest in cases of specific kinds of norms or in specific circumstances. But we said that fair opportunity requires that we appeal to contextually specific capacities, and it's not clear how a specific capacity—indexed to an agent, a time, a kind of moral demand, and a particular circumstance or situation—could fail to manifest itself.

1. To be compatible with determinism, the fair opportunity conception must appeal to normative capacities that are germane to responsibility but susceptible to performance errors.
2. Fair opportunity can appeal to general or specific capacities.
3. General capacities are susceptible to performance errors but are not germane to responsibility.
4. Specific capacities are germane to responsibility but are not subject to performance errors.
5. Hence, there is no conception of capacity that allows us to reconcile fair opportunity with determinism.

To defend fair opportunity, I think we should resist (4).

It's reasonably clear how quite general capacities that manifest themselves regularly across a wide range of demands and circumstances might fail to do so in particular circumstances involving certain kinds of demands or situational pressures and confounds. But if fairness requires that we focus on contextually specific capacities, is there still room for explaining performance

[9] For versions of this dilemma, see Whittle, "Dispositional Abilities" and Carolina Sartorio, "Situations and Responsiveness to Reasons" *Noûs* 52 (2018): 796–807.

error? Doesn't determinism imply that any putative performance error reflects a context-specific incapacity?

We need an example, and it might help to begin with a nonmoral one. Consider J.L. Austin's example of the short putt that he could and should have made but didn't.

> It is not that I should have holed it if I had tried: I did and missed it. It is not that I should have holed it if conditions had been different: that might of course be so, but I am talking about the conditions as they precisely were, and asserting that I could have holed it. There is the rub.[10]

A general capacity spans diverse circumstances, and it is not hard to see how different circumstances might produce different outcomes. But a specific capacity is keyed to particular circumstances, and determinism seems to ensure the same outcomes in the same circumstances. There is a causal explanation of why Austin's putt missed the hole. But if we assess Austin's specific capacity to hole the putt holding fixed *everything* about the case in which he missed the putt, it's hard to see how he had the specific capacity to hole the putt.

However, this can't be the right way to assess a capacity, even a specific one. In analyzing ascriptions of capacities, we are positing an actual psychological structure, but one which funds relevant counterfactual claims about how the agent would have behaved in other relevantly similar circumstances. If determinism is true, we don't think that the agent would behave any differently in circumstances *exactly* like the actual circumstances in *all respects*. Instead, we think that he could have acted differently in the actual circumstance if he would have acted differently in circumstances that were different but *relevantly similar*.[11] This means that capacities cannot be tied to the particular circumstances in which they are or are not exercised. Of course, relevant differences cannot be too great; otherwise, we will not be tracking specific capacities. Indeed, if we vary circumstances too much, we won't even be tracking an actual, rather than a potential, capacity. For instance, not being an especially skilled putter, I might not have made a 10-foot putt. We can't test whether I could have made the putt that I failed to make by asking whether I would have made the putt if I first became as good a golfer as Tiger Woods.

---

[10] J.L. Austin, "Ifs and Cans" reprinted in J.L. Austin, *Philosophical Papers* (Oxford: Clarendon Press, 1961), p. 166.
[11] See Daniel Dennett, *Freedom Evolves* (New York: Viking, 2003), pp. 75–76.

For this would appeal to a potential, rather than actual, capacity of mine. Exactly how to constrain the relevant counterfactuals is a complex matter, but it's reasonably clear that the relevant differences should be familiar and modest. And one counterfactual does not confirm or disconfirm a capacity. Incompetent golfers can make lucky putts once in a great while, and Tiger Woods occasionally misses putts that are for him makeable. What we should expect from someone who has a capacity is that in the relevant counterfactuals he will perform successfully on a *regular* basis. But by this test it seems plausible that good putters have the capacity to make short putts.

What is true of putting capacity is true of normative capacities. Specific normative capacities must not be tied to a complete description of the world in which they are not exercised; otherwise, there could never be a specific capacity that was not exercised. But it is the very idea of a capacity that it admits of performance failure. Even if we are focused on specific capacities, we can't constrain the specification of a capacity in a way that doesn't allow this. This means that in deciding whether an agent has a specific normative capacity that he didn't exercise on a particular occasion, we are allowed to ask whether he would have manifested the capacity in different but relevantly similar circumstances. In doing so, we should look to see if there is regular recognition and conformity to normative demands across these nearby or relevantly similar possible worlds. For instance, in trying to decide if an adolescent who bullied another student had the capacity to recognize that what he did was wrong, it is not relevant to ask whether he would have recognized this if he had been mature emotionally, but it is relevant to ask whether he would have perceived similar treatment of himself by another as wrong. In deciding whether someone who engaged in theft, knowing it to be wrong, because of an addiction he acquired by taking medically prescribed opioids is responsible, it is not relevant to ask if he would have stolen if he had not been addicted, but it is relevant to ask if he could have conquered or circumvented his craving.

This response to the capacitarian dilemma reconciles specific capacities with determinism by insisting that the relevant counterfactuals to consult in determining whether there was a specific capacity in a case involving a performance failure include circumstances that are different from, but relevantly similar to, actual circumstances. Perhaps the incompatibilist will claim that this is question-begging. But I don't see how we can avoid this assumption if we want to take seriously the distinction between competence and performance and the idea of a specific capacity or competence. From this perspective, refusing to consider counterfactuals in which there are any qualitative differences from actual circumstances is what is question-begging. Given the burden of proof the skeptic about responsibility must bear to sustain an error theory, this way of assessing specific capacities seems not unreasonable.

32. Capacitarian Compatibilism

The fair opportunity conception of responsibility grounds responsibility in an agent's capacities and opportunities. In particular, responsibility for wrongdoing involves capacities to have acted otherwise than one did. To ground responsibility, these capacities must be actual and not merely potential. Moreover, they should be reasonably specific and not too general. To determine if someone had this kind of capacity, we must answer counterfactual questions about how she would have behaved in relevantly similar circumstances. If an agent would perform the relevant action in a sufficient number of such relevantly similar circumstances, then she had the ability to do so in the actual circumstances, even though she did not. In such circumstances, we can ascribe to the agent a performance error against the backdrop of an underlying competence, capacity, or ability. How specific an ability we should test for, just which circumstances are relevantly similar, and how often she must act in a given way in those circumstances to possess the ability are all matters of degree. But the fact that the counterfactual test for capacities is scalar seems like a virtue, not a vice. Capacities can be more or less robust or fragile, and we should want an understanding of capacities that respects and explains, rather than ignores, this fact. This analysis of fair opportunity is compatibilist insofar as the truth of the relevant counterfactuals seems fully compatible with determinism.

It is worth distinguishing this compatibilist version of fair opportunity from a superficially similar compatibilist conception of free will that also relies on abilities and counterfactual conditionals. G.E. Moore and A.J. Ayer proposed a compatibilist conception of freedom and responsibility in terms of a conditional analysis of an ability to do otherwise.[12] The traditional conditional analysis of the ability to do otherwise claims that an agent had the ability to do x, even though she did not, provided that had she chosen to do x, she would have done it. Such counterfactual conditionals seemed compatible with determinism, because the conditional could be true, even if an agent was

---

[12] G.E. Moore, *Ethics* [1912] (Oxford: Clarendon Press, 1966), ch. 6 and A.J. Ayer, "Freedom and Necessity" in A.J. Ayer, *Philosophical Essays* (London: Macmillan, 1954).

determined to act otherwise. But the traditional conditional analysis of free-dom and responsibility is widely viewed as deeply problematic. At least two problems are worth mentioning. First, even when an agent possesses an ability, and chooses to exercise it, she may fail to manifest the ability due to interfer-ence, either external or internal. In such cases, the ability is *masked*. Second, the conditional analysis of freedom just pushes the threat of determinism backward. The antecedent of the conditional in the conditional analysis need not be true. After all, it is a counterfactual conditional. But it seems the antecedent must be possible. However, if determinism is true, it seems the antecedent of the conditional must be necessarily false. If I was determined to do x by choice, then I could not have chosen not to do x.

There are two important ways in which the counterfactual conditionals that define fair opportunity differ from the traditional conditional analysis of freedom and which avoid these two problems with the traditional analysis. The counterfactual analysis of the capacities required by fair opportunity has different *inputs* and *outputs* from the counterfactual analysis in the traditional conditional analysis. Whereas the traditional analysis asks what the agent would have done in the exact same circumstances if she had chosen differently, fair opportunity asks how the agent would have behaved in a range of relevantly similar circumstances in the presence of justifying reasons. Because fair opportunity appeals to behavior in a range of cases, it is fully able to recognize that abilities will not always manifest themselves because they might be masked by interfering factors. To screen off masking interfer-ence, we need to employ counterfactuals in relevantly similar circumstances that abstract from that interference. This solves the first problem with the traditional analysis. Because fair opportunity appeals to what the agent would do in the presence of justifying reasons in a range of circumstances, it does not turn on whether the agent could have chosen otherwise than she did. This solves the second regress worry about the traditional analysis.

This compatibilist interpretation of fair opportunity strikes me as fairly promising. Given the strong presumption against adopting an error theory about responsibility, this strikes me as good reason to work within this sort of compatibilist interpretation, refining and defending it. Should it turn out that the compatibilist interpretation cannot be defended, this would be reason to explore libertarian resources to ground the capacities and opportunities required by fair opportunity.

33. An Incompatibilist Manipulation Argument

We might conclude our discussion of the compatibilist interpretation of fair opportunity by considering Derk Pereboom's defense of incompatibilism that appeals to a four-case sequence of manipulation cases.[13] Pereboom's argument is worth our attention, even though I am not undertaking an exhaustive examination and refutation of incompatibilist arguments. This argument has been influential, and, more importantly, it brings out important issues about the connection between capacities and strong passions and desires that fair opportunity needs to address.

Pereboom wants to consider cases that meet various plausible compatibilist conditions of responsibility yet in which he thinks we will be inclined to deny that the agent is responsible. He believes that this is true of each of his cases, so that any one of them, considered individually, constitutes a counter-example to compatibilism. But he also recognizes that compatibilist opponents won't agree at the outset that determinism is inconsistent with responsibility. So he presents his cases in a sequence that begins from a case of manipulation in which he thinks it will be especially clear that the agent is not responsible, despite satisfying compatibilist conditions, and progresses in stages toward the familiar case of determinism. Because he thinks that it is difficult for us to draw a principled line between adjacent cases, he thinks that we are forced, by our intuitions that the agent is not responsible in the first manipulation case, to the conclusion that she is not responsible in the normal deterministic case, even if that wasn't antecedently clear.

To maximize the scope of his incompatibilist argument, Pereboom describes each case in a way that makes it appear to satisfy various plausible compatibilist conditions on responsibility, including various quality of will and capacitarian conceptions. Since I am interested in the bearing of Pereboom's argument on the fair opportunity conception of responsibility, I can ignore the way in which his four cases satisfy other compatibilist conceptions of responsibility.

Each case involves Professor Plum murdering White for selfish reasons. Pereboom stipulates both that Plum's selfish motives are strong and cause him to choose to murder White and that Plum remains reasons-responsive

[13] Pereboom introduced the manipulation sequence in Derk Pereboom, "Determinism *Al Dente*" *Noûs* 29 (1995): 21–45. He subsequently revised it in *Living without Free Will* (New York: Cambridge University Press, 2001) and again in *Free Will, Agency, and Meaning in Life*. I draw on the most recent formulation in *Free Will, Agency, and Meaning in Life*, pp. 74–82.

throughout his deliberations. Though sharing this common ground, the four cases are otherwise different.

1. *Proximate Neural Manipulation.* In this case, neuroscientists manipulate Plum's neural states just prior to his deliberations, inducing in him a strong selfish desire that leads him to kill White. Plum remains reason-responsive throughout.
2. *Distal Neural Manipulation.* In this case, neuroscientists set in motion a deterministic process at the beginning of Plum's life that induces in him at the time of action a strong selfish desire that leads him to kill White. Plum remains reason-responsive throughout.
3. *Bad Formative Circumstances.* In this case, a community ethos of individualism, encouraged by his parents and educators, leads Plum to form strong selfish desires and to kill White. Plum remains reason-responsive throughout.
4. *Determinism.* Plum lives in a deterministic universe with no neural interventions or bad formative circumstances and yet develops a strong selfish desire to kill White on which he (Plum) acts. Plum remains reason-responsive throughout.

Pereboom thinks that we might take any one of these four cases as counter-examples to compatibilist conceptions of responsibility, including any reasons-responsive conception, such as the fair opportunity conception. But he thinks that this is especially true of the first case and recognizes that not everyone would initially view (4) as a counter-example to compatibilism. Because he thinks we cannot draw any principled distinction among adjacent cases, he also thinks that the firm and universal conviction in the first case that Plum is not responsible can be leveraged to lead us to accept a similar verdict about the ordinary deterministic case (4). So, even if we were not initially inclined to treat (4) as we treat (1), the sequence forces us to do so.

Suppose that we began by thinking that the proximate manipulation in (1) prevented responsibility, despite reasons-responsiveness, but did not think that the determinism in (4) prevented responsibility, provided Plum was reasons-responsive. Should we revise our beliefs about (4) in light of our beliefs about (1) and the fact that we can't identify any one point in the progression where we think responsibility sets in? We might not for one of two reasons.

First, suppose we agree that the smooth progression among the cases forces us to reach similar verdicts in (1) and (4). Why think that consistency should force us to treat (4) the way we do (1)? We might equally well reverse the order of the sequence, beginning with (4) and progressing toward (1). But then consistency would force us to treat (1) the way we do (4). Why prefer assimilating (4) to (1), rather than assimilating (1) to (4)?[14]

Second, the very reversibility of the argument may make us suspect it. It seems relevantly like a Sorites argument. The Sorites argument is a step-wise argument designed to convince us that there are no such things as heaps of sand. One grain of sand is not a heap. Adding one grain of sand to something that is not a heap cannot produce something that is a heap. But then it follows that there is no number of grains of sand, however large, that constitutes a heap of sand. Though the exact diagnosis of where the Sorites argument goes wrong is controversial, it is widely viewed as fallacious, because it takes one from a true premise to a manifestly false conclusion. A further sign that something is fishy about the Sorites argument is that it is reversible. We might begin with something that is clearly a heap of sand. Subtracting one grain of sand from something that is a heap cannot produce something that is not a heap. But then it follows that there is no number of grains of sand, however small, that is not a heap. If the same argument can be used to support contradictory conclusions, it does not seem to be a good argument. Pereboom's argument seems suspiciously like a Sorites argument.

Interesting as these objections are, they are not the most important objections to Pereboom's argument. Pereboom assumes that if we excuse in (1) and hold responsible in (4), we will be unable to explain the difference. But there is an obvious difference between (1) and (4). (1) involves manipulation, whereas (4) does not. In fact, (1) and (2) both involve manipulation. Whether (3) does is less clear. Pereboom doesn't specify the unfortunate formative circumstances in (3) in enough detail to know whether we should view it as a case of social manipulation. The presence of manipulation in some but not all of the cases is, of course, by design. But mightn't it explain differential responsibility verdicts in the cases? Pereboom thinks not, because he thinks that manipulation, as such, will not affect reasons-responsiveness. That might be a reason to think that pure appeals to normative competence won't discriminate for the presence of manipulation, provided the cases all involve reasons-responsiveness. But the fair opportunity conception of responsibility supplements normative competence with situation control and treats the significant

---

[14] The reversibility of Pereboom's argument is also explored in Michael McKenna, "A Hard-line Reply to Pereboom's Four-Case Manipulation Argument" *Philosophy and Phenomenological Research* 77 (2008): 142–59.

impairment of either as excusing. Like duress, manipulation involves wrongful interference by another and, hence, may seem to violate situational control. If so, fair opportunity, unlike some other forms of compatibilism, has a straightforward explanation of why the differences between (1) and (4) matter for responsibility.

This reply depends on treating manipulation as relevantly like duress. Though both involve wrongful interference by another, there is a potentially significant difference as well. Whereas the prototypical case of duress involves coercion that interferes with the agent's choices in a way that wrongly opposes the agent's will, Pereboom's cases of manipulation operate upstream and co-opt her will. I'm not sure if this difference between duress and manipulation prevents us from viewing manipulation as an impairment of situational control. If it doesn't, then fair opportunity can explain the different responsibility verdicts in (1) and (4). But Pereboom may think that this difference is normatively significant, because manipulation affects the agent's psychology, rather than her options.

Let us grant this, for the sake of argument, and consider only the resources that fair opportunity shares with reasons-responsive conceptions. (1) is supposed to be the strongest case for denying responsibility, despite Plum's reasons-responsiveness. But the manipulation in (1) is a red herring. If Plum is reasons-responsive despite the existence of strong selfish desires, however they came about, then Plum is responsible. *A fortiori*, if Plum is reasons-responsive in (2)–(3), despite his strong desires, then he is responsible in those cases as well.

Plum's strong selfish desire might just as well have been caused, in some complicated way, by a large solar flare. It would still be true that if he remains fully reasons-responsive then he is responsible, despite his strong selfish desire. Pereboom might reply by distinguishing the manipulation and solar flare case. In the manipulation case, there is interference from another's agency, as there is not in the solar flare case. We might even think that this makes the manipulators responsible for Plum's actions. But *responsibility is not a zero-sum affair* in which we have to divide a fixed quantum of responsibility among the number of actors who contribute their agency. In a standard case of conspiracy, we don't divide responsibility by the number of conspirators, we *multiply* it by the number of conspirators. Whether or not we view the manipulators in (1) as having some responsibility for White's murder, we can and should view the manipulators' creation of a selfish desire as making a suggestion to Plum. As long as Plum remains fully reasons-responsive, he has the capacity to resist this suggestion and so bears responsibility for White's murder.[15]

---

[15] For a similar response, see Vargas, *Building Better Beings*, p. 291.

If we experience hesitancy about ascribing responsibility to Plum in any of these cases, I think that it is because we perceive an actual or potential tension between ascribing strong contra-moral desires to Plum and treating him as fully reasons-responsive. Pereboom writes as if these are completely unrelated facts about Plum that can easily occur together. If that is so, then Plum's strong desires don't excuse, because they don't affect his reasons-responsiveness. This is as true in (1) as in (4).

But our hesitancy might reflect recognition that strong desire and reason-responsiveness are not completely independent factors. Strength of desire and reasons-responsiveness are potentially connected, because degree of responsiveness depends on degree of difficulty in recognizing or conforming to justifying reasons, which in turn can depend on strength of one's desire, especially if these are normatively recalcitrant desires. Normative competence involves reasons-responsiveness, which is itself a matter of degree. As we have seen, this can be measured counterfactually—one is more responsive the greater the range of circumstances in which one would recognize and conform to the relevant norms, and less responsive the greater the range of circumstances in which one would not recognize or conform to those norms. The more normatively competent agent is responsive cognitively and volitionally to the relevant norms in a greater range of possible circumstances, and the less competent agent is responsive in a smaller range of possible circumstances. Moreover, competence can be understood as ease or facility of performance, and incompetence as difficulty of performance.[16] The limiting case of difficulty is impossibility, and degree of incompetence can be understood in terms of comparative difficulty of performance. This means that reasons-responsiveness and, hence, normative competence are inversely related to degree of difficulty. Irresistible desires are impossible to resist and so fully excusing. Strong desires, though not irresistible, may be difficult to resist. So, the existence of strong contrary desires may compromise reasons-responsiveness and normative competence somewhat. This is what makes Pereboom's stipulation (in all cases) that Plum acts on strong desires but is fully reasons-responsive potentially problematic, and it may explain some of our ambivalence about these cases.

Pereboom's stipulation need not be incoherent. He doesn't say enough about the strength of Plum's selfish desire. On the one hand, if it is just a

---

[16] For one development of this view, see Dana Nelkin, "Difficulty and Degrees of Moral Praiseworthiness and Blameworthiness" *Noûs* 50 (2016): 356–78. We will return to issues about partial responsibility in Chapter 15.

temptation that he succumbs to, whatever its source, this may be compatible with him remaining substantially reasons-responsive. In such cases, Plum is weak-willed but responsible, and that verdict is fully consistent with fair opportunity. On the other hand, Plum's selfishness may be deep-seated and borderline pathological, in which case, even if his selfish desire is not literally irresistible, it may be powerful enough to substantially compromise his reasons-responsiveness. If we allow responsibility and excuse to be scalar and partial, then, in such a case, fair opportunity implies that Plum is no more than partially responsible and merits a partial excuse. If we insist that there must be a threshold of responsiveness below which an agent is fully excused and above which she is fully responsible, then we cannot yet tell what fair opportunity implies about Plum's case without a more precise calibration of the strength of his selfish desire and of the responsiveness threshold between excuse and responsibility. But then there is no precisification of the strength of Plum's desires that causes problems for fair opportunity.

We can now put together our responses to Pereboom's manipulation argument and its assumptions about the significance of manipulation. In effect, Pereboom faces a dilemma.

1. Either the manipulation of Plum's desires impairs his normative capacities or it doesn't.
2. If the implanted desires do not impair Plum's reasons-responsiveness, then Plum is responsible for murdering White, even if he did so as the result of strong desires.
3. If the implanted desires do impair Plum's reasons-responsiveness, then Plum is excused insofar as he is not fully reasons-responsive.
4. Either way, manipulation of Plum's desires does not give us reason to abandon the fair opportunity conception of responsibility.

This diagnosis of what is problematic in Pereboom's stipulations about the cases explains why we might be ambivalent about what to say in some of his cases but why we shouldn't draw any incompatibilist morals from those cases. It also illustrates a theme about the interdependence of recalcitrant desire and normative competence that will be an important issue going forward in our discussion of the implications of fair opportunity for cases of partial responsibility.

5

Fair Opportunity and History

So far, we have motivated the fair opportunity conception of responsibility by appeal to our reactive attitudes and practices, especially those involving excuse, and defended its basic architecture and demands. We have also explored a compatibilist interpretation of its assumptions about capacities and morally relevant alternatives and possibilities. This conception, articulated so far, says that an agent is responsible for wrongful conduct iffi that conduct was the result of her choices and at the time of action she was normatively competent and possessed situational control.

This formulation of fair opportunity has an important *synchronic* quality. Responsibility is a function of structural features of the agent at the time of deliberation and action. There is a question about how big this synchronic window is. A narrow version of the window would be a minimal time slice including facts about the agent only at the very moment of action. A broader version of the window would extend backward from this time slice to any proximate aspects of her situation, psychology, and deliberation that have a direct bearing on her action. According to fair opportunity, our interests in responsibility and excuse will be affected by her capacities and opportunities at the time of action, which requires a broader version of the synchronic temporal window. There may remain some vagueness or indeterminacy about just how broad this synchronic window is. But a synchronic version of fair opportunity can and should live with this indeterminacy. At least, present purposes don't require reducing this indeterminacy.

However, a synchronic conception of responsibility might seem inadequate. Responsibility and excuse may seem to be essentially *historical* concepts. We may think that we can't reliably determine responsibility and excuse by appeal to synchronic or structural facts alone. In some cases, it may seem to matter how those structural facts came into existence. Is an agent who was reasons-responsive at the time of action responsible for her action if she was reasons-responsive only through the manipulation of others, or does the history of manipulation defeat her responsibility? A synchronic version of fair opportunity says that sufficient normative incapacity is excusing, but is it excusing in cases of culpable incapacity in which the agent bears responsibility for

Fair Opportunity and Responsibility. David O. Brink, Oxford University Press (2021). © David O. Brink.
DOI: 10.1093/oso/9780198859468.003.0005

becoming incapacitated? Can an agent be responsible for her actions if she does not have a history of taking responsibility for her actions and instead views herself as buffeted about by external forces? Should we recognize an excuse, whether full or partial, when we learn that a culpable wrongdoer was the victim of systematic abuse and neglect during her formative years?

These questions are interesting in their own right. But they raise the further question about whether our conception of responsibility should have an historical dimension and, hence, whether fair opportunity should take an historical form. Fair opportunity can take an historical form, if need be. So, although it's worth knowing whether fair opportunity should take an historical form, the answer to this question does not affect the plausibility of the fair opportunity conception. Fair opportunity, as far as I can see, does not have a horse in this race. Having said that, my provisional view is that an ahistorical version of fair opportunity has the resources to explain cases and intuitions that might seem to call for historical analysis. If so, I think we should prefer this sort of deflationary analysis of the historical dimensions of responsibility. If my case for an ahistorical treatment of fair opportunity does not convince some readers, they are welcome to develop an historical version of fair opportunity.[1]

34. Manipulation

In Chapter 4, we examined Pereboom's arguments for incompatibilism that appeal to several cases involving manipulation. He assumes that manipulation undermines responsibility and claims that we can't distinguish cases of manipulation from cases involving ordinary deterministic forces. Crucially, he assumes that the manipulation in question focuses on the agent's desires, leaving his normative capacities fully intact. Though that assumption, we saw, is questionable, here we do want to focus on cases in which manipulation plays a role in whether or not the agent is normatively competent.

Many forms of proximate manipulation excuse by compromising situational control. If so, their significance can be accommodated by a synchronic conception of fair opportunity. The interesting question is whether distal, rather than proximate, manipulation might compromise responsibility. In principle, there are two kinds of cases to consider—cases in which an agent

---

[1] In this chapter, I am especially conscious of debts to discussion with Craig Agule, Michael McKenna, and Dana Nelkin.

who was previously competent is psychologically manipulated so as to render him incompetent and cases in which an agent who was previously incompetent is manipulated so as to render him competent. The first are cases of *incapacitating manipulation*, whereas the second are cases of *enabling manipulation*. It is important that the manipulation not be subtle or engage the person's own agency, perhaps taking the form of suggestions or education, but that it involves completely bypassing the person's agency to produce profound change in the agent's normative capacities.

Presumably, the reason manipulation might be relevant to assessments of responsibility is that prior manipulation seems subversive of responsibility. If so, we are not equally interested in cases of incapacitating and enabling manipulation. Cases of incapacitating manipulation are not relevant, because historical and ahistorical conceptions won't disagree in their verdicts about them. An historical conception will or can excuse subsequent wrongful conduct insofar as it is the product of prior manipulation, and an ahistorical conception will excuse subsequent wrongful conduct insofar as the agent was not reasons-responsive at the time of action.

A more relevant case would involve enabling manipulation. To fix ideas, consider the case of Professor Fig. Imagine that Fig developed a form of psychosis, which rendered her insufficiently reasons-responsive. In this condition, she developed various paranoid delusions that Professor Plum was a threat to her, but let's assume that she was too incompetent to act on this false belief. Now, imagine that Fig is transformed by manipulation that bypasses her agency into someone who is reasons-responsive. Imagine that without Fig's knowledge or consent, doctors give her an experimental drug that cures her psychosis. However, she retains a few of her old attitudes, including her distrust of Plum. In her reasons-responsive state, Fig kills Plum. Is Fig responsible for killing Plum, or is she excused because the manipulative intervention of others subverts her responsibility? Here, historical and ahistorical conceptions would seem to disagree—ahistorical conceptions would treat Fig as responsible, whereas historical conceptions would treat Fig as excused.

Once we are clear about the case of enabling manipulation, an ahistorical analysis seems preferable. If at the time of killing Plum Fig is fully reasons-responsive, then she is responsible for killing him. We are assuming that her false belief about Plum's being a threat is now a cognitive performance error and does not undermine her reasons-responsiveness. She is no more excused than someone who had always been reasons-responsive but killed out of dislike or distrust.

Of course, enabling manipulation does block responsibility in one way. Though Fig is responsible for killing Plum, she is not responsible for becoming competent. This is due to manipulation that bypassed her agency. This means that responsible action does not require that one be responsible for being responsible. Enabling manipulation defeats responsibility for becoming responsible but not downstream responsibility for actions performed while competent. These plausible claims about enabling manipulation are not only consistent with, but in fact require, an ahistorical analysis.

35. Culpable Incapacity and Tracing

A more promising rationale for an historical conception of responsibility lies in cases of *culpable incapacity*. An ahistorical version of fair opportunity claims that one is excused for wrongdoing just in case one lacks sufficient normative competence or sufficient situational control at the time of action. But this structural claim may seem implausible, because incapacity and lack of opportunity are not sufficient for excuse. They are not sufficient for excuse, because neither is excusing if the agent is responsible and, hence, culpable for the incapacity or lack of opportunity. For example, we believe that the drunk driver is culpable for harm he does to others (e.g. vehicular homicide), even though he is intoxicated and incompetent at the time he causes the harm, provided that he was responsible earlier for drinking too much in conditions when he was likely to drive. Someone not responsible for being intoxicated, say because another person slipped a roofie into his soda without his knowledge, would presumably not be responsible for subsequent harms he causes. The idea that one is responsible for wrongs committed while culpably incapacitated but excused for wrongs done while non-culpably incapacitated is intuitive. Such intuitions receive expression in the criminal law in the Model Penal Code's refusal to recognize an excuse for "voluntary intoxication" and its recognition of an excuse for "involuntary intoxication" (MPC §2.08).[2] A similar restriction applies to the conditions under which lack of situational control excuses. The Model Penal Code does not recognize duress as excusing if the agent who is subject to duress is substantially responsible for bringing about the circumstances of his own duress (MPC §2.09). For instance, if

---

[2] Though voluntary intoxication does not excuse, it can negate a *mens rea* element of wrongdoing, such as intent. This qualification will be explained in Chapter 7, when we examine *actus reus* and *mens rea* and their roles in criminal liability.

I conspire with others to commit a crime and then am subject to duress when I try to back out at the last minute, I cannot plead a duress excuse if I engage in the wrongdoing in response to duress from my co-conspirators. Together, these intuitive and doctrinal constraints on excuse support the general proposition that conditions that would otherwise constitute an excuse are not excusing when the agent is substantially responsible for bringing about these conditions. Though this general principle applies both to excuses of incapacity and lack of opportunity, it will be convenient to focus on incapacity excuses. Here, the operative principle is that incapacity excuses when and only when it is non-culpable.

It looks like the relevance of prior culpability to defeating an incompetence excuse in cases of culpable incapacity is evidence against ahistorical or structural versions of fair opportunity and supports the idea that there is an essential historical dimension to responsibility. The most common way of conceptualizing this historical dimension of responsibility is by appeal to *tracing*. Fischer and Ravizza introduce the concept, which allows that someone might be responsible for an action, even though she is not reasons-responsive at the time of action, provided we can trace responsibility backward from that point to some point earlier in the etiology of the action when she was suitably reasons-responsive.[3] In effect, adding tracing to a reasons-responsive conception makes that conception *disjunctive*—proximate responsibility requires proximate or distal reasons-responsiveness. Tracing seems to accommodate cases of culpable incapacity well. If fair opportunity adds a tracing element to situational control as well, it could also accommodate cases in which a duress excuse is unavailable to an agent, despite her lack of situational control, because her earlier culpable actions exposed her to duress. In addition, tracing seems to explain how we can be responsible when we act on automatic or habitual scripts, which do not seem to be reasons-responsive. These scripted actions can be responsible provided that at some earlier point the agent deliberately cultivated the habits from which she later acts.

This appeal to tracing seems to solve problems that ahistorical conceptions of responsibility face and to provide evidence that responsibility is essentially an historical concept. But before we accept tracing, we should ask if it is needed to solve these problems with ahistorical accounts and if it is otherwise plausible. There is reason to be skeptical on both fronts.

It is not clear that tracing is necessary to explain why culpable incapacity is not excusing. Tracing anchors proximate responsibility, at the time of

---

[3] Fischer and Ravizza, *Responsibility and Control*, pp. 49–51, 194, 201–02.

incapacity, in distal responsibility. In the case of voluntary intoxication, tracing funds responsibility for vehicular homicide when the agent is incapacitated by grounding it in her earlier reasons-responsive decision to drink in circumstances when she was likely to drive. But there is an ahistorical explanation of the agent's culpability in cases of culpable incapacity. On this alternative explanation, the agent does not act responsibly at the time of incapacitation, but she is responsible for the reasonably foreseeable consequences of her earlier reasons-responsive decision to drink in circumstances in which she was likely to drive. Though the exact details of whom she harms and how may not have been reasonably foreseeable, it was reasonably foreseeable that drinking in circumstances in which she may drive (e.g. has made no alternative provisions for transportation) poses non-negligible risk to herself and others. This makes her decision to drink in such circumstances reckless, and so the ahistorical conception holds her responsible for reckless endangerment and its reasonably foreseeable consequences. This is a deflationary explanation of culpable incapacity that seems to accommodate such cases while relying on fewer independent assumptions about the nature of responsibility.[4]

In fact, we might find that the tracing explanation of culpable incapacity is not only unnecessary but actually problematic.[5] Whereas the ahistorical explanation denies that the drunk driver is excused from vehicular homicide because she is responsible for her earlier recklessness and its consequences, the tracing explanation anchors her later responsibility in her earlier responsibility for recklessness. But then the ahistorical explanation finds her responsible for one wrongdoing—earlier recklessness and its consequences—whereas tracing finds her *doubly responsible*—both for the earlier recklessness and for the homicide she causes while intoxicated. But then tracing implies that she is responsible and, hence, blameworthy for two separate wrongs—reckless endangerment and vehicular homicide. This looks like double counting. Culpable incapacity should not be excused, but neither should it be blamed

---

[4] My ahistorical explanation of culpable incapacity shares some features in common with other forms of skepticism about tracing, including Matt King, "Traction Without Tracing: A (Partial) Solution for Control-Based Accounts of Moral Responsibility" *European Journal of Philosophy* 22 (2104): 463–82 and Craig Agule, "Resisting Tracing's Siren Song" *Journal of Ethics and Social Philosophy* 10 (2016): 1–24.

[5] In *Essays on the Active Powers of the Human Mind* Reid discusses responsibility in cases of culpable incapacity, claiming that such agents are responsible for the foreseeable consequences of their earlier choices to become incapacitated, but are not responsible at the time they are incapacitated (*Essays* IV vii).

and punished twice over. If so, it's not just that we can make do without tracing but also that we are better off without it.

What about the apparent virtue of tracing's ability to explain how we can be responsible for habitual and scripted actions, which seem not to be the result of explicit reasoning but which are the products of habits deliberately cultivated at an earlier time? Here too, tracing is not necessary to explain what's important. First, the previous point also applies here. Instead of recognizing both proximate and distal responsibility, as tracing does, we could recognize only distal responsibility in cultivating habits and their reasonably foreseeable manifestations. It's true that one might not foresee the details of the particular manifestations of habits one has cultivated, but one might be responsible for any of the kind of reasonably foreseeable manifestations of habits one has cultivated.[6] Second, and really more importantly, there is really nothing incompatible about acting on habit or scripts and being reasons-responsive. As we saw in our discussion of reasons-responsiveness and deliberation (§20), reasons-responsiveness does not require express deliberation. Much action can be reasons-responsive provided that it tracks reasons or values reliably without the actor consciously representing her conduct under the guise of the good or the right and without engaging in conscious deliberation about alternatives. To be morally responsible, it may be that agents have to have the capacity to reason about the merits of alternatives and regulate their conduct in accordance with these deliberations. But what's necessary for responsibility is the capacity, not its exercise. The fact that I act on automatic or System 1 processes does not show that I lack the capacity to reason about the merits of these processes or to suspend them when appropriate.

Despite the initial attraction of historical appeals to tracing as a way of explaining why culpable incapacity is not excusing and of explaining how agents can be responsible for scripted behavior, tracing's historical claims are unnecessary to explain what's important in such cases. In fact, tracing may actually bring unwelcome normative commitments. If so, we don't yet have a good reason to abandon an ahistorical conception of fair opportunity or to embrace tracing.

---

[6] Vargas is also skeptical about tracing. See Manuel Vargas, "The Trouble with Tracing" *Midwest Studies in Philosophy* 29 (2005): 269–91. But his skepticism is different from mine. Tracing also requires that the downstream consequences of one's earlier reasons-responsive decisions be reasonably foreseeable. In the tracing cases Vargas discusses, he disputes that the unwelcome downstream consequences of one's earlier reasons-responsive behavior are reasonably foreseeable. But this is because he assumes that one must foresee the details of these consequences, whereas I do not. Recklessness requires only that the agent be able to anticipate the general kinds of risks one poses to others.

36. Taking Responsibility

Fischer and Ravizza think that responsibility is historical in another way as well. They claim that responsible agents must *take responsibility* for their own actions.[7] Because their conception of reasons-responsiveness is mechanism-based, rather than agent-based, they formulate this historical claim as the thesis that taking responsibility is part of making a mechanism one's own. But even they think that it is agents who take responsibility, and we have already explained why it is better to formulate fair opportunity in terms of the responsiveness of persons or agents, rather than mechanisms (§28). Their proposal can be translated into a claim about persons taking responsibility and ownership of their actions. Taking responsibility for one's actions, on this view, involves regarding oneself as the cause of one's actions and as a fair target of the reactive attitudes insofar as one is in fact reasons-responsive.[8] Taking responsibility for one's actions means regarding oneself as both having a kind of moral value and as accountable to others. It involves seeking opportunities for choice and control and a willingness to bear the consequences for one's choices. Coming to regard oneself as accountable and coming to be regarded by others as accountable are mutually reinforcing processes that are part of the normal maturation of children into adolescents and adolescents into adults who are responsible for their actions. If so, taking responsibility might seem essential to responsible agency.

Notice that whereas taking on board tracing made the resulting conception of responsibility *disjunctive*, requiring that agents take responsibility for their actions makes the resulting conception of responsibility *conjunctive*. In effect, tracing implies that responsibility can be original or derived. But taking responsibility is an additional requirement of responsibility, over and above reasons-responsiveness. On Fischer and Ravizza's eventual conception of responsibility, reasons-responsiveness and taking responsibility are individually necessary and jointly sufficient for responsibility.

Their *developmental* claim is quite plausible. Part of the process of becoming a responsible agent involves viewing oneself as accountable for one's actions and accepting the consequences of one's decisions. The individual who does not view himself as accountable for anything that happens within his own life or for things he does that help or harm others, and views the

---

[7] Fischer and Ravizza, *Responsibility and Control*, ch. 8.
[8] Fischer and Ravizza, *Responsibility and Control*, pp. 210–14.

outcomes for himself and others as just so much good or bad fate, is unlikely to develop the sort of normative competence that is necessary for responsibility. But this is a causal claim about how agents mature and develop normative powers, not a separate ingredient in responsibility. It might be very unlikely that someone would become sufficiently reasons-responsive without a healthy sense of personal accountability. It may even be true that once one is reasons-responsive one cannot *sustain* those capacities if one ceases entirely to view oneself as accountable, though notice that this is a forward-looking, rather than backward-looking, claim. But these causal claims do not gainsay the claim that if an agent is reasons-responsive, he does not also need to take responsibility for his actions in order to be responsible for them. For this, being reasons-responsive and having situational control are sufficient. If an agent were to perform intentional actions for which he was reasons-responsive, that would make him accountable for the foreseeable consequences of those actions, whether or not he viewed himself as accountable and saw himself as the legitimate target of reactive attitudes in that case. He would not be excused by failing to take responsibility for those actions.

Fischer and Ravizza consider this sort of objection.[9] They respond to cases of genuine failure to take responsibility by insisting that responsibility really does require viewing oneself as accountable. This may sound like table-thumping on their part. However, I think that they can be read as suggesting that one can't sustain reasons-responsiveness without generally viewing oneself as accountable. This claim has some plausibility, but it falls short of what's necessary to defend an independent historical requirement on responsibility in several ways. At most, it shows that one couldn't remain reasons-responsive while *systematically* refusing to accept responsibility for one's actions. It wouldn't show that a reasons-responsive agent couldn't *selectively* fail to take responsibility for some actions for which she was accountable while remaining reasons-responsive. Moreover, it wouldn't show that you need an historical condition *in addition* to reasons-responsiveness.

A general practice of taking responsibility has some plausibility as a causal hypothesis about how best to develop and maintain reasons-responsiveness. It has considerably less plausibility as a thesis about the need for an additional constituent of responsibility, over and above reasons-responsiveness and situational control.

---

[9] Fischer and Ravizza, *Responsibility and Control*, pp. 220–21.

37. Unfortunate Formative Circumstances

Another potential rationale for regarding responsibility as an ineliminably historical concept appeals to the importance of an agent's *formative circumstances* to our moralized reactive attitudes. We can explore these issues in the context of Watson's rich and suggestive essay "Responsibility and the Limits of Evil," especially his discussion of the Robert Harris case. In this essay, Watson develops Strawsonian themes about the ways in which the reactive attitudes of praise and blame are "forms of address" to members of our moral community. Watson distinguishes sharply between excuse and exemption and understands exemption as a generalized suspension of the reactive attitudes for individuals not within our moral community, such as children or adults under severe stress. He extends this analysis to those who are evil, suggesting that their evil may put them outside our moral community ("beyond the pale") and disqualify them as legitimate targets of blame.[10]

Watson illustrates these issues in an extremely interesting discussion of the case of Harris, who had a violent adolescence and was convicted later of killing two boys in cold-blood as part of a carjacking. Harris killed with pleasure, showing no remorse whatsoever.[11] Harris was given a death sentence and eventually executed. Watson notes that on learning the heinousness of his crime, which he relates in some detail, we find ourselves applying the reactive attitudes toward Harris and treating him as a paradigm case of a culpable wrongdoer apt for blame. Indeed, we might treat Harris's lack of remorse and indifference to human life as an *amplifier* of our blame and as an *aggravating condition* at sentencing. But then Watson describes Harris's history of physical and emotional abuse and neglect at the hands of his parents. His siblings described him as a child who was initially very sensitive and desperate for affection but as the result of parental neglect and abuse became hardened and sadistic, torturing and killing animals. Later, he was arrested several times and sent to youth detention centers, where he was raped on multiple occasions and tried to commit suicide.

Watson notes that when we learn about Harris's unfortunate formative circumstances prior to his commission of the crime for which he was convicted and executed our reactive attitudes are likely to change and soften. We will likely blame him less severely and may favor some kind of mitigation of

---

[10] Watson, "Responsibility and the Limits of Evil," p. 235.
[11] However, in a 2004 postscript Watson adds that Harris did express remorse to the father of one of his victims at his 1992 execution.

his sentence. Or, at least our blaming responses will co-exist with a newfound sympathy and understanding, in which our responses are ambivalent, rather than moderated. Either way, our reactive attitudes have altered, and we experience some tendency toward suspending them in light of Harris's abuse and neglect. Watson suggests that Harris's incapacity for relationships with others is what underlies this change.[12]

What should we conclude about the Harris case, and does it offer any support to the call for an independent historical condition on responsibility, over and above normative competence and situational control? People's reactive attitudes vary, but I find Watson's claims resonate with me. When I contemplate Harris's rotten formative circumstances, my blaming response is moderated somewhat or at least becomes ambivalent. For purposes of discussion, I will assume that this is a common and not unreasonable response. The question is what it shows.

Should it affect our views about Harris's responsibility for his crime? That might depend on how we understand Strawson's thesis linking the reactive attitudes and responsibility. As we saw (§13), Strawson's thesis can be interpreted in two very different ways, depending on whether we assign explanatory priority to the reactive attitudes or to responsibility. On a response-dependent interpretation, there is no response-independent justification of our attributions of responsibility or the reactive attitudes. Responsibility judgments simply reflect those settled dispositions to respond to others that are constitutive of various kinds of interpersonal relationships. By contrast, a realist interpretation stresses the way that the reactive attitudes make sense in light of and so *presuppose* responsibility. A realist reading promises to justify the reactive attitudes in a way in which a response-dependent reading cannot, but the realist reading also makes the justification of the reactive attitudes hostage to the existence of a plausible conception of responsibility that can be specified independently of the reactive attitudes. Fortunately, fair opportunity answers the need to provide a response-independent conception of responsibility.

If one were to accept a response-dependent interpretation of Strawson's thesis, linking the reactive attitudes and responsibility, doubts about whether the reactive attitudes apply to Harris would imply doubts about whether Harris is responsible. Even if we find only that learning Harris's history moderates our attitudes, this would require us to diminish his responsibility for the crime. Watson clearly reads Strawson as accepting response-dependence,

---

[12] Watson, "Responsibility and the Limits of Evil," p. 242.

though Watson is less clear whether he endorses respondence-dependence himself. However, we have defended a realist reading of Strawson's thesis as a philosophical (rather than interpretive) proposal, against the response-dependent reading. According to the realist, we can't read someone's responsibility off of our reactive attitudes toward his actions. The reactive attitudes are justified iff the target is responsible. This requires us to identify a plausible response-independent conception of responsibility. That inquiry supported the fair opportunity conception of responsibility. How might Harris's formative circumstances be related to the requirements of fair opportunity?

On the one hand, the record available to us suggests that Harris did not receive a systematic psychiatric evaluation and did not enter a plea of insanity, which might lead us to assume that his normative competence was not significantly impaired. On the other hand, abuse and neglect, especially at an early age, have been correlated with the development of affective deficits, such as empathy deficits, and later conduct disorder.[13] We need to be careful not to assume that such correlations demonstrate incapacity, but the correlations are nonetheless suggestive. As we will see in Chapter 11, empathy deficits are one characteristic of psychopathy. Though Harris was never diagnosed as a

[13] For discussion of early neglect and abuse and disorders of attachment, see, e.g., John Bowlby, "The Influence of Early Environment in the Development of Neurosis and Neurotic Character" *International Journal of Psycho-Analysis* 21 (1940): 154–78, John Bowlby, "Forty-four Juvenile Thieves: Their Characters and Home-Life" *International Journal of Psycho-Analysis* 25 (1944): 107–28, and John Bowlby, *Attachment and Loss,* Vol. II (New York: Basic Books, 1973); Kim Chisholm, "A Three Year Follow-Up of Attachment and Indiscriminate Friendliness in Children Adopted from Romanian Orphanages" *Child Development* 69 (1998): 1092–106; Alan Schore, *Affect Regulation and the Origin of the Self: The Neurobiology of Emotional Development,* 2d ed. (New York: Routledge, 2016), esp. chs. 27–28; Christina Saltaris, "Psychopathy in Juvenile Offenders: Can Temperament and Attachment Be Considered as Robust Developmental Precursors?" *Clinical Psychology Review* 22 (2002): 729–52; Grazyna Kochanska and Sanhag Kim, "Toward a New Understanding of Legacy of Early Attachments for Future Antisocial Trajectories: Evidence from Two Longitudinal Studies" *Development and Psychopathology* 24 (2012): 783–806; Mario Mikulincer and Phillip Shaver, *Attachment in Adulthood: Structure, Dynamics and Change,* 2d ed. (New York: Guilford, 2016), ch. 13; and Tsachi Ein-Dor and Guy Doron, "Psychopathology and Attachment" in *Attachment Theory and Research: New Directions and Emerging Themes,* ed. J. Simpson and W.S. Rholes (New York: Guilford, 2015). For some other developmental perspectives on childhood abuse and neglect, see, Dante Cicchetti and Sheree Toth, "Child Maltreatment" *Annual Review of Clinical Psychology* 1 (2005): 409–38; Joshua Mersky and Arthur Reynolds, "Child Maltreatment and Violent Delinquency: Disentangling Main Effects and Subgroup Effects" *Child Maltreatment* 12 (2007): 246–58; Terrie Moffitt and Avshalom Caspi, "Evidence from Behavioral Genetics for Environmental Contributions to Antisocial Conduct" in *Handbook of Socialization,* ed. J. Grusec and P. Hastings (New York: The Guilford Press, 2007); Carl Maas, Todd Herrenkohl, and Cynthia Sousa, "Review of Research on Child Maltreatment and Violence in Youth" *Trauma, Violence, and Abuse* 9 (2008): 56–67; Emily Paterson, *Child Maltreatment across the Life-Course: Links to Youth Offending* (Ph.D. Thesis, Griffith University, 2015); and Jonathan Glover, *Alien Landscapes?* (Cambridge, MA: Harvard University Press, 2014), ch. 3, 25. Many thanks to Gail Heyman and Monique Wonderly for suggestions about the developmental literature.

psychopath, he displays some aspects of a psychopathic profile. Though I shall later express some skepticism about whether the empathy deficits of psychopaths should be excusing, at this stage it's not unreasonable to think that Harris's history of abuse and neglect might have impaired some aspects of his normative competence.

If Harris's history did impair his competence, then his wrongdoing should be excused in whole or in part. Here, history would matter, but only because it might causally affect whether Harris was competent at the time of wrongdoing, not as an independent element of responsibility. Alternatively, if Harris's history did not impair his competence, then it does not affect his responsibility. That doesn't mean that his unfortunate formative circumstances might not matter. We have already suggested that blame and punishment are fitting responses to culpable wrongdoing—wrongdoing for which the agent is responsible—in the sense that culpable wrongdoing creates a strong *pro tanto* case for blame and punishment (§2). We will return to these issues in Chapter 6. On this sort of broadly retributive conception of blame and punishment, the *pro tanto* case for blame and punishment must sometimes compete with various sorts of reasons to blame or punish less than desert demands. Sympathy for undeserved hardship might support calls for mercy in some cases, which might temper the demands of retributive justice. A case for mercy does not undermine responsibility and blame and so is not an excuse. Rather, the case for mercy and for blame co-exist, and each moderates the demands of the other.

But if this analysis is right, we can offer a constructive dilemma to show that Harris's unfortunate formative history does not give us reason to treat responsibility as an historical concept.

1. Either Harris's history of abuse and neglect impaired his normative competence at the time of the commission of his crime or it did not.
2. If Harris's history did affect his competence, this fact excuses or at least mitigates his wrongdoing, just because it causally affects his reasons-responsiveness at the time of action.
3. If Harris's history did not affect his competence, then he is responsible and, hence, blameworthy for his wrongdoing.
4. However, a history of abuse and neglect may justify compassion, which does not gainsay his responsibility and blameworthiness, but may justify mitigation on grounds other than desert.
5. Hence, in neither case does Harris's unfortunate history justify recognizing an historical condition on responsibility, over and above normative competence and situational control.

Interesting as the Harris case is, it does not support historicism about responsibility, as we have been understanding that doctrine.[14]

38. Ahistoricism

Should our conception of responsibility as fair opportunity depend only on synchronic facts about the capacities and opportunities of agents at the time of action, or should it treat responsibility as an essentially historical concept, assigning historical conditions about the origins of the agent's capacities and opportunities an independent constitutive role in responsibility, over and above the requisite capacities and opportunities? In principle, fair opportunity could be developed as either a synchronic and structural conception or as an historical conception. Our examination of possible rationales for treating responsibility as an historical concept has not been exhaustive. Nonetheless, it supports provisional skepticism about whether fair opportunity should be developed as an historical conception. There are familiar reasons to think that some kinds of histories enable, cultivate, and sustain normative competence and situational control and that other histories impair normative competence and situational control. How could it be otherwise if we approach fair opportunity in a psychologically realistic and naturalistic manner? But the fact that history can causally affect normative competence and situational control does not show that we want to treat historical conditions as constituents of responsibility, beyond their role in creating and maintaining the relevant capacities and opportunities. The etiology of putative excuses, such as incapacity or duress, does affect whether those conditions genuinely excuse, because culpable incapacity or duress does not excuse. But this important fact can be explained on a synchronic or structural conception by grounding responsibility for later outcomes in earlier choices that were competent and not subject to duress. For these reasons, in what follows, I will formulate fair opportunity as a synchronic or structural conception. Historicists, who remain unconvinced, are free to develop an historicist version of fair opportunity.

---

[14] This conclusion agrees with parts of the analysis in Michael McKenna, "The Limits of Evil and the Role of Moral Address: A Defense of Strawsonian Compatibilism" *The Journal of Ethics* 2 (1998): 123–42 and Craig Agule, *Responsibility, Reasons-Responsiveness, and History* (University of California, San Diego, Ph.D. Dissertation, 2017), chs. 6–7.

6

Blame, Punishment, and Predominant Retributivism

In thinking about responsibility and, in particular, accountability, it is useful to focus on blame and other negative reactive attitudes and practices. When we hold people accountable, it is usually for some kind of wrongdoing, whether in action or attitude. Moreover, it is reasonable to count criminal law principles and doctrines as among our reactive attitudes and practices insofar as they reflect our practices of holding wrongdoers accountable. So, the criminal law is essentially concerned with negative, rather than positive, reactive attitudes and practices involving blame. Blame and punishment are closely related insofar as punishment involves both censure and sanction. Realism about Strawson's thesis about the connection between the reactive attitudes and responsibility supports a broadly retributive conception of blame and punishment that sees blame and punishment as *deserved* or *fitting* responses to culpable wrongdoing, that is, misconduct for which the agent is responsible in the accountability sense.[1] Indeed, culpable wrongdoing just is the basis of desert for blame and punishment. Some kind of retributivist conception of punishment explains important features of the criminal law, including the two main affirmative defenses in the criminal law—justifications and excuses. These two defenses deny different elements in the retributivist analysis of desert. Justifications deny wrongdoing, whereas excuses deny responsibility or culpability for wrongdoing. Some form of retributivism is plausible, once we understand retributivist essentials and avoid common misconceptions about retributivism. The most plausible form of retributivism is a mixed conception

---

[1] Chapter 7 will distinguish three conceptions of culpability. *Narrow* culpability corresponds to the elemental sense of *mens rea*, which provides the mental or subjective dimension of criminal wrongdoing. *Broad* culpability is the responsibility condition in virtue of which the agent's wrongdoing is blameworthy and without which she would be excused. *Inclusive* culpability is the combination of wrongdoing and responsibility that together make the agent blameworthy and deserving of blame and punishment. Each kind of culpability plays an important role in a broadly retributive rationale for the criminal law that predicates blame and punishment on the fair opportunity to avoid wrongdoing. Here, my focus is on broad culpability. Indeed, unless context indicates otherwise, my discussion of culpability concerns broad culpability.

Fair Opportunity and Responsibility. David O. Brink, Oxford University Press (2021). © David O. Brink.
DOI: 10.1093/oso/9780198859468.003.0006

of punishment that combines backward-looking and forward-looking rationales for punishment but in which the element of desert predominates.

39. Blame, Blameworthiness, and the Ethics of Blame

Blame and related attitudes—censure, condemnation, and reproach—are commonplace in public and private life. We blame governmental officials and other public figures for high crimes and misdemeanors, unjust policies, and various kinds of indiscretion. We blame private citizens we don't know for misconduct that becomes public. We blame friends and acquaintances if we find their conduct or attitudes fall short of reasonable expectations, as when one censures a friend for being indiscreet with confidential information one shared with him. And we engage in self-reproach when we realize that we have behaved poorly, let others down, or been negligent, for instance, when one blames oneself for not being more considerate and supportive of a friend when she was struggling through a difficult personal problem.

Blameworthiness is essential to blame. But what exactly is the relationship between them? Blame is a *psychological* attitude or action that an appraiser takes toward someone on account of the target's actions or attitudes, whereas blameworthiness is a *normative* concept in which a person is an appropriate or fitting object of blame on account of facts about her and her actions or attitudes. On the one hand, blame seems *conceptually prior* to blameworthiness insofar as the normative notion presupposes the psychological notion— blameworthiness is suitability for blame. On the other hand, blameworthiness seems to be *normatively prior* to blame insofar as only the blameworthy should be blamed. A target is blameworthy just in case she *merits* or *deserves* blame, blame is *suitable, apt, fitting*, or (in an eighteenth-century idiom) *meet*.

Different conceptions of blameworthiness offer different accounts of the conditions under which a target is a suitable or fitting object of blame. On some views, the grounds for blameworthiness are *forward-looking*. On these views, blame is appropriate because of some good that it would bring about— for instance, the expression of the appraiser's attitudes, the affirmation of norms that have been breached, moral uptake in the target, or the reconciliation of the appraiser or victim and the target. On other views, the grounds for blameworthiness are *backward-looking*. On such views, blame is fitting or deserved for some kind of past offense or failing for which the agent in question was culpable or responsible.

Different backward-looking conceptions of blameworthiness result from different conceptions of responsibility. The view defended here is the fair opportunity conception of responsibility. On this conception, responsibility and, hence, culpability require that at the time in question the agent had the relevant capacities—normative competence—and the fair opportunity to exercise these capacities—situational control. Normative competence itself factors into cognitive competence—the ability to recognize the relevant norms—and volitional competence—the ability to conform one's conduct to this normative knowledge. Normative competence and situational control are individually necessary and jointly sufficient for responsibility, because significant impairment of either condition compromises the agent's fair opportunity to avoid wrongdoing. Though I will draw on the fair opportunity conception of responsibility, different backward-looking conceptions of blameworthiness could be funded by different conceptions of responsibility.

Following Strawson, we might view any purely forward-looking conception of blameworthiness as problematic because it appeals to the *wrong sort of reason* for blame. It would be unfair and inappropriate to blame someone in the absence of wrongdoing or for wrongdoing for which the agent was not responsible, no matter how much good might come from doing so. A purely forward-looking conception of blameworthiness might be the best we could do if we were skeptics about responsibility.[2] But, if we are not skeptics about responsibility, then a purely forward-looking rationale for blame is the wrong sort of reason. This means that we should explore the resources of backward-looking and mixed conceptions of blameworthiness. In particular, we should pursue a conception of blameworthiness in which *desert*, based on an offense for which the agent is responsible, is necessary and sufficient for blameworthiness.

However, it is important to add that blameworthiness is necessary but not sufficient for blame being *fully* justified—that is, on-balance or all-things-considered justified. Some blameworthy actions should not be blamed, perhaps because doing so would be hypocritical or counter-productive or cause more harm than good or because blame should be tempered with mercy or forgiveness. But if blameworthiness does not entail justified blame, how are the two connected? If something is blameworthy, then there is a *pro tanto* case for blaming it. This *pro tanto* case for blame implies that blame should be withheld only for sufficient countervailing reasons. If so, blameworthiness is

---

[2] See, e.g., Pereboom, *Living without Free Will* and *Free Will, Agency, and Meaning in Life.*

always a reason to blame, even if in particular cases that reason is overridden by countervailing considerations against blaming. This means that while desert is necessary and sufficient for blameworthiness, it is necessary, but not sufficient, for justified blame.

When we should blame raises issues about the *ethics of blaming*. If culpable wrongdoing or failing is always a *pro tanto* reason to blame, what kinds of considerations interfere with and possibly defeat the *pro tanto* case for blaming the blameworthy? In principle, there could be many kinds of countervailing considerations, and it would be difficult to catalog all of them. Here are a few salient possibilities.

First, *blame might be costly* emotionally or otherwise. Sometimes the costs are borne by the appraiser, sometimes by the target, sometimes both, and even sometimes by third parties. We are all familiar with the adage that one must pick one's battles, and this advice applies no less to the practice of blame. Presumably, the balance of reasons to blame depends on both the degree to which the target is blameworthy and the costs of blaming, especially to the appraiser and third parties.

Second, forgiveness seems to involve the *forswearing of blame*, and so the ethics of blaming will interact with the ethics of forgiving. Forgiveness itself seems to presuppose blameworthiness. It makes no sense to forgive another unless one regards the target of forgiveness as blameworthy. If an agent has committed no wrong or is fully excused for that wrong, there is nothing to forgive. Forgiveness raises important issues about who has standing to forgive, the conditions under which forgiveness is appropriate, whether forgiveness is ever mandatory or always remains discretionary, how, if at all, the decision of one party to forgive affects the decision of other parties to forgive, and how to measure the strength of the reasons to forgive.[3] These are complex and difficult issues. Though they interact with the ethics of blaming, they lie largely outside the focus of this book, and I will not have much further to say about forgiveness.

Third, it is sometimes said that some people lack the *standing to blame* in particular cases.[4] In the law, standing depends on whether a party has a

---

[3] For good discussions of some issues about forgiveness, see Paul Hughes and Brandon Warmke, "Forgiveness" *Stanford Encyclopedia of Philosophy* (2017) and Per Milam, "Forgiveness" in *The Oxford Handbook of Moral Responsibility*, ed. D. Nelkin and D. Pereboom (Oxford: Clarendon Press, 2021).

[4] See, e.g., Scanlon, *Moral Dimensions*, pp. 175–79; Macalester Bell, "The Standing to Blame: A Critique" in *Blame: Its Nature and Norms*, ed. D.J. Coates and N. Tognazzini (New York: Oxford University Press, 2012); and Gary Watson, "Standing in Judgment" in *Blame: Its Nature and Norms*, ed. Coates and Tognazzini.

sufficient *stake in* or *relation to* a legal matter to bring suit. Standing to blame would seem to involve the question of whether someone has a sufficient stake in or relation to an offense to blame the wrongdoer. If someone lacks standing in relation to a wrong and a target, that presents a reason why that person should not blame the target. For instance, it is sometimes said that hypocrites lack the standing to blame others for sins of which they themselves are guilty. One might claim that it was hypocritical for President Trump to blame Al Franken for sexual misconduct, because there is strong evidence that Trump is himself a serial sexual harasser. If so, Trump lacked standing to blame Franken for sexual assault. Though it's plausible that hypocrites and those complicit in an offense lack standing to blame, it's not clear who does have standing. Standing to blame may vary with the nature of the wrong or failing. If the wrong has a victim, the victim may have some special standing to blame. But if the wrong is a moral wrong, then it may be that any member of the moral community has some standing to blame, even if the victims of the wrong have special standing to blame. There might be a presumption in favor of standing, which has specific defeaters, such as hypocrisy or complicity. It's important to note that standing to blame is appraiser-relative, so that one person's lack of standing need not imply that another person lacks standing. Hypocrites might lack standing to blame, but others do not. Moreover, even if others lack standing to blame, that does not mean that the culpable wrongdoer is not blameworthy. Indeed, it might be that the disqualification for blaming that lack of standing generates itself is only *pro tanto* reason not to blame. If there is a serious wrong for which a wrongdoer is fully culpable, and there is no one free from sin to blame him, it might be permissible for a fellow sinner to blame the target, especially if in so doing the appraiser acknowledges that she is not free from sin herself. In such cases, it might be better for blame to come from a remorseful and reformed sinner than to forego blame altogether. Some of these issues about the standing to blame and punish will be important in Chapter 9.

Moreover, the nature and strength of reasons that might compete against the *pro tanto* case to blame the blameworthy will undoubtedly depend on how we understand blame itself. If blame has an essential function, such as norm enforcement or facilitating reconciliation, then there may be special reasons not to blame in particular cases if that would not be conducive to reinforcing norms or facilitating reconciliation. So, the ethics of blame returns us to issues about what is essential to blame.

40. The Core and Syndrome of Blame

Blame is familiar and common and implicated in important ways with other practices, attitudes, and values. Yet blame is remarkably difficult to analyze, and there have been many different conceptions of blame, each of which has things to recommend it but which seems susceptible to objection or counter-example.[5] It is common to try to analyze blame in terms of necessary and sufficient conditions as a way of capturing what is essential to blame. Different conceptions of blame have been proposed, and most build on familiar and common dimensions of blame. Some of these conceptions conceive of blame in terms of the appraiser's state of mind, focusing on her negative evaluation of the target and the target's conduct as blameworthy or her negative emotions and reactive attitudes, such as resentment and indignation, toward the target and her conduct. For example, some have claimed that blame consists in a *negative evaluation* of the target's conduct or attitudes.[6] But this sort of cognitive account seems to leave out the emotional engagement characteristic of blame. Strawsonians view it as essential to blame that the appraiser adopts certain *reactive attitudes*, such as anger or resentment toward a target.[7] However, such reactive attitude accounts may seem to ignore the important social or interpersonal role that blame can have. But Strawsonians are also interested in the interpersonal role of the reactive attitudes. So it is open to them to say that blame essentially involves some kind of *moral communication or address*.[8] Some forms of communication are unilateral expressions of blame, perhaps in the form of *protest*.[9] But often blame is expressed communication by the appraiser that addresses the target or others. Sometimes, the appraiser seeks to *open a dialogue* or *initiate a normative exchange* with the target.[10] Blame might be a way of signaling to the target and others that the target has acted in ways that display *insufficient regard* for the interests or rights of the appraiser or others and that involve a breach of trust.[11] Sometimes, an expressive or communicative analysis incorporates a *functional*

---

[5] See the essays in *Blame: Its Nature and Norms*, ed. Coates and Tognazzini.

[6] See, e.g., Watson, "Two Faces of Responsibility," p. 266.

[7] See, e.g., R. Jay Wallace, "Rightness and Responsibility" in *Blame: Its Nature and Norms*, ed. Coates and Tognazzini.

[8] See, e.g., Watson, "Responsibility and the Limits of Evil," p. 230.

[9] See, e.g., Angela Smith, "Moral Blame and Moral Protest" in *Blame: Its Nature and Norms*, ed. Coates and Tognazzini.

[10] See, e.g., Michael McKenna, *Conversation and Responsibility* (Oxford: Clarendon Press, 2012) and "Directed Blame and Conversation" in *Blame: Its Nature and Norms*, ed. Coates and Tognazzini; Miranda Fricker, "What's the Point of Blame? A Paradigm Based Explanation" *Noûs* 50 (2016): 165–83.

[11] See, e.g., Scanlon, *Moral Dimensions*, ch. 4.

dimension, as when blame is understood to involve forms of interpersonal address that have the function of *norm enforcement*.[12] While each of these forms of expression and communication is important, none seems essential to blame inasmuch as it seems possible for blame to be *private*—that is, an internal mental act of censure or reproach that does not receive verbal or other communicative expression.

Perhaps the problem with these traditional analyses is that each latches on to a partial truth and takes that to be essential. If so, the remedy might be to offer a more *multi-dimensional* analysis. One possibility is to treat blame as a *cluster concept* in which some threshold number of elements are both necessary and sufficient for the application of the concept, even though no one element must be a part of this cluster.[13] However, the cluster approach seems unable to explain what makes any cluster of elements sufficient or how the elements of the cluster hang together. A different, but related, approach is to treat blame as a *prototype concept*, which identifies a *paradigm* or *stereotype* that combines all recurring elements and then measures putative cases of the concept in terms of their *approximation* or *resemblance* to the paradigm or stereotype.[14] While a prototype conception may be the most promising multi-dimensional approach, it still fails to explain what unifies the elements of the prototype.

At this juncture, one might despair of providing any kind of analysis or conception of blame. Perhaps we should approach blame the way Justice Potter Stewart approached obscenity, when he famously despaired of defining obscenity but said "I know it when I see it."[15] Perhaps blame is *sui generis* and unanalyzable.

However, there is reason to be more sanguine about blame than Potter Stewart was about obscenity. The key to progress lies in seeing that there is a *core* to blame that is present in all cases, even purely private mental instances of blame. The core, which is both necessary and sufficient for blame, is an aversive attitude toward the target that is predicated on the belief or judgment,

---

[12] See, e.g., Cass Sunstein, "Social Norms and Social Roles" *Columbia Law Review* 96 (1996): 903–68; Victoria McGeer, "Civilizing Blame" in *Blame: Its Nature and Norms*, ed. Coates and Tognazzini; Bertram Malle, Steve Guglielmo, and Andrew Monroe, "A Theory of Blame" *Psychological Inquiry* 25 (2014): 147–86; and Fiery Cushman, "The Scope of Blame" *Psychological Inquiry* 25 (2014): 201–05.

[13] For discussion of cluster concepts, see Hilary Putnam, "The Analytic and the Synthetic" reprinted in Hilary Putnam, *Philosophical Papers, Volume 2: Mind, Language, and Reality* (New York: Cambridge University Press, 1979), p. 52.

[14] For discussion of prototype-related approaches to concepts, see Eleanor Rosch, "Principles of Categorization" in *Cognition and Categorization*, ed. E. Rosch and B. Lloyd (Hillsdale, NJ: Erlbaum, 1978) and Edward Smith and Douglas Medin, *Categories and Concepts* (Cambridge, MA: Harvard University Press, 1981).

[15] *Jacobellis v. Ohio*, 378 U.S. 184 (1964), at 197 (Stewart J. concurring).

perhaps tacit, that the target is blameworthy. Once we identify this core, we can work outward toward familiar expressions, manifestations, and functions of blame. Because blame involves the belief that the target is blameworthy, which involves wrongdoing for which the agent was responsible, it is natural for appraisers not just to register private mental acts of blame but also to be disposed to manifest this blame in various private and public ways in suitable circumstances. In particular, blamers are disposed to express their blame to the target and others, to protest the target's behavior or attitudes, to engage the target in a normative exchange that acknowledges breached relations and can provide the target with an opportunity to express remorse and make amends, and to reaffirm and enforce the norms that have been breached. These are all normal expressions of blame that constitute a *non-accidental syndrome*, but they lie *downstream* from the core of blame. As with any psychological disposition, blame's dispositions may not manifest themselves in particular circumstances due to the operation of other dispositions and other forms of psychological interference. For instance, though a victim may blame her abuser and be disposed to rebuke him, she may not express her blame to her abuser in contexts in which she believes that blame is likely to lead to retaliation from her abuser and an escalation of the abuse. So, although elements of the syndrome non-accidentally co-occur with the core of blame, it is quite possible for there to be blame without one or more of these downstream expressions of blame.[16]

The tricky part in this account is specifying the core of blame. What exactly does it involve? Blame seems to involve a cognitive element insofar as an attitude won't count as blame unless the appraiser regards the target as blameworthy, which we said involves two components—the belief that the target acted wrongly or poorly and that the target was responsible for her wrongdoing or failing. Culpable wrongdoing is the desert basis of blame, and blame seems to presuppose the belief, express or tacit, that the target is blameworthy. There can be blame without the target actually being blame-worthy if the appraiser is unaware of the fact that the target did not commit the wrong or was not responsible for it. But it seems the appraiser has to believe that the target is blameworthy. Blame tends to dissipate or transform into other reactive attitudes when appraisers recognize that the target is not blameworthy.

---

[16] For one interpretation of a syndrome as a non-accidental cluster of elements, no one of which is necessary to the concept or kind, see Boyd's discussion of homeostasis in Richard Boyd, "Homeostasis, Species, and Higher Taxa" in *Species: New Interdisciplinary Essays*, ed. R. Wilson (Cambridge, MA: MIT Press, 1999).

Could the judgment of blameworthiness be all there is to blame? Some have objected to such cognitive views of blame because they are too detached and not emotionally engaged. However, at this point, it's not clear that emotional detachment is a good objection, because emotional engagement might just be part of the normal downstream manifestations of blame. Though it might seem possible to take a detached clinical view of blame, normally the belief that someone has acted badly leads to feelings of indignation, resentment, or disappointment and associated behaviors. If emotional engagement is downstream from the core, cases of emotionally detached blame needn't be counterexamples to a purely cognitive conception. Indeed, one might appeal precisely to emotional detachment, for instance, when one blames fictional characters or historical individuals from bygone eras, to motivate the purely cognitive account of the core.

Though one might defend a purely cognitive conception of the core of blame in this way, it seems more plausible that blame does involve some kind of aversive attitude or emotion in addition to the judgment of blameworthiness. In effect, this would be to express doubt that there are genuine cases of completely emotionally detached blame. The precise reactive attitudes involved in blame no doubt vary from case to case. The reactive attitudes that one experiences in blaming fictional characters or historical figures are no doubt milder than the reactive attitudes one experiences in blaming one's spouse for infidelity or one's friend for betrayal of trust. But there seems to be a kind of aversive attitude present in all cases of blame, even when one blames a fictional character or a long-dead historical figure. Consider some such blaming responses—our disapproval of Agamemnon for sacrificing his daughter Iphigenia to ensure safe travel to Troy, our aversive reaction to the character Edward Casaubon in George Eliot's *Middlemarch* for his self-absorption and his failure to appreciate Dorothea's promise and passions, our blame for Neville Chamberlain for his attempts to appease Hitler, and our condemnation of Hitler himself for the atrocities of the Holocaust. In our blaming responses in these cases, we are not just recording an evaluation to which we might be indifferent. In these and similar cases, we experience negative reactive attitudes ranging from disappointment, dismay, and frustration to indignation, repulsion, disgust, and horror. These reactive attitudes will not be tied as tightly to action as the emotions in otherwise similar non-fictional or non-historical cases, but they are there, which is partly why fiction and history can move us. There may be no single emotional response common to all cases of blame, but they all seem to involve some negative or aversive emotional reaction, if only a fairly mild one. This suggests that the core of blame consists in some kind of aversive attitude toward a target that is based on an assessment of the target as blameworthy.

The core of blame gives us a traditional analysis of blame that promises to be immune to counterexample, but the syndrome explains what is attractive in various multi-dimensional approaches, especially cluster and prototype approaches.[17]

41. The Relation between Blame and Blameworthiness

However, there is a worry about the cognitive aspects of the core of blame. Because the core of blame involves a belief or judgment that the target is blameworthy, this threatens to make the analysis circular. It's true, as we saw, that blame and blameworthiness are distinct concepts. In particular, blame is a psychological concept, whereas blameworthiness is a normative concept. But blameworthiness involves fitness or aptness for blame. So, if we analyze blame even partly in terms of blameworthiness, blame occurs both in the analysandum and in the analysans. That's a kind of circularity.

Perhaps it's an innocent or at least acceptable kind of circularity. Presumably, circularity would be problematic in a *reductive* analysis. But we might eschew a reductive analysis of blame, preferring instead a *commentary* or *elucidation* that employs the concept under investigation or cognate concepts.[18]

Though commentaries and elucidations can be informative, even if circular, we can avoid circularity altogether. Though different conceptions of blameworthiness offer different substantive conceptions of when one is a fitting or apt target of blame, we have seen the plausibility of a backward-looking conception that focuses on desert and identifies the desert basis of blame with wrongdoing (or other failing) for which the target is responsible. If so, the concept of blameworthiness can be eliminated from the analysans of blame in favor of the combination of wrongdoing and responsibility.

However, this may seem only to enlarge, rather than remove, the explanatory circle. As we saw (§13), Strawson's thesis links responsibility and the

---

[17] This core and syndrome analysis of blame is articulated and defended at greater length in Brink and Nelkin, "The Nature and Significance of Blame."

[18] Here, I have some sympathy with David Wiggins, who views circularity as a defect in a definition or analysis, but not in the sort of commentary or elucidation that he claims to offer. See David Wiggins, "A Sensible Subjectivism?" in David Wiggins, *Needs, Values, and Truth* (Oxford: Blackwell, 1987), pp. 188–89.

reactive attitudes. If we were to accept a response-dependent reading of Strawson's thesis, this would make our analysis of the cognitive dimension of blame circular. For, on this reading, blame would presuppose blameworthiness, which would depend on responsibility, which, in turn, would depend ultimately on blame, that is, our blaming practices.

However, we avoid this kind of circularity on the realist reading of Strawson's thesis. According to the realist reading, the appropriateness of the reactive attitudes is explained by responsibility, not the other way around. Indeed, if we want to take seriously the fallibility of the reactive attitudes and offer a justification of them, then we need to embrace a response-independent conception of responsibility. Though the plausibility of the realist interpretation of Strawson's thesis depends on a promissory note to provide a plausible response-independent conception of responsibility, the fair opportunity conception of responsibility fulfills this promise. If this or some other response-independent conception of responsibility can be defended, then the correct conception of responsibility can be explained in a way that does not presuppose blame, and we can give an account of the ground of blameworthiness that appeals to wrongdoing and responsibility, not blame itself. This allows us to make use of blameworthiness in the analysis of blame in a way that can, in principle, be eliminated, and this allows our analysis of the core of blame to avoid the charge of circularity.

42. Criminalization, Blame, and Punishment

On this analysis, blame is an aversive reactive attitude that presupposes that its target is blameworthy—that the target is culpable or responsible for some kind of wrongdoing, whether that is a shortcoming in action or attitude. *Punishment* combines blame or censure and sanction of some kind. It has a condemnatory function in which breach of norms makes one a legitimate target of censure. If so, punishment involves blame and so presupposes that the target of punishment is blameworthy. Blameworthiness consists in wrongdoing for which the agent is responsible. But punishment involves sanction, as well as censure. Punishment goes beyond blame and attaches sanctions of various kinds to especially significant forms of culpable wrongdoing.

Punishment can be *informal* when sanctions are imposed by private parties, either as individuals or as groups, to perceived wrongdoing. Informal punishment might involve public rebuke and various forms of social distancing. Punishment is *official* when the state has a *system* of sanctions that it imposes for violations of its rules. *Legal* punishment is official punishment in which a legal system systematically imposes sanctions for violations of legal rules by its members. Informal punishment and legal punishment are distinct, and there are, no doubt, interesting differences between them.

There are important issues about moral blame and punishment that is informal, rather than official and legal, some of which we will address eventually. However, I want to focus, for now, on the nature and justification of legal blame and punishment. I believe that many issues about moral and legal blame and punishment are parallel, as we should expect given the way that the criminal law draws on entrenched moral ideas about wrongdoing, blame, responsibility, and excuse and in turn affects the way we think about those moral ideas. However, there are special issues involved in legal punishment that deserve our attention, especially insofar as we want to engage criminal law principles and doctrines about responsibility and excuse.

One question for any theory of punishment is what the state should criminalize and why. One possible approach to this topic is *legal moralism*. The legal moralist claims that moral wrongdoing is both necessary and sufficient for criminalization. Moralism contrasts with the *harm principle*, which claims that the only legitimate reason for the state to restrict the liberty of its citizens is to prevent harm to others. Though much wrongdoing involves conduct that harms others, there is harmful conduct that is not wrong because it is justified (e.g. self-defense) and there are wrongs that do not harm others, because they exploit others or treat them unfairly without harming them. Though there will be overlap in the demands of legal moralism and the harm principle, the overlap is imperfect, with the result that the harm principle and legal moralism are not only different principles about the limits of the criminal law but also extensionally non-equivalent.

Legal moralism combines the claims that wrongdoing is necessary and sufficient for criminalization. It is the sufficiency claim that is controversial. In *On Liberty* John Stuart Mill famously embraces the harm principle and rejects legal moralism.[19] Many liberals, such as Joel Feinberg, agree with Mill, treating the rejection of legal moralism as a constitutive commitment of liberalism.[20] Some wrongs are *personal*, occurring within personal or family

---

[19] John Stuart Mill, *On Liberty* [1859] in *The Collected Works of John Stuart Mill*, vol. XVIII. For discussion of these issues, see Brink, *Mill's Progressive Principles*, chs. 6–9.

[20] See Joel Feinberg, *The Moral Limits of the Criminal Law*, 4 Vols. (Oxford: Clarendon Press, 1984–88), esp. vol. IV. Feinberg conceives of himself as a Millian liberal, with the exception that he wants to recognize some forms of offense regulation as permissible. Whether Feinberg has understood Mill correctly is another matter.

relationships and involving betrayals of trust or ingratitude. Though these personal wrongs are regrettable, we may not want the state interfering in our private lives to prevent them. Moreover, we may not want the criminal law to penalize all vice or enforce all virtue. Sloth, lust, envy, and gluttony are sins, but provided they do not harm others, it is not clear that we think they are the business of the criminal law. One might infer that these liberal conclusions require rejecting legal moralism. If there are any cases in which we should reject the enforcement of morality, that might seem to undermine legal moralism, because immorality is not sufficient to justify regulation.

However, this anti-moralist argument is too quick. The legal moralist can and should distinguish stronger and weaker claims.

- *Strong Legal Moralism.* Wrongfulness is a sufficient reason to regulate conduct.
- *Weak Legal Moralism.* Wrongfulness is sufficient to establish a *pro tanto* reason to regulate conduct.

Strong legal moralism says that it is always on-balance or all-things-considered right to regulate immoral conduct. By contrast, weak legal moralism says only that immorality establishes a *pro tanto* case for regulation. In particular, weak moralism allows that this *pro tanto* case might be overridden if legal sanctions are an ineffective way to curb vice and encourage virtue or the costs of legal intrusion are too great. If so, liberals can and should reject strong legal moralism but need not reject weak legal moralism.[21]

Even if weak legal moralism is more plausible than strong legal moralism and is compatible with some liberal strictures on the moral limits of the criminal law, we might still wonder if it is true. Is immorality per se a *pro tanto* reason for the state to criminalize conduct? Not if the state has *limited authority and functions* that do not include a generalized duty to enforce and promote the whole of morality.

The criminal law might have the more limited function to enforce important *elementary* moral, social, and political requirements, not morality per se. We might think of elementary normative requirements in terms of *natural* and *civic duties*. Natural duties are owed to other human beings, as such, and enjoin serious wrongs against the person, such as murder, assault, rape, theft,

---

[21] See Moore, *Placing Blame*, chs. 16, 18. Moore thinks that retributivism entails legal moralism. I reconstruct and assess this claim in David O. Brink, "Retributivism and Legal Moralism" *Ratio Juris* 25 (2012): 496–512.

and fraud. By contrast, civic duties obtain among members of cooperative schemes and social practices and involve obligations to do one's fair share to comply with the cooperative scheme and to support the social practice. For instance, paying one's taxes and honoring one's contractual commitments are civic duties. The exact boundary between natural and civic duties may not always be clear, but a rough sense of the nature and scope of natural and civic duties might be enough for present purposes. The general observance of natural and civic duties is mutually beneficial, affording each citizen security of her personal rights and in her social dealings with others. This gives us some reason to think that a social contract among free and equal persons would agree to a system of criminal norms that enforced elementary normative requirements by requiring compliance with fundamental natural and civic duties.

The distinction between natural and civic duties overlaps with a familiar distinction in the criminal law between crimes *mala in se*—wrongs in themselves—and *mala prohibita*—wrongs by virtue of prohibition. Crimes *mala in se* are typically treated as more serious than crimes *mala prohibita*. Beyond this, it is unclear if there is a consensus about the extensions of two categories of crimes. Some crimes *mala in se* violate natural duties and include wrongs against the person, such as murder, rape, assault, theft, and fraud. It is commonly thought that crimes *mala prohibita* do not violate natural duties and can include crimes of prostitution, drug use, gambling, tax evasion, traffic violations, loitering, and truancy. I'm not sure if the category of crimes *mala prohibita* is well conceived. In some cases of alleged crimes *mala prohibita*, it is arguable that the activities are wrong in themselves or at least that their wrongness depends on moral principles that do not themselves depend on social recognition for legal enactment. For example, even if paying one's taxes is a civic, rather than a natural, duty, it seems clear that tax evasion is wrong, because it is unfair, independently of the enactment of rules prohibiting tax evasion. Also, though traffic regulations often have an important conventional element designed to facilitate coordination among motorists and between motorists and other members of the public, the reason for these rules is to promote transportation safety, which is not itself a conventional good. If so, we might think that these examples of alleged crimes *mala prohibita* were better understood as crimes *mala in se*. Other examples, such as loitering and truancy, are harder to interpret as crimes *mala in se*. But precisely for this reason, we might wonder if they should be criminalized. I won't try to settle the question of whether the criminal law should recognize crimes *mala prohibita*. If so, they are likely to be peripheral parts of the criminal law.

Our focus will be on central provisions of the criminal law that enforce elementary natural and civic duties and seem best understood as specifying crimes *mala in se*.

We need not decide between weak legal moralism and this more limited function for the criminal law, because both are likely to agree that the focus of legitimate criminalization, which can be justified all-things-considered, should be restricted to important natural and civic duties and crimes *mala in se*. For the weak legal moralist, this is a conclusion supported by the balance of reasons, whereas for the anti-moralist this will be a more foundational restriction on the scope of the criminal law.

This is the beginning of an explanation of what conduct the state should criminalize and why. A reasonably just criminal justice system will focus on crimes *mala in se* and the violation of important natural and civic duties. But why should the state sanction and not merely censure criminal wrongdoing? We do well to remember that sanctions can include a diverse array of restrictions on the rights and privileges of citizenship, ranging from fines, probationary status, community service, to incarceration. Sanctions of some sort are needed as a supplement to censure to ensure adequate levels of compliance with natural and civic duties. In a reasonably just legal system, citizens have good moral reasons to comply with these duties and avoid crimes *mala in se*. But moral reasons are not always sufficient to ensure adequate levels of compliance. Some individuals lack moral motivation entirely, for others moral motivation is weak, and those for whom moral motivation is usually strong are nonetheless prone to occasional weakness. A system of legal sanctions provides imperfect moral beings with prudential motivation that supplements and reinforces, rather than replaces, moral reasons for compliance.[22]

In the case of legal punishment, the state claims authority to censure and sanction for culpable violation of duly enacted norms. As such, punishment can be contrasted with other forms of social control that involve *detention*— both *prospective* detention in which an agent is civilly committed or quarantined, prior to wrongdoing, because he is a danger to himself or others, and *reactive* detention in which the agent has engaged in wrongdoing for which he is not culpable and, hence, is excused, but nonetheless poses an ongoing danger to himself or others. Detention, of either kind, involves neither blame nor sanction. Moreover, punishment can also be contrasted with forms of social control that do employ sanctions but not in response to

---

[22] See Andreas von Hirsch, *Censure and Sanctions* (Oxford: Clarendon Press, 1993), ch. 2.

culpable wrongdoing. The state might employ sanctions to control the attitudes and behavior of citizens in legal or extralegal ways, for instance, to
encourage loyalty and discourage legitimate dissent. What seems crucial to
punishment is that it is a public response to a perceived breach of legally
promulgated norms.

43. Justifying Punishment

The discussion so far has focused on our reasons for wanting to have criminal
norms that enforce mutually beneficial natural and civic duties and that attach
censure and often sanctions of some kind to culpable noncompliance. This is
perhaps enough background for us to raise the question of what justifies the
imposition of punishment for noncompliance. It's tempting to say that the
same reasons for having criminal laws, including sanctions for noncompliance, justify the imposition of sanctions for noncompliance. Indeed, I think a
simple version of this story is plausible. But we can appreciate this better once
we've looked at some familiar ways of justifying punishment.

Theories of punishment answer various questions about the justification of
punishment, including (1) *Whom* should we punish? (2) *Why* should we
punish? (3) *How much* should we punish? and (4) *How* should we punish?
A satisfactory theory of punishment should provide an answer to all these
questions (and perhaps more). How we answer one question may affect how
we can answer other questions. Different rationales for punishment approach
these issues differently, sometimes conceptualizing crime differently and
focusing on different aims of punishment.

1. *Deterrence*: Punishment aims to promote compliance with legal norms,
   and it does so by achieving deterrence, both specific and general—
   deterring the individual who is punished from further wrongdoing and
   other potential criminal wrongdoers.
2. *Rehabilitation*: Criminal conduct is an expression of social dysfunction,
   and punishment should aim to rehabilitate and re-socialize criminals,
   equipping them with psychological and social skills and other resources
   for being law-abiding and productive members of society.
3. *Norm reinforcement* and *communication*: Because criminal conduct
   breaches important social norms, punishment serves to express,
   reinforce, and communicate those norms.

4. *Restorative justice*: Criminal conduct breaches community norms and often wrongs a victim, in which case punishment should provide a mediation among the wrongdoers, the victims, and the larger community with the aim of restoring moral community and securing reconciliation.

5. *Retributive justice*: Criminal misconduct involves culpable wrongdoing— that is, wrongdoing for which the agent is responsible. Culpable wrongdoing is the desert basis of punishment. Punishment should aim to hold criminals accountable based on and in proportion to their desert.

These rationales are not exhaustive, but they are representative. Notice that rationales for punishment can be *pure*, appealing to a single factor or aim to justify punishment, or *mixed*, if they appeal to combinations of factors. Notice also the first four rationales are broadly *forward-looking*, appealing to some good consequence of punishment, whereas the last rationale is *backward-looking*, appealing to the historical notion of desert. Here too, conceptions of punishment can be purebreds or hybrids.[23]

We can test rival rationales by assessing their systematic comparative plausibility. We should see how well they answer these different questions about justified punishment, in particular, by measuring their commitments on these questions against our own considered convictions about these matters, and by comparing their theoretical virtues. Of special concern, when assessing the adequacy of any rationale, is whether its account of whom to punish is under-inclusive—failing to justify punishment of those who seem to merit punishment—or over-inclusive—justifying punishment of those who do not seem to merit punishment. A conception or rationale for punishment is problematic insofar as it is either under-inclusive or over-inclusive. The English jurist William Blackstone famously claimed that it is worse to punish the innocent than to let the guilty go free.[24] A corollary of Blackstone's asymmetry is that, all else being equal, it is worse to over-punish than to

---

[23] If, as I believe, restorative justice is most plausible when it incorporates, rather than eliminates, accountability, then restorative justice is best understood as a mixed conception, incorporating both a backward-looking (retributive) focus on desert and a forward-looking focus on reconciliation. For this sort of treatment of restorative justice, see R.A. Duff, *Punishment, Communication, and Community* (Oxford: Clarendon Press, 2001), pp. 92–106; R.A. Duff, "Restoration and Retribution" in *Principled Sentencing*, 3d ed., ed. A. von Hirsch, A. Ashworth, and J. Roberts (Oxford: Hart Publishing, 2009); and Lucy Allais, "Restorative Justice, Retributive Justice, and the South African Truth and Reconciliation Commission" *Philosophy & Public Affairs* 39 (2012): 331–63.

[24] Blackstone's version of this asymmetry involves a 10:1 ratio: "better that ten guilty persons go free than that one innocent party suffer." See William Blackstone, *Commentaries on the Laws of England* (London: Strahan & Woodfall, 1791) Book IV, Chapter 27, p. 358. Benjamin Franklin thought the ratio is 100:1. See Benjamin Franklin, "Letter to Benjamin Vaughn, March 14, 1785" in *The Writings of*

under-punish and, hence, that, all else being equal, it is a bigger vice in a theory of punishment to be over-inclusive than to be under-inclusive.

Most normative conceptions combine *accommodation* of our pre-theoretical normative commitments and *reform* of those commitments. Insofar as a conception subsumes and explains considered normative convictions, it accommodates them. But insofar as a conception conflicts with considered normative convictions, it calls for reform or revision. We should not expect perfect accommodation, because our moral judgments are incomplete, inconsistent, and subject to various kinds of bias and distortion. But complete reform is no more plausible than complete accommodation. Indeed, complete reform threatens to introduce a change in subject matter and should be explored only as a last resort, only if we conclude that our considered normative convictions are hopelessly muddled. Typically, reform is like the hole in a doughnut, made possible by a surrounding substance of accommodation. We accept local reforms as part of a process of global accommodation. This means that reform is always, or at least typically, partial. But to say that reform is partial does not imply that it cannot be significant. How revisionary a conception can be is something we cannot decide in advance of looking at the conception, its degree of accommodation, and the nature of its reforms.

So too with blame and punishment. Our pre-theoretical beliefs about blame and punishment are not sacred; they may be biased, incomplete, or inconsistent and may require revision. So, while it is some evidence against a conception that it is under-inclusive or over-inclusive, that evidence may not be decisive. The most compelling conception of punishment may be revisionary in some respects if it fits our other beliefs sufficiently well.

By these standards, we have reason to be skeptical of purely forward-looking conceptions of punishment, because they promise to be both under-inclusive and over-inclusive. Purely forward-looking conceptions will be under-inclusive, because they imply that we have no reason to punish when doing so would not secure the relevant good consequences. No doubt, punishment often does or at least can promote deterrence, rehabilitation, norm reinforcement and communication, and reconciliation. But we can imagine circumstances in which punishment would not secure these goods—in which rehabilitation was not possible and in which punishment could not be publicized or would be widely, but falsely, regarded as illegitimate. In such circumstances, someone who was fully responsible for a serious wrongdoing would go

---

Benjamin Franklin, ed. A. Smyth (New York: Macmillan, 1906), vol. 9, p. 293. It is the asymmetry itself, rather than any particular ratio, that is important for our purposes.

unpunished. Nonetheless, many of us would think that there was at least some reason to punish culpable wrongdoers in such circumstances. These would be cases of under-punishment. Moreover, purely forward-looking conceptions will be over-inclusive, because they imply that we have reason to punish in the absence of culpable wrongdoing if doing so would promote the relevant forward-looking values. Perhaps such cases would be rare or merely hypothetical, but they are problematic because they violate the norm that we should punish only the guilty. In such cases, purely forward-looking conceptions of punishment are over-inclusive. If we accept Blackstone's asymmetry, then, all else being equal, the sin of over-inclusiveness is more serious than the sin of under-inclusiveness.

We saw that Strawson criticizes instrumentalist conceptions of responsibility that justify ascriptions of responsibility and the reactive attitudes in purely forward-looking terms, by appeal to deterrence, norm reinforcement, and the like as invoking the wrong sort of reason for thinking someone responsible and applying the reactive attitudes (§1, 9). Adapting Strawson's point, we might say that purely forward-looking conceptions of punishment provide the *wrong sort of reason for punishment*. We should not punish for purely forward-looking reasons, in the absence of culpable wrongdoing, because the proper target of punishment is wrongdoing for which the agent is responsible. This is the claim that culpable wrongdoing is a necessary condition of justified punishment. This is an important insight of retributive conceptions, whether pure or mixed.

Perhaps we don't yet have a conclusive refutation of purely forward-looking conceptions of punishment. Every conception of punishment might prove revisionary, in which case we would need to determine the least revisionary conception, and until we've examined the implications of other conceptions, we don't know that some purely forward-looking conception won't be least revisionary. This is already reason to examine other conceptions, but there is reason to expect that retributive rivals, whether pure or mixed, will be less revisionary and, hence, more plausible than purely forward-looking conceptions.

44. Punishment and Responsibility

Retributive conceptions of punishment, whether pure or mixed, limit punishment to cases of culpable wrongdoing. Culpable wrongdoing is wrongdoing for which the agent is responsible. This means that legitimate punishment is conditional on the agent's responsibility for her wrongdoing. In the context of punishment, the relevant kind of responsibility is accountability, not attributability (§14). Recall that Watson associates attributive responsibility with action that expresses the agent's real self, with an aretaic perspective on her action, and with her own evaluative commitments or orientation. By contrast, he thinks that accountability involves liability to sanctions, raises questions about the fairness of imposing sanctions, and presupposes that the agent had control and a fair opportunity to avoid sanctions. We explained attributability in terms of quality of will and accountability in terms of the agent's capacities and opportunities. If that is right, it is doubtful that we can explain moral responsibility and blame entirely in terms of attributability and quality of will without invoking accountability and fair opportunity. In any case, criminal responsibility and punishment clearly require accountability and fair opportunity.

If punishment presupposes realism about responsibility and accountability, that means that punishment is threatened by skepticism about responsibility, conceived in terms of accountability. In this way, punishment is tied to traditional debates about whether we are ever responsible for our actions.

Skeptics about responsibility have reason to be skeptical about punishment. They could still accept purely forward-looking conceptions of punishment— defending punishment because it does or can promote various goods, such as deterrence, rehabilitation, norm enforcement and communication, and reconciliation. These rationales do not presuppose that the agent is responsible for her misconduct. But punishment involves both censure and sanction, which are attitudes and practices that seem to presuppose wrongdoing for which the target is responsible. This is why purely forward-looking conceptions seem to appeal to the wrong sort of reason for punishment. If we accept this link between legitimate punishment and responsibility, then skeptics about responsibility should be *abolitionists* about punishment. Nonetheless, they can seek to *replace* punishment with forms of social control that do not presuppose censure, sanction, and responsibility. In the criminal law, we acquit wrongdoers who are not responsible for their wrongdoing by reason of insanity. But if they remain a danger to themselves or others, they can be subject to *involuntary commitment*, during which they should receive psychiatric treatment designed to render them non-dangerous and to make them suitable for reintegration into society. Involuntary commitment is a form of *reactive detention*. We engage in *pre-emptive detention* when we *quarantine* people who are potential dangers to themselves or others, even in the absence of having acted wrongly or caused harm. The skeptic about responsibility might be an abolitionist about punishment but a proponent of involuntary commitment and quarantine.[25]

A realist reading of Strawson's thesis linking the reactive attitudes and responsibility stresses the way that the reactive attitudes make sense in light of and so presuppose responsibility. As such, the reactive attitudes are *evidence* about when to hold people responsible, but not something that *constitutes* them being responsible. The realist interpretation of Strawson's thesis promises to ground and justify the reactive attitudes in a way in which the response-dependent reading cannot. If we focus on wrongdoing, the realist can and should appeal to the working hypothesis about the inverse relation between responsibility and excuse in order to leverage our understanding of excuses to provide insight into the nature of responsibility. If hard determinism were true, we should excuse everyone, because no one is responsible. But the criminal law and our moralized reactive attitudes are *selective* about when to excuse. We excuse for particular kinds of incapacity, such as insanity, immaturity, or duress. But then our reactive attitudes and associated practices of excuse presuppose some version of compatibilism.

45. Retributive Essentials

Realism about Strawson's thesis says that our reactive attitudes are correct or justified insofar as they track the responsibility of their targets. Blame and punishment are reactive attitudes and practices. On the realist interpretation, Strawson's thesis represents some of the negative reactive attitudes, including blame and punishment, as fitting responses to wrongdoing for which the agent is responsible or culpable. This is a *retributivist* thesis about blame and punishment being *fitting* or *deserved* insofar as the agent is responsible or culpable for her wrongdoing.

What are the essentials of retributivism? Retributivism says that blame and punishment ought to be proportional to desert, which is itself the product of two independent variables—wrongdoing and responsibility or culpability.[26]

---

[25] See, e.g., Pereboom, *Free Will, Agency, and the Meaning in Life*, chs. 6–7 and Greg Caruso, "Skepticism about Moral Responsibility" *Stanford Encyclopedia of Philosophy* (2018) and "The Public Health-Quarantine Model" in *The Oxford Handbook of Moral Responsibility*, ed. D. Nelkin and D. Pereboom (New York: Oxford University Press, 2021).

[26] Here, I adapt some ideas in Robert Nozick, *Philosophical Explanations* (Cambridge, MA: Harvard University Press, 1981), pp. 363–66. My formula resolves some ambiguities and inconsistencies in his discussion.

$$P \propto D(= W \times R)$$

On this view, desert is the product of the magnitude of wrongdoing and the degree of responsibility. This is an ecumenical conception of desert insofar as it relies on the concepts of wrongdoing and responsibility (accountability) and does not seem to require any particular conception of either concept, though it fits naturally with the fair opportunity conception of responsibility. Notice that retributivism does not require more than this ecumenical conception of desert; in particular, it does not require a conception of desert that is either *sui generis* or presupposes libertarianism.[27]

In principle, different wrongs can be arranged on a scale of seriousness. Presumably, the magnitude of a wrong is often influenced by the amount of harm it produces or risks, though we probably shouldn't reduce wrongness to harmfulness, because there are harms that are not wrong (e.g. cases of self-defense and necessity) and because some wrongs may not be harmful (e.g. unfair free-riding). Degree of responsibility should be thought of as a percentage of full responsibility, which we could represent on a 0–1 scale. Thus, an agent would deserve punishment commensurate with the magnitude of the wrong she has committed just in case she is fully responsible for her wrongdoing and fractional punishments corresponding to reduced responsibility.

It will be helpful to distinguish three retributivist claims about punishment.

1. Desert in the form of culpable wrongdoing is a necessary condition of blame and punishment.
2. Proportionate justice sets an upper limit on permissible blame and punishment.
3. Blame and punishment are fitting responses to culpable wrongdoing in the sense that there is a strong *pro tanto* case for blame and punishment that is proportionate to desert.

---

[27] The conception of desert that I am working with is ecumenical in the sense that it consists in the moral quality of one's conduct and one's responsibility—understood as accountability—for that conduct. Chapter 7 will identify the desert basis for retributivism with inclusive culpability. In several writings Pereboom expresses skepticism about "basic" desert. See Pereboom, *Free Will, Agency, and the Meaning in Life*, chs. 6–7 and "Responsibility, Regret, and Protest." I'm not sure how basic desert, in his sense, is related to desert in my ecumenical sense. If basic desert is just ecumenical desert, then we disagree about the prospects for a compatibilist version of fair opportunity to explain desert. If basic desert requires that desert be *sui generis* or libertarian, then we should ignore basic desert and focus on ecumenical desert.

First, to avoid punishing the innocent, even when doing so would have consequentialist value, we must recognize retributivism as at least part of the truth about blame and punishment. Specifically, we must recognize desert as a necessary condition on blame and punishment. Second, proportionate just deserts track culpable wrongdoing and set an upper limit on the amount of punishment that is permissible in individual cases. These two claims—(1) and (2)—make up the *negative* retributivist thesis. Desert is a necessary condition for blame and punishment, because both are impermissible in the absence of culpable wrongdoing, and desert places an upper limit on permissible punishment, which must not exceed what would be proportional to desert. Pure and mixed retributive theories embrace the negative retributive thesis.

But many forms of retributivism, both pure and mixed, insist that desert is not just a constraint on blame and punishment but also provides an important *rationale* for these attitudes and practices. This is sometimes called the *positive* retributivist thesis.[28] According to the positive retributivist thesis, blame and punishment are fitting responses to culpable wrongdoing in the sense that culpable wrongdoing is sufficient for a strong *pro tanto* case for blame and punishment. Other things being equal, we should blame and punish culpable wrongdoers proportionate to their desert. Whether proportionate blame and punishment are always all-things-considered appropriate responses will depend on the balance of reasons and whether our conception of retributivism is pure or mixed.

Whether blame and punishment are fitting responses to culpable wrongdoing may depend on whether the wrongdoing in question is moral or legal. *Moral retributivism* says that blame and punishment are fitting responses to culpable *moral wrongdoing*. This is plausible insofar as persons are moral agents who are accountable for their conduct. Respecting persons as persons means that they should be held accountable for their responsible decisions and that it is fitting that they be blamed and punished for wrongdoing for which they are responsible. Realism about Strawson's thesis lends support to moral retributivism. *Legal retributivism* says that blame and punishment are fitting responses to culpable *legal wrongdoing*. However, it is less clear that culpable legal wrongdoing always deserves blame and punishment if only because legal norms and moral norms are distinct and legal wrongdoing is not necessarily moral wrongdoing. Where legal wrongdoing is not morally wrong, it is less clear that blame and punishment are deserved, even *pro tanto*.

---

[28] Duff discusses the negative and positive retributive desert theses in *Punishment, Communication, and Community*, pp. 12, 19.

One might conclude that there is a *pro tanto* case for punishing legal wrongdoing when and only when legal wrongdoing is also moral wrongdoing. But one might suppose that there can be a *pro tanto* case for punishing legal wrongdoing even in cases in which the legal norms being transgressed are morally problematic provided that the moral flaws in the law are fairly minor, do not occur too often, and do not have systematically disparate impact on citizens. On this view, the duty to obey the law is part of a *package deal*, arising from a sufficiently or reasonably just social compact. This echoes part of Herbert Morris's justification of punishment in "Persons and Punishment."[29] Morris argues that basic provisions of the criminal law against murder, rape, assault, theft, fraud, and trespass are norms the general observance of which is mutually beneficial. Culpable wrongdoers are those who free-ride, enjoying the benefits of others' compliance with these norms without incurring the costs of doing their part to maintain the system from which they benefit. But free-riding on mutually beneficial social practices is *unfair*. The wrongdoer claims more than his fair share, and fairness demands that he be punished according to the terms announced in advance as the penalty for noncompliance.

The mutually beneficial character of the laws of a reasonably just legal system extends to laws prohibiting crimes *mala in se* and *mala prohibita*. In the case of crimes *mala in se*, laws do not make the conduct wrong but rather *declare* it be wrong, legally reinforcing the wrongful status of wrongs against persons. In the case of crimes *mala prohibita*, the laws make the conduct wrong through *enactment*. In both cases, the prohibitions tend to be mutually beneficial, making noncompliance a *public wrong*, calling for state censure and sanction. In the case of crimes *mala in se* but not *mala prohibita*, the conduct is wrong independently of legal enactment. So in the case of crimes *mala in se* there are two kinds of reason for censure and sanction—reasons to enforce natural and civic duties and reasons of fairness—whereas in the case of crimes *mala prohibita* there is just one kind of reason for censure and sanction—reasons of fairness.

This appeal to fairness to help anchor desert has an important *scope limitation*—it applies only to social practices that are sufficiently just and mutually beneficial. If the social scheme does not meet this condition, then noncompliance may not be unfair. In particular, if one lives in a sufficiently unjust social scheme in which the benefits and burdens of social cooperation

[29] Herbert Morris, "Persons and Punishment" *The Monist* 52: 475–501 and reprinted in Herbert Morris, *On Guilt and Innocence* (Berkeley: University of California Press, 1976).

are not distributed fairly, then noncompliance with the scheme's norms—legal wrongdoing—need not be morally wrong and, hence, blame and punishment may not be deserved. In such systems, blame and punishment of crimes *mala in se* will still be fitting, but blame and punishment of some crimes *mala prohibita* may not be fitting. We will return to these issues about the bearing of structural injustice on responsibility, excuse, and punishment in Chapter 9.

When the scope condition is satisfied, legal, as well as moral wrongdoing, for which the agent is responsible merits punishment in the sense that there is a strong *pro tanto* reason to punish culpable wrongdoing. Retributivism that is suitably qualified in these ways not only has considerable intuitive appeal but also fits well with important parts of criminal jurisprudence. For instance, it explains well the two main kinds of affirmative defense a defendant can offer—justifications and excuses.[30] Justifications and excuses each deny one of the two elements in the retributivist desert basis for blame and punishment—wrongdoing and responsibility. Justifications, such as self-defense or necessity, deny wrongdoing, whereas excuses, such as insanity or duress, deny culpability or responsibility.

46. Misconceptions about Retributivism

Though some form of retributivism is, I think, the dominant conception of punishment in the criminal law, it has a mixed reputation in other quarters. Some of these misgivings may reflect concerns about the pure retributivist thesis that desert is the only factor affecting blame and punishment and that desert is always sufficient to justify punishment whatever the costs or moral perplexities. Mixed conceptions of punishment that recognize desert as only part of the justification of punishment may avoid worries directed at pure retributivism. However, there are other concerns about retributivism that would seem to apply to any form of retributivism, whether pure or mixed.

1. Retributivism is implausibly committed to *lex talonis*, which involves punishing wrongdoers in kind (e.g. an eye for an eye).

---

[30] While justifications and excuses are the two main affirmative defenses available to defendants, there are also policy-based exemptions, such as prosecutorial immunity for diplomats. See, e.g., Paul Robinson, *Structure and Function in the Criminal Law* (Oxford: Clarendon Press, 1997), pp. 96–124, 204–07 and Mitchell Berman, "Justification and Excuse, Law and Morality" 53 *Duke Law Journal* (2003): 1–77. We will return to issues about the architecture of affirmative defenses in Chapter 8.

2. Retributivism is implausibly committed to harsh punishments, such as those found in mass incarceration—trying juveniles as adults, three strikes laws, significant mandatory minima, long sentences for non-violent crime, and significant post-incarceration penalties, such as disenfranchisement, loss of public assistance, and requirements to disclose one's criminal record to potential employers.
3. Retributivism is implausibly committed to valuing the suffering of the wrongdoer.
4. Retributivism is implausibly committed to viewing retribution as an intrinsic good.
5. Retributivism is implausibly committed to basing sentences for individual crimes on the individual's total history of moral desert.

Some, if not all, of these concerns reflect misunderstandings of retributivist essentials or accretions in the retributivist tradition.

(1) Retributivism requires proportionate justice, not punishment in kind. There are some ways that the state ought not to treat its citizens, even if they have committed very serious crimes. For instance, even in the Unites States, where we allow capital punishment and permit various severe punishments, we have a constitutional prohibition on cruel and unusual punishment, which can plausibly be interpreted as a prohibition on severely inhumane and disproportionate punishments. There is room for debate about the implications of the Eighth Amendment prohibition on cruel and unusual punishments and, in particular, how far-reaching a constraint it places on permissible punishment. But it is widely agreed that the state ought not to torture torturers or rape rapists; such punishments would constitute cruel and unusual punishment. We can still punish *proportionately* without punishing in kind. *Lex talonis* might allow for swift but inhumane punishments in the case of rape or torture; proportional punishments that are humane might take longer.

(2) Some writers lay the problems associated with mass incarceration at the door of the retributivist.[31] We will discuss mass incarceration more fully in Chapter 9. Among the troubling aspects of mass incarceration are trying juveniles as adults, steep mandatory sentencing minima, long prison sentences, brutal prison conditions, and post-incarceration penalties, such as disenfranchisement, the inability to serve on juries, the loss of public

---

[31] See, e.g., Erin Kelly, "Doing Without Desert" *Pacific Philosophical Quarterly* 83 (2002): 180–2015; "Criminal Justice Without Retribution" *Journal of Philosophy* 106 (2009): 419–39; and *The Limits of Blame: Rethinking Punishment and Responsibility* (Cambridge, MA: Harvard University Press, 2018).

assistance, and the duty to report all felony convictions to potential employers. Moreover, a prominent dimension to mass incarceration is the racially disparate impact of these over-punitive practices. These are some of the aspects of the war on drugs and mass incarceration that have led to calls for criminal justice reforms.[32] If retributivism were responsible for the ills of mass incarceration, that would be reason to be skeptical of retributivism. But retributivism is not to blame for excesses in the criminal justice system. Retributivism can require accountability and proportionate punishment without requiring or even permitting these penal practices. There's no reason to assume that retributivism supports these practices or opposes criminal law reform. Indeed, it is natural to frame calls for criminal justice reform by saying these aspects of mass incarceration imprison people out of proportion to their deserts. But this justification of reform presupposes, rather than condemns, retributive ideas.

What proportionality clearly requires is *comparative* just deserts. This gives us only *ordinal* information about the magnitude of just deserts until we have *anchors* for the ordinal scale. A natural way to provide anchors is to determine the most severe punishment permissible for the most serious crimes (e.g. serial murder and torture) and the mildest form of sanction for the most minor infractions (e.g. jaywalking). There is room for disagreement about what quantum of punishment is appropriate for the anchors, especially at the maximum. Norway sets the maximum at 21 years, even for Anders Breivik, who killed 77 people in terrorist attacks, including 69 participants at the Social Democratic Youth League summer camp. The United States currently permits states to set the maximum at capital punishment. We might wonder whether capital punishment is compatible with retributive justice, especially because it forecloses the possibility of discovering wrongful convictions and because it has proven difficult to administer capital punishment in a way that is not racially unjust. Perhaps the top end of the scale should be life in prison without the possibility of parole (LPWP). But even if LPWP is the top end of the scale, most other crime, including even much violent crime, deserves considerably less punishment. We also need to distinguish the *length* and *manner* of punishment. We tend to think of punishment in terms of incarceration. But incarceration is only one form punishment can take. It can also take the form of diversionary treatment (such as house arrest, counseling, and/or community service), fines, and restitution. When punishment does involve incarceration, it need not be in over-crowded and inhumane conditions that endanger the health and safety of convicts and that provide little educational or

[32] See, e.g., Michelle Alexander, *The New Jim Crow* (New York: The New Press, 2010).

vocational training to equip prisoners to succeed in life outside of prison. It is open to retributivists to think that proportionality requires shorter periods of incarceration and more humane forms of incarceration for many crimes. Indeed, one might think that incarceration should be limited primarily to violent crime and serial offenders and that various kinds of diversionary treatment, such as community service and house arrest, would be appropriate for most forms of non-violent crime and first offenders.

In these ways, one can be a retributivist without endorsing the degree of punitiveness in the current American criminal justice system. Retributivists can and do think that prison conditions, criminalization for non-violent offenses, sentence length, and post-incarceration penalties are disproportionately punitive and violate just deserts.[33]

(3) What should the *currency* of proportionate punishment be? Both retributivists and their critics often assume that it is *felt suffering* and claim that retributivism is committed to the proposition that it is intrinsically or noninstrumentally good for culpable wrongdoers to suffer.[34] That's one form that retributivism might take. But it is not essential to retributivism. Retributivism is better understood, I submit, as the idea that desert demands *accountability*, where it is fitting to hold culpable wrongdoers accountable in ways that reflect the nature and gravity of their wrongs and their degrees of culpability. But the currency of accountability need not be suffering. Instead, it might consist in the *deprivation of certain rights and privileges of citizenship*, which would be temporary for all but the most serious forms of wrongdoing. As we have seen, retributivists endorse the idea that punishment is a fitting response to the culpable wrongdoer free-riding on the mutually beneficial social compact among citizens involved in the rule of law. The free-rider's noncompliance with the rule of law unfairly exploits the compliance of others. So, fairness requires punishing culpable wrongdoers who free-ride. But if this is part of the rationale for retributive deserts, then there's a strong case to be made that the appropriate currency of punishment should be some modification in the rights and privileges of citizenship, because it is the social compact among citizens on

---

[33] See, e.g., my retributivist critique of the juvenile transfer trend in Brink, "Immaturity, Normative Competence, and Juvenile Transfer" and in Chapter 12.

[34] See, e.g., Immanuel Kant, *The Metaphysics of Morals* [1797–98] in *Kant's Practical Philosophy*, trs. M Gregor (Cambridge: Cambridge University Press, 1997) (Prussian Academy pagination) 6: 331; W.D. Ross, *The Right and the Good* (Oxford: Clarendon Press, 1930), pp. 135–38; Hart, *Punishment and Responsibility*, pp. 234–35; Moore, *Placing Blame*, p. 163; Adam Kolber, "The Subjective Experience of Punishment" *Columbia Law Review* 109 (2009), p. 182; Victor Tadros, *The Ends of Harm* (Oxford: Clarendon Press, 2011), pp. 9, 25, 41, 66–78; and Mitchell Berman, "Rehabilitating Retributivism" *Law and Philosophy* 32 (2013), p. 87.

which the wrongdoer free-rides. Offenders have reason to regard the loss of rights and privileges of citizenship, even if temporary, as unwelcome and may well experience psychic costs and suffering as a result. If so, suffering may be a common by-product of punishment, but punishment should aim at accountability, measured in terms of the rights and privileges of citizenship, not suffering.

(4) Many of the same writers who link retributivism with suffering want to claim that imposing suffering on culpable wrongdoers is an intrinsic or non-instrumental good. Accountability does not require suffering, and the currency of retributivism should instead be loss of rights and privileges. If we avoid the mistake about suffering, should we then embrace the idea that retributivism treats accountability in the form of deprivation of rights and privileges for culpable wrongdoers as an intrinsic good? As long as we remember that the state of affairs is the complex one of being a deprivation of rights and privileges that is consequential on and proportionate to culpable wrongdoing, we might claim that retributivism is committed to viewing that as intrinsically or non-instrumentally good. But this should be understood as a *moral good*. For we could equally well say that what makes blame and punishment fitting responses to culpable wrongdoing is that they are *demands of justice*. This, after all, is why retributive essentials are often described in terms of *just deserts* or *proportionate justice*. It seems we can describe retributive outcomes either as a moral good or as a demand of justice. If the right is prior to the good, then the justice claim is prior in order of explanation to the moral goodness claim.

(5) Some moral retributivists, such as Kant and W.D. Ross, have suggested that as a matter of desert a person's overall happiness or welfare should be proportional to the net total amount of positive and negative desert he has accrued over the course of his life.[35] Though Kant and Ross seem to think that there is or would be a kind of fittingness to one's weal and woe tracking overall desert, it's not clear that either thinks that it is the job of the state to administer punishment by appeal to lifetime desert. However, some critics of retributivism have assumed that legal retributivism should take such a holistic form, apportioning punishment for individual crimes on the offender's overall moral desert.[36]

---

[35] Kant, *The Metaphysics of Morals*, 6: 331 and Ross, *The Right and the Good*, pp. 135–38.
[36] See Tadros, *The Ends of Harm*, pp. 68–73 and Adam Kolber, "The Time Frame Challenge to Retributivism" in *Of One-Eyed and Toothless Miscreants: Making the Punishment Fit the Crime?*, ed. M. Tonry (New York: Oxford University Press, 2019).

There seem to be both practical and conceptual problems with this sort of holistic legal retributivism. The practical problem is that the information required for calculating an individual's total moral desert is overwhelming and courts don't have resources or authority to make such assessments of an agent's total lifetime culpability. But there are conceptual worries as well. One worry is that holistic retributivism would allow people who had accrued sufficient moral credit over the course of their lives to commit crimes with impunity. Another worry is that if at each point in time blame and punishment are apportioned in light of an agent's total history of culpability, then past culpability will count more than once, indeed, indefinitely many times. But that seems like a form of double (multiple) jeopardy.

There are good reasons for retributivists to avoid these commitments. In particular, retributivists should distinguish between moral and legal forms of desert and between holistic and individualistic assessments of either kind of desert. Once we separate these issues, there is little reason to embrace this kind of holistic legal retributivism.

First, we need to observe the distinction between moral and legal retributivism. Moral retributivism predicates moral censure and sanction on culpable moral wrongdoing—that is, moral wrongdoing for which the agent is responsible—whereas legal retributivism predicates legal censure and sanction on culpable legal wrongdoing—that is, legal wrongdoing for which the agent is responsible. Moral blame and punishment should reflect culpable moral wrongdoing, whereas legal blame and punishment should reflect culpable legal wrongdoing. But then legal retributivism should base censure and sanction on desert for legal wrongdoing, not desert for moral wrongdoing. Moral assessments should track moral virtue in some way, but legal assessment should not.

Second, within either kind of desert, we need to distinguish holistic and individual assessment.[37] In the first instance, we assess desert, whether moral or legal, for individual actions, and its magnitude is a function of the magnitude of the wrongdoing and the degree of responsibility. Desert for individual actions can be aggregated, so as to yield cumulative desert assessments over periods of time, in the limit producing a holistic desert assessment for an agent's whole life. Holistic desert has a limited place in moral assessment. Moral praise and blame in response to particular actions should be individual,

[37] See, e.g., Joel Feinberg, *Doing and Deserving: Essays in the Theory of Responsibility* (Princeton, NJ: Princeton University Press, 1970), pp. 116–17 and Thomas Hurka, "Desert: Individualistic and Holistic" in *Desert and Justice*, ed. S. Olsaretti (Oxford: Clarendon Press, 2003), esp. p. 52.

rather than cumulative. Otherwise, we will engage in moral double-counting, triple-counting, etc. But moral assessment can focus on periods in a person's life, rather than individual actions. In such cases, moral assessment should be cumulative. The limiting case of this assessment of periods in a life is assessment of a whole life, in which one is interested in the agent's total history of moral desert. If there were a God, her moral assessment on Judgment Day would be holistic. Even in a secular world, agents can look back on their own lives and make holistic assessments of their own overall moral desert. If individual and holistic moral assessments are *mere* assessments and do not involve censure and sanction, then they can co-exist. But if they both involve proportional blame and punishment, that will produce double (multiple) moral accounting and be over-punitive.

When we turn from moral assessment to legal assessment, there is no form of cumulative or holistic assessment. We engage in legal censure and sanction only for individual offenses. We do not engage in legal censure and sanction for periods in a person's life, much less for her life as a whole. There are practical problems with punishing people for whole-life legal desert. There are obvious fact-finding difficulties. But also, by the end of a life, we would have run out of time in which to punish proportionately those who have significant negative net legal desert. If the assessments of legal desert are mere assessments, then we could make holistic legal assessments, as well as individual ones. But if these legal assessments involve censure and sanction, then there is the double (multiple) counting objection to combining individual and holistic assessments. If we punish for whole-life culpability in addition to individual culpability, we would be over-punishing. We avoid all these problems by insisting that legal retributivism focus on legal desert for individual wrongs and that it be individualistic, rather than holistic.[38]

47. Predominant Retributivism

So far, we have defended a conception of punishment with retributive elements, but we have been agnostic between pure retributivism and a mixed conception with important retributive elements. Pure retributivism claims

---

[38] I believe that this kind of individualist retributivism is compatible with letting a history of prior offenses play a limited role at sentencing. Such information can speak to dangerousness, evidence of remorse, and prospects for rehabilitation, which can all be non-desert factors that play a role in sentencing on mixed conceptions of punishment, such as predominant retributivism (discussed in §47).

that desert, understood in terms of culpable wrongdoing, is the only factor relevant to justifying punishment and that desert is both necessary and sufficient for punishment.[39] By contrast, a mixed conception of punishment combines retributive and forward-looking elements. There are different kinds of mixed conceptions, but most insist that desert is a necessary condition of punishment, because only that will avoid the most serious worries about over-inclusiveness afflicting pure forward-looking conceptions.

One mixed theory is a *disjunction* of desert and consequentialist values, claiming that either is sufficient to justify punishment. But disjunctivism inherits the problems of over-inclusiveness and under-inclusiveness of pure forward-looking conceptions, because it allows consequential values alone to justify punishment. A *conjunction* of desert and consequentialist values that treats desert and good consequences as individually necessary and jointly sufficient for punishment is more plausible, because it avoids the more serious over-inclusiveness   objection   to   pure   forward-looking   conceptions. Nonetheless, conjunctivism is still under-inclusive insofar as it doesn't recognize any reason to punish culpable wrongdoing when doing so does not have good consequences. If these were our only options, then pure retributivism might be the most plausible conception. But these are not the only kinds of mixed conceptions, and pure retributivism doesn't explain the persisting attractions of forward-looking considerations, such as deterrence, rehabilitation, norm enforcement and communication, and reconciliation.[40]

The most plausible formulation of retributive ideas is a mixed conception of punishment in which retributive ideas dominate, which we might call *predominant retributivism*. Any form of retributivism insists that culpable wrongdoing serves as a *constraint* on blame and punishment. This is the negative retributivist thesis. Desert is a necessary condition for blame and punishment, because both are impermissible in the absence of culpable wrongdoing, and desert places an upper limit on permissible punishment, which must not exceed what would be proportional to desert.

---

[39] See, e.g., Moore, *Placing Blame*, esp. pp. 88, 91, 154, but also see p. 174.

[40] Another mixed conception is the sort of rule consequentialist conception of punishment defended by Rawls in "Two Concepts of Rules" (see §12 above). There, he distinguishes between the prospective (legislative) perspective on a practice, specifying the reasons for having a practice, and the retrospective (judicial) perspective on that practice, applying the reasons within a practice. This allows him to claim that the reasons for having a practice of punishment are consequentialist but the reasons for deciding how to handle cases arising within the practice are retributive. However, as we discussed, it's not clear why Rawls thinks that prospective issues can be neatly sequestered from retrospective ones. It's doubtful that purely consequentialist reasons for having a practice will justify a practice that operates in an exclusively retributive fashion.

BLAME, PUNISHMENT, AND PREDOMINANT RETRIBUTIVISM   149

Both pure and predominant retributivism insist that desert is not just a constraint on blame and punishment but also provides an important *rationale* for these attitudes and practices. This is the positive retributivist thesis. Both claim that blame and punishment are fitting responses to culpable wrongdoing in the sense that culpable wrongdoing is sufficient for a strong *pro tanto* case for blame and punishment. Other things being equal, we should blame and punish culpable wrongdoers proportionate to their desert.

However, other things are not always equal. This is where predominant retributivism diverges from pure retributivism. Whereas the pure retributivist thinks that desert is the only factor affecting the decision to punish, predominant retributivism recognizes that there can be non-desert-based reasons not to punish proportionately, in particular, to punish less than required by desert. Such non-desert factors can include the costs of punishment, the prospects for rehabilitation, evidence of remorse and restitution, and the value of mercy, forgiveness, and reconciliation. The strong *pro tanto* case for blame and punishment based on desert must sometimes compete with these countervailing considerations and may not always carry the day. Because predominant retributivism allows that desert can compete with non-desert reasons against proportionate punishment, it is a mixed theory of punishment.

Predominant retributivism is also a mixed theory of punishment insofar as it allows desert and non-desert factors to address different questions about punishment. As we said, a complete theory of punishment should address *whom* to punish, *why* we should punish, *how much* we should punish, and *how* we should punish. Retributivism offers a unified answer to the first three questions: we should punish culpable wrongdoers; we should do so, because they deserve punishment for culpable wrongdoing; and we should punish them proportionate to their desert, that is, to their degree of culpable wrongdoing. Though desert may *constrain* how we punish, because it constrains how much we should punish, it leaves the manner of punishment largely *underdetermined*.[41] Provided that we punish all and only the guilty, punish them because they deserve punishment, and punish them in proportion to, or at least not in excess of, their just deserts, we are free to and should punish them in ways likely to promote various forward-looking values, such as deterrence, rehabilitation, norm enforcement and communication, and reconciliation. Indeed, I think that this is the most plausible way to understand the contributions of various forward-looking rationales for punishment—as claims

---

[41] See Also Doug Husak, "Kinds of Punishment" in *Moral Puzzles and Legal Perplexities*, ed. H. Hurd (Cambridge: Cambridge University Press, 2018).

about the manner, rather than the justification, of punishment. For instance, the most plausible communicative and restorative justice models of punishment presuppose that punishment should be reserved for culpable wrongdoers and that punishment should aim to hold culpable wrongdoers accountable. But they claim that the manner in which we should punish should reflect values of norm communication and reconciliation, and not just desert.[42]

Another way to reconcile forward-looking rationales for punishment and the retributivist backward-looking focus on desert is to allow consequentialist considerations to supplement considerations of desert in the determination of precisely how much to punish. Despite the apparent precision of the retributivist formula for punishment, desert may determine only an *interval*, rather than a precise quantum, of punishment. Indeed, interval sentencing is reflected in various sentencing guidelines, including the United States Federal Sentencing Guidelines.[43] Whether punishment intervals reflect genuine metaphysical indeterminacy in the desert basis of particular crimes or epistemological indeterminacy in our ability to track small but genuine differences in culpable wrongdoing is an interesting question, which we need not settle here. As long as there is limited indeterminacy in the desert basis for punishment, whether metaphysical or epistemological, there is a need to specify further a precise punishment value within the deserved interval. So, it is open to us to appeal to various consequentialist rationales to fine-tune the quantum of punishment within the space of punishments set by desert. Here, we might decide how much within an interval to punish a particular offense by considering the circumstances of the offense and the offender and appealing to forward-looking concerns with deterrence, rehabilitation, norm reinforcement and signaling, and the prospects for reconciliation.

Predominant retributivism is a conception of punishment that mixes a backward-looking focus on desert with various forward-looking rationales for punishment, but in which desert conditions forward-looking considerations in three ways. First, desert in the form of culpable wrongdoing is a necessary condition of blame and punishment. Second, retributive justice that is proportionate sets an upper limit on permissible blame and punishment. Third, blame and punishment are fitting responses to culpable wrongdoing in the sense that there is a strong *pro tanto* case for blame and punishment that is proportionate to desert. In some cases, there may be sufficient reason to

[42] For this sort of treatment of restorative justice, see Duff, *Punishment, Communication, and Community*, pp. 92–106 and Duff, "Restoration and Retribution" and Allais, "Restorative Justice, Retributive Justice, and the South African Truth and Reconciliation Commission."
[43] United States Sentencing Commission, *Guidelines Manual* (Nov. 2016).

punish less than just deserts, but this will be in spite of the demands of just deserts.

It might be helpful to review the path that led us to predominant retributivism. Punishment involves both blame and sanction. As such, it seems to presuppose that the targets of punishment are blameworthy—that is, that they are culpable or responsible for wrongdoing. This makes purely forward-looking conceptions of punishment that appeal to deterrence, rehabilitation, norm communication and reinforcement, or reconciliation and permit punishment in the absence of culpable wrongdoing, implausible. It favors conceptions that are retributive in holding that punishment should be proportional to desert, understood as the product of wrongdoing and responsibility. Realism about Strawson's thesis linking responsibility and the reactive attitudes encourages us to look to our practices of excuse to identify the nature of responsibility and culpability. When we follow this methodological advice, we can avoid skepticism about responsibility and are led to the fair opportunity conception of responsibility, which represents responsibility as consisting in suitable capacities—normative competence—and opportunities—situational control. Fair opportunity is a response-independent conception of responsibility of the sort required by realism about Strawson's thesis. This realist interpretation of Strawson's thesis supports some form of retributivism insofar as it implies that it is fitting to blame and sometimes punish wrongdoing for which the agent is responsible. Retributive justice seeks accountability, not suffering, and it condemns various aspects of mass incarceration as inconsistent with just deserts. However, this case for retributivism is agnostic between pure retributivism and mixed conceptions that include important retributive elements. Predominant retributivism is a mixed conception of punishment that can explain the appeal of forward-looking rationales for punishment while maintaining that they are constrained by desert. On this view, desert is a necessary condition on permissible punishment, sets an upper bound on permissible punishment in the form of proportionate justice, and provides a strong *pro tanto* case for blame and punishment that is proportionate to desert.

7

The Nature and Significance of Culpability

Now that we have motivated, articulated, and defended the fair opportunity conception of responsibility and its role in blame and punishment, we can examine worries that fair opportunity is socially fragile and explore its impli- cations for recognizing excuses in a variety of cases involving diminished competence and control. Though we can, and in some places must, distinguish questions of moral and criminal responsibility, there is *substantial overlap in moral and criminal law demands*, and there is *common architecture for responsibility and excuse* in the two domains. We have already exploited these parallels in motivating and articulating fair opportunity, and common architecture will form a defeasible working hypothesis in the discussion that lies ahead. As we consider challenges to and applications of fair opportunity, we can test and, if necessary, qualify or even reject the assumption of common architecture.

Substantial overlap and common architecture suggest that we can often look at the same cases and issues to explore moral and criminal responsibility. So, it will often be helpful to look at legal cases and doctrines, since these have both moral and jurisprudential dimensions. To do so, it will be useful to situate the claims of fair opportunity within the broader landscape of criminal law assessments for culpability, blame, and punishment. It will be helpful to locate issues about guilt and punishment in the larger context of a criminal trial, its phases, and possible outcomes. Then we can address issues about culpability in the guilt phase of a criminal trial. Culpability is an important part of a broadly retributive criminal jurisprudence, but it is not a unitary concept in the criminal law. To avoid confusion, it is important to distinguish different kinds of culpability and the division of labor among them in an adequate jurisprudence. This sort of conceptual clarity is important in its own right, but it also has wider significance. Different kinds of culpability map onto the philosophical distinction between attributability and accountability, and this fact illuminates both *relata* in the relation. Also, because strict liability can be understood as liability without culpability, different kinds of culpability imply the possibility of different forms of strict liability. This fact will reinforce concerns that strict liability violates demands of fair opportunity.

Fair Opportunity and Responsibility. David O. Brink, Oxford University Press (2021). © David O. Brink.
DOI: 10.1093/oso/9780198859468.003.0007

48. Criminal Trials

Criminal trials have two phases—the *guilt* phase and the *sentencing* phase. The guilt phase occurs first, and the sentencing phase occurs just in case the defendant is found guilty at the first phase of the trial. The guilt phase determines whether the defendant committed the offense and, if so, whether she has any affirmative defense that would justify acquittal. An offense has two dimensions: both the *actus reus*—the material elements of the offense, including the relevant conduct, effects, and attendant circumstances—and the *mens rea*—the mental elements of the offense, such as whether the agent intended the wrong, foresaw the wrong, was reckless with respect to the wrong, or was negligent with respect to the wrong.

Affirmative defenses concede that the defendant committed the offense but claim that she should be exempt from punishment nonetheless. Justifications, such as self-defense or necessity (choosing the lesser evil), deny that the violation was wrong all-things-considered. Excuses, such as insanity or duress, deny that the agent was responsible and, hence, blameworthy for the violation. Policy-based exemptions, such as diplomatic immunity, are non-exculpatory defenses that justify acquittal on extrinsic or pragmatic grounds.

Both the offense and defense parts of the guilt phase of the trial have associated burdens of proof. These burdens involve several distinctions. First, there is the burden of production or going forward. Second, there is a burden of persuasion on the issue going forward. We might think of the burden of production as establishing a *prima facie* case that the offense was committed or that the defendant has an affirmative defense. As a general rule, the burden of production for both offenses and defenses is addressed to the judge, whereas the burden of persuasion is addressed to the jury. For any burden of proof, we need to distinguish who bears the burden of proof and what the standard of proof is. It is the prosecution that bears the burdens of production and persuasion that the defendant committed the offense, and the standard of proof is quite high—beyond a reasonable doubt. By contrast, the burdens of proof associated with defenses are more variable. In general, it is the defense that has the burden of production in the case of affirmative defenses, such as justifications and excuses. Though it is common for the defense to have the burden of persuasion too, this is not always true. It will be simpler, for our purposes, to assume that with affirmative defenses the defense bears the burdens of both production and persuasion. Importantly, the standard of proof for affirmative defenses is lower—a preponderance of the evidence (more likely than not) or clear and convincing evidence (which is intermediate between preponderance of the evidence and beyond a reasonable doubt).[1]

American criminal law only recognizes two main outcomes at the guilt phase of a criminal trial—guilty or not guilty (acquittal). However, this conceals multiple possible outcomes and conceptual structure in a criminal trial (see Figure 7.1).

This is the basic structure of a criminal trial, focusing on the guilt phase.[2] Among other things, this underlying conceptual structure shows that the simple binary verdict of guilty or not guilty may obscure different possible reasons for a not guilty verdict. It would be clearer if courts were required to deliver one of five verdicts at the guilt phase of the trial: (1) no violation

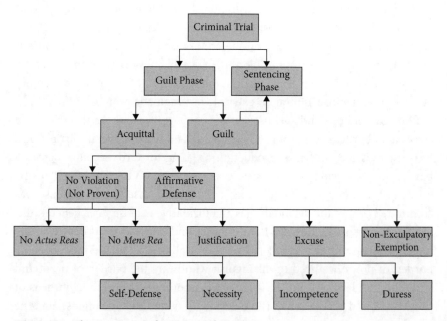

Figure 7.1 The Structure of a Criminal Trial

---

[1] For discussion, see Joshua Dressler, *Understanding Criminal Law*, 7th ed. (Lexis-Nexis, 2015), ch. 7.

[2] This overview omits mention of the provocation defense, which specifies conditions of adequate provocation and implies that suitably provoked homicides that would otherwise qualify as murder count as manslaughter and should be sentenced accordingly. The provocation defense is selective insofar as it applies only to homicide. Moreover, it is unclear whether provocation is best understood as a justification, mitigating the degree of wrongdoing, or as an excuse, mitigating the degree of responsibility or culpability. I address issues raised by the provocation defense in Chapters 8 and 14.

(violation not proven), (2) justified violation, (3) excused violation, (4) non-punishable violation, or (5) guilt.[3]

We will discuss most aspects of a criminal trial at one point or other. But we will be especially interested in the guilt phase of a trial and the role of the two variables in the retributivist desert basis—wrongdoing and culpability—in determining whether blame and punishment are appropriate. Justifications and excuses defeat blameworthiness in different ways—justifications deny or reduce wrongdoing, whereas excuses deny or reduce culpability or responsibility. We will examine the structure of affirmative defenses in more detail in Chapter 8. Much of the rest of our discussion will focus on responsibility and excuse, though we will see that it is not always clear whether a particular affirmative defense sounds in justification and excuse.

49. Culpability

Culpability is one concept shared by moral psychology and criminal jurisprudence and is intimately connected with our practices of blame and punishment. But while culpability is a concept recognized in moral philosophy, it is deployed more regularly within the criminal law. As we have seen, culpability plays an important role in the criminal law and in a broadly retributive justification of punishment, which understands the desert basis of criminal censure and sanction to consist in culpable wrongdoing. However, culpability is not a unitary concept in the criminal law. We can and should distinguish three different kinds of culpability within a retributive criminal jurisprudence.

First, one kind of culpability is an ingredient in wrongdoing itself, describing the agent's elemental *mens rea*—for instance, whether she intended the wrong, foresaw it, was reckless with respect to causing it, or was negligent with respect to causing it. These different mental states of the wrongdoer are thought to create a *hierarchy* of wrongdoing, ranging from intent to negligence. We might call this *narrow culpability*. Second, there is the kind of culpability that forms a proper part of the retributive desert basis of censure and sanction. Culpable wrongdoing—that is, wrongdoing for which the agent is responsible and blameworthy—is a condition of criminal censure and sanction. Wrongdoing that is not culpable in this sense is excused. We might call this *broad culpability*.

---

[3] Robinson makes an argument for the beneficial effects of this sort of conceptual clarity in his discussion of the backlash against the not-guilty verdict in the Rodney King case. See Robinson, *Structure and Function in the Criminal Law*, pp. 118–21, 145–46.

Third, we can and do identify culpability with the retributivist desert basis itself—the combination of wrongdoing and responsibility or broad culpability. This is how we understand culpability when we claim that the criminal law should punish only the culpable. We might call this *inclusive culpability*.

These different kinds of culpability correspond to different senses of *mens rea* or guilty mind. In recent criminal jurisprudence *mens rea* typically has a narrow sense, signifying *the mental elements of an offense* (intent, knowledge, recklessness, and negligence), complementing the objective dimension contributed by the specification of *actus reus* or guilty act. This is narrow culpability. But an older tradition of criminal jurisprudence conceives of *mens rea* broadly as signifying *blameworthiness*. An action might be wrong without being blameworthy if the agent is not responsible for her wrongdoing because she lacks the right sort of mental capacities to recognize wrongdoing or conform her behavior to these norms, or lacks freedom from wrongful interference by others. This would involve wrongdoing or offense without one kind of *mens rea* and culpability. When thinking about *mens rea* as blameworthiness, we might focus on the kind of responsibility that makes wrongdoing blameworthy—broad culpability—or we might focus on the combination of wrongdoing and responsibility—inclusive culpability—that makes someone blameworthy. Because these three kinds of culpability appeal to narrow and broad *mens rea*, we might recognize narrow culpability and two species of broad culpability—broad and inclusive culpability. For some purposes, the bipartite distinction—between narrow and broad culpability—is the most important. For other purposes, the tripartite distinction—among narrow, broad, and inclusive kinds of culpability—is essential.

How are these different kinds of culpability related? Because they are different kinds of culpability, we might be tempted to think that they are rival conceptions of a common concept. But that can't be correct, because, as we will see, they play different roles in an adequate criminal jurisprudence. If so, these different kinds of culpability are complementary, and it is important to distinguish them clearly and identify their different roles in the criminal law.

However, discussions of culpability have not always been clear about separating these different culpability concepts and their roles in the criminal law.[4] Even some very sophisticated writers fail to distinguish these kinds of culpability or make claims about culpability that can be reconciled only by

---

[4] Initially, I was puzzled by disparate claims made about the nature and significance of culpability in the criminal law literature that either employed the concept without analyzing it or asked it to do very different kinds of work. The reflections in this chapter began as an attempt to make sense of and reconcile these disparate claims within a unified framework.

distinguishing different kinds of culpability.[5] Other writers distinguish broader and narrower kinds of culpability but seem to suggest that they are rival conceptions of a common concept and focus only on the narrower kind of culpability associated with elemental *mens rea*, ignoring the broader kinds of culpability as blameworthiness.[6] Still others distinguish broad and narrow culpability and make consistent claims about their roles in the criminal law but are not as explicit as they might be about the exact division of labor between these kinds of culpability.[7]

We can remedy this situation by offering a unified account of these three kinds of culpability and their relationship to each other. On this account, narrow, broad, and inclusive culpability are complementary, rather than rival, conceptions. Narrow culpability corresponds to the elemental sense of *mens rea*, which provides the mental or subjective dimension of wrongdoing. Broad culpability is the responsibility condition in virtue of which the agent's wrong-doing is blameworthy and without which she would be excused. Inclusive culpability is the combination of wrongdoing and responsibility that together make the agent blameworthy and deserving of blame and punishment. Each kind of culpability plays an important role in a broadly retributive rationale for the criminal law that predicates blame and punishment on the fair opportunity to avoid wrongdoing.

50. Broad Culpability and Fair Opportunity

Retributivism asserts that culpable wrongdoing is the desert basis for punishment. In this formulation, culpable wrongdoing is wrongdoing for which the agent is responsible and blameworthy and without which she is excused. This is broad culpability and involves responsibility. Because the denial of responsibility is an excuse, responsibility and excuse are inversely related. Those responsible for their wrongdoing lack an excuse, and excused wrongdoing is wrongdoing for which the agent is not responsible. This relationship between

---

[5] See, e.g., Larry Alexander, Kimberly Ferzan, and Stephen Morse, *Crime and Culpability* (New York: Cambridge University Press, 2009), p. 171. Though culpability is the cornerstone of their theory of the criminal law (and part of the title of their book) and they make claims about the extension of the concept, they never analyze the concept and write as if the same concept can specify elemental *mens rea* and blameworthiness. I discuss their assumptions more fully below (§54), once I have explained the different kinds of culpability at work in the criminal law.

[6] See, e.g., Dressler, *Understanding Criminal Law*, pp. 118–19.

[7] See, e.g., Moore, *Placing Blame*, pp. 191–93, 403–19. In fact, I am sympathetic to Moore's bipartite claims about the culpability. One could see my project as making explicit the sort of division of labor among three different species of culpability that is implicit in his account.

responsibility and excuse allows us to model responsibility and, hence, broad culpability by attending to excuses.

As we saw in Chapter 3, when we do so, we are led to the fair opportunity conception of responsibility and, hence, broad culpability. The criminal law recognizes two main kinds of excuse: incompetence excuses, such as insanity, and duress excuses. Incompetence involves impairment of an agent's internal capacities. By contrast, duress involves a situational failing in which wrongful interference by another with the agent's options deprives her of the fair opportunity to act on her own deliberations about how to behave. In this way, standard excuses recognized by the criminal law reflect impairment of the agent's *capacities* or *opportunities*. If we treat excuse as a window onto responsibility, we might factor responsibility and, hence, broad culpability into two main conditions: the agent's internal capacities or normative competence and her opportunities or situational control. Normative competence itself involves a kind of reasons-responsiveness that factors into cognitive competence—the ability to recognize moral and criminal norms—and volitional competence—the ability to conform one's conduct to this normative knowledge. Normative competence and situational control are individually necessary and jointly sufficient for responsibility, because significant impairment of either condition results in an excuse. These forms of impairment are excusing, because blame and punishment are appropriate only when the agent had the fair opportunity to avoid wrongdoing.

The fair opportunity conception of responsibility provides a framework for understanding broad culpability as responsibility. It draws on resources familiar from philosophical discussions of moral responsibility and fair choice approaches to criminal responsibility and makes sense of the criminal law's conceptualization of excuses into impairment of capacities (incompetence) and impairment of opportunities (duress).

51. Narrow Culpability and Elemental *Mens Rea*

However, the predominant conception of culpability in the criminal law understands it in terms of *mens rea* and the specific mental states of agents that are ingredient in the idea of criminal offense. This conception of culpability appeals to half of a familiar division of labor between *actus reus* and *mens rea*.

The *actus reus* of an offense is often said to include the objective or material elements of the offense. The *actus reus* must be a voluntary act that brings about (causally or constitutively) wrongful conduct.[8] Wrongdoing can involve one or more of three material elements.

- *Conduct*: The proscribed conduct, independently of consequences or circumstances.
- *Results*: Some conduct is proscribed only when it causes certain results or consequences.
- *Attendant circumstances*: Some offenses build in attendant circumstances.

Every offense requires a conduct element.[9] Only some offenses require result or attendant circumstance elements. For instance, driving while intoxicated is a conduct offense that does not require specific results, such as an accident or injury. But some offenses do require specific results. Homicide requires conduct that results in death. If vehicular homicide due to intoxication were a separate crime, then it would have both conduct elements (driving while intoxicated) and result elements (when it led to death). Some offenses require specific attendant circumstances. For instance, the common law burglary offense requires that there be "breaking and entering of the *dwelling* of *another* at *nighttime*."[10]

These three elements can interact in ways that depend on how fine-grained the specification of conduct is. For instance, is a killing an action or a result? One could imagine describing the conduct in a comparatively thick way that includes the relevant results or circumstances, in which case many wrongs would simply be conduct crimes. Alternatively, one could specify the conduct thinly, such that the offense in question requires the addition of particular results or attendant circumstances, and not just conduct. It is not clear if anything substantive hangs on this question about how narrowly to construe conduct.[11]

---

[8] The voluntary act requirement of *actus reus* shows that the assumption that *actus reus* involves purely objective elements, in contrast to the subjective or mental elements of *mens rea*, is not strictly true.

[9] In principle, omissions could count as conduct, but in general they do not. An exception to this rule is when omissions occur in the capacity of someone with a defined role-responsibility. For instance, a lifeguard's conscious omission to save a drowning swimmer could count as conduct. The tendency not to recognize omissions as conduct is a contingent, rather than essential, feature of our doctrine of *actus reus*.

[10] See, e.g., Dressler, *Understanding Criminal Law*, p. 115.

[11] Robinson argues for construing conduct narrowly and for a correspondingly greater role for results and attendant circumstances in the specification of *actus reus*. See Robinson, *Structure and Function in Criminal Law*, pp. 25–27, 51.

The elemental sense of *mens rea* refers to the subjective or mental elements of an offense. It involves the agent's mental attitudes or relation toward the material elements of the wrong. Here, especially, common law doctrines are variable and idiosyncratic, and so it will be convenient to rely on the more systematic treatment of *mens rea* in the Model Penal Code (MPC §2.02), which has proven extremely influential. The Model Penal Code recognizes four culpable mental attitudes possible for each material element of the offense.

- The agent acts *purposely* if she intends the material element (conduct, result, or circumstance).
- The agent acts *knowingly* if she foresees that the material element is a certain or highly probable result of what she does, even if she does not intend it.
- An agent acts *recklessly* if she consciously disregards a substantial and unjustifiable risk that the material element exists or will result from her conduct.
- An agent acts *negligently* if she could and should have been, but was not, aware of a substantial and unjustifiable risk that the material element exists or will result from her conduct.

These categories reflect four grades of culpability from greater to lesser culpability and sometimes define distinct offenses. This can be readily appreciated in a case of harmful wrongdoing, such as homicide. Other things being equal, intending a wrongful harm is worse than foreseeing and causing it without intending it, which is worse than recklessly causing it, which is worse than negligently causing it. In the case of homicide, these different mental elements define different offenses. Murder is homicide with purpose or knowledge, manslaughter is reckless homicide, and negligent homicide is just that, homicide committed negligently.

This is the elemental sense of *mens rea*.[12] Insofar as offenses require *mens rea*, wrongdoers must possess some specified *mens rea* element—at least

---

[12] One advantage of focusing on the Model Penal Code is that it allows us to avoid the vexed common law distinction between general and specific intent. On one reading, specific intent crimes require the elemental *mens rea* of intent, whereas offenses that require one of the remaining three forms of elemental *mens rea* are general intent crimes. Alternatively, specific intent offenses are those that specify the possession of a further criminal intent, whereas general intent offenses do not. For instance, common law larceny is a specific intent crime, in this sense, because it involves the appropriation of the personal property of another *with the intent of permanently depriving the other of her property*. For discussion, see, e.g., Dressler, *Understanding Criminal Law*, pp. 137–39.

negligence—toward each material element of the offense. One kind of *strict liability* is any offense that does not require some form of *mens rea*—at least negligence—for some material elements of the offense. It is common to distinguish between mere *violations* and serious *crimes*, where crimes involve stigma and possible imprisonment and violations involve fines, rather than imprisonment, and do not carry stigma. Whereas it is not uncommon for there to be strict liability violations, strict liability crimes are rarer and more controversial. For instance, the Model Penal Code rejects the possibility of strict liability crimes, insisting that all crimes must have *mens rea* elements, at least negligence, with respect to the material elements of the offense (MPC §§2.02(1) and 2.05). We will explore the nature and wisdom of strict liability crimes later (§58 below).

52. Questions about Negligence and Elemental *Mens Rea*

For present purposes, there are two important points about elemental *mens rea*. The first claim is that there is a strong presumption that crimes must have a *mens rea* element, distinct from the material elements of the offense. The second claim is that these four mental elements—purpose or intent, knowledge, recklessness, and negligence—are the only ones that matter and that they differentially affect the seriousness of the offense. The first claim is more robust than the second and would survive revision to the list of four *mens rea* elements or their relative significance.

Some doubts about the fourfold hierarchy of purpose, knowledge, recklessness, and negligence concern the inclusion of negligence. For instance, some writers want to make do with fewer *mens rea* categories. In particular, some are skeptical about negligence as a *mens rea* category.[13] One reason sometimes offered for skepticism about negligence is that elemental *mens rea* picks out culpable mental states. But because the negligent person is unaware of the unjustifiable risk she runs she has no culpable mental state. If so, one might reason, negligence is not a well-motivated *mens rea* category.

But *mens rea* signifies culpable mind, and one can display a culpable state of mind by *not* having certain individual mental states. The person who is negligent displays a culpable state of mind insofar as she is insufficiently

---

[13] For example, in *Crime and Culpability* Alexander, Ferzan, and Morse reduce purpose and knowledge to special cases of recklessness and express skepticism about negligence as a form of elemental *mens rea*.

attentive to the risks she poses to others. As we will see (§56), there is a link between narrow culpability and quality of will. This allows us to say that the negligent person displays a problematic quality of will by virtue of being insufficiently attentive to the needs, interests, and rights of others. Even if there is no single culpable mental state that she possesses, her attitudes and evaluative orientation toward others are morally problematic. If so, this source of skepticism about negligence should be resisted.

Indeed, some have insisted on the importance of negligence and questioned the moral hierarchy in which negligence is less culpable than purpose, know-ledge, or recklessness.[14] For instance, it is worse to leave one's dog in the car on a hot day inadvertently than it is to tell a white lie intentionally. Of course, some cases of negligence will be worse than some cases of intentional wrong-doing if only because the consequences of negligence in some cases will be worse than the consequences of intentional misconduct in others. But the *mens rea* hierarchy should not be understood to assert, for example, that all cases of intent are worse than all cases of negligence, regardless of other differences in the cases and their consequences. Rather, the hierarchy asserts that *all else being equal* intent is worse than knowledge, which is worse than recklessness, which is worse than negligence. This hierarchy does not deny that some cases of negligence will be worse than some cases of purpose, knowledge, or recklessness, provided other things are not equal.

A different concern about negligence involves a puzzle about how to assess negligence. Negligence involves breach of a duty of care. In particular, negligence involves breach of a duty not to impose unjustifiable risks on others. Though the negligent agent was unaware that she posed an unjustifiable risk to others, she should and could have been aware of these risks. Avoiding negligence involves attention and vigilance with respect to unjustifiable risks. But there is a puzzle involving *lapses* of attention and vigilance.[15] Consider some ordinary duty of care, for instance, the duty to check one's blindspot in traffic before changing lanes. Satisfying this duty of care in ordinary circumstances involves modest, rather than heroic, attention and vigilance—a level of atten-tion and vigilance that ordinary competent drivers are capable of meeting. This seems to justify us in describing any driver who changes lanes without

---

[14] See Seana Shiffrin, "The Moral Neglect of Negligence" *Oxford Studies in Political Philosophy* 3 (2017): 197–228. Shiffrin is skeptical not about negligence but about its comparative importance. She thinks that the comparative culpability of negligence is frequently underestimated and that we should question the hierarchy in which purpose, knowledge, and recklessness are always worse than negli-gence.

[15] There is some related work in moral psychology on what are sometimes described as *slips*. See, e.g., Santiago Amaya, "Slips" *Noûs* 47 (2013): 559–76.

checking his blindspot as negligent. But while it seems realistic that for any given driver and lane change that the driver could and should have checked his blindspot, it does not seem realistic that drivers could go through their entire driving careers without ever failing to check their blindspot while changing lanes. This is just an instance of the familiar fact that an agent might be able to perform each individual task in an actual or potential series of tasks without being able to perform all the tasks in the series. On any given occasion for attention, I might be up to the task of being attentive without being up to the task of being attentive on all occasions. Individually, every negligent lapse might have been avoidable even if some negligent lapses were unavoidable.

This creates a puzzle about what to say about lapses, avoidability, and negligence. Perhaps individual avoidability is sufficient for negligence. On this view, we will all unavoidably be negligent at some point, and it may be a matter of moral luck whether this inevitable negligence proves consequential. But the idea of unavoidable negligence may seem problematic. Perhaps we should preserve the connection between negligence and avoidability and insist that one lapse is not sufficient for negligence. On one version of this view, only recurrent lapses would count as negligent. That would make findings of negligence depend on the agent's past conduct. But then we would fail to find someone guilty for first time negligence even when it was in fact avoidable.

I'm not sure how best to respond to this puzzle about lapses, avoidability, and negligence. I'm tempted to flag it as an issue *within* negligence, about what counts as negligence, and assume that it doesn't affect whether we want to recognize negligence as a form of elemental *mens rea*. But if the puzzle doesn't admit of a satisfactory response, that may threaten the coherence of negligence and whether we want to recognize it as a form of narrow culpability within the fourfold hierarchy of elemental *mens rea*. Though this is an interesting issue, our main concerns with fair opportunity do not depend on its resolution.[16]

Doubts about negligence sometimes motivate *contracting* the Model Penal Code's fourfold elemental *mens rea* hierarchy. I'm inclined to resist these

---

[16] Sripada appeals to a related puzzle to argue against capacitarian conceptions of responsibility, such as fair opportunity, and in favor of a quality of will conception. See, Chandra Sripada, "The Fallibility Paradox" *Social Philosophy & Policy* 36 (2019): 234–48. He assumes that the capacitarian must say that individual avoidability is sufficient for responsibility and that this is an unacceptable consequence of capacitarian views. But neither assumption is mandatory. Capacitarians could say that agents are responsible for individual lapses, even though they can't avoid some lapses overall, and embrace moral luck, or they could say that agents are only responsible for recurrent lapses, which were avoidable. Though I don't know which, if either, is the best solution, I don't think it's obvious that there is no acceptable capacitarian solution. The fact that this is a problem within the theory of negligence should provide reassurance that it is a puzzle for everyone and not one special to capacitarians.

reforms. A different reform would be to *expand* the hierarchy. Often, wrong-doing is done out of passion of some kind—for example, fear, jealousy, hatred, compassion, and even love. Perhaps recognition of the various passions and emotions that spur misconduct should make us broaden our conception of elemental *mens rea* to recognize additional morally significant psychological relations between an agent and her misconduct. In some cases, passion might seem to *mitigate* the agent's culpability, as when someone assists a suicide out of compassion for the suicide's suffering and autonomy. In other cases, passion might seem to *aggravate* culpability, for instance, when one person assaults or kills another as the result of racial animus. This seems to be the idea underlying sentence enhancements for bias motivated crimes. For these reasons, we might want to broaden the palette of elemental *mens rea*. Though this might be a well-motivated reform to our understanding of elemental *mens rea*, the same effect can be achieved by defining new offenses in terms of existing ones but adding particular passions or motivations as an attendant circumstance to the *actus reus* of the offense. Thus, one could define hate crimes by modifying the *actus reus* of existing crimes by adding hateful animus as an attendant circumstance. For our purposes, I'm not sure it matters what mechanism to use to achieve more fine-grained categorization of offenses—whether to modify *actus reus* or *mens rea*—but it's worth being clear that both mechanisms reflect the thought that there are more than four morally relevant culpable attitudes.

53. Combining Broad and Narrow Culpability

Now that we have examined narrow and broad culpability, we are in a better position to appreciate their roles in the criminal law. These two forms of culpability are distinct, but they are not rival conceptions of a common concept. Instead, they play complementary roles in the criminal law.

Broad culpability is the responsibility condition that makes wrongdoing culpable and without which wrongdoing is excused. Broad culpability is part of the retributivist idea that blame and punishment are fitting responses to culpable wrongdoing. This is wrongdoing for which the agent is responsible and, hence, blameworthy. It is the kind of culpability whose denial is an excuse. Moreover, it is the kind of culpability that requires both normative competence and situational control and implies that the agent had the fair opportunity to avoid wrongdoing.

Narrow culpability is culpability as elemental *mens rea*. Narrow culpability consists in different mental attitudes or relations that the agent might bear to the objective or material elements of the offense (its *actus reus*)—whether she intended the wrong, whether she foresaw and caused it without intending it, whether she was reckless in bringing it about, or whether she was negligent in bringing it about. These different forms of elemental *mens rea* represent different grades of culpability, from more to less, and help define different offenses.

These two kinds of culpability function quite differently in the criminal law. Along with wrongdoing, broad culpability is one of two independent variables in the retributivist desert basis for blame and punishment. By contrast, narrow culpability is the subjective element in wrongdoing insofar as elemental *mens rea* is a constituent of the offense itself. But then the two different kinds of culpability have different kinds of significance in the justification of blame and punishment. Whereas narrow culpability is part of the wrongdoing itself, broad culpability is a separate condition that has to be met if the wrongdoing is to be blameworthy.

We can see that these are different kinds of culpability by seeing how they typically require different burdens of proof. As an element of the offense itself, the prosecution bears the burden of proof for establishing elemental *mens rea* and, hence, narrow culpability, and that burden is proof beyond a reasonable doubt. While the prosecution bears the burden of proof that the defendant has committed wrong, including narrow culpability, it does not have the burden of proof of establishing broad culpability. Denying broad culpability or responsibility is an excuse, and, as with all affirmative defenses, the defense typically has the burden of establishing the excuse by either a preponderance of the evidence or a clear and convincing case (depending on the jurisdiction). The different burdens of proof associated with the two kinds of culpability (and their denials) is a signal that they play very different roles within the criminal law.

Another way to see the difference between these two forms of culpability is to see how they are not equivalent. They are not equivalent if one might possess narrow culpability without broad culpability. This is the familiar possibility that an agent might have done everything necessary to commit the wrong, including the required elemental *mens rea*, without being broadly culpable, because she is excused, either by reason of insanity or duress. Sometimes what disqualifies one from being broadly culpable also disqualifies one from being narrowly culpable, as when a particular form of normative incompetence prevents the agent from forming the elemental *mens rea* required by the offense. But this is not generally true. It is not true in traditional insanity or duress defenses in which the defendant does not deny any element of wrongdoing and, in fact, intends the wrong, but alleges an excuse based on normative incapacity or duress.

These considerations testify to the different roles that narrow and broad culpability play in the criminal law. We can represent these different roles propositionally.

1. Elemental *mens rea*—narrow culpability—and *actus reus* are individually necessary and jointly sufficient conditions of wrongdoing.[17]
2. Only agents who are responsible and, hence, blameworthy for their wrongdoing are apt targets of blame and punishment.

We could also represent these different roles diagrammatically (see Figure 7.2).

This shows clearly the different roles that narrow and broad culpability play in the determination of retributive desert.

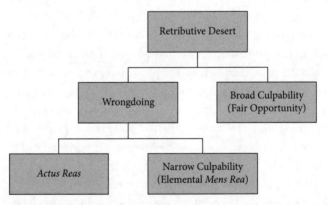

Figure 7.2 Broad and Narrow Culpability

---

[17] Strictly speaking, elemental *mens rea* (narrow culpability) and *actus reus* are individually necessary and jointly sufficient conditions for *pro tanto* wrongdoing. A justification denies wrongdoing, but it does not deny that the material and mental elements of the offense have been met. This implies that justifications deny *all-things-considered* wrongdoing, not *pro tanto* wrongdoing. So, elemental *mens rea* and *actus reus* are necessary and sufficient for *pro tanto*, rather than all-things-considered, wrongdoing. Another way to make this point is to distinguish *violation* and *wrongdoing*, which is an unjustified violation. Then we might say that *actus reus* and elemental *mens rea* are individually and jointly sufficient for a violation but individually necessary and not jointly sufficient for wrongdoing.

54. Inclusive Culpability

The retributivist formula treats culpable wrongdoing as the desert basis of blame and punishment. This is broad culpability and consists in responsibility, which can and should be modeled in terms of fair opportunity. Only wrongdoing that is responsible is blameworthy, and wrongdoing for which the agent is not responsible or broadly culpable is excused.

But whereas only wrongdoing that the agent is responsible for is culpable or blameworthy, we often apply the concepts of culpability and blameworthiness to the *combination* of wrongdoing and responsibility or broad culpability. When we describe an actor as culpable, we often signify *both* that she acted badly and that she was responsible for having done so. When we say that criminal law should punish only the culpable, we mean they should punish only wrongdoers who were responsible or broadly culpable for their wrongdoing. The combination of wrongdoing and responsibility or broad culpability is *inclusive culpability*. In fact, inclusive culpability is wrongdoing that is neither justified nor excused. Hence, it is wrongdoing that is both narrowly and broadly culpable. Though related to the other forms of culpability, this is plainly a distinct kind. Indeed, inclusive culpability just is the retributive desert basis for blame and punishment (see Figure 7.3).

We can now see clearly that these three kinds of culpability are different. But they are not rival conceptions of a common concept. Rather, they play essential but distinct roles in a broadly retributive criminal jurisprudence. To avoid confusion, it is important to distinguish these kinds of culpability clearly

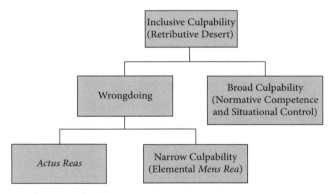

Figure 7.3 Inclusive Culpability

and be clear about their different roles in the division of labor in the foundations of criminal liability.[18]

55. Bipartite and Tripartite Culpability

We can and should distinguish narrow, broad, and inclusive culpability. Each plays an important role in a broadly retributive conception of the criminal law. This tripartition allows us to avoid asking one concept to play fundamentally different roles and to avoid talking past each other when we make what would otherwise be incompatible claims about culpability. For some purposes, it is important to insist on the tripartition among the three kinds of culpability; only in this way will we avoid asking one concept to perform three different tasks. By doing so, we gain clarity about the role of culpability in the criminal law. However, for other purposes, it is the bipartite distinction between narrow and broad culpability that is important. This bipartite culpability distinction helps clarify other debates in moral psychology and the criminal law.

First, the bipartite culpability distinction allows us to understand the difference between responsibility as attributability and responsibility as accountability as tracking the difference between narrow and broad culpability. Agents are attributively responsible for wrongdoing when it reflects their quality of will, and the different forms of elemental *mens rea* track a hierarchy among different qualities of will. By contrast, agents are only blameworthy for their wrongdoing and, hence, broadly culpable insofar as they are accountable for it.

---

[18]   I am now in a position to explain more fully my reservations about the treatment of culpability in Alexander, Ferzan, and Morse, *Crime and Culpability*. Despite the central role that culpability plays in the argument (and title) of their book, they never analyze the concept and make conflicting claims about its extension, writing as if the same concept can specify elemental *mens rea* and blameworthiness. (1) They appeal to culpability as the desert basis for their retributivist justification of punishment (p. 9). Then (2) they defend a novel theory of culpability as recklessness or unjustifiable risk creation, in opposition to the Model Penal Code's fourfold conception of elemental *mens rea* (chs. 2–3). Subsequently, (3) they conclude that culpability as recklessness is both necessary and sufficient for culpability as blameworthiness (p. 171). (1) and (2) are compatible only if (1) is understood as a claim about inclusive culpability and (2) is understood as a claim about narrow culpability. (3) cannot be defended. Narrow culpability cannot be sufficient for blameworthiness if only because elemental *mens rea* is part of wrongdoing and is not sufficient for blameworthiness if wrongdoing is excused by virtue of insanity or duress. These problems are remediable according to the model of culpability advocated here, provided Alexander, Ferzan, and Morse relativize (1) and (2) to different kinds of culpability and abandon (3). Moreover, these problems are independent of the merits of their other interesting and provocative claims (e.g. their claim that criminal responsibility reduces to unjustifiable risk creation, which implies skepticism about the need for a special part of the criminal code, defining particular crimes; their claim that the narrow culpability categories of purpose and knowledge are special cases of recklessness; their skepticism about negligence as a form of culpability; and their skepticism about resultant luck and insistence that completed crimes should be punished no differently than attempts).

The denial of accountability is an excuse, and the fair opportunity to avoid wrongdoing requires that agents only be blamed and punished for wrongdoing for which they are accountable.

Second, the bipartite culpability distinction also allows us to make better sense of the nature and permissibility of strict liability crimes. Narrow strict liability offenses are forms of liability without narrow culpability—in which there is no elemental *mens rea* requirement, not even negligence, with respect to at least one element of the wrongdoing. By contrast, broad strict liability offenses would be forms of liability without broad culpability—in which there is no requirement of responsibility or possibility of excuse. These are distinct kinds of strict liability.

56. Narrow Culpability and Attributability

As we saw (§14), Watson distinguishes two faces of responsibility— attributability and accountability.[19] We ascribe responsibility in the attributive sense to agents for their actions insofar as those actions reflect the quality of their wills. By contrast, we ascribe responsibility in the accountability sense to agents for their actions insofar as it is fair to blame them for those actions; they are not accountable for actions for which they are excused. The distinction between attributability and accountability tracks the distinction between narrow and broad culpability. Attributability tracks aspects of quality of will that are reflected in narrow culpability or elemental *mens rea*, whereas accountability tracks broad culpability as fair opportunity.

Earlier, we contrasted different conceptions of quality of will in terms of consistent character traits, a mesh between the agent's motivating attitudes and her higher-order attitudes, and a proper regard for the rights and interests of others. We defended a conception of quality of will in terms of proper regard for others.[20] For the most part, this conception of attributive responsibility fits well with narrow culpability, because different grades of elemental *mens rea* seem to reflect morally significant differences in the agent's quality of will. In assessing an agent's quality of will when she causes harm to another person, we think it matters whether she intended the harm, tolerated the harm as an acceptable byproduct of what she did intend, was aware of the unjustifiable risks she posed to others and was indifferent, or was not aware of unjustifiable risks she posed to others when she could and should have been.

[19] Watson, "Two Faces of Responsibility."   [20] Scanlon, *Moral Dimensions*, ch. 4.

Narrow culpability treats these mental elements as part of the wrongdoing itself. It is a controversial proposition in normative ethics that the agent's intentions or other mental states can affect the deontic status or valence—especially the permissibility—of his actions. Some deny the proposition, while others affirm it.[21] Proponents appeal to the doctrine of double effect and other ways in which an agent's intentions seem to affect the permissibility of her actions. For instance, proponents of the doctrine of double effect claim that, all else being equal, it is morally worse to intend harm than merely to foresee it as a byproduct of one's actions. Opponents insist on a sharp distinction between assessments of the deontic valence of actions and assessments of the agent's motives and character. Though Scanlon denies that narrow culpability can affect the permissibility of actions—that is a purely objective matter—he does allow that it can affect their meaning and blameworthiness. The criminal law seems to disagree insofar as elemental *mens rea* is an ingredient in most wrongdoing, at least in those offenses that are not strict liability offenses. Moreover, elemental *mens rea* is relevant not only to the criminalization of conduct but also to grading offenses in terms of their seriousness. Other things being equal, first-degree murder is a more serious offense than reckless homicide, and reckless homicide is a more serious offense than negligent homicide. For instance, under Model Penal Code doctrine, homicide with intent to kill is murder, whereas reckless homicide (not manifesting extreme indifference to the value of human life) is the lesser offense of manslaughter, whereas negligent homicide is the still lesser offense of negligent homicide (MPC §210.1–4). It is true that the criminal law distinguishes objective and subjective elements of criminal offenses and treats the objective elements as prior to and independent of the subjective elements, inasmuch as the subjective elements are specified in relation to particular objective elements. But the subjective and objective elements are individually necessary and jointly sufficient for the offense or wrongdoing. So, the criminal law conception of wrongdoing affirms the relevance of the agent's intentions and other mental attitudes to the deontic valence of her actions.

---

[21] Those who deny the relevance of intention and other mental states to deontic valence include Judith Thomson, "Physician-Assisted Suicide: Two Moral Arguments" 109 *Ethics* (1999), pp. 497, 517 and Scanlon, *Moral Dimensions*, ch. 1. Those who affirm the relevance of intention and other mental states to deontic valence include proponents of the doctrine of double effect, such as Warren Quinn, "Actions, Intentions, and Consequences: The Doctrine of Double Effect" *Philosophy & Public Affairs* 18 (1989): 334–51; Dana Nelkin and Samuel Rickless, "Three Cheers for Double Effect" 89 *Philosophy and Phenomenological Research* 89 (2014): 125–58; and Steven Sverdlik, *Motive and Rightness* (Oxford: Clarendon Press, 2011).

If narrow culpability tracks an agent's quality of will, it also tracks her normative *performance*, because her wrongdoing manifests the improper use of her normative competence in different possible ways, involving intentional wrong, foreseen but unintended wrong, recklessness, or negligence. This means that narrow culpability and attributability are concerned with the agent's actual normative performance, not her normative competence.

57. Broad Culpability and Accountability

There may be senses of responsibility and blame—attributability senses—that track narrow culpability. But there are also important senses of responsibility and blame—accountability senses—that require more. Consider a case in which A intends to violate B's rights to bodily integrity or property. This licenses us in attributing harmful agency to A and would justify B's anger and hard feelings toward A. Perhaps this would even license B to blame A in a way. But suppose that we learn that A did not in any relevant sense have a fair opportunity to do otherwise, perhaps because he was insane or immature and lacked basic normative competence to recognize or conform to the relevant norms forbidding this kind of rights violation. Insanity and duress are excuses and imply that the agent was not at fault for the harm he did. It is natural in such circumstances to say that A was not responsible for the wrongs he committed. But since by hypothesis he was attributively responsible for the harm he caused, the sense in which he is not responsible must be a different sense of responsibility. This is Watson's sense of responsibility as accountability. It is also natural to say in these circumstances that A is not blameworthy for his wrongdoing. It would be unfair to punish A for wrongdoing that he did not have an adequate opportunity to avoid.[22] But blame is typically a sanctioning response, even if it is usually less severe than punishment, and so it would also be unfair to blame A for wrongdoing that he did not have adequate opportunity to avoid. Broad culpability requires the agent to be responsible—accountable—for his wrongdoing for blame and punishment to be fair.

Broad culpability is tied to responsibility, understood as accountability, and it is plausibly modeled by the fair opportunity to avoid wrongdoing. Broad culpability conditions appropriate reactive attitudes and practices in a way that

---

[22] Of course, while blaming and punishing normatively incompetent wrongdoers might be unfair, civil commitment might nonetheless be appropriate if they pose a significant danger to themselves or others.

narrow culpability does not.[23] Retributivism insists that narrow culpability is insufficient for punishment and that only broadly culpable wrongdoing—wrongdoing for which the agent is accountable—is a fit object of punishment. These relationships can also be viewed from the perspective of excuse. Excuses deny accountability, but not all excuses deny attributability, since agents who are attributively responsible for wrongdoing may still be excused if they are incompetent, for instance, insane or immature. Earlier, we noted that responsibility and excuse are inversely related such that those responsible for wrongdoing are not excused for it and those excused for wrongdoing are not responsible for it. But only responsibility as accountability, not responsibility as attributability, bears this inverse relationship to excuse. This suggests an important respect in which the criminal law's concern with censure and sanction tracks responsibility as accountability. Though there is a role for attributability to play in specifying the kind of wrongdoing at stake in a given case, when the criminal law addresses the sort of responsibility ingredient in broad culpability, it is concerned with accountability, not attributability.[24] We can summarize this conclusion by noting that broad culpability and accountability presuppose the sort of normative *competence* required by fair opportunity, not normative performance.

58. Two Kinds of Strict Liability

Our discussion of different kinds of culpability provides an interesting perspective on issues about the nature and wisdom of strict liability offenses. Strict

---

[23] I take myself to be disagreeing with Scanlon about paradigmatic forms of blame being predicated on attributability. However, it's hard to know how deep this disagreement is, because it's hard to know when he thinks attributability is sufficient for blame and punishment. On the one hand, he seems to predicate blame, as such, on attributability and quality of will. On the other hand, he allows that "hard treatment" and punishment require accountability and fair opportunity, and not just attributability and quality of will. See Scanlon, *Moral Dimensions*, pp. 202–04. If Scanlon accepts this second claim, he can admit that attributability is not sufficient for accountability and claim that whereas blame requires only attributability and quality of will, punishment requires accountability and fair opportunity. Even this weaker set of claims would be problematic if, as I believe, central expressions of blame, and not just punishment, are apt iffi the agent is accountable and had the fair opportunity to avoid wrongdoing.
[24] In his discussion of responsibility and excuses, Wallace mistakenly follows Austin in claiming that excuses represent actions as inadvertent, rather than intentional. See J.L. Austin, "A Plea for Excuses" reprinted in Austin, *Philosophical Papers* and Wallace, *Responsibility and the Moral Sentiments*, ch. 5. But this confuses narrow and broad culpability and attributive responsibility and accountability. Intention is a *mens rea* element of the wrongdoing itself, but excuses are affirmative defenses that concede wrongdoing but nonetheless claim that the agent was not responsible—accountable—for the wrongdoing. Standard excuses, including both insanity and duress, apply to intentional wrongdoing but nonetheless excuse as not blameworthy.

liability can be understood as liability without culpability.[25] Our distinction between narrow and broad culpability allows us to formulate two different forms of strict liability—one without narrow culpability and one without broad culpability.

Strict liability is usually understood to involve liability without narrow culpability. On this view, strict liability offenses do not have an elemental *mens rea* component, not even negligence. Because elemental *mens rea* can apply to any element of the *actus reus*—the conduct, the results, or the attendant circumstances—we can understand strict liability offenses as offenses that contain *at least one* material element for which there is no *mens rea* requirement.[26] Because this form of strict liability is defined in terms of the absence of narrow culpability, we might call it *narrow strict liability*.

Tort law recognizes strict liability offenses—liability without a requirement of negligence—in connection with the design, manufacture, and handling of dangerous materials and products. The justification for strict liability in tort law is usually some combination of deterrence—discouraging risky activity altogether or encouraging special care and diligence in risky pursuits—and administrative efficiency—avoiding the difficulties and costs of trying to ascertain whether there has been negligence. These benefits of strict liability in tort may seem acceptable in part because tort law can be seen as a pricing system for behavior that does not attach imprisonment and stigma for liability. Some requirements of the criminal law, concerning things such as parking and licensure, are primarily regulative in nature and do not attach condemnation or imprisonment to their violation. We might call these *violations* and distinguish them from *crimes* for which one is liable for stigma and incarceration. The distinction between violations and crimes is important, even if it isn't always easy to draw. Criminal violations are more like tort offenses, and it is not uncommon to see strict liability violations in the criminal law. However, strict liability crimes are less common and typically viewed as more

---

[25] For useful discussions of strict liability in the criminal law, to which I am indebted, see Kenneth Simons, "When Is Strict Liability Just?" *Journal of Criminal Law & Criminology* 87 (1997): 1075–1137 and "Is Strict Criminal Liability in the Grading of Offenses Consistent with Retributive Justice?" *Oxford Journal of Legal Studies* 32 (2012): 445–66 and the essays in *Appraising Strict Liability*, ed. A.P. Simester (Oxford: Clarendon Press, 2005)—especially Stuart Green, "Six Senses of Strict Liability: A Plea for Formalism"; A.P. Simester, "Is Strict Liability Always Wrong?"; Doug Husak, "Strict Liability, Justice and Proportionality"; and Alan Michaels, "Imposing Constitutional Limits on Strict Liability: Lessons from the American Experience."

[26] See, e.g., Andrew Ashworth, *Principles of Criminal Law* (Oxford: Clarendon Press, 1991), pp. 135–36 Green, "Six Senses of Strict Liability," pp. 2–4; Simester, "Is Strict Liability Always Wrong?," p. 22.

problematic, precisely because culpability seems important where stigma and incarceration hang in the balance. While the Model Penal Code permits strict liability violations, it categorically rejects strict liability crimes (MPC §§2.02(1) and 2.05).[27] Nonetheless, strict liability crimes are recognized in some jurisdictions. One example would be a statutory rape statute that made it a crime for an adult to have consensual intercourse with someone who is in fact a minor, regardless of whether the adult reasonably believed the minor to be another adult. In this case, the statute may require that sexual intercourse be intentional, but it would not require any elemental *mens rea*—not even negligence—with respect to the age of one's sexual partner. Another example is the felony murder rule that allows conviction for murder for any participants in a felony when death results from conduct pursuant to the underlying felony.[28] So, for example, though the underlying felony, such as armed robbery, may require intent or knowledge, any participant in the robbery is guilty of murder, regardless of whether he participated in or was aware of the killing. Yet another example is the use of Proposition 21, passed in California in 2000, in order to prosecute anyone who associates with gang members and who "willfully promotes, furthers, assists, or benefits" from criminal gang activity, even rap artists who are not themselves gang members and whose music concerns gang culture but who did not participate in and had no knowledge of the criminal activities of the gang.[29]

Narrow strict liability offenses are morally problematic. The most serious complaint about them is that they are *unfair*. Because strict liability offenses, in this sense, do not require elemental *mens rea*—not even negligence—they make one liable despite all reasonable efforts to avoid wrongdoing. This violates the norm that blame and sanctions be imposed only for conduct that the agent had a fair opportunity to avoid. In "Legal Responsibility and Excuses" Hart suggests that the criminal law conditions liability on culpability out of respect for "the efficacy of the individual's informed and considered

---

[27] The limitation of strict liability offenses to violations that do not potentially result in stigma and imprisonment is reflected in Justice Blackmun's opinion in *Holdridge v. United States* 282 F.2d 302, 310 (8th Cir. 1960).

[28] See, e.g., CAL. PEN. CODE §189. Also see Dressler, *Understanding Criminal Law*, pp. 517–18.

[29] See CAL. PEN. CODE §182.5. Recently, rapper Brandon Duncan (aka Tiny Doo), who had no criminal record, was prosecuted under the provisions of Proposition 21 for participating in criminal gang activity by virtue of benefiting from the sales of his album *No Safety*. Duncan's album displays a loaded revolver on the cover, and his lyrics refer to gang life. He did not otherwise participate in or have knowledge of the gang's criminal activities. Had he been convicted, he would have faced up to 25 years in prison. The charges were ultimately dismissed on the ground that Duncan could not be charged with conspiracy without a specific underlying crime. However, this ruling does not preclude conviction for conspiracy by virtue of benefiting from the criminal activity of others in which one had no direct involvement in cases where there is a specific underlying crime.

choice in determining the future."[30] A corollary of this concern with individual autonomy is the demand for the fair opportunity to avoid wrongdoing. This principle is at work in support of the fundamental legal principle of *legality*. Legality is the doctrine that there should be no punishment in the absence of public notice of a legal requirement. The principle of legality is usually defended as part of fair notice. *Ex post facto* or retroactive criminal law would be unfair, because it would punish those for failing to conform to behavioral expectations of which they had not been apprised in advance. *Ex post facto* law thus threatens individual autonomy and its demand of fair opportunity to avoid wrongdoing. But a similar rationale is at work against strict liability offenses. Just as it would be unfair to convict actors for failing to conform to standards that had not been promulgated in advance, so too it would be unfair to convict actors for failing to conform to standards (promulgated in advance) that they did everything within their power to obey. Conviction without culpability denies the fair opportunity to avoid wrongdoing.

We tolerate this unfairness in the case of strict liability torts and in the case of strict liability violations, for the sake of deterrence and administrative efficiency, where stigma and incarceration do not hang in the balance. But the willingness to sacrifice fairness to the defendant for the sake of deterrence and efficiency is harder to justify in the criminal law where there is the prospect of blame and punishment and not just financial liability. Strict liability violates the norm that censure and imprisonment be imposed only for conduct that the agent had a fair opportunity to avoid. This is why strict liability crimes, as distinct from violations, are anomalous within the criminal law and viewed as morally problematic. Principles of fairness support the position of the Model Penal Code, which tolerates strict liability violations but otherwise categorically rejects strict liability crimes (MPC §§2.02(1), 2.05).

So much for narrow strict liability crimes. However, because we distinguished narrow and broad culpability, there is potentially another form of strict liability. This would be liability without broad culpability or blameworthiness. Because wrongdoing that is not blameworthy is excused, this would be liability without excuse. We might call this *broad strict liability*.

Hart's own discussion mixes broad and narrow strict liability together. For instance, he conflates broad and narrow culpability.

In the criminal law of every modern state responsibility for serious crimes is excluded or "diminished" by some of the conditions we have referred to as

---

[30] Hart, "Legal Responsibility and Excuses" p. 46.

"excusing conditions." In Anglo-American criminal law this is the doctrine that a "subjective element," or "mens rea," is required for criminal responsibility, and it is because of this doctrine that a criminal trial may involve investigations into the sanity of the accused; into what he knew, believed, or foresaw; or into the questions whether or not he was subject to coercion by threats or provoked into passion, or was prevented by disease or transitory loss of consciousness from controlling the movements of his body or muscles.[31]

Here, Hart runs together narrow culpability requirements—the importance of elemental *mens rea*—and broad culpability requirements—the conditions of responsibility and blameworthiness, without which wrongdoing is excused. Later, he explains why strict liability is problematic in the criminal law, which he regards as imposing liability without the possibility of excuse. This is where he invokes the idea that criminal liability is predicated on the fair opportunity to avoid wrongdoing, which requires that wrongdoers only be held liable when they had the capacities and opportunities that make them responsible and, hence, blameworthy for their wrongdoing.[32]

Other commentators have been more careful to distinguish narrow and broad strict liability. They sometimes distinguish *formal* and *substantive* conceptions of strict liability.[33] Most commentators who draw this distinction focus on formal or narrow strict liability, although Doug Husak has insisted on the significance of substantive or broad strict liability as a separate form of strict liability. It's important to see what broad strict liability would involve. Because broad culpability involves wrongdoing for which the agent is responsible and, hence, blameworthy, it is culpability without which the agent would be excused for her wrongdoing. But then broad strict liability would involve criminal liability without responsibility and the possibility of an excuse. Being clear about broad strict liability allows us to make two important points.

First, there are no broad strict liability crimes insofar as the excuses are perfectly general affirmative defenses, applicable to any form of wrongdoing. We noted that excuses factor into incompetence (e.g., insanity) and duress. While there could, in principle, be broad strict liability crimes, there are in fact none. Indeed, the Model Penal Code treats insanity and duress as perfectly general defenses (MPC §§4.01(1), 2.09(1)). So, whereas narrow strict liability

---

[31] Hart, "Legal Responsibility and Excuses," p. 31.
[32] Hart, "Legal Responsibility and Excuses," pp. 43–49.
[33] See, e.g., Green, "Six Senses of Strict Liability," p. 10; Simester, "Is Strict Liability Always Wrong?" p. 23; and Husak, "Strict Liability, Justice and Proportionality," pp. 86–93.

crimes are somewhat anomalous and morally problematic, there do not appear to be any broad strict liability crimes.[34]

Second, we can explain why there are no broad strict liability crimes. Broad strict liability crimes would involve liability without a requirement of responsibility or the possibility of an excuse. Indeed, as we saw, responsibility and excuse are inversely related—if an agent is responsible for wrongdoing, she has no excuse for it; and if she is excused for her wrongdoing, she is not responsible for it. If we attend to the criminal law's conception of excuse as involving incompetence or duress, we can see that responsibility requires both normative competence and situational control. The explanation for recognizing normative competence and situational control is that significant impairment of either compromises the fair opportunity to avoid wrongdoing. This is one way of articulating Hart's point about why responsibility and excuses are central to criminal liability.

The same fairness norm that predicates blame and punishment on the fair opportunity to avoid wrongdoing is at work in explaining what is problematic about both broad and narrow strict liability crimes. This provides an explanation and partial vindication of Hart's conflation of narrow and broad strict liability. We do need to distinguish narrow and broad culpability, as he does not, and this will allow us to distinguish narrow and broad strict liability, as he does not. But Hart may not distinguish them, as he should, because he sees that both narrow and broad culpability speak to the criminal law's concern with requirements of fairness and that strict liability crimes, whether narrow or broad, offend against the fair opportunity to avoid wrongdoing, though in different ways. Narrow strict liability criminalization is unfair because it does not require any elemental *mens rea*—not even negligence—as a part of wrongdoing and so makes agents liable despite reasonable care to avoid wrongdoing. Broad strict liability criminalization is unfair, not because of how it conceives wrongdoing, but because it doesn't recognize the way in which excuses defeat responsibility for wrongdoing and, hence, blameworthiness. Incompetence and duress excuses are important, because they compromise the agent's fair opportunity to avoid wrongdoing.

---

[34] Doris and Murphy appeal to situationist psychology to claim that we should offer a wide-ranging excuse for wartime wrongdoing. See John Doris and Dominic Murphy, "From My Lai to Abu Ghraib: The Moral Psychology of Atrocity" *Midwest Studies in Philosophy* 31 (2007): 25–55. They try to avoid the unwelcome consequences of this kind of promiscuity about excuse by endorsing a form of strict liability that would punish despite the existence of an excuse. But this compounds one mistake—an insufficiently discriminating conception of excuse—with another—the failure to recognize that excuse is a true defense that justifies acquittal. We can easily avoid the second mistake by not making the first one. For discussion, see David O. Brink, "Situationism, Responsibility, and Fair Opportunity" *Social Philosophy & Policy* 30 (2013): 121–49 and Chapter 10 below.

8

Affirmative Defenses

Principles and Puzzles

In subsequent chapters, we will assess whether the fair opportunity conception of responsibility is socially fragile—whether it still applies and provides guidance about blame and punishment in circumstances of structural injustice and given pervasive situational influences on human behavior. If fair opportunity survives these challenges, we will test its implications for cases of partial responsibility involving incompetence and psychopathy, immaturity, addiction, and crimes of passion. These challenges and applications often raise questions about whether agents are justified or excused for their offenses. Both justifications and excuses are affirmative defenses that concede that the agent committed the offense but nonetheless support acquittal. Justifications deny wrongdoing, whereas excuses deny that the agent was responsible or culpable for her wrongdoing. Before we can sensibly evaluate whether a particular offense should be justified or excused, we need a better sense of the different affirmative defenses and how they are related to each other. That is the task of this chapter. In particular, this chapter aims not only to describe these defenses as they are usually understood but also to raise theoretical questions and puzzles about how their underlying structure is best understood. I hope and believe that my descriptive claims are reasonably accurate. My theoretical and normative claims are offered in a more speculative spirit.

59. The Architecture of Defenses

We can build on the picture of affirmative defenses introduced in Chapter 7's account of the structure of a criminal trial (§48). That picture was incomplete, because it did not recognize different forms of defensive force justifications and did not include the provocation doctrine, which raises difficulties that weren't especially relevant then but will be directly relevant to the discussion in Chapters 14 and 15. We can start with a diagrammatic representation of

Fair Opportunity and Responsibility. David O. Brink, Oxford University Press (2021). © David O. Brink.
DOI: 10.1093/oso/9780198859468.003.0008

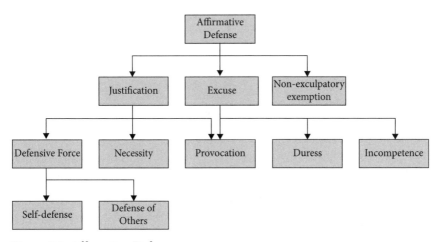

Figure 8.1 Affirmative Defenses

affirmative defenses, as they are usually understood, for instance, in the Model Penal Code (see Figure 8.1).

Affirmative defenses are part of the guilt phase of a criminal trial. The guilt phase determines whether the defendant committed the offense or violation and, if so, whether she has any affirmative defense that would justify acquittal. As we saw, an offense has two dimensions: both the *actus reus*—the material elements of the offense, including the relevant conduct, effects, and attendant circumstances—and the *mens rea*—the mental elements of the offense, including intent, knowledge, recklessness, and negligence. Affirmative defenses concede that the defendant committed the offense but claim that she should be exempt from punishment nonetheless. Justifications, such as self-defense or necessity (choosing the lesser evil), deny that the violation was wrong all-things-considered. Excuses, such as insanity or duress, deny that the agent was responsible and, hence, blameworthy for the violation. Both justifications and excuses are exculpatory, defeating blameworthiness and inclusive culpability, though in different ways. By contrast, some affirmative defenses are non-exculpatory, because they justify acquittal without providing exculpation. For example, there are policy-based exemptions, such as diplomatic immunity, which do not deny that the violation was wrong or culpable but deny that the violation should be punished for broadly pragmatic reasons. Though policy-based exemptions are a diverse class and raise some interesting issues, they involve conduct that is both wrong and culpable. As such, they are non-exculpatory and, hence, are not central parts of the moral foundations of the criminal law. Our focus will be on the two main kinds of exculpatory defenses—justifications and excuses.

As we saw in Chapter 7, the details concerning burdens of proof are complicated, involving the distinction between burdens of production and burdens of persuasion, who has the burden, and what the standard of proof is. It is the prosecution that bears the burdens of production and persuasion that the defendant committed the offense, and the standard of proof is quite high—beyond a reasonable doubt. By contrast, it is the defense that has the burden of production in the case of affirmative defenses, such as justifications and excuses. Though it is common for the defense to have the burden of persuasion too, this is not always true. It will be simpler, for our purposes, to assume that with affirmative defenses the defense bears both the burdens of production and persuasion. Importantly, the standard of proof for affirmative defenses is lower—a preponderance of the evidence (more likely than not) or clear and convincing evidence (which is intermediate between preponderance of the evidence and beyond a reasonable doubt).

Though the criminal phase of a trial delivers binary verdicts of guilty or not guilty, there are, in effect, five possible verdicts at the guilt phase of the trial: (1) no violation (violation not proven), (2) justified violation, (3) excused violation, (4) non-punishable violation, or (5) guilt.

Our discussion of exculpatory defenses will focus on justifications and excuses. The main justifications are self-defense and necessity, and the main excuses are incompetence or insanity and duress. Provocation is an unusual defense along several dimensions. Most justifications and excuses have two features. First, they are typically *general* defenses that apply to all kinds of crime—including, for instance, homicides, rapes, assaults, and property crimes. This generality is a distinctive feature of the Model Penal Code, as we will see. Second, American criminal law is, for the most part, *bivalent* about justifications and excuses—an agent's offense is either fully justified or impermissible and an agent is either fully responsible for his wrongdoing or he is fully excused. The underlying conditions that tend to justify or excuse violations may be scalar, but, if so, then there is some threshold for these conditions above which the agent is justified or excused and below which he is not. By contrast, the provocation defense shares neither of these two features. The provocation defense is not general; it applies only to homicides. It specifies conditions of adequate provocation for homicides and claims that suitably provoked homicides that would otherwise qualify as murder count only as manslaughter and should be sentenced accordingly. Moreover, unlike other affirmative defenses, provocation does not justify acquittal. Instead, it reduces the severity of the crime and sentence from what it would be without provocation. This is why provocation is often cited as the one counterexample to the generalization that in American criminal law the guilt phase of a trial is bivalent. Finally, as we shall see in Chapter 14 when we assess the provocation defense more fully, it is not entirely clear whether to conceptualize the provocation defense as a partial justification or as an excuse. This depends on whether adequate provocation makes the crime *less wrong* or whether it makes the agent *less responsible* and, hence, *less blameworthy* for committing a wrong. In fact, we will see reason to regard some provocation defenses as partial justifications and some as partial excuses.

I now want to sketch the requirements of these different affirmative defenses and explore some issues about whether we should accept this conventional wisdom about their underlying structure.[1]

Federal criminal law deals with crimes enacted by Congress pursuant to federal powers specified in the Constitution, regulating, among other things, drugs, immigration, national security, and interstate commerce. But much criminal law is regulated by the states, pursuant to their police powers under the Constitution. American criminal law is based, in significant part, on the common law—criminal law principles recognized by courts in England and imported to the colonies and, eventually, to states. In most states, these common law principles and doctrines have now been superseded by statutory regulation. Because many state penal codes adopt common law principles, there is an extended sense in which many criminal codes can still be viewed as reflecting the common law. However, the Model Penal Code represents another source of influence on criminal law doctrine in many states and on criminal law theory. As I explained earlier, the Model Penal Code represents a principled set of reforms to common law doctrines that reflect best practices developed by a team of prominent judges, lawyers, and legal academics. The Model Penal Code defines general principles of criminal liability and affirmative defense, as well as definitions of specific offenses and sentencing provisions. Though few, if any, jurisdictions have adopted the Model Penal Code wholesale, nonetheless, it has proved enormously influential on many issues in many jurisdictions. For the most part, the Model Penal Code has been a force for progressive reform. We shall have occasion to see its progressive influence on several doctrines, including necessity and insanity, though we will also see

---

[1] Other useful discussions of the underlying structure of justifications and excuses can be found in Kim Ferzan, "Justification and Excuse" and Joshua Dressler, "Duress" both in *The Oxford Handbook of the Philosophy of Criminal Law*, ed. J. Deigh and D. Dolinko (Oxford: Clarendon Press, 2011).

that its interpretation of the provocation defense is in many respects regressive, rather than progressive. In explaining the affirmative defenses, it is important for us to attend to differences between common law and Model Penal Code versions of these defenses, even if, for the most part, we choose to focus on the Model Penal Code versions. I begin with a summary of the defenses, as understood by the common law and the Model Penal Code, and then proceed to ask several questions about the architecture of these defenses.[2]

60. Self-defense and Defense of Others

Criminal law recognizes conditions under which what would otherwise be unlawful force is justified.[3] The more familiar case is self-defense, but the criminal law also recognizes cases in which defense of others is justified. We will begin with self-defense, since defense of others is parasitic on self-defense.

The standard case of self-defense involves the use of defensive force to protect oneself against threats by a culpable aggressor. There are interesting questions that can be asked about non-standard cases where, for example, the aggressor is non-culpable or where the person employing defensive force later initiated the conflict originally. I will focus on the standard case of the use of defensive force by a non-aggressor to protect himself against culpable aggression by another.

At common law, a non-aggressor is justified in using force against another iffi he reasonably believes that such force is necessary to protect himself from imminent use of unlawful force by another and the defensive force he uses is proportional to the unlawful force that is threatened. The agent employing self-defense must reasonably believe three things:

1. Defensive force is necessary to protect himself from threats to his bodily integrity.
2. The threat posed to which self-defense is a response is imminent.
3. Defensive force is proportional and not excessive in relation to the harm threatened.

---

[2] Here, as elsewhere, my summary owes a significant debt to Dressler, *Understanding Criminal Law*.

[3] There is potential overlap between criminal law discussions of the use of defensive force in self-defense and defense of others and recent work in the morality of war and killing discussing the conditions under which individuals make themselves liable to the use of defensive force by others. An example of this just war approach is Jeff McMahan, *Killing in War* (Oxford: Clarendon Press, 2009). I find the traditional focus on the actor's justification, rather than the victim's liability, to be more intuitive. However, as far as I can see, the same issues can be raised from either perspective.

A special case of self-defense involves the use of deadly force. The common law understands deadly force as force likely to result in death or serious bodily injury and claims that deadly force is justified iffi the agent reasonably believes that its use is necessary to prevent imminent and unlawful use of deadly force by the aggressor.

The Model Penal Code builds upon but modifies common law doctrines. It says that an agent is justified in using force against another iffi he reasonably believes such force is immediately necessary to protect himself from the use of unlawful force by the other (MPC §3.04(1)). Deadly force is justified only in response to a threat of deadly force, where deadly force includes force necessary to prevent (1) death, (2) serious bodily injury, (3) forcible rape, or (4) kidnapping (MPC §3.04).[4] Significantly, the Code drops the common law temporal requirement of imminence in favor of necessity, and it offers a fuller specification of the nature and forms of deadly force.

The main point at which self-defense will be relevant to issues that lie ahead will be when we explore comparisons between the role of self-defense in battered person defenses and the provocation defense in Chapter 14. In some battered person killings, an abused person kills her abuser while he sleeps in a case of *pre-emptive* self-defense, claiming that she reasonably believed that deadly force was necessary to protect herself from a genuine threat that was not imminent. Such a claim would not satisfy the common law conception of self-defense, which requires imminence, but it might satisfy the Model Penal Code conception of self-defense, which focuses on necessity, rather than imminence.

As a general rule, defensive force to protect a third party is justified when the third party would be justified in exercising self-defense. According to the Model Penal Code, defensive force by A against B to protect C is justified iffi it would be reasonable for A to believe that anyone in C's situation is justified in exercising self-defense against B's threat (MPC §3.05(1)). Justified defense of another may also be relevant to some battered person cases in which the abused enlists the aid of another to defend her against credible threats from an abuser.

With all justifications, it's not just that the conduct being justified is in fact permissible. Justified conduct would otherwise be wrong but is made permissible in virtue of the agent acting on good reasons.[5] An act is justified iffi it is

---

[4] The Model Penal Code requires only that the agent believe that proportional force is necessary to prevent unlawful force, but MPC §3.09 makes the self-defense excuse unavailable if the agent's beliefs were false and reckless or negligent. My description in the text combines these two conditions.
[5] Thanks to Gabe Mendlow for encouraging me to make this qualification explicit.

pro tanto wrong but nonetheless on-balance permissible because the agent acted on sufficiently good countervailing reasons. This is true in the case of self-defense and defense of others. In calling these defenses justifications we are saying that force that would otherwise be impermissible is made permissible by virtue of the agent having good reason to use defensive force to protect innocent parties, whether himself or another.

61. Necessity

In addition to self-defense and defense of others, the criminal law recognizes cases in which circumstances necessitate and so justify the choice of a lesser evil. Consider two examples. Adapting an example from Aristotle's *Ethics*, we might think that the captain of a ship who encountered an unexpected storm was justified in throwing overboard his client's cargo, rather than risk the destruction of his ship and crew (*NE* III 1). Here, the captain does something that would otherwise be illegal in order to avert a greater harm to innocent parties. Or suppose that we are hunting in a remote area, that you accidentally incur a self-inflicted gunshot wound, and that I reasonably believe that the only way to get you timely medical attention is to call Emergency Medical Services using the phone in the only cabin within miles. The cabin is unoccupied. My trespass, though otherwise unlawful, is justified in order avoid possible loss of life. In both cases, actions that would otherwise be illegal are justified as instances of the agent choosing a lesser evil.

As with self-defense, a standard necessity justification involves more than conduct being permissible. It also involves the idea that the conduct in question would otherwise be wrong but is made permissible in virtue of the agent acting on good reasons, choosing the lesser evil. An act is justified as a case of necessity iffi it is *pro tanto* wrong but nonetheless on-balance permissible because the agent acted on sufficiently good countervailing reasons, avoiding greater evils. Though the details of common law conceptions of necessity are variable, these seem to be common essentials, with respect to which the agent has to have reasonable belief.

1. The agent must be faced with a clear and imminent danger.
2. The cause of the danger must be a natural (non-human) factor or circumstance.
3. There must be no alternative legal way of avoiding the danger in question.

4. The consequences of not violating the law must be worse than those of wrongdoing.
5. The actor must not be substantially responsible for bringing about the necessity.
6. The necessity defense does not extend to homicide.

The importance of (4) explains why the necessity defense involves the choice of a *lesser evil*. Though necessity is clearest in cases in which the unlawful option is a *substantially* lesser evil, the definition of necessity requires only that it be the lesser evil.

Though the Model Penal Code also understands necessity in terms of choosing a lesser evil, it modifies the common law conception in significant ways.

(1) Conduct which the actor believes to be necessary to avoid a harm or evil to himself or to another is justifiable, provided that: (a) the harm or evil sought to be avoided by such conduct is greater than that sought to be prevented by the law defining the offense charged; and (b) neither the Code nor other law defining the offense provides exceptions or defenses dealing with the specific situation involved; and (c) a legislative purpose to exclude the justification claimed does not otherwise plainly appear. (2) When the actor was reckless or negligent in bringing about the situation requiring a choice of harms or evils or in appraising the necessity for his conduct, the justification offered by this Section is unavailable in a prosecution for any offense for which recklessness or negligence, as the case may be, suffices to establish culpability.   [MPC §3.02]

The Model Penal Code broadens the necessity defense at common law in three interesting ways.

First, as with self-defense, the Code does not require that the threatened harm that the agent seeks to avert be imminent, provided that the agent reasonably believes that what would otherwise be unlawful harm is necessary to avoid greater harm. In this way, the Code rejects (1) in the common law doctrine.

Second, the Model Penal Code does not require that the necessity be caused by natural (non-human) factors, rejecting (2) of the common law doctrine. As we will see, this removes an important distinguishing mark at common law between necessity and duress. Both involve defenses that appeal to a hard choice the agent faces. Duress is hard choice that originates in the wrongful agency of another. The insistence in the common law necessity doctrine that hard choice must have natural origins meant that duress could not count as necessity. The Model Penal Code removes this obstacle. What that might mean for the relation between necessity and duress is something we will explore shortly (§68).

Third, whereas the common law limits the kinds of wrongdoing that admit of necessity defenses, the Model Penal Code does not, treating necessity as a general justification. In particular, the common law excluded a necessity defense in cases of homicide. This issue was famously raised in *Regina v. Dudley and Stephens* (1884), in which three adult survivors of a shipwreck practiced the maritime "custom of the sea," killing and eating a sick cabin boy in order to survive.[6] To the surprise of many, the survivors were convicted and sentenced to death, despite their necessity plea and the custom of the sea. At trial, Lord Coleridge expressed concern about allowing necessity defenses involving homicide. However, one might reasonably think that the same rationale that applies in non-homicide necessity cases can carry over to homicide cases. This would be to reject (6) in the common law necessity defense, as the Model Penal Code does.

62. Incompetence

Justifications and excuses deny different elements in the retributivist desert basis for punishment. Whereas justifications deny wrongdoing, excuses deny culpability or responsibility. We said that the criminal law understands excuses to involve impairments of the agent's capacities or opportunities. Here, we focus on incompetence excuses.

Whereas moral assessment is open to the possibility that normative competence might be impaired in various ways, including mental illness, immaturity, and addiction, the main incompetence excuse recognized in the criminal law is insanity, though the diminished competence of adolescents is one central rationale for a separate juvenile court, which we will discuss in Chapter 12. If we think of insanity as confined only to certain kinds of mental illness—for instance, paranoid psychosis—we might worry that the criminal law has an

---

[6] *Regina v. Dudley and Stephens* 14 Q.B.D. 273 (1884). However, the sentences of the prisoners were commuted after six months imprisonment. For discussion of the case, see A.W.B. Simpson, *Cannibalism and the Common Law: The Story of the Tragic Last Voyage of the Mignonette and the Strange Legal Proceedings to which it Gave Rise* (Chicago, IL: University of Chicago Press, 1984) and Neil Hanson, *The Custom of the Sea* (London: Doubleday, 1999).

overly narrow conception of incompetence. However, if insanity just is normative incompetence, then there may be many kinds of insanity that could be
excusing. Because we will examine incompetence and insanity in greater detail
in Chapter 11, my discussion here will focus on a few essential contrasts. For
present purposes, the two most important conceptions of insanity are the
M'Naghten common law conception and the Model Penal Code conception.

It's not entirely clear if M'Naghten treats moral ignorance as sufficient for
excuse or whether it requires cognitive incapacity. Earlier, we defended the
view that cognitive incapacity is required (§§16–17). Performance errors only
excuse when they reflect an underlying incompetence. Moreover, this capacitarian interpretation of M'Naghten is a common one, reflected, for example, in
the Federal insanity test.

> It is an affirmative defense to a prosecution under any Federal statute that, at
> the time of the commission of the acts constituting the offense, the defend-
> ant, as a result of a severe mental disease or defect, was unable to appreciate
> the nature and quality or the wrongfulness of his acts. Mental disease or
> defect does not otherwise constitute a defense.[7]

With insanity, as with other affirmative defenses, the Model Penal Code
expands common law conceptions of the defense.

> (1) A person is not responsible for criminal conduct if at the time of such
> conduct as a result of a mental disease or defect he lacks substantial capacity
> either to appreciate the criminality [wrongfulness] of his conduct or to
> conform his conduct to the requirements of law. (2) As used in this
> Article, the terms "mental disease or defect" do not include an abnormality
> manifested only by repeated criminal or otherwise anti-social conduct.
>
> [MPC §4.01]

Like M'Naghten, the Model Penal Code requires that the relevant incapacities
be due to mental disease or defect and that there be independent evidence of
this disease or defect, apart from the wrongdoing itself. Despite these commonalities, the Model Penal Code test is conceptually broader than
M'Naghten. We will examine the differences between M'Naghten and Model
Penal Code conceptions of insanity at greater length in Chapter 11. For
present purposes, the most important difference is that whereas M'Naghten

---

[7] 18 U.MPCS.C. §1 (a) (2005).

has a purely cognitive conception of responsibility, the Model Penal Code conception is cognitive and volitional. Earlier, we argued that normative competence has both cognitive and volitional dimensions—the ability to recognize normative requirements and the ability to conform one's conduct to this normative knowledge (§§16–18). The Model Penal Code agrees. Because *both are required for responsibility*, significant *impairment of either is excusing*, with the result that the Code's conception of insanity is conceptually broader than the M'Naghten conception, which recognizes only cognitive impairments as excusing.

Here, as on many issues, the Model Penal Code was influential in leading to reforms in state criminal codes. Prior to adoption of the Model Penal Code, the purely cognitive M'Naghten test was the dominant conception of insanity in American criminal law. But, under the influence of the Model Penal Code, many states came to adopt its broader conception of insanity. However, this trend changed dramatically in the wake of John Hinckley's acquittal in 1982 on grounds of insanity for the attempted murder of President Ronald Reagan. Public outcry over the verdict led to a backlash against any perceived broadening of the insanity defense and a return in many jurisdictions to a narrower M'Naghten-style conception of insanity.

63. Duress

A duress defense is generally regarded as excusing, rather than justifying, though we shall see that this consensus is open to question. At common law, duress involves six conditions.

1. Another person threatened death or grievous bodily injury to the agent or a relative of the agent unless she committed the offense.
2. The threat was credible.
3. The threat was imminent.
4. There was no reasonable alternative to compliance as a way of avoiding the threat.
5. The actor was not responsible for being subject to the threat.
6. The defense does not apply to homicides.

As with other defenses, the Model Penal Code understands duress as a more inclusive defense.

(1) It is an affirmative defense that the actor engaged in the conduct charged to constitute an offense because he was coerced to do so by the use of, or a threat to use, unlawful force against his person or the person of another, which a person of reasonable firmness in his situation would have been unable to resist. (2) The defense provided by this Section is unavailable if the actor recklessly placed himself in a situation in which it was probable that he would be subjected to duress. The defense is also unavailable if he was negligent in placing himself in such a situation, whenever negligence suffices to establish culpability for the offense charged.   [MPC §2.09(1)]

The Model Penal Code conception of duress is more inclusive in three ways. First, the Code says that duress must involve a threat of unlawful force but denies that the threat need involve death or grievous bodily harm, and it need not be directed at the agent herself or a close associate, revising both aspects of (1) in the common law doctrine. Moreover, the threat need not be imminent, contrary to condition (3) in the common law. The Model Penal Code does not mention the lack of permissible alternative ways of avoiding the threat, but it does insist that the threat should be such that a person of reasonable firmness would not or could not resist, and one might think that the latter condition includes the former condition. Finally, there is no restriction on the kind of wrongdoing to which duress is a defense. In particular, duress can be a defense to homicide, contrary to (6) in the common law doctrine.

64. Provocation

As we noted above (§59), provocation is a selective, rather than general, defense, because it applies only to homicides. Moreover, it is only a partial defense, because, even when successful, it does not justify outright acquittal, but instead results in conviction and sentencing for a lesser offense. Homicide that would otherwise count as murder counts as manslaughter when suitably provoked.

The common law recognizes adequate provocation in cases of homicide that satisfy several conditions.

1. The homicide must be committed in a sudden state of passion.
2. The agent did not have a reasonable amount of time to cool off.
3. Adequate provocation must be such as would provoke a reasonable (or perhaps ordinary) person.

4. Provoking events must belong to one of the following categories: (a) aggravated assault and battery, (b) mutual combat, (c) commission of a crime against a close relative of the defendant, (d) illegal arrest, and (e) direct observation of spousal adultery.

Historically, the common law required that provoking events must be category-specific, as specified in (4). However, these strict categorical requirements have eased, with the result that many jurisdictions leave the determination of adequate provocation to the jury.[8]

The Model Penal Code defines provocation as part of its conception of manslaughter.

(1) Criminal homicide constitutes manslaughter when: (a) it is committed recklessly; or (b) a homicide which would otherwise be murder [i.e. a homicide that it is intentional, foreseen, or the result of extreme indifference to human life] is committed under the influence of extreme mental or emotional disturbance for which there is a reasonable explanation or excuse. The reasonableness of such explanation or excuse shall be determined from the viewpoint of a person in the actor's situation under the circumstances as he believes them to be. (2) Manslaughter is a felony of the second degree.

[MPC §210.3]

Here too, the Model Penal Code expands the scope of the defense. Notice that it does not limit the provocation defense to specific categories of provocation. Crucially, the Model Penal Code conceptualizes provocation in terms of *extreme emotional disturbance* and relativizes what counts as excusing emotional disturbance to the agent's actual perspective, however unreasonable that might otherwise seem to be. As we will see in Chapter 14, reforms in the Code's conception of the provocation defense threaten to make it a regressive doctrine in its application to some crimes of passion in which disappointed lovers and stalkers kill the object of their affections or others and claim provocation.

65. Are the Standards Ingredient in the Defenses Objective or Subjective?

Both justifications and excuses require that certain conditions be satisfied for the defense in question to obtain, and sometimes these conditions appeal to

---

[8] See Dressler, *Understanding Criminal Law*, pp. 539–41.

beliefs, attitudes, or behavior of the defendant or of a reasonable person. This raises the question of whether and, if so, how the law should relativize these conditions to the perspective of the defendant. Commentators sometimes contrast *objective* and *subjective* approaches. For instance, an objective approach to self-defense might claim that defensive force is permissible iffi it is necessary to avert an unlawful threat and employs proportionate force. Here, both necessity and proportionality are construed objectively, that is, independently of the agent's beliefs. By contrast, a subjective approach might claim that defensive force is permissible iffi the agent believed that defensive force was necessary and that the force he employed was proportional. Both the common law and the Model Penal Code adopt an *intermediate* position on self-defense, making the availability of the defense conditional on the agent's *reasonable* beliefs about necessity and proportionality. This gives us three different ways we could understand the conditions of the self-defense justification. What is true of self-defense is true of necessity as well. For instance, we can approach the question of whether criminal offense was necessary to avert a greater evil from an objective, subjective, or intermediate perspective. Whereas some common law formulations seem to appeal to objective necessity, the Model Penal Code appeals to subjective necessity, in particular, the agent's beliefs about the necessity of unlawful action to avert a greater harm. The Model Penal Code conceptions of duress and provocation both appeal to claims about the responses of reasonable actors. In the case of duress, this looks like an appeal to an intermediate standard, but the provocation defense understands reasonable provocation from the perspective of the agent's actual beliefs and attitudes.

This raises a general question about how, if at all, to relativize the defenses. This issue has both *descriptive* and *normative* dimensions—how, if at all, *are* various defenses relativized and how, if at all, *should* they be relativized. These are complicated issues that outstrip my expertise and that, I hope, need not be resolved for purposes of this book. I suspect that there is no uniform answer to the descriptive question about what kind of relativization we find for various defenses in different jurisdictions, and even for a given defense there may be variation between common law conceptions and the Model Penal Code. However, it may be worth framing the normative issue, if only briefly.

We can usefully recast the distinction between objective and subjective approaches in terms of *relativity* to different sets of considerations.[9] In

---

[9] My tripartite proposal is adapted from Parfit's useful tripartition of reasons and, hence, justifications into those that are *fact-relative*, *belief-relative*, and *evidence-relative*. See Derek Parfit, *On What Matters*, 2 vols. (Oxford: Clarendon Press, 2011), vol. I, ch. 7. Evidence-relativity can be understood as an intermediate value on a continuum in which fact-relativity and belief-relativity are the poles. I adapt

particular, we can recognize three kinds of relativity—*fact-relativity*, which makes the defense relative to the actual facts or circumstances in question, whether the agent is in a position to recognize them or not; *attitude-relativity*, which makes the defense relative to the agent's actual beliefs or attitudes about a situation; and *capacity-relativity*, which makes the defense relative to the cognitive and volitional capacities of the agent in those circumstances. We can think of these as three salient points on a scale of objectivity from fact-relativity to capacity-relativity to attitude-relativity. Indeed, there is a sense in which fact-relativity involves no real relativization since it depends on how things objectively are, not on how they are from some more restricted perspective.

The normative proposal that strikes me as plausible is that, for the most part, the conditions for justifications should be fact-relative and the conditions for excuse should be capacity-relative. The basis for this proposal lies in the division of moral labor between justifications and excuses. Justifications and excuses deny different elements of inclusive culpability, which is the retributivist desert basis for punishment. Justifications deny wrongdoing, whereas excuses deny responsibility and, hence, blameworthiness or broad culpability. Permissibility denies wrongdoing, and permissibility seems to depend on objective facts, such as the existence and magnitude of threats and risks and the means to avoid or minimize them, not the agent's ability to recognize such facts. By contrast, blameworthiness does seem to depend on an agent's ability to recognize an action as wrong and to conform her conduct to that knowledge. This is the heart of the fair opportunity claim—capacity and opportunity constrain blame but not wrongdoing. If so, then justifications, such as self-defense and necessity, should be formulated in a fact-relative way. In cases in which the agent had false but reasonable beliefs, given the circumstances and evidence available to her, that her use of defensive force was necessary and proportional to avert an unlawful threat or that her unlawful behavior was necessary to avert a greater evil, her unlawful conduct should be excused, rather than justified. Excuses, generally, should be based on the agent's capacities and opportunities, not on her actual beliefs, attitudes, and conduct.[10] The agent's actual beliefs and attitudes seem relevant only to the requirements of elemental *mens rea*. If so, this may contribute to doubts

Parfit's tripartition, because I think defenses are sometimes relativized to non-epistemic attitudes and capacities.

[10] This proposal about how to relativize justifications and excuses is broadly similar to ideas in Robinson, *Structure and Function in Criminal Law*, pp. 100–24.

about the Model Penal Code's attitude-relative conception of the provocation defense, which we will take up in Chapter 14.

This normative proposal for making justifications fact-relative and excuses capacity-relative has some plausibility. Whether it would be plausible to implement this proposal consistently across all dimensions of each defense and how revisionary such a proposal would be are complicated issues, which I cannot address here. However, such a proposal seems to fit with our understanding of the difference between justifications and excuses, which will play a role in our subsequent analysis.

66. Is Self-defense a Special Case of Necessity?

Should we accept this conventional picture of the structure of justifications? In particular, should we accept the idea that defensive force and necessity are two coordinate but independent forms of justification? There is certainly a loose and popular sense of "necessity" in which defensive force is permissible only because of necessity. We might ask if we could treat defensive force as a special case of necessity in the stricter sense at work in the criminal law. I will discuss this issue with reference to whether self-defense is a special case of necessity, but presumably many of the same relations will obtain between defense of others and necessity.

Necessity involves the choice of an otherwise unlawful option that is the lesser of two evils. One obstacle to assimilating self-defense to necessity is that self-defense is justified in cases that might not satisfy the lesser evil condition. A natural way to understand lesser evil is by reference to a *balance of evils* in a broadly consequentialist fashion that ranks outcomes according to their moral seriousness and by the number of such outcomes. On such a view, all else being equal, murder is worse than rape, which is worse than simple assault, which is worse than theft; and two murders are worse than one, three murders are worse than two, and so on. But if necessity appeals to such a consequentialist analysis of the balance of evils, self-defense cannot always be assimilated to necessity. Self-defense, at least as conceived by the Model Penal Code, justifies the use of lethal force in cases that would not satisfy this version of the lesser evils test. The Code implies that justified self-defense extends to cases of killing one to save oneself, killing to prevent grievous bodily injury, killing to prevent forcible rape, and killing to prevent kidnapping. These are cases in which self-defense is justified but does not seem to involve a lesser evil, because it involves comparable or even somewhat greater evils.

However, we have reason to question this interpretation of the balance of evils. If we accepted it, there would be a necessity defense for any action that minimized harm. But the necessity defense would not justify a surgeon killing one healthy patient to transplant his organs into the bodies of two patients awaiting life-saving transplants of different organs. Moreover, we might be inclined to think that preventing a lesser but substantial harm to a loved one should perhaps justify doing something unlawful that would involve moderately greater total harm, spread across several people. If so, we might doubt that lesser evil in this consequentialist sense is either necessary or sufficient to qualify for the necessity defense.

The potentially problematic feature of this consequentialist analysis of the balance of evils is its *agent-neutral* character. An *agent-neutral* reason is one that can be specified without any essential reference to the agent who has it, and, as a result, all else being equal, every agent has the same agent-neutral reasons. By contrast, *agent-relative* reasons do make essential reference to the agent who has them, as a result of which different agents have different agent-relative reasons. A reason to promote happiness generally or minimize harm is an agent-neutral reason, whereas a reason to promote my own happiness or minimize my own pain is an agent-relative reason. It is common to recognize agent-relative *constraints* on the agent doing harm to others, even if this is necessary to minimize total harm, and to recognize agent-relative *options* to perform suboptimal actions, out of special concern for the agent's own interests or the interests of others who stand in special relationships to him, such as his loved ones and friends. This suggests the possibility of a *moralized* balance of evils test that recognizes agent-relative reasons. For then we can explain why some cases of killing two to save one might satisfy the necessity defense and why some cases of distributing a greater total harm among several people for the sake of avoiding individual harm to oneself or a loved one might satisfy the necessity defense.

A sensible agent-relative morality employs constraints and options that are *moderate, rather than absolute.*[11] Constraints are absolute if it is always wrong to treat others in certain ways (e.g. violating their rights), no matter how much good could be achieved or harm avoided by doing so. By contrast, constraints are moderate if there is some sufficient amount of good to be produced or harm to be avoided that would make it permissible to violate the constraint.

[11] For discussions of moderate agent-relative morality, see, e.g., Thomas Nagel, "War and Massacre" reprinted in Thomas Nagel, *Mortal Questions* (New York: Cambridge University Press, 1979); Moore, *Placing Blame*, pp. 721–25; Shelly Kagan, *Normative Ethics* (Boulder, CO: Ridgeview Press, 1998), p. 79; and Larry Alexander, "Deontology at the Threshold" *San Diego Law Review* 37 (2000): 893–912.

A moderate constraint could explain why it would be wrong for the surgeon to kill one patient to save two without implying that one innocent could never be killed to save very large numbers of innocents. Likewise, options are absolute if they permit the agent to prefer his own good or that of a loved one to the good of others, no matter how great the cost to others. By contrast, options are moderate if there is some amount of good that could be achieved or harm prevented that would defeat the agent-relative option. A moderate option could explain why I am permitted not to sacrifice significant goods in my life for the sake of marginally greater goods to strangers without implying that I could refuse to save the lives of many when I could save them at little or no cost to myself. Though moderate agent-relative morality implies that there is some point at which constraints and options give way to the increasing agent-neutral opportunity costs of respecting them, there is no reason to expect that there is some precise point on the consequentialist scale where constraints and options lapse, any more than there must be some precise point at which accumulating grains of sand constitutes a heap. As far as I can see, it could be indeterminate at what point moderate constraints and options lapse or fail.[12]

If we moralize the balance of evils test by appeal to some such moderate agent-relative morality, we might be able to salvage self-defense as a special case of necessity in one of two ways. First, insofar as we focus on cases in which an agent uses lethal force against a culpable aggressor who threatens a lesser agent-neutral evil, such as rape or kidnapping, an agent-relative balance of evils allows us to treat the interests of the culpable aggressor as less morally significant than the otherwise comparable interests of the innocent threatened party. This rationale promises to explain cases involving culpable aggressors, but it wouldn't extend to more controversial cases of self-defense against non-culpable aggressors.[13] Second, we get a more robust assimilation of self-defense to necessity if our moralized balance of evils test appeals to an agent-relative morality that recognizes constraints and options, for this allows us to treat self-defense against significant but lesser agent-neutral threats as the

[12] Cf. Tom Dougherty, "Vague Value" *Philosophy and Phenomenological Research* 89 (2014): 352–72.

[13] Whereas self-defense against culpable aggressors provides a justification, there is a case for treating self-defense against non-culpable aggressors as providing an excuse. Culpable aggressors arguably waive their right not to be harmed in a way that non-culpable aggressors do not. In the case of defense against culpable aggressors this eliminates the wrongness of defensive harm and so paves the way for justification. However, in the case of defense against non-culpable aggressors, the wrongness of defensive harm remains, which suggests perhaps that defensive force in such cases does not justify the use of force but renders it non-blameworthy or less blameworthy.

choice of a lesser moralized evil if the threat falls on oneself or a close relation. If successful, this would apparently allow us to represent legitimate cases of self-defense as cases of necessity. So, necessity would be the unifying principle of justifications. We could even distinguish *defensive* and *non-defensive* necessity.[14]

67. Should We Recognize Partial Justification?

What should we say about defensive violations that prevent significant harms to the agent or her loved ones that do not satisfy this moderate agent-relative balance of evils? For instance, suppose I act to save a loved one from a significant but non-lethal threat by using lethal defensive force. As long as such violations are not appropriately moralized lesser evils, presumably they do not constitute genuine justifications. We might call these *imperfect justifications*.

If we accept the assumption of bivalence—that an agent's offense is either fully justified or impermissible and an agent is either fully responsible for his wrongdoing or he is fully excused—imperfect justifications can have no bearing on the guilt phase of a trial. However, imperfect justifications might still be relevant at the sentencing phase of a trial. Provided that a guilty verdict determines only a morally permissible interval of punishment and there is suitable discretion about the precise quantum of punishment to impose, imperfect justifications might be accommodated at sentencing. As we will see in Chapter 15, this treatment of imperfect justifications will be problematic insofar as there are significant mandatory minima and sentencing discretion is severely constrained.

Alternately, we might reject bivalence and conceptualize imperfect justifications as *partial justifications*. Partial justification runs counter to the conventional assumption that permissibility and, hence, justification are all or nothing.[15] But once we accept the picture of agent-relative morality underlying the balance of evils test sketched above, we have some reason to rethink this assumption.

---

[14] However, if self-defense, as well as necessity, involves a moralized balance of evils test that appeals to a moderate agent-relative morality, this may raise questions about whether defense of others is permissible everywhere that self-defense would be permissible, because the agent-relative options and constraints that shape the contours of self-defense and defense of others to whom the agent stands in special relationships won't apply to defense of others to whom one stands in no special relationship.

[15] See, e.g., Sachar Eldar and Elkana Laist, "The Misguided Concept of Partial Justification" *Legal Theory* 20 (2014): 157–85.

1. Violations are justified when they opt for a determinately lesser evil.
2. The balance of evils should be moralized in accord with a moderate agent-relative moral conception.
3. Hence, a violation protected by a constraint or option is justified only when the constraint or option determinately overrides agent-neutral moral opportunity costs.
4. But imperfect justifications include cases in which it is indeterminate whether constraints or options are overridden by moral opportunity costs.
5. In such cases, it is indeterminate whether or not the constraint or option overrides its moral opportunity costs.
6. Though violations in such cases are not lesser evils, neither are they greater evils.
7. In such cases, imperfect justifications should be partial justifications.

If we accept (7) and allow partial justification in cases of imperfect justification involving indeterminate permissibility, we might want to go further and recognize partial justification in cases of imperfect justification in which the moral case for the violation is determinately overridden by considerations of moral opportunity cost. The intuitive idea is that the moral reasons for the violation don't cease to be relevant by being overridden. When the balance of reasons determinately favors one option over another, that may settle the question of what one ought to do all-things-considered, but it doesn't imply that there was nothing favoring the other option. We might only want to recognize partial justification in cases in which the case for violation was substantial, though overridden, or we might want to measure the degree of partial justification in a way that reflects the degree to which the case for violation falls short of being sufficient. On this version of partial justification, there are degrees of wrongness and when an agent has a non-negligible but insufficient necessity justification what she does is less wrong and merits a partial justification.[16]

We might also try to capture partial justification within the net of *provocation*. As we noted, provocation is usually regarded as the primary exception to the generalization that American criminal law is bivalent about guilt. Though provocation is often conceptualized as an excuse, this assumption deserves

---

[16] See, e.g., Douglas Husak, "Partial Defenses" *Canadian Journal of Law and Jurisprudence* 11 (1998): 167–92 and Thomas Hurka, "More Seriously Wrong, More Importantly Right" *Journal of the American Philosophical Association* 5 (2019): 41–58.

scrutiny. It may not always be clear whether provocation excuses or justifies. If suitable provocation leaves the wrongness of the act unaffected and reduces the responsibility or blameworthiness for the wrong, then it partially excuses. But if suitable provocation reduces the wrongness of the act, then it partially justifies. If there are moral factors that present in sufficient degree would fully justify, then why can't those same factors present to a reduced degree, reduce the wrongness of the agent's conduct? If so, there could be cases in which provocation might function as a partial justification. We will return to these issues in §69 and Chapter 14.

68. Questions about Necessity and Duress

Conventional wisdom says that necessity is a justification and duress is an excuse. But we might wonder if this contrast holds up to closer scrutiny.[17] There are some doctrinal differences between the two defenses. Whereas the necessity defense requires that the violation be a lesser evil, duress requires that the violation be such that a reasonable person could or would not resist. But when would a reasonable person not resist? Perhaps just when the coercion reflects a lesser evil. Also, at least at common law, whereas necessity has to have a natural source, duress has its source in the wrongful agency of another person. But even this contrast is muted by the Model Penal Code, which drops the common law requirement that the origin of necessity be natural, rather than man-made. This opens the possibility that at least some cases of duress might qualify as necessity defenses under the Model Penal Code, at least if the threatened harm is worse than the violation in question. Moreover, there are other similarities. Both necessity and duress involve hard choice for the agent, forcing her into a violation in which she would otherwise not engage. Moreover, both defenses commonly assume that the violation is necessary to avoid the alternative, that is, that there is no legal way to escape the hard choice.

Given the similarities between necessity and duress, we might question the claim that one justifies while the other excuses. Even if we were skeptical of this sharp contrast, that wouldn't tell us how best to eliminate the contrast. If we had to treat all necessity defenses and all duress defenses the same, we might revise conventional wisdom either by treating necessity as an excuse or by

---

[17] Some of the issues I raise and conclusions I defend in this section overlap with the discussion in Dressler, "Duress," which I find quite useful.

treating duress as a justification.[18] Alternatively, we might think that each could count as *both* justification and excuse. Necessity could both justify and excuse, as could duress. If so, either defense would overdetermine acquittal, but I'm not sure what's problematic about that. But there is still another possibility—that not all necessity defenses and not all duress defenses are of a piece. Perhaps some necessity defenses sound more in justification, some sound more in excuse, and some sound in both. Similarly, perhaps some duress defenses sound more in excuse, some sound more in justification, and some sound in both.

Let's reconsider necessity. Perhaps the clearest case for thinking of necessity as a justification is our example of a hunter breaking into an unoccupied cabin to use the phone to call for emergency medical assistance for a critically injured friend. It's easy to assume this violation is fully justified. But we might instead think that it is excused, rather than justified. The hunter violates the property rights of the owner of the cabin, and, especially if she has to do property damage in order to gain entry, she will owe the owner compensation. So, even in this case, we might be tempted to say that she has done wrong, but is excused and, hence, not blameworthy. Other cases of necessity seem to provide even more compelling cases of excuse. Despite the existence of agent-relative constraints, it might be the lesser moralized evil to harm one person to save many, for instance, killing a sick cabin boy to save many shipwreck survivors. We could deny that the survivors who practiced the custom of the sea acted wrongly, but it seems at least as plausible to say that they did wrong but were not blameworthy for the wrong they did because of their dire circumstances. Or consider a variation on our hunting example in which the hunter has to twist the arm of a small child to induce the owner of the cabin to let him in to use the phone to call for emergency medical assistance for his injured hunting companion. This too would seem to satisfy a plausible mor-alized balance of evils test. Do we want to say that it is permissible for the hunter to assault the child? It seems at least as plausible to say that the circumstances excuse the hunter's wrongdoing, changing not the act's deontic valence but rather its blameworthiness.

But if necessity excuses, what does this imply about self-defense? If self-defense is or can be understood as a special case of necessity, does this imply that self-defense is also an excuse, rather than a justification? That would be a

---

[18] For interesting defenses of the claim that duress should be understood as a justification, see Peter Westen and James Mangiafico, "The Criminal Defense of Duress: A Justification, Not an Excuse—And Why It Matters" *Buffalo Criminal Law Review* 6 (2003): 833–950 and Peter Westen, "Does Duress Justify or Excuse?" in *Moral Puzzles and Legal Perplexities*, ed. H. Hurd.

surprising result. But we're not forced to that conclusion if not all cases of necessity excuse. We just said that this mixed verdict might track differences in whether necessity involves the violation of significant rights or not. Necessity seems more like an excuse when it sanctions the violation of someone else's important rights. Otherwise, we can view it as a justification. In fact, there might be an even stronger case for thinking of defensive necessity in terms of justification, rather than excuse. The standard case of self-defense is against a culpable aggressor. But we might regard the culpable aggressor as having waived or surrendered or forfeited his right against harm by the defender. If so, that removes the principal reason for regarding defensive necessity as an excuse. There is no right the aggressor has that self-defense violates, which suggests that self-defense in such cases is permissible, rather than wrong but excused. We have not discussed the use of defensive force against non-culpable aggressors. If we recognize a defense that applies to defensive force against non-culpable aggressors, then we might want to treat that defense as an excuse, rather than a justification. For we wouldn't have the same reason to think that non-culpable aggressors had waived or surrendered their rights. This would be more like the necessity cases in which the lesser evil does involve rights violations. I don't know if it's mandatory to view these cases as excusing, rather than justifying. But that description has plausibility and a rationale.

What about duress? As we noted, there are similarities between paradigmatic cases of duress and paradigmatic cases of necessity. Both involve hard choice that is not the agent's fault and that leaves no legal alternatives to avoiding the difficulty. Whereas necessity traditionally involves hard choice with natural origins, duress involves hard choice arising from the wrongful agency of another. But we might think that the origins of hard choice are not morally significant, provided the agent is not responsible for being subject to hard choice. Indeed, the Model Penal Code drops the common law requirement on necessity that the hard choice have natural origins, clearing the way to assimilating duress to necessity. But, equally, we might think that there's no good reason to restrict duress to hard choice originating from another's agency.

I don't see that this yet gives us reason to reduce duress to necessity or to regard duress as a justification, rather than an excuse. If we separate duress and necessity by the origins of hard choice, then they look like coordinate defenses. We can assimilate duress to necessity if we relax the assumption that necessity can only involve hard choice with natural origins, but equally we can assimilate necessity to duress if we relax the assumption that duress can only involve hard choice with origins in the agency of others. So far, the situation of duress and necessity seems symmetrical. Even if we do asymmetrically assimilate (reduce) duress to necessity, it's not clear that this makes duress a justification, rather than an excuse. For, as we have just seen, the necessity defense can often be treated as an excuse, rather than a justification.

Consider some cases of duress that might otherwise satisfy necessity requirements. Because necessity involves the choice of lesser evil, we need to consider cases of duress in the context of a moralized balance of evils test that is or can be sensitive to a plausible agent-relative morality. It is useful to distinguish two kinds of cases.

- *Duress without Harm.* A wrongfully threatens B (or B's loved one) with grievous bodily harm if B doesn't engage in harmless wrongdoing, such as prostitution or drug-trafficking.[19]
- *Duress with Harm.* A wrongfully threatens B (or B's loved one) with grievous bodily harm unless B participates in wrongful harm against C in which the harm to C is significant but significantly less than the harm threatened to B (or B's loved one). Perhaps A uses the threat to enlist B's help to assault C, embezzle from C, or extort C.

Both Duress without Harm and Duress with Harm look to satisfy a suitably moralized balance of evils test. If so, they could be cases of necessity too, provided necessity does not require hard choice with natural origins. But that doesn't force us to reduce duress to necessity or to say that duress justifies, rather than excuses. We might allow that Duress without Harm sounds in justification, rendering the duressed actor's violation permissible or justified. I'm not sure this interpretation as justification, rather than excuse, is mandatory, but it has some plausibility. However, insofar as the justification interpretation is plausible, this may reflect underlying doubts about whether the activities in question—prostitution and drug trafficking—ought to be criminalized in the first place. If we turn to Duress with Harm, the justification reading looks less compelling. In such cases, it's less tempting to view B's violation of C's rights as permissible. It seems more plausible to treat B's violation of C's rights as not blameworthy, that is, as excused. The duress does not seem to change the fact that B wrongs C, and if B wrongs C, it's arguable

---

[19] I recognize that both prostitution and drug-trafficking can be harmful activities, but it is arguable that most of the harms are consequential on criminalization. There's a case to be made that, suitably regulated, these activities should not be criminalized.

that he acts wrongly. It may not be incoherent to think that an agent can wrong someone while acting permissibly, but I don't see what recommends this interpretation of the Duress with Harm cases.

One reason to think that duress does not always justify appeals to a *permissible resistance test*.[20] One diagnostic for whether an otherwise wrongful action is justified or excused is whether it would be permissible for the victim or others to resist the action that might be the object of a defense—if resistance is impermissible, the action in question is permissible and justified; if resistance is permissible, that suggests that the action is not justified, in which case any defense would have the flavor of excuse. I'm inclined to think that in some cases of duress resistance is permissible, which suggests that the duressed action is not justified. If A threatens B to harm B's daughter unless B harms my daughter, it's permissible for me to resist B harming my daughter. Contrast this case with the hunting case in which A trespasses to save B's life when this was the only means of doing so—it would not be permissible for the homeowner or another to stop A. If so, we should not treat all cases of duress as cases of justification.

Moreover, there may be cases that do or should satisfy the duress defense that don't satisfy a moralized balance of evils test.

> *Greater Evil Duress.* A threatens B (or B's loved one) with a significant evil that falls just short of what is necessary to make it the lesser evil on a suitably moralized balance of evils test. Perhaps A threatens to break the arms of B's loved one unless B participates in bringing about the complete financial ruin of several of A's business rivals.

It's hard to describe such cases with certainty, because it's hard to specify the details of the right form of moderate agent-relative morality that should inform our moralized balance of evils cases. I think that this one is plausible, but the reader is free to substitute one that strikes her as more plausible. Presumably, Greater Evils Duress cases qualify for the duress defense. There is no bar to recognizing a duress defense in such cases at common law, provided A does not enlist B in killing others. There is no bar to recognizing a duress defense in such cases under the Model Penal Code, provided a person of reasonable firmness would be unable to resist the threat to his loved one. If the duress defense applies in such cases, they must excuse, since, by hypothesis, they do not justify.

---

[20] I owe this suggestion to Larry Alexander.

Wrongful coercion to enlist the agent in committing offenses that fail a moralized balance of evils test substantially, rather than marginally, might not qualify for the duress defense. Such cases would be cases of *imperfect duress*. Imperfect duress might provide a partial excuse or mitigation. If criminal defenses are treated bivalently, then imperfect duress could be relevant as a mitigator at sentencing, provided there is sufficient discretion at sentencing. Alternately, we might reject bivalence and recognize at least some cases of imperfect duress as *partial excuses*.

Where does this discussion leave us about the relationship between necessity and duress and the question of whether either justifies or excuses? There are certainly some cases that might count as either necessity or duress, especially if we are willing to relax traditional requirements about the sources of hard choice for necessity and duress, requiring only that the agent non-culpably faces a hard choice that would satisfy a suitably moralized balance of evils test. But it's not clear what this overlap between necessity and duress shows.

It's not obvious that it supports reducing either to the other or eliminating either in favor of the other. Moreover, it's not clear why individual cases couldn't qualify under both defenses. This might involve duplication, but it doesn't pose any problem, as long as either is sufficient for acquittal.

Nor is it clear that this forces us to view necessity as an excuse, rather than a justification, or duress as a justification, rather than an excuse. Recall that this is the question of whether either defense denies wrongdoing or denies blame-worthiness for the wrong. Though necessity is traditionally treated as a justification, it's not clear that necessity should always be viewed as a justification, rather than an excuse. This is especially so in cases in which harm to others satisfies the lesser evils test. Similarly, duress that harms third parties seems more naturally viewed through the lens of excuse than the lens of justification.

Moreover, even if there is overlap between necessity and duress, the overlap seems imperfect. Greater Evils Duress cases can satisfy the demands of duress without satisfying the lesser evils demands of necessity. If so, those cases of duress cannot be assimilated to necessity, and they clearly sound in excuse, rather than justification.

The traditional sharp contrast between necessity and duress is over-simple, and we might want to rethink the assumptions that necessity always sounds in justification and never in excuse and that duress always sounds in excuse and never in justification. However, I don't think we have seen reason to reduce one to the other or eliminate one in favor of the other or to reject the claim that in some cases necessity justifies and that in some cases duress excuses.

69. Is there a Distinct Duress Excuse?

If we put together questions raised in the last two sections—whether justifications can be partial and whether duress can sometimes be treated as a case of necessity—we can raise the question whether there really is or should be a distinct duress excuse. I don't mean to cast doubt on whether duress is a defense or even the claim that duress might be excusing. But there is a question whether duress is a separate and distinct kind of excuse. Call this conclusion *eliminativism about duress as an excuse.*

We need to start with some assumptions, motivated by the previous discussion. Let's stipulate, for the sake of argument, that where duress satisfies the relevant moralized balance of evils test that duress provides a justification. Let's also stipulate that where the threat falls just short of satisfying the moralized balance of evils test we can treat duress as providing partial justification. Finally, let's assume that in a minority of cases duress excuses by creating incompetence or extreme emotional disturbance. Though we said that in most cases acceding to duress involved a reasoned response to a wrongful threat to oneself or a loved one, there may be cases in which the threat to oneself or a loved one significantly impairs one's normative competence, making it difficult either to appreciate one's reasons or to bring oneself to act on this knowledge. These three assumptions provide the context for the eliminativist argument about whether duress is a distinctive excuse.

There seem to be three possibilities. (1) Duress that does satisfy the balance of evils test is a justification. (2) Duress that falls short of the lesser evil is a partial justification. (3) Duress that clouds judgment and produces temporary incapacity is an incapacity excuse. In none of these cases is duress a distinctive excuse. In (1) and (2), duress is a justification, whether full (1) or partial (2). In (3), duress is an excuse, but it's a special case of an incompetence or insanity excuse. If so, duress is a defense, and in some cases it excuses, but in no case is it a separate and distinct kind of excuse.

This argument for eliminativism about duress merits attention, but I'm not sure we need accept it. For one thing, it depends crucially on the assumption that there are partial justifications and that duress defenses that come up just short of the moralized balance of evils test should be regarded as partial justifications. This requires denying bivalence about justification. In this respect, some see an asymmetry between justification and excuse. Whereas it's common to deny bivalence about excuse and recognize partial excuse, it's less common to deny bivalence about justification and recognize partial justification. Against this asymmetry, we might claim that there are degrees of wrongness and that when an agent has a non-negligible but insufficient necessity justification what she does is less wrong and merits a partial justification. Until we resolve this issue about partial justification, the eliminativist argument against duress remains inconclusive.

Moreover, for the eliminativist argument to succeed, understanding duress in terms of another category of justification or excuse must *preclude* recognizing duress as an excuse in its own right. But we've already questioned that assumption, suggesting that a given defense might *both* justify and excuse. In such cases, exculpation might be overdetermined, but it's not obvious why that would be problematic.

Finally, however the issue of partial justification is resolved, the eliminativist argument only succeeds if treating duress as a justification or an incompetence excuse *exhausts* its significance as a defense. But we might doubt this. Consider case (2) again, in which there is a non-negligible lesser evil defense but it falls short of satisfying the moralized balance of evils test. Providing examples of such cases can be contentious precisely because the exact contours of a moralized balance of evils test can be contentious. One such case might involve a defendant who participates in an armed robbery that leads to homicide as the result of duress in which gang members threaten significant but non-lethal harm to one of the defendant's loved ones. Even if we want to treat this as a case of partial justification, we might think that it provides a full excuse. Though wrong and at most partially justified, we might think that the agent who participates in the armed robbery in such circumstances is not blameworthy and should be fully excused. If so, partial justification would not capture the full significance of duress as a defense. In particular, this would give us reason to treat duress as a distinctive excuse that resists assimilation to partial justification.[21]

70. Is Provocation a Justification or an Excuse?

We saw that provocation is an unusual defense along at least two dimensions. Whereas most defenses are general defenses—applying to all kinds of crimes—provocation is a selective, rather than general, defense, because it applies only to homicides. Moreover, whereas American criminal law is generally bivalent about justification and excuse, provocation is only a partial defense, since, even

[21] For a different take on how duress can be a distinctive defense, see Craig Agule, "Distinctive Duress" *Philosophical Studies* 177 (2020): 1007–26.

when successful, it does not justify outright acquittal, but instead results in conviction and sentencing for a lesser offense. Homicide that would otherwise count as murder counts as manslaughter when suitably provoked.[22]

There are two apparently distinct questions worth asking about provocation. First, what counts as adequate provocation? Second, whatever counts as provocation, is that partial defense best understood as a justification or as an excuse? In fact, the questions are connected. I don't think we can answer the second question independently of the first.

In §64 we outlined differences between the narrow categorical conception of provocation in the common law and the extreme emotional disturbance conception in the Model Penal Code. We need to examine the different implications of these two conceptions in more detail, which we will do in Chapter 14 in the context of discussing battered person defenses and crimes of passion. What we will see is that there are different kinds of cases to which the provocation defense might apply. If so, we shouldn't assume that there's a univocal answer to the question whether provocation justifies or excuses. In some cases, a suitably provoked homicide might reduce what would otherwise be its degree of wrongness; if so, in those cases provocation might function as a partial justification. But, in other cases, the provoked homicide really reflects an unreasonable response on the part of the agent grounded in impaired normative competence. Such cases are really cases of partial competence, perhaps temporary in nature, and are best conceptualized as partial excuses, rather than partial justifications. This refusal to provide a uniform answer to the question of whether provocation justifies or excuses is promising. Making good on that promise will have to await the analysis in Chapter 14.

71. Revisiting the Architecture of Defenses

Our discussion of the architecture of affirmative defenses has been complex and defies easy summary. It has had both descriptive and potentially revisionary dimensions. The descriptive claims will be important at various points in the discussion ahead as we assess different challenges to and applications of

---

[22] An alternative conceptualization of provocation that bears consideration is that it is neither a partial justification nor a partial excuse but rather an attendant circumstance in the specification of *actus reus*—that is, an attendant circumstance that precludes murder but can be an ingredient in manslaughter. This analysis, plausible as far as it goes, might seem unsatisfactory if we think that the explanation for this *actus reus* difference between murder and manslaughter rests on the thought that provocation provides a partial justification or excuse.

fair opportunity and the defenses, whether full or partial, available to offenders in various circumstances. Whereas I feel reasonably confident in something like this description of the main affirmative defenses, my attempt to re-examine the normative architecture of the defenses is somewhat revisionary and decidedly speculative. Five themes emerge from this re-examination that are worth highlighting.

First, some kinds of theoretical unification are more promising than others. I do think that there is an interesting case to be made for treating self-defense, and defensive force more generally, as a special case of necessity. That case depends on a moralized balance of evils test, funded partly by an agent-relative moral conception. Moreover, there is interesting but imperfect overlap between necessity and duress defenses. The imperfect overlap means that neither defense could be reduced to or eliminated in favor of the other. Even where they overlap, there seems to be no need to give explanatory priority to one or the other.

Second, traditional descriptions of the defenses often assume that the defenses can be neatly categorized as justifications or excuses. However, on closer inspection, some of these categorizations might seem more problematic. I don't see any reason to challenge the usual view that incompetence defenses, such as insanity, function as excuses, rather than justifications. Nor do I think that there is any compelling reason to challenge the traditional view that defense against culpable aggressors functions as a justification, rather than an excuse. But I do think that it is much less clear whether defense against non-culpable aggressors, necessity, duress, and provocation function as justifications or as excuses. It's not clear that particular defenses couldn't have dual functions, even if this overdetermines acquittal. Moreover, we may find that there is no unitary answer for any particular defense whether it justifies or excuses, but that the cases falling under that defense partition into classes some of which sound more naturally in justification and some of which sound more naturally in excuse.

However, this willingness to fit at least some cases of necessity and provo-cation under the rubric of excuse may seem to raise questions about our working hypothesis that responsibility and excuse are inversely related. But that is not a serious worry. Remember that responsibility, according to fair opportunity, involves both normative competence and situational control. Duress compromises situational control. But the cases of necessity that excuse are like cases of duress in that they involve hard choice for which the agent is not culpable, though they can arise from natural as well as agential causes. But then it's not a big stretch for fair opportunity to include some cases of necessity among the excuses; these will be cases of hard choice, for which the agent is not responsible, that impair situational control. Moreover, my suspicion is that the cases in which provocation (partially) excuses, rather than justifies, will be cases in which the agent's normative competence is partially and perhaps temporarily impaired. If so, the variety of potential excuses is no threat to our working hypothesis about the inverse relationship between responsibility and excuse.

Third, we should be cautious about generalizing across and within defenses. We don't want to be Procrustean about unity and diversity within the defenses or about when they justify and when they excuse.

Fourth, our discussion of affirmative defenses raises questions about the exculpatory force of justifications and excuses. Though both justifications and excuses justify acquittal in an exculpatory fashion, they are exculpatory in different ways, because they deny different elements of inclusive culpability. Justifications deny wrongdoing, whereas excuses concede wrongdoing but deny that the agent was responsible for the wrongdoing, denying that the agent was blameworthy for her wrongdoing. This raises the issue of whether justifications or excuses provide more thorough exculpation. One way to think about this issue is whether a defendant shopping for an exculpatory defense has reason to prefer one defense over the other. On the one hand, one might think that justifications provide fuller exculpation than excuses. If one's conduct is justified, then it was permissible, not wrong all-things-considered. In this way, a justification seems to clear one's moral ledger fully. By contrast, an excuse concedes that one acted wrongly but insists that one is not blameworthy for the wrong, either because one's capacities or opportunities were impaired. Here, one might think that an excuse fails to clear one's moral ledger fully. On the other hand, justifications don't usually clear one's moral ledger completely. Justified violations are *pro tanto* wrong, but permissible all-things-considered in light of the circumstances and all relevant factors. In such cases, *pro tanto* wrongness is countervailed, but not eliminated. This is reflected in necessity justifications in which the justified conduct is described as a lesser evil. Though the lesser evil, it's still an evil. A similar analysis of self-defense seems plausible. The use of lethal force against a culpable aggressor seems wrongful, even if it is a lesser wrong than being killed by a culpable aggressor. This will follow trivially if self-defense can be represented as a special case of necessity. But then if all justifications involve choice of the lesser evil or wrong, they don't clear the defendant's moral ledger completely. It's not clear whether someone shopping for a defense should prefer justifications to excuses. Perhaps there is more to say about this comparative issue, but, for present purposes, I will assume that, all else being equal, justifications and excuses are equally exculpatory.

Finally, there is an important sense in which all of the defenses are animated by a concern with fair opportunity. In Chapters 3 to 5, we motivated, articulated, and defended the fair opportunity conception of responsibility and excuse. But there is a sense in which fair opportunity also animates defenses that are justifications. Lack of fair opportunity clearly explains the duress defense. Though that is often understood as an excuse, we claimed that some cases of duress might equally be conceived in terms of justification. If so, fair opportunity will explain these justifications as well. But fair opportunity also seems relevant to understanding self-defense and necessity. When I commit an offense as a lesser evil, I lack a fair opportunity to avoid the offense, and when I use self-defense to repel a culpable aggressor, he leaves me no fair opportunity to avoid harming him. In these ways, fair opportunity provides a rationale for defenses generally, and not just excuses.

9

Structural Injustice and Fair Opportunity

Predominant retributivism claims that there is a strong *pro tanto* case for punishing culpable wrongdoers. But that assumption might seem problematic when we consider the appropriate response to offenders who are the victims of social injustice in the sense that they have significantly lower life prospects and fewer social and economic opportunities than other members of their society. A society characterized by systematic structural injustice *marginalizes* some of its members. The marginalized might include groups with lower socio-economic status and prospects in which their relative lack of resources puts them at a significant competitive disadvantage with respect to members of higher socio-economic groups. Though lower socio-economic status is always a disadvantage, it is especially disadvantageous in societies with significant socio-economic inequality in which resources affect one's opportunities. The marginalized might also include out-groups whose members are the object of explicit or implicit discriminatory attitudes and treatment, because even on an otherwise level playing field members of out-groups will fare worse than their counterparts in the relevant in-groups. For instance, African Americans and Latinx Americans have significantly different economic and health prospects than their white counterparts, and it is now clear that the phenomenon of mass incarceration—from policing, to prosecution, to sentencing, to post-incarceration outcomes—has a racially disparate impact. The marginalized in a society do not benefit from the rule of law in the way that other members of their society do, which raises the question of whether we can justify punishing the marginalized in societies that experience structural injustice.

We might approach the issue of whether structural injustice compromises blame and punishment in one of two ways. First, we might focus on the state, asking if structural injustice compromises the legitimacy of the state or its authority to punish victims of structural injustice when they commit crime. Second, we might focus on the victims of injustice, asking if structural injustice makes the dispossessed less deserving of blame and punishment for their offenses. Perhaps these two approaches end up in the same place, but that's not obvious at the outset. Some writers focus primarily on the first approach. Some of these arguments are more promising than others. But a complete

Fair Opportunity and Responsibility. David O. Brink, Oxford University Press (2021). © David O. Brink.
DOI: 10.1093/oso/9780198859468.003.0009

discussion should also consider the second approach, especially the question of what the fair opportunity conception implies about the culpability of the marginalized for certain kinds of crimes. I will argue that structural injustice *selectively* compromises the state's authority to punish crimes by the marginalized that *result directly* from structural injustice and that this typically provides a *partial defense* or *mitigates*, rather than completely exculpates. This claim reflects both the moral limits of retributivism and the application of the fair opportunity conception of responsibility.

72. Sources of Structural Injustice

Structural injustice, as I understand it here, must be *systemic*. A society won't count as structurally unjust if inequalities in life prospects don't form persistent patterns and those disfavored by one policy or law are just as likely to be favored by other policies and laws. If local variations in people's life prospects even out over the long-run, the society is not structurally unjust.

Different theories of distributive justice might measure structural injustice differently insofar as they focus on different *currencies* of distributive justice— such as income, utility, well-being, primary goods, resources, capabilities, liberties, non-domination, and opportunities—and different distributive *principles*—such as maximization, equality, priority, sufficiency, and laissez-faire. A complete theory of justice has to address these and other foundational issues. Our purposes require much less philosophical infrastructure and allow us, I hope, to be reasonably philosophically ecumenical.

Opportunities are one important kind of currency affecting matters of social justice, and it is plausible that there should be *fair equality of important opportunities*. Opportunities need not be strictly equal, provided that there is fair equality of opportunity in the sense that some people's opportunities to succeed should not be so unequal as to significantly advantage some in relation to others in ways over which they have little control. Fair equality of opportunity is a comparatively ecumenical yardstick for measuring justice and injustice inasmuch as it is a norm embraced by many otherwise diverse conceptions of distributive justice. However, both *material inequality* and *discrimination* tend to compromise fair equality of opportunity in predictable ways.

Material inequality undermines fair equality of opportunity in morally arbitrary ways over time. This is easiest to see in an inter-generational case. Assume that there is initial comparative equality in Generation 1 but that over time, through a combination of hard work and luck, X1 prospers relative to Y1. Let's stipulate that X1 is entitled to her advantages. But if there are no significant restrictions on private spending or bequest, X1's children will start life at a significant material advantage relative to Y1's children. X1 can send X2 to private schools and hire tutors to help X2 prepare for college tests. X1 can ensure that X2 does not have to work a part-time job during school, which might detract from X2's academic performance. X1's choices allow X2 to attend a high school with smaller class sizes that provides AP classes, and a high percentage of X2's classmates will go to college, making X2 better prepared for admission to elite colleges or universities. X2 won't have to go into debt to attend college, and when X2 looks for internships and jobs, she can draw on X1's superior social and professional networks. X1 leaves most of her estate to X2. Now imagine that Y2 copes with social and economic deficits that mirror X2's advantages. X2 now has important advantages relative to Y2, and this makes a difference when X2 and Y2 meet in the marketplace. When they negotiate over the terms of social interaction, X2's comparative wealth allows her to hold out longer in negotiations with Y2 and so claim more favorable terms relative to Y2 than she could negotiating from a situation of equality. These are just a few of the ways in which advantages and deficits tend to be passed from one generation to the next. X2 and Y2 have inherited these advantages and deficits and are not responsible for them. But then, even if inequalities in Generation 1 are morally acceptable, inequalities in Generation 2 and subsequent generations won't be. And, of course, without significant constraints on bequest these inequalities tend to snowball over multiple generations.

Significant material inequality is problematic because of the way it adversely affects fair equality of opportunity over time.[1] It's possible to limit inequality's effect on opportunity by significant estate taxes, a progressive personal income tax, national healthcare, free quality primary, secondary, and tertiary

---

[1] This explanation of how material inequality erodes fair equality of opportunity over time owes its inspiration to Rawls's critique of laissez-faire and his defense of democratic equality. See John Rawls, *A Theory of Justice* (Cambridge, MA: Harvard University Press, 1971), §§12–13. Rawls argues that the effects of the *social lottery*, affecting the class into which one is born, are arbitrary from the moral point of view and that, hence, fair opportunity requires constraining the ways in which one may benefit from the social lottery. But, he claims, the effects of the *natural lottery*, affecting one's native talents and endowments, are equally morally arbitrary and, hence, fair opportunity constrains how one may benefit from their employment. This reasoning leads Rawls to abandon not just laissez-faire, which corrects for the social lottery in some ways, but also liberal conceptions of fair opportunity that correct for the social, but not the natural, lottery. Instead, it leads him to embrace democratic equality and its claim that fair opportunity must recognize both the natural and social lotteries as morally arbitrary and view the results of both lotteries as a common asset. If Rawls is right, fair opportunity might begin as an ecumenical constraint but proves to have robustly egalitarian implications.

education, rigorous enforcement of anti-nepotism and anti-cronyism policies, and other measures. But, without such measures, inequality compromises fair equality of opportunity, which in turns taints inequalities that are sustained and exacerbated by the lack of a level playing field. Of course, there are always exceptions—cases of individuals who, through good luck and hard work, rise above the disadvantages with which they start life. But the exceptions don't disprove the generalization or its disturbing character. It's harder for those who start at a disadvantage to succeed than it is for those who don't. This is a morally arbitrary difference that ramifies over time and that explains why those who start with advantages disproportionately succeed relative to those who do not.

Material inequality's negative impact on fair equality of opportunity need not involve discrimination. But discrimination, both explicit and implicit, also compromises fair equality of opportunity. When in-groups practice discrimination against out-groups in education, housing, school choice, employment, and social and professional networking, this denies fair equality of opportunity to members of the out-group. Discrimination can occur along many dimensions, including gender, race, ethnicity, religious affiliation, sexual orientation, and disability. All else being equal, discrimination will be worse for those at the *intersection* of multiple out-groups.

We can try to prevent these outcomes by adopting anti-discrimination laws. But such laws work better against explicit than against implicit bias. Especially if violations of anti-discrimination laws require a finding of discriminatory intent and not just differential impact, then there will be many forms of bias that elude the filter of anti-discrimination laws. Moreover, discrimination has its own inter-generational tendencies. *De jure* policies of segregation can limit housing and employment opportunities in an earlier generation, creating inequalities that have a self-perpetuating, often *de facto*, character.[2]

Those who lack fair equality of opportunity are marginalized. Social and economic inequality tends to marginalize, and explicit and implicit discrimination practiced by in-groups against out-groups also marginalizes. Moreover, we should expect to find even larger percentages of the marginalized at the *intersection* of these two groups—*members of lower socio-economic out-groups*.

Of course, we can ask the theoretical question of how significant social injustice would affect the morality of punishing the marginalized for criminal wrongdoing while remaining agnostic about whether our own society exhibits

---

[2] See, e.g., Richard Rothstein, *The Color of Law* (New York: Norton, 2017).

significant structural injustice. However, I take it to be obvious that there is significant structural injustice in the United States. Indeed, growing social and economic inequality strikes me as one of the greatest social problems we now face. There may be reasonable disagreement about just how much structural injustice there is today, but it is hard to deny that the poor and people of color tend to have fewer economic, social, and political opportunities than their white privileged counterparts. So, I think that this is not a purely academic question.

73. Mass Incarceration

When considering how structural injustice might affect the punishment of criminal offenses by marginalized members of society, we have reason to be especially concerned about injustices committed by the criminal justice system itself. This gives us reason to be especially concerned about injustices involved in *mass incarceration*. There is a growing consensus that the criminal justice system in the United States involves practices of mass incarceration that are overly punitive and in need of reform. Academics and activists have expressed these concerns over many years. The need for criminal justice reforms has become more salient recently, as have public demands for reform. Unfortunately, to date, reforms are comparatively few and modest. Reformers must play a long game.

Part of mass incarceration involves trial and sentencing protocols that are overly punitive in apparently non-discriminatory ways. Mass incarceration has many elements, including these:

- The adoption of steep mandatory minimum sentences for many crimes;
- The adoption of habitual offender statutes, such as three-strikes laws, that sentence repeat offenders to extremely long sentences, including life imprisonment without the possibility of parole, often for comparatively minor offenses;
- The trend to try juveniles in adult criminal court, which leads to longer and harsher sentences than those resulting from juvenile court; and
- Various post-incarceration penalties, including burdensome parole requirements, requirements to disclose convictions to potential employers, loss of public assistance (e.g. food stamps and housing assistance), and political disenfranchisement.

Earlier, we noted that these aspects of mass incarceration involve disproportionate punishment and so violate retributive essentials (§46). We will discuss
some of these worries more fully in Chapters 12 and 15.

But a significant part of the problem with mass incarceration involves its
racially disparate impact on the lives of people of color, especially African-
American and Latinx men. Mass incarceration involves a mix of conscious and
unconscious racial discrimination. This trend has been documented and
discussed by various sociologists and criminologists.[3] My summary draws on
the work of these scholars, especially Michelle Alexander, James Forman Jr.,
and Tommie Shelby.

Historically, the United States was not an outlier on the number of citizens
incarcerated and the length of their sentences. This began to change in the
mid-1970s in response to the war on drugs and the political decision to get
tough on crime. Our incarceration rates went from 100 to 700 persons per
100,000 people. African Americans make up 13 percent of the general population but, by some estimates, 50 percent of the prison population. In 2008, the
incarceration rate among black males was 3161 per 100K, which was 6.5 times
the rate for white males.[4] Though the war on drugs was the single biggest
contributor to mass incarceration and to disparate racial incarceration rates,
studies show that white and majority populations use and sell drugs at
approximately the same rates.[5] Despite comparable drug usage and sales
among the races, increases in incarceration rates for drug crimes differed
markedly for different racial groups between 1983 and 2000: the number of
white drug-related imprisonment increased eightfold; the number of Latinx
drug-related imprisonment increased 22 times; and the number of African-
American drug-related imprisonment increased 26 times.

How do racially disproportionate outcomes come about? In broad outline,
there are two kinds of factors to discuss. First, racially disproportionate
incarceration outcomes occur because of inequalities in social capital and
opportunities. We will discuss the significance of these factors later. Second,
discrimination occurs or is amplified at various points within the criminal

---

[3] See, e.g., Glenn Loury, *The Anatomy of Racial Inequality* (Cambridge, MA: Harvard University
Press, 2003); David Cole, "Turning the Corner on Mass Incarceration?" *Ohio State Journal of Criminal
Law* 9 (2011): 27–51; Alexander, *The New Jim Crow*; James Forman, Jr., "Racial Critiques of Mass
Incarceration: Beyond the New Jim Crow" *New York University Law Review* 87 (2012): 101–46 and
Locking Up Our Own: Crime and Punishment in Black America (New York: Farrar, Straus, and Giroux,
2017); and Tommie Shelby, *Dark Ghettos: Injustice, Dissent, and Reform* (Cambridge, MA: Harvard
University Press, 2016).
[4] See Cole, "Turning the Corner on Mass Incarceration?" p. 28.
[5] See Alexander, *The New Jim Crow*, pp. 7, 97.

justice process—from arrest, to prosecution, to sentencing, to post-imprisonment penalties.

Arrest. First, there are financial incentives for the police to make arrests in terms of resource allocation and confiscated property. Second, there are efficiencies to making arrests in urban, rather than more dispersed suburban, environments. Third, there are fewer political consequences to making arrests in poor urban neighborhoods, rather than wealthier suburban neighborhoods. Fourth, police have large discretion to stop and search people, provided they get consent, but they exercise this discretion in racially disparate ways. For instance, studies in New Jersey and Maryland show that despite comparatively low numbers of minority motorists (15 percent and 21 percent respectively) they were a much larger percentage of drivers stopped and searched in "random" stops (77 percent and 80 percent respectively). Fifth, there is some reason to think that implicit biases influence conduct and especially actors in situations that are not regulated and involve significant decision-making discretion. There is considerable discretion in the decision to arrest. For instance, an important meta-analysis found that non-white suspects were 30 percent more likely to be arrested than white suspects.[6] Finally, there is no effective way to challenge racially discriminatory law enforcement, because, under current law, courts require proof of discriminatory *intent*, and not just discriminatory impact.[7] These ways in which policing practices contribute to the discriminatory impact of mass incarceration are distinct from concerns about the unnecessary and disproportionate use of force, sometimes lethal force, by the police, especially against people of color, that have been the subject of recent protests.[8]

Prosecution. First, prosecutors have considerable discretion about which cases to prosecute, and proving discriminatory exercise of this discretion requires proof of intent to discriminate. Second, as we just noted, implicit biases can influence conduct, especially actors who are accorded significant decision-making discretion, as prosecutors are. Third, prosecutors can often *stack charges*, multiplying the number of charges that a single crime involves,

---

[6] Tammy Kochel, David Wilson, and Stephen Mastrofski, "Effect of Suspect Race on Officer's Arrest Decisions," *Criminology* 49 (2011): 473–512.

[7] *City of Los Angeles v. Lyons* 461 U.S. 95 (1983).

[8] I have in mind especially Black Lives Matter and related protests in Ferguson Missouri in 2014 and in response to the police killing of George Floyd in Minneapolis in 2020. Here, I am focusing on mass incarceration and its discriminatory impact, not police brutality. But unnecessary and disproportionate use of force by police is a serious criminal justice concern and should be part of a larger set of reforms. Moreover, the racially disparate character of both mass incarceration and police brutality likely has common causes and contributing factors.

thus magnifying the costs of conviction and increasing the incentives to settle for a plea deal that involves felony conviction. Fourth, poor defendants often have inadequate or over-worked legal counsel to apprise them of the consequences of plea deals and litigate their cases effectively, often resulting in clients accepting plea deals without fully realizing the consequences of felony pleas. Finally, the need to provide childcare or make provisions for a family often induce the accused to accept plea deals that will get them out of prison and back with their family sooner, despite the costs of a felony plea deal. In this connection, courts have considerable discretion in setting bail. But bail can be difficult to meet, especially for indigent defendants with jobs and families to protect, further incentivizing poor defendants to accept plea deals that they might otherwise not. For this reason, cash bail has unjust differential impact on the rich and poor. The criminal law needs to balance public safety and the presumption of innocence. It can do so without resort to cash bail, employing pre-trial detention or electronic monitoring in cases of violent offenders or offenders who pose a serious flight risk, especially where there is strong *prima facie* evidence of guilt.[9]

Sentencing. First, as we have seen, the sentences for all kinds of convictions have increased through mandatory minima, three strikes laws, etc. But given the disproportionate numbers of minority convictions, harsh sentencing requirements magnify the percentage of the prison population that is minority. Second, insofar as sentencing guidelines often give discretion to judges and juries, there are additional worries about the operation of implicit bias in discretionary sentencing, as is reflected in the racially disparate impact of death penalty sentences.

Post-incarceration. As we noted, considerable invisible sanctions follow former felons. First, these include burdensome parole requirements, which can be easy to violate and offer zero tolerance even for innocent violations. Second, felons are under requirements to disclose convictions to potential employers. Though such requirements make sense in the case of some felonies and some potential jobs, where the nature of the felony presents a disqualification for the particular job description, they lead to an unjustified burden on employment prospects in many cases. Third, felons lose rights to important

---

[9] In a potentially welcome development, in August 2018 California became the first state to abolish cash bail, reserving the right to use pre-trial detention or electronic monitoring for defendants who pose a demonstrable danger, to themselves or others, or flight risk. See "California is the First State to Scrap Cash Bail" *The New York Times* Aug. 28, 2018. For this to be a progressive development, procedures must be put in place to minimize the influence of discriminatory animus in the use of pre-trial detention.

forms of public assistance, including food stamps and housing assistance. The lack of employment and housing force many former felons into homelessness, which can breed desperation and further criminal activity. Finally, felons are often barred from voting and jury service, effectively disenfranchising them. For instance, the vast majority of states deny felons the right to vote while incarcerated, and most states deny paroled and former felons the right to vote for periods ranging from several years to a lifetime. This sort of disenfranchisement violates a norm of democratic legitimacy that the governed should have a say about the way in which they are governed.

Mass incarceration is sometimes analogized to the Jim Crow era. One might agree that mass incarceration has important racially discriminatory aspects while recognizing important disanalogies between mass incarceration and Jim Crow.[10] First, Jim Crow denied equal rights and opportunities to African Americans just in virtue of their race, whereas mass incarceration disproportionately affects people of color within the larger class of criminal offenders. Insofar as this is true, mass incarceration involves discriminatory sub-classification within the class of criminal offenders, rather than the discriminatory treatment of African Americans as such. Second, much of the literature on mass incarceration adopts a myopic focus on the war on drugs, suggesting that most incarceration is for non-violent crime. Drug-related offenses constitute one-quarter of the prison population, whereas violent offenders constitute one-half of the prison population.[11] Since a significant proportion of drug-related offenses involve violent crime, the ratio of violent to non-violent crime is even higher than the ratio of violent crime to drug-related offenses. Whereas there are significant disparities in arrest and sentencing along racial lines in drug offenses, a disproportionate amount of violent crime is committed by African Americans, typically against other African Americans.[12] Third, though incarceration rates for African-American males are disproportionately high, incarceration rates for whites and Latinx are significant—according to some studies, one-third of prison inmates are white and 20 percent are Latinx. If so, almost 60 percent of the

[10] Here, my discussion draws on Forman, "Racial Critiques of Mass Incarceration: Beyond the New Jim Crow" and *Locking Up Our Own*.

[11] Only in federal prisons are drug offenders a majority (52 percent), but federal prisons house fewer inmates, and federal criminal law focuses primarily on drug and immigration offenses for obvious reasons.

[12] The black arrest rate for murder is seven to eight times higher than it is for whites, and the black arrest rate for robbery is ten times higher than for whites. See Forman, "Racial Critiques of Mass Incarceration," pp. 124–25, citing Henry Ruth and Kevin Reitz, *The Challenge of Crime: Rethinking our Response* (Cambridge, MA: Harvard University Press, 2003), p. 75.

prison population is *not* African-American.[13] The common denominator for all incarcerated groups is *socio-economic* hardship and lack of fair equality of economic opportunity. An exclusive focus on discrimination against African Americans fails to make common cause with other affected groups in linking criminal justice issues with social and economic inequality. Finally, though middle-class and upper-class African Americans can be affected by policing that involves racial profiling, for the most part these groups are not subject to mass incarceration and are as supportive of accountability and incarceration as their white counterparts, as evidenced by policing and crime control policies in Washington, DC, where African Americans form a political majority.[14]

Whether or not we accept the Jim Crow analogy, we can agree that there is a problem of mass incarceration involving prison sentences that are too long; overcrowded and brutal prisons that encourage recidivism rather than serving as schools for the social sentiments; and post-incarceration forms of punishment that deprive former felons of social and political opportunities and privileges. Mass incarceration is especially troublesome insofar as it is directed at non-violent first-time offenders and involves discriminatory policing and sentencing. We need to distinguish sharply between violent and non-violent crime, and we should not whitewash violent crime, many of whose victims are African Americans. The target of our most vigorous criminal justice reforms should be non-violent offenders and recognizing and changing the conditions of socio-economic inequality that contribute to such crimes. Though we should recognize and combat the racially discriminatory aspects of current policing and sentencing practices, we should recognize that these issues do not affect African Americans exclusively and do our best to make the coalition for criminal justice reform inclusive.

74. Structural Injustice and Punishment

Structural injustice is a social evil that ought to be eliminated or at least minimized. This requires legal and political changes of various sorts designed to reduce social and economic inequality, to insulate fair opportunity from the effects of inequality, to combat discrimination, and to reform criminal justice in a way that makes it less punitive and less discriminatory. If we could eliminate structural injustice and engage in prison reform, predominant

---

[13] Forman, "Racial Critiques of Mass Incarceration," pp. 136–38.
[14] For discussion, see Forman, *Locking Up Our Own*.

retributivism would be a reasonable foundation for allocating just deserts. However, we have a long way to go to remove structural injustice. We need to ask how—in the meantime—facts about structural injustice affect the state's authority to punish the marginalized for their offenses and the culpability of the marginalized. In effect, this is a question of *transitional justice*, which belongs to *non-ideal theory*. Though transitional, it is not a temporary problem. This kind of non-ideal theory is a robust part of the context of criminal law in the United States and, to a lesser extent, other common law countries that contain significant social and economic inequality and discrimination.

To focus discussion, consider some crimes that the marginalized commit, such as drug-trafficking and prostitution. Though some drug trafficking and prostitution crimes involve the use of violence, many do not. Let's focus on non-violent versions of these crimes initially. Two issues stand out. First, when non-violent, these crimes may not involve significant harm to others. Much of the violence there is in the drug trade and prostitution is arguably the *result* of criminalization. This was true of Prohibition. Prohibition provided a weak deterrent for alcohol consumption, encouraged binge drinking, and gave rise to black markets, which not only increased the costs of alcohol but also led to organized crime, corruption, and violence. Prohibition was the wrong way to regulate the undesirable effects of alcohol consumption. Perhaps similar verdicts are appropriate about the criminalization of drugs and prostitution. If so, non-violent drug and prostitution crimes may be morally less problematic than other crimes. Second, criminalization of these activities creates underground economies or black markets that provide alternate forms of economic activity, especially to members of marginalized groups in certain regions. Structural injustice—in particular, the way it compromises fair equality of opportunity—often creates incentives for the marginalized to participate in underground economies as a way to survive economically in an environment of limited opportunities.

Though we shouldn't restrict our inquiry to blame and punishment for non-violent drug trafficking and prostitution committed by the marginalized, this will prove to be an important focus, because this will be where the retributive case for blame and punishment is weakest.

75. The Complicity Argument

Several writers who have claimed that structural injustice compromises punishment of marginalized offenders have appealed to claims about *complicity* to ground this claim.[15] Insofar as governmental action or inaction brings about the very social conditions that compromise fair equality of opportunity and incentivize participation in black markets, the state bears some responsibility for criminal conduct by the marginalized and so is complicit in their wrongdoing. If the state is complicit in criminal misconduct, it may lack authority to punish that wrongdoing.

However, state complicity on its own does not show that the defendant is not blameworthy or that the state lacks the authority to punish. For that, we need an independent argument that the marginalized are justified or excused. Complicity does not in general defeat blameworthiness. B's complicity in A's crime does not in general diminish A's culpability. We can't infer from the fact that the state is culpable that the marginalized are not. Culpability is not a zero-sum affair. For instance, we don't halve the normal sentence for murder when two conspire to commit murder; instead, we punish them each fully, thereby doubling the total sentence. We need a separate argument for thinking that state culpability diminishes the culpability of the marginalized.

One suggestion that has been made is that the state's complicity in structural injustice shows that it lacks *standing* to blame and punish the crimes of the marginalized. Earlier, we noted that standing is an aspect of the ethics of blame and, by extension, the ethics of punishment (§39). Even if someone is blameworthy, others may lack the standing to blame them. A common illustration of this is *hypocrisy*. Hypocrites lack the standing to blame others for sins of which they themselves are guilty. For instance, President Trump lacked standing to blame Al Franken for sexual misconduct, because he (Trump) is a serial harasser. Indeed, we might think that complicity is like hypocrisy insofar as it implies that the state shares responsibility for the very offense that it seeks to condemn and punish.

However, this use of complicity to criticize the state's standing to condemn and punish wrongdoing by the marginalized is non-exculpatory. Lack of standing to blame does not cancel blameworthiness. A hypocrite might lack the standing to blame, though the sinner remains blameworthy and can be legitimately blamed by others. Similarly, the state might lack standing to condemn crime in which it is complicit, though the marginalized remain blameworthy and can be legitimately blamed by others. Moreover, it's not clear that lack of standing is an absolute bar to blaming. Lack of standing

[15] See, e.g., Duff, *Punishment, Communication, and Community*, pp. 184–88; Victor Tadros, "Poverty and Criminal Responsibility" *The Journal of Value Inquiry* 43 (2009): 391–413; Gary Watson, "A Moral Predicament in the Criminal Law" *Inquiry* 58 (2015): 168–88; and Shelby, *Dark Ghettos*, pp. 244–48.

arguably makes it *pro tanto* wrong to blame. But one can imagine circumstances in which this *pro tanto* case against blame is overcome. If there is a serious wrong for which a wrongdoer is fully culpable, and there is no one free from sin to blame him, it might be permissible for a fellow sinner to blame the target, especially if in so doing the blamer acknowledges that she is not free from sin. In such cases, it might be better for blame to come from a remorseful and reformed sinner than to forego blame altogether. This might apply to the case in which the state is complicit in the wrongs of the marginalized, because the state is the only party authorized to punish.

I do not mean to deny the significance of complicity. If the state is complicit in structural injustice and structural injustice contributes to some criminal activity by the marginalized, this makes the state culpable and funds calls for reform. But the state's culpability does not show that marginalized offenders aren't also culpable and deserving of punishment. The more fundamental question, which complicity does not address, is whether the offenses of the marginalized are blameworthy.

76. The Moral Limits of Retributivism

As part of that inquiry, we would do well to remember the moral limits of retributivism and ask if structural injustice compromises the moral condition on retributivist essentials. Recall the way in which the retributivist case for punishing criminal offenders depends on the background justice of the legal system being enforced (§43). In discussing retributivism, we saw the need to distinguish the claims of moral and legal retributivism. Moral retributivism says that blame and punishment are fitting responses to culpable moral wrongdoing. This is plausible insofar as persons are moral agents who are accountable for their conduct; respecting persons means that it is *pro tanto* fitting that they be blamed and punished for wrongdoing for which they are responsible and that they merit or deserve blame and punishment. Legal retributivism says that blame and punishment are fitting responses to culpable legal wrongdoing. However, it is less clear that culpable legal wrongdoing always deserves blame and punishment if only because legal norms and moral norms are distinct and legal wrongdoing is not necessarily moral wrongdoing. But where legal wrongdoing is not morally wrong, it is less clear that blame and punishment are deserved, even *pro tanto*.

One might conclude that there is a *pro tanto* case for punishing legal wrongdoing only when legal wrongdoing is also moral wrongdoing. But one might suppose that there can be a *pro tanto* case for punishing legal wrong-doing even in cases in which the legal norms being transgressed are morally problematic provided that the moral flaws in the law are fairly minor, do not occur too often, and do not have systematically disparate impact on citizens. On this view, the duty to obey the law is part of a *package deal*, arising from a sufficiently reasonably just social compact. Basic provisions of the criminal law against murder, rape, assault, theft, and trespass are norms the general observance of which is mutually beneficial. Culpable wrongdoers are those who free-ride, enjoying the benefits of others' compliance with these norms without incurring the costs of doing their own part to maintain the system from which they benefit. But free-riding on mutually beneficial social practices is *unfair*. The culpable wrongdoer claims more than his fair share, and fairness demands that he be punished according to the terms announced in advance as the penalty for noncompliance. Recognizing the wrongdoer as a person, who is morally accountable, supports punishing him in accordance with the demands of fairness.

This appeal to fairness to anchor desert has an important *scope limitation*—it only applies to social practices that are sufficiently just and mutually beneficial. If the social scheme does not meet this condition, then noncompliance may not be unfair. In particular, if one lives in a sufficiently unjust regime in which the benefits and burdens of social cooperation are not distributed fairly, then noncompliance with the scheme's norms—legal wrongdoing—need not be morally wrong and, hence, blame and punishment may not be deserved. Structural injustice raises the question of whether the moral condition on retributivist essentials is met.

The answer to this question is complicated. While conceding that our society tolerates social and economic inequalities that compromise fair equality of opportunity, someone might claim that these are social and economic inequalities, not inequalities in the rule of law. We might think that the criminal law norms, the general observance of which is mutually beneficial, do apply equally. To that extent, we might wonder if social and economic inequality compromises the enforcement of criminal law norms.

However, this response to the worry about structural injustice is problematic. First, the criminal law does reinforce various social and economic inequalities insofar as it criminalizes noncompliance with tax laws that entrench these inequalities and criminalizes economic participation in black markets that provide alternative economic opportunities to the marginalized. In effect, it's difficult to separate out social and economic protections on the one hand, and criminal law protections on the other. Second, our discussion of mass incarceration and its racially disparate impact suggests that it's simply not true that criminal law norms are enforced in equitable and racially neutral ways. Policing, prosecution, sentencing, and post-sentencing protocols disproportionately target the poor and people of color.

Having conceded that there are significant injustices in the provision of criminal justice goods and other social and economic opportunities and prospects, it still seems true that everyone benefits from the provision and enforcement of criminal law norms—it's just that they don't benefit equally. Though the marginalized would be better off in a criminal justice system the burdens of which were distributed more equitably, it seems unlikely that they would be better off in the state of nature without the protection of the criminal law. The fact that the marginalized benefit, but unequally, from the rule of law suggests a *mixed verdict* on whether the moral conditions for retributivist essentials are satisfied in unjust regimes. This mixed verdict seems to *degrade but not eliminate* the fairness demands for punishing the marginalized. This might support recognizing a partial justification or excuse for the crimes of the marginalized or providing mitigation for their crimes at sentencing, a possibility we'll explore further in a moment.

Moreover, it's important to recognize the *restricted scope* of such potential exceptions to the state's authority to punish the marginalized. Structural injustice *selectively* compromises the state's authority to punish crimes by the marginalized that *result directly* from structural injustice. Injustice may mitigate non-violent crimes, such as black marketeering, fraud, and theft, that are directly responsive to inequality in opportunities, but it does nothing to mitigate crimes against persons, such as murder, rape, or assault. Shelby makes a related point when he distinguishes between *civic obligations* to other members of a cooperative scheme (e.g. duties to pay taxes and honor contractual commitments) and *natural duties* one owes to other human beings as such (e.g. duties not to kill or harm others).[16] He suggests that structural injustice might compromise civic obligations while leaving natural duties intact. This claim explains his later suggestion that even an unjust state retains the authority to enforce criminal laws that target crimes *mala in se*.[17] Here, he alludes to the criminal law distinction between crimes *mala in se*—wrong in themselves—and *mala prohibita*—wrong because they are prohibited. As we noted above (§42), crimes *mala in se* are typically morally more serious than crimes *mala prohibita*, though the distinction is supposed to turn on whether the crimes concern conduct that is wrong itself (e.g. murder, rape, assault,

---

[16]   Shelby, *Dark Ghettos*, p. 213.   [17]   Shelby, *Dark Ghettos*, p. 234.

theft), rather than wrong because it is prohibited (e.g. drug use, prostitution, traffic offenses, loitering). In recognizing an unjust state's duty to enforce laws against crimes *mala in se*, he may mean to suggest that though an unjust state loses the authority to enforce drug laws and other petty crimes, it retains the right to enforce laws against more serious crimes against persons and property that have the status of natural duties. If so, structural injustice mitigates the case for state punishment of the marginalized only when there is a suitable *nexus* between the injustice and the crime committed.

77. Injustice and Fair Opportunity

So far, our focus has mostly been on the state's authority to punish in conditions of structural injustice. But we might also focus on the desert and culpability of the marginalized in structurally unjust systems. Given the broadly retributive aspects of the criminal law, we should ask to what extent the marginalized are inclusively culpable for their offenses and whether they have the basis for any kind of affirmative defense. We have been focusing, for the most part, on non-violent crimes by the marginalized involving participation in underground economies, such as drug use or sale and prostitution, fraud, and theft. Might such offenses be either justified or excused? Neither a self-defense justification nor an incompetence excuse seems especially relevant to these offenses, at least not to paradigmatic cases. The most relevant defenses seem to be necessity and duress.

Does structural injustice provide the basis for a necessity or duress defense for offenses by the marginalized? Both necessity and duress are defenses based on hard choice and a lack of fair opportunity, and structural injustice may seem to create hard choices for the marginalized and impair their fair opportunity to avoid wrongdoing by making the paths to success that are available to their privileged counterparts less accessible for them. In assessing these claims, there are several questions we might distinguish. First, we might ask whether structural injustice raises questions of necessity or duress. Second, we might ask whether the appropriate defense would constitute a justification or an excuse. Third, however these questions are answered, we need to ask whether the conditions for the defense are satisfied or at least approximated. Let's address these questions in this order.

Does structural injustice sound more in justification or duress? Consider someone who engages in underground economies because of her limited opportunities, who steals food to feed her starving family, or who practices fraud in order to get medical attention for her sick child. In these cases, the marginalized offender seems to be responding to hard choice. That hard choice does not seem to be the product of the wrongful interference by another agent, as in a paradigmatic case of duress. Should we look to necessity instead? However, the marginalized offender in such cases may not seem to be responding to necessity either, inasmuch as the source of the hard choice does not seem to be natural circumstances, such as a natural disaster. We can still make out a case of duress, because even if the hard choice is not produced by a proximate threat from another individual, it is the result of *collective* action and inaction in the form of tax, education, healthcare, and criminal justice policies. If so, it's not clear why we couldn't try to frame a defense in terms of duress. That doesn't mean that it couldn't also be framed in terms of necessity, provided we accept the Model Penal Code conception of necessity, which allows the source of hard choice to be either natural or man-made. Moreover, if we step back from the details of the doctrines of necessity and duress in the common law and Model Penal Code, we can see that both involve a defense for agents who engage in an offense only because of a hard choice they face, for which they are not responsible. But then at least some offenses that the marginalized commit because of their limited opportunities can appeal to the principle that underlies necessity and duress defenses, whether or not they provide a perfect fit with either of those doctrines.

Insofar as some offenses committed in circumstances of structural injustice can appeal to principles ingredient in necessity and duress, should this be regarded as involving justification or excuse? That's a difficult question to answer, because, as we saw, though necessity is often regarded as a justification and duress is often regarded as an excuse, the line between justification and excuse here is obscure (§§68–69). There's a case for treating some cases of necessity and perhaps some cases of duress as justifications, which deny wrongdoing, and for treating other cases of necessity and duress as excuses, which deny responsibility or broad culpability. Whether either defense justifies or excuses may depend on whether the offense involves significant harm or wrong to others. Where the offense involves significant harm or wrong, the defense sounds more in excuse. Where this is not true, the defense may sound in justification. If so, then we'd need to determine whether the offenses of the marginalized involve significant harm or violations of rights to determine if the defense took the form of a justification or an excuse. If there is a necessity/duress defense for non-violent drug consumption or trafficking or prostitution, then that might be best understood as a justification, whether full or partial. If there is a necessity/duress defense for theft or fraud, then that might be best understood as an excuse, whether full or partial.

However, it's not clear how important it is to decide whether the defense, if any, sounds in justification or in excuse. When successful, both defenses justify acquittal. Indeed, as we saw, perhaps particular cases sound in *both* justification and excuse. That would overdetermine acquittal, but it's not clear why that need be problematic.

However we resolve these taxonomical issues, there remains the important substantive question about how strong these defenses are. On this issue, a mixed verdict seems appropriate. Central to common law conceptions of both necessity and duress is that the hard choice that the agent faces forces her hand to commit the offense because there is no legal alternative to violating the law in order to avoid the serious hardship for which she is not responsible. The absence of legal alternatives is also part of necessity doctrine under the Model Penal Code. It is arguably implicit in the Model Penal Code conception of duress, which requires that the threat be one that no reasonable person would resist, because a reasonable person presumably prefers legal to illegal alternatives to threats. This is where difficulty occurs in treating structural injustice as a complete defense, because the pressures to commit wrongdoing and the absence of viable alternatives typically do not foreclose all legal alternatives to wrongdoing. One can avoid peer pressure to join gangs and apply oneself diligently to one's studies in order to attend college and seek a professional vocation, even though few of one's peers do. One can avoid wrongdoing, but it often requires ignoring peer pressure and persevering on a long and difficult path with an uncertain promise of possible future reward, often without the support of family or friends. If necessity and duress defenses require the complete absence of legal alternatives to wrongdoing, then structural injustice will typically not be an affirmative defense that denies inclusive culpability.

However, we might want to deny that defenses need to be bivalent, that is, all or nothing. Though American criminal law tends to be bivalent at the guilt phase of a trial, the factors that tend to justify or excuse—necessity, duress, and incompetence—seem to be scalar. For instance, normative competence comes in degrees, with the result that impaired competence should also come in degrees, supporting the idea of partial excuse or mitigation when the impairment is significant but not complete. A similar idea seems to apply to the situational aspects of hard choice that underlie necessity and duress. Situational control also seems to be a scalar phenomenon, depending on the number and availability of alternatives to wrongdoing. When there is literally no alternative to wrongdoing, one completely lacks situational control. But

A might have less situational control than B if A has fewer viable alternatives to wrongdoing than B, with the result that it is harder for A to avoid wrongdoing than B. If we accept that situational control is scalar, then we might well conclude that structural injustice sometimes funds a partial defense or mitigation for wrongdoing insofar as it reduces the availability and feasibility of alternatives to wrongdoing for members of marginalized groups. If defenses are all or nothing and require complete incapacity or complete absence of permissible alternatives, then structural injustice will not excuse, but it might fund mitigation at sentencing, depending on the degree of difficulty of avoiding wrongdoing. If defenses can be scalar and partial, then structural injustice might in some circumstances fund a partial defense, again depending on the degree of difficulty of avoiding wrongdoing.

It bears repeating that if injustice is to provide partial defense or mitigation for wrongdoing, there must be the right nexus between the crime and the diminished opportunities. Economic hardship and reduced socio-economic opportunities do not fund a partial defense for crimes, such as murder or spousal abuse, that are not directly related to these limited opportunities.[18] By contrast, non-violent drug trafficking, prostitution, and fraud might, in the right circumstances, be more rational responses to the significantly reduced economic opportunity that the marginalized face. If so, this might fund a partial defense or mitigation for crimes that are a direct response to structural injustice.

Additionally, we can and should acknowledge the role of structural injustice in incentivizing certain kinds of crimes by reforming the *content* and *manner* of punishment. If certain crimes are understandable responses to reduced socio-economic opportunities, then this provides strong reason to make punishment incorporate educational and vocational opportunities and to ensure that punishment does not create new post-incarceration disabilities in public assistance, employment, and voting rights. There are good reasons to undertake these penal reforms anyway, but there is special reason to do so in the case of crimes that are directly responsive to structural injustice.

---

[18] This is why I couldn't agree with those students in my Philosophy of Law class in 1995 who responded to O.J. Simpson's acquittal in the face of overwhelming evidence of his guilt by saying, in effect, that racial oppression either justified or excused his killing his ex-wife Nicole Simpson and her friend Ron Goldman.

10

Situationism and Fair Opportunity

We tend to view ourselves and other normal, competent adult agents as having comparatively stable characters and as being responsible for our choices and their foreseeable consequences. We may not always behave consistently, if only because we experience occasional weakness of will, and our characters are not fixed but can and do change over time. Nonetheless, we think of ourselves as having relatively settled character traits that shape much of our behavior. Moreover, we assume that acting from character is compatible with being responsible for our actions. As long as our character has not been deformed in ways that deprive us of competence to recognize and respond to reasons, we assume that we are responsible both when we act within character and when we succumb to weakness of the will. Competent agents are responsible for their conduct, except in unusual circumstances in which they act under extreme duress, for instance, as the result of coercion.

The situationist literature in psychology may seem to challenge these assumptions about character and responsibility. Situationism claims that conduct is not determined by character and also reflects the operation of underappreciated aspects of the agent's situation or environment. For instance, several situationist studies suggest that our willingness to engage in compassionate behavior toward those perceived to be in need is determined to a very surprising extent by modest contextual factors influencing our mood. Context and situational factors, as well as character, explain behavior. Situationist studies in which behavior seems better explained by contextual than by characterological factors can be both surprising and unsettling. They may suggest that we don't understand ourselves and our motivations very well, and they may raise questions about our competence and responsibility for our conduct.

Recently, some philosophers have embraced situationist findings and drawn revisionary philosophical conclusions, expressing skepticism about the existence of stable character traits, the prospects for virtue ethics, and ordinary assumptions about moral responsibility.[1] John Doris has developed these

---

[1] See John Doris, *Lack of Character* (New York: Cambridge University Press, 2002); Gilbert Harman, "Moral Philosophy Meets Social Psychology: Virtue Ethics and the Fundamental

Fair Opportunity and Responsibility. David O. Brink, Oxford University Press (2021). © David O. Brink.
DOI: 10.1093/oso/9780198859468.003.0010

arguments about the revisionary implications of situationism for ethical theory and moral responsibility further than others.[2] In *Lack of Character* Doris summarizes situationist findings and argues that ordinary assumptions about character and its explanatory significance must be abandoned. He argues that this undermines any conception of virtue ethics that attaches moral significance to character and suggests that situationism challenges familiar conceptions of moral responsibility. Situationism raises quite general questions about responsibility. But it also raises questions about responsibility and excuse in particular circumstances in which agents engage in misconduct as the result of situation-specific environmental stress and social pressure. One example of this kind of case is wartime misconduct. In "From My Lai to Abu Ghraib: The Moral Psychology of Atrocity" Doris and Dominic Murphy appeal to situationist ideas to motivate a wide-ranging excuse for wrongdoing during wartime, significantly limiting the scope of moral responsibility.[3]

We need to assess whether and, if so, in what ways situationism should revise our assumptions about moral responsibility. Situationism is relevant to moral responsibility and may lead to some revisions in our assumptions about responsibility, especially in wartime. However, situationism's implications for responsibility are not as revisionary as these more radical claims suggest. The fair opportunity conception can take situationism on board without capsizing the boat.[4]

78. Situationism

The situationist literature contains a variety of experiments that seem to show that personality traits explain less behavior than we might have thought and that situational factors, sometimes apparently inconsequential ones, explain

---

Attribution Error" *Proceedings of the Aristotelian Society* 99 (1999): 315–31; and Peter Vranas, "The Indeterminacy Paradox: Character Evaluations and Human Psychology" *Noûs* 39 (2005): 1–42. For an earlier and less revisionary philosophical discussion of situationist findings, see Owen Flanagan, *Varieties of Moral Personality* (Cambridge, MA: Harvard University Press, 1991).

[2] Doris has developed the arguments that interest me the furthest, and so I will focus on his discussion. Much of my discussion of Doris applies, I think, to Harman. Vranas's discussion is narrower and in some ways more circumspect.

[3] Doris and Murphy, "From My Lai to Abu Ghraib."

[4] In this way, my response to Doris's situationist arguments differs from the response offered in Dana Nelkin, "Freedom, Responsibility, and the Challenge of Situationism" *Midwest Studies in Philosophy* 29 (2005): 181–206. Nelkin contrasts two ways of responding to the situationist challenge to responsibility—one is to measure the significance of situationist findings against a particular conception of responsibility, while another is to ask, prior to the adoption of a particular conception of responsibility, why situationist findings might seem to threaten responsibility and then to see if those worries are well founded. Whereas Nelkin pursues the second strategy, I pursue the first.

more behavior than is often supposed. This has led some psychologists to identify the so-called *Fundamental Attribution Error*, which Lee Ross and Richard Nisbett characterize as involving:

> People's inflated belief in the importance of personality traits and disposi-
> tions, together with their failure to recognize the importance of situational
> factors in affecting behavior.[5]

A series of situationist studies support the Fundamental Attribution Error. Many of these studies share general features. They examine character traits, such as compassion, that are assumed to be fairly common and widespread. They place subjects in situations that would seem likely to elicit the corres- ponding behavior, and they study ways in which apparently modest situational or contextual factors affect the behavior of subjects, inducing them to behave in unexpected ways. Here are a few landmark studies.

Group Effects. Solomon Asch performed experiments to test whether the tacit desire for conformity with one's peers would induce subjects to report obviously erroneous answers to perceptual questions.[6] In the Asch paradigm, a real subject was placed in a group with confederates of the experimenter and they were asked questions about the comparative lengths of various lines. The confederates answered first and gave the same answers as each other. After giving a few correct answers, the confederates began giving obviously wrong answers. In a control group, in which there was no pressure to conform, only one subject in 35 ever gave an incorrect answer. However, in cases in which confederates gave the wrong answer first, subjects gave incorrect answers 32 percent of the time. In fact, 75 percent of subjects gave an incorrect answer to at least one question in these circumstances.

Compassionate Behavior. Several studies have shown compassionate behav- ior to be correlated with modest situational factors. Alice Isen and Paula Levin performed an experiment in which they tested the helping behavior of subjects who had just made a telephone call in a public phone booth.[7] Some subjects found a dime that had been planted in the change slot by the experimenters; for other subjects, no dime was left. All subjects encountered a confederate of

[5] Lee Ross and Richard Nisbett, *The Person and the Situation* (Philadelphia, PA: Temple University Press, 1991), p. 4.

[6] Solomon Asch, "Effects of Group Pressures on the Modification and Distortion of Judgment" in *Groups, Leadership, and Men*, ed. H. Guetzkow (Pittsburgh, PA: Carnegie Press, 1951).

[7] Alice Isen and Paula Levin, "Effect of Feeling Good on Helping" *Journal of Personality and Social Psychology* 21 (1972): 384–88.

the experimenter while leaving the phone booth who dropped a folder full of papers, creating an opportunity for the subject to provide assistance. Only one in 24 subjects who did not find a dime helped; 16 of 18 who did find a dime helped. Jon Darley and Daniel Batson performed an experiment involving seminary students who had been invited to prepare and deliver a talk on either the parable of the Good Samaritan or possible employment opportunities for seminary students.[8] En route to the talk, the seminary students encountered a confederate of the experimenter slumped in a doorway and in apparent need of medical attention. Despite the subject of their talks, the best predictor of whether subjects would stop and help was whether they had been told they should hurry to get to their talk. Subjects told they were running ahead of time engaged in helping behavior 63 percent of the time; subjects told they were on time engaged in helping behavior 45 percent of the time; and subjects told they were running late helped only 10 percent of the time.

Authority. Among the most famous of situationist experiments is a series of experiments performed by Stanley Milgram in which subjects engage in apparently harmful behavior in response to non-coercive instructions from the experimenter.[9] Subjects were volunteers in an experiment ostensibly about memory and learning. An experimenter asked each subject to participate in an experiment with another person who was in fact a confederate of the experimenter. The confederate was to be the learner and was asked questions by the subject. In the basic format of the experiment, the learner was placed in another room, apparently hooked up via electrodes to a device that the subject was told would deliver shocks that the subject would be asked to administer in response to the learner's mistakes. The shocks were staged, not real. After each mistake, the subject was asked to administer a shock to the learner, increasing the magnitude of the shock after each successive mistake. The shocks were represented to the subject as ranging from slight (15–60 volts), to moderate (75–120 volts), to strong (135–180 volts), to very strong (195–240 volts), to intense (255–300 volts), to extremely intense (315–360 volts), and to dangerous (375–420 volts). In the standard format of the experiment, as the apparent voltage was increased, the confederate responded with increasing (feigned) distress and finally, and ominously, with silence. If subjects expressed concern about continuing to administer apparently more serious shocks, the experimenter responded by politely but firmly insisting that the experiment was

[8] Jon Darley and Daniel Baton, "From Jerusalem to Jericho: A Study of Situational and Dispositional Variables in Helping Behavior" *Journal of Personality and Social Psychology* 27 (1973): 100–08.
[9] Stanley Milgram, *Obedience to Authority* (New York: Harper & Row, 1969).

important and that the shocks were painful but not harmful. In the original study, 62.5 percent of subjects shocked their learners to the maximum allowable amount into the dangerous zone with intense protestation and screams from the confederate followed by silence. These results held up in numerous replications, though there were interestingly different results in some permutations of the original experiment, some of which I discuss below.

Role Playing. Equally infamous was Philip Zimbardo's Stanford Prison Experiment in which a simulated prison was set up in the basement of the Stanford Psychology Department and in which student volunteers were randomly assigned roles as prisoners and guards.[10] Though they were asked to play the roles of prisoners and guards, guards were instructed to avoid physical punishment and to treat their charges humanely. The experiment was to run for two weeks but had to be terminated after six days because the guards had become increasingly abusive and sadistic and prisoners were experiencing genuine psychological trauma.

In all these studies, people displayed surprising and unsettling patterns of behavior—treating others in ways that they had reason to believe were harmful or failing to respond compassionately to those in apparent need. There is reason to think that what explains these surprising results are situational or contextual factors, factors that we might not have thought would be so important. This is why situationists identify a Fundamental Attribution Error.

How robust are these situationist findings? The sciences collectively, including social sciences such as psychology, have been experiencing problems replicating some research findings, including some landmark psychological studies.[11] Does the replication crisis undermine confidence in situationist findings? We need to be fallibilists about scientific findings. If individual studies cannot be replicated, that provides reason to be skeptical of the results of those studies. Until a given study has been replicated in similar circumstances, we should not treat the results as settled science, especially if the results are surprising. So we should be cautious about relying on a few surprising studies. But where studies converge in their findings, and where meta-analysis of disparate studies upholds the findings, we should be reasonably confident in those results, even if this means distrusting particular studies. This seems to be the situation in situationist psychology. For instance, there has been some difficulty replicating the results in the Isen and Levin phone

---

[10] The Stanford Prison Experiment took place in the early 1970s. See Philip Zimbardo, *The Lucifer Effect* (New York: Random House, 2007).

[11] See, e.g., Harold Pashler and Christine Harris, "Is the Replication Crisis Overblown? Three Arguments Examined" *Perspective on Psychology* 7 (2012): 531–36.

booth study.[12] But, for the most part, there has been replication of several studies, including, importantly, the Milgram experiments; there is convergence in support of situationist claims; and meta-analyses confirm situationist influences.[13]

79. Situationism, Character, and Virtue

In *Lack of Character* Doris goes further than the Fundamental Attribution Error, not just claiming that situation is more important and character less important than we thought, but also expressing skepticism about the existence of stable character traits.[14] We might distinguish three possible situationist claims of increasing strength.

1. Character is less important and situational factors are more important than we thought in explaining human behavior.
2. Character is less important than situational factors in explaining human behavior.
3. There are no stable character traits.

The Fundamental Attribution Error makes the interesting but comparatively weak claim in (1). A stronger comparative claim would be (2). Neither of these comparative claims implies skepticism about character traits of the sort expressed in (3) and endorsed, at least sometimes, by Doris.

Doris's skepticism about character reflects three assumptions that he thinks are pervasive in characterological moral psychology.

1. *Cross-situational consistency*. Character traits are cross-situationally (or horizontally) consistent behavioral dispositions. If you have a trait, it should manifest itself consistently in a variety of different behavioral contexts.
2. *Diachronic Stability*. This is a temporal (vertical, rather than horizontal) behavioral consistency requirement, which is not cross-situational. If

---

[12] See, e.g., Gregory Blevins and Terrance Murphy, "Feeling Good and Helping: Further Phone Booth Findings" *Psychology Reports* 34 (1974): 326 and James Weyant and Russell Clark, "Dimes and Helping: The Other Side of the Coin" *Personality and Social Psychology Bulletin* 3 (1976): 107–110.

[13] See also Doris, *Talking to Our Selves*, pp. 44–49.

[14] I provide references to *Lack of Character* parenthetically in my text.

you have a situationally specific trait at one time, you are likely to have it at another time.

3. *Evaluative Integration.* If you have one morally relevant character trait, you are more likely to have others. The inseparability of the virtues, according to which if you have one virtue you must have all the others, would be an extreme version of evaluative integration.

Doris concludes that situationism undermines cross-situational consistency and evaluative integration but leaves diachronic stability intact (22–23). Most agents do not display cross-situationally consistent character traits, and they tend to be morally fragmented. Doris thinks that only diachronically consistent local traits exist (62–67). In effect, he thinks that agents do not exhibit cross-situationally consistent traits, but that they are consistent over time in the manifestation of narrow, situationally specific, traits.

Doris goes on to develop two different implications of situationism for ethical theory, one negative and one positive. The negative ethical conclusion is that virtue ethics and other forms of moral character evaluation are bankrupt because they rest on mistaken assumptions about the existence of robust character traits (107–19). The positive thesis is that it might be possible to remake a characterological moral theory that is sensitive to the findings of situationism (an empirically adequate characterological theory) or, if that is not possible, to fashion a non-characterological moral theory that helps facilitate better moral outcomes by attending to the importance of situational factors in behavior (120–21, 146, 163).

In *Lack of Character* Doris focuses primarily on the negative thesis.[15] But his positive thesis is independent of the negative thesis. We might want to modify our institutions, policies, and personal plans in light of a recognition of the importance of situational and contextual factors. For instance, the Fundamental Attribution Error might help me recognize that I am less likely to succeed in dealing with substance abuse problems by sheer willpower than by circumvention—altering the context of choice by removing the availability of the substance (e.g. throwing the liquor bottles out) and changing my patterns of association (e.g. no longer socializing with my drinking buddies in contexts in which alcohol is served). Situationism might also provide further support for ideas in behavioral economics about how the context or framework of choice can influence outcomes. For instance, Cass Sunstein and Richard Thaler advocate a regulatory approach that they call "libertarian

---

[15] Doris has more to say about the positive thesis in the second half of *Talking to Ourselves*.

paternalism," because it structures choice in ways that tend to lead to better welfare outcomes for those making choices but in ways that are non-coercive and do not limit choice.[16] We could *nudge*, rather than coerce. For instance, we could arrange for the healthy foods in the cafeteria to be more easily accessible, reserving the less accessible locations for less healthy foods. Sometimes, we can nudge just by changing the default options in a menu. In the case of defined contribution retirement plans, we could make the maximum annual contribution the default option, which the agent could change but only through deliberate choice. Changing default settings and opt-in to opt-out selections can improve outcomes, both prudentially and socially, without depriving people of options and choices. The way we manage the architecture of choice should take into account situational influences on choice.

80. Ethical Implications of Situationism

Doris's negative argument raises a number of issues. He infers skepticism about character from inconsistent behavioral manifestation. One might well question whether behavioral inconsistency undermines the ascription of character traits and whether familiar moral assumptions presuppose cross-situationally stable traits.

It is not clear that we should draw skeptical conclusions about character from data about behavioral inconsistency. In fact, a significant strand in the social psychology literature expressly resists this skeptical conclusion, treating situationist findings as motivating a situationally adequate and constrained conception of character, one in which character is not a simple behavioral disposition but a complex suite of dispositions to perceive and attend to certain aspects of one's situation, to feel certain emotions, and to react appropriately.[17]

Despite some disclaimers (15–16), Doris focuses almost exclusively on behavior and treats failures to manifest the trait in certain conditions as evidence that the person does not have a robust trait. But traits might manifest

---

[16] See Cass Sunstein and Richard Thaler, *Nudge: Improving Decisions about Health, Wealth, and Happiness* (New Haven, CT: Yale University Press, 2008) and Cass Sunstein, *Why Nudge?* (New Haven, CT: Yale University Press, 2014).

[17] See Walter Mischel, *Personality and Assessment* (Hoboken, NJ: John Wiley & Sons, 1968) and Ross and Nisbett, *The Person and the Situation*. For a philosophical analysis of this strand in the empirical work, see Daniel Russell, *Practical Intelligence and the Virtues* (Oxford: Clarendon Press, 2009), esp. chs. 8–9.

in other ways, for instance, in emotional responses, such as anxiety or regret, or in compensating behavior, such as apology, restitution, and might stimulate learning from mistakes.[18] For instance, it's noteworthy that most of the compliant subjects in Milgram experiments manifested visible signs of stress and anxiety as they complied with requests to administer shocks. These other forms of manifestation might serve as evidence of a character trait, even in the absence of invariant behavioral manifestations. We might wish that the character trait was stronger and manifested itself in compassionate behavior more reliably, but that does not show that the subject does not possess the trait of compassion.

Furthermore, traits might display a behavioral tendency and yet be *masked* by other traits. If traits are, in part, dispositions that tend to produce behavior when other things are equal and there are no interfering conditions, then we should not expect traits to manifest themselves behaviorally in situations in which there is significant situational interference. A given situation might engage more than one trait. If the traits tend toward incompatible courses of conduct, then at least one trait will not manifest itself behaviorally. For instance, in the Milgram experiments, should we conclude from failures of compassionate behavior, as Doris does, that those who fail to act compassion-ately are not compassionate, or should we conclude instead that people who are compassionate are also deferential to authority? Milgram interpreted his own experiments in the second way, as showing that deference is a real and powerful character trait. We might wish that the compassion of many subjects had been stronger and won out over their deference to authority, but the fact that they deferred does not itself mean that they are not compassionate. Similarly, the seminarian experiment need not show that the seminarians were not compassionate; instead, it may show that they recognized a special obligation to deliver their promised talks, perhaps assuming that others without special commitments could provide any needed assistance. Perhaps it's a condition of our ascribing a trait such as compassion to a person that it manifest itself behaviorally often enough. But how high that behavioral

---

[18] Several philosophers have raised questions about Doris's behavioral assumptions about character traits and his demand for cross-situational consistency. See, e.g., Robert Adams, *A Theory of Virtue* (Oxford: Clarendon Press, 2006), esp. ch. 8, and Russell, *Practical Intelligence and the Virtues*, esp. chs. 8–9. One would like to know whether some of Milgram's subjects thought about their choices in the experiment and behaved differently, going forward, as the result of the experiment and the debriefing afterward. There is no reason to expect this sort of effect in unconflicted subjects, but it would be a real possibility for conflicted subjects. Milgram reports that some subjects later reported having learned important things about themselves from the experiment. See *Obedience to Authority*, p. 200.

threshold should be is not clear, and it does seem clear that some failures to manifest the trait are compatible with possessing it.

We might also ask whether our normal assumptions about character and our ordinary moral discriminations are jeopardized by recognition that cross-situationally stable character traits are less common than we assumed.

First, situationist experiments don't show that no one has cross-situationally consistent traits, just that they aren't as common as we might have thought or hoped. We could hold onto the idea that traits must be manifested behaviorally and simply conclude that virtue is less common than some think. Though nearly two-thirds of Milgram's subjects delivered the maximum shock, a little more than one-third did not. This is only so much comfort, because some of these subjects supplied intense shocks short of the maximal shock. But 20 percent did refuse to administer strong shocks, and 15 percent refused to continue as soon as the learner protested and asked for the experiment to stop. It's not clear that we should think that virtues are more common than this.[19]

Second, situationism doesn't show that there aren't differences in the moral behavior of people. Even if few people are as consistent as we might have thought or hoped, *comparative* differences still exist among people in terms of the comparative robustness of their traits. But these comparative differences can ground moral discriminations among them and their degree of virtue. From the fact that few are consistently or perfectly virtuous, it does not follow that the rest of us are all equally virtuous or non-virtuous. If consistency and virtue are scalar, then we can still draw familiar moral distinctions among people based on their character, and even the frequency with which they manifest the trait in behavior, even if few exhibit perfect character or virtue.

Third, knowledge is power. Once people recognize ways in which they are prone to situational influences, they may become better at resisting them. Indeed, it is precisely here that the positive potential of recognizing the role of situational factors can be empowering. In this connection, Milgram notes that some subjects later reported having become more aware of their susceptibility to influence by authorities and better able to resist authority when it conflicts with conscience as the result of the experiment.[20]

---

[19] Cf. Rachana Kamtekar, "Situationism and Virtue Ethics on the Content of our Character" *Ethics* 114 (2004): 458–91.
[20] See Milgram, *Obedience to Authority*, p. 200.

These responses raise questions about whether situationist findings really do undermine our normal assumptions about character and its moral importance. They suggest that Doris's skepticism may be premature.

81. Situationism, Responsibility, and Fair Opportunity

In the penultimate chapter of his book, Doris explores the implications of situationism for our assumptions about responsibility. His claim is that situationism poses problems for various conceptions of responsibility, especially *characterological* and *normative competence* conceptions. However, Doris seems to think that if we adopt his favored *identificationist* conception of responsibility, the problems situationism poses are manageable.[21]

A characterological conception of responsibility has some *prima facie* plausibility. Hume expressed support for a characterological conception of responsibility in *An Enquiry Concerning Human Understanding*.

> The only proper object of hatred or vengeance is a person or creature, endowed with thought or consciousness; and when any criminal or injurious actions excite that passion, it is only by their relation to the person, or connection with him. Actions are by their very nature temporary and perishing; and where they proceed not from some *cause* in the character and disposition of the person who performed them, they can neither redound to his honour, if good; nor infamy, if evil. The actions themselves may be blameable; they may be contrary to all the rules of morality and religion: But the person is not answerable for them; and as they proceeded from nothing in him, that is durable and constant, and leave nothing of that nature behind them, it is impossible that he can, on their account, become the object of punishment or vengeance.   [§VIII, Part ii]

When someone acts in character, her actions express her settled beliefs and desires, and so seem to be attributable to her. By contrast, if an agent acts out of character, her actions don't express her true self, but perhaps the pressures of the situation or the influence of other people. So we might conclude that an agent is responsible for her action just in case it expresses her character or true self. One of the virtues of such a character theory is that it seems fully

---

[21] Interestingly, in "From My Lai to Abu Ghraib" Doris and Murphy rely exclusively on a normative competence conception of responsibility.

compatible with determinism, inasmuch as it makes responsibility a matter of a causal relation between actions and character. Responsible action not only can be but also *must be* caused by character, and character can itself be causally determined.

A characterological conception of responsibility will be problematic if it is committed to cross-situational consistency and if situationism shows that there are no such robust traits. If situationism supports only the moderate comparative claim contained in the Fundamental Attribution Error, then it may not support skepticism about character and so may not threaten characterological conceptions of responsibility. Even if situationism does support skepticism about global character traits, we might try to reformulate characterological conceptions of responsibility so that they do not presuppose cross-situational consistency.

However, there are other serious worries about characterological conceptions of responsibility that are completely independent of situationism.[22] The more serious worry is that characterological conceptions are both under-inclusive and over-inclusive about who is responsible and blameworthy. A characterological conception promises to be under-inclusive about whom to blame or punish, because it will exculpate people who are reasons-responsive and choose to do wrong, provided that choice is out of character. For instance, it will exculpate Richard Herrin for his deliberate murder of Bonnie Garland, on the ground that this was out of character for him, despite the fact that there was no evidence that he suffered from significant cognitive or volitional impairment.[23] The characterological conception of responsibility promises to be over-inclusive about whom to blame or punish as well, because it won't exculpate for wrongdoing that is in character, even if the agent's character lacks elementary capacities for reason-responsiveness.

Doris himself wants to integrate situationism with an identificationist conception of responsibility. An identificationist conception of responsibility is a version of quality will, which we examined earlier (§§14, 28). Frankfurt introduced the identificationist idea, claiming that agents are responsible just in case agents identify with their motivating desires, producing a mesh between their motivating desires and their second-order or aspirational desires.[24] Watson modified Frankfurt's proposal to claim that agents are responsible just in case their motivating desires mesh with their evaluative

---

[22] For an extended discussion with which I am sympathetic, see Moore, *Placing Blame*, ch. 13.

[23] The Herrin case is discussed, as part of a similar worry about the under-inclusiveness of characterological conceptions of responsibility, in Moore, *Placing Blame*, pp. 578–80.

[24] See Frankfurt, "Freedom of the Will and the Concept of a Person."

judgments about those desires.[25] Most agents identify with or endorse their determining motives, wanting to want what they want or regarding what they want as valuable. But in some cases agents may not approve or endorse what they want, as in the case of the unwilling drug addict. Perhaps many of the subjects in the Milgram or Stanford Prison experiments did not endorse their desires and actions. I don't think the experimental studies are clear about this, but it's possible. Would this mean that subjects in those studies were not responsible for their behavior and should be excused?

We should be skeptical of identificationist conceptions of responsibility. For one thing, they have a hard time holding agents who are weak-willed responsible. For in the case of weakness of will or akrasia, the agent acts contrary to what she judges best, because she is moved by good-independent appetite or desire. But then the akratic actor typically does not endorse or approve the desires that in fact determine her will when she is weak-willed. But we normally hold akratic actors responsible and do not in general treat weakness of will as an excuse. We do so on the assumption that at the time of action they were normatively competent and reasons-responsive.

In fact, given the worries about the under-inclusiveness and over-inclusiveness of characterological conceptions, which Doris seems to recognize (130–32), it is a little surprising that he wants to embrace an identificationist conception of responsibility. For it, like the characterological conception, threatens to be both under-inclusive and over-inclusive. It will be under-inclusive, because it will excuse when someone doesn't identify with her guiding motive, even if she was normatively competent for her choice of wrongdoing. Perhaps Richard Herrin didn't approve of his homicidal motives, but if he was competent and intended to murder Bonnie Garland, then he is responsible. It will be over-inclusive, because it will count wrongdoing as culpable, provided the agent endorses her motivations for wrongdoing, even if she was not reasons-responsive at the time.

Doris's introduction of a constraint of *narrative integration* into the identificationist proposal is supposed to make it less under-inclusive, because it will not excuse for failure to approve of one's determining motive if those motives are nonetheless part of a larger plan or narrative that guides one's life (142–46). But it's far from clear that narrative integration solves these problems. Indeed, like the characterological view, the narrative view invokes patterns in one's choices and behavior. But with the characterological view it was precisely the idea that anomaly, as such, was excusing that led to the

---

[25] See Watson, "Free Agency."

under-inclusiveness worry. So it's hard to see how narrative integration won't make the resulting identificationist view under-inclusive as well.

I've articulated these worries about both characterological and identificationist views against the backdrop of a conception of responsibility as the fair opportunity to avoid wrongdoing that requires choice by an agent who is normatively competent and has situational control. Doris does not address the fair opportunity conception per se, but he does discuss normative competence conceptions of responsibility, and normative competence is a proper part of fair opportunity. He claims that situationism poses serious challenges to normative competence conceptions, a claim that deserves our attention.

Before turning to the bearing of situationism on normative competence, it might be worth pausing over the implications of situationism for situational control. For one might have thought that this would be the aspect of responsibility that situationism challenged. Perhaps we only think that we possess situational control while we are in the grips of the Fundamental Attribution Error. Once we recognize the pervasive influence of situational factors on our behavior, perhaps we should conclude that situational control is an illusion or at least frequently impaired.

However, it is hard to see factors of the sort studied by situationists as compromising situational control. As we have seen, the paradigmatic excuse that denies situational control is duress. But in the criminal law duress requires an agent who accedes to wrongful coercion or threats by another agent and that leaves no reasonable alternative to wrongdoing. This standard is clearly not met in any of the situationist studies we have discussed. In many cases, there is no other agent intervening to apply pressure on the wrongdoers, except in the attenuated sense that all the studies involve situational features as part of the experimental design. The closest we come to coercion is the Milgram experiments in which the experimenter requests the subject to shock the learner to correct his mistakes. But there is no reasonable interpretation of coercion in which such a request is coercive, and it certainly leaves open reasonable and permissible alternatives to compliance with the request. Subjects were free to withdraw from the experiment, incurring at most the displeasure of the experimenter. Even if we drop the criminal law's demand that duress have its source in the coercive intervention of another agent and allow duress excuses in response to hard choices, whatever the cause, the situationist cases still won't involve duress. For the choice agents face when they engage in wrongful behavior in these studies is just not a sufficiently hard choice, and they all have reasonable and permissible alternatives to wrongdoing.

Because there is no plausible duress excuse for bad behavior in the situationist studies, we should instead see if situational factors compromise the agent's normative competence. This is the claim that Doris develops (133–34). He begins by claiming that situational factors compromise self-control and that they show that self-control is more the exception than the rule (134). But self-control is involved in normative competence, and so Doris concludes that situationism challenges the cognitive and volitional dimensions of normative competence (136). He claims that situational factors may impair the agent's ability to recognize reasons for action—perhaps the hurried seminarians don't even notice the slumping confederate—or may make it difficult for agents to sustain and implement their normative judgments—perhaps group effects compromise volitional capacities, and Milgram subjects are disabled from acting on their moral knowledge by their desire to comply with authority (136–38).

82. Distinguishing between Performance Errors and Incompetence

But most situational findings describe patterns, albeit surprising patterns, in behavior. They do not demonstrate *incapacity*. For instance, in the Milgram experiments we may be surprised to find that two-thirds of subjects fail to do the compassionate thing because of a desire, perhaps sub-conscious, to conform to the firm requests of the experimenter. But while many people did in fact act surprisingly badly, there's nothing in the situationist gloss on the Milgram experiments to suggest that subjects lacked the ability or capacity to resist the experimenter's suggestion. We might put this point by saying that situationism addresses situational patterns in *performance*, not issues of *competence*.

It seems extremely plausible that these situational factors affect performance, not competence. After all, the situationist paradigm precisely targets capacities and traits that we take to be commonplace, rather than exceptional or heroic. A significant number of subjects manifest this capacity in expected behavior, and, even those who don't, show signs of discomfort and stress that evidence the existence of the capacity for appropriate action.

Here, we need to draw on our earlier discussion of competence and capacity, as distinct from performance (§§16, 29–32). Life is replete with unexercised capacities of various kinds. In analyzing these ascriptions of capacities, we are positing an actual psychological structure, but one which funds relevant counterfactual claims about how the agent would have behaved in other circumstances. If determinism is true, we don't think that the agent would behave any differently in circumstances *exactly* like the actual circumstances *in all respects*. Instead, we think that he could have acted differently in the actual circumstance if he would have acted differently in circumstances that were *different but relevantly similar*. Of course, relevant differences cannot be too great; otherwise, we will be tracking potential, rather than actual, capacities. Exactly how to constrain the relevant counterfactuals is a complex matter, but it's reasonably clear that the relevant differences should be familiar and modest. And one counterfactual does not confirm or disconfirm a capacity. What we should expect from someone who has a capacity is that in the relevant counterfactuals he will perform successfully on a *regular* basis. But by this test it seems plausible that most subjects that did not display compassionate behavior could have.

Consider the Milgram experiment again. Would the compliant subjects have administered serious shocks if they had been given more time to consider their options, if they had been reminded that they were volunteers in an experiment, if they had been asked to justify their imposition of apparent harm, or if they had known the learners? If subjects would not have shocked in some of these circumstances, that provides evidence that those subjects had a capacity for recognizing reasons for compassion and for engaging in compassionate behavior or at least avoiding maleficent behavior.

However, it might seem that appealing to counterfactuals in different circumstances misses the point of the situationist challenge. Situationism, it might be claimed, shows that *general* capacities that are *contextually invariant* are not psychologically relevant and that we must appeal, instead, to *contextually specific* capacities.[26] It might seem that specific capacities are not subject to performance errors. A specific capacity is keyed to particular circumstances, and determinism seems to ensure the same outcomes in the same circumstances.

We should be interested in contextually specific capacities, not just because of situationist findings, but because accountability requires that the agent have had the relevant normative capacities at the time of action and in the situation she faced. But specific normative capacities must not be tied to a complete description of the world in which they are not exercised; otherwise, there could never be a specific capacity that was not exercised. But it is the very idea of a

---

[26] See, e.g., Vargas, *Building Better Beings*, ch. 7 and "The Social Constitution of Agency and Responsibility: Oppression, Politics, and Moral Ecology."

capacity that it admits of performance failure. Even if we are focused on specific capacities, we can't constrain the specification of a capacity in a way that doesn't allow this. This means that in deciding whether an agent has a specific normative capacity that he didn't exercise on a particular occasion, we are allowed to ask whether he would have manifested the capacity in slightly different but relevantly similar circumstances. In doing so, we should look to see if there is regular recognition and conformity to normative demands across these nearby or relevantly similar possible worlds.

Interestingly, several variations that Milgram himself devised in his basic experimental design reinforce these claims. Though the variations involve different subjects, they provide evidence about subjects in general. The counterfactuals that are most relevant to whether a given agent had a capacity to behave differently than she in fact did in actual circumstances ask how *she* would have behaved in relevantly different circumstances. But if we can't test how she would have behaved in such circumstances, we can nonetheless appeal to how other people do behave in such circumstances. Unless we have reason to believe that her capacities are unusual in this regard, the behavior of others in relevant circumstances can be defeasible evidence about how she would behave and what capacities she has. In a variation in which subjects had to place the learner's hand on an electronic plate in order for him to receive the (apparent) shock, only 30 percent of subjects administered the maximal shock, as compared with 62.5 percent in the original study.[27] In a later variation in which the experimenter left the room and gave instructions remotely, only 20 percent of subjects administered the maximal shock, even though this required the subject to lie to the experimenter about the shocks she administered.[28] Importantly, in a variation in which the subjects themselves determined the severity of the shock, 95 percent of subjects refused to administer shocks beyond the point at which the learner protested.[29]

These are reasons to think that appropriate counterfactual evidence would vindicate ordinary assumptions that most people have the capacity for recognizing and responding to reasons for compassionate behavior, even when they don't exercise these capacities. If situationist studies reveal facts about performance, rather than competence, then situationism does not compromise the sort of normative competence necessary for responsibility.

[27] Milgram, *Obedience to Authority*, pp. 34–35.   [28] *Obedience to Authority*, pp. 59–60.
[29] *Obedience to Authority*, pp. 70–72.

Of course, it may be that in some contexts situational factors genuinely do compromise cognitive or volitional aspects of normative competence. For instance, as we will see (§§83–84), there is a good case to be made that the normative competence of soldiers in the heat of battle is potentially compromised in several ways—by making high stakes decisions in split seconds often under significant uncertainty in circumstances in which their passions and instincts can be inflamed. The point is not that situational factors cannot affect normative competence but rather that situational factors do not, as such, compromise normative competence.

Doris suggests that situationism poses another "more insidious" problem for normative competence (138). Because people make the Fundamental Attribution Error, they are often ignorant of the influence of situational factors on their decision-making. To this extent, they don't understand their own cognitive processes (139).[30] Some degree of psychological transparency might be relevant to deliberations, especially deliberation designed to limit or counteract certain implicit biases and influences. But fair opportunity does not insist that psychological transparency is necessary for normative competence. Absent duress, agents are responsible for their conduct just in case they were normatively competent at the time and in the circumstances. Agents may often act wrongfully under the influence of situational factors, which they don't fully understand, but that doesn't show that they lack the capacity to do otherwise.

83. Situationism and Wartime Misconduct

Even if situationism does not in general compromise responsibility, it might be that the particular situational factors compromise normative competence or situational control. In "From My Lai to Abu Ghraib: The Moral Psychology of Atrocity" Doris and Murphy make this sort of more restricted argument when they argue that ideas from situationist psychology support excusing a large variety of wartime wrongdoing, including not only crimes committed by combatants, such as the killing of noncombatants and the use of disproportionate force, but also the commission of non-combat-related crimes committed during wartime by soldiers, such as crimes committed by guards in military prisons.[31] They do not explicitly frame their argument in terms of a

---

[30] This is also a theme in the first half of Doris, *Talking to Ourselves*.
[31] I provide references to this article parenthetically in the text.

particular conception of responsibility and excuse, but they do make appeals to the importance of normative competence, which is the relevant aspect of the fair opportunity conception of responsibility.[32]

Their argument appeals to both *distal* and *proximate* factors affecting the normative competence of soldiers under stress. They mention three distal influences (38–41).

- Military training reduces inhibitions on using violence.
- Military training reduces independence of judgment and increases respect for authority and following the chain of command.
- In various ways, military training demonizes the enemy, often representing them as morally inferior or sub-human.

But we must remember that military training also teaches soldiers to respect various constraints in war, such as the requirement to target combatants and not noncombatants, to use proportionate defensive force, and to minimize collateral harm. This means that the valence of distal factors is mixed.

This is one reason it is important to recognize, in addition to these distal influences on soldiers, several proximate factors potentially affecting the normative competence of soldiers in battle. Perhaps the most obvious proximate factor, which Doris and Murphy do not mention, is that often battlefield decisions have to be made instantaneously without the benefit of careful and dispassionate assessment. They cite other proximate factors that tend to corrupt judgment (35–38).

- The diffusion of responsibility that individuals experience in groups
- The onslaught of noise and other perceptual stimuli
- The filth and odors in battle that confound the senses and lead to a sense of pollution and contamination
- Exhaustion and lack of sleep
- The emotional toll of losing comrades to injury and death

Doris and Murphy claim that the combination of distal and proximate factors produce "moral drift" and impair normative competence.[33]

---

[32] It is interesting that Doris and Murphy frame their excuse for wartime wrongdoing by appeal to normative competence conceptions of responsibility, since, as we have seen, in *Lack of Character* Doris argues that situationism undermines normative competence.

[33] The military criminal code appears to rely on a M'Naghten-style cognitive conception of normative competence. See *Manual for Courts Martial* 2012, Rule 706, especially 706(c)(2)(A), and

When all or most of the distal and proximate factors are present, there is a plausible basis for a full or partial excuse for some forms of wrongdoing. Their argument is strongest when it applies to *inadvertent wrongdoing* by *combatants* in the *heat of battle*. Call this *hot combat*. The immediate context of battle calls for quick decision-making and contains a barrage of stimulus, both of which may compromise decision-making capacities that are central to normative competence (35–41). It will often be hard under battle conditions to make some discriminations between right and wrong, because it is hard to distinguish between combatants and noncombatants or to assess proportionate responses instantaneously and under chaotic conditions. And even if one can recognize what duty requires, it may be very hard to resist orders to act differently or to resist the pressures of comrades to follow their lead.

It is not clear whether wrongdoing under such circumstances should be afforded a full or partial excuse, that is, a genuine defense or mitigation. There's no reason to expect a general answer. Verdicts would have to be case-specific. One thing that is especially interesting about this kind of excuse for wartime wrongdoing is that it illustrates ways in which situational factors can compromise normative competence (§24). This is true whether the excuse provided is full or partial.

But notice two important limitations in this rationale for excuse. First, it depends heavily on the proximate factors present in hot combat; there is no reason to expect the excuse to obtain when these proximate factors are absent or significantly reduced. Second, even in cases of wrongdoing committed in the heat of battle and pursuant to the orders of superiors, there are limitations on what can be excused. In particular, even compliance with the orders of a superior does not excuse *manifest illegality*.[34] Manifest illegalities are actions that are wrong on their face and clearly exceed the bounds of justified force. Manifest illegalities would include the intentional targeting of noncombatants, the torture and execution of prisoners, and sexual assault on combatants or noncombatants.

However, Doris and Murphy are surprisingly promiscuous with excuses, extending excuses from these core cases in which understandable forms of inadvertent wrongdoing are committed in the heat of battle to various kinds of peripheral cases.

916(b)(2). My own view is that the failure to recognize a distinct volitional dimension to normative competence is a mistake here, as it is in the M'Naghten test (see §§16, 22, 86).

[34] See Model Penal Code §2.10 and Manual for Courts Martial 2012, Rule 916(d).

In particular, we need to say something about how far from the battlefield the kinds of excusing conditions we identify reach, and what behaviors they extend to. It might be thought that the scope of our argument is actually quite limited, covering only certain sorts of "unnecessary killing" during combat operations, and that the further from these central cases we look, the less plausible the argument becomes. This is certainly a reasonable position to adopt, and we agree that the further one strays from the manifestly *legal* killing of enemy soldiers actively engaged in combat, the more difficult it is to establish the presence of excusing conditions. However, we think that the scope of our argument is surprisingly broad...   [46]

Indeed, they think that the argument for excuse extends from hot combat to cases involving wrongdoing committed by soldiers outside of immediate combat situations. We might call these cases of *warm combat* in which soldiers who do spend time in combat commit wrongdoing in wartime but outside of immediate combat. One such case is the killing of at least 400 unarmed noncombatants by members of Charlie Company during the Vietnam War in 1968.[35] Most of the victims were women and children, some of whom were raped before being killed. Another such case is the killing of 24 unarmed civilians by U.S. Marines in Haditha in the Al Anbar province of Iraq in 2005. In both cases, the killings were widely held to be committed in retaliation for recently suffered combat casualties.

Doris and Murphy want to extend further the excuse for wartime wrong-doing to cases of *cold combat* involving soldiers away from battle acting as prison guards. The most visible such case involved the physical, psychological, and sexual abuse and torture of prisoners by military personnel in the U.S. Army at the Abu Ghraib Prison in Iraq in 2004.[36] Surprisingly, Doris and Murphy do not invoke the Stanford Prison Experiment in their argument for excuse at Abu Ghraib.[37] We might think that just as otherwise normal young men can become abusive toward others when given authority over them, so too can young men and women when they are made real, and not just pretend, prison guards with real, and not just pretend, authority. Indeed, we might expect that such abuse is all the more likely when practiced by members

---

[35] See Seymour Hersh, "The My Lai Massacre," a three-part article in the *St. Louis Dispatch* November 1969 and Michael Bilton and Kevin Sim, *Four Hours in My Lai* (New York: Viking, 1992).

[36] Seymour Hersh, "Torture at Abu Ghraib" *The New Yorker* May 10, 2004.

[37] By contrast, in *The Lucifer Effect* Zombardo explicitly notes and explores parallels between the Stanford Prison Experiment and wartime atrocities, especially at Abu Ghraib.

of the military, who have become desensitized to suffering, against real prisoners thought to be enemy combatants.

When we see how apparently ordinary people can in the right circumstances behave badly we can be impressed by circumstantial luck, both good and bad. Perhaps many of us who do not serve in the army would find ourselves behaving badly had we been assigned duty at Abu Ghraib. Reflecting on the Stanford Prison Experiments, we might be tempted to think: There, but for the grace of God, go I. Those not religiously inclined may think instead: There, but for the natural and social lotteries, go I. But it's not clear why this recognition of our own good circumstantial luck should lead us to excuse those with bad circumstantial luck. Instead, one might conclude that in other circumstances we too would be culpable for the sort of wrongdoing that would be a fitting object of blame and punishment.

Though they recognize the distinction between full and partial excuses or mitigation, they nonetheless argue that wartime atrocity should typically receive a full excuse, and not just mitigation (49). Furthermore, they think that in wartime it becomes extremely difficult to distinguish between manifest illegality and military necessity (42, 45). Doris and Murphy do not claim that all cases of wartime wrongdoing should be excused, but they do claim that the presumption should be in favor of excuse, rather than culpability (26, 46).

84. Toward a Discriminating Conception of Excuse for Wartime Misconduct

War crimes raise an interesting and important issue in applied responsibility, and it seems quite plausible that normative competence is sometimes compromised in hot combat, providing an excuse, whether full or partial, for inadvertent wrongdoing committed in such circumstances. We should be sympathetic toward soldiers who have to make life and death decisions in an instant amid an onslaught of confusing informational and sensory stimuli. Making fine moral discriminations in such circumstances can be like trying to drink from a fire hose. We should be prepared to excuse difficulty soldiers might have distinguishing combatants from noncombatants and from assessing what is proportionate force to be used in disabling potential aggressors. Moral mistakes, in such circumstances, would not be justified, but they might be excused. However, the full scope of Doris and Murphy's excuse for wartime wrongdoing is quite extraordinary in several respects.

For one thing, it is quite surprising that Doris and Murphy suppose that there should be a presumption in favor of excuse for wartime wrongdoing of various kinds. In the criminal law, the prosecution has the burden of proof for establishing the elements of the crime—*actus reus* and *mens rea*—beyond a reasonable doubt. But with affirmative defenses, which concede the elements of the offense but allege justification or excuse, it is the defense that typically has the burden of proof by a preponderance of the evidence or by clear and convincing evidence. So, in particular, it is the burden of the wrongdoer to show that he is entitled to an excuse, because either his normative competence or his situational control was significantly impaired. In part because defenses of justification and excuse are designed to be exceptional, it makes sense that those asserting such defenses should bear the burden of proof.

Moreover, it is peculiar that Doris and Murphy acknowledge that the rationale for the excuse in hot combat depends on distal and proximate factors that are either absent or greatly reduced in situations of warm combat and virtually non-existent in situations of cold combat. They recognize a distinction between full excuse and mitigation (or partial excuse) and recognize that excusing factors are scalar but nonetheless insist on defending full excuse in a wide range of cases. Because the plausibility of an excuse in the case of hot combat depends crucially on proximate factors in the heat of battle, we should not recognize excuses for wartime wrongdoing committed in circumstances in which these proximate factors are absent or significantly reduced. Furthermore, the killings in My Lai and Haditha and the torture and abuse at Abu Ghraib seem to include clear cases of manifest illegality that would fall outside the scope of excuse even in hot combat. The basis for excuse can't be absent or reduced without losing or reducing the excuse.

Consistent with Doris's argument in *Lack of Character*, Doris and Murphy conflate issues of competence and performance. Responsibility requires normative competence, and normative competence requires capacities to make normative discriminations and act on those normative judgments. Since responsibility requires these capacities, it is not compromised whenever they are not properly exercised. Indeed, if they were, we could never hold people for responsible wrongdoing. But situationism only says something about patterns in people's actual behavior, how situational factors tend to influence behavior. These facts about performance in no way indicate an inability to reason or act otherwise. The same is true in war. Situational evidence, by itself, only shows things about how soldiers behave and the influence of situational factors on their conduct. It does not demonstrate incapacity. In cases involving hot combat, this further claim might be warranted. It might well be that in

situations involving risk of serious personal harm and death in which decisions have to be made in an instant and in which there is a barrage of sensory
stimuli, the ability to tell right from wrong and to implement the right decision
despite distraction and countervailing passion is severely compromised. But
there is no reason to assume that this competence is seriously compromised in
warm and cold combat situations. All Doris and Murphy offer by way of
evidence for the extension is situationist claims about how common moral
drift is even in such situations. But unless we are to excuse all wrongdoing, we
have to distinguish between performance and competence and demand evidence of genuine incapacity.

Their support for a widespread excuse for wrongdoing in wartime should
strike us as promiscuous about excuse and insufficiently serious about
accountability. They try to meet these worries by adopting the surprising
position that a full excuse does not preclude criminal liability. In effect, they
urge that military tribunals recognize strict liability. That is, they conclude that
we should excuse the wrongdoers but punish them anyway. This is an extraordinary claim. For one thing, a broadly retributivist conception of blame and
punishment, according to which blame and punishment are deserved in
proportion to culpable wrongdoing, is very plausible and a deep feature of
the criminal law. Denying either wrongdoing or culpability rebuts the case for
blame and punishment. Whereas justifications deny wrongdoing, excuses
deny culpability or responsibility. So a full excuse that denies culpability or
responsibility altogether precludes guilt and punishment. This retributivist
argument is reflected in the criminal law insofar as excuses are affirmative
defenses, which, if successful, justify acquittal. Moreover, as we have seen
(§58), ensuring the fair opportunity to avoid wrongdoing renders strict liability in the criminal law deeply problematic. It is possible but controversial to
have strict liability crimes that don't require some *mens rea* element, at least
negligence, for some material element of an offense, but even crimes that are
strict liability in this sense admit of an excuse in terms of insanity or diminished competence. There are no strict liability crimes that do not admit of
excuse because of impairments to normative competence or situational control. As excuses, these conditions block blame and punishment. If we were to
accept Doris's and Murphy's argument that most wartime wrongdoing should
be excused, we would have to forego blame and punishment. The difficulty of
accepting that conclusion is not reason to embrace strict liability for war
crimes but rather reason to have a more discriminating conception of excuse.

Part of having a more discriminating conception of excuse involves taking
normative competence seriously and not excusing wartime wrongdoing in

which the soldier's cognitive and volitional capacities are not significantly compromised. Another part of a more discriminating conception of excuse might be to recognize the possibility of more fine-grained responses to wartime wrongdoing. Normative competence and, hence, responsibility are scalar phenomena, even if we sometimes employ thresholds and bright lines in our decisions about whom to hold responsible and whom to excuse. While a full excuse for wartime wrongdoing should presumably be exceptional and limited to wrongs that are not manifestly illegal and are committed in the heat of battle or under direct orders from a superior, not all combat situations compromise a soldier's normative capacities to the same degree. Consequently, we may have reason to recognize *partial* excuses even when a full excuse cannot be justified. In systems that do not recognize partial excuse, the same facts about diminished capacity that would otherwise justify a partial excuse can and should operate as mitigating factors at sentencing. A further resource for fine-tuning blame and punishment in situations of partial responsibility is the distinction between *censure* and *sanction*. The criminal law typically both censures and sanctions culpable wrongdoing. But these responses can come apart. In situations in which it may have been hard for a soldier to exercise good judgment that did not sufficiently impair her normative competence to qualify for a full excuse, we may nonetheless consider mitigation or the possibility of censuring her and her conduct without imposing sanctions.

85. Beyond Wartime Misconduct

If this more discriminating conception of responsibility and excuse for wartime wrongdoing makes sense, it might be adapted to misconduct in other contexts. The features of hot combat that make excuse, whether full or partial, plausible are potentially dangerous encounters and conflicts, uncertainty due to limited information and time to deliberate, inflamed emotions, and perceived pressure from superiors or peers to engage in misconduct. These factors have the potential to excuse individually or in concert. Some or all of these factors can be found in other contexts.

One context that displays some of these features is gang life and organized crime.[38] Gang activities and encounters with other gangs are potentially

---

[38] This comparison was suggested in a seminar I taught at the University of San Diego School of Law by a student who had spent time in the District Attorney's office working on cases involving the prosecution of gang activity.

dangerous, where decisions about the use of force often need to be made quickly and subject to limited information, and the collective and hierarchical structure of gangs brings pressure to engage in misconduct from superiors and peers. The consequences for not meeting demands for misconduct can be quite serious. In this respect, there can be an element of duress in some cases of gang misconduct. An obvious limitation in the comparison between gangs and the military is the legitimacy of the underlying activity. Even if military misconduct is illegal, military service, as such, is not. Legitimate military service is not just permissible but admirable. We've seen that it's generally true that even if one satisfies conditions that would otherwise excuse, one is not entitled to the excuse if one is substantially responsible for bringing about those conditions (§§35, 60, 62), and this is a subject to which we will return (§§88, 116, 126). Incapacity is not excusing when it is culpably acquired, as in the case of voluntary intoxication (MPC §2.08), and duress is not excusing when the duressed person is substantially responsible for his own duress (MPC §2.09). So one might think that gang misconduct could never be excused by duress. Perhaps this is typically true. But one would not be substantially responsible for gang activity if one's initial recruitment and subsequent role in gang activity were themselves the result of coercive duress, which presumably happens sometimes. Moreover, if structural injustice severely limits one's opportunities for success outside of participation in gang activity, this might provide partial excuse or justification for gang membership. Engaging in gang misconduct as the result of duress in these circumstances might merit partial excuse or mitigation, provided the conduct did not involve manifest illegality. If most gang activity involves manifest illegality, that will severely limit the parallel between military and gang misconduct.

Clearer parallels with military misconduct might involve misconduct by police and prison guards. Here too, we find actors involved in potentially dangerous encounters, where decisions about the use of force often need to be made quickly and subject to limited information and in the heat of passion. Both the police and prison security are organizations with collective and hierarchical structure that can bring pressure to engage in misconduct from superiors and peers, as well as pressure to cover up misconduct. Unlike gang activity and like military service, police and prison work are legitimate callings. Indeed, the similarities between the military, the police, and prison security officers are in many ways quite striking. These similarities support similar conclusions. We should rarely, if ever, excuse manifest illegality by police officers or security personnel, treating suspects or prisoners in ways that are clearly impermissible. We should be prepared to consider full or partial excuses for inadvertent misconduct only in the moral equivalent of hot combat—where police or prison guards make reasonable mistakes in the heat of the moment about the proportionate use of force. These objective mistakes, even though reasonable, are best conceptualized as excuses, whether full or partial, rather than justifications. They show the misconduct to be less than fully blameworthy, rather than justified.

These remarks about potential parallels between responsibility and excuse for wartime misconduct and misconduct that occurs in other contexts has been speculative and suggestive, at best. Defending such claims would require more careful engagement with the details and circumstances of misconduct in these contexts. But if the fair opportunity perspective on responsibility and excuse for wartime wrongdoing is plausible, these parallels would be worth exploring further and more fully.

11

Incompetence, Psychopathy, and Fair Opportunity

Recall our working hypothesis that responsibility and excuse are inversely related—responsibility for wrongdoing precludes excuse, and excuse denies responsibility for wrongdoing. Incompetence excuses, such as insanity, involve significant impairment of the agent's normative capacities. Insanity is the main incompetence excuse in the criminal law and provides a clear model for a moral excuse of incompetence. The fair opportunity conception of responsibility factors normative competence into both cognitive and volitional capacities and treats these two sets of capacities as individually necessary and jointly sufficient for the relevant sort of competence. The fair opportunity conception of responsibility supports a conception of excuse that treats either cognitive or volitional impairment as the basis of an excuse, and this claim about excuse has important implications for our understanding of insanity and incompetence. In particular, fair opportunity provides support, in broad terms, for the Model Penal Code conception of insanity as involving either cognitive or volitional impairment, rather than the M'Naghten purely cognitive conception.

However, even the Model Penal Code conception of insanity is under-inclusive in some ways and over-inclusive in others. On the one hand, it's not clear that we should require that incompetence be caused by a mental disease or defect, as all extant insanity conceptions do, at least if mental disease or defect is understood as a separate clinical category that would restrict the cases of incompetence qualifying for insanity. On the other hand, incompetence should not be excusing if the agent is culpable for being incompetent, as she might be if her incompetence is successfully managed by medication and, while competent, she chooses to go off her medication and ends up engaging in wrongdoing as the result of her incompetence.

Though the prototypical insanity excuse is one involving severe mental illness with psychotic episodes, the fair opportunity analysis of incompetence excuses should make us take seriously other potential incompetence excuses. One kind of potential incompetence excuse that has been the subject of much

Fair Opportunity and Responsibility. David O. Brink, Oxford University Press (2021). © David O. Brink.
DOI: 10.1093/oso/9780198859468.003.0011

discussion is *psychopathy*. Psychopathy is puzzling for several reasons. First, our reactive attitudes toward psychopaths are variable and sometimes ambivalent. On the one hand, the criminal law does not recognize psychopathy as an excuse. Psychopaths do not present themselves as traditional incompetents who are delusional or incoherent. They are typically alert, intelligent, and frequently socially at ease, even charming. Psychopaths can display cruelty and malice and typically show no remorse for the harm they do. These characteristics of psychopathy explain why many are inclined to treat it as an aggravating, rather than excusing or mitigating, factor. On the other hand, several writers have appealed to empirical studies of psychopaths and their psychological deficits to argue that they have significantly impaired normative competence that might justify excusing their wrongdoing. Our understanding of the responsibility of psychopaths is further complicated by the fact that empirical work on psychopathy is still evolving and is currently unsettled in several respects. For these reasons, it is hard to reach definitive conclusions about whether psychopathy should be excusing. But the fair opportunity conception of responsibility, incompetence, and excuse can help to frame the debate about whether psychopathy can excuse in a constructive way. Moreover, there is, I will argue, reason to be skeptical about whether we should recognize such an excuse at the present time, given what we now know about the nature of psychopathy.

If psychopathy were excusing, it would justify a fairly general excuse. But we might also consider more *selective* forms of incompetence. Though incompetence can be selective along several dimensions and for various reasons, I'd like to discuss cases in which agents are not otherwise normatively incompetent but nonetheless have a significant *moral blindspot*. In particular, I want to focus on misconduct that results from moral blindspots that an agent internalizes and that are reinforced by his community. A recurrent kind of case involves bias and discriminatory treatment of members of outgroups. Some examples involve historical injustices, both ancient and more recent, such as the institution of slavery in various historical periods, discrimination against African Americans in the Jim Crow South, discrimination against black South Africans during Apartheid, or the discrimination against homosexuals. Many of these forms of discriminatory misconduct resulted from culturally reinforced and entrenched moral beliefs. Are slaveholders, incorrigible racists, misogynists, and homophobes selectively incompetent? If so, are they less blameworthy for their mistaken attitudes and conduct? Though I don't rule out the possibility of misconduct that might be excused because of selective incompetence, I do think that the selective character of moral blindspots—the fact that blindspots occur in people who are otherwise normatively competent—means that these blindspots are typically corrigible and don't constitute genuine incompetence.

86. Conceptions of Insanity

Insanity is the paradigm incompetence excuse. There have been at least five separable insanity tests, each of which has had a day in the sun in American criminal law.[1]

1. The M'Naghten cognitive test, which excuses iffi the wrongdoer was unable to recognize the wrongness of his act due to mental disease or defect.
2. An irresistible impulse test, which excuses if the wrongdoing is the product of irresistible impulses resulting from mental disease or defect.
3. The Durham Product test, which excuses iffi the wrongdoing is the causal product of mental disease or defect.
4. The Model Penal Code test, which excuses iffi there is a substantial impairment of the defendant's ability (a) to appreciate the wrongness of his actions or (b) to conform his conduct to that appreciation due to mental disease or defect.
5. The Federal cognitive test, which excuses iffi the wrongdoer could not appreciate the wrongness of his action due to mental disease or defect.

Nonetheless, it is fair to focus on M'Naghten and the Model Penal Code. The irresistible impulse test was meant as a supplement to M'Naghten, not to serve as a self-standing test, and a version of it is incorporated in the Model Penal Code doctrine. The Federal test represents a common understanding of M'Naghten. Hence, only the Durham Product test is a real alternative to M'Naghten and the Model Penal Code, and it was widely recognized as providing a conception of excuse that was both under-inclusive and over-inclusive. If mental disease or defect does not cause incompetence, it should not be excusing, and incompetence should be excusing, whether or not it is caused by mental disease or defect. For these reasons, the Durham Product test is rightfully ignored.

---

[1] For discussion, see Dressler, *Understanding Criminal Law*, ch. 25 and Michael Moore, *Law and Psychiatry: Rethinking the Relationship* (Cambridge: Cambridge University Press, 1984).

The main debate has been whether sanity is just a matter of cognitive competence, with the result that the insanity excuse should involve a purely cognitive impairment, or whether sanity includes volitional competence as well, in which case insanity could take the form of cognitive or volitional impairment. These two different conceptions are represented by the M'Naghten test and by the Model Penal Code test, respectively.

M'Naghten tried to kill Prime Minister Robert Peel, inadvertently killing his secretary, Edward Drummond, instead. M'Naghten suffered from paranoid delusions. Lord Chief Justice Tindal formulated the charge to the jury this way.

> The question to be determined is whether at the time the act in question was committed, the prisoner had or had not the use of his understanding, so as to know that he was doing a wrong or wicked act. If the jurors should be of the opinion that the prisoner was not sensible, at the time he committed it, that he was violating the laws both of God and man, then he would be entitled to a verdict in his favour: but if, on the contrary, they were of the opinion that when he committed the act he was in a sound state of mind, then their verdict must be against him.[2]

The jury found M'Naghten not guilty by reason of insanity.

It's not entirely clear if M'Naghten treats moral ignorance as sufficient for excuse or whether it requires cognitive incapacity. Tindal's charge could perhaps be read either way. Earlier, we defended the view that cognitive incapacity is required (§§16–17). Performance errors only excuse when they reflect an underlying incompetence. Moreover, this capacitarian interpretation of M'Naghten is a common one, reflected, for example, in the Federal insanity test.

> It is an affirmative defense to a prosecution under any Federal statute that, at the time of the commission of the acts constituting the offense, the defendant, as a result of a severe mental disease or defect, was unable to appreciate the nature and quality or the wrongfulness of his acts. Mental disease or defect does not otherwise constitute a defense.[3]

With insanity, as with other affirmative defenses, the Model Penal Code expands common law conceptions of the defense.

---

[2] M'Naghten's Case, 10 Cl. & F.200, Eng. Rep. 718 (1843).   [3] 18 U.S. Code §17 (2005).

> (1) A person is not responsible for criminal conduct if at the time of such conduct as a result of a mental disease or defect he lacks substantial capacity either to appreciate the criminality [wrongfulness] of his conduct or to conform his conduct to the requirements of law. (2) As used in this Article, the terms "mental disease or defect" do not include an abnormality manifested only by repeated criminal or otherwise anti-social conduct.
>
> [MPC §4.01]

Like M'Naghten, the Model Penal Code requires that the relevant incapacities be due to mental disease or defect and that there be independent evidence of this disease or defect, apart from the wrongdoing itself.

Moreover, like M'Naghten, the Model Penal Code does not specify whether the wrongdoing that the agent must be able to recognize or appreciate is legal or moral wrongdoing, leaving this to be specified jurisdiction by jurisdiction. A natural assumption is that whereas moral responsibility requires competence with respect to moral requirements, criminal responsibility requires competence with respect to criminal law norms.

Despite these commonalities, the Model Penal Code test is conceptually broader than M'Naghten in three ways. First, the most important difference is that whereas M'Naghten has a purely cognitive conception of responsibility, the Model Penal Code conception is cognitive and volitional. Because the Code requires *both* forms of competence for responsibility, significant impairment of *either* is excusing, with the result that the Code's conception of insanity is conceptually broader than the M'Naghten conception, which recognizes only cognitive impairments as excusing.

Second, the Model Penal Code says that one is insane if one lacks a *substantial* capacity, whether cognitive or volitional. This contrasts with traditional understandings of M'Naghten that say, in effect, that one must be completely lacking in cognitive capacity to qualify as insane. Someone who had minimal cognitive competence might qualify as sane under M'Naghten but as insane under the Model Penal Code. The Code applies this same substantial capacity analysis to volitional, as well as cognitive, capacity.

Third, the Model Penal Code requires that the defendant be able to *appreciate* the wrongfulness of her conduct. It's not immediately clear if this is different from formulations of M'Naghten requiring that one be able to *recognize* the wrongfulness of her conduct. Interestingly, the Federal insanity defense is formulated in terms of appreciation. On the one hand, these could be viewed as equivalent formulations—one is able to appreciate that one's act is wrong just in case one is able to recognize that it is wrong. On the other hand, appreciation might go beyond recognition. On this view, appreciation requires at least a rudimentary understanding of *why*, as well as *that*, something is wrong. If so, whereas M'Naghten's knowledge requirement involves a fairly thin kind of understanding, the Model Penal Code's appreciation requirement arguably involves a thicker kind of understanding.

Here, as on many issues, the Model Penal Code was influential in leading to reforms in state criminal codes. Prior to adoption of the Model Penal Code, the purely cognitive M'Naghten test was the dominant conception of insanity in American criminal law. But, under the influence of the Model Penal Code, many states came to adopt its broader conception of insanity. However, this trend changed dramatically in the wake of John Hinckley's acquittal in 1982 on grounds of insanity for the attempted murder of President Ronald Reagan. Public outcry over the verdict led to a backlash against any perceived broadening of the insanity defense and a return in several jurisdictions to a narrower M'Naghten-style conception of insanity. This regressive backlash has reshaped the insanity defense in American jurisdictions with slightly more states now employing a version of the M'Naghten conception of insanity than a Model Penal Code conception.[4]

87. Fair Opportunity and the Model Penal Code

As between the Model Penal Code and M'Naghten conceptions of insanity, the fair opportunity conception of responsibility and excuse endorses something like the Model Penal Code conception, rather than the narrower M'Naghten conception.

First, the fair opportunity conception of responsibility rejects skepticism about the volitional dimension of normative competence (§§16, 18, 22). Normative competence requires more than cognitive competence. It also requires volitional capacities to form intentions based on one's practical judgments about what one ought to do and to execute these intentions over

---

[4] As of this writing, of the 43 states that employ either M'Naghten or the Model Penal Code, 22 employ M'Naghten and 21 employ Model Penal Code reforms. Nine states have no insanity defense or a different one. The post-Hinckley backlash was based on misunderstandings about the frequency of insanity pleas, the frequency of successful insanity pleas, and the consequences of successful insanity pleas. Though the frequency of insanity pleas and successful insanity pleas varies in different jurisdictions, the rates have always been quite low and were not substantially affected by adoption of a broader conception of insanity. See, e.g., Judge Rubin's dissent in *United States v. Lyons*, USCA 5th Cir., 731 F.2d 243, 739 F.2d 994 (1984). Moreover, it's not clear that Hinckley would have been found sane under M'Naghten.

time, despite distraction, temptation, and other forms of interference. Volitional impairment might take many forms—including compulsions or paralyzing phobias that are insistent and resist attempts to conquer or circumvent them; severe depression that might make it difficult to summon focus, attention, and resolve necessary to execute complex or difficult plans; and abnormalities in the prefrontal cortex of the brain that impair executive function. Because normative competence has both cognitive and volitional dimensions, the fair opportunity conception endorses the more inclusive conception of responsibility that recognizes both cognitive and volitional conditions and excuses for significant impairment of either.

Second, if we are going to treat responsibility and excuse as bivalent—all or nothing—then we must set some kind of threshold for responsibility, above which one is fully responsible and below which one is fully excused. If so, it is better to require substantial, rather than bare, capacity, such that excuse is triggered by substantial impairment, rather than complete incapacity. The Model Penal Code's claim that the competence threshold for responsibility should be substantial, rather than minimal, is plausible in its own right. But it is especially plausible if we accept Blackstone's asymmetry that it is worse to over-punish than to under-punish (§43). As we shall see in greater detail in Chapter 15, when the underlying facts about responsibility and excuse are scalar, bivalent verdicts produce failures of proportionate justice in the form of over-punishment and under-punishment. The lower the threshold for responsibility, the higher the percentage of over-punishment, relative to under-punishment. If over-punishment is worse than under-punishment, this gives us special reason not to make the responsibility threshold *de minimus*.

Third, it is harder to know what the fair opportunity conception of responsibility implies about the Model Penal Code requirement that the agent be able to appreciate the quality of his act and its wrongfulness, in part because it is hard to know whether appreciation should be understood as a further requirement beyond recognition of wrongfulness.[5] The greater the gap between the sort of understanding required by appreciation and recognition, the more significant the appreciation requirement. But the more significant the gap, the

---

[5] If appreciation involves understanding, this issue may be the same as the issue whether understanding is a distinct epistemic requirement from knowledge. Non-reductionists think that understanding is a further requirement, beyond knowledge, whereas reductionists deny this. For defense of non-reductionism about moral understanding, see Alison Hills, "Moral Testimony and Moral Epistemology" *Ethics* 120 (2009): 94–127 and "Understanding Why" *Noûs* 50 (2016): 661–88. For a defense of reductionism, see Paulina Sliwa, "Moral Understanding as Knowing Right from Wrong" *Ethics* 127 (2017): 521–52.

harder it is to justify a separate appreciation requirement. Fair opportunity requires agents to be able to discriminate right from wrong and recognize wrongdoing. Perhaps because fair opportunity requires that the agent be able to recognize when wrongdoing is justified, for instance, as permission to do the lesser evil, it may require that the agent be able to *grade* offenses as greater and lesser. So a recognitional capacity should perhaps include a rough gradeability capacity. But it is not clear that the fair opportunity to avoid wrongdoing requires any very subtle or sophisticated form of legal or moral understanding. I don't have to be a mechanic to be a competent driver. Similarly, it is not clear that I have to understand the normative basis of moral requirements to be competent about their deployment.

We might contrast *refined morality* and *basic morality*. Refined morality can be delicate, requiring a keen appreciation of the needs and signals of others and a deft touch. For instance, some demands of friendship and loyalty are refined. However, much of morality requires fairly basic honesty, cooperation, fidelity, restraint, and fair play and a capacity for moral triage. The requirements of the criminal law are even more elemental. Two points are worth making in light of this contrast. First, our focus here is on basic morality and the criminal law, whose demands are fairly similar. The cognitive capacities necessary to recognize basic morality and the criminal law will be more modest than those necessary to recognize refined morality. Second, even if we shift focus to refined morality, it is not clear why this should induce us to switch from recognition to appreciation. The norms of refined morality may be more complex or subtle than those of basic morality, which would affect the capacities necessary for recognizing the norms in question, but there is no apparent reason that this should affect the sort of cognitive relation the agent should bear to these norms. These considerations suggest caution about embracing an appreciation standard that is significantly more demanding than a recognitional standard, especially if we focus on basic morality and the criminal law. The fair opportunity conception of responsibility seems to require only a recognitional capacity and perhaps a gradeability capacity.

Consequently, there are at least two important respects in which the fair opportunity conception of responsibility favors the broader Model Penal Code conception of the insanity defense, as against the narrower M'Naghten conception. Responsibility requires both cognitive and volitional competence; and, if we accept bivalence about responsibility and excuse, substantial impairment of either should be excusing.

88. Beyond the Model Penal Code

Despite affinities between fair opportunity and the Model Penal Code, there are two ways in which fair opportunity might require modifications to the Code's understanding of insanity. If insanity should be understood as an incompetence excuse, there are at least two potential worries about the Model Penal Code conception. On the one hand, it might be too broad, providing an incompetence excuse in cases of culpable incapacity in which we shouldn't recognize an excuse. On the other hand, it might be too narrow, failing to recognize incompetence excuses in cases that we should.

As formulated, the Model Penal Code treats substantial cognitive or volitional impairment as sufficient for an incompetence excuse. Taken at face value, this conception of an incompetence excuse is over-inclusive. Though in many cases normative incompetence of the relevant kind should be sufficient for an excuse, not in all cases. In particular, in cases in which the agent is herself responsible for becoming incompetent, it seems she should not be afforded an excuse, at least not a full excuse.

We might want to insist that normative incompetence should be excusing only when it was non-culpably acquired (see Figure 11.1). Consider someone who suffers from a kind of mental disorder that renders her normatively incompetent but that can be effectively treated with medication. Assume that it is reasonably foreseeable that when she is incompetent she is prone to misconduct and poses a substantial risk to herself or others. Suppose that she is normatively competent when she is on her medication but that, while competent, she chooses to stop taking her medication, perhaps because she dislikes some of its side-effects. If so, while competent, she decides to risk making herself incompetent, foreseeing that this poses a substantial risk of misconduct. If she engages in wrongdoing after quitting her medication, she would, by hypothesis, not be competent at the time of her wrongdoing and so

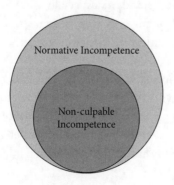

Figure 11.1 Only Non-culpable Incapacity Is Excusing

would qualify for the insanity defense if incompetence were sufficient for that excuse. Presumably, we want to say that the insanity or incompetence excuse should be unavailable to wrongdoers even if they were incompetent at the time of their wrongdoing if they were substantially competent and, hence, substantially responsible and culpable for becoming incompetent. Depending on how serious the side-effects of medication were, we might be willing to extend some mitigation to her at sentencing. But we should be reluctant to recognize an insanity excuse in such circumstances. This would introduce into the criminal law doctrine of insanity a restriction on the availability of the excuse when the agent is responsible for what would otherwise be excusing conditions.

This would be to treat insanity similar to the way in which the Model Penal Code already limits other excuses. For instance, culpable incapacity, such as voluntary intoxication, is not excusing (MPC §§2.08(4)–(5)(b)). An agent should be excused for misconduct resulting from intoxication if her intoxication was non-voluntary, for instance, if someone surreptitiously placed a roofie in her iced tea. But intoxication does not excuse if it results from the agent's clear-eyed consumption of alcohol or other drugs. Similarly, duress does not excuse when the agent is substantially responsible for being subject to duress (§2.09). If someone voluntarily enters into a criminal conspiracy and eventually commits the crime under duress from her co-conspirators after hesitating at the last minute, a duress excuse will be problematic.

Moreover, we said that fair opportunity can make sense of these limitations on excuse using historical or ahistorical resources. We can deny excuse in cases of culpable incapacity either (a) by recognizing responsibility at the time of wrongdoing by *tracing* it back to competent and responsible choice at an earlier point in time (e.g. the competent choice to go off medicine that maintains competence or the competent choice to drink in circumstances in which she might later drive) or (b) by holding the agent responsible for the reasonably foreseeable consequences of her earlier competent and responsible choices. Though I offered reasons to prefer the synchronic explanation of these limits on excuse (§35), present purposes allow us to be agnostic about the merits of historical and ahistorical explanations of these limits. Whereas we do want to recognize incompetence excuses for non-culpable incapacity, we should be reluctant to extend excuses to cases of culpable incapacity.

To block incompetence excuses for culpable incapacity, we need to narrow the Model Penal Code conception of incompetence excuses. But, in another way, the Model Penal Code conception may be too narrow and require broadening. Like M'Naghten and all other proposed insanity tests, the Model Penal Code restricts the insanity defense to wrongdoing that results from incapacity "due to mental disease or defect." Call this the *mental disease requirement*. On one reading of this requirement, it is a further condition beyond the relevant kind of incapacity, yielding a smaller class of excuses than the simple appeal to incapacity would. However, according to the fair opportunity conception of responsibility, significant impairment of normative competence should be excusing regardless of its cause, provided that the cause was non-culpable. This generates the worry that the Model Penal Code conception of insanity, with its mental disease requirement, is too narrow to serve as a general incompetence excuse.

This is a problem only if the Model Penal Code's mental disease requirement is supposed to function as an independent requirement, one constrained by independent psychiatric criteria. This would be to treat the concept of mental illness as a diagnostic *clinical category*, perhaps drawing its evidence from the current version of the *Diagnostic and Statistical Manual of Mental Disorders (DSM)*.[6] This clinical reading of the mental illness requirement would further limit the larger class of normative incapacity to the proper subclass of those whose normative incompetence is the product of clinically recognized mental illness or defect, and this would give rise to the worry that the Model Penal Code insanity test represents an under-inclusive incompetence excuse. According to this clinical reading of the mental disease requirement, insanity would be limited to the intersection of normative incompetence and conditions with origins in mental disease or defect (see Figure 11.2).

This clinical conception of the mental disease requirement threatens to be too restrictive. We can imagine significant impairments of cognitive or volitional competence that might not issue from a clinically well recognized

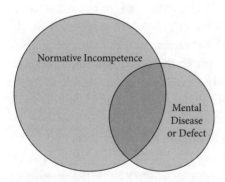

Figure 11.2 A Clinical Conception of Insanity

[6] American Psychiatric Association, *Diagnostic Statistical Manual of Mental Disorders* 5th ed. (Washington, DC: American Psychiatric Association, 2013).

mental disease or that issues from a condition about which there is significant clinical disagreement. If the case for significant impairment of normative competence can be made plausibly, and the agent is not himself culpable for the impairment, this should be sufficient for an incompetence excuse.

Consider cases of *coercive indoctrination* in which agents engage in misconduct as a result of moral ignorance resulting from coercive indoctrination and epistemic isolation. One well-known case of potential coercive indoctrination involved Patty Hearst, the heiress to the William Randolph Hearst publishing empire. In 1974, at the age of 19, Hearst was kidnapped by the Symbionese Liberation Army and subsequently participated in criminal activity organized by the SLA, including an armed bank robbery. She initially participated in SLA discussions and activities out of fear for her safety. Some facts in the case are contested, such as whether at the time of the bank robbery she was a willing convert to the SLA cause or whether she was acting under more conventional duress. At trial, her defense mixed elements of duress, coercive indoctrination, and Stockholm syndrome. The judge instructed the jury to consider only a duress defense. Her duress defense was unsuccessful, and she was convicted of armed robbery and eventually sentenced to seven years in prison. President Jimmy Carter commuted her sentence to time served in 1979, and in 2001 she was pardoned by President Bill Clinton.[7]

For our purposes, we needn't settle any of the contested aspects of Hearst's actual psychology or the best way to frame her defense. I'm interested in one way we might want to conceptualize an incompetence excuse in a case like Hearst's. So let's consider an interpretation of Hearst's case that did involve coercive indoctrination, whether or not that's ultimately the correct description of Hearst herself. On this version of events, Hearst eventually became a willing SLA participant, partly because her isolation and coercive indoctrination led her to believe that she had been abandoned by society and her family and that her survival depended on embracing the SLA. Even if her criminal activity could not be excused by duress, there's still a plausible case to be made that her wrongdoing was the result of temporary non-culpable cognitive incompetence. Her isolation and indoctrination arguably led her to mistakenly endorse the SLA cause and believe that her criminal activity was justified. If so, her capacity to discriminate between right and wrong at the time of her misconduct was arguably substantially impaired. Since the isolation and indoctrination followed on her kidnapping, Hearst would have been

---

[7] A recent account of the Hearst kidnapping and trial is Jeffrey Toobin, *American Heiress* (New York: Doubleday, 2016).

non-culpable for her incapacity. If so, on this version of events, she had a plausible claim for a temporary incompetence excuse.[8]

It's hard to square recognition of a non-culpable incapacity excuse due to coercive indoctrination with the clinical interpretation of the Model Penal Code's mental disease requirement. This is because coercive indoctrination is not a well-recognized clinical category. It's true that "identity disturbance due to prolonged and intense coercive persuasion" is mentioned in the *DSM*. But it's listed in the category Other Specified Dissociative Disorder, and this category is treated as marginal.

> This category applies to presentations in which symptoms characteristic of a dissociative disorder that cause clinically significant distress or impairment in social, occupational, or other important areas of functioning predominate but do not meet the full criteria for any of the disorders in the dissociative disorders diagnostic class.   [*DSM*, p. 306]

This makes it seem like incapacity due to coercive indoctrination is a disputed or marginal category within the *DSM*. At best, it is not clear that one could mount a successful insanity defense based on coercive indoctrination if we read the Code's mental disease requirement as a clinical category, no matter how clear the incapacity and how extreme the coercive indoctrination. There may well be other ways in which the clinical conception of the mental disease requirement is too restrictive, but coercive indoctrination provides one illustration.

But we don't need to interpret the mental disease requirement as a clinical category. Alternatively, we might interpret the mental disease requirement as having no independent significance. Perhaps any form of significant normative incompetence qualifies as a mental illness. This would be to treat the concept of mental illness, for purposes of the Model Penal Code, as a *forensic category*. If so, there is no problem of under-inclusiveness, because the mental illness requirement is not an independent requirement above and beyond the incompetence requirement. The mental illness requirement, on this forensic reading, does not pick out a proper subset of the class of normative incompetence.

---

[8] I've benefited from discussions of coercive indoctrination with Evan Tiffany and from his essay "Conceptualizing Coercive Indoctrination in Moral and Legal Philosophy" *Criminal Law and Philosophy* (forthcoming).

It is unclear how we are supposed to understand the mental disease requirement in the Model Penal Code insanity defense, in particular, whether we
should understand it as a clinical or forensic category. Of course, psychiatric
evidence will be relevant on either reading of the requirement—on the clinical
reading, as evidence that the defendant had a *bona fide* mental disease over
and above her incompetence, and, on the forensic reading, as evidence that she
is normatively incompetent. I suspect that most consumers of the Model Penal
Code understand the requirement as a clinical category.[9] If so, we should treat
its conception of insanity as only a proper part of an incompetence excuse.
This would be reason to abolish the insanity test and replace it with a more
general incompetence test that would include both cognitive and volitional
incompetence, whatever its (non-culpable) cause. Traditional abolitionists are
hard abolitionists, because they seek to remove the excuse provided by the
insanity defense. By contrast, the form of abolitionism that the fair opportunity conception of responsibility favors is *soft abolitionism*, inasmuch as it
rejects the clinical interpretation of the mental disease requirement in the
insanity defense and argues for a broader excuse of normative incompetence.

If we bear in mind these concerns about how the Model Penal Code
conception of insanity might be both over-inclusive and under-inclusive, we
could defend a qualified version of that conception as a general incompetence
excuse. As a first approximation, a fair opportunity incompetence excuse
might be formulated this way.

(1) A person is not responsible for criminal conduct if at the time of such
conduct she lacks substantial capacity either to appreciate the wrongfulness
of her conduct or to conform her conduct to these norms. (2) This defense is
not available to wrongdoers even if they were incompetent at the time of
their wrongdoing if they were substantially competent and, hence, responsible at an earlier time for becoming incompetent.

Some such conception of incompetence incorporates the virtues of the Model
Penal Code, while correcting for the respects in which its conception of excuse

[9] The fact that proponents of the now discredited product test thought that adopting its rule,
according to which wrongdoing is excused on grounds of insanity if the wrongdoing is the product
of mental disease or defect, was simpler than incapacity tests and by-passed issues about incapacity
suggests that they conceived of mental illness as distinct from normative incapacity and easier to
establish. However, the Durham product test was eventually interpreted so as to define mental disease
or defect as "any abnormal condition of the mind which substantially affects mental or emotional
processes and substantially impairs behavior controls." See *MacDonald v. United States*, 312 F.2d 847,
851 (D.C. Cir. 1962). While the product test may have begun with a clinical, rather than forensic,
conception of mental disease, it eventually came closer to a forensic conception.

is both too narrow and too broad. It is the sort of incompetence excuse supported by the fair opportunity conception of responsibility.

89. A Brief Case Study of Insanity: Andrea Yates

Andrea Yates is arguably a good illustration of a traditional insanity defense. For years, she had suffered with severe post-partum depression and psychosis and killed her five children by drowning them in the bathtub of the family home in Houston in 2001 under the belief that this was the only way to save their souls from Satan. Partly on the strength of problematic expert testimony for the prosecution by Park Dietz, Yates was convicted in 2002 of first-degree murder and received the mandatory minimum sentence of life imprisonment with the possibility of parole after 40 years. However, on appeal in 2006, her conviction was overturned and she was found not guilty by reason of insanity. She was committed to a high security mental hospital and in 2007 moved to a lower security facility.[10]

As in other jurisdictions, Texas had earlier broadened its conception of insanity under the influence of the Model Penal Code but then retrenched as part of the backlash against the Hinckley case. The Texas provision for insanity is a version of the M'Naghten test.

It is an affirmative defense to the prosecution that, at the time of the conduct charged, the actor, as a result of severe mental disease or defect, did not know that his conduct was wrong.[11]

Here, the test focuses on ignorance, not incapacity. But it's unlikely that culpable ignorance (e.g. willful ignorance) would be excused. If not, then it's really a test of cognitive incapacity. Moreover, it does not specify whether the requisite normative knowledge concerns legal or moral wrongdoing.

---

[10] *Yates v. Texas*, 171 S.W.3d 215, 218 (Tx. Ct. App. 2005). The Yates cases were much discussed in the media and legal circles. For academic discussion, see, e.g., Deborah Denno, "Who Is Andrea Yates? A Short Story about Insanity" *Duke Journal of Gender Law & Policy* 10 (2003): 1–60 and Phillip Resnick, "The Andrea Yates Case: Insanity on Trial" *Cleveland State Law Review* 55 (2007): 147–56. Denno's article was written after the first trial and before the second; though it provides extensive criticism of Dietz's testimony, it contains useful information about the facts of the case. Resnick provided expert psychiatric testimony at the second trial, rebutting key components of Dietz's testimony.

[11] Texas Penal Code, Annotated, §8.01.

The case was complicated in various ways. On the one hand, Yates claimed that she knew that it was legally wrong to kill her children and insisted that she be punished, indeed, executed. The killing itself had been premeditated, and Yates was apparently meticulous about the process, posing the bodies of the children in her bed afterward. When the police arrived and interviewed her, she seemed composed. She was resistant to the proposal that she mount an insanity defense. Despite her history of mental illness, Dietz testified that Yates knew that killing her children was both legally and morally wrong.

However, by Yates's own testimony, she had been visited by Satan, who threatened to take her children because of her own vices. This threatens to raise vexed issues about *deific decree*, which arises in cases in which the wrongdoer hears voices, which she takes to be divine commands, to kill. In some jurisdictions, deific decree is held to excuse because it shows that the accused did not satisfy the relevant standard of cognitive competence. It does not appear that Yates believed that God had commanded her to kill the children. So Yates does not present a clear case of deific decree.[12] However, if her religious hallucinations are to be credited, it seems that she thought that she herself had already been lost to Satan and that he was threatening her children. By killing them, she seems to have thought that she would condemn herself and yet save the children's souls from eternal damnation. If she thought she was protecting her children by killing them, it seems she did not know that what she did, in killing them, was morally wrong, though she may have known it was legally wrong. Even if she thought her killing of the children constituted a homicide offense, she might well have thought that her actions pursued a lesser evil and, hence, were justified. Even if she didn't know that what she was doing was wrong, it's a separate question whether she had sufficient capacity to realize this. But if her beliefs were this untethered from reality, there seems good reason to wonder if she could have been normatively competent at the time.

Dietz's confident assertion that Yates did know the difference between right and wrong was based on a single interview he conducted with Yates many

---

[12] Deific decree is puzzling. Even if an agent believes that God has told her to kill, there's an interesting question whether this shows that she lacks normative competence. On the one hand, bad advice from a perceived advisor does not automatically exculpate. I might have the capacity to recognize bad advice as bad and be expected to exercise that capacity, refusing to follow the advice. Perceived deities might be thought to be just especially influential spiritual advisors. A responsible agent should ask if it's more reasonable to accept the authority of voices instructing you to commit atrocities or to question the source of this advice. On the other hand, anyone who thinks that God is instructing her to commit atrocities may be so irrational that she couldn't be expected to question the authority of her visions.

months after the killings in a period in which her mental condition was improved due to supervised medication. Even if she was competent at the time of that interview, that wouldn't show that she was competent at the time of the killings. And it's not clear that her later more competent testimony would be a reliable window onto what her earlier less competent self was thinking.

Significantly, there was a history of mental illness in Yates's family that included both her father and her three siblings. Her own mental illness emerged after the birth of her first son in 1994. She was diagnosed with post-partum depression and psychosis, both recognized as psychological disorders in the *DSM* (§§298.8, 295.90). Because she had so many children in such a short period of time, she was either pregnant or nursing during most of the time from the birth of her first child to her killing of her five children. She became withdrawn and severely depressed, experienced paranoid delusions and self-loathing, and twice tried to kill herself. With Yates's mental history in mind, it's easy to doubt that she was normatively competent. One can reasonably doubt that she had the cognitive capacity to recognize right from wrong or that if she did form the right judgment that she had the capacity to conform her behavior to this knowledge amidst her depression and paranoid delusions.

90. Psychopathy

Whereas the sort of psychosis experienced by Andrea Yates presents a reasonably familiar model of insanity, psychopathy represents an interesting and difficult case for thinking about insanity and excuse. Psychopathy is difficult for several reasons. Our reactive attitudes toward psychopaths are variable and potentially ambivalent. On the one hand, the criminal law does not recognize psychopathy as an excuse. Psychopaths do not present themselves as traditional incompetents who are delusional, incoherent, catatonic, or suicidal. They are typically alert, intelligent, socially at ease, even charming. Psychopaths can display cruelty and malice and typically show little or no remorse for the harm they cause. These characteristics of psychopathy explain why many are inclined to treat psychopathy as an *aggravating*, rather than excusing or mitigating, factor. On the other hand, several philosophers and legal theorists have recently claimed that psychopaths have psychological deficits of various kinds that impair their normative competence and, hence, provide the basis for a potential excuse.[13] To address these issues, we also need to know something about the nature of psychopathy and then ask whether and, if so, why psychopaths lack normative competence.

Despite decades of research by psychologists, psychiatrists, cognitive scientists, neuroscientists, and criminologists, there is still much that is not known or that is contested about psychopathy, for instance, about its etiology and neuroanatomy. In what follows, I will try to focus on the syndrome of personality traits and behavior that is best understood and most directly relevant to assessments of normative competence.[14] Psychopathy is thought to depend on endogenous neurological and personality factors, even if its psychological and behavioral expression can sometimes be affected by nurture, education, and other environmental factors. Psychopathic personality and behavior in adults is usually traceable back to childhood, with adult onset being both rare and contested. Hervey Cleckley's pioneering work on psychopathy in *The Mask of Sanity* (1941) has been extremely influential and remains helpful. It is noteworthy that Cleckley's clinical observations included both unsuccessful or criminal psychopaths and so-called successful psychopaths whose deviance did not include criminal behavior or who had not been caught and convicted for criminal misconduct. As the title of Cleckley's book suggests, he was struck by the superficial appearance of normalcy in most psychopaths. Unlike familiar forms of mental illness that might qualify for an insanity defense, psychopaths do not usually present as obviously mentally disturbed. They are not delusional, incoherent, unusually anxious, or especially prone to suicide. In fact, psychopaths are usually quite intelligent and articulate and display superficial social skills. But if one looks beneath this veneer and examines their history, psychopaths display similar personality traits and behavior. They tend to be egocentric and to have shallow affect or emotion; they are insincere, untruthful, and manipulative; and they lack

---

[13] See Watson, "Responsibility and the Limits of Evil" and Gary Watson, "The Trouble with Psychopaths" in *Reason and Recognition: Essays on the Philosophy of T.M. Scanlon*, ed. S. Freeman, R. Kumar, and J. Wallace (Oxford: Clarendon Press, 2011); Cordelia Fine and Jeanette Kennett, "Mental Impairment, Moral Understanding, and Criminal Responsibility" *International Journal of Law and Psychiatry* 27 (2004): 425–43; Stephen Morse, "Psychopathy and Criminal Responsibility" *Neuroethics* 1 (2008): 205–12; Ishtiyaque, Haji "Psychopathy, Ethical Perception, and Moral Culpability" *Neuroethics* 3 (2010): 135–50; and Nelkin, "Psychopaths, Incorrigible Racists, and the Faces of Responsibility."

[14] My principal sources are Hervey Cleckley, *The Mask of Sanity* [first edition 1941] (St. Louis, MO: C.V. Mosby, 1955); Robert Hare, *Without Conscience* (New York: Simon & Schuster, 1993); James Blair, "A Cognitive Developmental Approach to Morality: Investigating the Psychopath" *Cognition* 57 (1995): 1–29 and Blair, Mitchell, and Blair, *The Psychopath*; and *Handbook of Psychopathy*, ed. C. Patrick (New York: Guilford Press, 2006).

remorse for their wrongdoing. These traits lead to various behavioral problems. Psychopaths regularly engage in antisocial behavior that causes hardship to others; this antisocial behavior is typically inadequately motivated and imprudent; they fail to learn by experience from their mistakes; their behavior is aimless and displays no life plan; and they are unable to sustain lasting and satisfying interpersonal relationships.[15]

Building on Cleckley's work, Robert Hare developed an extremely influential diagnostic tool for psychopathy—the Hare Psychopathy Checklist—Revised (PCL-R).[16] Developed in prison populations, it purports to be a general psychopathy construct but is perhaps best suited for diagnosing criminal psychopathy. The PCL-R tests the following traits and behaviors.

1. Glibness/superficial charm
2. Grandiose sense of self-worth
3. Need for stimulation/proneness to boredom
4. Pathological lying
5. Conning/manipulative
6. Lack of remorse or guilt
7. Shallow affect
8. Callous/lack of empathy
9. Parasitic lifestyle
10. Poor behavioral controls
11. Promiscuous sexual behavior
12. Early behavior problems
13. Lack of realistic, long-term goals
14. Impulsivity
15. Irresponsibility
16. Failure to accept responsibility for one's own actions
17. Many short-term marital relationships
18. Juvenile delinquency
19. Revocation of conditional release
20. Criminal versatility

The test is administered by trained professionals based on an extensive review of the subject's file and a structured interview with the subject. For each item, a

[15] See Cleckley, *The Mask of Sanity*, esp. pp. 380–81 and Christopher Patrick, "Back to the Future: Cleckley as Guide to the Next Generation of Psychopathy Research" in *Handbook of Psychopathy*, ed. Patrick.

[16] Robert Hare, *The Hare Psychopathy Checklist—Revised*, 2d ed. [first edition 1991] (Toronto: Multi-Health Systems, 2003).

subject will be scored between 0 and 2 points, with total scores ranging between 0 and 40 points. Adults scoring above 30 are deemed determinately psychopathic; those scoring below 20 points are deemed determinately non-psychopathic. The PCL-R was originally conceptualized as a two-factor model of psychopathy consisting of interpersonal and affective items and impulsive and anti-social lifestyle items.[17] The PCL-R has proven useful at predicting recidivism rates among criminal offenders and so is increasingly used for purposes of assessing suitability for parole and early release programs.

One important aspect of ongoing research on the nature of psychopathy involves distinguishing it from other sorts of psychological disorders. The American Psychiatric Association's *Diagnostic and Statistical Manual* (*DSM*) recognizes Conduct Disorder (CD) as a pattern of persistent conduct in which the rights of others or other social norms are violated (*DSM*, pp. 469–71). Individuals who are adults with CD and have a history of CD tracing back to adolescence are diagnosed with Antisocial Personality Disorder (ASPD) (*DSM*, pp. 659–63).[18] Though both CD and ASPD include psychopathic factors, neither requires the full range of psychopathic factors. In fact, CD and ASPD can cover many different kinds of antisocial behavior, many of which do not seem to threaten normative competence or justify an insanity or incompetence defense. However, psychopathy is a special case, worth distinguishing from this larger class. Recent work on psychopathy suggests several distinguishing marks of psychopathy.[19]

1. ASPD and CD can involve *reactive* aggression in which the subject responds with disproportionate anger and aggression to some kind of provocation. By contrast, psychopathy involves *instrumental* aggression in which the subject uses aggression to get what he wants, regardless of the importance or stability of these objectives.

2. Many individuals with CD experience guilt or remorse in response to the wrongs and harms they commit. By contrast, psychopaths do not experience guilt or remorse, typically blaming their victims.

3. ASPD need not involve significant emotional deficits. By contrast, psychopaths display shallow affect. They have significant empathy deficits;

---

[17] More recently, it has been reconceptualized as a three-factor model and, by Hare himself, as a four-factor model. The PCL-R has been adapted to a 12-item version (PCL: SV) for use in the MacArthur Risk Assessment Study and to a 20-item age-appropriate version (PCL: YV) for use with adolescents. See, e.g., Robert Hare and Craig Neumann, "The PCL-R Assessment of Psychopathy: Development, Structural Properties, and New Directions" in *Handbook of Psychopathy*, ed. Patrick.

[18] Also see the *DSM* alternate model for ASPD, *DSM*, pp. 764–65.

[19] See James Blair et al., *The Psychopath*.

they tend to display low situational social anxiety, as measured by electrodermal tests; and they display little fear and have difficulty with aversive learning in which behavior is modified in response to the prospect of punishment for noncompliance.

4. Psychopaths are alleged to have trouble distinguishing moral and conventional norms, where moral norms, unlike conventional norms, are supposed to be serious, invariant, and not conditional on local authorities and taboos.

5. ASPD and reactive aggression often involve prefrontal cortex abnormality; psychopathy often involves amygdala abnormality.

So, there is some consensus about the distinctive features of psychopathy. It is typified by a syndrome of personality and behavioral traits. Though superficially normal in intelligence and affect, psychopaths tend to have shallow affect and deficits in empathy, anxiety, and fear. They tend to be impulsive, engaging in dangerous and imprudent behavior, often for fleeting or insubstantial purposes. They do not pursue long-term objectives or life-plans. They are manipulative and pathological liars, using aggression instrumentally and experiencing little or no remorse for the harm they cause others. They are not able to sustain lasting interpersonal relationships. One of the most disturbing aspects of psychopathy is that no effective form of treatment has been identified.[20] However, some consolation can be taken in the fact that the duration of psychopathy tends to be limited, with the antisocial behavioral expressions of psychopathy dropping sharply after the age of 40.[21] Until we are better able to document the neuropsychological deficits of psychopaths and devise interventions or effective behavioral therapies, diagnoses of psychopathy will mainly be relevant to blocking the early release of psychopathic criminals and perhaps justifying civil commitment for especially dangerous psychopaths, at least until such time as they are no longer a significant threat to others.

[20] See, e.g., Grant Harris and Marnie Rice, "Treatment of Psychopathy: A Review of Empirical Findings" and Michael Seto and Vernon Quinsey, "Toward the Future: Translating Basic Research into Prevention and Treatment Strategies" both in *Handbook of Psychopathy*, ed. Patrick.

[21] R.D. Hare, L.N. McPherson, and A.E. Forth, "Males Psychopaths and their Criminal Careers" *Journal of Consulting and Clinical Psychology* 56 (1988): 710–14 and Grant Harris, Marnie Rice, and C.A. Cormier, "Psychopathy and Violent Recidivism" *Law and Human Behavior* 15 (1991): 625–37.

91. Should Psychopathy be Excusing?

We are now in a better position to address the question of whether and, if so, why psychopathy provides a legal or moral excuse. As I noted at the outset, views are mixed about whether psychopathy excuses. On the one hand, psychopathy is not recognized as an excuse under existing insanity doctrine, and many would regard psychopathy as an aggravating, rather than a mitigating, factor. The psychopath's apparent indifference to the suffering of others and lack of remorse for the wrongs he commits and harms he causes may seem to make him more deserving of blame and punishment. On the other hand, several philosophers and legal academics have argued that we should recognize psychopathy as an excusing condition. Because some of them have claimed or implied that psychopaths have impaired normative competence, their arguments engage the fair opportunity conception of responsibility and excuse defended here.

One reason that psychopathy is not recognized as a legitimate insanity defense may be that it is not recognized as a distinct personality disorder in the *DSM*, and all extant insanity tests require that the incapacity be the product of a mental disease or defect.[22] If we conceptualize that requirement as involving a distinct clinical diagnosis over and above the incapacity itself, that might explain reluctance to recognize psychopathy as a form of insanity. While this might explain reluctance to recognize an insanity defense for psychopathy, it would not be a good justification of that reluctance. For one thing, there is significant consensus, as we have seen, that psychopathy is an empirically valid construct, which is both narrower and more pathological than ASPD. Moreover, we saw that for purposes of assessing responsibility and excuse we should understand mental disease or defect as a forensic category that is not independent of normative incompetence. This is why the fair opportunity conception of the incompetence excuse drops the requirement that normative incompetence be the product of mental disease or defect, provided only that the agent is not herself responsible for being incompetent.

Watson offers one rationale for excuse in his discussion of the Robert Harris case, which we discussed earlier (§37). Harris was not diagnosed with

---

[22] A draft of *DSM-5* proposed to treat ASPD and psychopathy as coordinate labels, but the published version, like *DSM-IV*, employs only ASPD as the identifying label. Both *DSM-IV* and *DSM-5* indicate in passing that ASPD "has also been referred to as psychopathy, sociopathy, or dyssocial personality disorder" (*DSM*, p. 659). So psychopathy is not an official label for any *DSM* conduct or personality disorder. As noted above, though psychopaths satisfy some CD and ASPD criteria, one can satisfy CD and ASPD without being psychopathic.

psychopathy, but he fits the psychopathic profile well. He had a long history of violence and cruelty, before being convicted for killing two boys as part of a carjacking. Harris expressed no remorse for the killings and in fact seemed to enjoy the suffering of his victims.[23] After noting our revulsion toward characters, such as Harris, Watson suggests that their failure to recognize and respond to basic moral considerations may place them outside the community of participants in the reactive attitudes. This is a theme he develops and applies in particular to psychopathy in "The Trouble with Psychopaths." While acknowledging that psychopaths display a disregard for the interests of others that allows us to attribute wrongdoing to them, Watson expresses doubts about their accountability for wrongdoing. He claims that psychopaths are constitutionally disqualified as members of the moral community because they are "unreachable by the language of moral address." What needs explanation here is what would make psychopaths beyond the scope of moral address. The explanation required by the fair opportunity conception of responsibility, with which Watson expresses some sympathy, is that psychopaths lack normative competence, in particular, the ability to recognize and respond to reasons, especially moral reasons. But whereas Watson mostly assumes that psychopaths lack normative competence or, at least, moral competence, this is an issue we need to investigate.

We have conceptualized normative competence as involving both cognitive capacities—the ability to make normative discriminations and recognize wrongdoing—and volitional capacities—the ability to conform one's actions to this normative knowledge. Some early work on psychopathy suggested that it might compromise volitional, rather than cognitive, competence.[24] On the volitional interpretation of psychopathy, psychopaths recognize what they should and should not do but have affective or motivational problems acting on their normative beliefs and regulating their behavior as they recognize they ought. However, this view of psychopathy as involving volitional deficits has largely given way to the view that it involves primarily cognitive deficits. Certainly, this cognitive interpretation of psychopathy is the predominant view of those who advocate for excusing psychopaths. On this cognitive interpretation of psychopathy, psychopaths lack the ability to make suitable normative discriminations and recognize wrongdoing.

---

[23] Harris is reported to have expressed remorse at his execution, but this would have been unprecedented, and there is reason to question the sincerity of otherwise unattested expressions of empathy and remorse by psychopaths.

[24] See, e.g., Hare, *Without Conscience*, pp. 75–76.

92. Does Psychopathy Involve Cognitive Impairment?

This cognitive interpretation of psychopathic deficits fits with the common observation that psychopathy involves a kind of *normative blindness*, akin to color blindness, in which psychopaths just don't perceive normative, especially moral, issues the same way that cognitive normals or typicals do. It also fits with the claims of moral philosophers and criminal law theorists who advocate recognizing a M'Naghten-style excuse for psychopathy.[25] However, this cognitive conclusion is more often asserted than defended. It merits more careful assessment.

The most complete defense of a M'Naghten-style excuse for psychopathy of which I am aware is that offered by Cordelia Fine and Jeannette Kennett in their article "Mental Impairment, Moral Understanding and Criminal Responsibility: Psychopathy and the Purposes of Punishment." They accept, at least for purposes of argument, a M'Naghten-style conception of excuse as limited to cognitive incompetence, in part because this is a feature of the Australian criminal code that they want their arguments to engage.[26] They claim that the ability to know or appreciate that an act is legally wrong requires moral, and not just legal, understanding. Thus, they conclude that criminal cognitive competence requires moral cognitive competence. Fine and Kennett then defend the claim that psychopaths lack basic moral cognitive competence—the idea that psychopaths are morally blind—by appeal to psychological deficits exhibited in psychopathy—the alleged inability of psychopaths to distinguish between conventional and moral norms and their affective deficits, in particular, their empathy and fear deficits. Their argument has something like this structure.

1. Moral responsibility requires cognitive competence with respect to moral norms (cognitive moral competence).
2. Criminal responsibility requires cognitive competence with respect to criminal law norms.
3. Cognitive competence with respect to criminal law norms requires an ability to appreciate the illegality of one's actions.
4. Appreciation of the illegality of one's actions requires understanding the moral basis of criminal law norms.

---

[25] See, e.g., Morse, "Psychopathy and Criminal Responsibility" and Watson, "The Trouble with Psychopaths."
[26] Australian Criminal Code Act 1995 (Cth) §7.3(1).

5. Hence, criminal responsibility requires moral responsibility, because cognitive criminal competence requires cognitive moral competence.
6. Cognitive moral competence requires the possession of moral concepts.
7. Hence, criminal responsibility requires the possession of moral concepts.
8. The psychological deficits of psychopaths—their difficulty distinguishing moral and conventional norms, their empathy deficits, and their problems with aversive learning—prevent them from having moral concepts.
9. Hence, psychopaths are not morally responsible.
10. Hence, psychopaths are not criminally responsible.

Though Fine and Kennett conclude that psychopaths are neither morally nor criminally responsible, they recognize that psychopaths remain dangerous, which can justify the state in preventively detaining them. Unlike others who largely assert or stipulate that psychopaths are morally blind, Fine and Kennett argue for this claim. This is the right sort of argument for excusing psychopaths. The question is whether it is compelling. Closer inspection, I think, reveals grounds for skepticism.

There are interesting questions about the first part of the argument linking criminal responsibility with moral responsibility. The fair opportunity conception of responsibility insists that normative competence and, in particular, cognitive competence is necessary for responsibility. This implies that the ability to recognize moral wrongdoing is a necessary condition of moral competence and, hence, moral responsibility. So if psychopathy compromises cognitive moral competence, this raises serious questions about whether psychopaths should be held morally responsible. That's an interesting conclusion in its own right. But it is less clear that moral competence is necessary for criminal responsibility. Criminal responsibility, we said, would seem to involve a kind of normative competence to recognize and conform to norms of the criminal law. Criminal law doctrines of insanity sometimes fudge this issue by insisting only that the agent had the ability to recognize or appreciate that her conduct was wrong. This leaves unspecified whether the norms whose violation is in question are criminal or moral. But the criminal law only punishes violations of the criminal law, not moral wrongs per se. This is why many jurisdictions that address the ambiguity specify that the focus should be on the capacity for recognizing criminal wrongdoing. Even if we distinguish them, they could still be linked if appreciating legal norms requires understanding their moral basis. But that requires a thick conception of appreciation, whose rationale is not very clear. Moreover, if thick legal appreciation required knowing the basis of legal norms, it's not clear that this would require knowledge about the moral basis of legal norms. Knowing the basis of legal norms would require knowledge about what it takes for something to be a valid legal norm—the sort of thing H.L.A. Hart thinks would be provided by a rule of recognition.[27]

If so, we might dispute (3) and (4), and this means that even if Fine and Kennett are right that (6) and (8) force us to accept (9), (10) wouldn't follow. For then, we might conclude that psychopaths are morally excused but criminally responsible. This more limited conclusion is still quite interesting and worth investigating, whether or not it supports a legal excuse.

93. The Moral/Conventional Distinction and Cognitive Impairment

Fine and Kennett appeal to frequently cited studies claiming that psychopaths have trouble discriminating between moral and conventional norms. Elliott Turiel and colleagues found that psychological normals or typicals distinguish consistently and reliably between conduct that is morally wrong and conduct that is wrong by virtue of social convention.[28] Turiel's test depends on the idea that, in contrast with conventional transgressions, moral wrongs (1) are independent of local authority, (2) involve harm, rights violations, or unfairness, (3) are temporally and geographically invariant, and (4) are more serious. Moral prohibitions on murder or assault score higher on all four dimensions than rules of mere etiquette. Turiel found that the ability to make the moral-conventional distinction was well established even in very young children, who distinguish between moral prohibitions on hitting classmates and conventional requirements of classroom etiquette. In two studies, James Blair applied Turiel's Moral-Conventional Transgressions task (MCT) to subjects in prison populations and mental hospitals who had high scores on the PCL-R, concluding that psychopaths cannot discriminate reliably between moral and conventional norms and treat moral norms as if they were conventional

---

[27] See H.L.A. Hart, *The Concept of Law* (Oxford: Clarendon Press, 1916), esp. chs. 5–6.
[28] Elliot Turiel, *The Development of Social Knowledge: Morality and Convention* (New York: Cambridge University Press, 1983).

norms.[29] Fine and Kennett appeal to these results to suggest that psychopaths lack moral concepts and competence. This would tend to show that psychopaths lack the competence necessary for moral responsibility. If, as Fine and Kennett allege, criminal responsibility requires moral cognitive competence, then these results would also tend to show that psychopaths lack the competence necessary for criminal responsibility.

However, there are several places in this argument to express skepticism. For one thing, we have already questioned the assumption that criminal responsibility requires moral competence. If Fine and Kennett were right that psychopaths lack moral concepts and competence, this would help show that they were not morally responsible, which is itself an interesting and important conclusion. But this wouldn't show that psychopaths weren't criminally responsible. After all, on most jurisprudential views, there is an important conventional element in the law, because laws are social artifacts that depend on the relevant kind of social and institutional enactment. So, even if psychopaths treated moral norms as if they were conventional norms, this would not interfere with their ability to recognize legal norms, which are conventional in character.

Also, one might question the philosophical presuppositions of Turiel's work. The MCT seems to presuppose a sharp distinction between moral norms, which are historically and culturally invariant and authority-independent, and conventional norms, which are historically and culturally variable and authority-dependent. But some metaethical views might question this contrast. Some moral conventionalists or constructivists believe that moral requirements are the product of an agreement and can be culturally variable.[30] Others see some, if not all, moral demands as demands that agents make on each other, rendering these demands in some sense authority-dependent.[31] Though I am not especially sympathetic to these metaethical views,[32] we should be wary of empirical work if it depends on contested metaethical commitments. Whether Turiel's work does so depend is not clear. It requires distinguishing norms of etiquette that can depend on quite local and arbitrary authorities, with the result that the normative valence of conduct can be changed by fiat, and moral norms that are not similarly

[29] See Blair, "A Cognitive Developmental Approach to Morality: Investigating the Psychopath" and R.J. Blair, L. Jones, F. Clark, and M. Smith, "Is the Psychopath Morally Insane?" *Personality and Individual Differences* 19 (1995): 741–52.

[30] See, e.g., Gilbert Harman, "Moral Relativism Defended" *Philosophical Review* 84 (1975): 3–22.

[31] See, e.g., Stephen Darwall, *The Second-Person Standpoint* (Cambridge, MA: Harvard University Press, 2006).

[32] See David O. Brink, *Moral Realism and the Foundations of Ethics* (New York: Cambridge University Press, 1989).

dependent and variable. One might well accept this contrast even if one thought moral norms were conventional or authority-dependent at some more fundamental level and in some less arbitrary way. For this reason, I doubt that Turiel's MCT is philosophically problematic.

The bigger worry, I think, is not Turiel's distinction, but Blair's use of it.[33] In Blair's studies, psychopaths failed to distinguish moral and conventional norms along three of the four dimensions the MCT identified. Psychopaths did cite authorities in explaining why violations of moral and conventional norms are wrong (roughly, both are wrong just because they violate rules), whereas normals cited harm and rights-violations as the reasons that moral transgressions are wrong. But otherwise they scored moral and conventional transgressions similarly, saying both were contextually invariant, impermissible, and serious wrongs. An alternative interpretation of these findings is that in important respects psychopaths treated conventional norms as if they were moral norms. In other words, it's not so much that psychopaths assimilate moral norms to conventional ones as that they assimilate conventional norms to moral ones. Blair defended his different interpretation of the results as fitting his hypothesis that psychopaths lack moral concepts by claiming that the reason they treated conventional norms so seriously is that they wanted to manipulate experimenters by telling them what they (the psychopaths) thought they (the experimenters) wanted to hear. Though this is a possible confound in results that doesn't seem to support his interpretation, that hardly vindicates his interpretation. Blair's results should not be treated as confirming the hypothesis that psychopaths have trouble distinguishing moral and conventional norms and that they lack moral concepts.

In recent experiments designed to eliminate incentives for insincere reports, psychopathic offenders were not found to be any worse at distinguishing moral and conventional norms than non-psychopathic offenders.[34] Moreover, in related experiments, psychopaths were shown to track normal comparisons of the seriousness of offenses, treating murder, simple theft, prostitution, and

---

[33] For a similar verdict, see David Shoemaker, "Psychopathy, Responsibility, and the Moral/Conventional Distinction" *Southern Journal of Philosophy* 49 *Spindel Supplement* (2011): 99–124 and *Responsibility from the Margins*, ch. 6.

[34] See Eyal Aharoni, Walter Sinnott-Armstrong, and Kent Kiehl, "Can Psychopathic Offenders Discern Moral Wrongs? A New Look at the Moral/Conventional Distinction" *Journal of Abnormal Psychology* 121 (2012): 484–97 and Jana Schaich Borg and Walter Sinnott-Armstrong, "Do Psychopaths Make Moral Judgments?" in *The Oxford Handbook of Psychopathy and Law*, ed. K. Kiehl and W. Sinnott-Armstrong (Oxford: Clarendon Press, 2013).

dishonesty as forming a continuum from more to less serious offenses.[35] These experiments suggest that psychopaths have normal abilities to recognize moral wrongdoing and to grade offenses for their seriousness.

It is understandable that Fine and Kennett relied on Blair's claims that psychopaths cannot distinguish between moral and conventional norms, because at the time they were writing Blair's studies were the only ones available. However, the claim that psychopaths lack moral concepts and, hence, moral competence, because they treat moral norms as if they were conventional norms does not hold up well to closer inspection. The original studies do not support the conclusion that psychopaths have an impoverished conception of morality, rather than an inflated conception of conventional norms. Further experiments designed to distinguish these two interpretations show that psychopaths can distinguish moral and conventional requirements as well as non-psychopaths. In fact, these studies cast considerable doubt on the proposition that psychopaths lack moral concepts and moral competence. But then the literature on psychopathy and the moral/conventional distinction does not support a finding of cognitive incompetence that would provide a M'Naghten-style excuse for psychopaths.

94. Affective Deficits and Cognitive Incompetence

Fine and Kennett also appeal to well-documented affective deficits in psychopaths—involving empathy, fear, and situational anxiety—in support of their claim that psychopaths lack cognitive incompetence. One might wonder how an emotional deficit would establish a cognitive deficit. But one might well claim that empathy for victims and fear of sanctions for noncompliance are essential to learning moral norms and to detecting when they apply. In this way, affective deficits might be a source of cognitive incompetence.

Consider empathy first. Psychologists sometimes distinguish between *cognitive* and *affective* or *emotional* empathy. Whereas cognitive empathy involves the tendency to recognize and understand the attitudes and emotions of others, affective or emotional empathy involves the ability to experience the emotions of others oneself, perhaps in a less intense form. Though emotional empathy would normally produce cognitive empathy, it's possible to have cognitive empathy without emotional empathy.

---

[35] Paul Robinson and Robert Kurzban, "Concordance and Conflict in Intuitions of Justice" *Minnesota Law Review* 91 (2007): 1829–1907 and Borg and Sinnott-Armstrong, "Do Psychopaths Make Moral Judgments?"

It is plausible that there's some connection between moral knowledge and empathy.[36] After all, the most important norms of morality and law are concerned with harm prevention, and empathy seems to be a normal way for us to detect when our behavior is harmful and wrong and a normal way for us to be motivated not to harm others. The first fact about empathy represents it as having a role *upstream* from normative cognition and so potentially relevant to cognitive capacity, whereas the second fact about empathy represents it as having a role *downstream* from normative cognition and so potentially relevant to volitional capacity. Insofar as we are here concerned with the effect of psychopathy on cognitive competence, we are interested in this first epistemic role of empathy.

Do empathy deficits fund a M'Naghten-style excuse for cognitive incapacity? It's worth noting that an influential meta-study of research on empathy deficits and aggression finds that only 1 percent of the variation in aggression is caused by lack of empathy.[37] This shouldn't be surprising. If we were just looking for whether empathy deficits explain aggression, we might look at other conditions that involve empathy deficits, such as autism. But it's well established that autistic individuals are not prone to aggression. What explains why high scores on the PCL-R are predictive of aggression is that the PCL-R scores for both attitudinal and behavioral factors. Those determined to be psychopathic on the PCL-R have a history of conduct disorder. Empathy deficits are not predictive of conduct disorder, but past conduct disorder is predictive of future misconduct. Other attitudinal and behavioral aspects of the psychopathy construct are much better predictors of violence than empathy deficits.[38]

However, even if empathy deficits don't predict wrongful aggression, we might suppose that empathy can be a useful resource in moral cognition, providing those with normal capacities for empathy with a distinctive kind of epistemic access to moral norms and their application. But it doesn't follow from this fact alone that empathy is necessary for moral concepts or making moral discriminations. There could be other modes of access to moral knowledge and recognition of wrongdoing. It seems I could know that causing death

---

[36] For a defense of the connection between empathy and morality, see Simon Baron-Cohen, *The Science of Evil: On Empathy and the Origins of Cruelty* (New York: Basic Books, 2011). For criticisms, which I find compelling, see Paul Bloom, *Against Empathy: The Case for Rational Compassion* (New York: Harper Collins, 2016).

[37] David Vachon, Donald Lyman, and Jarrod Johnson, "The (Non)Relation Between Empathy and Aggression: Surprising Results from a Meta-Analysis" *Psychological Bulletin* 140 (2014): 751–73.

[38] For doubts about the importance of empathy, as distinct from rational compassion, in explaining moral knowledge and conduct, see Bloom, *Against Empathy*.

or bodily injury is harmful and, hence, wrong even if I didn't experience these facts empathetically. I could come to know these facts propositionally, rather than empathetically, and I could accept the authority of other members of my community about what actions were right and wrong, whether or not I had empathetic understanding of the harms caused to others by my wrongdoing. So, if the question is whether I have the capacity to recognize moral wrong-doing, empathy might be useful, but it does not seem necessary. If so, the psychopath's empathy deficits do not yet provide an excuse.

Cognitive capacity is sometimes analogized to a perceptual capacity, and, as we have seen, some are willing to count psychopathy as a form of moral or criminal blindness. We might explore the value of these metaphors by think-ing about colorblindness. Colorblind people, let us assume, are unable to distinguish between red and green. We might ask whether their incapacity provides them with an excuse for failing to obey traffic laws requiring them to stop their vehicles at red lights. It is true that colorblind people cannot experience the difference between red and green traffic lights phenomeno-logically, the way non-colorblind people can, and so cannot rely on these normal visual cues to recognize vehicular wrongdoing. But there are other ways of recognizing when the traffic light is red. The red light is the top light in a vertical display, whereas the green light is the bottom light (in a horizontal display, the red is leftmost and the green is rightmost), and colorblindness does not interfere with this sort of positional recognition. But this suggests that colorblindness would not excuse vehicular wrongdoing, because even if it deprives an agent of one familiar form of epistemic access to the facts in question, it leaves available other modes of access.

Similarly, we might think that a systematic lack of empathy might deprive psychopaths of one familiar form of epistemic access to the harmful and wrongful nature of their actions, but it wouldn't thereby deprive them of other forms of access to this information. One could learn that murder, rape, and assault were harmful and wrong without needing to identify them as wrong empathetically.[39]

---

[39] For comparison, consider Asperger's syndrome, which involves difficulties in social interaction and communication often traced, at least in part, to empathy deficits. People with Asperger's often have difficulty reading and responding appropriately to social cues. This makes it hard to relate to others normally. However, it is possible for some people with Asperger's to learn non-empathetically the significance of various social signals from others and the appropriate conduct in various recurrent contexts. In this way, some with Asperger's can construct a list of best practices that they can then try to internalize and follow. See David Finch, *The Journal of Best Practices* (New York: Simon & Schuster, 2012). The result is not always socially seamless, but it can approximate normal conduct. These best practices may not be learned in the normal comparatively effortless way, but they are learnable.

Notice that this skepticism about whether empathy deficits excuse relies crucially on the assumption that persons, rather than mechanisms, are the relevant units of responsibility and responsiveness, which we defended earlier (§21). The argument from empathy deficits to excuse tacitly assumes a mechanism-based conception of reasons-responsiveness, since it treats the normal empathy-based access to moral knowledge that is missing or compromised in the case of psychopaths as sufficient for excuse. We see here how mechanism-based conceptions of excuse are implausibly promiscuous. A defective empathy-based mechanism for recognizing moral norms does not block responsibility or excuse if psychopathic agents have available alternative mechanisms for accessing moral norms, including propositional knowledge about wrongful harm. We should be reluctant to excuse an agent if she had the capacity to recognize the limitations of her actual mechanisms and employ other reasons-responsive mechanisms to circumvent the non-responsive mechanism and avoid wrongdoing.

One might argue that empathy doesn't have to be necessary for moral knowledge for empathy deficits to excuse. If empathy is for normal agents a reliable way of acquiring moral knowledge, then lack of empathy might make the task of acquiring moral knowledge *harder*, even if it does not make it impossible. As Joseph Newman describes it,

> Whereas most people automatically anticipate the consequences of their actions, automatically feel shame for unkind deeds, automatically understand why they should persist in the face of frustration, automatically distrust propositions that are too good to be true, and are automatically aware of their commitments to others, psychopaths may only become aware of such factors with effort.[40]

If so, empathy deficits might still seem to excuse.

This assumes that empathy is the normal and preferred form of epistemic access to moral norms. That assumption is open to question.[41] But even if we make that assumption, it's still not clear that epistemic difficulty funds an excuse of cognitive incompetence. A deficit can make the acquisition of moral knowledge harder than it would otherwise be without making it hard (simpliciter), and even if the empathy deficit makes the acquisition of moral

---

[40] Joseph Newman, "Psychopathic Behavior: An Information-Processing Perspective" in *Psychopathy: Theory, Research, and Implications*, ed. Cooke, Forth, and Hare (Dordrecht: Kluwer, 1998).

[41] See, e.g., Bloom, *Against Empathy*.

knowledge hard (and not just harder), it's not clear that it makes it so hard as to deprive the psychopath of the fair opportunity to avoid wrongdoing. After all, if the psychopath has these other sources of moral knowledge, that might be opportunity enough. Not everyone finds it equally easy to avoid wrongdoing for a variety of reasons. Some situations pose more hardship for everyone than others, and some people experience more hardship in some situations than other people do. Many comparative difficulties don't rise to the level as to undermine the fair opportunity to avoid wrongdoing and, hence, don't serve as the basis for excuse. Unless empathy deficits substantially interfere with the ability of psychopaths to make normative discriminations, it's hard to see how such deficits could fund a M'Naghten-style excuse.

Another affective deficit that psychopaths possess involves fear. Because fear is thought to be an essential component of aversive learning, Fine and Kennett reason that a lack of fear would interfere with normal ways of learning the importance of legal and moral concepts. But this appeal to fear deficits to support cognitive incompetence also moves too fast. Psychopaths clearly find imprisonment disagreeable and are keen to be out of prison as soon as possible. It may be that they don't anticipate the disagreeable consequences of misconduct as much as they should or that this recognition does not operate as it should to produce impulse control. But this doesn't mean that they can't recognize intellectually that they risk unpleasant consequences when they engage in wrongdoing. Moreover, we should distinguish between norms, whether criminal or moral, and sanctions that might be attached for noncompliance. A failure to fear sanctions might affect one's motives for noncompliance, but there's no reason it should prevent one from recognizing the norms of conduct, especially when one sees others willingly conforming to these norms.

Recent studies on psychopathic performance on the MCT and on grading the seriousness of offenses strongly suggests that psychopaths do have normative knowledge. But what is actual must be possible. If so, psychopaths appear to be cognitively competent, at least with respect to the requirements of basic morality and the criminal law.[42] This does not address the downstream role of empathy in relation to normative cognition, which bears on the volitional, rather than the cognitive, dimensions of normative competence.

---

[42] For a similar assessment, see Heidi Maibom, "Responsibility in the Age of Neuroscience: Moral Understanding and Empathy in Psychopathy" in *The Oxford Handbook of Moral Psychology*, ed. J. Doris and M. Vargas (New York: Oxford University Press, 2021). One might concede that empathy is not necessary for cognitive access to the requirements of basic morality and the criminal law but claim that it is necessary for cognitive access to the requirements of refined morality. If so, psychopathy might fund a much narrower and specifically moral excuse. This depends, I think, on the plausibility of the claim that empathy is actually part of the content of the norms of refined morality. This is an interesting claim, which I cannot assess here.

95. Does Psychopathy Involve Volitional Impairment?

Recent writers who have treated psychopathy as excusing have tended to assume that psychopathy undermines cognitive competence. Those who have argued for this claim have appealed to alleged trouble psychopaths have distinguishing moral and conventional norms and their affective deficits, especially involving empathy and fear. But the evidence that psychopaths cannot distinguish moral and conventional norms is not compelling, and they seem quite reliable in grading the seriousness of offenses. Psychopaths do have affective deficits in empathy and fear. These deficits do not prevent the formation of moral concepts and the ability to recognize moral and criminal norms. If they don't, we lack sufficient reason to accept a M'Naghten-style excuse for cognitive incompetence for psychopathic wrongdoing. Empirical work on the nature of psychopathy is continuing and evolving, so it would be foolish to assume that this verdict couldn't change as we learn more about the cognitive capacities of psychopaths. But for now I think we should be skeptical about whether psychopathy excuses on cognitive grounds. If we assume that the defense should bear the burden of proof to establish an insanity defense, then we do not yet have sufficient reason to recognize psychopathy as providing an excuse of cognitive incompetence.

However, the fair opportunity conception of responsibility also recognizes a volitional dimension of responsibility and, hence, excuses based on volitional impairment. This raises the question of whether psychopathy significantly impairs an agent's ability to conform her conduct to her normative knowledge. Here, the downstream role of empathy and fear deficits might be relevant, explaining why psychopaths aren't more reliably moved to care about the harm they cause or to fear sanctions for noncompliance with moral and criminal norms. It is a distinctive feature of psychopathy that psychopaths are impulsive and often impose substantial costs on others and take substantial risks themselves for insubstantial and even whimsical ends. If they are able to recognize the relevant norms, this suggests a possible volitional, rather than cognitive, impairment.[43] Failures of empathy and fear might contribute to impulsive and undisciplined transgression of moral and criminal norms.

It is reasonably plausible that psychopaths do have volitional control problems of some sort. They don't seem to care enough about what they often recognize to be wrongdoing. Moreover, their moral and criminal

---

[43] See Maaike Cima, Franca Tonnaer, and Marc Hauser, "Psychopaths Know Right from Wrong But Don't Care" *SCAN* 5 (2010): 59–67.

transgressions are often spectacularly imprudent, suggesting that they can't even pursue their own self-interest reliably. But the crucial and difficult question is whether their failure to conform to the relevant norms represents a genuine incapacity to conform. Is it just that they often won't conform to norms that they recognize or that they can't? To distinguish can't and won't, we need to see if psychopaths are moderately reasons-responsive. It is clear that they conform their behavior to the reasons they recognize less often than normals do. But just as occasional weakness of will in normals does not show that they lack volitional competence, the more common and significant failings of psychopaths to conform do not automatically show that they lack volitional competence. To show genuine volitional incompetence, we would have to have evidence of systemic control problems. It would not be enough to know that they failed to conform in the case in which they committed wrong or even that they failed to conform in other cases in the past. One would have to show that conformity was exceptional. But psychopaths often seem able to conform to relevant norms with new acquaintances and when they know they are being watched and evaluated. So there is reason to think that they do have some significant volitional competence. To assess this volitional rationale for excusing psychopaths we would require more empirical evidence about the decision-making histories of psychopaths and the extent and causes of their problems with impulse control. While the best prospects for an excuse for psychopathy might lie with studying the extent and nature of their volitional impairment, I don't think the present state of our knowledge about psychopathy provides sufficient evidence for a volitional excuse.

96. Skepticism about whether Psychopathy Excuses

The fair opportunity conception of responsibility factors responsibility into conditions of normative competence and situational control. Normative competence factors into cognitive and volitional capacities that are individually necessary and jointly sufficient for someone to count as a responsible agent. This supports a conception of insanity or incompetence that recognizes substantial impairment of either cognitive or volitional competence as excusing, provided the agent is not substantially responsible for her own incompetence. We can use this fair opportunity conception of responsibility and excuse to help frame the question of whether and, if so, why psychopathy is excusing. The most common rationale for excusing psychopathy appeals to claims about cognitive incompetence. However, when this rationale is examined more closely, there are good philosophical and empirical reasons to be skeptical that psychopaths lack the relevant capacities to recognize and appreciate moral or criminal wrongdoing. There may be more to be said for a volitional rationale for excuse. The crucial question here is whether the problems psychopaths have with impulse control and conforming their behavior to the relevant moral and criminal norms are pervasive and systematic enough to demonstrate genuine volitional incompetence. The available empirical evidence, I think, should leave us (defeasibly) skeptical about the merits of this volitional rationale for excuse.

It might be helpful to locate my skepticism about whether psychopathy excuses in the space of alternatives. In "Psychopaths, Incorrigible Racists, and the Faces of Responsibility" Dana Nelkin takes up the question of whether psychopaths are responsible for their wrongdoing or should be excused.[44] Following Watson and others, she stipulates that psychopaths lack normative competence—are morally blind—and asks how this should affect our attitudes toward their responsibility. To answer this question, she invokes Watson's distinction between attributability and accountability. Recall that attributive responsibility is a function of the agent's quality of will, which is reflected in her evaluative orientation and the regard she has for the rights and interests of others, and that accountability is a matter of whether it is fair to blame and sanction the agent's conduct, whether she deserves blame and punishment, and whether she had the fair opportunity to avoid wrongdoing (§14). If psychopaths are morally blind, we can ask whether they are either attributively responsible or accountable for the wrongs they commit.

Nelkin contrasts two positions with her own. One possibility is reflected in Watson's distinction between attributability and accountability and his verdict that psychopaths are attributively responsible for their wrongdoing, because it reflects their true self and the quality of their will, but not accountable for their wrongdoing, because they lack normative competence without which it is unfair to blame and punish them. Another possibility is reflected in the views of the *new attributionists*, who claim that attributive responsibility is sufficient for accountability (§14). New attributionists, such as Angela Smith and Matt Talbert, would appeal to Watson's claim that psychopaths are attributively responsible and infer that they must be accountable as well.[45] Against these two positions, Nelkin wants to agree with Watson that the two

[44] Nelkin, "Psychopaths, Incorrigible Racists, and the Faces of Responsibility."
[45] Smith, "Control, Responsibility, and Moral Assessment" and "Attributability, Answerability, and Accountability: In Defense of a Unified Account" and Talbert, "Blame and Responsiveness to Moral Reasons: Are Psychopaths Responsible?" and "Accountability, Aliens, and Psychopaths."

kinds of responsibility are distinct and that attributability is not sufficient for accountability. However, against both Watson and the new attributionists, she wants to deny that psychopaths are even attributively responsible. Their moral blindness prevents them from having the sort of moral concepts necessary for attributive responsibility insofar as attributability reflects aretaic judgments of virtue and vice. So, although she agrees about the independence of attributability and accountability, she thinks psychopaths are responsible in *neither* sense.

1. Psychopaths are morally blind and so lack moral concepts necessary for normative competence.
2. Attributability depends on quality of will and does not guarantee accountability, which requires desert and the fair opportunity to avoid wrongdoing.
3. Ascriptions of quality of will reflect aretaic judgments about the agent's virtue or vice.
4. Ascriptions of accountability depend on the agent having the fair opportunity to avoid wrongdoing.
5. Moral blindness blocks the normative competence necessary for the fair opportunity to avoid wrongdoing.
6. Hence, psychopaths are not accountable for their wrongdoing.
7. Moral blindness blocks the possession of normative competence necessary for ascriptions of virtue or vice.
8. Hence, psychopaths are not attributively responsible for their wrongdoing.

On the surface, Nelkin's position would also contrast sharply with my own position, inasmuch as I agree about the independence of attributability and accountability but argue that psychopaths are responsible for their wrongdoing in *both* senses (or at least I claim that there is not good reason at this point in time to deny that they are responsible in both senses), resisting both (6) and (8).

With respect to psychopaths, we can ask if they are attributively responsible and whether they are accountable. We can map answers in a two-by-two matrix (see Figure 11.3).

My conclusion is like that of the new attributionists, that psychopaths are both attributively responsible and accountable, though the new attributionists infer accountability from attributability, as I do not. Since Nelkin says that

		Accountability	
		Yes	No
Attributability	Yes	Attributionists Brink	Watson
	No		Nelkin

Figure 11.3 Psychopathy, Attributability, and Accountability

psychopaths are neither accountable nor attributively responsible, her position looks diametrically opposed to mine. However, this sharp contrast may be misleading, since her verdict depends on the assumption or stipulation that psychopaths are morally blind, which is precisely the assumption that I dispute.

We can and should distinguish between treating psychopathy as a *philosophical construct* and as an *empirical construct*. Those who treat psychopathy as a philosophical construct are *stipulating* that psychopaths are morally blind or incompetent, and this leaves it as an open question whether there are in fact any psychopaths. By contrast, those who treat psychopathy as an empirical construct understand the nature and measures of psychopathy as psychologists, psychiatrists, and criminologists do and as I have explained here. Treating psychopathy as an empirical construct leaves it as an open question whether psychopaths are morally blind or normatively incompetent. If we aren't clear about distinguishing between philosophical and empirical conceptions of psychopathy, there's a danger of people talking past each other. Nelkin makes clear that her conclusion that psychopaths are neither attributively responsible nor accountable for their misconduct applies only to the philosophical construct of psychopathy, that is, to those who are assumed to be morally blind. But these claims may not apply to the empirical construction of psychopaths, since it remains to be seen whether they are morally blind. By contrast, I am explicitly concerned with the empirical construction of psychopathy, and I am expressing skepticism about whether they are in fact morally blind. As a result, our different verdicts about whether psychopaths are responsible and, if so, in what sense reflect fundamentally different assumptions about how to understand psychopathy and so need not express a fundamental disagreement. I reject (1), on which the argument for both (6) and (8) depends. In particular, I think that the emotional deficits that psychopaths are alleged to have do not fund an excuse of cognitive incompetence. The appeal to psychopaths' inability to distinguish moral and conventional norms is not a robust result, and the empathy deficits of psychopaths do not render them morally incompetent.

However, we may have a residual substantive disagreement over whether moral blindness would acquit psychopaths of attributive responsibility, inasmuch as I am inclined to agree with Watson that psychopaths would be attributively responsible even if they were morally blind, and Nelkin thinks not. The issue here, I believe, turns on what conception of quality of will is required for attributive responsibility. Nelkin appeals to one strand in discussions of attributability, viz. the idea that there are aretaic judgments about the virtue or vice displayed in the agent's choices and behavior. I think I am prepared to agree that if psychopaths were morally blind, where that means that they lack moral concepts or any conception of the moral standing of other people, then it would be more natural to interpret their behavior as amoral, rather than vicious. But they would still display other qualities of will that have figured prominently in discussion of attributive responsibility. For they harm others intentionally and willfully, sometimes with pleasure, and without remorse. Their wrongdoing would reflect stable character traits, which they endorse and do not disavow, and would reflect a settled disposition to ignore the interests and rights of others. I take these other aspects of quality of will to be sufficient to ground attributability, so I think that psychopaths would be attributively responsible even if they were morally blind, and even more so insofar as they retain some forms of moral acuity. In other words, because I am inclined to reject (3), I am inclined to think the argument for (8) would not go through, even if one conceded (1), for the sake of argument. Nonetheless, perhaps Nelkin and I are in agreement that there is a plausible argument for (8), but only if (1) and (3) are both true.

97. Selective Incompetence and Moral Blindspots

If psychopaths were normatively blind, they would have a quite general incompetence excuse. If so and if exemptions are comparatively general excuses (§11), then psychopaths would be exempt from blame and punishment, though possibly subject to civil commitment. I don't think that psychopaths are in fact normatively blind or exempt. More plausibly, some successful insanity pleas qualify as exemptions. Andrea Yates's severe post-partum depression and psychotic episodes impaired her normative competence in quite general ways that would justify treating her as generally or systematically incompetent and exempt.

However, incompetence need not be general or systemic and, hence, does not always support exemption. Incompetence can be *selective*. Incompetence can be selective along any number of dimensions. It might be selective temporally. Even temporally persistent incompetence will typically be limited temporally, having some point of onset and resolution. But how long it persists can vary. In Chapter 12 we will look at immature competence, which is eventually outgrown. Dehydration can induce dementia and delusions of a more temporary nature. As we will see in Chapter 14, extreme emotional disturbance can be thought of in terms of impaired competence, and it is often temporally fleeting. Provided the agent suffered substantially impaired competence at the time of action and was substantially non-culpable for her incompetence, she is entitled to an excuse, whether full or partial.

Incompetence can be selective along other dimensions as well. Perhaps one's cognitive competence is limited to certain subject matters or one's volitional competence is limited by certain kinds of passions or desires, but not others. Perhaps an addiction to gambling or various compulsive disorders involves impairments of cognitive or volitional capacities. But these impairments would be local, not global, and would not render the agents who suffer from these conditions exempt generally from the reactive attitudes, blame, and punishment. The crucial questions would be how significant the impairments were, how relevant they were to the misconduct in question, and whether the agent was culpable with respect to the impairments.

A full discussion of selective incompetence is beyond the scope of this book. But I do think that it would be worthwhile addressing one kind of potential incompetence that would be selective. Those who are not generally incompetent can have *moral blindspots* that lead them to engage in wrongdoing that is selective but nonetheless robust in character. I'm thinking especially of people who treat some people but not others unjustly out of a principled moral mistake about the moral standing and rights of others with whom they interact. Familiar examples involve bias and discriminatory treatment of members of outgroups. These include both historical and contemporary injustices, such as the institution of slavery in various historical periods, discrimination against African Americans in the Jim Crow South, Nazi genocide during the Holocaust, discrimination against black South Africans during Apartheid, and discrimination against homosexuals.

If these were just isolated acts of injustice, there might be no question about the competence and responsibility of the agents of injustice. But in many cases, these injustices reflect principled moral ignorance. In particular, in many such cases injustice is the product of moral blindspots that the agent learned and internalized from his family and community and that are deeply entrenched. Growing up in a tradition that normalized this blindspot might have made it hard to recognize this as a moral mistake or to persevere in correcting it. Without prejudging the matter, we need to ask whether these and other blindspots are genuinely incorrigible and, if so, whether such agents are entitled to some kind of excuse, full or partial, for their misconduct. On the one hand, we should recognize the existence of powerful psychological and social obstacles to identifying and correcting these blindspots in some cases. On the other hand, the fact that the blindspot is selective, rather than general, means that agents who are subject to blindspots already have at hand resources for correcting their mistakes.

One kind of example that is sometimes discussed in this sort of context is whether slaveholders in antiquity or in the Antebellum South were responsible for the wrong of owning slaves.[46] Since owning slaves in ancient Greece or the Antebellum South was not illegal at the time, the question that concerns us is whether slaveholders in these societies were responsible for moral misconduct.

Perhaps some slaveholders were akratic, embracing or tolerating slavery, despite recognition that it was wrong. Akratic misconduct manifests awareness that the conduct is wrong. Since the weak-willed person actually manifests moral knowledge, he possesses cognitive competence. So the only ground for excuse would be volitional impairment. Might the fact that a slaveholder lives in a society that not only tolerates but normalizes slavery be the source of volitional impairment? The akratic slaveholder might have reasons of financial self-interest for acquiescing in slaveholding, or he might experience pressure to conform with the opinions and conduct of his family and peers who have internalized slaveholding norms. But slavery is a profound wrong—a form of manifest immorality—and we don't normally think that self-interest or peer pressure are irresistible impulses that excuse manifest immorality.

Perhaps the more common and more difficult cases involve not akrasia, but ignorance. In such cases, slaveholders mistakenly believe that slavery is permissible, making their personal ownership of slaves permissible. Even if slavery is now generally recognized as an immoral violation of basic human rights, this was not always so. In antiquity and the Antebellum South, the practice of slavery was widespread and, we might suppose, widely viewed as permissible, either because of the (alleged) natural inferiority of slaves or as a

---

[46] The discussion of Ancient Slaveholders has become something of a trope in philosophical discussion of the epistemic conditions of responsibility. See, e.g., Rosen, "Culpability and Ignorance," claiming that slaveowners in antiquity should be excused for non-culpable moral ignorance. For more mixed verdicts, see, e.g., Gwen Bradford, "Hard to Know" in *Responsibility: The Epistemic Condition*, ed. P. Robichaud and J. Wieland (Oxford: Clarendon Press, 2017) and Alexander Guerrero, "Intellectual Difficulty and Moral Responsibility" in *Responsibility: The Epistemic Condition*, ed. P. Robichaud and J. Wieland (Oxford: Clarendon Press, 2017).

legitimate spoil of war. Individual slaveholders grew up in such societies in which slavery and its associated rationales were normalized. It was part of their way of life. Many of them will have seen their ownership of slaves as perfectly normal and permissible. Does this make their moral ignorance non-culpable?

It is sometimes assumed that slaveholders would have to have been aware of moral challenges to slavery for their ignorance to be culpable.[47] At least in some historical periods, perhaps abolitionist ideas were rare. But abolitionist ideas have been around as long as slavery has. In the *Politics* Aristotle notoriously defends slavery, claiming that some people can be enslaved justly because they are natural inferiors, incapable of the sort of deliberation required for proper management of their own affairs or those of the community (Book I, esp. 1254b20–24, 1260a12–22).[48] But even Aristotle was aware of abolitionist condemnations of slavery as contrary to nature (1253b20–23). Or consider Thomas Jefferson, who owned slaves and resisted calls for their unconditional manumission, even at the end of his life. Jefferson was a man of letters and a world traveler, who was aware of abolitionist ideas and of nations and states where slavery was illegal. Several of his contemporaries and friends called for the abolition of slavery (e.g. George Wythe, the Marquis de Lafayette, Edward Coles, William Short, and Thaddeus Kosciuszko) and took steps to emancipate their own slaves (e.g. Coles and Kosciuszko).[49] As a young man, Jefferson sometimes expressed skepticism about the institution of slavery and endorsed limitations on the expansion of slavery within the United States. In fact, as the principal author of *The Declaration of Independence*, he was committed to the proposition that *all* men are created equal and endowed with inalienable natural rights to life, liberty, and the pursuit of happiness. In these and countless other cases, slaveholders have been aware of abolitionist ideas.

In any case, awareness of abolitionist ideas is not necessary to have the capacity to recognize that slavery is wrong. If the wrongness of slavery can be

---

[47] Rosen, "Culpability and Ignorance" claims that moral ignorance excuses whenever it cannot be traced back to akratic behavior. If we are capacitarians, we should reject the assumption that awareness of wrongdoing is a condition of blameworthiness. See §17 above.

[48] Aristotle, *Politics* in *The Complete Works of Aristotle, The Revised Oxford Translation*, 2 vols., ed. J. Barnes. (Princeton, NJ: Princeton University Press, 1984).

[49] For useful discussions of Jefferson's compromised relation to slavery, see Paul Finkleman, "Thomas Jefferson and Antislavery: The Myth Goes On" *The Virginia Magazine of History and Biography* 102 (1994): 193–228 and *Slavery and the Founders: Race and Liberty in the Age of Jefferson*, 3d ed. (New York: Taylor & Francis, 2014), esp. chs. 7–8 and Henry Wiencek, *Master of the Mountain: Thomas Jefferson and his Slaves* (New York: Farrar, Strauss and Giroux, 2012). Also see Diane Jeske, *The Evil Within* (New York: Oxford University Press, 2018) and her discussion of the moral failings of Jefferson and others with significant moral blindspots. Her discussion is more focused on the moral failings themselves and the capacity for philosophical thinking to correct these failings than on responsibility per se, but the two issues are linked.

grasped based on moral and non-moral beliefs available to the slaveholder exercising modest epistemic diligence, then the slaveholder is cognitively competent. This is where the selective character of moral blindspots is important. The slaveholder recognizes interpersonal moral demands selectively, within his own race, ethnic group, class, or tribe. Because he recognizes the rights and interests of others within his own group, all he needs to do is to see that the scope limitations on which rights he recognizes are arbitrary.

For instance, a good case can be made that Aristotle's own assumptions about virtue and happiness could and should have led him to condemn slavery. Aristotle believed that human beings are rational animals, capable of adapting their emotions and actions to the demands of reason and virtue and that freedom and citizenship are appropriate for rational animals. But slaves are humans and, hence, rational animals too, with the potential for virtue and happiness, and so it is fitting that they too enjoy freedom and citizenship. In effect, Aristotle had good reason to extend the privileges of citizenship that he already recognized from propertied male Athenians to slaves and women.[50]

The case is even more straightforward with Jefferson. Jefferson was committed to a Lockean theory of natural and inalienable human rights to self-ownership and liberty. As human rights, these were rights all should enjoy. Moreover, his interaction with his own slaves, especially those he permitted to be educated and to work in his own house, gave him ample evidence of their intelligence, humanity, and emotional vulnerability. He had every reason to recognize the full implications of his commitment to natural rights. This was an obvious implication of the moral views he already held, not some radical exercise of moral imagination. Moreover, they were implications recognized by several of his contemporaries and friends.

These two cases illustrate the more general claim that when moral blindspots are selective they tend to be culpable because the agent already has underlying moral commitments in light of which the blindspot is corrigible. That there might be financial or social pressures reinforcing these blindspots does not make them incorrigible. These pressures might explain why those in the grip of a moral blindspot fail to correct their moral errors, but they do not show that the agent lacked the capacity to correct these errors. As we have seen

---

[50] For versions of this internal critique of Aristotle's claims about the natural inferiority of slaves and women, see David O. Brink, "Eudaimonism, Love and Friendship, and Political Community" *Social Philosophy & Policy* 16 (1999): 252–89 and Richard Kraut, *Aristotle's Political Philosophy* (Oxford: Clarendon Press, 2002), esp. chs. 7–8.

at several points (§§16, 29–32, 82), we should not mistake performance errors for incompetence.

Perhaps it will be claimed that at the time of the misconduct resulting from the moral blindspot, the fact that the blindspot is entrenched means that it is not corrigible then and there. But exercises of modest epistemic care can take place at many points, so there is no reason to assume that they weren't available at the very onset of misconduct. Moreover, if we are talking about owning or even just intellectually justifying slavery, these are events that persist over time. Even if the blindspot was not corrigible at some particular moment, agents have ample opportunity to consider the moral issues over time and to identify and correct their moral ignorance. Perseverance in misconduct can be culpable even if it wasn't initially culpable.

In effect, I'm arguing that in these particular cases of manifest immorality, moral blindspots don't support a finding of genuine incompetence and, hence, don't justify an excuse of selective incompetence. Strong financial or social pressures reinforcing these blindspots might provide some modest mitigation, at least making the misconduct somewhat less blameworthy than the misconduct would be absent these pressures. But they do not provide an excuse.

How robust are these claims about responsibility for misconduct resulting from moral blindspots? On the one hand, I think that these claims generalize naturally from a discussion of Aristotle and Jefferson to other cases of manifestly immoral conduct in which agents fail to see wrongdoing by failing to accept the full implications of moral principles that they already accept in their application to groups to which they belong. It's not hard to see how similar claims might be reached in cases involving genocide or discrimination against women, religious sects, or homosexuals.

On the other hand, verdicts will depend on the details of the case. We should be skeptical of an incompetence excuse in cases of misconduct in which the agent was otherwise competent and not unduly epistemically isolated. In such circumstances, blindspots seem corrigible. But one can imagine someone brought up in a very insular and homogeneous community and tradition who is taught to privilege the needs and interests of members of her community in relation to the needs and interests of outsiders. Suppose, moreover, that her community discourages questioning authority and that she has never encountered outsiders before and is disposed to treat them as having lesser moral status in ways that have been consistently reinforced within her community. If her epistemic isolation has been great enough, perhaps we should doubt that her discriminatory attitudes and conduct are sufficiently corrigible. Her situation might resemble, in some respects, the sort of coercive indoctrination that arguably impaired the normative competence of Patty Hearst. Whereas Hearst's incompetence was general but temporally limited, this person's blindspot would be limited to the treatment of outsiders. Perhaps her blindspots do indicate selective incompetence. If so, in her sort of case, we should take seriously an incompetence excuse, whether full or partial, at least initially. But as she gains more experience with the intelligence and humanity of these outsiders, she will grow more culpable if she persists in her moral ignorance and misconduct.

12

Immaturity and Fair Opportunity

In this chapter, we will focus on juvenile offenders and the questions of whether and, if so, why they deserve less blame and punishment than their adult counterparts. For the most part, our discussion will focus on teenage minors, who can and should be conceptualized as juveniles or adolescents, rather than as children or kids.[1] One issue that will concern us is whether we should recognize a *moral asymmetry* in our treatment of juvenile and adult crime such that, all else being equal, juvenile offenders deserve less punishment than their adult counterparts. Recognizing this kind of asymmetry between juvenile and adult offenders raises questions about the legitimacy of the trend to transfer juveniles to adult criminal court.

If we do recognize an asymmetry between juvenile and adult offenders, we need to ask what grounds this asymmetry. As we saw in our discussion of structural injustice in Chapter 9, we can in principle separate issues about the *political legitimacy of the state punishing certain offenders* and issues about the *desert of those offenders*. That distinction may prove helpful in assessing the treatment of juvenile crime as well. We can distinguish two different rationales for the asymmetry between juvenile and adult offenders. A *political rationale* claims that the disenfranchisement of juveniles compromises *the state's democratic authority* to punish juveniles in the same way it can punish adults. By contrast, a *developmental rationale* claims that juveniles *deserve* to be punished less than adults because their immaturity makes them less responsible and, hence, less culpable for their wrongdoing. These two rationales are not obviously inconsistent. But we might wonder about their comparative merits. Though there are some reasons to question the legitimacy of the state punishing offenders who are disenfranchised, it is the developmental rationale for the reduced desert of juvenile offenders that is more important, or so I shall argue.

---

[1] When we speak of children or kids, we often have in mind pre-teenage minors. Consequently, referring to the adolescent juveniles centrally implicated in debates about juvenile justice as either children or kids is misleading and perhaps patronizing.

Fair Opportunity and Responsibility. David O. Brink, Oxford University Press (2021). © David O. Brink.
DOI: 10.1093/oso/9780198859468.003.0012

Many would agree that adolescent juveniles are immature not just chrono-logically but normatively. Biological, cognitive, volitional, emotional, and social change and development are important parts of adolescence.[2] These developmental facts suggest that adolescents have diminished normative com-petence with the result that, all else being equal, they are less responsible and, hence, less culpable for criminal offenses than their normal adult counterparts. The fair opportunity conception of responsibility enables us to frame, assess, and explore the implications of this developmental rationale for the moral asymmetry of juvenile and adult offenders.

As we saw in Chapter 11, insanity and related incompetence excuses appeal to failures of normative competence and responsibility that have two features—they are pathological and they often are persistent, if not permanent. By contrast, immaturity is, of course, perfectly normal—every adult was once an adolescent—and is thus a transitional phase on the path from childhood to adulthood. Though different in these important ways from insanity, imma-turity also involves reduced competence, which should affect the responsibility of juveniles and our conception of juvenile justice.

The traditional juvenile court developed, in significant part, from the recognition of this developmental rationale for thinking that juvenile crime is special. After providing some background about the traditional juvenile court, we will look at the trend to bypass the juvenile court and transfer juveniles to adult criminal court that began in the 1980s and 1990s and continues today. Transfer to adult criminal court leads to longer and harsher sentences for juvenile crime. There may be special circumstances in which the transfer of juveniles to adult criminal court is permissible or even required by retributive principles. But central aspects of the transfer trend are deeply unjust. Explaining the developmental rationale for what is special about juvenile justice will allow us to contrast the fair opportunity perspective on juvenile justice with other perspectives on what is special about juvenile justice and how best to accommodate this difference.

Finally, we should examine an apparently antithetical trend in more recent Supreme Court decisions endorsing limitations on juvenile sentencing involv-ing capital and other serious offenses. Though constitutional sentencing limitations do recognize something special about at least some forms of juvenile crime, they only arise in cases in which juveniles are tried in adult court and thus reinforce aspects of the transfer trend. Moreover, the question

<hr>

[2] For one useful survey, see Laurence Steinberg, *Adolescence*, 11th ed. (New York: McGraw-Hill, 2017).

about whether to recognize categorical sentencing limits for juveniles raises interesting and important questions about the tension between categorical sentencing rules and individualized desert that require our attention.

98. The Juvenile Court

The concept of a special system of juvenile justice was largely a twentieth-century development.[3] Until the very late nineteenth century, Anglo-American law tended to treat children either as property or as little adults. Under the age of five or six, children were regarded as the property of their parents, to be treated, like other property, at the discretion of the owner. Once a child reached the age of five or six, the law generally regarded him as a legal person, holding most of the responsibilities and some of the rights of adults.

Industrialization and urbanization in the nineteenth century and the emergence of charitable organizations contributed to new ideas about the education and socialization of children, in general, and wayward children, in particular. This led to the development of houses of refuge and cottage reformatories that dealt with wayward children with a mix of discipline, education, and vocational training. In the United States in the late nineteenth century, jurisdictions in several states experimented with separate procedures of some kind in the criminal trials of juveniles. The first juvenile court was established in Cook County, Illinois in 1899. By the 1920s separate juvenile justice systems were established in nearly every state.

These juvenile courts differed from their adult counterparts in several ways. These differences reflected the assumptions that juveniles were not as mature as adults and that they were therefore both less responsible for their offenses and more corrigible than their adult counterparts. Procedurally, the juvenile courts were more informal and less adversarial. Substantively, they focused less on punishment and more on rehabilitation and socialization. Pursuing a doctrine of *parens patriae* (common guardianship), juvenile courts adopted a more paternalistic attitude toward juvenile offenders.[4] Consequently, the disposition of juvenile offenders was different. Separate juvenile correctional

---

[3] My sketch of some aspects of the juvenile justice background owes much to John Whitehead and Steven Lab, *Juvenile Justice*, 9th ed. (Boston, MA: Routledge, 2018) and Howard Snyder and Melissa Sickmund, *Juvenile Offenders and Victims: 2006 National Report* (Washington, DC: Department of Justice, Office of Juvenile Justice and Delinquency Programs, 2006), ch. 4.

[4] A classic statement of the *parens patriae* doctrine is Julian Mack, "The Juvenile Court" *Harvard Law Review* 22 (1909): 104–22.

facilities were created that stressed educational and vocational training, sentences were often shorter, courts made greater use of probationary and other diversionary alternatives to incarceration, and the criminal records of juvenile offenders were not made a matter of public record in order to prevent stigmatization that might interfere with their successful reintegration into society.

For some time, the paternalistic focus of juvenile courts lent itself to procedural informalities in which juvenile offenders were not accorded the same procedural safeguards before and during trial as their adult counterparts. This practice eventually led to due process concerns, and by the 1960s the Supreme Court was willing to recognize due process rights in juvenile proceedings. In *Kent v. United States* the Court insisted that in any judicial transfer of juvenile offenders from juvenile to adult criminal court the accused is entitled to a hearing, the assistance of counsel, and a statement of the reasons for the transfer.[5] In the case of *In re Gault* the Court held that juveniles enjoy the Fifth Amendment right against self-incrimination and the Sixth Amendment rights to notice of charges, to confront and cross-examine accusers, and to the assistance of counsel.[6] And in *In re Winship* the Court not only affirmed the requirement that adult criminals be convicted only by the standard of guilt beyond a reasonable doubt but also extended this evidential requirement to juvenile proceedings in which incarceration is a possible outcome.[7]

Contemporary juvenile jurisprudence distinguishes juveniles from adults and recognizes distinct forms of juvenile offense. For instance, the Model Penal Code identifies juveniles as those under 18. Though it requires juveniles under 16 to be tried in juvenile court, it provides for the possibility of judicial waiver of juveniles between the ages of 16 and 18 to adult criminal court on a case-by-case basis, in which the prosecution bears the burden of proof in justifying the waiver.[8] A substantial majority of states have followed the Model Penal Code in identifying juveniles as those under 18.[9] Juvenile courts recognize two main kinds of juvenile offense. *Juvenile crime* is simply criminal

---

[5] *Kent v. United States*, 383 U.S. 541 (1966).   [6] *In re Gault*, 387 U.S. 1 (1967).
[7] *In re Winship*, 397 U.S. 358 (1970).
[8] Model Penal Code §4.10 [Immaturity Excluding Criminal Conviction; Transfer of Proceedings to Juvenile Court] and Commentary.
[9] The age of majority was quite variable. In 2004, ten states (GA, IL, LA, MA, MI, MO, NH, SC, TX, WI) identified juveniles as those under 17 years of age, and three states (CT, NY, and NC) identified juveniles as those under 16 years of age. However, 18 years of age has become a more dominant standard, applying in all states except Alabama and Nebraska, where the age of majority is 19, and Mississippi, where the age of majority is 21. See <https://statelaws.findlaw.com/family-laws/legal-ages.html> (accessed 7-14-18).

activity committed by a juvenile. The rules for adult and juvenile crime are the same; the only difference is the age of the offender. By contrast, *status offenses* comprise acts whose legality depends upon the status of the actor. Juvenile status offenses involve acts that would be legal if performed by an adult but are illegal for juveniles, such as truancy, running away from home, curfew violations, smoking, drinking, and swearing. Consequently, the trend of trying juveniles as adults applies only to juvenile criminal conduct, not juvenile status offenses.

The juvenile court is different from adult criminal court in other ways too. Whereas defendants in adult criminal court can and often do elect to have jury trials, the trials in juvenile court are bench trials, conducted by judges with experience in juvenile justice. Defendants in juvenile court experience different sentencing and incarceration outcomes as well. Unless extended through the use of blended sentencing, sentences in juvenile court expire at the age of majority, and so can be much shorter than sentences for comparable offenses in adult court. Juvenile criminal records are sealed, whereas there is public access to the criminal records of adult offenders. Finally, juvenile offenders are sentenced to juvenile correctional facilities, which can be and often are less dangerous than adult correctional facilities and which are supposed to address the particular developmental nutritional, physical, educational, and vocational needs of juvenile offenders.

99. The Transfer Trend: Trying Juveniles as Adults

In response to perceived increases in violent youth crime, especially associated with drug trafficking, the 1980s and 1990s witnessed a national trend toward getting tough on youth crime and holding youthful offenders more accountable. Though the trend has abated somewhat, its legacy is still with us. A central element in this national trend is the transfer of juveniles to adult criminal court, where the consequences of conviction are in various ways much more severe than they are in juvenile court. Prosecutors have long had discretion to prosecute older, mature juveniles who are repeat offenders as adults, and judges in juvenile court have long had the power to issue waivers or transfers that reassign these kinds of juveniles to adult court after a hearing in juvenile court. But in the attempt to get tough on violent juvenile crime both the judicial waiver and prosecutorial discretion have expanded with the result that more juveniles are being transferred to adult court at younger ages for a broader variety of crimes.

The most traditional mechanism for trying juveniles as adults is the *judicial waiver* or transfer of the juvenile to adult criminal court. The judicial waiver occurs in a juvenile court hearing, decided on a case-by-case basis. Model Penal Code §4.10 contemplates that the waiver will occur only in cases in which the juvenile is at least 16-years-old. It does not specify the conditions in which such a waiver is appropriate. Traditionally, juvenile court judges have taken into consideration the age and maturity of the accused, the prior record of the accused (e.g. whether he is a repeat offender), and the severity or seriousness of the offense. Several states have passed legislation that affects the judicial waiver, effectively expanding its scope. For instance, several states have lowered the age at which the judicial waiver can be issued either as a general matter or for certain categories of offense. For example, in 1978 New York passed a Juvenile Offender law that made 13-year-olds eligible for trial for murder in criminal court and made 14-year-olds eligible for such trial in cases involving lesser violent offenses.[10] In effect, the judicial waiver, as traditionally conceived, creates a presumption in favor of trying the accused juvenile as a juvenile, a presumption which could only be rebutted on a case-by-case basis when it was shown that the juvenile was sufficiently mature and had already shown signs of sufficient incorrigibility as to justify treating him as an adult. Recently, several states have also expanded the scope of the judicial waiver by shifting the presumption from juvenile jurisdiction to adult jurisdiction for certain ages and categories of offense. Partly as the result of such statutory changes the scope of the judicial waiver has expanded considerably.

Another mechanism of transfer to adult court involves *prosecutorial discretion*. Recent legislation in several states gives prosecutors the authority, either as a general rule or in special circumstances relating to the age of the accused and the category of offense, to determine whether to bring the case in adult court. This mechanism allows the prosecutor to bypass the need for a judicial hearing and waiver. Recent legislation has simultaneously expanded prosecutorial discretion—expanding the pool of cases in which prosecutors can exercise their discretion to try juveniles as adults—and restricted it—by creating presumptions for transfer for certain ages and categories of offense. Both kinds of change in prosecutorial discretion have had the effect of increasing the number of transfers.

However, even with the legislative changes in these two transfer mechanisms, they do not mandate transfer. Even when there is a presumption in favor of transfer, it can be rebutted in individual cases. Perhaps the most significant

---

[10] 1978 N.Y. Laws, ch. 478 §2(h) (codified as amended at N.Y. Penal Law §30.00 (McKinney 1998)).

and disturbing aspect of the transfer trend is the legislative adoption in many states of *mandatory transfer* statutes that exclude certain cases that would otherwise go to juvenile court from going there and require such cases to be processed in adult criminal court, bypassing both judicial and prosecutorial scrutiny over the appropriate forum for the accused. Typically, mandatory transfers lower the age at which juvenile cases go to adult court either as a general rule or for special categories of violent offense, such as murder, rape, and aggravated assault. Many states have now adopted some kind of mandatory transfer legislation.

The situation in California, where juvenile transfer has been and is evolving, is instructive. Adoption of Proposition 21 in 2000 added a mandatory transfer to the California Welfare and Institutions Code §707(b) requiring that juveniles 14 years of age or older be tried as adults in cases where they are accused of murder or various sexual offenses, including rape, forcible sodomy, and lewd and lascivious acts with a child under the age of 14. Subsequently, the provisions of Proposition 21 and §707(b) were amended by the adoption of Proposition 57 in 2016, permitting the transfer of juveniles as young as 14 accused of §707(b) offenses to adult criminal court but making the transfer conditional on prosecutorial petition and judicial approval. Proposition 57 shows that enthusiasm for mandatory transfer has abated. But it still permits transfer, subject to prosecutorial and judicial discretion, of juveniles as young as 14. In 2018, Senate Bill (SB) 1391 went further than Proposition 57, eliminating authority to transfer juveniles who are 14 or 15. California Courts of Appeal have been divided on the constitutionality of SB 1391, and the California Supreme Court has agreed to review a case in which a Circuit Court upheld the constitutionality of SB 1391.[11] As California illustrates, attitudes toward the transfer trend are changing.[12] But in many other jurisdictions, the transfer trend is still strong, and even in California discretionary forms of juvenile transfer remain in effect.

The net result of such departures from the Model Penal Code provisions for juvenile transfer is that more juveniles are being transferred to adult court at younger ages for a broader variety of crimes.[13] Though enthusiasm for the transfer trend may have abated somewhat in the last decade, the legacy of the

---

[11] *People v. Superior Court* (S.L.), Court of Appeal of California, Sixth Appellate District (2019).

[12] Many thanks to Commissioner Robert Leventer for explaining developments in juvenile transfer in California since the adoption of Proposition 21 in 2000.

[13] The trend is well documented in P. Griffin, P. Torbert, and L. Szymanski, *Trying Juveniles as Adults in Criminal Court: An Analysis of State Transfer Provisions* (Washington, DC: Office of Juvenile Justice and Delinquency Prevention, 1998); Snyder and Sickmund, *Juvenile Offenders and Victims*, ch. 4; and Whitehead and Lab, *Juvenile Justice*, ch. 8.

transfer trend is still with us, especially in jurisdictions with mandatory transfer still on the books.

It is this broad trend to try juveniles as adults and, in particular, the trend to try ever-younger juveniles as adults on account of the seriousness of their offenses that ought to raise serious jurisprudential concerns. The transfer trend denies that there is anything special about juvenile justice. The extreme expression of this trend would be the *abolition* of the juvenile court altogether, treating juvenile offenders exactly the same as their adult counterparts. Those of us who think that the abolition of the juvenile court and the transfer trend are unjust need to explain what is special about juvenile justice. We need to explain the moral asymmetry between juvenile and adult offenders. Questions can be raised about the political legitimacy of treating juvenile offenders the same as adults when juveniles are politically disenfranchised, as adults are not. Though doubts about the democratic legitimacy of the transfer trend are interesting, I'm not sure that they can provide a fully satisfying rationale for what is special about juvenile justice. For that, we will need to appeal to the developmental rationale and its claim that juveniles tend to be normatively less competent than their adult counterparts. This will raise a series of important issues about how best to accommodate this developmental rationale institutionally.

100. Democratic Legitimacy and the Transfer Trend

There is a worry about the political legitimacy of abolitionism and the transfer trend given the fact that juveniles do not have the vote. Earlier, we noted that the disenfranchisement of former felons seems to violate norms of democratic legitimacy that insist that the governed be able to participate in the adoption of laws that affect them (§73). Likewise, treating juveniles exactly the same as adults seems to violate norms of democratic legitimacy insofar as juveniles lack the franchise that adults possess. Just as American revolutionaries appealed to democratic legitimacy in complaining about taxation without representation, so too juveniles might object to the transfer trend by complaining about incarceration without representation.[14]

---

[14] Disenfranchised felons might also complain about incarceration without representation. However, in their case, the franchise is lost as the result of conviction and incarceration. By contrast, juvenile offenders are incarcerated without ever having had the franchise.

Democratic principles give citizens a voice in determining institutions and policies that affect them, and we might say that institutions and decision-making mechanisms are democratic insofar as they reflect the will of the governed. For this reason, democratic principles favor extending the franchise and making it universal, or nearly so. Democratic principles are compelling, and can be defended from a wide variety of normative perspectives. Contractualists and others often defend democracy as a *fair procedure* for decision-making that treats citizens as free and equal persons. On this sort of view, democratic procedures reflect the interests of each citizen in autonomy and self-determination.[15] Consequentialists of various stripes defend democratic institutions as generally and non-accidentally producing *better outcomes* for its citizens. On this sort of view, political institutions are best when they are in the interest of the governed, and democratic processes better reveal the interests of the governed, by making governors accountable to the governed, and may promote the improvement of normative capacities for self-government and autonomy among citizens.[16] One can also offer *mixed* justifications of democracy that recognize both procedural and outcome-oriented justifications of democracy.[17] One can defend democratic principles by appeal to the civic republican tradition that values freedom conceived as non-domination.[18] Alternatively, one might defend them by appeal to the liberal tradition that posits a right to self-determination and seeks to protect individuals from wrongful interference by others.[19]

If we accept democratic principles for any of these reasons, we might doubt the political legitimacy of the transfer trend.

---

[15] Proceduralist justifications of democracy might be traced back at least to Rousseau. See Jean Jacques Rousseau, *A Discourse on the Origin of Inequality* [1755] and *The Social Contract* [1762] both in *Rousseau: The Basic Political Writings*, 2d ed., D. Cress (Indianapolis, IN: Hackett, 2012). A contemporary statement is Charles Beitz, *Political Equality: An Essay in Democratic Theory* (Princeton, NJ: Princeton University Press, 1989).

[16] Consequentialist and outcome-oriented justifications of democracy might be traced back to the Philosophical Radicals, especially James Mill and John Stuart Mill. See James Mill, *An Essay on Government* [1824] reprinted in *Utilitarian Logic and Politics*, ed. J. Lively and J. Rees (Oxford: Clarendon Press, 1978) and John Stuart Mill, *Considerations on Representative Government* [1861] in *The Collected Works of John Stuart Mill*, vol. XIX. A contemporary consequentialist about democracy is Richard Arneson, "Democracy is Not Intrinsically Just" in *Justice and Democracy*, ed. K. Dowding, R. Goodin, and C. Pateman (Cambridge: Cambridge University Press, 2004).

[17] See, e.g., Thomas Christiano, *The Rule of the Many* (Boulder, CO: Westview Press, 1996) and David Estlund, *Democratic Authority* (Princeton, NJ: Princeton University Press, 2007).

[18] An early republican justification of democracy is Richard Price, *Observations on the Importance of the American Revolution* (London: T. Cadwell, 1785). A modern statement of republican democratic principles is Philip Pettit, *Republicanism: A Theory of Freedom and Government* (Oxford: Clarendon Press, 1997).

[19] An influential liberal conception of democracy is found in John Stuart Mill, *On Liberty* [1859] in *Collected Works* vol. XVIII and *Considerations on Representative Government*.

1. The state can legitimately enforce only those laws against citizens who have had a say in enacting laws in the sense that they have had an opportunity to influence the adoption of those laws.
2. Juveniles lack the right to vote and so lack the opportunity to influence the adoption of laws that affect them.
3. Hence, the state is not justified in enforcing laws against juveniles as it is in enforcing laws against adults.

Do our democratic commitments compromise the political legitimacy of the state punishing juveniles the same as adults in this way? This is a promising suggestion. It is similar to the main line of argument developed in Gideon Yaffe's recent book *The Age of Culpability*,[20] though he focuses less on the issue of political legitimacy per se and more on a complicated argument from juvenile disenfranchisement to their reduced culpability. I will briefly address that wrinkle in his argument later (§105), but I think that the political legitimacy argument is best assessed, at least initially, independently of claims about desert. Despite the initial appeal of this argument from democratic legitimacy to explain what is special about juvenile justice, there are several problems that need to be worked out first. Some problems have potential solutions, but others may not be so easy to fix.

One worry about the democratic objection to the transfer trend is that it proves too much. If laws can be legitimately enforced only against those who have had a say in enacting them, then the disenfranchisement of juveniles might seem to imply that the state has *no authority* to enforce laws against juveniles. But this claim that democratic states lack legal authority altogether over disenfranchised juveniles is a very radical claim, much more radical than the moral asymmetry thesis that juveniles deserve to be punished less than their adult counterparts. We should be able to resist the transfer trend without completely relinquishing authority over disenfranchised youth.

However, this objection assumes that the vote is the only way that people can have a say over the laws that affect them. One might deny this assumption, pointing out that there are other opportunities to influence what laws are enacted or repealed besides voting. Political speech is also one way to affect political decision-making, and juveniles have First Amendment rights to political speech and assembly. They may not have the full complement of First Amendment rights that adults do, but they nonetheless have significant

---

[20] Gideon Yaffe, *The Age of Culpability: Children and the Nature of Criminal Responsibility* (Oxford: Clarendon Press, 2018).

expressive liberties. If so, juveniles, though disenfranchised, do not lack political influence altogether.

This reply might threaten to undercut the original argument providing a democratic rationale for thinking that juvenile justice is special. After all, if juveniles have forms of political say other than the vote, then it might seem that we've lost the democratic rationale against the transfer trend. The answer, as Yaffe notes, is to recognize that political say is *scalar*. While the First Amendment rights of juveniles ensure that they are not without political say entirely, it's nonetheless true that because they lack the franchise they have less political say than adults, who possess both First Amendment rights (indeed, less qualified expressive rights) and the franchise.[21] This means that the state enjoys *differential* democratic authority in relation to juveniles and adults. But this claim is precisely what's needed to explain how the state can have some authority over juveniles, though less than the authority they have over adults.

Another worry that the democratic argument against the transfer trend proves too much is that it would seem to apply equally well to other non-voting groups that nonetheless seem to be subject to the law, such as resident aliens, foreign nationals, and other visitors. Not only do foreign visitors lack the right to vote, but they also lack some, though not all, of the constitutional protections afforded to juvenile and adult citizens. Perhaps the expressive liberties that foreign visitors possess are enough to ensure that they don't lack political say altogether. Yet surely they have less political say than juvenile citizens, and even less political say than adult citizens. This would apparently imply that a democratic state has less authority to enforce its criminal law against foreign visitors than against its own citizens, both juvenile and adult. However, that seems like an unacceptable commitment.

The proponent of the democratic rationale for what is special about juvenile justice might claim that foreign visitors effectively agree to be subject to the host country's laws when they enter that country, thus waiving any complaint of democratic legitimacy that they might otherwise make later in response to prosecution for noncompliance with the laws of the host country.[22] According to this suggestion, host countries retain authority over foreign visitors by virtue of their consent to be subject to the laws of the host country.

However, it's not clear that this solves the problem with the democratic rationale. It seems that foreign visitors might not agree to be governed by some laws in the host country. Why assume that their decision to visit nonetheless

---

[21] For discussion of these issues, see Yaffe, *The Age of Culpability*, pp. 165–71.
[22] For a version of this reply, see Yaffe, *The Age of Culpability*, pp. 185–95.

312 FAIR OPPORTUNITY AND RESPONSIBILITY

constitutes consent to be governed by all the laws of the host country? We can't answer that this is the condition that the host country places on visitation. If that is an adequate answer here, then the proponent of the transfer trend has an answer to the appeal to democratic legitimacy. For the state can equally say that full criminal penalties are a condition that it places on noncompliance with the criminal law. Then, when a juvenile commits a crime, the state can say that the juvenile's noncompliance constitutes consent to be subject to the same penalties for noncompliance that adults are subject to. The stipulation about implied consent seems no more plausible in the case of foreign visitors than it is in the case of juveniles.[23] If so, this seems to be an unresolved problem in the democratic rationale for why juvenile justice is special and what is wrong with the transfer trend. If sound, it has very unattractive and revisionary implications about the legitimate authority of democratic states over foreign visitors. But if we abandon this argument, we can no longer appeal to democratic legitimacy to explain what is special about juvenile justice and to reject the transfer trend.

Finally, there is a worry about whether democratic legitimacy could constitute a free-standing rationale for the special treatment of juvenile justice that does not presuppose the plausibility of the developmental rationale. If the only thing wrong with the transfer trend is that disenfranchised juveniles are treated the same as enfranchised adults, there's an obvious solution. Give juveniles the vote. There are two problems with this proposal. First, anyone attracted to the developmental rationale will think that even if juveniles had the vote, there would still be reason to view many of them as deserving less punitive treatment on account of their immaturity and its presumed effect on their level of normative competence and desert. Second, even if we could be persuaded that it was legitimate to treat some 17-year-olds or perhaps even 16-year-olds as adults, provided they had the right to vote, most of us would be reluctant to think that it would be permissible to treat much younger juveniles as adults if only they had the right to vote. Surely, it would be objectionable to treat eight-year-olds as adults if only we gave them the vote. The importance of the developmental rationale explains both objections. We would think that there was something problematic about treating many juveniles as adults, even

---

[23] This concern about how the democratic rationale for the juvenile/adult asymmetry can avoid exculpating criminal wrongdoing by foreign visitors extends to Yaffe's willingness to assimilate juvenile disenfranchisement to the disenfranchisement of felons. Though I don't want to defend the political legitimacy of disenfranchising felons during, much less after, incarceration, it's not clear why the state couldn't equally well insist that disenfranchisement is part of the price of criminal offense, with the result that felons could be construed as having consented to forfeit the franchise when they choose to engage in criminal activity.

if they had the vote, because we believe that their immaturity explains their reduced normative competence and desert. Moreover, the same immaturity that explains why it would be wrong to treat enfranchised juveniles as adults explains why there are lower limits on how early the franchise should be granted. It may well be that 18 years of age is not the only plausible age threshold for the vote, but it seems quite plausible that eight-year-olds are developmentally below the threshold.[24]

Where does this leave us? The idea that the state might lack political legitimacy to treat juvenile offenders the same as adult offenders on account of juvenile disenfranchisement is certainly suggestive. However, there are unresolved worries about whether that argument proves too much to be acceptable. Moreover, even if these worries can be addressed, it seems unlikely that this democratic rationale for the different treatment of juvenile offenders can be free-standing, independent of the developmental rationale that many juvenile offenders are immature and so deserve lesser punishment. Even if we gave juveniles the vote, we would still be moved to treat them differently from their adult counterparts on account of their immaturity, and there are limits to how much we should lower the age threshold for the franchise that seem likely to track developmental aspects of normative competence. For these reasons, the case for treating juvenile offenders differently than their adult counterparts must rest primarily on the developmental rationale.

101. Immaturity, Fair Opportunity, and Desert

Proponents of transferring juveniles to adult criminal court appear to be moved by a level of violence in juvenile crime normally associated with adult crime. The motto seems to be that adult crime calls for adult penalties. But insofar as we are retributivists about whom to punish and how much to punish, we should see a problem with the trend to try juveniles as adults on account of the seriousness of their crimes. It is true that the retributive formula

---

[24] This worry that the democratic rationale for the differential treatment of juvenile offenders is not a free-standing rationale should be especially troubling for someone like Yaffe, who wants to accept the democratic rationale and reject the developmental rationale. Yaffe describes this kind of concern as "facile" (p. 8). I'm not sure he ever explains why it is facile. The only reply he seems to make is to defend a comparatively high threshold for the franchise by appeal to claims about the way in which parental interests in influencing the further future through legislation, constrained by equality of influence, militates against setting the franchise threshold substantially lower (pp. 172–82). I found this discussion both hard to follow and normatively problematic insofar as it posits a legitimate adult interest in having a say not just about present policy but also about further future policy.

implies that all else being equal—in particular, holding culpability constant—the worse the wrong the greater should be the punishment. But all else is not equal when we are comparing juvenile and adult crime. Wrongdoing or harm done and responsibility or culpability are *independent* factors in the retributivist desert basis for punishment. Juveniles can engage in the same crimes as adults, committing the same wrongs, but typically they bear less responsibility for the wrongs they commit. This is because for developmental reasons they typically possess reduced normative competence in relation to their adult counterparts. Insofar as they possess reduced normative competence, juveniles will be less responsible and, hence, less broadly culpable than adults. Insofar as they are less culpable for their wrongs, they deserve less blame and punishment. This is the retributive element in the developmental rationale for what is special about juvenile justice.[25]

The fair opportunity conception of responsibility recognizes that normative competence has both cognitive and volitional dimensions. Responsible agents must be able to recognize reasons bearing on their conduct and make suitable normative discriminations, and they must be able to conform their conduct to this normative knowledge. If so, normative competence involves a variety of psychological capacities. It involves cognitive capacities to recognize the relevant norms and to grade their comparative urgency, so as to navigate potential moral conflicts. It also involves volitional capacities, including capacities for impulse control necessary to implement one's judgments about what is best, despite temptation and distraction and independence from peer pressure for conformity. These capacities are *scalar* insofar as they can be possessed to different degrees. Of course, adults can vary in the degree to which they possess these capacities. But we believe that most normal adults have these capacities to a sufficient degree to make them responsible for their actions. By contrast, the gradual development of normative competence is what marks normal normative progress through childhood and adolescence to maturity. Though not all individuals mature at the same rate, and some individuals never mature, this sort of normative maturation is strongly correlated with age. The reduced normative competence of juveniles provides a retributive justification for reduced punishment for juveniles.

---

[25] Our focus here is on how immaturity affects normative competence, responsibility, and desert. A different concern is how immaturity affects the competence of juveniles to stand to trial—to understand the charges, to assist counsel in preparing a defense, and to make plea decisions. See, e.g., Richard Bonnie and Thomas Grisso, "Adjudicative Competence and Youthful Offenders" in *Youth on Trial: A Developmental Perspective on Juvenile Justice*, ed. T. Grisso and R. Schwartz (Chicago, IL: University of Chicago Press, 2000).

There is widespread agreement among developmental psychologists that the period between twelve and eighteen years of age is a time of very significant physical, cognitive, and emotional development.[26] Older adolescents may have many of the cognitive abilities that adults have, but they lack the wealth of experience and factual information that adults typically possess. Even when older adolescents share cognitive abilities with adults, they typically lack familiar forms of emotional and social maturity and control. They are less able to represent the future adequately, with the result that they are more impulsive and less risk-averse.[27] They also tend to be more susceptible to the influence of peers, with the result that they lack a key ingredient in normative competence.[28] Finally, there is emerging evidence that the neurological correlates of these cognitive, emotional, and social capacities are undergoing crucial development throughout adolescence and well into late adolescence.[29] If normative competence is a condition of responsibility, then the reduced or diminished normative competence of juveniles calls into question many of the punitive reforms to juvenile justice embodied in the transfer trend.

102. Immaturity and Forward-looking Rationales for Punishment

In this way, immaturity is directly relevant to the retributivist's backward-looking rationale for punishment. Immaturity involves reduced normative competence and, hence, reduced culpability and desert. All else being equal,

---

[26] See, generally, Steinberg, *Adolescence*; E. Scott, N. Reppucci, and J. Woolard, "Evaluating Adolescent Decision Making in Legal Contexts" *Law and Human Behavior* 19 (1995): 221–44 and Thomas Grisso and Robert Schwartz (eds), *Youth on Trial: A Developmental Perspective on Juvenile Justice* (New York: Oxford, 2000).

[27] See, e.g., P. Finn and B. Bragg, "Perception of the Risk of an Accident by Young and Older Drivers" *Accident Analysis and Prevention* 18 (1986): 289–98; M. Tester, W. Gardiner, and E. Wilfong, "Experimental Studies of the Development of Decision-making Competence" in *Children, Risks, and Decisions: Psychological and Legal Implications* (New York: American Psychological Association, 1987); and Scott et al., "Evaluating Adolescent Decision Making in Legal Contexts."

[28] See, e.g., T. Berndt, "Developmental Changes in Conformity to Peers and Parents" *Developmental Psychology* 15 (1979): 608–16; S. Steinberg and S. Silverberg, "The Vicissitudes of Autonomy in Early Adolescence" *Child Development* 57 (1986): 841–51; Scott et al., "Evaluating Adolescent Decision Making in Legal Contexts."

[29] See, e.g., S. Anderson, A. Bechara, H. Damasio, D. Tranel, and A. Damasio, "Impairment of Social and Moral Behavior Related to Damage in Human Prefrontal Cortex" *Nature Neuroscience* 2 (1999): 1032–37; F. Benes, "The Development of Prefrontal Cortex: The Maturation of Neurotransmitter Systems and their Interactions" in *Handbook of Developmental Cognitive Neuroscience*, ed. C. Nelson and M. Luciana (Cambridge, MA: MIT Press, 2001); and William Hirstein, Katrina Sifferd, and Tyler Fagan, *Responsible Brains: Neuroscience, Law, and Human Culpability* (Cambridge, MA: MIT Press, 2018), ch. 8.

juveniles tend to be less responsible than their adult counterparts. But immaturity is also relevant to the forward-looking rationales for punishment, especially those involving rehabilitation and deterrence. Recall that predominant retributivism allows consequential considerations to play three different roles in punishment—they can play roles in fine-tuning the quantum of punishment appropriate within the interval set by desert, determining the manner and forms of punishment, and providing reasons to punish less than the agent deserves (§47).

Rehabilitative goals have a legitimate role in adult criminal justice, in which offenders are fully responsible for their crimes. They have an even more important role in juvenile justice, in which the immaturity of offenders renders them simultaneously less responsible but more corrigible. Adolescence is a pivotal period both because it is a time of enormous cognitive and emotional growth and maturation and because it is a time when enduring intellectual, emotional, and social skills and habits are being established. This means that adoption of the rehabilitative stance toward juvenile offenders is not only especially appropriate but also especially consequential. This makes it imperative that juvenile offenders be sentenced to special juvenile facilities that avoid the brutality of adult prisons, that provide significant educational, vocational, and avocational training, and that make provisions for the special nutritional and developmental needs of adolescents. Adult correctional facilities rarely address rehabilitative goals with adult offenders. They are even more poorly suited to address the special rehabilitative needs and opportunities posed by juvenile offenders. But then the trend to try juveniles as adults and incarcerate them in adult correctional facilities runs afoul of rehabilitative ideals of punishment.

We can also see how immaturity changes the operation of deterrent values within juvenile criminal justice. Deterrence is usually understood in terms of sanctions that create incentives to comply with the law, thus deterring crime. By attaching sanctions to criminal activity, we make it less attractive; the greater the sanctions we attach to it, the more unattractive we make such activity. In the case of *specific* deterrence, applying sanctions to the wrongdoer is supposed to deter *him* from further criminal conduct. In the case of *general* deterrence, applying sanctions to the wrongdoer is supposed to deter *others* from criminal conduct.

Immaturity seems likely to affect the deterrent value, both general and specific, of sanctions for juveniles. The deterrent effect of sanctions crucially depends on potential criminals being rational calculators of expected utility. No doubt, this is an idealizing assumption even for some adults. But it is an especially unrealistic assumption for juveniles. Younger adolescents not only lack the cognitive capacities of adults, but also, and more importantly, they lack the ability to vividly represent the future and are prone to discount the significance of future benefits and harms out of proportion to their actual magnitude and, as a result, to engage in irrational risk-taking. But this means that sanctions that might, in principle, work for adults won't have the same deterrent value for juveniles. In fact, there is evidence from Florida and other states that use of harsher, adult criminal sanctions for minors actually increases recidivism rates.[30] If so, considerations of specific deterrence actually speak against the transfer trend. In the juvenile context, deterrence is more likely to be served by establishing better schools for the social sentiments both inside and outside of correctional facilities than by ratcheting up the severity of the sanctions for violating the law.

103. Two Tracks in Juvenile Justice

There is growing evidence that adolescence involves a period of increased risk-taking and anti-social impulses that are normally outgrown. The historically robust fact that juvenile crime constitutes a disproportionate amount of all crime committed means that most deviance is limited to adolescence.[31] Most deviant adolescents do not become deviant adults. Whereas most teenage offenders do not become career criminals, younger preteen arrest is the best predictor of career criminality. This suggests that the class of juvenile offenders divides roughly into two subclasses—a small number of juveniles whose anti-social tendencies begin before puberty who are strongly disposed to become career offenders, and a much larger number of juveniles whose deviance is confined to adolescence and who, under normal circumstances, would outgrow these deviant tendencies.[32] Whereas specifically adolescent deviance is more common and represents a temporary phase, significant preteen deviance is strongly correlated with cognitive and emotional disabilities and the presence of domestic dysfunction and other environmental stress

---

[30] See Donna Bishop, Charles Frazier, Lonn Lanza-Kaduce, and Lawrence Winner, "The Transfer of Juveniles to Criminal Court: Does It Make a Difference?" *Crime and Delinquency* 42 (1996): 171–91.

[31] See, e.g., Barry Feld, *Bad Kids: Race and the Transformation of the Juvenile Court* (New York: Oxford, 1999), pp. 221–22.

[32] See, e.g., Terrie Moffitt, "Adolescence-Limited and Life-Course-Persistent Antisocial Behavior: A Developmental Taxonomy" *Psychological Review* 100 (1993): 674–701 and Thomas Grisso, "Society's Retributive Response to Juvenile Violence: A Developmental Perspective" *Law and Human Behavior* 20 (1996): 229–47.

for which it is difficult to correct. Indeed, significant preteen violence is predictive of antisocial personality disorder and psychopathy (§90). This two-track model of juvenile deviance has implications for what is distinctive about juvenile justice.

On the one hand, few people think that normal preteens—those who suffer from no special cognitive, affective, or conative deficits—are fully responsible, and the trend to try juveniles as adults does not extend to preteens.[33] If preteen crime is mostly committed by children who suffer from severe psychological deficits, then there is even less reason to treat them as normatively competent and even less reason to treat them as responsible for the offenses they commit. The absence of responsibility for their offenses means that they do not meet the retributive condition for punishment. But preteen criminality, especially violent criminal conduct, demands intervention in the form of counseling, monitoring, and detention if the child poses a significant danger to himself or others.

By contrast, adolescence-specific deviance is potentially culpable, but at least with younger adolescents, we have reason to think that their normative competence is diminished. When we note that such deviant behavior is normally outgrown, this might incline us to view it as part of the process of normative maturation, experimentation, and education. This isn't to normalize juvenile criminal conduct, but it suggests that criminal conduct might be the manifestation of developmentally normal psychological mechanisms involving risk-taking and experimentation. Moreover, this isn't a reason not to hold juveniles accountable and punish their misconduct. Indeed, appropriate reactive attitudes, intervention, and punishment may be essential if juveniles are to learn important moral lessons and outgrow their deviance. But recognition that most juvenile crime is adolescence-specific gives us reason to respond to age-specific juvenile misconduct in ways that encourage moral learning and don't foreclose the possibility of a normal adult life.

---

[33] The earliest transfer, with which I am familiar, is the famous case involving Lionel Tate, who as a 12-year-old killed a six-year-old family friend in daycare, imitating what he had seen in professional wrestling on television. Tate was tried as an adult and convicted of first-degree murder, which in Florida carries a mandatory sentence of life in prison without the possibility of parole. Tate was offered a chance to plead to second-degree murder and a reduced sentence, but his mother insisted that he refuse the plea bargain on the ground that Lionel did not intend to kill his friend. In response to public outcry over Tate's sentence, he was granted a retrial and accepted substantially the same plea deal that he had earlier refused. See *Tate v. Florida*, 864 So. 2d 44, 46–47 (Fla. Dist. Ct. App. 2003). Another case involving 12-year-olds occurred in Wisconsin, when 12-year-olds Morgan Geyser and Anissa Weier tried to kill their friend Payton Leutner, stabbing her 19 times, in an attempt to appease the (fictional) Slender Man. Geyser and Weier were tried as adults but acquitted by reason of insanity and committed to psychiatric care for a minimum of 40 years (Geyser) and 25 years (Weier). See, e.g., "Teenager in 'Slender Man' Stabbing Gets 40 Years in Mental Hospital" *New York Times* February 1, 2018.

104. A Developmental Rationale for what is Special about Juvenile Justice

In the last three sections I have articulated a developmental rationale for the moral asymmetry thesis that, all else being equal, juveniles should be treated differently and punished less harshly than their adult counterparts.[34] This rationale for what is special about juvenile justice has fairly revisionary legal and policy implications, especially in undermining the legitimacy of many aspects of the transfer trend. Despite its reformist implications, the developmental rationale will seem familiar and plausible to many. Moreover, our commitments to the fair opportunity conception of responsibility and predominant retributivism help frame and inform this developmental rationale. Predominant retributivism insists on the importance of desert to understanding how we should respond to juvenile crime, and fair opportunity insists that we understand desert and broad culpability in terms of normative competence and situational control. Developmental psychology supports the claim that other things being equal juveniles, especially younger adolescents, tend to be less normatively competent than adults. Predominant retributivism also permits the operation of forward-looking considerations about how best to respond to juvenile offenders, provided these considerations are conditioned by backward-looking retributive considerations. Here too, developmental findings support treating juveniles differently than adults. Juveniles tend to be more corrigible and, hence, better candidates for rehabilitation; they tend to be less competent rationally, which diminishes the specific deterrent value of sanctioning them; and the fact that most criminal conduct is adolescence-specific suggests the importance of holding them accountable in ways that allow them to learn from their mistakes and pursue normal adult lives.

However, we need to be cautious about how exactly to frame the conclusion of the developmental rationale and what it implies about the ways in which juvenile justice is special. The idea that there is a moral asymmetry between juvenile and adult offenders is a useful generalization or slogan, but it requires various qualifications.

First, we should not expect the developmental rationale to provide a purely principled justification of a categorical asymmetry between juveniles and adults, without resort to pragmatic considerations. For instance, we are unlikely to be able to justify treating everyone over 18 in adult criminal

---

[34] For another version of the developmental rationale, see Elizabeth Scott and Larry Steinberg, "Blaming Youth" *Texas Law Review* 81 (2003): 799–840.

court and everyone under 18 in juvenile court without appeal to pragmatic factors. This is because when the underlying normatively relevant factors are scalar, thresholds and bright lines will be somewhat arbitrary, because they attach enormous significance to small differences straddling the threshold and ignore large differences above and below the threshold. There will typically be little difference in normative competence between a young 18-year-old and an older 17-year-old, though a categorical asymmetry would treat them very differently. Moreover, there will be individual variation, with some juveniles being more normatively mature for their age than other juveniles the same age and perhaps than other young adults. In order to maintain a categorical asymmetry between juveniles and adults, we would need to resort to pragmatic considerations. For instance, the case for a categorical asymmetry is stronger if the following claims are plausible.

1. Age is a generally reliable proxy for normative maturity.
2. Most 18-year-olds are sufficiently mature to be held responsible.
3. Normatively precocious juveniles are rare.
4. It is difficult to identify normatively precocious juveniles reliably.
5. Blackstone's asymmetry: mistakes of over-punishment are worse than mistakes of under-punishment.

Together, these claims make the best case for embracing a categorical asymmetry between juveniles and adults in which we treat all juveniles differently than adults. Because it relies on empirical claims, especially about our epistemic limitations, it is a partly pragmatic rationale for a simple categorical asymmetry between juveniles and adults.

Second, even if this is a reasonable pragmatic solution to handling individual variation, it does nothing to address reliable differences between older and younger juveniles and similarities between older juveniles and younger adults. If we assume that most 18-year-olds have reached a threshold of sufficient normative competence to be tried in adult court, we may wonder whether a categorical asymmetry between 18-year-olds and 17-year-olds makes sense, given their similarities. It's not clear if their modest differences in normative competence and Blackstone's asymmetry justify categorically different treatment. In this connection it is noteworthy that the Model Penal Code does not embrace a categorical asymmetry between juveniles and adults. As we have seen, the Model Penal Code presumes that all juveniles should be tried in juvenile court but allows that presumption to be rebutted in a case-by-case manner for juveniles between 16 and 18 years of age based on a judicial determination that the juvenile in question demonstrates culpability comparable to an adult (MPC §4.10). Because the judge has limited discretion and must rebut a presumption in favor of 16 to 17-year-olds being tried in juvenile court, this limited use of judicial waiver is a modest departure from categorical asymmetry, one that aims to better track developmental facts about competence and culpability.

Third, another well motivated departure from a categorical asymmetry between juvenile and adult crime concerns the selective use of *blended sentencing* that combines a juvenile sentence until the age of majority and an adult sentence subsequent to the juvenile one. Older mature adolescents will often be significantly, if not fully, normatively competent. This will be true of many 17-year-olds. So they can be largely, if not fully, responsible for committing crimes, both serious and less serious. Under the traditional juvenile sentencing rules that require juvenile sentences to expire by the age of majority, such offenders are unlikely to receive sentences commensurate with their desert. Indeed, there is a puzzle for the traditional juvenile sentencing system that the older and more responsible the offender—the closer to being 18 years old—the less time he can serve for his crimes. Blended sentencing provides a solution to this puzzle insofar as it allows mature adolescents who are substantially culpable for serious crimes to serve limited adult sentences in addition to their comparatively short juvenile sentences. I am not claiming that the actual use of blended sentencing has typically conformed to the retributive formula of proportionality, only that the retributive conception of proportionality endorses the selective use of blended sentencing.

Fourth, even if the developmental rationale is right that competence and culpability generally track immaturity, justifying lesser sentences for juveniles than adults, we might wonder if a youth discount should extend to especially heinous crimes, such as murder, torture, and aggravated sexual assault that wounds or maims the victim. Borrowing a concept from wartime wrongdoing, which we discussed earlier (§83), we might wonder whether the partial excuse that applies to many juvenile offenses should apply to *manifest illegality*, at least as committed by older adolescents. Manifest illegalities are actions that are wrong on their face and would be clearly wrong under any realistic circumstances.[35] If manifest illegality involves especially obvious wrongdoing, we might wonder if it requires the same normative acuity to recognize. We have treated wrongdoing and responsibility or (broad) culpability as independent variables in the retributive desert basis for punishment. For the most

---

[35] See Model Penal Code §2.10 and Manual for Courts Martial 2012, Rule 916(d).

part, this is both right and important. However, wrongdoing and culpability may not be completely independent in the case of manifest illegality, because we may think that it requires a fairly basic, rather than subtle, normative competence to recognize manifest illegality as wrong. If so, we can and should hold young adolescents less responsible for acts of manifest illegality, but we might doubt that we should extend a significant sentencing discount to 17-year-olds guilty of manifest illegality.[36] This limited departure from a categorical juvenile/adult asymmetry could be readily accommodated by the provisions for possible judicial waiver for 16-year-olds and 17-year-olds recognized in the Model Penal Code. Especially since judges have to rebut the presumption in favor of trying such cases in juvenile court, the waiver could be restricted to older adolescents in cases involving manifest illegality.

We could try to defend a simple categorical asymmetry between juvenile and adult crime by appeal to both the developmental rationale and pragmatic considerations. However, we should recognize that the developmental rationale does not support a simple categorical asymmetry. Seventeen-year-olds will often be as competent as young adults, especially for crimes involving manifest illegality. Moreover, a retributive understanding of the developmental rationale requires the selective use of blended sentencing for serious crimes committed by older adolescents. These are well motivated departures from a simple categorical asymmetry between juvenile and adult crime and are fully consistent with the Model Penal Code position that treats the asymmetry as a presumption that can be rebutted on a case-by-case basis for older adolescents and especially serious crimes. The developmental rationale should embrace these deviations from a strict asymmetry. However, the transfer trend far outstrips these modest departures from strict asymmetry, transferring young adolescents to adult court for a wide variety of offenses. That trend pushes the age at which normative competence might be established much further back, to ages where it strains credulity to think that the case for normative immaturity could be successfully rebutted. This is bad enough, but an important strand in the transfer trend actually inverts the presumption so that many juveniles accused of certain crimes now bear the presumption of showing that they should be tried in juvenile court. Worse still are the mandatory transfer laws that automatically transfer comparatively young juveniles accused of certain crimes to adult court. It is hard to see how such transfer policies could be defended by appeal to the scalar nature of normative competence

---

[36] Here, I revisit and express doubts about a position I defended in "Immaturity, Normative Competence, and Juvenile Transfer," pp. 1576–77.

and individual variability in normative maturation. An unrebuttable 18-year-old cut-off, which few endorse, would be problematic in some of its applications, but at least it would generally, if imperfectly, track the facts about normative competence that matter. To replace an unrebuttable 18-year-old threshold in favor of an unrebuttable 14-year-old threshold is ludicrous. It too fails to achieve individualized justice, but it also greatly multiplies the number of individual injustices. For while an 18-year-old threshold for adulthood will be both under-inclusive and over-inclusive at the margins, a 14-year-old test will be massively over-inclusive. This is bad enough. If we assume, as Blackstone does, that it is better to weight the criminal justice system so that errors of over-punishment are seen as worse than errors of under-punishment, then the transfer trend must seem especially unjust. This means that the appeal to accountability that is often made to support the trend to try juveniles as adults, so far from supporting that trend, actually undermines it.

105. Skepticism about Skepticism about the Developmental Rationale

I expect that many readers will find this developmental rationale for the reduced culpability and desert of juvenile offenders plausible. So it is perhaps worth saying briefly why I think we should resist Yaffe's skepticism about this sort of developmental rationale.[37] Yaffe reconstructs the developmental rationale in roughly the same terms that I have here, in §§101–104. However, though he accepts that adolescent development tends to make juveniles normatively less competent and culpable than their adult counterparts, he thinks that these developmental factors can't provide a principled rationale for a categorical asymmetry between juveniles and adults in which all juveniles are tried in juvenile court and all adults are tried in adult court. The problem is twofold. First, individual variation means that some mature adolescents are as culpable as normal adults, and some young adults are no more culpable than mature adolescents.[38] Second, the developmental rationale holds the special treatment of juveniles hostage to the truth of these empirical claims, whereas Yaffe regards the asymmetry between juvenile and adult offenders as a categorical one.[39]

---

[37] See Yaffe, *The Age of Culpability*, chs. 1–2.   [38] Yaffe, *The Age of Culpability*, pp. 24–30.
[39] Yaffe, *The Age of Culpability*, pp. 31–39.

Yaffe's skepticism assumes that we should be committed to a simple categorical asymmetry and that such a categorical difference between juveniles and adults cannot depend on empirical or pragmatic considerations. But the version of the developmental rationale developed here rejects these assumptions. The strong, but imperfect, correlation between age, maturity, and normative competence might be sufficient to justify a categorical asymmetry, but, if so, only on pragmatic grounds that appealed to the strength of the correlation, the infrequency of exceptions, and our inability to reliably identify the exceptional cases. But it is better to reject a categorical asymmetry and treat the chronological juvenile/adult threshold as establishing a rebuttable presumption about the treatment of individual cases that would permit the judicial transfer of older adolescents to adult criminal court when and insofar as sufficient competence and culpability could be demonstrated.[40] However, this use of the judicial waiver should be used sparingly and should not extend to younger juveniles, under the age of 16. Moreover, I don't see any reason why the rationale for treating juvenile misconduct as special should not rely on plausible empirical claims.

Yaffe criticizes the empirical character of the developmental rationale, noting that if it turned out, as an empirical matter, that girls were developmentally more mature than boys by, say, two years, then the youth discount that applies to boys would not extend to girls.[41] In this case, there would be a gender asymmetry in the sort of transfer that was permissible. Yaffe takes this to be a *reductio* of the deliberative rationale, describing the potential gender asymmetry as "laughable" and "morally intolerable."[42] But I don't see why this is laughable or morally intolerable. Given the importance of desert to punishment and competence to desert, I think we would need to take the gender asymmetry seriously *if but only if* we were confident that girls were more developmentally advanced than boys *in all normatively relevant* respects. But I don't believe that there is good evidence for this proposition, at least not at the present time. In the absence of such evidence, gender equality should be our norm. Indeed, given the pervasiveness of gender discrimination against girls and women, we might have sufficient reason to oppose the gender asymmetry even if there was good empirical evidence that girls are more mature than boys in all relevant respects. This would be an argument of overall justice, not a claim about individual responsibility and desert.

---

[40] Currently, there is no provision for transferring immature young adults to juvenile court. Their options would seem to be partial excuse or sentence mitigation in adult criminal court.
[41] Yaffe, *The Age of Culpability*, pp. 31–33.   [42] Yaffe, *The Age of Culpability*, pp. 39, 183.

Yaffe thinks he can provide a rationale for a categorical asymmetry between juveniles and adults that appeals to juvenile disenfranchisement. This is the central thesis of his book. His argument is not exactly the argument for the political illegitimacy of punishing disenfranchised juveniles, which we discussed critically before (§100). Rather, the main argument of his book is that because juveniles have less say over the laws that govern them they are less culpable for qualitatively identical crimes than adults commit, a result that in no way depends on developmental differences between juveniles and adults. This is an interesting and complex argument that defies easy summary. The structure of the argument is something like this.[43]

1. Legal culpability is a matter of one failing to track the legal reasons one has and can be measured by one's degree of departure from those reasons or norms.
2. Deserved punishment is a matter of legal culpability.
3. The weight of legal reasons one has is partly a function of whether one is entitled to have a say over the content of those reasons.
4. Because they are disenfranchised, juveniles have less say over the content of their legal reasons than their adult counterparts.
5. Hence, all else being equal, juveniles are less culpable and, hence, less deserving of punishment, than their adult counterparts.

Several steps in this argument deserve discussion.

First, notice that the comparative conclusion (5) does not itself establish a categorical difference between juvenile and adult criminal conduct that assigns juveniles to juvenile court and adults to adult criminal court. These differences may require some leniency toward juveniles, but it does not require all the features of juvenile court. Moreover, these differences may be offset by other factors affecting the culpability of individual offenders. We may have no reason to view a normatively precocious juvenile who is disenfranchised as less culpable overall than a normatively immature young adult who has the franchise. This is just to say that having the vote seems at best to be one element of culpability. The most that could be said is that other things being equal disenfranchised juveniles would be less culpable than their adult counterparts. This isn't sufficient to defend the claim that

---

[43] Though the argument is developed over four chapters, it is effectively summarized in *The Age of Culpability*, pp. 158–59.

juveniles, as such, deserve to be punished less, much less in juvenile court, rather than adult criminal court.

Second, we might wonder if having a say over the laws that govern one does affect the weight of one's legal reasons to comply, as (4) claims. Don't foreign visitors have the same legal reasons to comply with the laws of the host country as adult citizens do? Isn't that simply a matter of the state having legal authority to pass laws regulating the behavior of people within its borders? But this authority is the same in the case of adult citizens and foreign visitors. Similarly, it seems that there are the same legal reasons for juveniles and adult citizens to comply with the laws in place, which derives from the state's authority to pass laws regulating the behavior of individuals within its borders. It seems implausible to suppose that the legal reasons to refrain from first-degree murder are different for adults and juveniles.

Yaffe's claim that having a say in enacting the laws that govern one affects one's reasons for compliance seems especially implausible as applied to crimes *mala in se*. Crimes *mala in se* are wrongs in themselves, whereas crimes *mala prohibita* are wrongs by virtue of prohibition (§42). Crimes *mala in se* violate natural duties and include wrongs against the person, such as murder, rape, assault, theft, and fraud. Crimes *mala prohibita* do not violate natural duties and can include crimes of prostitution, drug use, gambling, tax evasion, traffic violations, loitering, and truancy. Because they involve crimes against the person that violate natural duties, crimes *mala in se* tend to be more serious offenses than crimes *mala prohibita*, which serve more to facilitate security, cooperation, and coordination. In the case of crimes *mala in se* the reasons for compliance do not depend on legal enactment. If so, it's not clear how failure to participate in enactment could change one's reasons for compliance.

Third, we have reason to question Yaffe's conception of culpability in (1). Here, we need to recall that the retributivist desert basis for punishment has two independent variables—wrongdoing and responsibility or culpability. The two main affirmative defenses—justification and excuse—deny different elements in this retributive desert basis. Whereas justifications deny wrongdoing, excuses deny responsibility or culpability. Partial defenses would reduce or mitigate wrongdoing or culpability. Partial justifications would reduce wrongdoing, whereas partial excuses would reduce responsibility or culpability. The developmental rationale conceives of culpability in terms of responsibility and, ultimately, fair opportunity and normative competence. The denial of culpability in this sense is an excuse. The developmental rationale in effect says that immaturity affects the normative competence and culpability of juvenile offenders, providing a partial excuse for juvenile wrongdoing. By contrast, Yaffe's conception of culpability is focused not on normative competence but on failure to track one's reasons. Juveniles, he thinks, are less culpable because there are fewer reasons for them to track than their adult counterparts. But this suggests that on Yaffe's conception of culpability juvenile crime is less wrong than its adult counterpart. That is to treat the reduced culpability of juveniles as sounding in justification, rather than excuse. That contrasts with the developmental rationale, which treats the asymmetry between juveniles and adults as sounding in excuse, rather than justification. Here, we have reason to agree with the developmental rationale's focus on excuse. Juvenile offenses, such as murder, are no less wrong than the same offenses committed by adults, but, other things being equal, juveniles are less responsible than their adult counterparts and, hence, less blameworthy.

Here, we might consider Yaffe's conception of culpability in (1) based on our earlier discussion of culpability, attributability, and accountability (esp. §§14, 49–57). Yaffe's conception of culpability involves a normative failing—a normative performance error—on the agent's part to attend properly to the reasons that bear on her conduct. As such, it speaks to how legally wrong the agent's conduct was, not how responsible she was for her conduct, which is a matter of her normative competence, not her performance. Yaffe's proposal may be relevant to narrow culpability and attributability, but not to broad culpability and accountability. The question of whether it is fair to punish juveniles as we punish adults is a question about accountability, not attributability. In particular, the claim that juveniles deserve a break, in relation to adults, is a claim about their reduced responsibility and broad culpability. We need to assess that claim by appeal to the fair opportunity conception of responsibility, and the test it imposes is one of normative competence, not performance.

106. The Juvenile Court and Soft Abolitionism

The developmental rationale for treating juvenile crime differently than adult crime on account of the generally reduced competence and accountability of juvenile offenders is robust. The normative immaturity of adolescents makes them less responsible for their wrongdoing than for otherwise similar wrongdoing by their adult counterparts. This makes them deserve less blame and punishment than their adult counterparts. Proportionate justice demands that, all else being equal, we blame and punish juveniles differently. The transfer trend overlooks this fact about comparative just deserts. In effect, the transfer trend represents a *blindspot* about the link between immaturity and culpability. Moreover, this broad-scale diagnosis of the blindspot responsible for the transfer trend is reinforced by some important jury studies involving assessments of the severity of punishment appropriate for crimes in which the assessments of respondents were surprisingly insensitive to information about the age of the wrongdoer. In such cases, respondents seemed to track the scale of the wrongdoing, largely ignoring differences in the degree of maturity and normative competence of the wrongdoer.[44]

The traditional juvenile court can be viewed as one way to correct for this bias. In the traditional juvenile court, we remove juvenile cases from superficially similar but importantly different cases involving adult offenders, disrupting the tendency to wrongly assimilate juvenile crime to adult crime. Trials in juvenile court are bench trials, and presiding judges have special training dealing with immature offenders. There is explicit instruction to consider the maturity and culpability of offenders in juvenile court, and, of course, juvenile penalties are shorter, served in different facilities, and records are sealed. The developmental rationale seems to support the traditional juvenile court, perhaps not in an unqualified form, but with modest qualifications that permit the use of blended sentencing and limited judicial waiver for older adolescents on a case-by-case basis.

However, we might ask if the developmental rationale really supports the traditional juvenile court, whether in an unqualified or qualified form. In this connection, we might want to consider Barry Feld's interesting proposal to abolish the juvenile court in *Bad Kids: Race and the Transformation of the*

---

[44] See C. Crosby, P. Britner, K. Jodl, and S. Portwood, "The Juvenile Death Penalty and the Eighth Amendment: An Empirical Investigation of Societal Consensus and Proportionality" *Law and Human Behavior* 19 (1995): 245–61. Their questionnaire contained descriptions of cases with defendants on trial for murder whose ages ranged from 10–19-years-old. The details of the cases included a description of the crime, probable culpability of all juveniles, level of remorse, and age of the defendant. The number of respondents willing to impose the death penalty for defendants were as follows: 96.3 percent of male respondents and 95.7 percent of female respondents were willing to impose the death penalty on the 19-year-old defendant; 92 percent of male respondents and 87 percent of female respondents were willing to impose the death penalty on the 16-year-old defendant; 87.5 percent of male respondents and 52.9 percent of female respondents were willing to impose the death penalty on the 15-year-old defendant; and 71 percent of male respondents and 52.4 percent of female respondents were willing to impose the death penalty on the 10-year-old defendant. Though the willingness among male respondents to impose the death penalty was not completely insensitive to immaturity, and the willingness among female respondents was more sensitive, the level of insensitivity in both men and women was striking. A similar finding about the comparative insensitivity of views about the severity of sentencing to degree of maturity and normative competence is made in S. Ghetti and A. Redlich, "Reactions to Youth Crime: Perceptions of Accountability and Competency" *Behavioral Sciences and the Law* 19 (2001): 33–52.

Juvenile Court. Together, the juvenile court and adult criminal court form a dual court system. Feld proposes to abolish the juvenile court and transfer all juveniles to adult criminal court. The unqualified adoption of a unitary system is a form of *hard abolitionism* that seeks to do away with separate treatment for juvenile crime, and it is the more systematic version of the transfer trend. As such, it is wildly at odds with the retributive concern with just deserts and proportionate justice. However, Feld's proposal is importantly different from traditional forms of hard abolitionism. It is a form of *soft abolitionism* that abolishes separate courts for juveniles and adults but tries to ensure proportionate justice for juveniles within a unitary system. He does this by proposing adoption of a *youth discount rate at sentencing.*

A separate juvenile court may function as a useful institutional antidote to case-by-case analysis of both youthful and adult offenders in a single criminal court. We have seen that there is a blindspot in which people fail to treat wrongdoing and culpability or responsibility as independent variables in the retributivist desert basis of punishment, effectively tracking degrees of wrongdoing but not degrees of culpability or responsibility. Both jury studies and the transfer trend itself testify to its prevalence in public opinion. A natural worry is that this blindspot about the effect of immaturity on culpability and of culpability on desert will have full range to operate in case-by-case treatment of juvenile offenders within a unified criminal court with the predictable result that juveniles will be treated like their adult counterparts more often than they deserve. Use of a separate juvenile court can be defended as a sort of institutional *precommitment* strategy to block the bias in assignment of just deserts that would result from the operation of the blindspot in a unified system.

Feld's abolitionist proposal contains its own precommitment strategy that might deal with this blindspot. Feld's proposal gives up case-by-case evaluation of juvenile offenders. Though he recognizes that the morally relevant variable is maturity, he proposes to treat age as an objective and administratively feasible proxy for maturity and to use age as the basis for a discount rate that is to be applied to the sentencing of juvenile offenders.

> This categorical approach would take the form of an explicit "youth discount" at sentencing. A 14-year-old might receive, for example, 25 to 33 percent of the adult penalty; a 16-year-old defendant, 50 to 60 percent; and an 18-year-old adult, the full penalty, as is presently the case. The "deeper discounts" for younger offenders correspond to the developmental continuum and their more limited opportunities to learn self-control and to

exercise responsibility. A youth discount based on reduced culpability functions as a sliding scale of diminished responsibility.[45]

Because Feld's youth discount rate is tied to age, it represents, as he notes, a categorical approach to juvenile sentencing that would precommit judges and prevent the operation of the blindspot in case-by-case evaluation within an integrated criminal justice system.

Though this proposal to abolish the juvenile court is in one way more radical than the transfer trend, which accepts the juvenile court but seeks to limit its role, its reforms are very different from the transfer trend. For the abolitionist reform preserves the traditionalist's insistence that, all else being equal, juveniles are less culpable for the wrongs they do than their adult counterparts and so are deserving of less punishment, whereas the transfer trend rejects this commitment to differential desert and punishment. From this perspective, the transfer reforms are much more radical than Feld's soft abolitionist reforms. Because the soft abolitionist reforms do not threaten differential desert and punishment, they are less threatening to the traditional rationale for a separate juvenile court. Feld's soft abolitionism represents an alternative to the traditional juvenile court, but one which preserves the juvenile court's recognition of the developmental rationale for treating juvenile crime differently than adult crime.

Whether soft abolitionism is an attractive alternative is another matter. To make it plausible, we might need to add additional qualifications to the treatment of juveniles within a unitary system. For we might want juveniles to serve their sentences at different facilities that are less harsh, more attuned to the psychological and nutritional needs of juveniles, and more committed to educational training than adult correctional facilities. We might also want the records of juveniles to be sealed after a certain point in time. Feld acknowledges the need for preserving these features of the traditional juvenile court, distinguishing between guilt and sentencing aspects of a trial.[46] However, separate correctional facilities introduce dual or parallel institutions into the criminal justice process. If we allow dual institutions at some points, we must give up on the goal of complete integration or unification, and it is less clear what the appeal of partial integration or unification is.

Moreover, we may worry that Feld's proposal gives up any attempt to pursue individual desert, since mitigation is tied to age, which is an imperfect proxy for maturity. For precisely this reason, Feld's proposal may be

---

[45] Feld, *Bad Kids*, p. 317.   [46] Feld, *Bad Kids*, pp. 325–26.

administratively simpler, but it gives up the aspiration that is otherwise part of the criminal law to predicate individual punishment on facts about an individual's desert—her actions, circumstances, mental states, and capacities. As we have seen, age is an imperfect proxy for normative maturity. Even if maturation is reasonably regular, so that there is a significant correlation between age and maturity, there will be individual variance. Some 16-year-olds will have as much normative competence as the normal 18-year-old, and some 16-year-olds will have as much normative competence as the normal 14-year-old. So adoption of a categorical age-based discount will be both under-punitive and over-punitive, relative to the demands of individualized justice.

Perhaps this is just the inevitable moral trade-off that has to be made between the demands of individualized justice and the need to correct for an over-punitive blindspot that operates in case-by-case analysis. But the traditional juvenile court as qualified by the Model Penal Code promises to precommit in a way that avoids the blindspot. For, in contrast with the unified system, it takes juvenile crime out of direct comparison with adult crime and thus circumvents the operation of the blindspot for the effects of immaturity on culpability and of culpability on desert. In doing so, it does impose one category, viz. the distinction between minors and adults. But, as we have seen, it treats this categorical distinction as creating a defeasible presumption. The availability of the judicial waiver allows judges to transfer a mature juvenile to criminal court on a showing in the individual case that the defendant is sufficiently mature to stand trial as an adult. Moreover, within juvenile court, judges can and do take account of the maturity levels of juveniles of different ages as factors in both guilt and sentencing phases.

Both the traditional juvenile court and soft abolitionism condemn the current punitive reforms embodied in the juvenile transfer trend. Though there is a surprising amount to be said in favor of the abolitionist proposal, the traditional separate juvenile court has the advantages of preserving immaturity's relevance to responsibility and excuse and of making punishment sensitive to maturity in a way that does not sacrifice individualized justice.[47]

---

[47] Perhaps the abolitionist who favors the age-based discount schedule could try to accommodate the demands of individualized justice by treating that schedule as establishing rebuttable presumptions about sentencing. It is an empirical question whether making the presumptions rebuttable in a unified system that allows direct comparison with adult offenders would give too much room for the blindspot to operate. Hirstein, Sifferd, and Fagan, *Responsible Brains*, pp. 172–74 suggest partitioning adolescence into four grades of diminished capacity. Only two of their four categories involve categorical discounts; the other two involve rebuttable presumptions.

107. Constitutional Limits on Juvenile Sentencing

In the context of jurisprudential doubts about the trend to try juveniles as adults and their reduced culpability, it is worth discussing issues raised in comparatively recent Supreme Court decisions that address and uphold sentence limitations on juvenile crime in capital and other cases involving serious crimes. We will focus on three cases. First, *Roper v. Simmons* (2005) interprets the Eighth Amendment's prohibition on cruel and unusual punishments to impose a categorical prohibition on capital punishment for juveniles convicted of homicide.[48] Second, *Graham v. Florida* (2010) interprets the Eighth Amendment to impose a categorical prohibition on life sentences without the possibility of parole (LWOP) for juveniles convicted of non-homicide offenses.[49] Third, *Miller v. Alabama* (2012) interprets the Eighth Amendment to prohibit mandatory LWOP sentences for juveniles convicted of capital crimes.[50]

These cases dealing with sentence limitations for juveniles bear an interesting relation to the transfer trend. On the one hand, because they recognize a developmental rationale for differential sentencing for juveniles and adults, these cases resist at least the most extreme implications of the transfer trend. On the other hand, the issues addressed in these cases would not even arise without the transfer trend, because they all involve appropriate sentences for juveniles who have been tried in adult criminal court. When juveniles are tried in adult court, they become subject to sentencing possibilities—including mandatory sentencing—that run afoul of the reduced culpability of juvenile offenders recognized in these cases.

To appreciate the significance of these cases, it might be helpful to rehearse some of the relevant constitutional background, in particular, cases that stake out previous doctrine about the constitutionality of juvenile sentencing and evolving doctrine about the sentencing of those with mental disability. Though obviously and importantly different, both involve limitations on permissible sentencing of those with some degree of diminished capacity.

In *Thompson v. Oklahoma* (1988), a plurality opinion declared that the Eighth Amendment does not permit the execution of offenders under 16 (in this case a 15-year-old) at the time of the crime.[51] The Court's reasoning appealed to both societal standards and the Court's own judgment about proportionate punishment, claiming that the same reasons that 15-year-olds

---

[48]   *Roper v. Simmons*, 543 U.S. 551 (2005).   [49]   *Graham v. Florida*, 130 S.Ct. 2011 (2010).
[50]   *Miller v. Alabama*, 132 S.Ct. 2455 (2012).   [51]   *Thompson v. Oklahoma*, 487 U.S. 815 (1988).

are not given various social responsibilities explain why they are less responsible and culpable.

In *Stanford v. Kentucky* (1989), a majority opinion appealed to societal standards of decency and ruled that the Eighth Amendment does not prohibit the death penalty for criminal offenders between the ages of 16 and 18. The Court rejected the idea that it should bring its own opinion to bear in deciding the constraints imposed by the cruel and unusual punishment clause.[52]

In *Penry v. Lynaugh* (1989), decided on the same day as *Stanford*, the Court appealed to societal standards to conclude that the Eighth Amendment does not require a categorical exemption from the death penalty for those with mental disabilities.[53]

Thirteen years later, in *Atkins v. Virginia* (2002), the Court appealed to both societal standards, as measured by legislative action and penal practice, and its own independent judgment, ruling that the Eighth Amendment does preclude the execution of mentally disabled offenders, thus overruling *Penry*.[54] The Court appealed to lesser competence and culpability of those with mental disabilities and the Eighth Amendment's retributive concern with proportionate punishment.

In *Roper*, 17-year-old Christopher Simmons and a friend kidnapped a woman from her home and threw her off a bridge, where she drowned. Simmons was tried as an adult, and under Missouri law was sentenced to death. Kennedy's majority opinion interprets the Eighth Amendment to impose a categorical prohibition on capital punishment for juveniles convicted of homicide, thus overruling *Stanford*. He appeals to societal consensus against the use of the death penalty for juveniles, as reflected in legislative changes in state criminal codes that have in many cases eliminated the possibility of the death penalty for juveniles and changes in penal practice of sentencing juveniles to the death penalty even in jurisdictions where that is permissible. But Kennedy also relies on the Court's own reading of the evidence about juvenile culpability to argue that the Eighth Amendment's demand for proportionate punishment precludes the execution of offenders who were juveniles at the time of their crimes. Kennedy embraces a version of the developmental rationale for treating juveniles differently than adults, citing reduced impulse control, reduced independence of judgment (reduced ability to resist peer pressure), and underdeveloped character as factors reducing

---

[52] *Stanford v. Kentucky*, 492 U.S. 136 (1989).   [53] *Penry v. Lynaugh*, 492 U.S. 302 (1989).
[54] *Atkins v. Virginia*, 536 U.S. 304 (2002).

juvenile culpability and undermining deterrence rationales for capital punishment. On this basis, he defends a categorical ban on capital punishment for
juveniles while conceding that some juveniles may be as mature as normal
adults, appealing to our inability to identify these exceptional cases reliably.
Kennedy also appeals to the consensus elsewhere in the world that capital
punishment for juveniles is disproportionate, presumably not because constitutional law in the United States must follow the law of other countries, but as
evidence about what is proportionate and disproportionate punishment, for
purposes of the Eighth Amendment.

In dissent, O'Connor questions the appropriateness of adopting categorical
bans on capital punishment for juveniles when it is conceded that some older
juveniles are sufficiently culpable to justify capital punishment. She claims that
categorical rules are in tension with the commitment to individualized justice
in sentencing.

Terrance Graham was 16 when he attempted armed robbery in Florida.
Graham was tried as an adult, but he expressed remorse and a resolve to do
better and was sentenced to probation. However, while on probation, he
committed additional crimes in which his companions used firearms. His
probation was revoked, the trial court judge claimed he was incorrigible, and
he was sentenced on the earlier charges to LWOP. Kennedy's majority
opinion mostly follows the script of *Roper*. He appeals to both societal
consensus, as reflected in legislative changes and penal practice, and to the
Court's own reading of the evidence about juvenile culpability to argue that
the Eighth Amendment's demand for proportionate punishment precludes
LWOP for juvenile offenders in non-homicide cases. Here, Kennedy concedes that legislative history is not definitive evidence of societal condemnation. But he appeals again to penal practice (the fact that such punishments,
though available in many jurisdictions, are often not used) and the uniform
direction of legislative change toward the refusal to permit the death penalty
for juveniles. Kennedy says the same developmental factors that reduced
juvenile culpability in *Roper*—reduced impulse control, lack of independence
of judgment, and underdeveloped character—also reduce culpability for
non-homicide offenses. Perhaps more clearly here, Kennedy defends a categorical ban, while conceding that some older juveniles may be sufficiently
mature to be tried as adults, by appeal to our inability to reliably identify
these exceptional cases. Again, Kennedy appeals to the consensus elsewhere
in the world that such sentencing practices for juveniles are disproportionate. Here he makes especially clear that this fact is evidential about the moral
issue about proportionality, not dispositive.

Roberts concurs in the conclusion that Graham's sentence was constitutionally disproportionate without agreeing with—in fact, rejecting—the majority's categorical ban. Roberts points out that Graham's sentence of LWOP for attempted robbery is far more severe than comparable crimes by adults. Moreover, he agrees with the developmental claim that immaturity does in general diminish culpability and so should be relevant to proportional sentencing. But Roberts claims that there are some cases—involving especially heinous offenses and older juvenile offenders who are sufficiently mature and competent—in which LWOP is as fitting for juveniles as for adults. He focuses on cases in which the crimes are serious and involve manifest immorality, the juvenile is 17, and there is no reason to believe that there is significant lack of culpability. In such cases, he thinks, LWOP can be proportionate for juveniles.[55] Roberts assumes that we will know the exceptional cases in which defendants are mature enough to be treated the same as adults when we see them.

Miller involved two Alabama cases in which 14-year-olds were tried and convicted as adults for homicide. Under mandatory sentencing laws in Alabama, they were sentenced to LWOP. In one case, the youth (Jackson) was convicted of homicide under the felony-murder rule—when Jackson and friends went to rob a video store, he stayed outside, and his friend shot the store clerk. Kagan writes for the majority, interpreting the Eighth Amendment to prohibit mandatory LWOP sentences for juveniles convicted of capital crimes. She says that the result here is the product of two distinct lines of cases—the categorical bans in *Roper* and *Graham* and other cases that call for individualized sentencing. Kagan says that the categorical ban in *Graham*, though it applied there only to non-homicides, applies here to homicides, citing factors diminishing culpability that have wider application, including to homicides. In principle, that might support a categorical ban on LWOP sentences for any juvenile offender in any type of crime, including homicide. But she does not draw that stronger conclusion. Instead, she notes that proportionate sentencing must consider the potentially reduced culpability of juvenile offenders. So whereas *Graham* adopted a categorical ban on LWOP in non-homicide cases, *Miller* requires that such sentences cannot be categorically required in homicide cases. The result in *Miller* does not prevent sentencing some juvenile killers to LWOP, but it does say that this cannot be mandatory and can happen only after explicit consideration of the maturity

---

[55] Roberts discusses three such cases. See *Graham*, at 2041–42.

of the juvenile defendant and in light of the way in which immaturity can diminish responsibility.

Roper and *Graham* both involve categorical limits on juvenile sentencing, whereas *Miller* rejects a categorical limit in favor of individualized sentencing. But the three cases are united by a concern about the danger of over-punishing juvenile offenders, in relation to adult offenders, on account of their reduced normative competence. Whereas the first two cases find that reduced juvenile competence is sufficient to justify categorical bans on the most severe punishments, the third case appeals to the same facts to justify consideration of reduced normative competence among juveniles as part of the sentencing process for homicides by juveniles. Kagan's rationale in *Miller* attempts to be ecumenical. The principles in *Roper* and *Graham* argue for categorical bans on the most extreme sentences for homicide and non-homicide cases. Elsewhere and in general, the Court believes that proportionate sentencing must be individualized. Even if the first view argues for extending *Graham*'s categorical ban to juvenile homicide, both views can agree that the sort of mandatory life sentences without parole in Alabama are disproportionate and unconstitutional.

108. The Tension between Categorical Rules and Individual Desert

Our discussion of juvenile justice—both the transfer trend and constitutional limits on juvenile sentencing—has endorsed the developmental rationale for thinking that other things being equal punishment of juvenile crime should be less severe than for comparable adult crime. Though forward-looking considerations about rehabilitation, deterrence, and the adolescence-specific character of crime support this asymmetry between juvenile and adult crime, the primary factor in the developmental rationale is retributive. It is because adolescents are cognitively and volitionally immature that they deserve to be punished less for their crimes than their adult counterparts. The traditional juvenile court is one way to recognize this asymmetry and guard against the blind spot the general public seems to have for the independence of wrongdoing and culpability. These same developmental considerations underlie Supreme Court cases recognizing sentence limitations that apply to juveniles that do not apply to adults.

However, the factors that underlie the developmental rationale are all scalar and allow for variation among juvenile cohorts (17-year-olds, 16-year-olds,

15-year-olds, etc.) and among individuals within a given cohort. This fact raises questions about whether the categorical rule for assignment to juvenile or adult court and the categorical rules imposing sentence limitations for juveniles are consistent with individual just deserts. We may be confident that normal 14-year-olds are developmentally immature in relation to normal 19-year-olds in ways that are normatively significant and justify differential treatment, but the differences between 17-year-olds and 18-year-olds are less sharp, especially as only one day might separate members of these two cohorts. Moreover, given individual variation, some 17-year-olds will be at least as normatively competent as some 18-year-olds. How then can their categorically different treatment be squared with the criminal law's interest in individual desert? Won't this result in some older adolescents being under-punished and some young adults being over-punished? To some extent, these concerns about individual desert animate both Yaffe's concerns about the developmental rationale and O'Connor's and Roberts' concerns about categorical limits on juvenile sentencing.

Let's focus for a moment on the worry about under-punishing adolescents. As we have seen, one could try to defend categorical differences between juveniles and adults in their application to all juveniles on partly pragmatic grounds. One might insist we need bright lines here, even if the underlying factors are scalar. To maintain a categorical asymmetry between juveniles and adults, we could argue that (1) age is a generally reliable proxy for normative maturity; (2) most 18-year-olds are sufficiently mature to be held responsible; (3) normatively precocious juveniles are rare; (4) it is difficult to identify normatively precocious juveniles reliably; and (5) mistakes of over-punishment are worse than mistakes of under-punishment. If these conditions are met, there is a reasonably strong pragmatic rationale for a simple categorical asymmetry between juveniles and adults. Indeed, we might claim that by following this categorical rule about assignment to juvenile or adult court, we are likely to maximize just deserts overall, even if it means that in some cases we would under-punish. This is fairly clearly the sort of argument that Kennedy advances against O'Connor and Roberts.

However, even if this pragmatic rationale explains why we should be firm about not treating younger adolescents as adults, it does not explain why we should treat older adolescents, for instance 17-year-olds, so differently from young adults. This is where we invoked departures from the categorical asymmetry between juveniles and adults involved in the use of blended sentencing for older adolescents and the Model Penal Code provision for judicial waiver for older adolescents. Especially if the presumption is in favor of trying older adolescents as juveniles, the selective use of blended sentencing or the judicial waiver must rebut that presumption on a case-by-case basis and for cause. Why not similarly treat the constitutional limits on juvenile sentencing as rebuttable presumptions, rather than categorical limits? In effect, *Miller* does treat the prohibition on LWOP sentences for all crimes, even homicide, as a rebuttable presumption, insofar as it claims that LWOP cannot be mandatory, even for murder, and in the case of murder must be conditioned on an assessment of the juvenile's maturity and normative competence. So the question is whether the rules laid down in *Roper* and *Graham* would be better construed as rebuttable presumptions, rather than categorical rules. I suspect that sympathy with the categorical versions of these sentence limitations is fueled by doubts about whether capital punishment is ever, or at least usually, a justified response to homicide and whether LWOP is ever, or at least usually, a justified response to crimes that are not homicides. Of course, this would raise questions about the permissibility of these punishments for adults too. If we *stipulate* that capital punishment is sometimes justified for homicides such as murder and that LWOP is sometimes justified for crimes other than homicides for adults, then I think we have reason to recognize the possibility that such punishments might be deserved for some older adolescents, and we should treat the rules forbidding such punishments as rebuttable presumptions.

This analysis requires some comment about the treatment of young adults and the use of significant mandatory minima for adults. If we are going to allow departure from rules about the differential treatment of juveniles when we are dealing with older juveniles and allow that the presumption against treating them as adults can be rebutted if they can be shown to be normatively competent, shouldn't we allow adults, including young adults, the opportunity to show that they should not be subject to full adult punishments if their normative competence is impaired in some way? Perhaps the presumption should be that all adults should be subject to punishment specified for crimes that are neither justified nor excused, but this should be a rebuttable presumption. More generally, this is a problem for all mandatory sentencing schemes for adults, such as mandatory minima and three strikes laws, because they prevent the consideration of reduced culpability. If so, the reform of juvenile justice suggests broader reforms for criminal law more generally. We will return to these more general issues about partial responsibility and excuse in Chapter 15.

13

Addiction and Fair Opportunity

In this chapter, we focus on the questions of whether and, if so, how and to what degree addiction might affect responsibility and constitute an excuse.[1] We can and should assess potential excuses for addiction by appeal to the fair opportunity conception of responsibility. To do this, we will need to see how addiction might affect the will of addicts and their normative competence and situational control. We need to assess not just whether addiction significantly impairs the capacities and opportunities of addicts but also whether addicts might bear some responsibility for such impairment.

Assessing excuses, whether full or partial, for addiction depends in part on *what* we might be excusing. The *purchase and consumption* of certain addictive drugs can itself be illegal, but this is not always so, as in the case of caffeine, alcohol, and, in some jurisdictions, marijuana. Moreover, it is controversial whether the sale and consumption of many or most drugs ought to be criminalized.[2] So it will be helpful to focus on cases in which addiction plays some role in explaining wrongful conduct, but in which the wrongful conduct is independent of the consumption of the addictive substance, such as theft or prostitution to support a habit or child neglect or endangerment in the process of procuring drugs.

The consumption of some addictive substances can produce *intoxication*, which can involve incapacity. As we will see, under some criminal law theories it is controversial whether people can be guilty of *status*, rather than *conduct*, crimes. We may doubt that people should be blameworthy for status per se, as opposed to the conduct to which that status may lead. For this reason, it will be useful to restrict our attention to conduct crimes for which addiction might serve as a full or partial excuse. Our focus will be on whether addicts should be excused, in full or in part, for wrongful conduct they perform due to their substance addiction. This would include wrongs committed in service of the addiction, such as theft, prostitution, or child neglect. It could also include

---

[1] In this chapter, I am especially conscious of debts to discussion of these issues with Cami Koepke.
[2] See, e.g., Douglas Husak, *Legalize This! The Case for Decriminalizing Drugs* (London: Verso, 2002) and *Overcriminalization: The Limits of the Criminal Law* (Oxford: Clarendon Press, 2008).

Fair Opportunity and Responsibility. David O. Brink, Oxford University Press (2021). © David O. Brink.
DOI: 10.1093/oso/9780198859468.003.0013

wrongs committed by addicts while high or intoxicated, such as assaulting someone while under the influence of the drug to which they are addicted. Here, we can ask whether intoxication from addiction might excuse wrongful conduct in a way in which voluntary intoxication does not.

109. Addiction as a Clinical Category

Of course, what we say about whether addicts are responsible for the wrongs they commit in the service of their addiction depends on how we understand addiction. One place to start is with the American Psychiatric Association's *Diagnostic and Statistical Manual.* The *DSM* discusses these issues as Substance-Related and Addictive Disorders.

The *DSM* focuses on *substance-related* disorders but also discusses gambling as a *behavioral* addiction. Though substance addiction to drugs such as alcohol, cocaine, and heroin provide our clearest examples of addiction, some researchers want to extend models of addiction from substances to behaviors, such as gambling, sex and the consumption of pornography, and high risk-reward activities. It is unclear if all of these substance and behavioral syndromes form a unitary kind, but there is consensus that pathological gambling exhibits strong neurobiological, as well as behavioral, correlates with substance addiction.[3] Many of our claims about responsibility and excuse in cases of substance addiction will have implications for cases involving behavioral addiction, especially pathological gambling. But it will simplify an already complex discussion to focus primarily on substance addiction.

The *DSM* offers a general analysis of substance-related disorders and then applies that analysis to specific substances, including alcohol, caffeine, cannabis, hallucinogens, inhalants, opioids, sedatives, stimulants, and others. Our immediate interest is in the *DSM*'s general analysis. The criteria for addiction are analyzed along four dimensions—control, social impairment, risk, and pharmacology—and each dimension has multiple criteria. Control issues arise when an individual is led to consume larger quantities of the substance than originally intended; there is a persistent but unsuccessful desire to consume less; inordinate amounts of time are spent obtaining and consuming the substance and recovering from consumption; and the individual experiences

---

[3] D. Ross, C. Sharp, R. Vuhnich, and D. Spurrett, *Midbrain Mutiny: The Picoeconomics and Neuroeconomics of Disordered Gambling* (Cambridge, MA: MIT Press, 2008) and Jennifer Bellegarde and Marc Potenza, "Neurobiology of Pathological Gambling" in *What is Addiction?*, ed. D. Ross, H. Kincaid, D. Spurrett, and P. Collins (Cambridge, MA: MIT Press, 2010).

cravings that are triggered by conditioned cues. Social impairment takes place when substance procurement and use interferes with personal, professional, and social goals and responsibilities. Risk involves the recurrent use of the substance in which this poses significant risk to the addict or others. The pharmacological dimension of addiction pertains to both increasing tolerance of the drug and the need of the addict for larger doses of the substance and increasing withdrawal symptoms when cravings are not satisfied.

The *DSM* treats addiction as a cluster of these criteria in which no individual criterion is necessary and in which the number of criteria exhibited and the degree to which they are exhibited are both variable. In this respect, the *DSM* should perhaps be interpreted as treating addiction as a cluster or prototype concept (§40). The stereotypical or paradigmatic case of addiction would involve all of these criteria to a high degree. Actual cases of substance abuse could then be conceptualized and assessed as addictions or disorders insofar as they approximate this prototype.

Some substances appear to be more addictive than others. Opioids, including heroin and prescription pain killers, cocaine, and methamphetamine are more addictive than other drugs, such as alcohol, marijuana, LSD, nicotine, and caffeine. If so, we need to be careful about generalizing about whether addiction excuses. Claims that are plausible about some kinds of addicts and addictions may be less plausible about others.

Drawing proper normative conclusions about addiction depends on the details of the science of addiction. That science is complex and evolving, and my understanding of it is imperfect.[4] I'll try to raise normative issues that depend on general and fairly ecumenical functional assumptions about addiction, but it is important to remember that our normative theorizing here, as elsewhere, is hostage, at least in part, to details and changes in the underlying empirical literature.

The *DSM* associates addiction with a cluster of symptoms. Perhaps this is an adequate analysis. But it would be nice to have a conception of addiction that explained how these symptoms are caused and naturally occur together. It will be helpful to explore two specific models of addiction. One views addiction as a kind of recurrent dynamic instability in the agent's beliefs or preferences. The other treats addiction as an impairment of the agent's cognitive and volitional control. These two models are potentially complementary.

---

[4] Two recent collections of essays that provide diverse perspectives on the science, psychology, and philosophy of addiction are *What is Addiction?*, ed. Ross, Kincaid, Spurrett, and Collins (Cambridge, MA: MIT Press, 2010) and *Addiction and Self-Control*, ed. N. Levy (Oxford: Clarendon Press, 2013).

110. Akrasia and Dynamic Instability in Attitudes

One approach to understanding addiction begins by thinking about the nature of akrasia or weakness of will. Akrasia occurs when an agent knows or believes that one option (A) is better than another (B) all things considered, she can do either A or B, but she nonetheless chooses to do B. Akrasia is puzzling insofar as it is unclear why agents would freely choose an option they deem inferior, and it challenges standard models of rationality that treat agents as expected utility maximizers (optimizers). In the course of developing the fair opportunity conception of responsibility, we have several times noted that akrasia does not normally defeat ascriptions of responsibility or excuse. Akrasia is relevant to addiction insofar as some theories of addiction model it as a special kind of akrasia, treating addiction as recurrent or systematic akrasia.

Plato's *Protagoras* provides a useful framework for thinking about akrasia. There, Socrates denies the possibility of akrasia or weakness of will—the phenomenon of acting contrary to one's better judgment. Those who believe in akrasia say that the akrates is overcome by pleasure. Socrates argues that if hedonism is true this description of akrasia becomes incoherent, because it means that the putative akrates holds inconsistent beliefs about comparative value and pleasure of his options. That is an interesting and complex argument that I won't address here. But part of the Socratic diagnosis of what goes wrong in putative cases of akrasia is relevant here. Socrates focuses on cases in which one's judgment about what is best is overcome by pleasure, in particular, proximate pleasure (*Protagoras* 356a–357e). He suggests that our judgments about what is best are inappropriately influenced by the proximity of pleasures and pains. The proximity of pleasures and pains leads to inflated estimates of their magnitude. This kind of temporal bias, Socrates thinks, produces *instability* in the agent's beliefs about what is best. For instance, in a *cool prospective moment* an agent might judge that a short-term indulgence should be forsaken for the sake of a later greater good. But as the indulgence becomes imminent—in the *heat of the moment*—its proximity changes the agent's estimate of the magnitude of the pleasure associated with the indulgence, leading him to conclude that the indulgence is actually worth the cost. But in a *cool retrospective moment*, when his passions no longer inflame his judgment, he sees that he purchased the indulgence at too high a cost and experiences regret. There is no genuine weakness of will, on this interpretation of events, because the agent's beliefs about what is best actually change and he acts in accord, rather than against, his beliefs about what is best that he holds at the time of action. Though Socrates denies that the agent acts akratically, he does think that he acts irrationally, allowing temporal proximity to affect his beliefs about the magnitude of the benefits and harms associated with his options. One sign of the irrationality of the bias is the instability temporal proximity induces in the agent's beliefs and preferences. The fact that the hot judgment is preceded and followed by contrary cool judgments is evidence that the hot judgment is not to be trusted.

One needn't accept Socratic skepticism about weakness of will in order to accept his attack on temporal bias. Socrates believes that we are optimizers and that our desires and passions reflect our beliefs about what is best. He interprets temporal proximity as inducing a change of belief about what is best, which means that the putative akrates does not act contrary to his practical beliefs at the time of action. But we might believe, instead, that agents are not always optimizers and can and do act on autonomous desires and passions that do not always track beliefs about what is best. On this alternative interpretation, we might think that temporal bias influences the agent's actions, not by changing her beliefs about what is best, but by triggering or inflaming good-independent desires or passions. This picture of akrasia reflects Plato's own claims in *Republic*, Book IV.

The Platonic interpretation of akrasia appeals to conflicting desires, whereas the Socratic interpretation appeals to conflicting beliefs or judgments. This makes the Platonic interpretation *conative*, in contrast to the Socratic inter-pretation, which is *cognitive*. The Socratic cognitive interpretation is skeptical about akrasia; it implies that the putative akrates does not in fact act contrary to his judgments about what is best, because these have shifted as the result of temporal bias. By contrast, the Platonic conative interpretation of dynamic instability accepts akrasia; at the time of action, the akrates is moved by inflamed non-optimizing or good-independent desires, as a result of which he acts against what he knows or believes to be best. If we are realists about akrasia, we have reason to prefer the Platonic to the Socratic interpretation of dynamic instability.

However, both Socratic and Platonic interpretations can treat the instability of our attitudes in cases of putative akrasia as resting on an irrational form of temporal bias. They can agree that temporal proximity does not affect the magnitude of goods and harms and therefore should not affect their signifi-cance. Moreover, we might treat the diachronic instability of the bias as evidence of its irrationality: the brief hot attitude and assessment appears anomalous against the background of prospective and retrospective cool attitudes and assessments.

111. From Akrasia to Addiction

In *Breakdown of Will*, George Ainslie develops this picture of weakness of will as involving dynamic inconsistency by modeling it as involving *hyperbolic*, rather than exponential, temporal discounting.[5] Whereas exponential discounting involves a constant rate of discounting goods and bads based on their temporal proximity, hyperbolic discounting involves steeper discounting in the near future and lesser discounting in the further future. Ainslie treats addiction as a species of weakness that involves *recurrent* hyperbolic discounting and dynamic instability of preferences. He treats this as a problem for traditional utility theory but also as a kind of irrationality insofar as it frustrates the agent's stable long-term preferences. He implies that it is also a sign of irrationality insofar as recurrent hyperbolic discounters can be turned into money-pumps.

> The greater bowing [in a hyperbolic discount curve] means that if the hyperbolic discounter engaged in trade with someone who used an exponential curve, she'd soon be relieved of her money. Ms. Exponential could buy Ms. Hyperbolic's winter coat very cheaply every spring, for instance, because the distance to the next winter would depress Ms. H's valuation of it more than Ms. E's. Ms. E could then sell the coat back to Ms. H every fall when the approach of winter sent Ms. H's valuation of it into a high spike. Because of this mathematical pattern, only an exponential discount curve will protect a person against exploitation by somebody else who uses an exponential curve.[6]

As far as I can see, Ainslie's main claims are agnostic as between the cognitive (Socratic) and conative (Platonic) interpretations of hyperbolic discounting. However, insofar as he sees himself as modeling how weakness of will is possible, he seems committed to the Platonic, rather than the Socratic, interpretation of dynamic inconsistency in attitudes.[7]

---

[5] See George Ainslie, *Breakdown of the Will* (Cambridge: Cambridge University Press, 2001). This develops his earlier claims in *Picoeconomics: The Strategic Interaction of Successive Motivational States within the Person* (Cambridge: Cambridge University Press, 1992) and "A Research-Based Theory of Addictive Motivation" *Law and Philosophy* 19 (1998): 77–115.

[6] Ainslie, *Breakdown of the Will*, pp. 30–31.

[7] Neil Levy appeals to Ainslie's work to argue for a cognitive interpretation of the sort of oscillation or dynamic instability in the attitudes of the addict. See Neil Levy, "Addiction as a Disorder of Belief" *Biology and Philosophy* 29 (2014): 337–55. But I don't think he makes a strong case for the cognitive, rather than conative, interpretation of the oscillation, and I don't see that anything he wants to claim

I don't know if the conception of addiction as involving dynamically inconsistent attitudes provides an equally plausible model of all kinds of addiction. But it does seem very plausible as applied to many forms of addiction. The crucial question from the point of view of the fair opportunity conception of responsibility is whether these inconsistencies in attitude result from impaired cognitive or volitional capacity.

112. Between Compulsion and Control

The picture of addiction as recurrent akrasia, involving dynamically inconsistent attitudes, leaves out something important about addiction. It doesn't explain why or how the pattern recurs—why the agent repeatedly shifts her preferences in ways that make her worse off in the long-run. To explain this, we need to explain how addiction operates on the will.

In a very useful analysis of addiction, Richard Holton and Kent Berridge contrast two different models of addiction: *choice* and *compulsion*.[8] A choice or control model views addicts as rational actors who possess self-control but have unusual beliefs and preferences—either false beliefs about the consequences of their consumption, abnormally strong desires for consumption, or utility functions that display steep temporal discounting (even hyperbolic discounting) of future benefits and harms. By contrast, the compulsion model views addiction as a disease that renders addicts subject to irresistible desires that undermine self-control and, by extension, normative competence. Holton and Berridge note that there is some truth to each model but maintain that neither model is plausible as it stands.

On the one hand, the control model gets some things right about addiction. The consumption preferences of many addicts are intelligent insofar as they are sensitive to the costs of drugs or the difficulty of acquiring them or consuming them. Many addicts are able to resist and quit in the face of sufficient, and sufficiently salient, rewards and penalties—for instance, witness the success of airline pilots and doctors whose addiction has been detected and are subject to random drug testing as a condition of continued professional

---

about addiction hangs on the truth of the cognitive interpretation, unless perhaps he thinks that cognitive excuses are more robust than other sorts of excuses.

[8] Richard Holton and Kent Berridge, "Addiction Between Compulsion and Choice" in *Addiction and Self-Control*, ed. N. Levy. My discussion is also indebted to Richard Holton's treatment of addiction in his Uehiro Lectures on mental illness and the social self in Oxford during Trinity Term 2018.

practice. Many addicts break the cycle of dynamically inconsistent attitudes without the help of clinical assistance, and others break their dependency with the help of counseling and reliance on circumventing cues and opportunities for consumption, rather than brute exercises of willpower.[9]

On the other hand, the compulsion model is right to notice that the brains, psychology, and behavior of addicts are different than those of non-addicts and that addiction gives rise to cue-driven cravings and to lasting vulnerability to cravings. In addition, there is a significant genetic component to the development of addiction.[10] Because genetic factors are not within the agent's control, they suggest that there is an element of addiction that lies outside the agent's control. Research on addiction is often focused on two syndromes: *craving-consumption-reward* and *craving-non-consumption-withdrawal* syndromes. Drug use produces dopamine spikes that give rise to a reward system that produces strong and insistent desires for consumption and drug-related behavior. Initially, drug consumption produces pleasurable experiences. Contextual cues are established by the reward system, triggering consumptive desires. However, the reward system induces desires for consumption whose strength or effectiveness is out of proportion to judgments about the value or even the pleasure expected from drug use. In this way, addiction gives rise to *wanting* that eventually outstrips *liking*. These cravings give rise to consumption and withdrawal syndromes. While unsatisfied, the desires produce discomfort and pain and, when satisfied, typically, but not always, produce satiation and contentment. The disposition to form such desires can persist even after the addict has stopped using the substance and no longer experiences withdrawal.

In these ways, the rival models of control and compulsion each gets some things right about addiction, but each misses insights of the rival model. Addiction gives rise to consumptive desires that are strong and insistent and resistant to deliberative influence, and, hence, it poses problems of self-control. But because addictive syndromes can be controlled with effort and various kinds of pre-commitment strategies that rely on circumventing, rather than

---

[9] Ross, Don and Kincaid, Harold. "Introduction: What is Addiction?" in *What is Addiction?*, ed. Ross, Kincaid, Spurrett, and Collins, pp. vii–viii.

[10] M. Kreek, D. Nielsen, and K. LaForge, "Genes Associated with Addiction: Alcoholism, Opiate, and Cocaine Addiction" *Neuromolecular Medicine* 5 (2004): 85–108; A. Saxon, M. Oreskovich, and Z. Brkanac, "Genetic Determinants of Addiction to Opioids and Cocaine" *Harvard Review of Psychiatry* 13 (2005): 218–32; D. Lobo and J. Kennedy, "The Genetics of Gambling and Behavioral Addictions" *CNS Spectrums* 11 (2006): 931–39; C. Hailie, T.R. Kosten, and T.A. Kosten, "Genetics of Dopamine and Its Contribution to Cocaine Addiction" *Behavioral Genetics* 37 (2007): 119–45; and J. MacKillop, J. McGeary, and L. Ray, "Genetic Influences on Addiction: Alcoholism as an Exemplar" in *What is Addiction?*, ed. Ross, Kincaid, Spurrett, and Collins.

conquering, the cravings, addiction does not preclude self-control. On this kind of view, addiction lies between compulsion and control and appears to impair, without destroying, reasons-responsiveness.[11]

113. Addiction and the Law

We should distinguish the issue about whether addiction excuses from different, if related, questions about whether drug use and intoxication excuse. Even if drug use or intoxication does not excuse per se, it might be that the situation of the addict is different and involves control problems not present in all cases of drug use or intoxication. If possession or use of the substance itself is illegal, the question can arise whether the addict is responsible for the wrongdoing constitutively involved in her addiction, namely, her drug possession and use. Though this is one kind of case in which addiction might potentially function as an excuse for wrongdoing, it is a special case, both because some addictive drugs are not illegal to possess or use (e.g. alcohol), and because addiction can be causally implicated in wrongdoing that is not partly constitutive of addiction, as when the addict engages in trespass, theft, assault, prostitution, or child neglect to procure drugs.

As a general rule, American criminal law does not recognize addiction as an excuse. There are several cases that deal with the legal treatment of addiction. We should examine the principles articulated there to see if they are compatible with fair opportunity and whether they preclude addiction excuses altogether.

Robinson v. California (1962) involved a California statute making it a crime to be addicted to narcotics.[12] Writing for a majority, Justice Stewart claims that the statute violates the Eighth Amendment prohibition on cruel

---

[11] A similar verdict is reached by other writers, including R. Jay Wallace, "Addiction as a Defect of the Will" *Law and Philosophy* 18 (1999): 621–54; Gary Watson, "Excusing Addiction" reprinted in Watson, *Agency and Answerability*; Timothy Schroeder and Nomy Arpaly, "Addiction and Blameworthiness" in *Addiction and Self-Control*, ed. N. Levy; and Hannah Pickard, "Responsibility without Blame for Addiction" *Neuroethics* 10 (2017): 169–80. Though I agree with Pickard that addiction does not preclude responsibility, I am skeptical of the responsibility without blame framework that she wants to apply to addiction. It is unclear what conception of responsibility or accountability she employs. Also, we can distinguish blame and blameworthiness and recognize the possibility of responsibility without blame. However, it's hard to recognize responsibility without blameworthiness, and special countervailing considerations need to be adduced for why we should not blame the blameworthy (§§39, 41). Several of Pickard's arguments against blame assume that it must be mean-spirited or express contempt and that it cannot be accompanied by compassion. But I don't see why we need to make any of these assumptions. For instance, we can hold loved ones and friends accountable, and even blame them, with compassion and without rancor or contempt.

[12] *Robinson v. California*, 370 U.S. 660 (1962).

and unusual punishment. On the one hand, Stewart emphasizes that this criminalizes a status, rather than conduct, and that this is inconsistent with basic criminal law demand to focus on voluntary acts as part of *actus reus*. On the other hand, Stewart also suggests that what makes it wrong to criminalize status is that addiction involves a disease, which can in principle be contracted innocently or involuntarily. Though addiction might be innocently acquired in the case of addiction to medically prescribed pain killers or in cases where the addicts developed the addiction during adolescence, addiction is not always or even usually innocently or involuntarily acquired. This is an issue to which we will return later (§116).

Powell v. Texas (1968) involved a Texas statute forbidding intoxication in public places.[13] Powell pleaded that chronic alcoholism impaired his ability to limit his alcohol intake and avoid being drunk in public, making the Texas statute unconstitutional under the Eighth Amendment. In rejecting Powell's claim, Justice Marshall distinguished *Powell* and *Robinson*, claiming that the latter punished status, whereas the former punished conduct—the act of being drunk in public—thus focusing on the status/action distinction, raised in *Robinson*. We may wonder whether being drunk in public is an act, rather than a status. But, even if it is an act, Powell might still claim that his alcoholism impaired his ability to stay sober and that his intoxication impaired his ability to stay out of public spaces. Marshall says that medical science is too divided over whether and to what degree alcoholism is addictive and impairs capacities necessary for responsibility to accept Powell's argument. Moreover, Marshall points out that Powell's own expert admits that even if Powell lacked control after several drinks, he did not lack control before taking the first one. Concurring, Justice White notes that the Texas statute punishes acts, rather than status, but points out that this doesn't settle the question of whether alcoholics are addicts who suffer from substantial impairment of control. However, since he favors reversal of the lower court findings, it seems that he must think that the evidence of substantial impairment is not compelling.

On the one hand, we now have evidence that alcoholics do experience control problems. On the other hand, we have said that addiction impairs, without precluding, competence and control. So it may not be clear that alcoholics are sufficiently incompetent as to justify an incompetence excuse. If we recognized partial excuses that track degree of incompetence, then alcoholics might be entitled to a partial excuse of some kind. But, as we have seen, American criminal law is generally bivalent about responsibility and

---

[13] *Powell v. Texas*, 392 U.S. 514 (1968).

excuse—treating them as all or nothing—and assuming that substantial capacity is sufficient for responsibility and only severe impairment is sufficient for excuse. If so, then we might think that the science of addiction does not yet show that alcoholics are sufficiently impaired as to warrant an excuse. Moreover, even if alcoholism did constitute sufficient impairment as to excuse, it still won't excuse if the agent is substantially responsible for becoming addicted. This appeals to the general principle that conditions that would otherwise be excusing are not excusing when the agent is substantially responsible for that condition obtaining and to the special case of this principle that says that incompetence that would otherwise be excusing is not excusing when it is incompetence for which the agent is culpable (§§35, 88). Marshall invokes this principle to provide an additional ground for denying Powell an incompetence excuse in *Powell*. In *Robinson*, Stewart recognizes that there might be circumstances in which an addict might not be culpable for her incapacity, in which case incompetence might be excusing—provided the impaired competence was significant enough.

In *United States v. Moore* (1973) the Fifth Circuit Court of Appeals rejected a heroin addict's claim that his addiction impaired his self-control and led him to procure and possess heroin in violation of the statute.[14] Judge Wilkey delivered the majority opinion, rejecting this claim on the ground that it would excuse too many because many kinds of wrongdoers had powerful incentives to commit wrongdoing. Judge Leventhal's concurring opinion stresses that a self-control excuse would excuse too many and that the law is set up so that excuses have to be exceptional, rather than common, and for this reason accepts impairment of self-control only when it is substantial and the result of a mental disease or defect.

United States v. Lyons (1984) is a significant Fifth Circuit case, which we encountered earlier (§22).[15] Part of the background to *Lyons* is another Fifth Circuit case *Blake v. United States* (1969) in which the court relied on a Model Penal Code insanity test, recognizing both cognitive and volitional dimensions of competence.[16] Lyons was indicted for obtaining controlled narcotics by fraud and pleaded that his addiction rendered him insane by substantially compromising his ability to *conform* his conduct to the law, thus appealing to the volitional prong of the Model Penal Code insanity test. Judge Gee writes the majority opinion and rejects Lyons's incompetence argument, making two main claims.

[14] *United States v. Moore*, 486 F.2d 1139 (1973).
[15] *United States v. Lyons*, 731 F.2d 243 (1984).   [16] *Blake v. United States*, 407 F.2d 908 (1969).

First, he claims that addiction per se is not excusing, even under the Model Penal Code insanity test, and others concur in this claim. But this is ambiguous between two different rationales: (a) addiction does not satisfy the mental disease or defect requirement for insanity, and (b) addiction does not constitute substantial impairment. Gee allows Lyons to introduce evidence that his addiction caused physical and/or psychological damage that rendered him substantially incapacitated. Here, Gee says that mental disease or defect is a forensic, rather than clinical, category, because whatever produces incompetence qualifies as a mental disease or defect. This agrees with our earlier claims that fair opportunity supports a more inclusive conception of insanity that treats the mental disease requirements as a forensic category or abolishes the mental disease requirement altogether (§88). That means that Gee appeals to (b), claiming that addiction does not, as such, constitute sufficient impairment so as to excuse.

Second, Gee rejects *Blake*'s adoption of the Model Penal Code conception of insanity, arguing that we should focus only on cognitive competence and eschew volitional competence, on the ground that current medical science does not allow us to distinguish incapacity and capacity not exercised—that is, doesn't allow us to distinguish can't and won't.

The concurring opinions (by Judges Rubin, Williams, Politz, Tate, and Higginbotham) are interesting. They accept Gee's first rationale for ruling against Lyons but reject his second rationale as unnecessary and over-broad. That means that there is only a majority on Gee's first rationale—that addiction is not sufficiently impairing to excuse—and Gee's second rationale is not controlling.

Gee's skepticism about the volitional dimension of normative competence is just dicta and is not a controlling part of the opinion. Nonetheless, it's worth addressing. Gee's skepticism about volitional competence is like the skepticism we encountered in Morse earlier.[17] Both claim that we can't distinguish between can't and won't. However, there are several reasons to be skeptical about this sort of skepticism about the volitional dimension of normative competence (§22). First, this is an evidentiary problem, not a claim about the ingredients of normative competence. Moreover, this evidentiary problem seems no worse than the one for the cognitive dimension of normative competence, which requires us to distinguish between a genuine inability to recognize something as wrong and a failure to form correct normative beliefs

---

[17] Morse, "Uncontrollable Urges and Irrational People."

or attend to normative information at hand on particular occasions. Neither Morse nor Gee questions the importance of cognitive competence because of the difficulty of distinguishing can't and won't there. Why should these difficulties pose a greater problem for volitional competence? Making the distinction between can't and won't is a challenge, but not an insurmountable one, in either the cognitive or volitional case. Counterfactual evidence is relevant to establishing both cognitive and volitional competence, and among the evidence for the truth of these counterfactuals is evidence about an agent's responsiveness in the past. We decide whether an agent had cognitive or volitional capacity on a given occasion in part by seeing if he recognized the relevant norms in the past and conformed his conduct to them previously. Past history does not always answer questions about current capacity definitively, but it is certainly relevant and probative. If an agent has a history of control problems, then that is defeasible reason to think that he might suffer from volitional impairment. If there is little or no such history and no other reason to suspect volitional impairment, that would be defeasible evidence that current volitional failure does not reflect volitional incapacity. Moreover, there are various empirical tests of volitional engagement; for instance, there are neurophysiological tests for various forms of affective, as well as cognitive, sensitivity, such as electrodermal tests of empathetic responsiveness. Finally, the empirical literature on addiction shows that addicts experience difficulties with control that non-addicts do not.

Because there is no good reason to be skeptical about volitional competence, the important question is whether the majority is right that there is inadequate evidence that addiction involves sufficient cognitive or volitional impairment so as to excuse. If excuse requires complete incompetence, then the evidence that addiction involves compromised competence may not be sufficient to excuse. But we said that fair opportunity arguably requires substantial, rather than bare, capacity and should excuse for significant, and not just complete, incapacity (§87). If so, there is a better case for recognizing an excuse for some forms of addiction. If addiction still falls short of the required degree of impairment for a full excuse, then one might think that addiction could at least qualify for a partial excuse. Of course, American criminal law is generally bivalent about affirmative defenses, treating them as all or nothing. We will see reason to question bivalence in Chapter 15. But if we accept bivalence, if only for pragmatic reasons, we should recognize the relevance of addiction to potential mitigation at sentencing.

114. What's Wrong with a Duress Model

If we are to take seriously the argument that addiction should be excusing in whole or in part, we need to explain how addiction impairs fair opportunity. Several writers have likened addiction to duress, treating it as a kind of inner compulsion.[18] If so, addiction might be taken to impair situational control, as duress excuses do. How plausible is a duress model for excusing addiction?

There are several problems with treating addiction as a duress excuse. Earlier, we examined common law and Model Penal Code conceptions of duress (§63). Simplifying some important differences between the common law and the Model Penal Code, we might identify these features as essential to duress.

1. Another person threatens wrongful harm to the agent or another unless the agent engages in wrongdoing.
2. The threat is credible.
3. There is no legal alternative that avoids the threat.
4. An agent of reasonable firmness would be unable to resist this threat.
5. The agent is not culpable or responsible for being exposed to the threat.

If these are the essentials of a duress excuse, then there are several obstacles to treating addiction as a duress excuse.

First, duress requires that the compulsion result from unlawful threats by another agent. Addiction does not satisfy this condition. Of course, one might claim that the relevant issue is hard choice and that the source of the hard choice is not directly relevant. Whatever the merits of that as a moral claim affecting moral responsibility, it's a serious obstacle to treating addiction as satisfying the requirements of the legal excuse of duress.

Second, duress requires that there exist no legal alternatives that avoid the threat. Though this is often true in standard cases of coercion by another, it's not true in the case of addiction. The addict is free not to consume the substance in question and not to engage in wrongdoing in furtherance of that consumption.

---

[18] See Doug Husak, "Addiction and Criminal Liability" *Law and Philosophy* 18 (1999): 655–84; Stephen Morse, "Hooked on Hype" *Law and Philosophy* 19 (2000): 33–49; and especially Watson, "Excusing Addiction."

Third, duress compromises the situational dimension of responsibility, compromising fair opportunity to avoid wrongdoing. By contrast, addiction is an internal condition of the agent, which may compromise normative competence, compromising either cognitive or volitional capacities. If so, addiction looks more like an incompetence than a duress excuse.

Fourth, in cases of duress, the agent has no impairment of competence, just lacks the fair opportunity to avoid wrongdoing, because of the wrongful threat by another. In the case of addiction, there only seems to be the promise of excuse if normative competence is compromised.

Fifth, in the standard duress case, the threats of another oppose the agent's own will. By contrast, in many cases of addiction, it seems that the compulsion co-opts the agent's assessment of her options and directs her will.[19]

Sixth, few seem to think that the desires of addicts are irresistible. An addict's appetites may be insistent, give rise to cravings, and produce discomfort when not satisfied, and that may make it harder for the addict to avoid wrongdoing than for someone not addicted, but that does not make them irresistible. Indeed, if Watson is right that we should think of addiction as involving acquired appetites, then addiction is no more irresistible than other strong appetites. This poses the question of whether the standard for volitional incompetence should be irresistible desires or something weaker, such as substantial volitional difficulty.

Finally, the Model Penal Code denies a duress excuse to someone who placed herself in a situation in which she would likely be subject to duress (MPC §2.09(2)). This limitation on duress is similar to the limitation on incapacity excuses that says that incapacity does not excuse when it is culpable incapacity (§§35, 88). As long as the addict is responsible for becoming addicted, it seems she would not have a duress defense. Of course, not all addicts are responsible for their addiction, for instance, if their addiction results from taking prescription narcotics for a legitimate medical condition or if the addiction is acquired in adolescence, prior to the agent being fully responsible. However, even here, we must be careful. An addict might not be responsible for her *initial* addiction in these circumstances, but she might nonetheless be culpable or responsible for *remaining* addicted over time and not seeking effective treatment. This is not to say that there couldn't be cases of non-culpable addiction, which then might be excusing if addiction involves sufficient impairment of normative competence, but it does suggest that the

---

[19] See Gary Watson, "Disordered Appetites: Addiction, Compulsion, and Dependence" reprinted in Gary Watson, *Agency and Answerability*, p. 66.

cases in which this excuse could potentially arise are special and that addiction per se cannot fund a duress excuse.

115. Addiction as Impaired Competence

The differences between addiction and duress make it difficult to see addiction as providing a duress excuse. It is more plausible to see addiction as potentially threatening normative competence. Addiction can impair judgment and the will, and so might produce some significant degree of normative incompetence.

Does it involve cognitive or volitional impairment, and is either kind of impairment great enough to fund an excuse or at least partial excuse or mitigation? On the one hand, addiction compromises *volitional* competence insofar as it impairs the agent's capacity to translate her deliberative judgments into intentions that she is able to implement despite distraction and temptation.[20] On the Platonic interpretation of dynamic inconsistency in attitude, the addict knows that what he is doing is wrong but cue-based cravings produce serious problems conforming his conduct to this knowledge. On the other hand, addiction might compromise *cognitive* competence insofar as the addict's insistent desires occupy his attentional field in a way that makes it difficult to attend to those aspects of a situation that normally signal wrongdoing. On the Socratic interpretation of dynamic inconsistency in attitude, cue-based cravings actually induce false beliefs about the merits of the agent's options. Addiction can co-opt the agent's evaluation of his options.

But while the psychological syndrome of the addict can disrupt the operation of the addict's knowledge or will, it's not clear how this is different from weakness in the form of strong appetites, which we do not normally think of as demonstrating substantial incapacity or as excusing. Put another way, it's not clear that this amounts to substantial incapacity, as required by our understanding of insanity and other incompetence excuses. If, contrary to fact, we had a doctrine of partial responsibility, there might be a case for recognizing a partial excuse for addicts who experience significant cognitive or volitional impairment. However, this would require showing partial or significantly compromised normative competence that did not apply equally to cases of putative akrasia in the face of strong appetites. If this is difficult to make out,

---

[20] See Wallace, "Addiction as a Defect of the Will," pp. 629, 640.

this might incline us to view addiction more as a mitigator than as a partial, much less full, excuse.

116. Addiction and Culpable Incapacity

However, this argument for partial excuse or sentence mitigation in cases of addiction overlooks the important limitation on incompetence excuses that they should not extend to cases where the agent is responsible for her own incapacity. As we have seen, as a general matter, affirmative defenses do not extend to conditions that would otherwise justify or excuse if the agent is substantially responsible for bringing about those conditions. This is true of excuses, as well as justifications, and, in particular, of both incompetence and duress excuses. Incapacity excuses only when it is non-culpable, and culpable incapacity does not excuse (§§35, 88).

So even if we could show that addiction impairs cognitive or volitional competence beyond the way that strong desires do, addiction could under-write partial excuse or mitigation only if it was non-culpable. Because many addictions are acquired voluntarily and responsibly, this will severely limit the excuse that addiction might otherwise fund. However, as we noted, there could be cases in which the addict is not culpable or at least not fully culpable for her addiction. For instance, some addicts might not be responsible for their addictions if they arose from taking necessary prescription medications, as Lyons alleges, or were acquired during adolescence when the addict was, by hypothesis, less responsible.

But, even here, we must be careful. An addict might not be responsible for her initial addiction in these circumstances, but she might nonetheless be culpable or responsible for remaining addicted over time and not seeking effective treatment. This means that even addicts who were not culpable for becoming addicted will often be culpable for remaining addicted, and this will undercut the excuse that their impairment might otherwise provide. This is not to say that there couldn't be cases of non-culpable addiction, which then might be excusing if addiction involves sufficient impairment of normative competence. Perhaps the best case would be one in which the addict non-culpably acquired the addiction and has a history of relapse despite diligent treatment efforts.

Fair opportunity provides a conceptual framework for assessing whether and, if so, when and how much addiction excuses. On the one hand, the fair opportunity framework implies that addiction is not per se excusing. A full excuse would typically be unjustified because the cravings of addicts are not irresistible. Addiction typically involves cognitive or volitional impairment, not complete loss of control. Moreover, even if addiction was otherwise excusing, it won't be excusing if the addict is substantially responsible for her addiction. On the other hand, the fair opportunity perspective does explain how addiction can in principle excuse, at least partially. The impairment to normative competence would have to be substantial, beyond the possession of strong desires, and the addict would have to be non-culpable for acquiring the addiction and remaining addicted. The difficult question is when these conditions are met. That's likely to depend a lot on the details of the case—what substance is involved, its effects on the cognitive and volitional capacities of the addict, how the addict acquired the addiction, and what steps the addict has taken and what obstacles she has encountered in seeking effective treatment. Assessing these matters will often be a difficult, partly empirical, matter and will be sensitive to changes and improvements in our understanding of addiction.[21]

---

[21] For a somewhat more skeptical conclusion about whether addiction can excuse, see Michael Moore, "Addiction, Responsibility, and Neuroscience" *University of Illinois Law Review* (2020): 375–470.

14

Battered Persons, Provocation, and Fair Opportunity

Often, wrongdoing is done out of passion of some kind—for example, fear, jealousy, hatred, compassion, and even love. A wrongdoer's passion might affect her narrow culpability or elemental *mens rea*, for instance, revealing that she didn't intend to act wrongfully or was negligent, rather than reckless. It's also possible that recognition of the various passions and emotions that spur misconduct should make us broaden our conception of elemental *mens rea* to recognize additional morally significant psychological relations between an agent and her misconduct. For the most part, the passions with which crimes are committed are treated as affecting the agent's inclusive culpability by affecting the wrongness of her conduct or her responsibility for those wrongs. In some cases, passion seems to *mitigate* the agent's inclusive culpability, providing some degree of justification or excuse, for instance when a battered woman kills her abuser pre-emptively out of reasonable fear for her safety. In other cases, passion seems to *aggravate* culpability, for instance when one person assaults another as the result of racial animus.

This chapter focuses on two kinds of crimes of passion and associated defenses—battered person cases and provocation cases. Battered person cases often involve an abused person killing his or her abuser out of fear, often reasonable, for his or her own safety. Provocation cases typically involve someone who has been emotionally provoked killing or harming his or her provoker. Historically, provocation cases included violent responses to assault, crimes against those near and dear, illegal arrest, and direct observation of spousal adultery. More recently, provocation centers on cases involving distraught or enraged lovers. Speaking colloquially, all such cases might be described as crimes of passion or cases of provocation. The victim of abuse who kills his or her abuser is certainly provoked and acts out of passion, typically fear. Likewise, the person who kills after being assaulted or the spouse who kills immediately after witnessing spousal betrayal and adultery is provoked and acts out of passion. We needn't condone such conduct to recognize it as a result of provocation or as a crime of passion, but this fact about the

Fair Opportunity and Responsibility. David O. Brink, Oxford University Press (2021). © David O. Brink.
DOI: 10.1093/oso/9780198859468.003.0014

origin of the conduct may mitigate our reactive attitudes and practices with respect to it.

The criminal law recognizes possible defenses, whether full or partial, for battered person and provocation cases. The defense usually associated with battered person cases is justification, in particular, self-defense, though we will see reasons to qualify this focus on justification and self-defense. But it is also possible to examine some battered person cases through the lens of provocation. As we have noted before, within the criminal law, provocation is a selective, rather than general, defense, because it applies only to homicides. Moreover, it is only a partial defense, because, even when successful, it does not justify outright acquittal, but instead results in conviction and sentencing for a lesser offense. Homicide that would otherwise count as murder counts as manslaughter when suitably provoked. There are two distinct questions worth asking about provocation. First, what counts as adequate provocation? Second, whatever counts as provocation, is that partial defense best understood through the lens of justification or excuse?

So far, we have framed the discussion of battered persons and provocation, as we should, in gender-neutral terms. Abusers can be men or women, as can the abused. Likewise, provokers can be men or women, as can the provoked. However, this apparent gender neutrality conceals an important gender asymmetry that we need to recognize and bear in mind. Battered person cases are typically battered women cases in which the abuser is a man and the victim of abuse is a woman. By contrast, under the influence of the Model Penal Code, provocation cases typically involve an aggrieved man killing a female love interest or others with whom she is romantically involved or associating. There seems to be general agreement about this gender asymmetry.[1] Though it's complicated to get reliable statistics,[2] one useful study of data from the FBI and National Center for Health Statistics made estimates of the gender breakdown in intimate homicides during the period 2010–17 and found that men kill women in 77.9 percent of the cases, women kill men in 19.7 percent of

---

[1] For instance, Nourse reports "In the cases I have studied, men are by far the most frequent victimizers, and women the most frequent victims." See Nourse, "Passion's Progress," p. 1335.

[2] One complication is that in homicide databases there is often incomplete information about the offender or the relationship between the victim and the offender. For instance, from 1993 to 2010 the relationship between the victim and the offender was unavailable in 24–32 percent of homicides involving female victims and 40–51 percent of homicides involving male victims. See Bureau of Justice Statistics, "Intimate Partner Violence: Attributes of Victimization, 1993–2010," November 2013 (https://www.bjs.gov/content/pub/pdf/ipvav9311.pdf). Another complication is that in these databases battered person cases are not typically distinguished from other cases of self-defense.

the cases, men kill men in 1.9 percent of the cases, and women kill women in .5 percent of the cases.[3]

By itself, this gender asymmetry is significant. It takes on additional significance when we note that courts are parsimonious in recognizing battered person defenses but comparatively liberal in recognizing provocation defenses. This leads to a potential *double standard* in the criminal law's treatment of crimes of passion involving men and women in which violence against women is treated less seriously than violence against men. A principled criminal jurisprudence should find any such double standard problematic.

Within this context, this chapter will examine crimes of passion involving battered persons and provocation, trying to make sense of each kind of crime and associated defense in its own terms but also trying to compare the treatment of each to make sure that together they provide a principled package. In the process, we should explore the proper form of each defense and whether, properly understood, that defense is full or partial and whether it justifies or excuses. Though our focus will be on two special cases of crimes of passion, involving battered persons and provocation, some of the lessons learned in these two cases may have wider significance for our understanding of crimes of passion more generally.

117. Defenses for Battered Persons and Battered Woman Syndrome

We do well to remember that men, as well as women, can be battered persons and that any defense that we recognize as applying to the criminal conduct of battered women should apply, in principle, to men as well. Nonetheless, it is important to focus on cases involving battered women. As we just noted, the overwhelming majority of cases involving crimes committed by battered persons are cases involving battered women, rather than battered men. Such cases take place against a background history of abuse. Again, in the overwhelming majority of cases, the abuser is male and the abused is female. Indeed, one of the defenses that has been offered for some crimes in response to abuse—*Battered Woman Syndrome* (BWS)—is specifically formulated so as to apply to women, rather than men. We will discuss BWS defenses shortly. Whatever the merits of a BWS defense, the currency of the BWS category

---

[3] See Emma Fridel and James Fox, "Gender Differences in Patterns and Trends in U.S. Homicide, 1976-2017" *Violence and Gender* 6 (2019): 27–36, esp. p. 29.

reminds us of the important fact that the central cases involving battered persons involve women who are victims of abuse by men.

Many crimes committed by victims of abuse reflect the operation of reasonable fear on the part of the abused that otherwise they will suffer further, possibly lethal, abuse. This fact seems to provide some defense, whether full or partial. But how should we understand such defenses? Are they full or partial defenses? Whether full or partial, are these defenses best understood as justifications or excuses? And what are the grounds for recognizing justifications or excuses in such cases? We will see that there is no one simple template for battered person defenses.

Before discussing the variety of cases involving battered women and battered women defenses, we need to discuss BWS. BWS describes a proposed clinical categorization of relationships characterized by a three-phase cycle. In the first phase, there are minor incidents of physical and/or verbal abuse in which the abused tries to appease her abuser. In the second phase, the abuse escalates in frequency and severity. In the third phase, the abuser expresses remorse and contrition, asks for forgiveness, and promises to reform. BWS involves the repetition of this cycle and is claimed to breed "learned helplessness" in the abused in which she feels trapped, unable to exit the relationship, and emotionally paralyzed.[4] BWS describes a post-traumatic stress disorder in which the history of abuse and fear impair the abused person's assessment of her options and her ability to act on her judgments about what would be best. So understood, BWS arguably involves some degree of impaired competence, which implicates a possible incompetence excuse.

Use of the BWS category has proven methodologically and morally controversial.[5] There is a tendency to associate all battered women defenses with BWS. But that is deeply misguided inasmuch as many crimes committed by battered women are perfectly rational responses to real and ongoing abuse and threats in which exit is not a realistic option or at least is a very risky option. As we will see, such cases raise the possibility of defenses of self-defense, duress, and provocation—none of which require appeal to impaired capacity. Perhaps some victims of abuse do suffer the sorts of cognitive and volitional impairments described by BWS, but there is no reason to assume that this is the norm. Moreover, to do so is morally offensive, insofar as it relies on a

---

[4] Lenore Walker, *The Battered Woman* (New York: Harper & Row, 1979).

[5] See, e.g., U.S. Department of Justice, *The Validity and Use of Evidence Concerning Battering and Its Effects in Criminal Trials* (Washington, DC, 1996) and Marilyn McMahon, "Battered Women and Bad Science: The Limited Validity and Utility of Battered Woman Syndrome" *Psychiatry, Psychology, and Law* 6 (1999): 23–49.

patronizing view of women as helpless victims, rather than rational actors, defending their rights.

This means that we have to be very careful about whether and, if so, how to appeal to BWS in battered women defenses. First, we can't assume that there is BWS wherever there is an abusive relationship; BWS requires evidence of impaired normative competence and not just abuse. Second, introduction of BWS into other defenses, such as self-defense or duress, threatens to derail those discussions, because they do not depend on incompetence. Incompetence is an excuse that admits wrongdoing but appeals to agential incapacity to block blameworthiness. Neither self-defense nor duress appeals to agential incapacity, and actors who act in self-defense or under duress would likely resent the suggestion that their behavior is the product of incapacity. One general moral to draw is that BWS should be only one part of the discussion of battered women, and perhaps a fairly small part at that.

118. Abuse and Duress

Many discussions of battered persons focus on cases in which the abused person in an abusive relationship kills or harms her abuser.[6] Such cases naturally raise questions of self-defense. These are important cases and can raise interesting issues. We shall discuss them shortly. But if we focus exclusively on such cases, we ignore an important class of cases that raise different possibilities of defense. In an important range of cases, the abused might engage in wrongdoing not directed at the abuser but because of a real or perceived threat from the abuser. For instance, an abused spouse or partner might participate in drug trafficking or prostitution because of a perceived threat from the abuser. Such cases in which the abused engages in wrongdoing at the behest of the abuser make possible a duress defense.

Recall our earlier discussion of duress (§63). At common law, a duress defense must satisfy six conditions.

1. Another person threatened death or grievous bodily injury to the agent or a relative unless she committed the offense.
2. The threat was credible.
3. The threat was imminent.

---

[6] See, e.g., Dressler, *Understanding Criminal Law*, pp. 242–48. Though I depart from Dressler's treatment here and elsewhere, I've learned much from his discussion.

4. There was no reasonable alternative to compliance as a way of avoiding the threat.
5. The actor was not responsible for being subject to the threat.
6. The defense does not apply to homicides.

The Model Penal Code understands duress as a more inclusive defense, modifying (1), (3), and (6).

> (1) It is an affirmative defense that the actor engaged in the conduct charged to constitute an offense because he was coerced to do so by the use of, or a threat to use, unlawful force against his person or the person of another, which a person of reasonable firmness in his situation would have been unable to resist. (2) The defense provided by this Section is unavailable if the actor recklessly placed himself in a situation in which it was probable that he would be subjected to duress. The defense is also unavailable if he was negligent in placing himself in such a situation, whenever negligence suffices to establish culpability for the offense charged.   [MPC §2.09(1)]

The Code says that duress must involve a threat of unlawful force but denies that the threat need involve death or grievous bodily harm, and it need not be directed at the agent herself or a close associate, revising both aspects of (1) in the common law doctrine. Moreover, the threat need not be imminent, contrary to condition (3) in the common law. The Model Penal Code does not mention the lack of permissible alternate ways of avoiding the threat, but it does insist that the threat should be such that a person of reasonable firmness would not or could not resist, and one might think that the latter condition includes the former condition. Finally, there is no restriction on the kind of wrongdoing to which duress is a defense; in particular, duress can be a defense to homicide, contrary to (6) in the common law doctrine.

We noted the conventional wisdom that duress is an excuse, denying responsibility or culpability for wrongdoing, rather than a justification, which denies wrongdoing. However, we also noted that there is reason to question this conventional wisdom. Some duress defenses can qualify as necessity defenses, which are typically regarded as justifications, rather than excuses. But it's not clear if this partial overlap between duress and necessity disqualifies duress as an excuse. Moreover, we saw some cases of duress that don't seem to satisfy necessity conditions. However, these questions about duress need not affect a duress defense for battered persons who engage in largely non-harmful wrongdoing, such as drug trafficking or prostitution, because of threats from an abuser.

In cases in which an abuser credibly threatens imminent harm to the abused or her loved ones if she doesn't engage in wrongful activity then and there, there seem to be all the elements for a duress defense. Of course, the defendant would have the burden of establishing that there was a credible threat, but that is a burden that can often be met, and, indeed, the history of abuse can be relevant evidence in that case. If such cases involve non-harmful wrongdoing, then a lesser evils test would be satisfied, qualifying the conduct for a necessity defense, as well. Though the common law assumes that necessity must result from naturally occurring events, rather than the wrongful agency of another, as in cases of coercion and duress, the Model Penal Code, we saw (§§61, 68–69), does not place this etiological restriction on necessity defenses (MPC §3.02). If so, it's not clear if a defense in this case sounds more in justification, excuse, or both. It doesn't look like we need to decide this issue to recognize a duress defense in such cases.

However, one might question whether a duress defense applies in circumstances otherwise like these in which the threat by the abuser is not imminent, perhaps because there is a significant interval of time between the threat and the point at which the abuser expects the abused to engage in wrongdoing at his request. In such a case, neither the imminence condition nor the absence of legal alternatives conditions required by the common law duress defense would be satisfied. Though the Model Penal Code does not require imminence, its reasonable person test arguably fails to be met in cases where there are perfectly legal ways for the agent to avoid both wrongdoing and the threat. This might seem relevant, because we might think that in such a case there are perfectly legal alternatives to compliance with the threat, such as ending the relationship with the abuser or reporting the abuser to authorities. If these were real alternatives to both wrongdoing and the threat, that would make it more difficult to sustain a duress defense. But in many such cases we have reason to doubt if these are real alternatives. They may be alternatives to engaging in the wrongful activity as directed by the abuser, but not to avoiding the threatened harm from the abuser. Abusers often track down the abused, after the abused has tried to exit the relationship, inflicting further violence, which can be lethal. Authorities can arrest the abuser and impose restraining orders against the abuser, but arrest can lead to bail, and arrest is no guarantee of conviction. Restraining orders are routinely violated, often with tragic results for victims of abuse whom they are supposed to protect. Women in abusive relationships have good reason not to trust alleged alternatives to acceding to the threats of their abusers. If so, a duress defense is reasonable in most cases in which an abuser credibly threatens a victim of abuse with serious harm if she fails to engage in drug trafficking, prostitution, and other forms of wrongdoing.[7]

How, if at all, might BWS be relevant to such a duress defense? Notice that a duress defense does not rely on any kind of impaired competence on the part of the duressed. On the contrary, a duress defense assumes that wrongdoing can be a reasonable response to credible threats. So, not only does a duress defense in such cases not presuppose BWS, in fact, BWS muddies the waters, confusing duress with incompetence. Now there might be cases that would not otherwise meet the requirements of duress to which BWS could be relevant. Suppose that the abuser's threat was not in fact credible—suppose he had a history of making idle threats—or that there were in fact genuine alternatives to wrongdoing and the threatened harm, such as exiting the relationship without repercussions. Nonetheless, if a history of prior abuse, perhaps occurring in a different, earlier relationship, left an agent unable to reliably assess her options and the credibility of threats, then perhaps there would be a basis for an excuse. But notice that this would now be an incompetence, rather than a duress, excuse, and, as such, the defendant would have the burden of establishing that she was impaired in relevant ways and to a sufficient degree.

119. Abuse and Self-defense

We can now turn to cases in which the battered person kills or harms her batterer. Not all such cases in which the abused harms the abuser involve homicides, successful or attempted. For instance, there is the famous case of Lorena Bobbitt. In 1993, after having endured years of psychological and physical abuse from her husband, John, including spousal rape, Lorena Bobbitt responded to his abuse and threats by cutting off his penis while he was sleeping.[8] This does not seem to be a case in which the abused sought to

---

[7] Discussions of the application of the Model Penal Code duress standard sometimes raise the question of whether the reasonable person test should be relativized to a reasonable woman standard. See, e.g., Dressler, *Understanding Criminal Law*, pp. 321–22. My suspicion, for which I won't argue here, is that there is no need to relativize the reasonable person standard. Any sensible application of that standard should be to the circumstances of the case, which can and should include facts about power differentials between the abuser and abused, the history of abuse, and the credibility and significance of the threat. I would have thought that this would include all the normatively relevant features of a gender-relativized standard.

[8] The Bobbitt case was odd in several ways. First, Lorena Bobbitt disposed of the severed penis after fleeing the scene, but experienced remorse and contacted authorities, who located it, after which it was

defend herself by attempting to kill her abuser. Interesting as such cases are, it will be convenient to focus on cases in which the abused kills her abuser. Such cases raise issues of self-defense.

It will be useful to partition the set of cases in which the abused kills her abuser into three subsets: *immediate self-defense*, in which the abused kills the abuser in response to an imminent threat; *pre-emptive self-defense*, in which the abused kills the abuser in response to a non-imminent threat, for example, when the abuser returns home or is sleeping; and *assisted self-defense*, in which the abused enlists the help of a third-party to kill the abuser in response to a non-imminent threat. A defense of self-defense is most straightforward in cases of immediate self-defense; it is less straightforward and more controversial in cases of pre-emptive self-defense and assisted self-defense.[9]

To assess these defenses, we need to recall the outlines of self-defense and defense of others (§60). Self-defense is generally regarded as a justification, denying wrongdoing, rather than an excuse, which concedes wrongdoing but denies responsibility or (broad) culpability for the wrongdoing. Deadly force is force likely to result in death or serious bodily injury and can be used in self-defense when necessary to protect oneself from the unlawful threat of deadly force by another. The common law requires that self-defense be used in response to an imminent threat, whereas the Model Penal Code requires only that self-defense be necessary to protect oneself from the unlawful threat of deadly force (MPC §3.04(1)). As a general rule, defensive force to protect a third party is justified when the third party would be justified in exercising self-defense. For instance, the Model Penal Code claims that defensive force by C against B to protect A is justified iff A would be justified in exercising self-defense against B's threat (MPC §3.05(1)).

When an abused person kills her abuser in immediate self-defense it is justified provided that it meets the conditions for self-defense employing deadly force. It would be the burden of the defendant to establish the elements of immediate self-defense, but there seem to be no special problems or issues associated with this defense in the case of battered persons. Indeed, a history of abuse including physical violence should make it even easier to establish the credibility of the abuser's threats of violence.

surgically reattached. Second, her defense mixed elements of self-defense and temporary insanity, and she was ultimately acquitted on insanity grounds, oddly appealing to "irresistible urges." Third, though the issues in the Bobbitt case are quite serious, some elements of the case are bizarre. The Bobbitt surname is certainly ironic, and after John Bobbitt's severed penis was reattached surgically, he went on to form a band called The Severed Parts.

[9] Dressler distinguishes "confrontational" and "nonconfrontational" cases and then discusses cases of "solicitation"—see Dressler, *Understanding Criminal Law*, p. 243.

Notice that there is no need to appeal to BWS in cases of immediate self-defense. In fact, appeal to BWS would just cloud the relevant issues in a case of immediate self-defense, because that would confuse a straightforward self-defense justification with an incompetence excuse. This would be a conceptually problematic mixing of distinct defenses. But it would also be morally problematic in conceding that the battered person acted wrongly, but absolving her from culpability by virtue of incompetence. A person who acts in immediate self-defense responds rationally and acts permissibly. Where BWS could be relevant, if it could be established, would be in cases wrongly believed by the abused to be cases of immediate self-defense. Conceivably, a threat that was not credible might be perceived by a victim of abuse with BWS as a credible and imminent threat that required deadly force in response. But in that case, BWS would be funding an insanity excuse, rather than a self-defense justification.[10] Such cases would presumably be unusual and make special evidentiary demands on the defense.

What about cases of pre-emptive self-defense in which a victim of abuse uses deadly force against an abuser who has credibly threatened deadly force against the abused but in which the threat is not imminent? The most common such cases involve the battered woman killing the abuser when he returns home or falls asleep.[11] Pre-emptive self-defense of this kind would not satisfy the imminence requirement of the common law. However, this wouldn't be an obstacle to self-defense under the Model Penal Code, because the Code requires only necessity, not imminence. But one might think that lack of imminence implies lack of necessity. For if the threat is not imminent, that seems to make available means of avoiding deadly force without employing deadly force, which might seem to render the use of deadly force unnecessary. For instance, the victim of abuse not subject to imminent violence could leave the abuser, ending their relationship, and/or report the abuser to authorities, bringing criminal charges against the abuser and seeking a restraining order against him. If these were genuine options for avoiding the abuser's threats, they would disqualify cases of pre-emptive defense from being genuine cases of self-defense. This has led some commentators to treat pre-emptive self-defense as sounding in excuse, rather than justification. One might try to liken non-imminent threats to duress.[12] However, it's not clear that duress can

---

[10] For a similar observation, see Stephen Morse, "The 'New Syndrome Excuse' Excuse" *Criminal Justice Ethics* (1995), pp. 12–13.

[11] See, e.g., *State v. Norman*, 366 S.E.2d 586 (N.C. Ct. App. 1988).

[12] See, e.g., Joshua Dressler, "Battered Women Who Kill Their Sleeping Tormenters: Reflections on Maintaining Respect for Human Life while Killing Moral Monsters" in *Criminal Law Theory* (Oxford:

provide relief where self-defense cannot. If the existence of alternatives to deadly force make self-defense unavailable, they arguably make duress unavailable as well, inasmuch as the existence of legal alternatives to wrong-doing that avoid the threat disqualify a duress defense. This is clearly true under common law conceptions of duress and arguably true under the Model Penal Code conception of duress. Alternatively, one might invoke BWS in the case of non-imminent threats, arguing for an incompetence excuse.

However, we don't need to treat pre-emptive self-defense as an excuse, rather than a justification. The Model Penal Code correctly distinguishes between imminence and necessity. If a threat of deadly force is sufficiently certain, it shouldn't matter if the execution of the threat lies in the future. If the only way I can prevent a villain from detonating a doomsday device in three days is to kill him now, before he activates the device, then it is both necessary and permissible to kill him now. Though necessity and imminence often go together, they can come apart, and, when they do, it is necessity, rather than imminence, that is important. Do necessity and imminence come apart in cases involving battered persons and pre-emptive self-defense? It certainly seems like they could. This involves recognizing that in many such cases the alleged means of avoiding deadly force without employing deadly force are not real options or at least very risky options. As we noted in discussing related issues about the duress defense, abusers often track down the abused after the abused has tried to exit the relationship, inflicting further violence, sometimes lethal. Moreover, authorities can arrest the abuser and impose restraining orders against him, but arrest can lead to bail, and arrest is no guarantee of conviction or imprisonment. Restraining orders are often violated, with griev-ous consequences for victims of abuse whom they are supposed to protect. Women in abusive relationships have good reason not to trust alleged alter-natives to the use of deadly force in response to non-imminent threats of deadly force. For these reasons, we should take seriously pre-emptive self-defense as a potential form of self-defense justification. Such claims need to be assessed on an individual basis, in light of the facts of the case, as with any other self-defense claim.

What about assisted self-defense in which the victim of abuse subject to credible threats from her abuser receives the assistance of a third party in using deadly force against her abuser? Third parties might engage in defense of the abused unilaterally or at the request of the abused. In special cases, the abused

Clarendon Press, 2002) and "Battered Women and Sleeping Abusers: Some Reflections" *Ohio State Journal of Criminal Law* 3 (2006): 457–71.

might hire a third party to provide defense. Third party involvement will have special value when the abuser is physically stronger than the abused and would likely prevail in a one-on-one defensive contest, as will often be the case when the abuser is male and the abused female. Such cases raise issues both of indirect self-defense by the abused and of defense of others by the third party. There could be such cases involving third-party response to imminent threats from an abuser directed at the abused. If such cases involve non-spontaneous involvement by third parties, they are likely to involve a third-party response to a non-imminent threat to the abused. In either case, the Model Penal Code rule should be operative—C is justified in protecting A against B's credible threats, and A is justified in enlisting C's defense, iffi A would be justified in using self-defense against B in these circumstances. These conditions can in principle be satisfied both in cases of immediate assisted defense and in cases of pre-emptive assisted defense.

120. Abuse and Provocation

Finally, we might consider a provocation defense of battered persons who kill their abusers. We will explore the provocation defense more fully in a moment. Here, we are interested in its potential application to battered person defenses. To address this issue, we need to remind ourselves of the essentials of a provocation defense. As we noted above (§64), provocation is a selective, rather than general, defense, because it applies only to homicides. Moreover, it is only a partial defense, because, even when successful, it does not justify outright acquittal, but instead results in conviction and sentencing for a lesser offense. Homicide that would otherwise count as murder counts as man-slaughter when suitably provoked.

The common law recognizes adequate provocation in cases of homicide that satisfy several conditions.

1. The homicide must be committed in a sudden state of passion.
2. The agent did not have a reasonable amount of time to cool off.
3. Adequate provocation must be such as would provoke a reasonable or perhaps ordinary person.

Historically, the common law required that provoking events were limited to one of the following categories: (a) aggravated assault and battery, (b) mutual combat, (c) commission of a crime against a close relative of the defendant, (d) illegal arrest, and (e) direct observation of spousal adultery. However, these strict categorical requirements have eased, with the result that many jurisdictions leave the determination of adequate provocation to the jury.[13]

The Model Penal Code defines provocation as part of its conception of manslaughter.

(1) Criminal homicide constitutes manslaughter when: (a) it is committed recklessly; or (b) a homicide which would otherwise be murder [i.e. a homicide that it is intentional, foreseen, or the result of extreme indifference to human life] is committed under the influence of extreme mental or emotional disturbance for which there is a reasonable explanation or excuse. The reasonableness of such explanation or excuse shall be determined from the viewpoint of a person in the actor's situation under the circumstances as he believes them to be. (2) Manslaughter is a felony of the second degree.

[MPC §210.3]

The Model Penal Code expands the scope of the provocation defense. It does not limit the provocation defense to specific categories of provocation. Moreover, the Code conceptualizes provocation in terms of extreme emotional disturbance and relativizes what counts as excusing emotional disturbance to the agent's actual perspective, however unreasonable that might otherwise seem to be.

Provocation is a partial defense. As we will see, it is somewhat unclear whether provocation is best understood as a partial justification, reducing the degree of wrongdoing, or as a partial excuse, conceding wrongdoing but reducing the degree of responsibility or culpability for wrongdoing. The consensus view is that provocation sounds in partial excuse, rather than partial justification.[14] However, we will have occasion to question that conventional wisdom later.

Provocation is not a natural defense for battered persons who kill their abusers. At first sight, it might not be clear why, since immediate self-defense, pre-emptive self-defense, and assisted self-defense could all, in the right circumstances, satisfy either the common law or Model Penal Code conceptions of provocation. However, there is a clear pragmatic reason for treating provocation as a defense of last resort in such cases. This is because provocation is only a *partial* defense, reducing murder to manslaughter, whereas

---

[13] See Dressler, *Understanding Criminal Law*, pp. 530–41.
[14] See, e.g., Dressler, *Understanding Criminal Law*, pp. 537–40, esp. 539.

self-defense, duress, and insanity are all *full* defenses, justifying acquittal when successful. When shopping for defenses, a justification, such as self-defense, is the first-best option, because it provides a full defense, justifying acquittal, and implies that one acted permissibly and did no wrong. Duress is a second-best option, because it also provides a full defense, justifying acquittal, and it has some elements of justification, at least when it satisfies the conditions of necessity. Even if duress is conceptualized as an excuse, rather than a justification, it locates the excuse in the way that the wrongful agency of another forces one's hand to commit wrong; it treats the wrongful use of deadly force as a rational response to abuse, rather than as a manifestation of the incompetence of the abused. Incompetence is a third-best option, because it provides a full defense, justifying acquittal, but one which represents the defendant as a compromised agent. If understood as an excuse, involving partial competence, provocation is probably a fourth-best option. In cases in which the conditions of immediate self-defense, pre-emptive self-defense, assisted self-defense, and duress are met, there is little reason to pursue a provocation defense, even if its conditions could be satisfied.[15]

121. Provocation and Crimes of Passion

Many crimes might be categorized as crimes of passion. There are so many different passions—including love, lust, loyalty, envy, ambition, greed, jealousy, a sense of betrayal, fear, insecurity, anger, hatred, misogyny, racial animus, and homophobia—that can be the occasion and trigger for wrongful conduct. Crimes that are not crimes of passion might be the exception, rather than the rule. Crimes of passion that are responses to provocation narrow this category somewhat. Depending on how provocation is understood, however, this sub-category is still potentially large and heterogeneous.

Two general features of the provocation defense that we have already encountered narrow its domain somewhat. First, whereas most defenses are general defenses—applying to all kinds of crimes—provocation is a selective, rather than general, defense, because it applies only to homicides. This provides some restriction on the domain of crimes of passion. Second, whereas American criminal law is generally bivalent about justification and excuse,

---

[15] However, the difficulties that women who pre-emptively kill their abusers encounter in successfully pleading self-defense or duress may make a provocation defense look like the best option. See Caroline Forell, "Gender Equality, Social Values, and Provocation Law in the United States, Canada and Australia" *Journal of Gender Social Policy and Law* 14 (2006): 27–71, esp. pp. 33–37.

provocation is only a partial defense, since, even when successful, it does not justify outright acquittal, but instead results in conviction and sentencing for a lesser offense. Homicide that would otherwise count as murder counts as manslaughter when suitably provoked. This means, as we noted before, that provocation is a defense of last resort, because it provides less relief than other defenses. Justifications, such as self-defense and necessity, and excuses, such as incompetence and duress, when successful, provide full defenses, justifying acquittal. All else being equal, a defendant shopping for potential defenses has reason to prefer full defenses to partial defenses. While these two general features of the provocation doctrine restrict its domain somewhat, they still leave its domain potentially wide.

The traditional common law conception of provocation would impose significant restrictions on the domain of that defense, limiting provocations to one of the following categories: (a) aggravated assault and battery, (b) mutual combat, (c) commission of a crime against a close relative of the defendant, (d) illegal arrest, and (e) direct observation of spousal adultery. Though some common law jurisdictions retain some version of this categorical approach, the general tendency has been to relax categorical restrictions. The Model Penal Code rejects categorical restrictions on potential provocation, conceptualizing provocation in terms of extreme emotional disturbance and relativizing what counts as excusing emotional disturbance to the agent's actual perspective. There are two main issues about provocation that we will address.

First, we must ask what counts as provocation. Here, we will be especially interested in differences between the common law and Model Penal Code conceptions. Whereas the common law emphasizes the conduct of the provoker, the Model Penal Code emphasizes the sensibility of the provoked. Given the way the Code focuses on extreme emotional disturbance and relativizes the reasonable person standard to the actual sensibility of the provoked, this leads to practical differences between the two conceptions. The Model Penal Code conception of provocation produces a defense with wider scope than the common law, and this breadth of scope has some troubling implications.

Second, there is the question of what sort of defense provocation is. In particular, is it best conceived of as a justification or as an excuse? The answer to this question is bound up with the answer to the question about what counts as provocation. When we look more closely at potential provocation conceptions and applications, we will see that there are different kinds of cases to which the provocation defense might apply. If so, we shouldn't assume that there's a univocal answer to the question of whether provocation justifies or excuses. In some cases, what's crucial is the nature of the provocation, and a suitably provoked homicide might reduce what would otherwise be its degree of wrongness, in which case provocation functions as a partial justification. But, in other cases, the provoked homicide really reflects an unreasonable response on the part of the agent. If this response is grounded in impaired competence, such cases are really cases of partial competence, perhaps temporary in nature, and are best conceptualized as potential partial excuses, rather than partial justifications.

122. Two Conceptions of Provocation

Because the traditional common law conception of provocation focuses on specific forms of provocation, its focus is on the provoker or act of provocation. It's true that the common law also requires that such provocations be such as to provoke a reasonable or ordinary person to violent response. But it requires a kind of provocation to which a violent response is reasonable or understandable. In this way, its focus is in significant part on the provoker and provocation. For this reason, the traditional common law conception of provocation sounds most naturally in justification, rather than excuse. In these cases, there is a provocative act that tends to elicit violent responses, even in reasonable people. Here, the provoker bears some of the blame for the resulting wrongdoing. Of course, it's not that provocation makes the act permissible. It's at most a partial justification. But it does make the resulting wrongdoing somewhat less morally objectionable or less wrong.

By contrast, the Model Penal Code places no restrictions on what can count as provocation and conceives of it as involving extreme emotional disturbance on the part of the provoked person. The Code does require that the sensibility of the disturbed person be reasonable, which could have thrown the focus back on the act of provocation. But the Code interprets a disturbed sensibility on the part of the provoked person, not in terms of an objective standard of reasonableness, but rather by the provoked person's actual perspective and sensibility. In effect, this removes any objective standard against which to measure the reasonableness of the provoked person's reaction. This really shifts the focus away from details about the provoker and the act of provocation to the perspective of the provoked person. Because it focuses on the disturbed sensibility of the provoked, the Model Penal Code conception of provocation often sounds most naturally in excuse, specifically incompetence, rather than justification. Of course, provocation, so understood, is not a full incompetence excuse, justifying acquittal. But it can function as a partial, and perhaps temporary, insanity excuse, reducing the agent's responsibility and culpability for his homicide.

The common law conception of provocation, with its categorical approach and its focus on provocation, tends to be more selective and disciplined about the defenses it supports. By contrast, the Model Penal Code conception of provocation—which eschews a categorical approach, focuses on the provoked, and relativizes its reasonable person standard to the agent's actual perspective—tends to be more promiscuous about the defenses it supports.

123. The Regressive Character of the Model Penal Code's Provocation Defense

The contrast between common law and Model Penal Code conceptions of provocation is a central theme in Victoria Nourse's important article "Passion's Progress: Modern Law Reform and the Provocation Defense."[16] In particular, she is interested in homicide cases involving actual or potential romantic partners and the differential treatment of such cases under the two conceptions of provocation. Whereas the typical battered person homicide involves a battered woman killing her abusive male partner, the typical crime of passion case involves a male killing his female love interest or her associates. Moreover, whereas the typical battered person case involves a violent response to wrongful battering, the violent response in crimes of passion homicides need not be a response to genuine misconduct on the part of the killer's female partner. This is because the Code relativizes the standard for assessing the killer's violent response to his actual perspective, rather than an objective standard. The Model Penal Code conception of provocation, Nourse argues, leads to the normalization of violence against women. In most areas of the criminal law, the Model Penal Code has been a progressive influence, presenting a more principled and humane conception of agency, responsibility, and culpability than what is often found in the common law. But when it comes to the provocation defense and crimes of passion, Nourse argues, the Model Penal Code is strikingly regressive.

Nourse did a comparative analysis of crimes of passion homicide cases from 1980 to 1995 in common law, Model Penal Code, and mixed jurisdictions,

---

[16] Nourse, "Passion's Progress."

looking not at trial outcomes but at jury instructions about the conditions under which they could consider a provocation manslaughter verdict, rather than a murder verdict. Whereas the traditional common provocation defense would recognize a provocation defense in such cases only when the provoked party was a direct witness to spousal infidelity, cases in Model Penal Code reform jurisdictions expanded the reach of provocation considerably. In reform jurisdictions, the killer and his victim need not have been married; the killer and his victim need not have been involved in a relationship at the time of the homicide; there need not have been actual infidelity, directly perceived; there need not have been even perceived infidelity; the killer may have responded to an apparent affront from the victim; the victim may have engaged in flirtatious behavior with another; the victim may have only signified an interest in dissolving the relationship; and the victim may have sought a protective order against an abusive partner. As Nourse points out, the range of cases in which juries have been allowed to consider the Model Penal Code provocation defense is shockingly permissive in several respects. First, it provides partial defense for trivial slights, such as the woman who turns her back on her partner after sex.[17] Second, it provides partial defense for homicides that were provoked by perfectly legal acts by the victim, such as separation, divorce, and dating others after separation or divorce. Third, it provides a partial defense in response to the victim's perfectly legal attempts to leave abusive relationships. In such cases, the killer has a defense despite the fact that he was responsible for the alleged provocation through his own prior culpable wrongdoing. Fourth, it provides partial defense in situations where there is no semblance whatsoever of proportionality between the alleged provocations (for example, infidelities, slights, departure) and the wrongdoing (homicide). Fifth, it assesses the reasonableness of the killer's response, not by a reasonable person's assessment of the provocation and its significance but by the killer's own perspective, at least as determined by his own beliefs, whether reasonable or not. In fact, when the extreme emotional disturbance standard is measured by the defendant's own perspective, we seem to be appealing to his actual response, not his capacity for self-control. These are all extraordinary exculpatory departures not just from the traditional common law doctrine of provocation but also from traditional and Model Penal Code standards for duress, which appeal to an objective reasonable person standard. A provocation defense that mitigates killings that are this easily provoked risks treating every crime of passion as one of provocation.

---

[17] *People v. Wood* 568 N.Y.S, 2d 651 (App. Div. 1991).

In many of these cases, the Model Penal Code seems to reward unreasonable attitudes and sensibilities on the part of the defendant. It's true that provocation is only a partial defense, so that provoked killers are still held accountable and punished. But their crimes are mitigated by provocation, and we may think that the crimes of those who kill from unreasonable attitudes should not be mitigated. Perhaps some of these men would be as easily provoked by the actions of other men in other contexts. If so, they might be easily provoked in an equal opportunity fashion. But otherwise there is reason to believe that in crimes of passion the killer is easily provoked by virtue of his victim's gender. The man who kills a woman for exercising her rights or for spurning his attentions not only acts unreasonably but displays misogynistic attitudes, not recognizing the agency and rights of women. Why isn't this misogyny an *aggravating* factor, rather than a mitigating one? Why aren't crimes of passion in such circumstances hate crimes?

124. A Double Standard for Battered Women and Provocation

A provocation defense is only one possible defense for battered women who kill their abuser and, for reasons canvassed above, a defense of last resort. Nonetheless, ordinary language allows us to describe both battered women who kill their abusive male partners and enraged men who kill their female partners as committing crimes of passion in response to provocation. While battered women who kill in immediate self-defense and can establish that fact can claim a full justification for their actions, it is much more difficult for women who kill in pre-emptive self-defense to prevail. I have criticized skepticism about pre-emptive self-defense in such cases. But it is a fact about battered women defenses. This skepticism about pre-emptive self-defense for battered women reflects doubts about whether their abuse constitutes adequate provocation. This stingy conception of provocation in cases of partner abuse contrasts sharply with the overly permissive view of provocation under the Model Penal Code in cases of enraged men who kill women under conditions of extreme emotional disturbance. This constitutes a double standard in the criminal law in which violence by men against women is tolerated in ways that violence by women against men is not.

This double standard is bad enough, but it is made worse when we factor in the *moral asymmetry* in what counts as provocation in the two contexts. Women who kill their male abusers are responding to wrongful violence in which their own rights are violated. By contrast, in many cases of provocation, men who kill their female romantic interest are responding to perfectly innocent actions of their female victims, who are merely exercising their legal rights. This moral difference in the kinds of provocation in the two contexts should make pre-emptive self-defense by battered women more defensible than many crimes of passion in which men kill women. This makes the actual double standard in which pre-emptive self-defense is more problematic than crimes of passion *doubly perverse*.

125. When Provocation Justifies and when it Excuses

Having discussed issues and problems about what constitutes provocation, we can now turn to the issue about whether provocation is best understood as a partial justification, reducing wrongdoing, or as a partial excuse, reducing responsibility and (broad) culpability. We shouldn't assume that there is a single invariant answer to this question.

One possible conceptualization of provocation is to treat it as an attendant circumstance in the specification of *actus reus*. On this conceptualization, we would be treating homicide that has been provoked—where that might be understood either in categorical terms or as committed under conditions of extreme emotional disturbance—as an attendant circumstance that precludes murder but can be an ingredient in manslaughter. This proposal has some plausibility, but I'm not sure that it really allows us to avoid the issues about justification and excuse. For an explanation of *why* there should be such an *actus reus* difference between murder and provocation manslaughter would presumably require saying that homicides committed as the result of provocation are either less wrong or less culpable. Insofar as *actus reus* is part of the specification of the offense or wrong, this might incline us to treat provocation as sounding in partial justification, rather than partial excuse.

The traditional common law conception of provocation is categorical, focusing on particular kinds of provocation and reasonable responses to those provocations. This might lend support to the idea that provocation should be understood as a partial justification, indicating that homicide, though wrong, is less wrong when provoked in specific ways that exceed the powers of a reasonable person to resist. If I kill someone who has raped my daughter, what I do is less wrong than if I kill that person for profit instead. Common law provocation's focus on the provoker may not exclude a partial excuse analysis, but at least it seems to permit a partial justification analysis.

By contrast, the Model Penal Code conception of provocation places no significant constraints on the content of provocation but does focus on the mental states of the provoked party. By focusing on the mental disturbance in the provoked party, the reform conception of provocation has apparent affinities with an incompetence excuse, such as insanity. It's possible to see its appeal to extreme mental or emotional disturbance as like an appeal to partial and temporary insanity.[18] Incompetence and insanity are excuses, as we have seen, so we might treat the Model Penal Code provocation defense as a partial excuse, rather than a partial justification.

However, the Model Penal Code conception of provocation makes for a problematic excuse of partial incompetence. This is because it appeals to the emotional disturbance of the provoked party without requiring that this disturbance significantly impairs his normative competence, cognitively or volitionally. One can imagine that sometimes emotional disturbance does cloud one's judgment or present problems of impulse control. But not all emotional disturbance results in significant cognitive or volitional incapacity, any more than strong emotions or desires necessarily incapacitate. If the reform conception of provocation is to provide a partial incompetence excuse, then it must be modified so that it appeals not just to emotional disturbance, but to lack of competence and control. Alternatively, we might treat the fact that it appeals to facts about the psychological states, rather than capacities, of the provoked as like a *mens rea* feature of the wrongdoing, affecting its degree of wrongness. This would make reform provocation sound in justification, rather than excuse. But that's not plausible, because reform provocation doesn't have to meet any objective standard of reasonableness. Indeed, reform provocation can apply to patently unreasonable responses on the part of the provoked to perfectly innocent behavior on the part of the victim. But then the Model Penal Code conception of provocation, as it stands, is not a plausible partial defense, whether conceived as an excuse or as a justification.

126. Provocation and Responsibility for Unreasonable Sensibilities

The reform conception of provocation would have some plausibility as a partial incompetence excuse if it required not just emotional disturbance but

---

[18] See, e.g., Joshua Dressler, "Provocation: Partial Justification or Partial Excuse?" *Modern Law Review* 51 (1988): 467–80.

significant loss of normative competence and control. Then and only then might extreme emotional disturbance be partially excusing as a kind of limited and temporary insanity.

However, it is a general principle in the criminal law that one cannot responsibly create the conditions of one's own excuse.[19] That is, an agent cannot claim an excuse in conditions that would otherwise merit an excuse when the agent is responsible and culpable for bringing about those conditions. An offender cannot claim an excuse in such cases, because it's not true that he lacked the fair opportunity to avoid wrongdoing. We've seen this principle at work in Model Penal Code restrictions on excuses involving intoxication (MPC §§2.08(4)–(5)(b)) and duress (MPC §2.09). We argued that this principle requires recognizing similar restrictions on an excuse of incompetence or insanity, making what would otherwise count as an excuse of incompetence or insanity unavailable if the agent was substantially responsible for becoming incompetent (§88). If we apply this principle to provocation, understood as a partial incompetence excuse, we should not recognize a provocation excuse where the provoked person is substantially responsible and, hence, culpable for his incapacity.

But this threatens to severely limit the scope of the Model Penal Code provocation defense, because many crimes of passion committed by emotionally disturbed men whose competence is temporarily impaired are responsible and, hence, culpable for the unreasonably volatile and violent sensibilities from which they kill women. There's no reasonable sensibility that sees homicide as a reasonable reaction to a woman exercising her rights of association. These crimes of passion reflect the operation of a volatile sensibility that is too easily provoked and responds with disproportionate violence, ignoring the rights of others. It may well be that particular manifestations of this kind of volatile sensibility lie outside the control of the person who has the sensibility at the very moment they occur. If so, his control may be genuinely impaired at the time he kills. But if he is responsible for acquiring the sensibility or for not modifying it, then his incapacity is culpable and is not excusing. As with our earlier discussion of culpable incapacity (§35), we can explain why such a killer has no excuse either by tracing responsibility for the homicide back to his earlier responsibility for acquiring or maintaining the unreasonable sensibility or by insisting that he is responsible for acquiring or maintaining the

---

[19] For discussion of the more general principle that one cannot cause the conditions of one's own defense, see Paul Robinson, "Causing the Conditions of One's Own Defense: A Study in the Limits of Theory in Criminal Law Doctrine" *Virginia Law Review* 71 (1985): 1–63.

unreasonable sensibility and its foreseeable consequences, which include susceptibility to unjustified violent reactions.

Are people responsible for acquiring or maintaining unreasonably volatile sensibilities? Perhaps some people are temperamentally volatile in the sense that they were born that way or developed such a sensibility at an early age and are literally incorrigible. In such a case, we might need to recognize a provocation defense, even if not an insanity defense. This would be a partial excuse. But such a person is obviously a danger to others, and this could justify civil commitment too.

However, if genuinely incorrigible volatility exists, it is the exception, rather than the rule. We expect people to be able to control and moderate their passions and assume that most adults can learn to do so with adequate attention and effort, which in some cases may require therapy and counseling. This is part of our view that people can change and that they are mostly responsible for their stable character traits. If people are not mostly responsible for their character traits, the criminal law has no business blaming and punishing wrongdoers. So if the criminal law is justified at all in its practices of holding people accountable, as I have argued that it is, then most crimes of passion do not merit a provocation defense, understood as a partial incompetence excuse, because even if that defense requires impaired capacity, it is not available to those who are responsible for their persistent incapacity. In most cases in which crimes of passion result from unreasonably volatile sensibilities, the offender cannot credibly say that he lacked the fair opportunity to do otherwise.

15

Partial Responsibility and Excuse

As we have seen, the criminal law is broadly retributive insofar as it predicates censure and sanction on culpable or responsible wrongdoing. Wrongdoing for which the agent is not responsible and, hence, not broadly culpable is excused. We spent considerable time motivating, articulating, and defending the fair opportunity conception of responsibility. Because responsibility and excuse are inversely related, fair opportunity has implications for excuse as well as responsibility; excuses correspond to ways in which the fair opportunity to avoid wrongdoing might be non-culpably impaired.

We also saw that fair opportunity informs criminal law principles governing culpability and various affirmative defenses. Whereas narrow culpability is an element of wrongdoing itself, broad culpability is the responsibility condition on wrongdoing, without which wrongdoing is excused. As such, broad culpability should be modeled by fair opportunity. Fair opportunity norms explain what is problematic about both narrow and broad strict liability crimes. The fair opportunity conception of responsibility helps us understand the architecture of affirmative defenses that are excuses, such as incompetence and duress. But fair opportunity principles also explain affirmative defenses that justify, such as self-defense and necessity, insofar as these are circumstances in which an agent lacks the fair opportunity to avoid committing offenses.

Fair opportunity is potentially socially fragile, but turns out to be surprisingly robust. Though the scope of fair opportunity can be limited by significant structural injustice, it still has significant application, even in conditions of structural injustice. Structural injustice only provides an excuse for selected offenses in which the marginalized have compromised opportunities, and even in these cases that excuse seems to be a partial excuse. With some limited exceptions, situationist psychological influences affect an agent's performance, rather than her competence, and so leave her fair opportunity intact. In cases of inadvertent wrongdoing committed in the heat of battle, situational factors may well compromise fair opportunity and so fund a full or partial excuse. However, this limited excuse for wartime wrongdoing does not generalize far.

In the last four chapters, we have applied the fair opportunity conception to various cases of potentially diminished capacity and opportunity—involving

Fair Opportunity and Responsibility. David O. Brink, Oxford University Press (2021). © David O. Brink.
DOI: 10.1093/oso/9780198859468.003.0015

incompetence and psychopathy, immaturity, addiction, and crimes of passion. Our verdicts in these cases were complex and defy easy summary. Sometimes, fair opportunity should lead us to be skeptical about recognizing excuses, for instance, in the case of psychopaths and their psychological deficits; addicts who are culpable for acquiring or maintaining their addictions; and crimes of passion in which men with unreasonably volatile sensibilities kill their romantic interests for perfectly innocent behavior on the part of the victim. However, excuses, whether full or partial, seem appropriate in other cases. Fair opportunity supports a revised version of the Model Penal Code insanity defense and its application to cases like Andrea Yates. Juvenile justice rightly recognizes that immaturity involves reduced normative competence and so tends to make adolescents less responsible for their wrongdoing than their adult counterparts. Immaturity implies partial responsibility, which provides the basis for criticizing the transfer trend, which treats juvenile crime the same as adult crime. Addiction often involves impaired self-control, with the result that addicts who are not substantially responsible for their addictions should be able to make a case for at least a partial excuse. Even if the Model Penal Code provocation defense is implausibly permissive from the point of view of fair opportunity, fair opportunity will recognize both justifications and excuses in cases of battered women who kill their abusers and crimes of passion in which genuinely wrongful behavior by the victim provides adequate provocation to homicide. In some of these cases, defenses might be partial in nature. Genuine provocation is a partial defense, and in cases in which battered persons kill, despite the existence of real, and not merely notional, alternatives to homicide, a battered person defense should also be partial.

Throughout the course of this discussion we have noticed that the capacities and opportunities required by the fair opportunity conception of responsibility are *scalar* phenomena, because normative competence and situational control can be matters of degree, as can be their impairment. Ideally, both blame and punishment would aim to deliver just deserts in cases of partial responsibility, making censure and sanction *proportional* to the degree of culpable wrongdoing. I believe that our ordinary assessments of moral responsibility, at least when they are reflective and measured, are already sensitive to the scalar nature of responsibility and excuse. The idea of partial responsibility and excuse is something most of us are prepared to recognize in our assessments of moral responsibility. However, the criminal law, especially American criminal law, is less hospitable to the possibility and significance of partial responsibility and excuse. With some qualifications, American criminal law is *bivalent* about responsibility and excuse. It treats responsibility as all or nothing, and it is stingy with excuse, in effect treating many cases of partial responsibility as if the individuals were fully responsible. It is normatively problematic to treat responsibility and excuse as bivalent when the underlying facts about them are scalar in nature.[1] This makes the criminal law *overly punitive* in significant ways. In this final chapter, I want to explain this concern about the bivalent character of American criminal law, take partial responsibility seriously, and explore some realistic alternatives to bivalence about excuse.

127. Partial Responsibility and Ideal Theory

Our discussion of partial responsibility and excuse will be abstract and conceptual, focusing on general features of the criminal law's assumptions about desert, responsibility, and excuse. But it will nonetheless be helpful to have some potential examples of partial responsibility in mind. Drawing on our discussion of incompetence, immaturity, addiction, and provocation, we might identify the following cases of potential partial responsibility:

1. A mother experiencing severe post-partum depression who commits infanticide, though knowing it to be wrong;
2. An adolescent who commits a property crime under pressure from gang members in his neighborhood;
3. An addict who commits a non-violent crime to support his addiction, which he acquired while taking medically prescribed pain medication or as an adolescent before he was fully responsible;
4. A battered woman who engages in prostitution or drug-trafficking at the behest of her abuser but not in response to a specific threat.

Whether any of these cases would be best understood as cases of full responsibility, full excuse, or partial responsibility would, no doubt, depend on further details of the cases. But it shouldn't be too hard to imagine ways of filling out the details that would raise issues of partial responsibility.

---

[1] Larry Alexander, "Scalar Properties, Binary Judgments" *Journal of Applied Philosophy* 25 (2008): 85–104 discusses related issues in ethics about difficulties using scalar input to justify binary verdicts. For more general discussions of the normative gap between scalar input and bivalent outcomes in the criminal law, see Husak, "Partial Defenses" and Adam Kolber, "The Bumpiness of Criminal Law" *Alabama Law Review* 67 (2016): 855–86.

Intuitively, responsibility is *scalar*, admitting of degrees. This intuitive observation is supported by the fair opportunity conception in which both normative competence and situational control are matters of degree. This claim is reinforced by noting that their impairment can be a matter of degree.

Consider normative competence. Normative competence involves reasons-responsiveness, which is itself a matter of degree. We said that capacities can be measured counterfactually—one is more responsive the greater the range of circumstances in which one would recognize and conform to the relevant norms, and less responsive the greater the range of circumstances in which one would not recognize or conform to those norms (§§19, 29–33). A more normatively competent agent is responsive cognitively and volitionally to the relevant norms in a greater range of possible circumstances, and a less competent agent is responsive in a smaller range of possible circumstances. Moreover, competence can be understood as ease or facility of performance and incompetence as difficulty of performance. The limiting case of difficulty is impossibility, which implies that degree of incompetence can be understood in terms of comparative difficulty of performance.[2] The harder it is for an agent to track her reasons cognitively or volitionally, the less normatively competent she is.

What is true of normative competence is also true of situational control. The fair opportunity to act on one's deliberations and choices free from wrongful interference by others, which is required by situational control, is also a matter of degree. This is because the impairment of situational control—clearest in cases of duress—involves hard choice, and hard choice comes in degrees. In particular, duress can make conforming to normative requirements more or less difficult. All else being equal, the greater the degree of difficulty that duress imposes on an agent, the greater a claim she has to a duress excuse.

This means that excuse is directly proportional to (non-culpable) difficulty in tracking reasons and that responsibility is inversely proportional to difficulty in tracking reasons. Though partial excuse makes sense for both incompetence and duress excuses, I will focus on partial incompetence excuses here. I adopt this focus for ease of exposition. The main conclusions we reach about partial incompetence excuses could be adapted, with suitable changes, to partial duress excuses.

If we focus on normative competence and hold the magnitude of wrong-doing constant, then, other things being equal, blame and punishment should

[2] For one development of this view, see Nelkin, "Difficulty and Degrees of Moral Praiseworthiness and Blameworthiness."

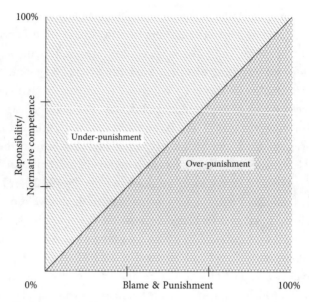

Figure 15.1 Proportionate Justice

be directly proportional to the degree of responsibility, as measured by the degree of normative competence, which is itself inversely related to degree of difficulty (see Figure 15.1).

As a matter of ideal theory, responsibility and excuse ought to be *continuously scalar* or, we might say, *analog*, thereby achieving *proportionate* desert and justice. Here, proportionate justice is represented by the diagonal. Punishment to the left of the diagonal is under-punishment, whereas punishment to the right of the diagonal is over-punishment. The degree of under-punishment or over-punishment can be measured by its distance from the diagonal.

128. Bivalence about Responsibility and Excuse

However, for the most part and with some qualifications, American criminal law treatment of responsibility and excuse is bivalent, recognizing a threshold of competence and responsibility below which one is fully excused and above which one is fully responsible.

An exception to this trend toward bivalence is the doctrine of provocation, under which intentional homicides committed with adequate provocation reduce to an offense of voluntary manslaughter (§§64, 70, 120–26). But the scope of this exception is quite limited, restricted as it is to homicides resulting from provocation. Moreover, even in this limited domain, it is not clear if this is a true exception, inasmuch as it is unclear whether provocation is best conceptualized as a partial excuse (partial responsibility) or as a partial justification (lesser wrongdoing). As we saw, some cases of provocation are best understood as partial justifications, whereas other cases are best understood as partial excuses (§125).

A potentially significant qualification to this trend toward bivalence involves a division of jurisprudential labor within criminal trials. As we have seen, criminal trials are *bifurcated* into guilt and sentencing phases (§48; see Figure 15.2). The guilt phase combines determinations of wrongdoing and affirmative defenses, such as excuse. The prosecution bears the burden of proof (beyond a reasonable doubt) for the elements of wrongdoing—both the objective elements (*actus reus*) and the mental elements (*mens rea*). Once wrongdoing is established, the defense has the opportunity to prove affirmative defenses, such as justification or excuse, and it typically has the burden of proof, either by preponderance of the evidence or clear and convincing evidence. So, in effect, a determination of offense creates a presumption of culpability for wrongdoing, which the defense can attempt to rebut, establishing an excuse. If wrongdoing is established and no defense is proven at the guilt phase, the trial proceeds to sentencing. In principle, mitigation at sentencing can include both desert factors relevant to, but not sufficient for, excuse and non-desert factors, such as remorse or reform.

Even if the guilt phase of a trial is bivalent, one might claim that the sentencing phase is scalar, rather than bivalent. Indeed, one might claim that the scalar nature of the sentencing phase makes up for the bivalence of the guilt phase.

However, though the possibility of sentence mitigation can sometimes soften the edges of bivalence about excuse, it is often an imperfect way to do

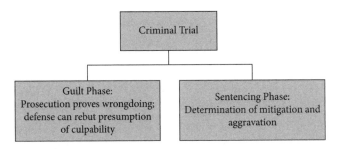

Figure 15.2 A Bifurcated Trial

so. First, there is often little or no discretion at sentencing. Mandatory minima and sentence enhancements often eliminate or severely restrict discretion at sentencing. Second, even when sentencing discretion exists and is wide, it is nonetheless discretionary. Failure to mitigate where there is lesser culpability is not seen as wronging the defendant or a failure of criminal justice. But on a broadly retributive jurisprudence that insists on proportional punishment, mitigation, when appropriate, should be mandatory, rather than discretionary. Finally, sentence mitigation is imperfect conceptually as well as practically. Excuse is an affirmative defense denying one element of the retributivist desert basis for punishment and is determined at the guilt phase. But partial responsibility and excuse concern the same dimension of desert and so arguably ought to be assessed at the guilt phase too, leaving non-desert considerations to inform sentencing.

With these qualifications in mind, it is fair to say that American criminal law is *predominantly bivalent*, rather than scalar, about responsibility and excuse and that sentence mitigation is an imperfect remedy for the concerns that bivalence at the guilt phase of a trial raises. For the most part, American criminal law treats responsibility and excuse as all or nothing, setting a fairly low threshold above which one is fully responsible (see Figure 15.3).

It's hard to know how best to operationalize the criminal law threshold for normative competence and responsibility. Given how many criminal

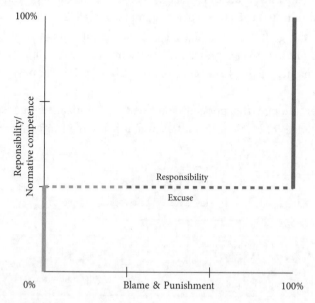

Figure 15.3 Bivalence

offenders suffer from some form of mental illness and impairment, how infrequently defendants plead insanity, and how infrequently these pleas are successful, one might think that the threshold is quite low. For purposes of illustration, I have set the threshold at 33 percent competence. In doing so, I believe that I have, if anything, understated how inclusive the bivalent conception of responsibility is.

129. Bivalence and the Failure of Just Deserts

We can now see how bivalence results in punishment that deviates significantly from just deserts by combining the first two figures (see Figure 15.4). By comparing bivalent and proportionate verdicts, we can see that a bivalent system introduces regions of under-punishment and over-punishment. These areas of under-punishment and over-punishment reflect the degree of unjust deserts, because the distance between actual punishment and the diagonal is proportional to the degree of under-punishment or over-punishment.

With a comparatively low threshold for responsibility, the region of over-punishment is large both absolutely and in relation to the region of under-punishment. This is bad enough. But if we agree with Blackstone that it is

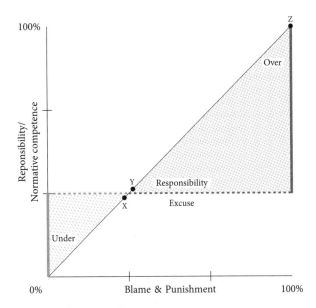

Figure 15.4 How Bivalence Produces Injustice

worse to over-punish than to under-punish (§43), we should be especially troubled that the ratio of over-punishment to under-punishment is so high.[3]

These comparisons hold, all else being equal, and make no assumptions about the frequency of cases at different points on the responsibility axis. If, as seems plausible, many offenders not qualifying for a full excuse have impaired competence to some degree, this will aggravate the worry about over-punishment.

Normative thresholds are arbitrary when the relevant underlying factors are scalar. Thresholds attach enormous normative significance to small differences straddling the threshold and ignore large differences above and below the threshold. For instance, in Figure 15.4 X and Y are responsible and, hence, blameworthy to similar degrees, whereas Z is blameworthy to a much higher degree. Their comparative just deserts are represented on the diagonal. However, the bivalent system with a responsibility/excuse threshold treats them very differently. X is fully excused, and Y is fully responsible, though their underlying levels of normative competence are very similar. Moreover, Z is treated as just as responsible and, hence, blameworthy as Y, even though Z is significantly more culpable than Y. These are significant failures of just deserts.

130. Non-ideal Theory won't Rescue Bivalence

If a broadly retributive conception of blame and punishment, such as predominant retributivism, is correct, then a *perfect moral accountant*—for instance, God—would employ a fully scalar conception of just deserts, assigning blame and punishment on a case-by-case basis and making them proportionate to culpable wrongdoing. A perfect moral accountant's determinations would conform to the diagonal.[4]

---

[3] Blackstone's version of this asymmetry involves a 10:1 ratio: "better that ten guilty persons go free than that one innocent party suffer," Blackstone, *Commentaries on the Laws of England*, Bk. IV, Ch. 27, p. 358. It might be tempting to think that Blackstone's asymmetry is already recognized in the fact that the prosecution bears a high burden of proof (beyond a reasonable doubt). But that burden concerns proof of wrongdoing, not culpability or responsibility. Once wrongdoing is established, it is typically the burden of the defense to prove that the defendant is not culpable, because incompetent. So, the procedure for proving responsibility and excuse does not reflect Blackstone's asymmetry.

[4] There is a problematic gap between scalar moral worth and bivalent divine verdicts—divine penalties and rewards—if God assigns all souls to Heaven or Hell, which are non-comparatively good or bad. See Ted Sider, "Hell and Vagueness" *Faith and Philosophy* 19 (2202): 58–68. This problem is reduced, though perhaps not eliminated, if Dante is right that there are levels (circles) in Heaven and Hell corresponding to a person's degree of moral worth.

However, our judiciary and juries are staffed by mortals who are *imperfect* moral accountants, with the result that attempts to implement just deserts sometimes lead to over-punishment or under-punishment. Implementing proportionate justice may prove problematic if it's very difficult to track differences in culpability reliably. Earlier (§106), we took note of jury studies suggesting that juries tend to focus on the seriousness of the wrongdoing and are insufficiently sensitive to factors that reduce culpability, thus leading to significant over-punishment.[5] If difficulties in reliably tracking diminished responsibility are great enough, that might provide a rationale for bivalence. Even if just deserts in ideal theory would be analog, perhaps difficulties in tracking just deserts reliably encountered by fallible appraisers in the real world justify adoption of a bivalent system as part of non-ideal theory.

It may seem odd to make the distinction between ideal and non-ideal theory within criminal jurisprudence, because we might think that the criminal law is essentially part of non-ideal theory. After all, criminal law necessarily involves partial compliance with norms of just behavior, and some people take partial compliance to be a dimension of non-ideal theory.[6] But we can distinguish within the theory of partial compliance between how ideally the system ought to respond to noncompliance of various kinds and how it ought to do so in light of human fallibility and considerations of feasibility. For this reason, we can and should distinguish between ideal and non-ideal aspects of criminal jurisprudence. This distinction allows us to make sense of a defense of bivalence restricted to non-ideal theory.

This defense of bivalence raises two distinct issues about tracking degrees of responsibility. First, it might be claimed that it is hard for imperfect moral accountants to recognize and track small differences in culpability. This is the problem of *epistemic granularity*. Second, even when we stipulate small differences in culpability, our normative responses might not always track those differences. Suppose that A and B both succumb to temptation and do wrong but A's temptation is slightly greater than B's. Perhaps God would blame B (a little) more than A, but most of us wouldn't. This is the problem of *normative*

---

[5] See Crosby et al., "The Juvenile Death Penalty and the Eighth Amendment." Their questionnaire contained descriptions of cases with defendants on trial for murder whose ages ranged from 10–19 years-old. The details of the cases included a description of the crime, probable culpability of all juveniles, level of remorse, and age of the defendant. Though the willingness among male respondents to impose the death penalty was not completely insensitive to immaturity, and the willingness among female respondents was more sensitive, the level of insensitivity in both men and women was striking. A similar finding about the comparative insensitivity of views about the severity of sentencing to degree of maturity and normative competence is made in Ghetti and Redlich, "Reactions to Youth Crime."

[6] See, e.g., Rawls, *A Theory of Justice* §39.

granularity. Both epistemic and normative granularity seem to be departures from the ideal of proportionate justice.

These are real difficulties implementing analog justice for non-ideal circumstances. However, they don't support adoption of the current bivalent system even as part of non-ideal theory. Any optimal rule, principle, or norm can be misapplied. We don't show that a norm is suboptimal just because some of its applications are individually suboptimal. Instead we have to show that there is another norm whose adoption would produce fewer suboptimal outcomes overall or whose suboptimal outcomes would be less unjust. But then difficulty with reliably producing just deserts by an analog method is not good reason to prefer a bivalent method unless bivalence produces fewer cases of unjust deserts or ones that involve less injustice. But since the bivalent system ignores all but the most extreme forms of incompetence, it is likely to generate greater injustice, in particular, more cases of more pronounced over-punishment.

131. Implementing Proportionate Justice

Non-ideal circumstances raise issues about epistemic and normative granularity, which are, in part, empirical issues. As a result, the optimal decision rules for non-ideal theory are a complex and partly empirical matter. Any recommendations have to be somewhat speculative and defeasible. Nonetheless, it is reasonably clear that bivalence with a low responsibility threshold will produce numerous and sometimes serious deviations from the ideal of proportionate justice. In particular, bivalence will lead to significant over-punishment.

It's also clear that the application of proportionate justice in non-ideal circumstances will yield some verdicts that are suboptimal in terms of just deserts. But proportionate justice is likely to yield fewer suboptimal results than bivalence, and when it does produce injustices, these are likely to involve smaller departures from just deserts than bivalence. Moreover, it won't be as prone as bivalence to over-punish. For these reasons, it is very likely that attempts to implement proportionate justice will more accurately track just deserts than bivalence.

There are two different points in a criminal trial at which one might try to implement proportionate justice—at the guilt phase or at the sentencing phase. One possibility would be to recognize diminished responsibility at the sentencing phase of a trial in the form of *mitigation.* On this approach, diminished responsibility would only become relevant once a defendant was found guilty. Consider a defendant with diminished responsibility. After the prosecution satisfied its burden of proving the elements of the offense, the defense would have the opportunity to establish an excuse. If the defense does not attempt to establish an excuse or tries but fails, the defendant will be found guilty. The very same facts that were relevant to establishing an excuse but judged insufficient at the guilt phase of the trial could then become relevant to sentencing, arguing for a reduced sentence, commensurate with partial responsibility.

Earlier (§128), I mentioned some obstacles to treating partial responsibility and excuse at the sentencing phase of a trial. One such obstacle is that sentence mitigation is generally conceived of as discretionary. Failure to mitigate where there is lesser culpability is typically not seen as wronging the defendant or a failure of criminal justice. But on a broadly retributive jurisprudence that insists on proportional punishment, mitigation, when appropriate, should be mandatory, rather than discretionary. To correct this problem, we would need to make culpability assessments at sentencing *mandatory*. Recall that in *Miller v. Alabama* Kagan's majority opinion precludes sentencing juveniles guilty of homicides to LWOP without explicit consideration of the way in which immaturity might reduce culpability and call for a lesser sentence (§§107–08). In effect, this strategy for implementing proportionate justice at sentencing would require similar consideration for reduced sentences for any case in which the defense could meet its burden for establishing diminished responsibility. A mandatory determination of culpability at sentencing would overcome the worry that sentence mitigation is discretionary.

However, this would not remove all the obstacles to recognizing partial responsibility and excuse at the sentencing phase. A further practical obstacle to implementing proportionate justice at sentencing is that often there is little or no discretion at sentencing. Mandatory minima and sentence enhancements often eliminate or severely restrict discretion at sentencing. To implement proportionate justice at sentencing, these restrictions on sentencing discretion would need to be eliminated. Mandatory minima would have to be abandoned to make way for gradient sentencing.

However, even if we removed these practical obstacles to implementing proportionate justice at sentencing, there would be a conceptual problem. Excuse is an affirmative defense denying one element of the retributivist desert basis for punishment and is determined at the guilt phase. But impaired responsibility that does not cross the threshold for a full excuse concerns the same dimension of desert as a full excuse would. But then it's arguable that partial responsibility and excuse ought to be assessed at the guilt phase too, leaving non-desert considerations to inform sentencing.

This suggests an alternative strategy for implementing proportionate justice that locates mandatory culpability grading prior to sentencing. This could be done as part of the existing guilt phase of a trial. Doing so would add to the possible verdicts about excuse, allowing a verdict of partial excuse as an alternative to excuse and no excuse. Indeed, to be fully scalar, this proposal would allow for a scale of excuses ranging from 0–100 percent. Moreover, we could make culpability assessments mandatory, rather than treating them as opportunities for establishing an excuse. This would better reflect the retributivist basis of punishment in culpable wrongdoing. The guilt phase of the trial would first require the prosecution to prove the elements of the offense beyond a reasonable doubt. Assuming wrongdoing is proven and there is no justification for the violation, the court would then make a culpability determination in which the defense would bear the burden of proof by either a preponderance of the evidence or clear and convincing evidence. On this version of proportionate justice, the court could find a violation not excused, fully excused, or partially excused to various degrees.

This would, in effect, replace a bifurcated trial with a *tripartite* trial in which determinations of wrongdoing and culpability or responsibility are separated and mandatory (see Figure 15.5).

On this proposal, once wrongdoing was proven, there would be a mandatory culpability determination, where the defense would have the burden of establishing an excuse, whether full or partial. Assuming that a full excuse was not established, there would be a separate sentencing phase where further considerations of mitigation and aggravation, including non-desert factors, would be assessed.[7]

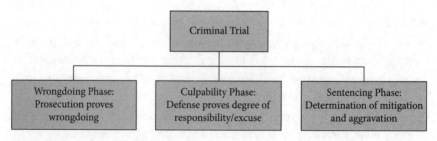

Figure 15.5 A Tripartite Trial

---

[7] I would like to think that this proposal for a trifurcated trial is similar in spirit to Robinson's elegant proposals to make the process and verdicts of the criminal law better reflect the underlying normative structure of criminal liability. For instance, Robinson argues that the simple binary verdict of guilty or not guilty obscures the different possible reasons for a not-guilty verdict. It would be better if courts were required to deliver one of five verdicts at the guilt phase of the trial: (1) no violation, (2) justified violation, (3) excused violation, (4) non-punishable violation, or (5) guilt. See Robinson, *Structure and Function in Criminal Law*, esp. pp. 204–07.

Though proportionate justice could in principle be achieved through modifications to either sentencing or guilt phases of the trial, I have offered some reasons for preferring the implementation of just deserts through modifying the guilt phase of criminal trials, rather than by modifying the sentencing phase.

132. Proportionate Justice and Blackstone's Asymmetry

However, we must remember that efforts to achieve proportionate justice via an analog method are subject to mistaken assessments of an offender's degree of responsibility. If we accept Blackstone's asymmetry in which over-punishment is worse than under-punishment, we might consider modifying proportionate justice so as to reduce the chances of over-punishment. Over-punishment often results from the blindspot about culpability, in which moral accountants aren't sufficiently sensitive to the bearing of reduced responsibility on inclusive culpability. We might modify determinations of proportionate justice by discounting punishment downward. One could operationalize such a discount in different ways. For purposes of illustration, I employ a 20 percent discount on punishment that tapers to 0 percent (see Figure 15.6).

In relation to the original conception of proportionate justice (Figure 15.1), this modified conception would make use of a smaller range of punishments

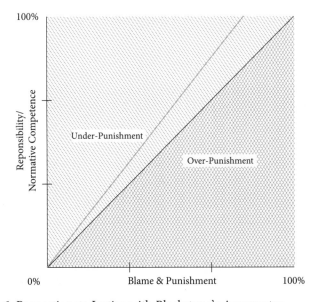

Figure 15.6 Proportionate Justice with Blackstone's Asymmetry

than under the original conception in an attempt to accommodate Blackstone's asymmetry and reduce the risk of over-punishment.

Though it is reasonably clear that proportionate justice, whether unmodified or modified, is superior to bivalence, it is less clear if either form of proportionate justice, even within a trifurcated trial, is optimal. That depends on the size and nature of the epistemic and normative granularity problems. If these problems are significant enough, that might be reason to explore alternatives that employ some kind of discontinuous assessment of responsibility or culpability that is more coarse-grained than proportional justice but more fine-grained than the bivalent system.

133. Trivalence

One such alternative would be a *trivalent* culpability assessment that allowed for verdicts of fully responsible, partially responsible, and non-responsible. Here, American criminal law might take a page from some other criminal justice systems that are trivalent about excuse. Criminal laws in England and Wales, Scotland, Ireland, and Australia recognize a defense of diminished responsibility to homicide, reducing what would otherwise be the sentence for murder to one of manslaughter.[8] For instance, in England §2 of the Homicide Act of 1957 provided this partial excuse for homicides committed by those with diminished capacity.

> Where a person kills or is a party to a killing of another, he shall not be convicted of murder if he was suffering from such abnormality of mind (whether arising from condition of arrested or retarded development of mind or any inherent causes or induced by disease of injury) as substantially impaired his mental responsibility for his acts and omissions in doing or being party to the killing.

§52 of the Coroners and Justice Act 2009 in England and Wales modified this provision, reducing an offense of murder to manslaughter in cases in which the defendant killed another as the result of "diminished responsibility" arising from a medical condition that impaired the defendant's ability "to understand

---

[8] For useful comparative data, see *Loss of Control and Diminished Responsibility*, ed. A. Reed and M. Bohlander (Farnham: Ashgate Publishing, 2011). The contributions to that volume by Ronnie Mackay, "The New Diminished Responsibility Plea," John Stannard, "The View from Ireland," and James Chalmers, "Partial Defences to Murder in Scotland" are especially useful.

the nature of his conduct, to form a rational judgement, or to exercise self-control."[9]

These trivalent conceptions of excuse apply only to homicides. But the issues about partial responsibility and excuse are perfectly general. For this reason, we might *generalize* this recognition of partial responsibility and excuse from homicides to all crimes. For instance, the German Criminal Code affords a full excuse for any offense to anyone who lacks normative competence and a partial excuse in cases of diminished responsibility in which normative competence is substantially, but incompletely, impaired (§§20–21 StGB).[10]

§20 Insanity. Any person who at the time of the commission of an offence is incapable of appreciating the unlawfulness of their actions or of acting in accordance with any such appreciation due to a pathological mental disorder, a profound consciousness disorder, debility or any other serious mental abnormality, shall be deemed to act without guilt.

§21 Diminished Responsibility. If the capacity of the offender to appreciate the unlawfulness of his actions or to act in accordance with any such appreciation is substantially diminished at the time of the commission of the offence due to one of the reasons indicated in §20, the sentence may be mitigated pursuant to §49(1).

This would be to introduce into American criminal law a *generic partial excuse defense*.[11] If trivalence is motivated by concerns about our inability to make the more fine-grained determinations of responsibility required by analog justice, then we might want to constrain such assessments within a finding of partial responsibility. We might insist that the punishment appropriate for partial

---

[9] The Scottish recognition of partial excuse to homicide dates at least to *HM Advocate v. Dingwall* (1867) 5 Irv 466 and was enacted into statute in Criminal Justice and Licensing (Scotland) Act 2010 §168. Though its conception of incompetence is not as clear as it might be, the Scottish conception is arguably similar to that in The Model Penal Code and the Coroners and Justice Act 2009, recognizing both cognitive and volitional incompetence.

[10] See Michael Bohlander, "When the Bough Breaks—Defences and Sentencing Options Available in Battered Women and Similar Scenarios under German Law" in *Loss of Control and Diminished Responsibility*, ed. Reed and Bohlander.

[11] For interesting discussion, to which I am indebted, see Stephen Morse, "Undiminished Confusion in Diminished Capacity" *The Journal of Criminal Law and Criminology* 75 (1984): 1–55 and "Diminished Rationality, Diminished Responsibility" *Ohio State Journal of Criminal Law* 1 (2003): 289–308. Interestingly, Morse's defense of partial excuse in the later paper reverses his skepticism about partial excuse in the earlier paper.

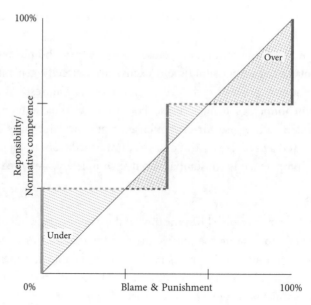

Figure 15.7 Trivalence

responsibility should be *half* of what would be appropriate for full responsibility. Here is one way to operationalize this proposal (see Figure 15.7).

Not surprisingly, if we compare the trivalent and bivalent systems correctly applied—the outcomes of conforming to their principles—the trivalent system is superior. It equalizes the ratio of over-punishment to under-punishment and reduces the magnitude of injustice done in individual cases (which reflects distance from punishment imposed to the diagonal).

Because trivalent culpability assessments make a tripartition of culpability intervals, we might conceptualize them as substantially responsible, partially responsible, and substantially non-responsible. We could also represent these as percentage intervals of full responsibility—0–32 percent responsible, 33–66 percent responsible, and 67–100 percent responsible. We could understand these relationships between qualitative and quantitative assessments of culpability in one of two ways depending on which we take to be explanatorily primary. We could treat the qualitative assessments as mutually exclusive and jointly exhaustive and then treat the percentage of responsibility as a way of operationalizing these qualitative differences. Alternately, we could treat the percentage of censure and sanction as reflecting percentage of culpability and the qualitative assessment of culpability as reflecting a perception of this percentage. For our purposes, I think we can remain agnostic about whether the qualitative or quantitative assessment should be explanatorily primary.

However, if we accept the Blackstone asymmetry that over-punishment is worse than under-punishment, we might want to modify the trivalent model so that we don't over-punish relative to the amount of responsibility, in effect, rounding punishment downward so that 67–100 percent responsibility would warrant 67 percent of the maximum punishment under proportionate justice; 33–66 percent responsibility would warrant 33 percent of the maximum punishment under proportionate justice; and 0–32 percent responsibility would warrant no punishment (see Figure 15.8).

This modification of trivalence makes use of only 67 percent of the scale of proportionate justice. Though it increases the degree of under-punishment somewhat, it eliminates the sins of over-punishment, at least when trivalence is correctly applied.

134. Beyond Trivalence?

Are we capable of more fine-grained culpability discriminations than a trivalent system allows? We might think that more subtle discrimination is possible. In particular, we might think that the category of partial responsibility and excuse lumps together significantly different degrees of responsibility. It will include both those barely below the threshold of full excuse and those

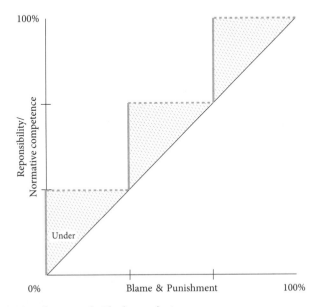

Figure 15.8 Trivalence with Blackstone's Asymmetry

barely above the threshold of no excuse. We might think that we can and should be allowed to distinguish among these different grades of partial responsibility. But if we want to avoid the full-blown scalar nature of the analog approach to responsibility and excuse, we need some categories.

One possibility would be responsibility quintiles. This would be a *pentavalent* system of responsibility and excuse. However, the experience in the Netherlands might make us cautious about embracing pentavalence. Section 39 of the Dutch Criminal Code provides for an insanity excuse when the offender was not responsible by reason of mental disease or defect.[12] Based on expert testimony, the judge would categorize the defendant's degree of responsibility in quintiles: (1) fully responsible, (2) somewhat diminished responsibility, (3) diminished responsibility, (4) severely diminished responsibility, or (5) insanity. This pentavalent responsibility assessment was not part of the Dutch Criminal Code itself, but evolved as the way to understand and implement partial responsibility. However, guidelines proposed for forensic psychiatric evaluation in 2012 recommended abandoning pentavalent assessments as unworkable, in favor of trivalent assessments. As a result of this proposal, Dutch practice seems to have switched from pentavalence to trivalence.[13] Though the Dutch experience is not dispositive, it might give us pause about pentavalence.

But there is space between trivalence and pentavalence. Perhaps the Goldilocks standard of granularity would be a *tetravalent* system that divides culpability into quartiles. We could conceptualize the quartiles qualitatively— (1) competent and responsible, (2) substantially competent and responsible, (3) substantially incompetent and not responsible, and (4) incompetent and not responsible. Alternately, we could conceptualize the quartiles as percentages of full responsibility—75–100 percent, 50–74 percent, 25–49 percent, and 0–24 percent. As before, we can remain agnostic about whether qualitative or quantitative assessment is explanatorily primary.

If we accept the Blackstone asymmetry that over-punishment is worse than under-punishment, we might seek to avoid over-punishment relative to responsibility quartiles by rounding punishments downward so that 75–100

---

[12] Dutch Criminal Code (1881, amended 2012).

[13] For discussion of the Dutch insanity defense, see, e.g., Susanna Radovic, Gerben Meynen, and Tova Bennet, "Introducing a Standard of Legal Insanity: The Case of Sweden Compared to the Netherlands" *International Journal of Law and Psychiatry* 40 (2015): 43–49 and Tijs Kooijmans and Gerben Meynen, "Who Establishes the Presence of Mental Disorder in Defendants? Medicolegal Considerations on a European Court of Human Rights Case" *Frontiers in Psychology* 8 (2017): 1–6. Radovic et al. are primarily interested in proposing an insanity defense for Sweden. Sweden had an insanity defense, which was abolished in 1965, leaving courts discretion to mitigate at sentencing so as to reflect diminished responsibility. Governmental commissions in 2002 and 2012 have proposed reinstating an insanity defense, modeled on the Model Penal Code.

percent responsibility would warrant 75 percent of the maximum punishment under proportionate justice; 50–74 percent responsibility would warrant 50 percent of the maximum punishment under proportionate justice; 25–49 percent responsibility would warrant 25 percent of the maximum punishment under proportionate justice; and 0–24 percent responsibility would warrant no punishment (see Figure 15.9).[14]

By comparison with trivalence, tetravalence would utilize a larger percentage of the scale of proportionate justice—75 percent. While it would still produce under-punishment, it would limit its severity. Also, though it would be less punitive than proportionate justice, it would eliminate over-punishment entirely, in recognition of Blackstone's asymmetry.

Whether tetravalence is more feasible or reliable than pentavalence or trivalence remains to be seen. Indeed, the Goldilocks standard of granularity that is psychologically realistic is a complex and partly empirical question, which might be best resolved in light of experimentation with different discontinuous measures of responsibility and normative competence. Until those experiments have been performed, the most plausible proposals might be trivalence and tetravalence.

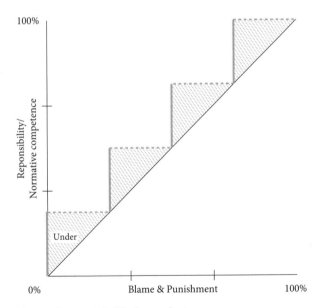

Figure 15.9 Tetravalence with Blackstone's Asymmetry

---

[14] This tetravalent conception of responsibility and excuse parallels the tetravalent measurement of the completion of criminal attempts that I outline in David O. Brink, "The Path to Completion" *Oxford Studies in Agency and Responsibility* 4 (2017): 183–205.

135. Taking Partial Responsibility Seriously

A retributive concern with just deserts should take partial responsibility and excuse seriously. There are questions for both ideal and non-ideal theory about how best to handle partial responsibility and excuse. We have briefly explored five options.

1. A bivalent system of responsibility and excuse with a comparatively low threshold for responsibility operative in American criminal law.
2. A trivalent system operative in some criminal justice systems, including a variation that would be responsive to Blackstone's asymmetry.
3. A pentavalent system, of the sort that was operative for a while in the Netherlands.
4. A tetravalent system, intermediate between trivalence and pentavalence, which could include provisions responsive to Blackstone's asymmetry.
5. A fully scalar analog system that aims at proportionate justice, including a variation that employs a discount on culpability assessments in response to Blackstone's asymmetry.

A bivalent criminal justice system significantly fails to deliver just deserts. This is clearly true of ideal theory, but it is also very plausible for non-ideal theory, because bivalence ignores all but the most extreme forms of impaired normative competence. This means that we should reject bivalence and embrace partial responsibility and excuse for both ideal and non-ideal criminal jurisprudence.

One question is *where* to do this. In principle, it could be done at sentencing, at the guilt phase of a trial, or at a separate culpability phase, which would occur after the determination of wrongdoing but before sentencing. If culpability grading were to occur during sentencing, mandatory minima and enhancements would need to be eliminated or severely restricted. Moreover, culpability grading would have to be mandatory, rather than discretionary. Even so, there would still be something conceptually problematic about separating determination of full and partial excuse into separate phases of a trial, insofar as they both bear on the same dimension of the retributivist desert basis for blame and punishment, namely, responsibility. It makes better sense, I think, to include a determination of partial excuse at the same point at which full excuses are assessed. This could be part of the guilt phase of a trial, after the prosecution establishes wrongdoing, which is where affirmative defenses are now assessed. However, it should be a mandatory assessment. Alternatively, one might introduce a separate culpability phase in trials, after a wrongdoing phase. Whereas the prosecution would be required to establish wrongdoing, the defense would be required to establish degree of culpability. On either proposal, wrongdoing for which the agent bears some responsibility would then pass to the sentencing phase of the trial, which would be restricted to non-desert factors.

Another question is *how* to implement partial responsibility and excuse. We examined four main possibilities. Analog or proportionate justice sets the standard for ideal theory, in which judges and juries reliably track the elements of inclusive culpability, in particular, both wrongdoing and responsibility. However, it is an open question whether trying to achieve proportionate justice is best in non-ideal circumstances in which there are problems of epistemic and normative granularity. Proportionate justice is clearly superior to bivalence with a low responsibility threshold, even in non-ideal circumstances. Whether proportionate justice is optimal for non-ideal circumstances is a complex, partly empirical question. But it also depends on the existence and attractions of alternative ways of assessing culpability. One alternative would be to apply a uniform discount to the findings of proportionate justice, in recognition of Blackstone's asymmetry and in an attempt to reduce the real threat of over-punishment.

If the difficulties of implementing proportionate justice reliably, arising from epistemic and normative granularity, are severe enough, we might want a discontinuous system that is more fine-grained than bivalence. We looked at trivalent, tetravalent, and pentavalent systems. Since their comparative merits are partly an empirical matter, ideally there would be experimentation among and even within different criminal justice systems. Until those experiments have been conducted, the experience in the Netherlands might give us caution about pentavalence. This leaves a choice between trivalence and tetravalence as the Goldilocks standard for a discontinuous, categorical approach.

Taking partial responsibility and excuse seriously at the institutional level is a difficult, partly empirical matter that requires fuller exploration and assessment. It is unclear whether to prefer a fully analog approach to proportionate justice, trivalence, or tetravalence. But it's clear that predominant retributivism and fair opportunity require some conception of partial responsibility and excuse.

Bibliography

For the most part, this Bibliography contains entries cited in the text and notes. In addition, it lists a few entries that are relevant to themes discussed here that are not otherwise cited.

Adams, Robert. *A Theory of Virtue* (Oxford: Clarendon Press, 2006).

Agule, Craig. "Resisting Tracing's Siren Song" *Journal of Ethics and Social Philosophy* 10 (2016): 1–24.

Agule, Craig. *Responsibility, Reasons-Responsiveness, and History* (University of California, San Diego, Ph.D. Dissertation, 2017).

Agule, Craig. "Distinctive Duress" *Philosophical Studies* 177 (2020): 1007–26.

Aharoni, Eyal, Sinnott-Armstrong, Walter, and Kiehl, Kent. "Can Psychopathic Offenders Discern Moral Wrongs? A New Look at the Moral/Conventional Distinction" *Journal of Abnormal Psychology* 121 (2012): 484–97.

Ainslie, George. *Picoeconomics: The Strategic Interaction of Successive Motivational States within the Person* (Cambridge: Cambridge University Press, 1992).

Ainslie, George. "A Research-Based Theory of Addictive Motivation" *Law and Philosophy* 19 (1998): 77–115.

Ainslie, George. *Breakdown of the Will* (Cambridge: Cambridge University Press, 2001).

Alexander, Larry. "Deontology at the Threshold" *San Diego Law Review* 37 (2000): 893–912.

Alexander, Larry. "Scalar Properties, Binary Judgments" *Journal of Applied Philosophy* 25 (2008): 85–104.

Alexander, Larry, Ferzan, Kimberly, and Morse, Stephen. *Crime and Culpability* (New York: Cambridge University Press, 2009).

Alexander, Michelle. *The New Jim Crow: Mass Incarceration in the Age of Colorblindness* (New York: The New Press, 2010).

Allais, Lucy. "Restorative Justice, Retributive Justice, and the South African Truth and Reconciliation Commission" *Philosophy & Public Affairs* 39 (2012): 331–63.

Alvarez, Maria. "Agency and Two-Way Powers" *Proceedings of the Aristotelian Society* 113 (2013): 101–21.

Alvarez, Maria. "Reasons for Action: Justification, Motivation, Explanation" *Stanford Encyclopedia of Philosophy* (2016).

Amaya, Santiago. "Slips" *Noûs* 47 (2013): 559–76.

American Law Institute. *Model Penal Code and Commentaries* (Philadelphia, PA: ALI, 1985).

American Psychiatric Association. *Statement on the Insanity Defense* (Washington, DC: APA, 1982).

American Psychiatric Association. *Diagnostic and Statistical Manual of Mental Disorders*, 5th ed. (Washington, DC: APA, 2013).

Anderson, S., Bechara, A., Damasio, H., Tranel, D., and Damasio, A. "Impairment of Social and Moral Behavior Related to Damage in Human Prefontal Cortex" *Nature Neuroscience* 2 (1999): 1032–37.

Aranella, Peter. "Character, Choice, and Moral Agency: The Relevance of Character to Our Moral Culpability Judgments" *Social Philosophy & Policy* 7 (1990): 59–83.

Aranella, Peter. "Convicting the Morally Blameless: Reassessing the Relationship Between Legal and Moral Accountability" *UCLA Law Review* 39 (1992): 1511–1622.

Aristotle. *Politics* in *The Complete Works of Aristotle, The Revised Oxford Translation*, 2 vols, ed. J. Barnes (Princeton, NJ: Princeton University Press, 1984).

Aristotle. *Nicomachean Ethics*, trs. T. Irwin (Indianapolis, IN: Hackett, 2019).

Arneson, Richard. "Democracy Is Not Intrinsically Just" in *Justice and Democracy*, ed. K. Dowding, R. Goodin, and C. Pateman (Cambridge: Cambridge University Press, 2004).

Asch, Solomon. "Effects of Group Pressures on the Modification and Distortion of Judgment" in *Groups, Leadership, and Men*, ed. H. Guetzkow (Pittsburgh, PA: Carnegie Press, 1951).

Ashworth, Andrew. *Principles of Criminal Law* (Oxford: Clarendon Press, 1991).

Austin, J.L. "Ifs and Cans" reprinted in Austin, *Philosophical Papers*.

Austin, J.L. "A Plea for Excuses" reprinted in Austin, *Philosophical Papers*.

Austin, J.L. *Philosophical Papers* (Oxford: Clarendon Press, 1961).

Ayer, A.J. "Freedom and Necessity" in A.J. Ayer, *Philosophical Essays* (London: Macmillan, 1954).

Baron-Cohen, Simon. *The Science of Evil: On Empathy and the Origins of Cruelty* (New York: Basic Books, 2011).

Beitz, Charles. *Political Equality: An Essay in Democratic Theory* (Princeton, NJ: Princeton University Press, 1989).

Bell, Macalester. "The Standing to Blame: A Critique" in *Blame: Its Nature and Norms*, ed. D. Coates and N. Tognazzini.

Bellegarde, Jennifer and Potenza, Marc. "Neurobiology of Pathological Gambling" in *What is Addiction?*, ed. Ross, Kincaid, Spurrett, and Collins.

Benes, F. "The Development of Prefontal Cortex: The Maturation of Neurotransmitter Systems and their Interactions" in *Handbook of Developmental Cognitive Neuroscience*, ed. C. Nelson and M. Luciana (Cambridge, MA: MIT Press, 2001).

Berman, Mitchell. "Justification and Excuse, Legality and Morality" *Duke Law Journal* 53 (2003): 1–26.

Berman, Mitchell. "On Interpretivism and Formalism in Sports Officiating: From General to Particular Jurisprudence" *Journal of the Philosophy of Sport* 38 (2011): 177–96.

Berman, Mitchell. "Let 'em Play: A Study in the Jurisprudence of Sport" *The Georgetown Law Journal* 99 (2011): 1325–69.

Berman, Mitchell. "Rehabilitating Retributivism" *Law and Philosophy* 32 (2013): 83–108.

Berndt, T. "Developmental Changes in Conformity to Peers and Parents" *Developmental Psychology* 15 (1979): 608–16.

Bilton, Michael and Sim, Kevin. *Four Hours in My Lai* (New York: Viking, 1992).

Bishop, Donna, Frazier, Charles, Lanza-Kaduce, Lonn, and Winner, Lawrence. "The Transfer of Juveniles to Criminal Court: Does It Make a Difference?" *Crime and Delinquency* 42 (1996): 171–91.

Blackstone, William. *Commentaries on the Laws of England*, 4 vols. (London: Strahan & Woodfall, 1791).

Blair, James. "A Cognitive Developmental Approach to Morality: Investigating the Psychopath" *Cognition* 57 (1995): 1–29.

Blair, James, Mitchell, Derek, and Blair, Karina. *The Psychopath: Emotion and the Brain* (Oxford: Blackwell, 2005).

Blair, R.J., Jones, L. Clark, F., and Smith, M. "Is the Psychopath Morally Insane?" *Personality and Individual Differences* 19 (1995): 741–52.

Blevins, Gregory and Murphy, Terrance. "Feeling Good and Helping: Further Phone Booth Findings" *Psychology Reports* 34 (1974): 326.

Bloom, Paul. *Against Empathy: The Case for Rational Compassion* (New York: Harper Collins, 2016).

Bohlander, Michael. "When the Bough Breaks — Defences and Sentencing Options Available in Battered Women and Similar Scenarios under German Law" in *Loss of Control and Diminished Responsibility*, ed. Reed and Bohlander.

Bonnie, Richard and Grisso, Thomas. "Adjudicative Competence and Youthful Offenders" in *Youth on Trial: A Developmental Perspective on Juvenile Justice*, ed. Grisso and Schwartz.

Borg, Jana Schaich and Sinnott-Armstrong, Walter. "Do Psychopaths Make Moral Judgments?" in *The Oxford Handbook of Psychopathy and Law*, ed. Kiehl and Sinnott-Armstrong.

Bowlby, John. "The Influence of Early Environment in the Development of Neurosis and Neurotic Character" *International Journal of Psycho-Analysis* 21 (1940): 154–78.

Bowlby, John. "Forty-four Juvenile Thieves: Their Characters and Home-Life" *International Journal of Psycho-Analysis* 25 (1944): 107–28.

Bowlby, John. *Attachment and Loss*, Vol. II (New York: Basic Books, 1973).

Boyd, Richard. "Homeostasis, Species, and Higher Taxa" in *Species: New Interdisciplinary Essays*, ed. R. Wilson (Cambridge, MA: MIT Press, 1999).

Bradford, Gwen. "Hard to Know" in *Responsibility: The Epistemic Condition*, ed. P. Robichaud and J. Wieland (Oxford: Clarendon Press, 2017).

Brink, David. *Moral Realism and the Foundations of Ethics* (New York: Cambridge University Press, 1989).

Brink, David. "Moral Conflict and Its Structure" *Philosophical Review* 103 (1994): 215–47.

Brink, David. "Eudaimonism, Love and Friendship, and Political Community" *Social Philosophy & Policy* 16 (1999): 252–89.

Brink, David. "Immaturity, Normative Competence, and Juvenile Transfer" *Texas Law Review* 82 (2004): 1555–85.

Brink, David. "The Significance of Desire" *Oxford Studies in Metaethics* 3 (2008): 5–46.

Brink, David. "Retributivism and Legal Moralism" *Ratio Juris* 25 (2012): 496–512.

Brink, David. *Mill's Progressive Principles* (Oxford: Clarendon Press, 2013).

Brink, David. "Responsibility, Incompetence, and Psychopathy" *Lindley Lecture* 53 (2013): 1–41.

Brink, David. "Situationism, Responsibility, and Fair Opportunity" *Social Philosophy & Policy* 30 (2013): 121–49.

Brink, David. "Originalism and Constructive Interpretation" in *The Legacy of Ronald Dworkin*, ed. S. Sciaraffa and W. Waluchow (Oxford: Clarendon Press, 2016).

Brink, David. "The Path to Completion" *Oxford Studies in Agency and Responsibility* 4 (2017): 183–205.

Brink, David. "Partial Responsibility and Excuse" in *Moral Puzzles and Legal Perplexities*, ed. H. Hurd.

Brink, David. "The Nature and Significance of Culpability" *Criminal Law and Philosophy* 13 (2019): 347–73.

Brink, David. "The Moral Asymmetry Between Juvenile and Adult Offenders" *Criminal Law and Philosophy* 14 (2020): 223–39.

Brink, David. "Responsibility, Punishment, and Predominant Retributivism" in *The Oxford Handbook of Responsibility*, ed. D. Nelkin and D. Pereboom (New York: Oxford University Press, 2021).

Brink, David and Nelkin, Dana. "Fairness and the Architecture of Responsibility" *Oxford Studies in Agency and Responsibility* 1 (2013): 284–313.

Brink, David and Nelkin, Dana. "The Nature and Significance of Blame" in *The Oxford Handbook of Moral Psychology*, ed. J. Doris and M. Vargas (New York: Oxford University Press, 2021).

Butler, Joseph. *Fifteen Sermons Preached at Rolls Chapel* [1726] reprinted in *Fifteen Sermons Preached at Rolls Chapel and A Dissertation on the Nature of Virtue*, ed. W. R. Matthews (London: G. Bell & Sons, 1953).

Butler, Joseph. *Dissertation on the Nature of Virtue* [1736] reprinted in *Fifteen Sermons Preached at Rolls Chapel and A Dissertation on the Nature of Virtue*, ed. W.R. Matthews (London: G. Bell & Sons, 1953).

Caruso, Greg. "Skepticism about Moral Responsibility" *Stanford Encyclopedia of Philosophy* (2018).

Caruso, Greg. "The Public Health-Quarantine Model" in *The Oxford Handbook of Moral Responsibility*, ed. D. Nelkin and D. Pereboom.

Chalmers, James. "Partial Defences to Murder in Scotland" in *Loss of Control and Diminished Responsibility*, ed. A. Reed and M. Bohlander.

Chisholm, Kim. "A Three Year Follow-Up of Attachment and Indiscriminate Friendliness in Children Adopted from Romanian Orphanages" *Child Development* 69 (1998): 1092–1106.

Christiano, Thomas. *The Rule of the Many* (Boulder, CO: Westview Press, 1996).

Cicchetti, Dante and Toth, Sheree. "Child Maltreatment" *Annual Review of Clinical Psychology* 1 (2005): 409–38.

Cima, Maaike, Tonnaer, Franca, and Hauser, Marc. "Psychopaths Know Right from Wrong but Don't Care" *SCAN* 5 (2010): 59–67.

Clarke, Randolph. "Dispositions, Abilities to Act, and Free Will: The New Dispositionalism" *Mind* 118 (2009): 323–51.

Clarke, Randolph. "Abilities" *Philosophy Compass* (2015): 1–12.

Cleckley, Hervey. *The Mask of Sanity* [first edition 1941] (St. Louis, MO: C.V. Mosby, 1955).

Coates, D.J. and Tognazzini, N., eds. *Blame: Its Nature and Norms* (New York: Oxford University Press, 2012).

Cole, David. "Turning the Corner on Mass Incarceration?" *Ohio State Journal of Criminal Law* 9 (2011): 27–51.

Crosby, C., Britner, P., Jodl, K., and Portwood, S. "The Juvenile Death Penalty and the Eighth Amendment: An Empirical Investigation of Societal Consensus and Proportionality" *Law and Human Behavior* 19 (1995): 245–61.

Cushman, Fiery. "The Scope of Blame" *Psychological Inquiry* 25 (2014): 201–05.

Damasio, Antonio. *Descartes' Error: Emotion, Reasons, and the Human Brain* (New York: Putnam, 1994).

Dancy, Jonathan. *Practical Reality* (Oxford: Clarendon Press, 2000).

Darley, Jon and Baton, Daniel. "From Jerusalem to Jericho: A Study of Situational and Dispositional Variables in Helping Behavior" *Journal of Personality and Social Psychology* 27 (1973): 100–08.

Darwall, Stephen. *The Second-Person Standpoint* (Cambridge, MA: Harvard University Press, 2006).

Deigh, John and Dolinko, David (eds). *The Oxford Handbook of the Philosophy of Criminal Law* (Oxford: Clarendon Press, 2011).

Delgado, Richard. "Rotten Social Background: Should the Criminal Law Recognize a Defense of Severe Environmental Deprivation?" *Law and Inequality* 9 (1985): 9–90.

Dennett, Daniel. *Freedom Evolves* (New York: Viking, 2003).

Denno, Deborah. "Who is Andrea Yates? A Short Story about Legal Insanity" *Duke Journal of Gender Law & Policy* 10 (2003): 1–60.

Doris, John. *Lack of Character* (New York: Cambridge University Press, 2002).

Doris, John. *Talking to Our Selves: Reflection, Ignorance, and Agency* (Oxford: Clarendon Press, 2015).

Doris, John and Murphy, Dominic. "From My Lai to Abu Ghraib: The Moral Psychology of Atrocity" *Midwest Studies in Philosophy* 31 (2007): 25–55.

Doris, John and Vargas, Manuel (eds). *The Oxford Handbook of Moral Psychology* (New York: Oxford University Press, 2021).

Dougherty, Tom. "Vague Value" *Philosophy and Phenomenological Research* 89 (2014): 352–72.

Dressler, Joshua. "Provocation: Partial Justification or Partial Excuse?" *Modern Law Review* 51 (1988): 467–80.

Dressler, Joshua. "Battered Women Who Kill Their Sleeping Tormenters: Reflections on Maintaining Respect for Human Life while Killing Moral Monsters" in *Criminal Law Theory* (Oxford: Clarendon Press, 2002).

Dressler, Joshua. "Battered Women and Sleeping Abusers: Some Reflections" *Ohio State Journal of Criminal Law* 3 (2006): 457–71.

Dressler, Joshua. "Duress" in *The Oxford Handbook of the Philosophy of Criminal Law*, ed. J. Deigh and D. Dolinko.

Dressler, Joshua. *Understanding Criminal Law*, 7th ed. (New York: LexisNexis, 2015).

Duff, R.A. *Punishment, Communication, and Community* (Oxford: Clarendon Press, 2001).

Duff, R.A. "Restoration and Retribution" in *Principled Sentencing*, 3d ed., ed. A. von Hirsch, A. Ashworth, and J. Roberts (Oxford: Hart Publishing, 2009).

Dworkin, Ronald. *Law's Empire* (Cambridge, MA: Harvard University Press, 1986).

Ein-Dor, Tsachi and Doron, Guy. "Psychopathology and Attachment" in *Attachment Theory and Research: New Directions and Emerging Themes*, ed. J. Simpson and W.S. Rholes (New York: Guilford, 2015).

Eldar, Sachar and Laist, Elkana. "The Misguided Concept of Partial Justification" *Legal Theory* 20 (2014): 157–85.

Estlund, David. *Democratic Authority* (Princeton, NJ: Princeton University Press, 2007).

Fara, Michael. "Masked Abilities and Compatibilism" *Mind* 117 (2008): 843–65.

Feinberg, Joel. *Doing and Deserving: Essays in the Theory of Responsibility* (Princeton, NJ: Princeton University Press, 1970).

Feinberg, Joel. *The Moral Limits of the Criminal Law*, 4 vols. (Oxford: Clarendon Press, 1984–88).

Feld, Barry. *Bad Kids: Race and the Transformation of the Juvenile Court* (New York: Oxford University Press, 1999).

Ferzan, Kim. "Justification and Excuse" in *The Oxford Handbook of the Philosophy of Criminal Law*, ed. J. Deigh and D. Dolinko.

Finch, David. *The Journal of Best Practices* (New York: Simon & Schuster, 2012).

Fine, Cordelia and Kennett, Jeanette. "Mental Impairment, Moral Understanding, and Criminal Responsibility" *International Journal of Law and Psychiatry* 27 (2004): 425–43.

Fingarette, Herbert and Fingarette, Ann. *Mental Disabilities and Criminal Responsibility* (Los Angeles, CA: University of California Press, 1979).

Finkleman, Paul. "Thomas Jefferson and Antislavery: The Myth Goes On" *The Virginia Magazine of History and Biography* 102 (1994): 193–228.

Finkleman, Paul. *Slavery and the Founders: Race and Liberty in the Age of Jefferson*, 3d ed. (New York: Taylor & Francis, 2014).

Finn, P. and Bragg, B. "Perception of the Risk of an Accident by Young and Older Drivers" *Accident Analysis and Prevention* 18 (1986): 289–98.

Fischer, John and Ravizza, Mark. *Responsibility and Control* (New York: Cambridge, 1998).

Fischer, John and Tognazzini, Neil. "The Truth about Tracing" *Noûs* 43 (2009): 531–56.

Flanagan, Owen. *Varieties of Moral Personality* (Cambridge, MA: Harvard University Press, 1991).

Foot, Philippa. *Virtues and Vices* (Los Angeles, CA: University of California Press, 1978).

Forell, Caroline. "Gender Equality, Social Values, and Provocation Law in the United States, Canada and Australia" *Journal of Gender Social Policy and Law* 14 (2006): 27–71.

Forman, James Jr. "Racial Critiques of Mass Incarceration: Beyond the New Jim Crow" *New York University Law Review* 87 (2012): 101–46.

Forman, James Jr. *Locking Up Our Own: Crime and Punishment in Black America* (New York: Farrar, Straus, and Giroux, 2017).

Frankfurt, Harry. "Alternate Possibilities and Moral Responsibility" *Journal of Philosophy* 66 (1969): 829–39.

Frankfurt, Harry. "Freedom of the Will and the Concept of a Person" *Journal of Philosophy* 68 (1971): 5–20.

Franklin, Benjamin. "Letter to Benjamin Vaughn, March 14, 1785" in *The Writings of Benjamin Franklin*, ed. A. Smyth (New York: Macmillan, 1906).

Fricker, Miranda. "What's the Point of Blame? A Paradigm Based Explanation" *Noûs* 50 (2016): 165–83.

Fridel, Emma and Fox, James. "Gender Differences in Patterns and Trends in U.S. Homicide, 1976–2017" *Violence and Gender* 6 (2019): 27–36.

Gardner, John. "The Gist of Excuses" *Buffalo Criminal Law Review* 1 (1998): 575–98.

Ghetti, S. and Redlich, A. "Reactions to Youth Crime: Perceptions of Accountability and Competency" *Behavioral Sciences and the Law* 19 (2001): 33–52.

Glover, Jonathan. *Alien Landscapes?* (Cambridge, MA: Harvard University Press, 2014).

Green, Stuart. "Six Senses of Strict Liability: A Plea for Formalism" in *Appraising Strict Liability*, ed. A.P. Simester.

Green, T.H. *Prolegomena to Ethics* [1883], ed. D. Brink (Oxford: Clarendon Press, 2003).

Green, T.H. *Collected Works*, 5 vols, ed. P. Nicholson (Bristol: Thoemmes, 1997).

Griffin, P., Torbert, P., and Szymanski, L. *Trying Juveniles as Adults in Criminal Court: An Analysis of State Transfer Provisions* (Washington, DC: Office of Juvenile Justice and Delinquency Prevention, 1998).

Grisso, Thomas. "Society's Retributive Response to Juvenile Violence: A Developmental Perspective" *Law and Human Behavior* 20 (1996): 229–47.

Grisso, Thomas and Schwartz, Robert (eds). *Youth on Trial: A Developmental Perspective on Juvenile Justice* (New York: Oxford, 2000).

Guerrero, Alexander. "Intellectual Difficulty and Moral Responsibility" in *Responsibility: The Epistemic Condition*, ed. P. Robichaud and J. Wieland (Oxford: Clarendon Press, 2017).

Hailie, C., Kosten, T.R., and Kosten, T.A. "Genetics of Dopamine and Its Contribution to Cocaine Addiction" *Behavioral Genetics* 37 (2007): 119–45.

Haji, Ishtiyaque. "On Psychopaths and Culpability" *Law and Philosophy* 17 (1998): 117–40.

Haji, Ishtiyaque. "The Emotional Depravity of Psychopaths and Culpability" *Legal Theory* 9 (2003): 63–82.

Haji, Ishtiyaque. "Psychopathy, Ethical Perception, and Moral Culpability" *Neuroethics* 3 (2010): 135–50.

Hanson, Neil. *The Custom of the Sea* (London: Doubleday, 1999).

Hare, Robert. *The Psychopathy Checklist Revised*, 2d ed. [first edition 1991] (Toronto: Multi-Health systems, 2003).

Hare, Robert. *Without Conscience* (New York: Simon & Schuster, 1993).

Hare, R.D., McPherson, L.N., and Forth, A.E. "Male Psychopaths and their Criminal Careers" *Journal of Consulting and Clinical Psychology* 56 (1988): 710–14.

Hare, Robert and Neumann, Craig. "The PCL-R Assessment of Psychopathy: Development, Structural Properties, and New Directions" in *Handbook of Psychopathy*, ed. C. Patrick.

Harman, Elizabeth. "Does Moral Ignorance Exculpate?" *Ratio* 24 (2011): 434–68.

Harman, Gilbert. "Moral Relativism Defended" *Philosophical Review* 84 (1975): 3–22.

Harman, Gilbert. "Moral Philosophy Meets Social Psychology: Virtue Ethics and the Fundamental Attribution Error" *Proceedings of the Aristotelian Society* 99 (1999): 315–31.

Harris, Grant and Rice, Marnie. "Treatment of Psychopathy: A Review of Empirical Findings" in *Handbook of Psychopathy*, ed. C. Patrick.

Harris, Grant, Rice, Marnie, and Cormier, C.A. "Psychopathy and Violent Recidivism" *Law and Human Behavior* 15 (1991): 625–37.

Hart, H.L.A. *The Concept of Law* (Oxford: Clarendon Press, 1961).

Hart, H.L.A. *Punishment and Responsibility* (Oxford: Clarendon Press, 1968).

Hart, H.L.A. "Legal Responsibility and Excuses" reprinted in Hart, *Punishment and Responsibility*.

Hart, H.L.A. "Negligence, Mens Rea, and Criminal Responsibility" reprinted in Hart, *Punishment and Responsibility*.

Hersh, Seymour. "The My Lai Massacre" in three parts, *St. Louis Dispatch* November 1969.

Hersh, Seymour. "Torture at Abu Ghraib" *The New Yorker* May 10, 2004.

Hills, Alison. "Moral Testimony and Moral Epistemology" *Ethics* 120 (2009): 94–127.

Hills, Alison. "Understanding Why" *Noûs* 50 (2016): 661–88.

Hirstein, William, Sifferd, Katrina, and Fagan, Tyler. *Responsible Brains: Neuroscience, Law, and Human Culpability* (Cambridge, MA: MIT Press, 2018).

Holton, Richard and Berridge, Kent. "Addiction: Between Compulsion and Choice" in *Addiction and Self-Control*, ed. N. Levy.

Hughes, Paul and Warmke, Brandon. "Forgiveness" *Stanford Encyclopedia of Philosophy* (2017).

Hume, David. *An Enquiry Concerning Human Understanding* [1748], ed. P.H. Nidditch (Oxford: Clarendon Press, 1975).

Hume, David. *An Enquiry Concerning the Principles of Morals* [1751], ed. P.H. Nidditch (Oxford: Clarendon Press, 1975).

Hume, David. *A Treatise of Human Nature* [1738], ed. P.H. Nidditch (Oxford: Clarendon Press, 1978).

Hurd, Heidi (ed.). *Moral Puzzles and Legal Perplexities* (Cambridge: Cambridge University Press, 2018).

Hurka, Thomas. "Desert: Individualistic and Holistic" in *Desert and Justice*, ed. S. Olsaretti (Oxford: Clarendon Press, 2003).

Hurka, Thomas. "More Seriously Wrong, More Importantly Right" *Journal of the American Philosophical Association* 5 (2019): 41–58.

Husak, Douglas. "Partial Defenses" *Canadian Journal of Law and Jurisprudence* 11 (1998): 167–92.

Husak, Douglas. "Addiction and Criminal Liability" *Law and Philosophy* 18 (1999): 655–84.

Husak, Douglas. *Legalize This! The Case for Decriminalizing Drugs* (London: Verso, 2002).

Husak, Douglas. *Overcriminalization: The Limits of the Criminal Law* (Oxford: Clarendon Press, 2008).

Husak, Douglas. "Strict Liability, Justice, and Proportionality" in *Appraising Strict Liability*, ed. A.P. Simester.

Husak, Douglas. *Ignorance of Law* (Oxford: Clarendon Press, 2016).

Husak, Douglas. "Kinds of Punishment" in *Moral Puzzles and Legal Perplexities*, ed. H. Hurd.

Hutcheson, Francis. *Illustrations on the Moral Sense* [1730], ed. B. Peach (Cambridge, MA: Harvard University Press, 1971).

Isen, Alice and Levin, Paula. "Effect of Feeling Good on Helping" *Journal of Personality and Social Psychology* 21 (1972): 384–88.

Jeske, Diane. *The Evil Within* (New York: Oxford University Press, 2018).

Kagan, Shelly. *Normative Ethics* (Boulder, CO: Ridgeview Press, 1998).

Kahan, Dan and Nussbaum, Martha. "Two Conceptions of Emotion in the Criminal Law" *Columbia Law Review* 96 (1996): 269–374.

Kahneman, Daniel. *Thinking, Fast and Slow* (New York: Farrar, Straus, and Giroux, 2011).

Kamtekar, Rachana. "Situationism and Virtue Ethics on the Content of our Character" *Ethics* 114 (2004): 458–91.

Kane, Robert. *The Significance of Free Will* (New York: Oxford University Press, 1996).

Kant, Immanuel. *The Groundwork for the Metaphysics of Morals* [1785] in *Kant's Practical Philosophy*, trs. M. Gregor (Cambridge: Cambridge University Press, 1997) (Prussian Academy pagination).

Kant, Immanuel. *The Critique of Practical Reason* [1788] in *Kant's Practical Philosophy*, trs. Gregor (Prussian Academy pagination).

Kant, Immanuel. *The Metaphysics of Morals* [1797–98] in *Kant's Practical Philosophy*, trs. Gregor (Prussian Academy pagination).

Kelly, Erin. "Doing without Desert" *Pacific Philosophical Quarterly* 83 (2002): 180–2015.

Kelly, Erin. "Criminal Justice Without Retribution" *Journal of Philosophy* 106 (2009): 419–39.

Kelly, Erin. *The Limits of Blame: Rethinking Punishment and Responsibility* (Cambridge, MA: Harvard University Press, 2018).

Kiehl, Kent and Sinnott-Armstrong, Walter (eds). *The Oxford Handbook of Psychopathy and Law* (Oxford: Clarendon Press, 2013).

King, Matt. "Traction Without Tracing: A (Partial) Solution for Control-Based Accounts of Moral Responsibility" *European Journal of Philosophy* 22 (2014): 463–82.

Kochanska, Grazyna and Kim, Sanhag. "Toward a New Understanding of Legacy of Early Attachments for Future Antisocial Trajectories: Evidence from Two Longitudinal Studies" *Development and Psychopathology* 24 (2012): 783–806.

Kochel, Tammy, Wilson, David, and Mastrofski, Stephen. "Effect of Suspect Race on Officer's Arrest Decisions" *Criminology* 49 (2011): 473–512.

Kolber, Adam. "The Subjective Experience of Punishment" *Columbia Law Review* 109 (2009): 182–236.

Kolber, Adam. "The Bumpiness of Criminal Law" *Alabama Law Review* 67 (2016): 855–86.

Kolber, Adam. "The Time Frame Challenge to Retributivism" in *Of One-Eyed and Toothless Miscreants: Making the Punishment Fit the Crime?*, ed. M. Tonry (New York: Oxford University Press, 2019).

Kooijmans, Tijs and Meynen, Gerben. "Who Establishes the Presence of Mental Disorder in Defendants? Medicolegal Considerations on a European Court of Human Rights Case" *Frontiers in Psychology* 8 (2017): 1–6.

Kornblith, Hilary. *On Reflection* (Oxford: Clarendon Press, 2012).

Kraut, Richard. *Aristotle's Political Philosophy* (Oxford: Clarendon Press, 2002).

Kreek, M., Nielsen, D., and LaForge, K. "Genes Associated with Addiction: Alcoholism, Opiate, and Cocaine Addiction" *Neuromolecular Medicine* 5 (2004): 85–108.

Kripke, Saul. *Wittgenstein on Rules and Private Language* (Oxford: Blackwell, 1982).

Kurth, Charlie. *The Anxious Mind: An Investigation into the Varieties and Virtues of Anxiety* (Cambridge, MA: MIT Press, 2018).

Levy, Neil. "Autonomy and Addiction" *Canadian Journal of Philosophy* 36 (2006): 427–47.

Levy, Neil (ed.). *Addiction and Self-Control* (Oxford: Clarendon Press, 2013).

Levy, Neil. "Addiction as a Disorder of Belief" *Biology and Philosophy* 29 (2014): 337–55.

Lobo, D. and Kennedy, J. "The Genetics of Gambling and Behavioral Addictions" *CNS Spectrums* 11 (2006): 931–39.

Locke, John. *An Essay Concerning Human Understanding* [1690], ed. P.H. Nidditch (Oxford: Clarendon Press, 1979).

Loury, Glenn. *The Anatomy of Racial Inequality* (Cambridge, MA: Harvard University Press, 2003).

Lowe, E.J. "Substance Causation, Powers, and Human Agency" in *Mental Causation and Ontology*, ed. A. Gibb, E.J. Lowe, and R. Ingthorsson (Oxford: Clarendon Press, 2013).

Maas, Carl, Herrenkohl, Todd, and Sousa, Cynthia. "Review of Research on Child Maltreatment and Violence in Youth" *Trauma, Violence, and Abuse* 9 (2008): 56–67.

Mack, Julian. "The Juvenile Court" *Harvard Law Review* 22 (1909): 104–22.

Mackay, Ronnie. "The New Diminished Responsibility Plea" in *Loss of Control and Diminished Responsibility*, ed. A. Reed and M. Bohlander.

MacKillop, J., McGeary, J., and Ray, L. "Genetic Influences on Addiction: Alcoholism as an Exemplar" in *What is Addiction?*, ed. Ross, Kincaid, Spurrett, and Collins.

Maibom, Heidi. "Responsibility in the Age of Neuroscience: Moral Understanding and Empathy in Psychopathy" in *The Oxford Handbook of Moral Psychology*, ed. J. Doris and M. Vargas (New York: Oxford University Press, 2021).

Malle, Bertram, Guglielmo, Steve, and Monroe, Andrew. "A Theory of Blame" *Psychological Inquiry* 25 (2014): 147–86.

McGeer, Victoria. "Civilizing Blame" in *Blame: Its Nature and Norms*, ed. Coates and Tognazzini.

McKenna, Michael. "The Limits of Evil and the Role of Moral Address: A Defense of Strawsonian Compatibilism" *The Journal of Ethics* 2 (1998): 123–42.

McKenna, Michael. "A Hard-line Reply to Pereboom's Four-Case Manipulation Argument" *Philosophy and Phenomenological Research* 77 (2008): 142–59.

McKenna, Michael. *Conversation and Responsibility* (Oxford: Clarendon Press, 2012).

McKenna, Michael. "Directed Blame and Conversation" in *Blame: Its Nature and Norms*, ed. Coates and Tognazzini.

McKenna, Michael. "Reasons-Responsiveness, Agents, and Mechanisms" *Oxford Studies in Agency and Responsibility* 1 (2013): 151–83.

McKenna, Michael and Warmke, Brandon. "Does Situationism Threaten Free Will and Moral Responsibility?" *Journal of Moral Philosophy* 14 (2017): 698–733.

McMahan, Jeff. *Killing in War* (Oxford: Clarendon Press, 2009).

McMahon, Marilyn. "Battered Women and Bad Science: The Limited Validity and Utility of Battered Woman Syndrome" *Psychiatry, Psychology, and Law* 6 (1999): 23–49.

Mele, Alfred. "Irresistible Desires" *Noûs* 24 (1990): 455–72.

Mele, Alfred. *Autonomous Agents* (New York: Oxford, 1995).

Mersky, Joshua and Reynolds, Arthur. "Child Maltreatment and Violent Delinquency: Disentangling Main Effects and Subgroup Effects" *Child Maltreatment* 12 (2007): 246–58.

Michaels, Alan. "Imposing Constitutional Limits on Strict Liability: Lessons from the American Experience" in *Appraising Strict Liability*, ed. A.P. Simester.

Mikulincer, Mario and Shaver, Phillip. *Attachment in Adulthood: Structure, Dynamics and Change*, 2d ed. (New York: Guilford, 2016).

Milam, Per. *Abolitionism about the Reactive Attitudes* (UCSD Ph.D., 2013).

Milam, Per. "Forgiveness" in *The Oxford Handbook of Moral Responsibility*, ed. D. Nelkin and D. Pereboom.

Milgram, Stanley. *Obedience to Authority* (New York: Harper & Row, 1969).

Mill, James. *An Essay on Government* [1824] reprinted in *Utilitarian Logic and Politics*, ed. J. Lively and J. Rees (Oxford: Clarendon Press, 1978).

Mill, John Stuart. *Collected Works of John Stuart Mill*, 33 vols., ed. J. Robson (Toronto: University of Toronto Press, 1965–91).

Mill, John Stuart. *A System of Logic* [1843] in *The Collected Works of John Stuart Mill*, vols. VII–VIII.

Mill, John Stuart. *On Liberty* [1859] in *The Collected Works of John Stuart Mill*, vol. XVIII.

Mill, John Stuart. *Utilitarianism* [1861] in *The Collected Works of John Stuart Mill*, vol. X.

Mill, John Stuart. *Considerations on Representative Government* [1861] in *The Collected Works of John Stuart Mill*, vol. XIX.

Mischel, Walter. *Personality and Assessment* (Hoboken, NJ: John Wiley & Sons, 1968).

Moffitt, Terrie. "Adolescence-Limited and Life-Course-Persistent Antisocial Behavior: A Developmental Taxonomy" *Psychological Review* 100 (1993): 674–701.

Moffitt, Terrie and Caspi, Avshalom. "Evidence from Behavioral Genetics for Environmental Contributions to Antisocial Conduct" in *Handbook of Socialization*, ed. J. Grusec and P. Hastings (New York: The Guilford Press, 2007).

Moore, G.E. *Ethics* [1912] (Oxford: Clarendon Press, 1966).

Moore, Michael. *Law and Psychiatry: Rethinking the Relationship* (New York: Cambridge, 1984).

Moore, Michael. *Placing Blame* (Oxford: Clarendon Press, 1997).

Moore, Michael. *Causation and Responsibility* (Oxford: Clarendon Press, 2009).

Moore, Michael. "Addiction, Responsibility, and Neuroscience" *University of Illinois Law Review* (2020): 375–470.

Morris, Herbert. "Persons and Punishment" *The Monist* 52: 475–501 and reprinted in Herbert Morris, *On Guilt and Innocence* (Berkeley, CA: University of California Press, 1976).

Morse, Stephen. "Undiminished Confusion in Diminished Capacity" *Journal of Criminal Law and Criminology* 75 (1984): 1–55.

Morse, Stephen. "Excusing the Crazy: The Insanity Defense Reconsidered" *Southern California Law Review* 58 (1985): 777–836.

Morse, Stephen. "Culpability and Control" *University of Pennsylvania Law Review* 142 (1994): 1587–660.

Morse, Stephen. "The 'New Syndrome Excuse' Excuse" *Criminal Justice Ethics* 14 (1995): 3–15.

Morse, Stephen. "Immaturity and Irresponsibility" *Journal of Criminal Law and Criminology* 88 (1997): 15–67.

Morse, Stephen. "Hooked on Hype" *Law and Philosophy* 19 (2000): 33–49.

Morse, Stephen. "Uncontrollable Urges and Irrational People" *Virginia Law Review* 88 (2002): 1025–78.

Morse, Stephen. "Diminished Rationality, Diminished Responsibility" *Ohio State Journal of Criminal Law* 1 (2003): 289–308.

Morse, Stephen. "Psychopathy and Criminal Responsibility" *Neuroethics* 1 (2008): 205–12.

Nagel, Thomas. "War and Massacre" reprinted in Thomas Nagel, *Mortal Questions* (New York: Cambridge University Press, 1979)

Nelkin, Dana. "Freedom, Responsibility, and the Challenge of Situationism" *Midwest Studies in Philosophy* 29 (2005): 181–206.

Nelkin, Dana. "Responsibility and Rational Abilities: Defending an Asymmetrical View" *Pacific Philosophical Quarterly* 89 (2008): 497–515.

Nelkin, Dana. *Making Sense of Freedom and Responsibility* (Oxford: Clarendon Press, 2012).

Nelkin, Dana. "Psychopaths, Incorrigible Racists, and the Faces of Responsibility" *Ethics* 125 (2015): 357–90.

Nelkin, Dana. "Difficulty and Degrees of Moral Praiseworthiness and Blameworthiness" *Noûs* 50 (2016): 356–78.

Nelkin, Dana and Pereboom, Derk (eds). *The Oxford Handbook of Responsibility* (New York: Oxford University Press, 2021).

Nelkin, Dana and Rickless, Samuel. "Three Cheers for Double Effect" 89 *Philosophy and Phenomenological Research* 89 (2014): 125–58.

Newman, Joseph. "Psychopathic Behavior: An Information-Processing Perspective" in *Psychopathy: Theory, Research, and Implications*, ed. Cooke, Forth, and Hare (Dordrecht: Kluwer, 1998).

Nourse, Victoria. "Passion's Progress: Law Reform and the Provocation Defense" *Yale Law Journal* 106 (1997): 1331–1448.

Nozick, Robert. *Philosophical Explanations* (Cambridge, MA: Harvard, 1981).

Parfit, Derek. *On What Matters*, 3 vols (Oxford: Clarendon Press, 2011–17).

Pashler, Harold and Harris, Christine. "Is the Replication Crisis Overblown? Three Arguments Examined" *Perspective on Psychology* 7 (2012): 531–36.

Paterson, Emily. *Child Maltreatment across the Life-Course: Links to Youth Offending* (Ph. D. Thesis, Griffith University, 2015).

Patrick, Christopher. "Back to the Future: Cleckley as Guide to the Next Generation of Psychopathy Research" in *Handbook of Psychopathy*, ed. C. Patrick.

Patrick, Christopher (ed.). *Handbook of Psychopathy* (New York: Guilford Press, 2006).

Pereboom, Derk. "Determinism Al Dente" *Noûs* 29 (1995): 21–45.

Pereboom, Derk. *Living without Free Will* (New York: Cambridge University Press, 2001).

Pereboom, Derk. *Free Will, Agency, and Meaning in Life* (Oxford: Clarendon Press, 2014).

Pereboom, Derk. "Responsibility, Regret, and Protest" *Oxford Studies in Agency and Responsibility* 4 (2017): 121–40.

Pettit, Philip. *Republicanism: A Theory of Freedom and Government* (Oxford: Clarendon Press, 1997).

Pickard, Hannah. "Responsibility without Blame for Addiction" *Neuroethics* 10 (2017): 169–80.

Pink, Thomas. *Self Determination* (Oxford: Clarendon Press, 2016).

Plato, *Complete Works*, ed. J. Cooper (Indianapolis, IN: Hackett, 1997).

Price, Richard. *Observations on the Importance of the American Revolution* (London: T. Cadwell, 1785).

Putnam, Hilary. "The Analytic and the Synthetic" in Hilary Putnam, *Philosophical Papers, Volume 2: Mind, Language, and Reality* (New York: Cambridge University Press, 1979).

Quinn, Warren. "Actions, Intentions, and Consequences: The Doctrine of Double Effect" *Philosophy & Public Affairs* 18 (1989): 334–51.

Radovic, Susanna, Meynen, Gerben, and Bennet, Tova. "Introducing a Standard of Legal Insanity: The Case of Sweden Compared to the Netherlands" *International Journal of Law and Psychiatry* 40 (2015): 43–49.

Railton, Peter. Practical Competence and Fluent Agency" in *Practical Reason*, ed. D. Sobel and S. Wall (Cambridge: Cambridge University Press, 2009).

Railton, Peter. "The Affective Dog and Its Rational Tale: Intuition and Attunement" *Ethics* 124 (2014): 813–59.

Railton, Peter. "Learning as an Inherent Dynamic of Belief and Desire" in *The Nature of Desire*, ed. J. Deona and F. Lauria (Oxford: Clarendon Press, 2017).

Rawls, John. "Two Concepts of Rules" *Philosophical Review* 64 (1955): 3–32, reprinted in John Rawls, *Collected Papers*, ed. S. Freeman.

Rawls, John. *A Theory of Justice* (Cambridge, MA: Harvard University Press, 1971).

Rawls, John. *Collected Papers*, ed. S. Freeman (Cambridge, MA: Harvard University Press, 1999).

Reed, Alan and Bohlander, Michael (eds). *Loss of Control and Diminished Responsibility* (Farnham: Ashgate Publishing, 2011).

Reid, Thomas. *Essays on the Active Powers of the Human Mind* [1788] (Cambridge, MA: MIT Press, 1969).

Resnick, Phillip. "The Andrea Yates Case: Insanity on Trial" *Cleveland State Law Review* 55 (2007): 147–56.

Robinson, Paul. "Criminal Law Defenses: A Systematic Analysis" *Columbia Law Review* 82 (1982): 199–291.

Robinson, Paul. "Causing the Conditions of One's Own Defense: A Study in the Limits of Theory in Criminal Law Doctrine" *Virginia Law Review* 71 (1985): 1–63.

Robinson, Paul. *Structure and Function in Criminal Law* (Oxford: Clarendon Press, 1997).

Robinson, Paul and Kurzban, Robert. "Concordance and Conflict in Intuitions of Justice" *Minnesota Law Review* 91 (2007): 1829–1907.

Rosch, Eleanor. "Principles of Categorization" in *Cognition and Categorization*, ed. E. Rosch and B. Lloyd (Hillsdale, NJ: Erlbaum, 1978).

Rosen, Gideon. "Culpability and Ignorance" *Proceedings of the Aristotelian Society* 103 (2003): 61–84.

Ross, Don and Kincaid, Harold. "Introduction: What is Addiction?" in *What is Addiction?*, ed. D. Ross, H. Kincaid, D. Spurrett, and P. Collins.

Ross, D., Kincaid, H., Spurrett, D., and Collins, P. (eds). *What is Addiction?* (Cambridge, MA: MIT Press, 2010).

Ross, D., Sharp, C., Vuhnich, R., and Spurrett, D. *Midbrain Mutiny: The Picoeconomics and Neuroeconomics of Disordered Gambling* (Cambridge, MA: MIT Press, 2008).

Ross, Lee and Nisbett, Richard. *The Person and the Situation* (Philadelphia, PA: Temple University Press, 1991).

Ross, W.D. *The Right and the Good* (Oxford: Clarendon Press, 1930).

Rothstein, Richard. *The Color of Law* (New York: Norton, 2017).

Rousseau, Jean Jacques. *A Discourse on the Origin of Inequality* [1755] in *Rousseau: The Basic Political Writings*, 2d ed., D. Cress (Indianapolis, IN: Hackett, 2012).

Rousseau, Jean Jacques. *The Social Contract* [1762] in *Rousseau: The Basic Political Writings*, D. Cress.

Rudy-Hiller, Fernando. "A Capacitarian Account of Culpable Ignorance" *Pacific Philosophical Quarterly* 98 (2017): 398–426.

Russell, Daniel. *Practical Intelligence and the Virtues* (Oxford: Clarendon Press, 2009).

Russell, John. "Are Rules All an Umpire Has to Work With?" *Journal of the Philosophy of Sport* 26 (1999): 142–60.

Russell, Paul. *The Limits of Free Will* (Oxford: Clarendon Press, 2017).

Ruth, Henry and Reitz, Kevin. *The Challenge of Crime: Rethinking our Response* (Cambridge, MA: Harvard University Press, 2003).

Saltaris, Christina. "Psychopathy in Juvenile Offenders: Can Temperament and Attachment Be Considered as Robust Developmental Precursors?" *Clinical Psychology Review* 22 (2002): 729–52.

Sartorio, Carolina. "Situations and Responsiveness to Reasons" *Noûs* 52 (2018): 796–807.

Saxon, A., Oreskovich, M., and Brkanac, Z. "Genetic Determinants of Addiction to Opioids and Cocaine" *Harvard Review of Psychiatry* 13 (2005): 218–32.

Scanlon, T.M. "The Significance of Choice" *The Tanner Lectures on Human Values* 8 (1988).

Scanlon, T.M. *Moral Dimensions: Permissibility, Meaning, and Blame* (Cambridge, MA: Harvard University Press, 2008).

Schlick, Moritz. *Problems of Ethics* (New York: Prentice Hall, 1939).

Schopp, Robert. *Automatism, Insanity, and the Psychology of Criminal Responsibility* (New York: Cambridge, 1991).

Schore, Alan. *Affect Regulation and the Origin of the Self: The Neurobiology of Emotional Development*, 2d ed. (New York: Routledge, 2016).

Schroeder, Timothy and Arpaly, Nomy. "Addiction and Blameworthiness" in *Addiction and Self-Control*, ed. N. Levy.

Scott, Elizabeth and Steinberg, Larry. "Blaming Youth" *Texas Law Review* 81 (2003): 799–840.

Scott, E., Reppucci, N., and Woolard, J. "Evaluating Adolescent Decision Making in Legal Contexts" *Law and Human Behavior* 19 (1995): 221–44.

Seto, Michael and Quinsey, Vernon. "Toward the Future: Translating Basic Research into Prevention and Treatment Strategies" in *Handbook of Psychopathy*, ed. Patrick.

Shelby, Tommie. *Dark Ghettos: Injustice, Dissent, and Reform* (Cambridge, MA: Harvard University Press, 2016).

Shiffrin, Seana. "The Moral Neglect of Negligence" *Oxford Studies in Political Philosophy* 3 (2017): 197–228.

Shoemaker, David. "Attributability, Answerability, and Accountability: Toward a Wider Theory of Responsibility" *Ethics* 121 (2011): 602–32.

Shoemaker, David. "Psychopathy, Responsibility, and the Moral/Conventional Distinction" *Southern Journal of Philosophy, Spindel Supplement* 49 (2011): 99–124.

Shoemaker, David. *Responsibility from the Margins* (Oxford: Clarendon Press, 2015).

Shoemaker, David. "Response-Dependent Responsibility; or, A Funny Thing Happened on the Way to Blame" *Philosophical Review* 126 (2017) 481–527.

Sider, Ted. "Hell and Vagueness" *Faith and Philosophy* 19 (2002): 58–68.

Sidgwick, Henry. *The Methods of Ethics*, 7th ed. (London: Macmillan, 1907).

Simester, A.P. "Is Strict Liability Always Wrong?" in *Appraising Strict Liability*, ed. A.P. Simester.

Simester, A.P. (ed.). *Appraising Strict Liability* (Oxford: Clarendon Press, 2005).

Simons, Kenneth. "When Is Strict Liability Just?" *Journal of Criminal Law & Criminology* 87 (1997): 1075–1137.

Simons, Kenneth. "Is Strict Criminal Liability in the Grading of Offenses Consistent with Retributive Justice?" *Oxford Journal of Legal Studies* 32 (2012): 445–66.

Simpson, A.W.B. *Cannibalism and the Common Law: The Story of the Tragic Last Voyage of the Mignonette and the Strange Legal Proceedings to which it Gave Rise* (Chicago, IL: University of Chicago Press, 1984).

Skinner, B.F. *Science and Human Behavior* (New York: Macmillan, 1953).

Sliwa, Paulina. "Moral Understanding as Knowing Right from Wrong" *Ethics* 127 (2017): 521–52.

Smart, J.J.C. "Free Will, Praise, and Blame" *Mind* 70 (1961): 291–306.

Smith, Adam. *The Theory of the Moral Sentiments* [1759], ed. D.D. Raphael and A.L. Macfie (Oxford: Clarendon Press, 1976).

Smith, Angela. "On Being Responsible and Holding Responsible" *The Journal of Ethics* 11 (2007): 465–84.

Smith, Angela. "Control, Responsibility and Moral Assessment" *Philosophical Studies* 138 (2008): 367–82.

Smith, Angela. "Attributability, Answerability, and Accountability: In Defense of a Unified Account" *Ethics* 122 (2012): 575–89.

Smith, Angela. "Moral Blame and Moral Protest" in *Blame: Its Nature and Norms*, ed. Coates and Tognazzini.

Smith, Angela. "Responsibility as Answerability" *Inquiry* 58 (2015): 99–126.

Smith, Edward and Medin, Douglas. *Categories and Concepts* (Cambridge, MA: Harvard University Press, 1981).

Snyder, Howard and Sickmund, Melissa. *Juvenile Offenders and Victims: 2006 National Report* (Washington, DC: Department of Justice, Office of Juvenile Justice and Delinquency Programs, 2006).

Srinivasan, Amia. "The Aptness of Anger" *The Journal of Political Philosophy* 26 (2018): 123–44.

Sripada, Chandra. "The Fallibility Paradox" *Social Philosophy & Policy* 36 (2019): 234–48.

Stannard, John. "The View from Ireland" in *Loss of Control and Diminished Responsibility*, ed. A. Reed and M. Bohlander.

Steinberg, Laurence. *Adolescence*, 11th ed. (New York: McGraw-Hill, 2017).

Steinberg, S. and Silverberg, S. "The Vicissitudes of Autonomy in Early Adolescence" *Child Development* 57 (1986): 841–51.

Strawson, Peter. "Freedom and Resentment" *Proceedings of the British Academy* 48 (1962): 187–211, as reprinted in *Free Will*, ed. Watson.

Sunstein, Cass. "Social Norms and Social Roles" *Columbia Law Review* 96 (1996): 903–68.

Sunstein, Cass. "Moral Heuristics" *Behavioral and Brain Sciences* 28 (2005): 531–73.

Sunstein, Cass. *Why Nudge?* (New Haven, CT: Yale University Press, 2014).

Sunstein, Cass and Richard Thaler. *Nudge: Improving Decisions about Health, Wealth, and Happiness* (New Haven, CT: Yale University Press, 2008).

Sverdlik, Steven. *Motive and Rightness* (Oxford: Clarendon Press, 2011).

Tadros, Victor. *Criminal Responsibility* (Oxford: Clarendon Press, 2005).

Tadros, Victor. "Poverty and Criminal Responsibility" *The Journal of Value Inquiry* 43 (2009): 391–413.

Tadros, Victor. *The Ends of Harm: Moral Foundations of Criminal Law* (Oxford: Clarendon Press, 2011).

Talbert, Matt. "Blame and Responsiveness to Moral Reasons: Are Psychopaths Blameworthy?" *Pacific Philosophical Quarterly* 89 (2008): 516–35.

Talbert, Matt. "Accountability, Aliens, and Psychopaths" *Ethics* 122 (2012): 562–74.

Talbert, Matt. "Attributionism" in *The Oxford Handbook of Moral Responsibility*, ed. D. Nelkin and D. Pereboom (New York: Oxford University Press, 2021).

Tester, M., Gardiner, W., and Wilfong, E. "Experimental Studies of the Development of Decision-making Competence" in *Children, Risks, and Decisions: Psychological and Legal Implications* (New York: American Psychological Association, 1987).

Thomson, Judith. "Physician-Assisted Suicide: Two Moral Arguments" 109 *Ethics* (1999): 497–518.

Tiffany, Evan. "Conceptualizing Coercive Indoctrination in Moral and Legal Philosophy" *Criminal Law and Philosophy* (forthcoming).

Timpe, Kevin. "Leeway vs. Sourcehood Conceptions of Free Will" in *The Routledge Companion to Free Will*, ed. K. Timpe, M. Griffith, and N. Levy (New York: Routledge, 2017).

Todd, Patrick. "Strawson, Moral Responsibility and the Order of Explanation: An Intervention" *Ethics* 127 (2016): 208–40.

Toobin, Jeffrey. *American Heiress* (New York: Doubleday, 2016).

Turiel, Elliot. *The Development of Social Knowledge: Morality and Convention* (New York: Cambridge University Press, 1983).

U.S. Department of Justice. *The Validity and Use of Evidence Concerning Battering and Its Effects in Criminal Trials* (Washington, DC, 1996).

Vachon, David, Lyman, Donald, and Johnson, Jarrod. "The (Non)Relation Between Empathy and Aggression: Surprising Results from a Meta-analysis" *Psychological Bulletin* 140 (2014): 751–73.

Vargas, Manuel. "The Trouble with Tracing" *Midwest Studies in Philosophy* 29 (2005): 269–91.

Vargas, Manuel. *Building Better Beings* (Oxford: Clarendon Press, 2013).

Vargas, Manuel. "Situationism and Moral Responsibility: Free Will in Fragments" in *Decomposing the Will*, ed. T. Vierkent, J. Kiverstein, and A. Clark (New York: Oxford University Press, 2013).

Vargas, Manuel. "The Social Constitution of Agency and Responsibility: Oppression, Politics, and Moral Ecology" in *The Social Dimensions of Responsibility*, ed. M. Oshana, K. Hutchinson, and C. Mackenzie (New York: Oxford University Press, 2017).

Vihvelin, Kadri. "Free Will Demystified: A Dispositional Account" *Philosophical Topics* 32 (2004): 427–50.

Vihvelin, Kadri. *Causes, Laws, and Free Will* (New York: Oxford University Press, 2013).

von Hirsch, Andreas. *Censure and Sanctions* (Oxford: Clarendon Press, 1993).

Vranas, Peter. "The Indeterminacy Paradox: Character Evaluations and Human Psychology" *Noûs* 39 (2005): 1–42.

Walker, Lenore. *The Battered Woman* (New York: Harper & Row, 1979).

Wallace, R. Jay. *Responsibility and the Moral Sentiments* (Cambridge, MA: Harvard, 1994).

Wallace, R. Jay. "Addiction as a Defect of the Will" *Law and Philosophy* 18 (1999): 621–54.

Wallace, R. Jay. "Rightness and Responsibility" in *Blame: Its Nature and Norms*, ed. D. Coates and N. Tognazzini.

Watson, Gary (ed.). *Free Will* (New York: Oxford University Press, 2003).

Watson, Gary. *Agency and Answerability* (Oxford: Clarendon Press, 2004).

Watson, Gary. "Free Agency" reprinted in Watson, *Agency and Answerability*.

Watson, Gary. "Responsibility and the Limits of Evil: Variations on a Strawsonian Theme" reprinted in Watson, *Agency and Answerability*.

Watson, Gary. "Two Faces of Responsibility" reprinted in Watson, *Agency and Answerability*.

Watson, Gary. "Disordered Appetites" reprinted in Watson, *Agency and Answerability*.

Watson, Gary. "Excusing Addiction" reprinted in Watson, *Agency and Answerability*.

Watson, Gary. "Reasons and Responsibility" reprinted in Watson, *Agency and Answerability*.

Watson, Gary. "The Trouble with Psychopaths" in *Reason and Recognition: Essays on the Philosophy of T.M. Scanlon*, ed. Freeman, Kumar, and Wallace (Oxford: Clarendon Press, 2011).

Watson, Gary. "The Standing to Blame: A Critique" in *Blame: Its Nature and Norms*, ed. D. Coates and N. Tognazzini.

Watson, Gary. "A Moral Predicament for the Criminal Law" *Inquiry* 58 (2015): 168–88.

Westen, Peter. "Does Duress Justify or Excuse?" in *Moral Puzzles and Legal Perplexities*, ed. H. Hurd.

Westen, Peter and Mangiafico, James. "The Criminal Defense of Duress: A Justification, Not an Excuse — And Why It Matters" *Buffalo Criminal Law Review* 6 (2003): 833–950.

Westlund, Andrea. "Selflessness and Responsibility for Self: Is Deference Compatible with Autonomy" *Philosophical Review* 112 (2003): 483–523.

Weyant, James and Clark, Russell. "Dimes and Helping: The Other Side of the Coin" *Personality and Social Psychology Bulletin* 3 (1976): 107–110.

Whitehead, John and Lab, Steven. *Juvenile Justice*, 9th ed. (Boston, MA: Routledge, 2018).

Whittle, Ann. "Dispositional Abilities" *Philosophers' Imprint* 10 (2010): 1–23.

Wiencek, Henry. *Master of the Mountain: Thomas Jefferson and his Slaves* (New York: Farrar, Strauss and Giroux, 2012).

Wiggins, David. "A Sensible Subjectivism?" in David Wiggins, *Needs, Values, and Truth* (Oxford: Blackwell, 1987).

Williams, Bernard. "Moral Luck" reprinted in Williams, *Moral Luck*.

Williams, Bernard. *Moral Luck* (Cambridge: Cambridge University Press, 1981).

Williams, Bernard. *Ethics and the Limits of Philosophy* (Cambridge, MA: Harvard University Press, 1985).

Wolf, Susan. "Sanity and the Metaphysics of Responsibility" in *Responsibility, Character, and the Emotions*, ed. F. Schoeman (Cambridge: Cambridge University Press, 1987).

Wolf, Susan. *Freedom within Reason* (New York: Oxford, 1990).

Yaffe, Gideon. *Attempts* (Oxford: Clarendon Press, 2010).

Yaffe, Gideon. *The Age of Culpability* (Oxford: Clarendon Press, 2018).

Zimbardo, Philip. *The Lucifer Effect* (New York: Random House, 2007).

Zimmerman, Michael. *Living with Uncertainty: The Moral Significance of Ignorance* (New York: Cambridge University Press, 2008).

Zimring, Franklin. *American Youth Violence* (New York: Oxford University Press, 1998).

Index

For the benefit of digital users, table entries that span two pages (e.g., 52–53) may, on occasion, appear on only one of those pages.